ENGLISH RECUSANT LITERATURE
1558—1640

Selected and Edited by
D. M. ROGERS

Volume 184

JOHN BRERELEY
The Lyturgie of
the Masse
1620

JOHN BRERELEY
*The Lyturgie of
the Masse*
1620

The Scolar Press
1974

ISBN o 85967 160 7

Published and printed in Great Britain by
The Scolar Press Limited, 59–61 East Parade,
Ilkley, Yorkshire and
39 Great Russell Street,
London WC1

1795527

THE
LYTVRGIE OF
THE MASSE:

WHEREIN ARE TREATED THREE
PRINCIPAL POINTES OF FAITH.

Bib: Theol

1. { *That in the Sacrament of the Eucharist are truly and really contained the body and bloud of Christ .*
2. { *That the Masse is a true and proper sacrifice of the body and bloud of Christ, offered to God by Preistes .*
3. { *That Communion of the Eucharist to the Laity vnder one kind is lawful .*

The ceremonies also of the Masse now vsed in the Catholicke Church, are al of them deriued from the Primitiue Church.

BY JOHN BRERELEY
PREIST.

Ex lib.

Harf.   Dr.

From the rysing of the sunne euen to the going downe, great is my name among the Gentils, and in euery place there is sacrifycing, and there is offered to my name a cleane oblation, becanse my name is great among the gentiles.
Malachie . 1 . 11 .

printed at Colen .   1620 .

Q Vid crediblius dicere intelligitur, quam quod ad participationem mensæ huius pertinet, quam Sacerdos ipse mediator Testamenti noui exhibet secundum ordinem Melchsadech de corpore et sanguine suo? Id enim sacrificium successit omnibus illis sacrificijs veteris Testamenti, quæ immolabantur in vmbra futuri &c. Pro illis omnibus sacrificijs et oblatio-nibus corpus eius offertur, et participantibus ministratur. Aug. de ciuit. Dei. l. 17. c. 20.

TO THE HIGH AND NOBLE
CHARLES, Prince of Wales, Duke of Cornewal,
Earle of Chester, and heire apparant to the Crowne and
Monarchie of great Britaine, his gratious Lord
al happines.

MOST GRATIOVS PRINCE,

IF I should onely cast dow*ne* mine eyes vpon the earth and slyme
of my vnworthines, and should not so much presume as to lift them
vp for the ioyful behoulding of those clearest beames which your knowen graces and vertues, of loue, bounty, & magnificence, do vouch-
saffe to send dow*ne* vpon earth most barraine, I should certainly haue
forborne to haue presented vnto your highnes any of the best flowers
or fruictes which so vnfructful a ground could possibly bring forth.

But when I further consider your selfe to be the sweetest flower in
our Britaine garden, springing from that roote which with most fra-
grant odoures of learning and wisdome refresheth and delighteth remotest nations, or more compendiously, that you are the sonne of
such a father, who (as to my greatest comforth I haue heard) not only
daigned to peruse some of my former laboures, but withal appointed
(as thinking them not altogether worthy of al contempt and neglect)
that seueral Doctors shoud be selected for the vndertaking and making of some satiffyable answeare, one of whom though my professed
aduersary, ingeniously confessing of them, *that they seeme both in the prefaces and pro-*
gresse, to haue deserued his Maiesties most fauo-
rable acceptance, this I say, being remembred,
& the whole world seeing that with your Princely bloud God & nature,
ha th deriued vnto you as hereditary your Fathers vertues, I cannot
but rest in hope, that at your leasurable houres this my vnworthy
worke shal somtimes receiue from your clearest eyes a gratious aspect.

And the more, when your highnes shal once perceiue, that as to
your Fathers greatest Maiesty I haue already conuinced ingeneral, that
the faith and religion which the Present Catholicke Roman Church
beleeueth and professeth, is one and the same with that faith and religion which Christ him selfe planted, his Apostles preached, the Fathers of the Primitiue times practised, and the Cristian Church euer
since

videlicet The Protestants Apology for the Roman Church

D. *Morton in his appeale*
epist. *to the Kinges Maie-*
sty.

since vniuerfally haith deliuered, and ai this by no meaner proofe then the free grauntes of the learnedst Protestantes them selues. So likwise I deme it now most expediet to geue the like accompt vnto your Highnes for some particular, but most principal pointes of faith at this day controuerted and disputed betweene the auncient Catholicke, and the moderne Protestant.

Amongst which what can be proposed more proper for so generous and heroical a spirit, or so pleasant and delightsome for so perfect an image of our great God, as the liuely portrature and true description of that highest honour and religion, which solely and peculiarly is by Christians to be exhibited to the first *Prototypon* of diuine maiesty. Seeing God it is that *made the world, and al thinges that are in it, he being Lord of heauen and earth, geuing life vnto al, and breathing and al thinges,* and this with so absolute a dependance as that the greatest Potentates in him alone *do liue, do moue, and be,* what more necessary to be knowen, or more diligently to be practised then the due exhibition of that highest honour, which so soueraigne a Maiesty exacteth at our handes?

Act. 17. 24. 25. 28.

Now this is that most puissant Prince, whereof I presume to make my present by this treatise following: it is true, proper, and external sacrifice, by which God alone is to be adored and serued as our soueraigne Lord maister of life and death, and author of al our good; this is the highest honour that can be geuen, proper to God and vncommunicable to any creature, as onely due to the diuine maiesty. And seeing that al true religion is instituted for the soueraigne acknowledgement and seruice of God, it is necessary that in his Church which is his kinkdome and monarchy, there should be a publicke worship of supreme honour, by which men assembled in one body and society might professe their faith, duty, and loyalty towardes him; so that religion without sacrifice is no other then a monarchy without homage, or a creature without a creator.

And for this very cause the Church of God, the onely saife keeper of true religion, euen from her first natiuity, vntil these her decrepit dayes, haith euer had proper and external sacrifice, and Preistes appropriated by their office to administer the same. The most famous sacrifice in the law of nature, was, that of *bread* and *wine* offered by the high Preist & king *Melchisadech*: in the law of *Moyses* there were

many, and

many, and thofe ordained and commaunded by God him felfe; in the law of grace Chrift eftablifhed one alone in the place of al the aunci-ent, adumbrated by them al, and alone more fufficient then them al, afwel by reafon of the thing offered, to wit the body and bloud of Chrift which are of infinite price, as alfo in reguard of the dignity of the offerer, who is the fonne of God, the Preiſt being only his Vicar: So that the facrifice of Chriftians, is the facrifice of the body and bloud of Chrift, inftituted & offered by him felfe at his laft fupper, with peculiar charge to his Apoſtles & their fucceſſors for their like obla-tion thereof.

Al which fucceeding ages haue fo abundantly accomplifhed, as that M. *Caluin* auoucheth that *al Kinges of the earth, and people, from the higheſt to the loweſt were made drunke with the golden Chalice of the Maſſe:* and that *Satan had blinded almoſt the wholeworld that it might beleeue the Maſſe to be a facrifice and oblation for the obtaining forgeuenes of finnes.* But though *Cal-uin* thus truly acknowledging the vniuerſal beléefe and vſage of the Maſſe, blafphemoufly imputeth the fame to Satans inchauntments; yet *Luther* directly to the contrary moft fincerely confeſſeth that Satan it was who with many argumentes difwaded him from faying of Maſſe, as being in the deuils doctrine and religion, *horrible Idolatry.*

Inſtit .l . 4 .c . 18 . parag . 18.

Ibidem . parag . 1 .

Now this impugning of the Maſſe by *Satan* , and *Luthers*, and his Proteſtant miniſtery, defiſting to fay Maſſe vpon Satans illuſions, and deceiptful argumentes, are fo clearely recor-ded to al poſterity in *Luthers*, and his fcholers bookes and writinges, as that the higheſt ho-nour of the Maſſe, and the ireligious infamy of the impugners therof, may truly be faid to be thereby written *with an Iron pen, and in plate of leade, or with ſteele grauen in flint-ſtone* neuer (*Iob . 19 . 24 .*) to be blotted out by fucceeding times.

See hereafter pag. 369. &c.

And as this holy facrifice you fhal here perceiue to haue beene plain-ly foretold by the auncient Prophets, to haue beene inftituted and offered by Chrift our redeemer, to haue beene vfed and practifed by his bleſſed Apoſtles and their fucceſſors, the learned and holy Bi-fhoppes, and Preiſtes of the pureſt times of the Primitiue Church; fo fhal you likewiſe clearely fee our religious obſeruance thereof to haue beene fo fcrupulous and fearful, as that the very ceremonies

¶ ¶ ¶   therein

therein vfed by vs at this day are truly fuch as are lawfully and lineally defcended from our noblelt progenitors the auncient Fathers.

But feeing that which is offered in this facrifice, is that which is moft pretious, to wit, the facred humanity of Chrift our Sauiour, here fhal you likewife fee it moft euidentiy euicted, and that by al arguments conuincing true faith and religion, that in the facred Euchariſt Chriſtes body is not onely by way of figure or remembrance, according to *Suinglius*, neither only by faith and fpiritually, as *Caluin*, neither conioyned with bread as *Luther*, but that the bread and wine according to their fubſtances and natures, are truly and really chaunged into the body and bloud of Chriſt, then which, what more grateful can be offered to God, what more honourable can be left to his Church, or what more profitably and comfortable can be beſtowed vpon the foules of the iuſt.

This then, moſt noble Prince, being the heauenly foode which I humbly prefume to offer vnto your excellencies moſt ſweeteſt taiſt and contemplation, I fhal reſt in hope that the dilicacy thereof wil fo ſtrongly poſſeſſe your fenſes with liking and admiration, as that therby pardon wil be pleaded for fo daring attempt, as the prefuming to write to fo great a foueraigne. In confidence whereof I wil remaine.

Your highnes humble feruant,
and denoted Orator

IOHN BRERELEY.

THE PREFACE TO
THE READER.

For so much (good Reader) as it is vsuall with certaine of our aduersaries, being preſſed with teſtimonies of the auncient Fathers, to deny at pleaſure ſundry of their writinges, reiecting them for counter-faite; I haue (for the better ſatisfaction, and in preuention thereof) thought it not vnneceſſary to geue proofe of ſuch of them as, being alledged in this enſuing treatiſe, are by our ſaid aduerſaries moſt wronged in this behalfe: In which courſe to beginne firſt with the wrongfully (*) reiected epiſtles of *Ignatius*, who confeſſedly (a) *was S. Iohns Scholer and liued in Chriſts time*: It is euident that (b) *Euſebius* & (c) *Hierom* do not onely make expreſſe mention of ſundry of them by name, as namely of *his Epiſtles to the Epheſians, to the Magneſians, to the inhabitantes of Trallis, to the Romans, to the Philadelphians, to the Smyrnenſes and to Polcarpus*; but doe alſo recite and alledge particularly out of them, ſundry (d) ſayinges or ſentences which are accordingly found

(*)
Caluin l. 1. inſtitut. c. 13. ſect. 29. ante med. ſaith: *nihil naniæ illis quæ ſub Ignatij nomine editæ ſunt putidius.*

(a)
So ſaith M. Whitguiſt in his defence of the anſwere to the admonition &c. pag. 408. circa med.

(b)
Euſebius hiſt. l. 3. c. 30. maketh expreſſe mention of the ſeueral Epiſtles writen by *Ignatius to the Churches of Epheſus, of Magneſia, the Trallian, Roman & Philadelphian Churches: to the Churches of Smerna, and to Policarpus*.

(c) Hierom in Catalog. Scriptorum Eccleſiaſt. ſaith *Ignatius, ſcripſit vnam epiſtolam ad Epheſios, alteram ad Magneſianos, tertiam ad Trallenſes, quartam ad Romanos, & inde egrediens ſcripſit ad Philadelphios; & ad Smyrnenſes, et proprie ad Policarpum, commendans illi Antiochenſem Eccleſiam*. (d) Euſebius vbi ſupra telleth how *Ignatius in his epiſtle to the Epheſians maketh mention of Oneſimus the Paſtor there: that in his Epiſtle to the Magneſians he remembreth Damas who was Biſhop there: that in his Epiſtle to the Church of Trallis he nameth Polibius who gouerned there:* Alſo he and *Hierom* (vbi ſupra) alledge a whole ſentence out of his epiſtle *ad Smernenſes* & a whole paſſage *verbatim* out of his epiſtle to the

A   Romans

Romanes: al which are found accordingly in the Epistles now extant.

(e)
Eusebius hist. l. 5. c. 6. initio saith; *Hunc (Ireneum) in eunte ætate Policarpi auditorē fuisse cognominus*: and *Hierom* in Catal. saith; *constat autem Policarpi Ireneum fuisse discipulum*.

(f)
See this in Eusebius hist. l. 3. c. 30. versus finem.

verbatim in the Epistles now extant: Before *Eusebius* and *Hierom*, did *Ireneus* (e) the Scholer of *Policarpe* almost 1500. yeares since, alledge (f) a saying of *Ignatius* which is yet to be found in his now Epistle to the *Romans*: Before him again S. *Policarpe*, who was (g) of great familiaritie with the Apostles as being (h) Scholer to S. *Iohn*, doth in his vndoubted (i) Epistle, make (k) mention not only of *Ignatius* his foresaid *Epistle sent to him*, but also of *Ignatius* his other *Epistles*: which antiquitie, & credit of *Ignatius* his foresaid *Epistles* is a thing so vndoubted, that they are accordingly cyted, & acknowledged for his *Epistles* by (l)

and in Ireneus him self l. 5. versus finem. (g) Eusebius hist. l. 3. c. 30. initio saith *Policarpus magna fuit cum Apostolis familiaritate & notitia coniunctus. &c.* (h) *Hierom in catol.* saith: *Policarpus Ioānis Apostoli discipulus, & ab eo Smirnæ Episcopus ordinatus &c.* (i) Concerning *Policarpus* his *Epistle ad Philippenses* it is mentioned by *Ireneus* l. 3. c. 3. fine in these wordes, *Est autem & Epistola Policarpi ad Philippenses scripta perfectissima*: and a part therof, as it is now extant, is specially alledged vnder the title of *Policarpus his Epistle to the Philippenses*, by Eusebius hist. l. 3. c. 30. prope finem. & l. 4. c. 13. fine. Eusebius in the latter place saying further therof, *Adhuc extat*: and *quibusdam prioris Epistolæ diui Petri testimonijs vtitur*: which is accordingly yet to be seene in the Epistle now extant. Lastly S. *Hierome in Catal.* saith; *scripsit Policarpus ad Philippenses valde vtilem Epistolam, quæ vsq; hodie in Asia conuentu legitur.* (k) *Policarpus in Epistola ad Philippenses, prope finem,* saith; *Scripsistis mihi, & vos, & Ignatius &c. Epistolas Ignaty quæ transmissæ sunt nobis habeo, & alias quantascunq; apud nos habuimus, transmisimus vobis &c. Continent enim Fidem, Patientiam, & omnem ædificationem &c.* And see this verie last recited sentence, specially recited & alledged, from & vnder the title *of Policarpus his Epistle ad Philippenses* by *Eusebius, hist. l. 3. c. 30. fine.* (l) *Chemnitius* in his examen, part. 3. pag. 57. a. ante med. saith *Ignatius auditor Iohannis in Epistola ad Philadelphienses, de cælibatu & coniugio, more prorsus Apostolico loquitur: Gratulor inquit &c.*

Chemnitius

Chemnitius, Maister (m) *Whitguift*, M. (n) *Carthwright* and D. (o) *Bancroft* And an other Protestant writer not doubting to charge his Puritan brethren with (p) *impudencie* for their denyal of the said Epistles: hitherto breifly concerning their proofe.

(2) Now concerning the obiections pretended against them: wheras (q) *Chemnitius* surmyseth (but without any alledged proofe) that though the said Epistles be writen by *Ignatius*, they haue yet certaine late vnworthy-additiõs inserted into thē; I wil examine breifly the examples most pretended in this behalfe. *Chemnitius* and *M. Whitaker* do (r) alledge to this end, these sayinges now extant in *Ignatius*; (s) *whosoeuer shal fast vpon the Lords day*

-m-
M. *Whitguift* in his defence &c. pag. 343. *prope finem* saith, *Ignatius immediatly after the Apostles time, calleth the Bishope the cheife Preist, in Epistola ad Smirnenses.* And againe, pag. 408. *circa med. Ignatius who was S. Iohns Scholer, & liued in Christes time in his Epistle ad Trallianos, speaketh thus.* And a litle after in the same place, he further saith, in proof of these Epistles.

These Epistles doth Eusebius make mention of, 1.3. c. 36. *and Hierom de viris illustribus.* (n) M. *Carthwright*, against whom *Ignatius is in* the last cyted place alledged, doth not in his answere therto (set downe there pag. 408. *prope finem*. and 409; *paulo post initium*) take exception to the said Epistles; but as acknowledging their antiquity answereth otherwise making onely question of the meaning of *Ignatius* his wordes, him selfe not doubting to alledge there pag. 99. *fine* from some of *Ignatius* his said Epipstlles. (o) M. *Bancroft* in his Suruey of the pretended holy discipline pag. 330. *post med.* noteth the Puritanes saying, concerning *Ignatius*, that with them *the poore old Father is straight way reiected as a counterfaite and vaine man.* (p) The Protestant author of the booke entituled *Quarimonia Ecclesiæ*, pag. 91. *poulo post med.* saith; *Epistolas ergo tuas Sanctissime Ignati adulterinas esse contendunt, in id enim impudentiæ diuerticulum &c.* (q) *Chemnitius* in his examen part. 1. pag. 94. a. *versus finem.* saith hereof *Admixta vero sūt et alia non pauca quæ profecto non referūt grauitatē Apostolicā & ibid. b. ante med.* he further saith *Epistolæ Ignatij trãsformatæ vidētur in multis locis ad stabiliendum statū regni Pontificij.* (r) *Chemnitius vbi supra*, immediatly next after saith: *Et diuinitus iudico esse factum, quod adulterina quædam assumensia suo se iudicio probant: nam in epist. ad Philip. ita hodie legimus,*

alledging

alledgeing fo the fen-
tences recited here in
the text, adding, *fed hæc
effe fuppofititia non eft dubium &c*. And fee the ve-
ry fame obiection made
in like forte by M. *Whi-
taker de facra Scriptura
queft.6.pag.652.* (s)
*Ex Epiftola Ignatij ad Phi-
lippenfes.* (t) *Ex eadē
Epiftol.* (u) M. Falke
in his anfwere to a coun-
terfaite Catholicke pag.
35. faith, *Iuftinus was in
this error that he thought
Angels lufted after women:
Ireneus affirmeth that our
Sauiour liued here* 50.

or *the Saboath is the killer of Chrift*. Againe,
(t) *whofoever fhal obferue Eafter with the Iewes
is Coopartner with them that killed our Lord:*
wherto I anfweare, firft that though this were
true in the fence pretended, and therupon erroneous, yet this no more proueth thefe fentences or the refidue of the Epiftles now que-
ftionable not to be writen by *Ignatius*, then
thofe other greater fuppofed errors wherwith our aduerfaries doe charge the moft
auncient (u) *Ireneus Iuftine Papias, the difciple of Iohn*, and fundry of the (x) *Apoftles
them felues* do proue the doctrines or writinges by thē publifhed, to be none of theirs.
Secondly I aufweare, that thefe are not errors,
nor doctrines improper to thofe times: for if
the phrafe of *killing Chrift* do caufe diflike,
it is to be taken as fpoken of killing Chrift

yeares: *alfo both he and Papias the difciple of Iohn, are charged by Hierom
to haue held this error, that Chrift fhould raigne a thoufand yeares after the
refurrection, here in the flefh.* (x) Brentius in Apolog. Confef.
Witenberg.c. de concilijs faith: *S. Peter the cheife of the Apoftles, &
alfo Barnabas, after the holy Ghoft receiued, together with the whole Church
of Hierufalem erred.* Alfo the Centurie writers of Magdeburge Cent.
1. col. 580. poft med. do fay; *Paul is perfwaded by Iames and the reft,
that for the offended Iewes he fhould purify him felfe in the Temple, whereunto
Paul yeeldeth, which certainly was no fmale flyding of fo great a Doctor, as
not hauing* (or vnderftanding) *fufficiently the reafons of Moyfes Law being abrogated.* And M. Whitaker *de Ecclefia Controu.* 2. quaft. 4. pag.
223. initio faith; *Imo poft Chrifti Afcenfionem et illum fpiritus fancti in
Apoftolos defcenfum, Ecclefiam totam erraffe Conftat de vocatione gentium,
non vulgus tantum Chriftianorum fed ipfos etiam Apoftolos.* And *ibid. circa
med.* he further faith, *Imo etiam Petrus errauit de legis cæremonialis
abrogatione,* (&c) *et hæc erat res fidei, et in hac errauit Petrus: preterea
in moribus etiam errauit, &c. hi magni errores erant, et hos tamen in
Apoftolis fuiffe videmus, etiam poftquam fpiritus Sanctus in illos difcenderat.*
and fee the like further in M. Fulke againft the Rhemifh Teftament in,

by way

by way of fignification, or in a like fober fence, as when the Apoftle affirmeth of greuous finners, that (y) *They crucifie againe to them felues the Sonne of God:* if the matter offend, it proceedeth onely from ignorance in antiquitie: for concerning firft the firfter example of not *fafting vpon the Saboath,* being the day of our Sauiours refurrection, and therfore called (z) *The Lords day,* and fo withal, to vs a day of ioy and comforth, rather then of mourning & fafting, that it was very aunciently (a) prohibited to faft therupon, is frequently affirmed by the Fathers: As alfo for the like reafon, a like auncient (b) cuftome was, not to faft vpon Chriftmas day, (c) *not* (faith *Epiphanius*) *though it doe chaunce vpon wednefday or fryday.* This prohibition not to faft vpon the Saboath is fo vndoubtedly auncient, that it is accordingly confeffed and alledged as from this very forefaid faying of *Ignatius* both by M. (d) *Whitguift,* and M. (e) *Carthwright*; M. (f) *Hooker* alfo not onely alledging, but likewife

Gallat. 2. fol. 322. b. *fine*. And Gualter in Act. 21.

(y)
Heb. 6. 6.
(z)
Apoc. 1. 10.
(a)

See teftimonie of this prohibition in *Tertulian de Corona militis.* And in *Concil. Gangrenfi. Can.* 18. & in *Concil. 4. Carthag. Can.* 64. and in *Epiphanius l. 3. contra harefes prope finem.* and *har.* 75. *ante med.* where he feteth downe *fafting vpon the Lords day* as one of the condemned errors peculiar to *Arius:* A thing fo euident that our learned aduerfarie *Lambertus Danaus l. de harefibus fol.* 118. *a. poft med.* confeffeth faying. *die dominico Ieiunare nefas omnino veteres existimabant.* (b) Not to faft vpon Chriftmas day is affirmed by S. *Leo Epift.* 93. *ad Turbium Asturienfem cap.* 4. (c) *Epiphanius l. 3. contra harefes har. vlt. fine* faith: *Neq, in die Epiphaniorum, hoc est apparitionis et aduentus, quando natus eft in carne Dominus, ieiunare licet, etiamfi contingat vt fit quarta aut pro fabatum.* (d) See this in M. *Whitguiftes* defence pag. 102. *ante et circa med.* (e) M. *Carthwright* in his words alledged there pag. 99. *fine* faith; *I could oppofe Ignatius and Tertulian, wherof the one faith, it is* nefas *a deteftable thing to faft vpon the Lords day:* the other faith *that it is to kil the Lord,* Tertul. *de Coron. milit. Ignat. in Epift. ad Philip.* (f) See Maifter *Hooker* in his Ecclefiaftical Polecie l. 5. Sect. 72. pag. 209. *circa med.*

withal defending in particuler the foresaid saying and doctrine therof, as the doctrine & saying of *Ignatius* to whose defence thereof made more at large I do refer the Protestant Reader.

(3) Now as concerning thother foresaid obiection of not (g) *keeping Easter with the Iewes:* against which M. (h) *Whitaker* obiecteth the example of *Policarpus* and *Policrates* who did keepe Easter with the Iewes. In explication therof I say, that as in those firster times Circumcision and sundry other like Iudaizing ceremonies, were in some Churches for the time (i) tollerated in reguard of the (*) weaknes of the Iewes, so likewise was for the time tollerated this foresaid (k) obseruation with them of Easter day, the which being afterwards by some obserued & defended as a matter of (l) necessitie (as in like maner also was (m) Circumcision) then did *Ignatius* in his foresaid alledged saying, earnestly impugne the same (euen as the Apostle did also vpon the like ground (n) impugne Circumcisió:) which example of *Ignatius*, was not long afterwardes imitated by (o) *Victor* who our very (p) aduersaries doe reuerence and by the Fathers of the most

(g) Mentioned next before at. t.

(h) M. *Whitaker* de sacra Scriptura pag. 652. saith, *Constat Policarpum & Policratem cum Iudæis Pascha celebrasse.*

(i) Paul *circumcised Timothee* Act. 16. 3. *shore his owne head in Cencris* Act. 18.18. *was purified in the Temple* Act. 24. 18. & 31. 26. and *kept the feast at Hierusalem* Act. 18. 21. whereto adde the decree for *abstinence from bloud and that which is strangled.* Act. 15. 29.

(*) See M. D. *Fulke* against the Rhemish Testament in Act. 15. fol. 213. a. circa med. sect. 9.

(k) *Osiander in his Epitome* hist. Ecclef. Centur. 2.1. 3. c. 2. pag. 51. paulo post med. saith hereof, *Iohannes et Phillippus* apostoli pascha celebrauerunt, quo tempore Iudæi &c. idq, Apostoli haud dubie fecerunt in gratiam Iudæorum qui nuper ad fidem conuersi fuerunt, vt plures Iudæos Christo lucri facerent: &c. (l) Of this affirmed necessitie see Eusebius hist. l. 5. c. 22. initio & c. 23. (m) Then came downe certaine from Iudæa, and taught the brethren saying, except ye be circumcised after the maner of Moyses you cannot be saued. (n) If you be circumcised Christ shal profit you nothing. Gal. 5. 2. (o) Concerning *Victor* see Eusebius hist. l. 5. c. 24. initio. (p) M. *Whitguift* in his defence &c. pag. 510. versus finem saith, *Victor*

A 4   famous

famous *Nicene* (q) *Councel*. In so much as the defenders of this Iudaizing opinion in the obseruation of Easter, were therfore at last reputed for (r) heretickes, and condemned as being (according to the meaning of *Ignatius* his foresaid wordes) guiltie (s) *in obseruing custome with them who were the authors of our Lords death*.

(4)   An other obiection (made by Doctor (t) *Whitaker* and (u) others against these Epistles of *Ignatius*) is that (x) *Theodoret* & (y) *Hierome* do alledge certaine testiomonies from *Ignatius* (*Theodoret* withal naming his Epistle *ad Smyrnenses*) which are not found either in that or in any other of *Ignatius* his Epistles now extant: wherto I answere, first, that the auncient Fathers haue in like maner (z) cyted this sentence *regnauit a ligno Deus*, as the saying of *Dauid* in his *Psalmes*, which yet is at this day wanting in them: as in like maner sundry sayinges are alledged from *Tulli*

was a godly Bishop and Martyr, (and) *not long after the Apostles times*.

(q)
Concerning the Nicene Councel against the obseruation of Easter with the Iewes, see *Athanasius in Epistola de sinodis Arimni & Seleuci*. And *Eusebius de vita Constantini l. 3. c. 5. 17. 18. Ephiphanius hær. 69.* and the Centurie writers *Cent. 4. c. 9. Col. 650. line 37. & Conc. Antiochenum Cant. 1.* (r) *Tertulian l. de præscript. fine* saith, *Est præterea etiam his omnibus Blastus accedens*

qui latenter iudaismumvult introducere, Pascha enim dicit non aliter custodieudum esse nisi secundum legem Moysi. 14. meusis &c. And that not onely *Blastus*, but also others were by the Church censured for Heretickes, for defending the foresaid obseruation of Easter with the Iewes: see further *Ephiphanius hær. 50. initio*. And *Aug. hær. 29.* and *Theodoret l. 3. hæret. Fab.* and *Damacene l. de hæresibus*. In so much as *Osiander Centur. 2. l. 4. c. 10. pag. 97. circa med.* saith hereof, *Inter hæreticos numerati et quartodecimani vocati sunt &c.* & vide *Centur. 5. l. 1. c. 22. pag. 95.* (s) Constantine the great (*apud Eusebium de vita Constantini l. 3. c. 18 .initio*) speaking of the obseruation of Easter saith therof *nihil nobis cum consuetudine Paricidarum, et illornm qui necis Domini authores extiterunt sit commune &c.* (t) Whitaker *contra Durœum l. 5. pag. 360. ante med.* (u) Chemnitius in his examen part. 1. pag. 94. a. *fine* & b. *initio*. & part. 4. pag. 127. b. *fine*. & pag. 128. a.   (x) Theodoret Dial. 3. (y)   Hierome Dial. 3. *contra Pelag.*   (z)   Cyted by S. Augustine in Psalme

in Psalme 95. and by
Tertulian, who in *libro
aduersus Iudæos versus finem* saith, *vnde et ipse Dauid regnaturum ex ligno
Dominum dicebat* and by
Iustine Martyr *in Colloquio cum Triphone iudæo
circa med.*

(a)
Paul wrote seueral E-
pistles to *Timothee*, the
Thessalonians, and to the
Corinthians: wherof one
mentioned 1. Cor. 5.
9. is now lost, as thin-
keth *Vrsinus* in his Co-
mentar. *Cattech*. pag.
33. (b) hereof see *Po-
licarpus in Epistola ad Phi-
lippeuses fine*. and *apud
Eusebium hist. l. 3. o.
30. fine*. (c) hereafter
*tract. 2. sect. 2. subdi-
uision. φ.* at u in the text.
(d) See this hereafter
*tract. 2. sect. 2. subdi-
uision.* 6. in the margen
vnder u. (e) Abraham
Scultetus in his medulla
Theologiæ pag. 440.
ante med. reiecteth this
obiection saying thereof,
*Nec obstat quod citatum
a Theodoreto ex Epistola
ad Smyrnenses testimonium*

pag. 226

and *Plato*, and the same not to be found in
their writinges now exstant: This therfore
only argueth that certaine partes of *Ignatius* his *Epistles* may be lost, but maketh nothing
against those now remaining. Secondly, I
further say concerning that obiected *sentence*
(touching the Eucharist) which *Theodoret*
alledgeth from *Ignatius* his *Epistle ad Smyrnenses*, that this ministreth no suspition of that
Epistle to be now forged, for it may be that
Ignatius did write moe *Epistles ad Smyrnenses*
then one, (according as S. *Paul* did write
seueral (a) *Epistles* to the same persons) as
in like maner also *Policarpus* affirmeth that
Ignatius wrote to him (b) *Epistles* in the
plural number, wheras we finde but one now
exstant: furthermore I say, that the foresaid
sentence cyted from *Ignatius* by *Theodoret*,
being the sentence alledged (c) hereafter,
is accordingly found in a certaine auncient
copie (d) mentioned by two Protestant
writers *Hammelmannus* and *Chemnisius*: in so
much as our learned aduersarie *Abraham Scultetus* (e) reiecteth this foresaid obiection
for vnworthy: As also D. Whitguift the
same notwithstanding, alledgeth and (f) al-
loweth euen that very foresaid Epistle now
extant *ad Smyrnenses*, which this foresaid obiection doth onely and most concerne: And
thus much breifly in behalfe of *Ignatius* his
Epistles.

(5) Next after *Ignatius* followeth to be
examined the writinges of *Dionisius Areopagita*, reiected likewise by our aduersaries
as being but counterfaited: Concerning

contra hæreticos de Eucharistia in nostris exemplaribus non legitur &c.
(f) M. Whitguift in his defence &c. pag. 343. *prope finem.*
which pointe

which point, it is to be obserued, that the writinges now extant vnder his name, haue bene specially alleaged, as being his vn- doubted writinges, by (g) *Nicephorus*, (h) *Euthimius*, (i) *Suydas*, (k) *Damascene*, (l) *Maximus*, (m) *Nicholas the first*, (n) *Martin the first* (o) *Anastasius*, by the second (p) *Nicene Councel*, and aboue 900 yeares since, in the *sixt Synode*, by the Bishopes of seueral Nations, as namely of (q) *Rome*, (r) *Ierusalem*, (s) *Antitioch*, (t) *Alexandria*, and (v) *Constantinople*. also by *Michael* (x) *Singelus of Ierusalem*, who numbreth vp *Dionisius* his bookes, and wrote a special Treatise of his praise, wherof (y) *Suidas* maketh mention; by S. *Gregorie the great*, who alledging this Author, calleth him (z) *Dionisius Ariopagita, the auncient and reuerend Father*: & by that auncient author of the booke of (a) *Questions to Antiochus* attributed by M. (b) *Parkins* his relation from the 7. synode to *Leontius*: In so much as M. *Whitaker* and *Peter Martir*, do both of them (c) acknowledge that in S. *Gregories* time (being now aboue a thousand yeares since) these writinges were extant, and then reputed for the writinges

alleaged heretofore in his preface, sect. 1. in the mergent at m.

(g) *Nicephorus hist*. l. 2. c. 20.

(h) *Euthimius in Panoplia*, part. 1. tit 2.

(i) *Suydas in collect*.

(k) *Damascen de fide orthodox*. l. 1. c. 12. & l. 2. c. 18. & l. 3. c. 6.

(l) *Maximu:, ser*. 57.

(m) *Nicholaus primus in epist. ad Michaelem Imperatorem*.

(n) *Martinus Primus in concilio Romano contra Monothelitas*.

(o) *Anastasius Bibliothecarius in epist. ad Carolum Caluum*. (p) *Concil*. 2. *Nicenum Can*. 2. & vide ibid. *Act*. 6. *Tom*. 3. (q) *Concil*. 6. *Constatinop. Act*. 4. *Agatho* being then Bishop of *Rome*. (r) By *Sophronius* Bishop of Hierusalem, ibidem *Act*. 11. (s) By *Macharius* Bishop of Antioch. *Act*. 8. (t) By *Cyrus* Bishop of Alexandria *Act*. 13. (u) By *Pirrus* Bishop of Constantinople, *Ibid*. (x) *Michael Singelus in Eucomio*. See this in *Alosius Lipomanus de vitis Sactorum*, part. 1. *in vitam Dionisy Areopagiti*. (y) *Suydas in collectam* saith hereof, *laudationem in magnum Dionisium scripsit Michael Singelus Hierosolomitanus &c*. (z) *Greg. in Euang. hom*. 34. (a) In the questions of *Antiochus, Quaest*. 8. it is extant in *Athanasius* workes, printed *Argent*. 1522. (b) *Parkins in problem. pag*. 17. versus fine (c) *Whitaker*.

B

de sacra

de sacra Scriptura. Contro-
uer. 1. quast. 6. pag.
660. fine, saith of *Dioni-*
sius his bookes now ex-
tant: *Non sunt recentes fa-*
teor nec contemnendi. &c.
Gregorius quidem magnus
illorum meminit &c. And
see the like in Peter Martir in 1. Cor. 15.
(d) *Humfredus in Iesui-*

writinges of *Dionisius Areopagita,* and M.D.
Humfrey, Philip Morney, the Century writers, &
others, in reguard of other more auncient testimonie geuen of them, do *(d)* confesse them
to be as yet more auncient. In more ful có-
firmation wherof *S. Gregory* (e) *Nazianzen*
alledgeth as from an auncient author before
his owne time, that which is accordingly
found in the writinges of *Dionisius* (f) now
extant. And the no lesse (g) auncient

tismi. part. 2. Rat. 5. pag. 514. *initio.* saith, *Hunc Areopagitam:*
Suydas, Adon, Michael Singelus, Gregorius Turonensis, & alij, Pauli andi-
torem credunt fuisse illum Scriptorem cælestis, et ecclesiastica Hierarchiæ. And
Philip Morney in his Treatise against the Masse, englished, l. 4. c. 5.
initio, pag. 432. paulo ante med. vndertaking to discourse *of the*
beleef of the Fathers in the matter of the supper, from the first Nicene coun-
cel, til Gregory the great, addeth immediatly, and next afterwardes saying; *let vs proceede according to the order of time and succession of the Fathers.*
S. Denis pretended the Areopagit (for we haue said that he may seeme to haue
liued about this time) did not otherwise vnderstand &c. And then afterwardes alledgeth *Chrisostom, Ambros, Basile, &c.* as in order of time poste-
rior to this *Dionise.* Also the Centurie writers *in Centur.* 4. c. 7. Col.
559. lin. 27. do place him in the beginning of *the fourth hundreth*
yeares after Christ, saying, *Author libri qui Dionisy Areopagitæ titulo vulgo*
venditatur, quem hoc seculo vixisse suo loco dicimus &c. In like maner M.
D. *Bridges* in his defence of the gouernement &c. pag. 967. *post*
med. saith, *I deny not this Dionsius to haue bene of some antiquitie, whom al-*
so I take to haue bene before Basile, though a counterfaite &c. And the Protestant writer *Hermanus Pacificus* in his Theses &c. pag. 139. *fine,* maketh these writinges of *Dionisius, much auncient to Chrisostom* saying;
quæ misteriorum explicatio consentit cum ijs quæ multo ante Chrisostomum, Di-
onisius de hoc rescripsit, cum ait, liber de ecclesiastica Hierachia &c. (e) *Nazi-*
anzen orat. in initiu. Christ. speaketh *of Sancta Sanctorum,* which (saith he)
are couered with Seraphines, and glorified with three sanctifications which do a-
gree in one domination and Deitie, euen as a certaine other author before vs,
baith reasoned most wisely & diuinely: these wordes cannot be meant of a-
ny author of his owne time (in whose writinges also now answerable

examlpe

example of this kind is alledged) but of an author to him self auncient.
(f) See *Dionfius de caleft*. *Hierarch*. c. 4. & 6. & 10. 11. & 12.
And fee *Budæus in Comentar. lingua Græc*.   (g) No lefse auncient;
for thefe homilies *In diuerfos &c*. were tranflated into Latine by *Rufinus*, as thinketh *Erafmus* in prefat. in 2. part. *operum Originis*. printed at Bafile 1545. in fo much as M *Parkins* in *Problem*. pag. 13.
initio faith, *homiliæ diuerfos*, *in ijs mentio Arianorum & Manicheorum*,
ex ijs, *fi quæ fuut ab Origine fcriptæ*, *corrupit eas Rufinus*:

homilies which goe vnder *Origens* name, do
(h) alledge and cyte exprefly from *Dionifius*
that which is likewife to be (i) found in his
now writinges : wherto might be added like
further teftimonie geuen of them by S. (k)
Chrifoftome, *Cirillus*, (l) *Alexandrinus*, and (*)
others. A thing fo euident, that M. D. *Fulke*,
though denying this author to be the true *Dionifius*, thinketh him yet no lefse auncient then
(m) *Dionifius Bifhop of Alexandria who fuccee-*
ded *Origen*, and florifhed (n) *Anno*. 250. Furthermore that euen this forefaid *Dionifius Alexandrinus* (who liued fo long fince) did him felf
write certaine *Annotations* vpon thefe other
writinges of *Dionifius Areopagita* is affirmed by
(o) *Anaftafius Antiochenus* who florifhed *Anno Dom*. 570. And the faid auncient Annotations of *Dionifius Alexandrinus* are yet further
mentioned (p) and alledged by *Pachimeres*, &
alfo (aboue 800. yeares fince) by *Maximus*.
Onely now I do further adde in ful conclufion,
that in reguard of fo euident premifses, fundry
other of our learned aduerfaries haue not doubted to acknowledge the due and anfwearable

(h)
Hom. 2. *in diuerf*.
faith, *in ipfo enim vt os*
loquitur diuinum, *viui-*
mus, mouemur et fumus,
vt ait magnus Dionifius
Areopagita, efse omnium
eft fupereffentia & diuini-
tas.   (i) In cap. 4.
de calefti Hierchia.
(k) *Anaftafius Biblio-*
thecar. in Epift. ad
Carolū Caluū affirmeth
that this author was
knowen to *Chrifoftome*,
who tearmed him in
reguard of his high diui-
nity, *Peteinon* ~~Fou Ou-~~ τȣ ȣρκȣ
~~ranȣ~~, the heauēs birde.
(l) It appeareth by
Liberatus (who liued
Anno 540.) that *Ciril*
Alex. alledged thefe
writinges of *Dionifius*
againft *Diofchorus* ,

whereof fee *Liberatus in Breu*. cap. 10.   (*) *Andræas Cretenfis* (manie
ages fince) in his fpecial writing of this *Dionifius*, & his bookes alledgeth in teftimonie of them *Methodius*, *Athanafius*, *Eugenius* , *Gregorius*
Turonenfis &c. (m) M. *Fulke* againft the Rhemifh Teftament *in*

B 2   2. Thef.

2. Thes. 2. vers. 15. fol. 361. b. paulo ante med. saith, *Dionise was not the Areopagite, but of latter time, by likelihood the Bishop of Alexandria who succeeded Origen.*   (n) See M. *Mores* Table pag. 112. at the yeare 250.   (o) ~~Athanasius~~ in libro cuius est titulus, *En to olego*; see this author and booke to this purpose alledged by *Maximus* in his breife commentary vpon *Dionisius.*   (p) Mentioned and alledged by *Pachimeres*, and *Maximus* in their scholies or brife commentaries vpon

Anastasius

Dionisius Areopagita.
(q)
M. *Whitguift* in his answere to the admonition pag. 105. sect. vlt. alledgeth him saying, *interrogatories ministred to the infante are of great antiquity, for Dionisius Areopagita de cælesti Hierarchia cap. 7. saith &c.*
(r)
M. *Sutlife* de Presbit. cap. 13. pag. 91. prope finem. alledgeth his Epistle *ad Demophilum*, and his *Hierarch. l. 1.* saying withal of him, *Dionisius antiquitatis optimus sane testis, videtur enim esse antiquissimus &c.*

antiquitie of these writinges now made questionable, as namely M. (q) *Whitguift* D. (r) *Sutlife* and (s) others. In further probabilitie of which their acknowledgement, I but adde how vnlike it is that a writer (confessedly in (t) M. *Fulkes* opnion no lesse auncient then thirteene hundred yeares since) should falsely vndertake the name and person of *Dionisius Areopagita* vnlesse (as certaine auncient heretickes did to such like purpose counterfaite the Apostles names) it were thereby to geue colour of defence to some singuler heretical opinion of those times; frō al suspition whereof, these writinges now in question are so clearely free (forbearing as improper to be aledged, but the only pointes of our Catholicke Religion, whereof these writinges geue abundant testimonie) that our very aduersaries are not, in other matters confessed

Puritan printed 1605. fol. G. 2. on the firster side *ante med.* saith, *I refer you to Tertulian, Iustine martir, Ciprian, &c. But what do I cite these fathers, Dionisius Areopagita who liued in the Apostles times maketh mention of the Crosse in Baptisme, de Ecclesiastica Hierarchia cap. de Baptismo.* And see further there fol. G. 2. on the other side *fine.* Also the Protestāt Treatise entituled *Consensus Orthodoxus* printed in folio Tiguri. 1578. fol. 198. b. *initio*. alledgeth *Dionisius Areopagita de Ecclesiastica Hierarchia Anno Christ. 96.* See M. *Cowper* late Superintendent of *Winchester* in his *Dictionarium Historicum* annexed to his *Thesaurus*

confessed and out of question, able to charge them so much as with the least pretence or colour of any one such defended error. Hitherto in proofe of the said writings.

(6) As concerning now the obiections pretended against them, wherin our aduersaries haue greatly laboured in reguard the said writinges make so directly with vs & against them. First it is obiected that *Eusebius* & *Hierō*, make no mention of them; wherto I say, that *Eusebius* and *Hierome* do both of them (x) confesse that there were many authors & bookes which neuer came to their knowledge: A thing not vnlike, if we but remember as incident to those precedent times the knowen want of printing, and great dificultie of manuscriptes through the violent persecutions which then raged: therfore I further geue in answere that which *Maximus* aboue 800. yeares since answered in defence of these writinges to this very obiection saying, *I* (y) *could recite the writinges of many* (which *Eusebius* knew not as namely) *of Hymeneus and Narcissus Bishops of Hierusalem, neither did Eusebius mention the workes of Pantenus, neither the workes of Clement of Rome* (*two Epistles of his excepted*) *nor of many others*. Thus for *Maximus*. And in like maner was this said obiection against these writinges further, specially answered by *Theodorus* (z) *Præsbiter*, who liued aboue 1000 yeares since: wherto I onely adde that which is heretofore in behalfe of these writinges

saurus, printed 1578. at the word *Dionisius Areopagita*. (t) See next before at the letter m.

(x)

Eusebius hist. l. 5. c. 29. saith, *etsi complura certe apud multos veteres Ecclesiasticorum scriptorum qui tum vixerunt eximiæ virtutis & exquisita diligentia monumenta huiusǫ, reseruantur; tamen quæ ipsi vidimus sunt hæc solum quæ sequitur.* So plainely doth he signifie him self to mention but *those onely workes which he him self sawe*, acknowledging as before *many* others besides: and see him further there in *fine capitis*, and see *Eusebius* in *græco Codice* l. 6. c. 12. In like maner doth S. *Hierome* in Catal. prope initium say, *Si quid de his hodie scriptitant a me in hoc volumine prætermissi sunt &c. quod*

tinges *alijs forsitan sit notū mihi in hoc terrarum angulo fuerit ignotū*. (y) *Maximus* in *Dionisium*. (z) *Photius* almost 800. yeares since in *Bibliotheca* saith, *Legimus Theodori Presbiteri librum quo demonstrat ea quæ S. Dionisij habemus opera Germana esse nec Pseudephigrapha: quatuor etiam obiectiones soluit: quarum prima &c. Secunda quod Eusebius Pamphilus opera a sanctis Patribus conscripta recenses de S. Dionisij operibus nec verbum quidem dam: Tertia &c. Quarta, quod loquitur de beati Ignatij Epistola cum sanctus Dionisius Apostolorum temporibus floruerit, Ignatius vero sub traiano Martirij certamen perfecerit qui paulo ante obitum Epistolam conscripsit de qua apud S. Dionisium est sermo. Has igitur quatuor obiectiones soluere conténdens Theodorus, pro viribus nititur demonstrare Germana esse sancti Dionisij opera.*

(a)
Heretofore sect. 5. at e h.

(b)
Heretofore sect. 5. at m.

(c)
Concerning the anti-quitie of *Dionisius A- lexdrinus*, *Eusebius*, and *Hierome*, and in which seueral ages each of thē liued, see M. *Mores* Table at their seueral names, & M. *Coupers* Cronicle.

(d)
This obiection is vrged by M. D. *Raynoldes* in his conference &c. pag. 488. by M. D. *Whitaker contra Duræum* l. 5. pag. 357. By M. *Fulke* against Purgatory pag. 353. (e) M. *Raynoldes* in his conference &c. pag. 488. (f) 1. Cor. 11. 18.

tinges, so euidently (a) alledged from *Nazianzen*, & others who liued in, or before *Eusebius* time, that M. D. *Fulke* (b) acknowledgeth them to haue bene extant in the time of *Dionisius Alexandrinus* almost (c) a hundreth yeares before *Eusebius*, who yet was auncient to *Hierome*; so plainly is refelled this so often (d) repeated obiection taken from *Eusebius* & *Hierome*.

(7) Secondly M. D. (e) *Raynoldes* obiecteth that *Dionisius* maketh mentiō of *Churches and Chauncels therein seuered with such sanctification from the rest of the Church, that laye men might not enter thereinto*, directly as M. *Rynoldes* pretendeth against the condition of those times, in which by reason of the persecution then raging, the faithful then were (as he vrgeth) glad to make their assemblies in priuate houses: wherto I answere, that the Apostle mentioning the people (f) *Comming together into the Curch*, insinuateth that in those times speciall places were apointed for publique prayer, which places the Apostle tearmeth *Churches*, expresly withal in his many sayinges (g) distinguishing them from the priuate houses of   the

(g) *Haue you not houses to eat and drinke in, or contemne you the Church of God. 1. Cor. 11, 22. If any be hungry let him eat at home that you come not together vnto iudgement. 1. Cor. 11. 34. Let women hould their peace in the Churches, if they would learne any thing let them aske their husband at home, for it is a foule thing*

for

for a woman to speake in the Church. 1. Cor. 14. 24. 25. 26. In so much
as M. Hooker l. 5. sect. 12. pag. 21 paulo post med. affirmeth that
this Apostle (hereby) teacheth, what difference there should be made, be-
twene house and house &c. the Apostle could not suffer, that the Church
should be made an Inne. (h) *Ignatius in Epist. ad Magnesios (proued*

the faithful; In further proofe of which
Churches, are not improper the testimonies of (h) *Ignatius, Clemens, & Philo*; as
also the (i) *auncient edifices* for praier, aug-
mented in building to be greater Churches
vpō the increase of Christiãs, & afterward
(k) demolished or pulled downe by Dioclesian, do yet further (l) proue the same.
And so likewise do the other yet more aū-
cient (m) examples affirmed from the old
heathen writers, though enemies of our
Christian profession. Hitherto of Churches. Now as concerning the foresaid
Chancels, seuered from the rest of the
Church into which Lay persons might not
come, as this is but agreable with the succeding testimonies of the other auncient
Fathers hereafter (n) in that behalfe more
specially alledged: So allo the wordes of
Dionisius do onelie but import a *Seueral-*
tie of the place where the Altar standeth,
which seperation might in those beginning
times, be in some places made and obserued without anie outward shew thereof,
by external building. And that yet also

heretofore *sect*. 1. saith. *Om-*
nes adunati, ad Templum
Dei concurrite &c. Clemens
the Apostles scholer, in his
booke of Recognitions, l.
10. *circa finem*, maketh like
mention of material Chur-
ches: and that this booke
of *Recognitions*, was aboue
1200 yeares since translated by *Rufinus*, is witne-
sed by *Rufinus in præfat. ad*
Gaudentium and by *Genna-*
dius de script. ecclef. & de
vir. illust. cap 17. In the
same time also doth *Philo*
make like mentiō of Chur-
ches, as apphareth by *Eu-*
sebius hist. l. 2. c. 16. an-
te med. and see S. *Clemeut*
describing the building, &
fashion of the Church al-
ledged hereafter *tract*. 1.
sect. 2. in the margin, at
6. next before l.

(i) *Eusebius hist. l. 8. ca. 1. circa med.* saith *Cum in antiquis illis ædificiis,*
non satis loci haberent, ampliores Ecclesias in vniuersis vrbibus fūdametis
dilatatis earum ad maiorem laxitatem erexerunt (k) *Eusebius ibidem, c. 2.*
initio affirmeth Dioclesiãs demolisiō of these Churches. (l) For if long
before Dioclesians time, Churches aunciently builded, were, in reguard of the peoples increase, pulled downe and reedified with enlargement, and the same being so enlarged, were in manie places then afterwards

terwardes demolished by Dioclesian : doth not this sufficiently proue the answearable antiquitie of them? (m) see in Baronius *Annal. to.* 1. printed 1601. Col. 618. the testimonies for Churches alledged of *Lucian* in *Traianes* time ; of *Lampridius,* in Alexanders time ; and of *Flauius Vopiscus, in* Valerians time. (n) hereafter *tract.* 1. *sect.* 2. *subdiuision.* 1. in the margin at o.

it might be then in some places by seperation of outward building , appeareth aswel by that which is here formerly aledged concerning the publike Churches of those times, as also in that it is certaine how that there were as then some Princes or Magistrates (o) conuerted to the faith, and others, who greatly (p) fauored the same, the multitude of Christians being then before (q) *very great,* & the Apostles being then also suffered to dispute or preach aswel openly (r) *in the Synagogue* as also (s) elswhere *and* (t) *without prohibition :* In which respect it is not so incredible that the faithful should be then permitted to erect Churches.

(8) Thirdly M . D . *Raynoldes* (u) obiecteth that *Dionisius* maketh mention of *Monkes* which (as he thinketh) were not then in being: To which purpose he alledgeth our S . *Thomas Aquinas* affirming (x) *that there was not then a-ny certaine sorte of Religious men :* whereto I answere, first cocerning *Thomas,* that he speaketh but of the distinct peculier Orders of Religious persons, as the *Benedictes* (and such like) which beganne aboute (y) *Anno Dom.* 518 him self otherwise expresly affirming *Monkes* in gene-ral, and to that end (z)alledgeing also the verie

(o)
The *Proconsul of Ciprus* conuerted. Act. 13. 12. and *Crispus cheife ruler of the Sinagougue with al his house.* Act. 18. 8.

(p)
Act. 26. 28. and see *Eusebius* hist. l. 4. c. 8. concerning Adrian & l. 3 . c. 15 .*fine* concerning *Nerua :* & l. 3 . c . 27 . concerning *Traiand.* & l. 5 . c. 5 . cocerning *Marcus Au-relius.* And see further l. 2. c . 2 .*fine.* & l. 4. c . 23 .*post med .*

(q)
Act. 16 . 5 . & 11 . 24. & 17 . 13 . & 21 . 20.

(r)
Act. 13 . 14 . 15 . 42 & 17 . 2 . & 18 . 4 . & 19 . 8 . (s) *In the mar-ket place.* Act. 17 . 17.

(t) Act. 28 . 31. (u) M. *Raynoldes* in his conference pag. 288 . *post med.* (x) Ibid. (y) *Hanmer* in his Chronographie annexed to the english translation of *Eusebius* fol. 54. col. 9. (z) D. *Thomas in secunda secunda quæst.* 184. Art. 5.

(a)

nie testimonie (now in question) of *Dionisius* so euidently is S. *Thomas* alledged against his owne meaning. Secondly if M. *Raynolds* thinke that the word *Monke* was not then in vse, why doth he not then likewise reiect *Philo*, who though huing in the same time haith yet the word (a) *Monasterion*. Thirdly if he thinke the thing signifyed to be improper to those times, do not our very aduersaries the Centurie writers confesse euen of the remotest nations in *Constantines* time, that (b) *vnder him were Monkes throughout Syria, Palestine, Bithinia, and the other places of Asia:* and also (c) *throughout Africke:* which their being then so generally dispersed through the whole Christiã world, argueth that the interim or meane time of their first beginning could be no lesse aunciet then the time in which *Dionisius* liued; as appeareth more plainly by the yet further answerable testimonies of *Eusebius* and (d) *Hippolitus,* and also of *Theophilus* (e) *Antiochenus,* who florished *Anno* 170. whereto I adde the knowen domesticall example of (f) *Glastenbury monastery* begunne in the Apostles times, and the cófessed (g) *Colliges of virgins professing as then perpetu-*

(a) *Philo apud Eusebium hist.* l. 2. c. 16.

(b) Centur. 4. col. 1294. line 50.

(c) *Ibid.* col. 1306. line 19. and *Eusebius* hist. l. 8. c. 20. maketh mention of one Peter before Constantines reaigne by him there termed *Religiosus vel Monachus vitam solitariam & meditationi dedicam secutus.*

(d) *Hipolitus in orat. de cõsumatione mundi* mentioneth *Monckes.*

(e) *Theophilus Antiochenus in libro* 1. *allegoriarum in Math. erunt duo in lecto* mentioneth *Mona-*

al chos alienos a tumultu generis humani & Domino seruientes. (f) *Camden* in his *Britannia* printed 1590. pag. 157. saith, *Monasterium glastenburiæ antiquam repetit originem a Iosepho Arimathensi qui Christi corpus sepulchro mandarat &c. hoc enim et antiquissima huius Monasterij monumenta testatur & Patricius Hiberniensium Apostolus in sua Epistola prodidit, nec est cur de hac re ambigamus.* (g) The Protestant writer *Abraham Scultetus* in his *medulla Theologiæ* pag. 450. *circa med.* alledgeth *Ignatius* saying *in Epist. ad Philadelph. Saluto Collegium virginum:* wherupon he immediately inferreth saying: *Ergone in illo Ecclesiæ flore fuerunt quæ castitatem & continentiam perpetuam profiterentur virgines fuerunt omnino.* And the Centurie writers likewise say, *ex Epistolis Ignatij apparet homines iam tum paulo impensius cæpisse amare & venerari virginitatis studium*

C *nam*

nam in Epiſtola ad Antioch. ait, virgines videant cui ſe conſecrauerunt:
Centur. 2. c. 4. col. 64. line 40. *et vide* Centur. 2. col. 167. line
24. Alſo *Ignatius* mentioneth further virgines, *ſacras virgines conſe-*
crated to God tearming therfore profeſſed Widowes *ſacrarium Dei (in E-*
piſt. ad Tarſenſes) as alſo doth S. *Policarpe in Epiſt. ad Philipenſes:* of
which religious profeſſion of Widowes in the Apoſtles times ſee more
hereafter *Tract. 1. ſect. 4. ſubdiuiſion. 1.* at b. c. d. e. f. g. And ſee like
anſweatable auncient teſtimonie *of ſacred virgines, in Tertalian de velan-*
dis virginibus. and in *Ciprian* l. 1. Epiſt. 11. *& de habitu virginū.* wherof ſee alſo the *Centuriſtes* Centur. 3. col. 140. line 17. & 27.

& col. 176. line 39.
(h)
Philo de vita Contemplati-
ua.

(i)
Euſebius hiſt. l. 2. c. 16.
paulo poſt initium ſaith
hereof, *principio illos fa-*
cultates ſuaſq, opes abijcere
& ſimul ac in hanc diuinam
viuendi rationem ſe abdere

al Chaſtitie. As alſo the *Monaſteries* & Chriſtian monaſtical profeſſors therin liuing, of
whom (h) *Philo* (who liued in the Apoſtles
time) ſpeaketh, tearming them *Eſſees,* deſcri-
bing their profeſſed (i) *ſolitarines,* (k) *forſaking*
of their goodes, (l) *faſting* from fleſh and wine,
their drinking of (m) only *water,* other wonderful (n) auſteritie of leaſt, and the ſame ſo
plainly that M. (o) *Raynoldes* in preuention
therof, would vpon weake (p) ſurmiſes. enforce

incipiunt, ſuis ſe bonis & fortunis omnibus prorſus exuere (Philo) teſtatur: de-
inde quibuſq, vitæ curis depoſitis depulſiſq, extra vrbium inania progreſſos in locis
ſolitarijs & hortis a populi conſpectu remotis domicilia rerum ſuarum collocare.
(k) *Euſebius vt ſupra.* (l) *Euſebius ibid. fine,* ſaith from Philo, *vinum*
non omnino guſtant Imo nec carnibus nec a liquo genere cibariorum quod ſit ſan-
guinis particeps veſcantur, et quod aqua ſola illis potio ſit. (m) *Euſebius* as
next before at l. (n) *Euſebius ibid. circa med.* ſaith from Philo, *vix ſemel*
toto triduo cibi recordantur &c. and a litle after, *vix tantum ſex diebus exple-*
tis Alimentum neceſſarium deguſtant: & ſomewhat afterward neare the end
he further ſaith, *Toros ſtramineos humi poſitos vſurpant &c. Sale et Hyſſopo*
pro obſonio et pane vtuntur. (o) M. *Raynoldes* in his conference pag.
488. *fine.* (p) *Ibid.* pag. 492. *circa med.* vpon ſurmiſe that wheras Philo ſaith, *Sex dies ſeorſum quiſq, in illis ſuis modo dictis Monaſterijs*
Philoſophantur, non progredientes foras, Imo ne proſpicientes quidem, ſeptima
vero conueniunt in cætum comunem: M. D. *Raynoldes* hereupon inferreth
that they obſerued *Saturday* for their Saboath, and therefore were not
Chriſtians

Christians but Iewes. whereto I say, that *Philo* his thus mentioning here (*not the seuenth day in the weeke as* M. *Raynoldes* pretendeth but) *the seauenth day after those Sixe* in which they kept priuate, inferreth no necessarie sequele that Saturday was their Saboath, for (notwithstanding those wordes) that foresaid *Seauenth day* after those *Sixe* might aswel fale out to be on our *Sonday* as vpō the Iewish Saturday. Secondly admit that these *Esses* being but lately conuerted, did as yet Iudaize in this point (as many likewise did in some thinges Iudaize in the Apostles times. (whereof see heretofore sect. 2. in the margin at x. and sect. 3. at h. i. m.) doth this proue that they were not Christians? prouidently therefore and as it were in preuention hereof S. *Hierome in Catal. in marco* saith, *videns Philo iudæorum disertissimus primam Ecclesiam adhuc Iudaizantem, quasi in laudem suæ gentis librum super eorum conuersatione conscripsit*. And our aduersaries *the Centurie writers* do collect from sundry places in the actes by them alledged, that the Apostles themselues obserued for a time the day of the Iewish saboath, concluding & saying, *quo autem tempore Christiani se a Iudæis disiunxerint & diem dominicum feriari cæperint non est memoriæ proditum, sed hoc seculo alios diem Sabbati alios diem Dominicum feriatos esse testabuntur &c*. Cent. 1.1.2. c.6.

force *Philos* meaning not to be at al of any Christian professors, but onely of Iewish *Essenes* mentioned by (q) *Iosephus*, from which indeed these other *Essees* of whom *Philo* here speaketh did wholly (r) *differ* in so much as *Philo* hauing

Col. 503. *circa et post med*.

(q)

Iosephus Antiquitat. Iudaic. l. 18. c. 2. et Iosephus de bello Iudaico l 2. c. 7. (r) *Wholly differre*: for if we compare together the sayinges of *Philo*, and *Iosephus*, it wil appeare that *Philos Essees* were farr more rigid and austere in life then *Iosephus* his *Essenes*, wherof some dwelled in Cities others maried, they also dyned and supped daily, differing as in the premisses, so likewise in their better dyet from *Philos Esses*. Also it appeareth by *Iosephus* that his *Essenes* were about *foure thousand in number* and commorant onely in *Iudæa*, which thing is affirmed also of them by *Philo* him selfin his booke *quod liber sit omnis sapiens*: wheras to the contrary *Philo* in his booke *de vita contemplatiua*, saith of the *Esses*, *Hoc genus reperitur in multis orbis Regionibus merito vt absolutæ probitatis receptum a Græcis atq̃, Barbaris maxime tamen in Ægipto frequentatur &c*. So euidently were they in many nations dispersed according to the the

C 2 dispersion

dispersion of the Gospel.
(s)
Hereof see *Eusebius* hist.
l.2.c.15. where it is
said of *Philo fama est in
Colloquium Petri qui Ro-
manis eodem tempore ver-
bum Dei prædicabat venis-
se &c.* whereupon (as
saith there *Eusebius*) he
afterwardes wrote (as
before of Christian pro-
fessors.

(t)
Next afterwardes in the
place before cyted.
(u)
*Philo de vita Contemplati-
ua* saith, *vocantur Thera-
pentæ &c.* and *Dionisius
de Eccle. Hierarch. c. 6.*

(s) hauing bene affected by conference then
before had with *S. Peter* to our Christiã profession, did (t) thereupon then afterwardes
write as before said of our Christian *Monkes*,
whom he doth (as likewise doth *Dionisius
Areopagita*) tearme *Therapentas* very plainly
by such their agreement in name peculier
to those first times, signifying them selues
to meane one and the same profession of life:
A thing so euident, that *Epiphanius*, *Hierom*,
and others do (x) affirme for cleare that *Philo* wrote of Christian professors: *Eusebius*
not doubting to charge the denyers thereof
(and therein M. D. *Raynoldes*) with (y) *ob-
stinacie*, sundry of our very aduersaries not for
bearing in so cleare a case to make their like
answearable (z) acknowledgement in this
behalfe: whereunto (were this place capable
therof) I could particularly further demonstrate

saith, *sancti præceptores nostri diuinis eos appel-
lationibus sunt prosecuti, partim Therapeutes &c. partim Monachos &c.*
(x) *Epiphanius hær.*29. *circa med.* saith of Philo *Monasteria ipsorum
in vicinia circa Mariam paludem recenjens non de alijs narrauit quam de
Christianis*; And *Hierome in Catal. in Philone* after his shewing that
Philo spake of Christians, concludeth saying, *Ex quo apparet talem primam Christo credentium fuisse Ecclesiam quales nunc Monachi esse nituntur &
cupiunt.* And that *Philo* spake of Christians is yet further affirmed by
Sozomen. hist. l.1.c.12. *fine*: & by *Cassianus* l.2.c.5. *de inst. cænob.*
(y) *Eusebius* hist.l.2.c.16. *versus finem* saith, *Ista Philonis tam per-
spicua testimonia de nostra religionis viris solum tradita esse pro certo arbitra-
mur: quod si quisquam adeo obstinato animo sit vt hisce etiam voluerit refraga-
ri sic tamē euidentioribus argumentis &c.* (z) Their late B.M. *Couper* in
his additiõ to *Languets* Cronicle (which endeth at fol.92. saith, *Philo wrote diuers thinges in praise of Christian Religion, wherfore of Hierome
he is numbred among the Ecclesiasticall writers fol.97,a. initio.* So fully
doth he agree in opinion herein with *Hierome*. And see M. *Hanmers*
like acknowledgment in his Cronagraphie annexed to his translation
of

of *Eusebius* pag. 18. in his Columne of *the Fathers of the Church*. And *Chemnitius* in his examen part. 4. pag. 124. a. vnderstandeth *Philo-*

strate and adde the three principal pointes of perfection perteyning to *Monachisme* as namely *Austeritie of life* in the examples of S. Iohn (a) Baptist, S. (b) *Iames*, and (c) *Timothee : vowed Chastity*, in the other example S. *Paules* professed (d) *Widdowes* and *voluntary pouerty* in the example of the first beleeuers mentioned in the (e) *Actes :* whereby would appeare that the pro-

as speaking of Christian professors.

(a)

The new testament mentioneth S. Iohn Baptists liuing *in the deserte Math* . 3 . 1 . 3. & 11 . 7. his course *Rayment of Camels haire*

and Gerdle of a skinne. Math. 3. 4. and his great abstinence from meate other then *Locustes and wilde honie: Math.* 3. 4. in respect whereof it is said of him that *he came neither eating nor drinking Math.* 11. 18. being therefore called *the Prince or author of Monasticall profession* by *Chrisostome, homil.* 1. *in Marcum,* and hom. *de Iohanne Baptista.* by *Hierom- and Eustoch. de Custod. virg.* by *Cassianus Collat.* 18. *c.* 6. by *Sozomen hist. l.* 1. *c.* 12. and by *Isidor. l.* 2. *de diuin. offic.* (b) The Centurie writers Cent. 1. l. 2. *c.* 10. Col. 582. *prope med.* reporting the historie of S. *Iames* from the testimory of *Egesippus,* say of S. Iames, *vinum et sycerem non bibebat &c.* wine *and sycer he did not drinke, he did not feede of any liuing creature, the Barbers Razer did not trimme him, his body was not annointed with oyle, nor washed in bathes, he wore not wolues garmentes but was attyred in Syndon, he prayed so continually vpon his knees, that Camellike he had lost the sence of feeling :* where to *Epiphanius hær.* 78. *circa med.* addeth that *(calceamentum non induit) he went bare-footed.* see also *Eusebius hist. l.* 2. *c.* 22. (c) *Timothies austeritie* was so great that S. *Paul* 1. *Tim.* 5. 23. admonisheth him saying *drinke not water, but vse a litle wine for thy stomakes sake and often infirmitie.* wherevpon *Caluin* (in 1. Tim. 5. 23. pag. 784. b.) saith, *apparet Timotheum victu austerum fuisse vt qui ne valitudini quidem suæ parceret.* and pag. 785. a. he further saith, *Continentiæ studio erat abstemius : at quam pauci hodie sunt quibus necesse sit aqua interdicere.* (d) Concerning the confessed *vowed Chastitie* of these Professed Widowes, see fully hereafter *Tract.* 1. *sect.* 4. *subdiuision* 1. at b. c. d. e. f. g. (e) Concerning *voluntary pouerty:* wherof example is geuen in the faithful peoples geuing away of their goodes mentioned *Act.* 4. 34. 37. & *Act,* 5. 2. that the same was not of commaundement, but voluntary and of perfection, appeareth *Act. 5. 4.* where it is said *remaning did not remaine to thee, and being sould was it not in thine owne power.* whereupon euen M. *Raynoldes* him selfe inferreth (in his Conference Cronicle pag. 492. *fine*) that, *the beleeuers at Hierusalem might keepe their owne if they listed as Peter said to Ananias Act. 5. 4.* and M. *Hooker* in his ecclesiasticall pol. *l. 2. sect. 4. pag. 103. circa med.* saith, *it was indifferent for Ananias to haue sould, or held his possessions til his solemne vow vnto God had strictly bound him one onely way:* and the like is affirmed by M. *Fenton* preacher at *Grayes Inne* in his Sermon of Symonie and Sacraledge printed 1604. pag. 46. & 47. in so much as M. D. *Couel* in his defence of M. *Hooker* pag. 52. *fine.* acknowledgeth in expresse tearmes *Willing pouerty:* though yet M. *Willet* in his Synopsis pag. 245. do impugne it: And our Sauiour expresly signifieth (*Math. 19. 21.*) the high perfection therof saying, *if thou wilt be perfect, goe sel the thinges thou hast and geue to the poore &c.* which councel S. *Peter* professeth thereto follow *versus 27.* wherto our Sauiour replyeth with promise of great reward *versus 28.* directly against the other euasory answeare that *our Sauiour did not councel this perfection, but* (said so) *onely to discouer the hipocrisie and confidence of the party* to whom he so spoke, affirmed by M. *Fulke* against the Rhemish Testament in *Math. 19. sect. 9. fol. 38. b.* & others.

(f) M. *Raynodes* in his conference pag. 489.

(g) *Dionisius de diuinis nominibus cap. 3.*

(h) Act. 9. 5.

(i) Gallat. 1. 18.

(k) Gallat. 1. 21.

profession of *Monachisme* is nothing so improper to the Apostolike times as M. D. *Raynoldes* and others would enforce.

(9) Fourtly M. D. *Raynoldes* (f) obiecteth that this *Dionisius* (g) affirmeth him self to haue bene present with *Timothie* and *Hierotheus* at the death of our blessed Lady, who dyed as the *Rhemistes* recken the fifteenth yeare after *Christes Ascention* which was *An. Dom.* 48. wheras saith D. *Raynoldes* the true *Dionisius* was not conuerted before the 17. yeare after Christs Ascention: In proofe whereof he alledgeth from the text, that S. *Paul* who conuerted *Dionisius,* was (h) not him self couerted til after Christes Ascention: and that (i) *then after three yeares he came to Hierusale* & thence (k) went into the coast of *Syria* & *Cilicia* &c.

(1)

(l) *Then after fourteene yeares he came againe to Hierusalem.* and after sundry other meane (m) trauailes came at last to (n) *Athens* where he conuerted (o) *Dionisius Areopagita* : where vpō M. D. *Raynoldes* inferreth that the said *three yeares and foureteene yeares,* doe euidently proue that it was 17. or 18. yeares (at the least) after Christes Ascension before the true *Dionisius* was conuerted. Thus farre his obiection consisting vpon these two pointes : the first that our Ladyes death was the 15. yeare after Christes Ascension, The second that *Dionisius* was not conuerted til after the 17. yeare after his Ascention, if either of which faile, the obiection then so much insisted vpon with al faileth. As concerning the first the *Rhemistes* onely tel what (p) *the comon opinion is of her 63. yeares of age :* which they neither allow nor reiect, but what is this to proue the certaine truth of her age? the yeare of our Sauiours (¶) birth is houlden incertaine, his passion also is diuersly reported, some saying he suffered the (q) 30. yeare of his age, others the (r) 33. others the (s) 34. others the (t) 50. as also the day and moneth of his passion is yet to vs (u) incertaine, how much more vncertaine then is the very yeare of the blessed virgines departure, especially considering that there is not so much as one special mention made of it during the first 300 yeares after Christ, so as in respect therof S. *Epiphanius* (x) thinketh her death to be incertaine and vn-

(l)
Gallat. 2. 1.
(m)
Act. 15. 4. & 16. 1.
6. 7. 10.
(n)
Act. 17. 15.
(o)
Act. 17. 34.
(p)
The *Rhemistes* in Act. 1. 14. saith, *the comon opinion is that she liued 63. yeares in al.*
(¶)
M. *Hanmer* in the preface of his Cronagraphia telleth that touching the yeare of the world when Christ was borne diuers men be of diuers opiniōs : to which purpose he reckneth the seueral opinions of *Eusebius,* the Hebrewes, Epiphanius, Carion, Luther, &c.
(q)
Vide Clementem Alexandrinum l. 1. *Strom.* & *Lactantium* l. 4. diuin. *institut.* c. 10.

(r) *Vide Ignatium in Epist. ad Tralianos : et Eusebium in Cronico...* (s) Hereof see *Omiphrius* and *Mercator.* (t) *Ireneus* l. 2. c. 39. *post med.* wherof M. *Fulke* in his answere to a counterfaite Catholicke pag. 35. cicca med. saith, *Ireneus affirmeth that our Sauiour Christ liued here 50. yeares* (u) *Vide Clement.* l. 1. *Strom.* (x) *Ephiphanius har. 78. contra Antidicomarianitas* saith *siue igitur mortua est non nouimus :* and af-

wardes

wardes: *siue mortua est*
sancta Virgo et sepulta &c.
siue sublata est &c. siue
māsit, nā non est impossibile
deo facere omnia quæ vult,
finis enim ipsius nemiui no-
tus est.

(y)
Epiphanius Presbiter. ser.
de Deipar. græc. & Ce-
dren. in compend. in tib.

(*)

M. *Hammer* in his Cro-
nagraphie annexed to
Eusebius translation in
english fol. 20. col. 3.
setting downe the yeare
of our Lord 56. placeth
ouer againſt it our La-
dies death saying, *Ma-*
ry the mother of our Lord
aboute that time departea
this life which implyeth
that she was aboute 72.
yeares aged before she
dyed. (z) M. *Raynolds*
in his conference pag.
489. *circa med.*   (a) As in the firſter place by theſe wordes, *then after*
three yeares I came to Hierusalem, he meant the third yeare after his conuerſion, ſo alſo in the latter place by his like phraſe *then after* 14. *yeares*
I went vp againe to Hierusalem he likewiſe meant as before the 14. yeare
after his conuerſion. (b) *Caluin in omnes Pauli Epiſt. in Gallat. 2. verſ.*
1. *fine.* ſpeaking of the ſaid 3. and 14. yeares ſaith, *porro quatuorde-*
cim auros accipio non ab vna profectione ad alteram, verum vt supputatio sem -
per a Pauli conuerſione incipiat, ita vndecim anni inter duos ascensus fuerunt:
So plainly doth he alſo diſſolue M. *Raynoldes* argument. (c) *Lubber-*
us in libro de Papa Romano printed 1594. pag. 814. geueth ſundry
examples againſt the argument framed from the computation of times
saying

unknowne to any: Adde herenuto that *Cedrenus,*
& *Epiphanius Presbiter* report (from teſtimony
before their times) that ſhe was (y) 72. *yeares*
aged before ſhe dyed: that alſo our learned
aduerſary M. (*) *Hammer* accordingly ſetteth
downe her death to be *Anno Dom.* 56. both
which afford *Dionysius* time enough to be after
his conuerſiō preſent at the Virgins death ſuppoſing his ſaid conuerſion had beene (z) *sea-*
uenteene or eighteene yeares at the leaſt after Chriſts
Ascention as M. *Raynoldes* vpō the ſecond poinſ
of his inferring premiſes vrgeth : now as concerning the ſaid ſecond point, that this alſo is
as incertaine as the firſt, appeareth in that no
neceſſity is that the foreſaid *three yeares* and
fouretene yeares ſhould be ſeueral, the (a) phraſe
rather arguing to the contrary, that both of
them do relate from the time of *Paules* conuerſiō, & thatſo the latter number being the greater doth comprehend the firſt, accordingly
euen as (b) *Caluin* him ſelf expoundeth the
ſame, ſo diuerſly and eaſily is diſſolued this
maine pretended obiection drawn from the
computation of time : A kind of argnment in
it ſelf otherwiſe ſo incertaine that our learned,
(c) aduerſaries them ſelues do in other ſpecially matter

*saying, Inter vos Papiſtas non conuenit quo tempore Petrus Romam venerit &c.
inter vos non conuenit quiſquam Petro ſucceſſerit &c. inter vos non conuenit
quo tempore Iudith Holophernem occiderit &c. Inter Prophanos hiſtoricos
non conuenit quo tempore bellum Troianum geſtum ſit &c. inter ſcriptores Ec-
cleſiaſticos non conuenit quo tempore Propheta vixerint &c. doceri non poteſt*

ally reiect it.

(10) Fiftly it is obiected by M. *Whitaker*
and M. *Raynoldes*, firſt that in *Dioniſius* b is writinges now extant is (d) *cited a ſaying of Ignatius out of an Epiſtle which he wrote to the Romanes
as he was going to ſuffer martyrdome* (2) *in the time
of Traiane:* wheras *Dioniſius him ſelfe was deade before* (3) *in the time of Domitian:* Secondly when
Ignatius wrote it (4) *Oneſimus was Biſhop of Epheſus, who ſucceded Tymothie,* wheras this counterfaite
Dioniſius alledgeth it (5) to Tymothie Biſhop of E-
pheſus, either after his deceaſe or before it was written. Thus farre M. *Raynoldes* wherto I anſwere
in order, and concerning the firſt, which conſi-
ſteth wholly vpon ſuppoſal that *Dioniſius* was
deade in the time of *Domitian* and *Ignatius* afterwardes dead in the time of *Traian,* In anſwere
therto (as lamenting the want of (*) *Theodorus
presbiters* booke mentioned by *Photius* which
would geue great light to this matter) I further
ſay, that for ſo much as confeſſedly there was
but (e) *one yeare two Monethes and eight dayes* betweene the ſeueral raignes of *Domitian* & *Traian*
during which meane time *Nerua* reigned ſuccee-
ding *Domitian,* the witnes alledged by M. *Raynoldes* to proue the ſeueral deathes of *Ignatius* &
Dioniſius
ſuppoſed title or inſcription of that booke. (*) See heretofore ſect.
6. in the margent at 7. *Photius* his teſtimony of *Theodorus Presbiter*
concerning the fourth obiection there recited (e) M. *Couper* late Biſhop of *Wincheſter* in his Cronicle *fol.* 106. a. *fine* ſaith, *Nerua* followed *Domitian in the Empire and reigned one yeare, two monethes, & eirht dayes,*

quo tempore *Iob fuit, an
propterea nunquam fuit?*
apagé has nugas.
(d)
M. *Raynoldes* in his cō-
ference pag. 488. *pau-
lo ante med.* and M.
*Whitaker de ſacra Scrip-
tura controu.* 1. *quaſt.*
6. Pag. 658.
(2)
M. *Raynoldes* alledgeth
for this *Euſebius in Cronico.*
(3)
For this, *Methodius in
Martyrio Dioniſy.*
(4)
For this, *Ignat. in E-
piſt. ad Epheſ.*
(5)
For this, *Dioniſius Are-
opagit. Epiſcopus Athe-
narum ad Timotheum
Epiſcopum Epheſi.* be-
ing M. *Raynodes* his

D   &c

&c. *Traian a Spaniard borne, after Nerua was admitted to the Emperial authority*.

(f)

M. *Foxe* Act. and Mon. printed 1576. pag. 38. a. *initio*. profeſſing to write of the martyrdom of thoſe who ſuffered in the firſt perſecutiõs, excuſeth him ſelf before hand ſaying, *it is impoſſilbe to keepe perfect order and courſe of yeares and tymes &c. eſpecially ſeeing that the authors them ſelues do diſagree in the times & kinde of martyrdõme of them that ſuffered*.

(g)

Suydas de vita Dioniſy apud Lipom. de vitis Sanctorum ſaith, *prouecta iam & decrepita ætate Dioniſius ſpiritus*

Dioniſius liuing ſo long after their deceaſes might incurre, or rather could not auoide, a farre greater miſtaking of the time of their ſeueral deaths, or at leaſt (which would ſuffice againſt this obiection) of the death of thone of them, then the foreſaid ſhort interim betweene the reigne of *Domitian* and *Traian*, doth amount vnto : A thing ſo euident that M. (f) *Foxe* confeſſeth the variable incertianty of the late reporters of thoſe auncient times : As alſo *Suydas* reporteth (and as is like vpon credit of auncient teſtimony before his time) that (g) *Dioniſius dyed in the time of Traian* : And the ſame is alſo affirmed by *Michael* (h) *Syngelus*, wheras others namely S . *Beda* and *Ado* drawe it yet further to the (i) time of *Adrian*, who ſucceeded *Traian* : *Ado* (k) alledging in profe therof an auncient writer of thoſe firſter times called *Ariſtides*, mentioned by S. (l) *Hierom*. In reſpect of which ſo variable premiſes M. D. *Humfrey* ſaith, (m) *The time of Dioniſius martyrdome is not agreed vpon among the Hiſtoriographers*: And may then this foreſaid obiection, (at the beſt, but
of

martyrio pro Chriſto conſummatur Traiano Cæſare imperante . (h) *Michael Syngelus in orat. de Dioniſio apud Lipomanum de vitis Sanctorum* ſaith, *Beatum Dioniſy agonem in poſtremis Traiani regni diebus fuiſſe accepimus* . (i) *Dioniſius Areopagita ſub Adriano principe poſt clariſſimam confeſſionem fidei, poſt grauiſſima tormentorum genera, glorioſo martyrio Coronatur. ſee this apud Bedam et Adonem die 3. Octobr* . (k) *Ado* addeth in profe therof ſaying, *vt Ariſtides Athenienſis vir fide ſapientiaq̃ mirabilis, teſtis eſt in eo opere quod de Chriſtiana religione compoſuit* . (l) *Hierom. in Catal. in Ariſtide* ſaith, *Ariſtides Athenienſis philoſophus, et ſub priſtino habitu diſcipulus Chriſti, volumen noſtri dogmatis rationem continens, eodem tempore quo et Quadratus Adriano principi dedit apologeticam pro Chriſtianis* . Therefore this *Ariſtides*, being, as was *Dioniſius*, of *Athens* and a Philoſopher, and in the ſame time with him, doth in his foreſaide booke
mentioned

mentioned likewise by S. *Hierome*, afforde much stronger proofe of *Dionisius* his death to be in *Adrians* time, then doth M. *Raynoldes* latter testimony to proue it to haue bene in *Domitians* time . (m) *Humfred. in Iesuetismi part . 2 . rat . 5 . pag . 513 . fine* . speaking of *Dionisius* his death saying, *Inter Historicos non constat de martyrij tempore* .

of great incertainty) afford any certaine argument against the so long time receiued writinges of *Dionisius*? Or is not the feeling weakenes of this kind of argument thus drawen from the variable reportes of Historiographers in their computation of times by our aduersaries (n) confessed, and otherwise made familiarlly knowen by the like domestical examples euery where occurring in our owne (o) Cronicles: And thus much of this firster pointe, wherto if neede were, might be added yet further answere . Concerning now the Second pointe of obiected repugnancie, which is, that when *Ignatius* wrote his foresaid Epistle cited by *Dionisius*, *Timothie was deade*, (p) *Onesimus being then Bishop of Ephesus*, and succeeding *Timothie*, wheras *Dionisius* directeth after *Timothies* death, his said booke wherin he so cyteth *Ignatius* euen to *Timothie* (him self as being then) *Bishop of Ephesus* . In answeare hereof, ouer and besides that which haith bene (q) already said concerning the great incertianty of argument taken from the computation of times, especially concerning thinges hapned in the Apostolicke age, wherof is not now extant any one special history or obseruatiō made within the first 300 . *yeares* after Christ: I further say only now as admitting that

(n)
Heretofore sect. 9 . in the margine at c .

(o)
This is euident in the variable report made by our Cronicles of King *Iohns death* : wherof see *Holinshead* in his last Edition the 3 . volume. pag . 194. b .)

(p)
Whereas M . *Raynoldes* obiecteth *Ignatius Epist . ad Ephes.* this indeede mentioneth that *Onesimus* was then Bishop there, but yet not that *Timothie* was then deade .

(q)
See heretofore sect. 9 . in the margen at c . & sect. 10 . in the margen at f . and o .

Timothie had bene deade whē *Ignatius* wrote his said Epistle to the Romans : First it doth not appeare that *Timothie* to whom *Dionisius*, directed his said booke *de diuinis nominibus*, was the same *Timothie* that was scholer to *Paul* & Bishope of Ephesus ; for that foresaid title or inscription seemeth to haue beene but the addition of some later scribe or publisher

lisher

(r)
This is the title of his booke *de Ecclesiastica Hierarchia.*

(s)
So he tearmeth him in the very first beginning of his booke *de Ecclesiastica Hierarchia*, & in the very end of that booke he further saith, *Hæc a me fili tam multa tamq, præclara &c.*

(t)
That there was then others of that name appeareth by examples of one *Timothie* who being sonne to the noble Roman senator *Pudens*, was Preist and disciple to S. *Paul* of whom mention is made in *Martirol. Ro.* 20. *Iun.* and more aunciently, *in actis Praxedis & Puden. apud Baronium* at *An.* 159. *sect.* 8.

(u)
Dionisius Alexandrinus apud Euseb. hist. l. 7. c. 20. *Paulo post med.* saith concerning S. *Iohn, multi propter singularem amorem quo erga illum affecti erant &c. & propter æmulatione qua ad illum imitandum flagrabant &c. etiam istam appellationem amplexati, sunt quemadmodum nomina Pauli & Petri fideliū liberi crebro ferunt.*

lish, vpon coniecture that there was then no other of that name but onely the foresaid *Timothie:* wheras the true title, as appeareth by his other next precedent booke directed likewise to the same *Timothie*, was but (r) *compresbitero Timotheo Dionisius presbiter:* whom he also tearmeth (s) *Sanctissime fili Timothee*; therby signifying some (t) other yonger person vpon whom was perhaps (in honour or loue of the other) imposed the name of *Tomothie*, the like wherof was in these times very (u) vsual: Secondly I say as supposing now yet further that *Dionisius* his booke had beene written to *Timothie* Bishop of *Ephesus*, that it is not incredible that *Dionisius* hauing written his said booke to the said *Timothie* should yet afterwardes enlarge the same with new additions, for as S. (x) *Hierome* wel obserueth, euery writer hath power ouer their owne writhinges to renew and amend them at their owne pleasure, in which case of addition or enlargement vpon renewing, *Dionisius* might wel after *Timothies* death alledge or cite *Ignatius* his foresaid Epistle to the Romanes: like (y) examples in which agreeing of latter incerted additions improper and not agreeing to the time of the firster edition of the same bookes are daly fresh and occuring: Thirdly wheras the whole difficulty of his receiued repugnancie doth consist vpon supposal that *Dionisius* should cite the foresaid sentence of *Ignatius* out of his Epistle to the Romans, at the writing wherof we suppose *Timothie* to haue bene deade: The obiection hereof is much lesse forcible in that *Dionisius* onely alledgeth the sentence vnder the

(z)

the name of *Ignatius* in general, without naming or cyting therefore in particuler the foresaid Epistle to the Romans, or any other place of *Ignatius* his writinges: So as it is not (for sundry (z) reasons) so clearely certaine, that *Dionisius* cyted those wordes as from *Ignatius* his Epistle to the Romans, which is the onely cheife pointe now questionable: so many waies is the supposed certanty of the foresaid obiection made incertaine; and so thereby auoided. In which course of obiecting such like seeming repugnancies, if a curious and vnsatisfied witte should yet further labour against the knowen writinges of the other Fathers, or (which is more) against the sacred Scriptures, what like knowen seeming difficulty (though against the (a) Scriptures them selues) might

(z)
For like as the Apostle repeateth in seueral places this one sentence of *our burial with Christ through Baptisme*, Rom. 6. 4. & Colos. 2. 12. also this other, *a litle leauen doth leauen the whole lumpe*. (1. Cor. 5. 6. & Gal. 5. 9.) in like maner this third, *he that reioyceth let him reioice in the Lord*, 1. Cor. 1. 31. & 2. Cor. 10. 17.) wherto might be added diuers others, as

Ephes. 5. 15. 16. & Colos. 4. 5. and elswhere. So likewise it may wel be that *Ignatius* did in like maner often repeate in his writinges the foresaid sentence, *my loue is crucified*, and so much the rather, by how much it is more then ordinarily passionate as flowing from the sacred abundance of his enflamed heart: And though the said sentence be not as now extant in any of his writinges, other then his said Epistle to the Romans, yet that enforceth not, as appeareth, not onely by example of certaine other confessed sentences of *Ignatius* not to be found in his writinges now extant, wherof see hertofore *sect.* 4. throughout: but also by further testimonie that *Ignatius* his writinges be not al of them now extant: for that he wrote more Epistles then we now haue, appeareth by these wordes: *Ego scribo omnibus Ecclesijs & omnibus mando, quia voluntarie pro Deo morior, si vos non prohibueritis. (in Epist. ad Romanos ante med.)* And *Eusebius hist. l. 3. c. 30.* (and after *M. Hanmers* translation l. 3. c. 32.) signifyeth a special treatise of his concerning *Apostolicke Traditions*. (a) To geue a taste hereof by some few examples in the Scriptures: in *Math. 27. 9.* are wordes alledged vnder the name of *Hieremie*, which are not found in *Hieremie*, but in *Zacharie*, 11. 13. Also in *Marc. 15. 25.* our Sauiour is said to be crucified *in the third hower*, wheras in S. *Iohn. 19. 14.*

Pilate

Pilate fate in iudgement vpon him *aboute the fixt hower*, likewife S. *Luke*
3. 35. 36. affirmeth *Sale, to be the fonne of Caynan, and Caynan the fonne*
of Arphaxad, and fo *Arphaxad* was Grandfather to *Sale*. But in Genefis 11. 12. it is faid that, *Arphaxad liued* 35. *yeares and begate Sale*,
vpon which faid laſt dificulty, though *Beza in Nou. Teſt.* of 1556. to
reconcile *Luke* with *Genefis* doth in the faid 3. Chapter of *Luke*
verf. 36. alter S. *Lukes* greeke text, leauing out thefe wordes,
who was the fonne of Caynan, and is therin defended by M. *Fulke* in his
defence of the Englifh tranflations againſt M. *Martin* in the preface
feɕ̃. 18. *pag.* 41. and by him alfo in that omiſſion imitated in his
tranflation placed with the *Rhemiſtes:* yet the Englifh Bibles of 1576.
and others dare not fol-
low his bould example | might thence arife I leaue to the confiderati-
therein. | on of thofe that be learned.

<table>
<tr><td>

(b.)
The *Centuriſts Centur.* 1.
l. 2. c. 10. col. 637.
line 57. faith, *primum e-*
nim quis non miretur tan-
tum Pauli difcipulum et A-
poſtolum beneficij couerfionis
& amicitiæ cum Preceptore
tam omnino potuiſſe obliuifci,
vt ne vno quidem in loco
Pauli meminerit, aut eius
authoritate qnæ tradit fe
fcribere, teſtetur.

(c)
Dionifius in libro de Ecclef.
Hierarch. c. 2. alled-
geth S. *Paul* to *Timothie*
faying, *vt enim chariſſimus*
præceptor noſter dicit &c.

</td><td>

(11) Sixtly it is obiected by the *Centu-*
riſtes, that *Dionifius* in thefe his writinges (b)
neuer remembreth his maiſter S. Paul, nor pro-
feſſeth to write by his authority: whereto I an-
fweare, that if this were true and not miſta-
ken, yet were it but an obiection fcarce fo
much as coniectural, rather then prouing.
Secondly I fay it is vntrue, for *Dionifius* ma-
keth fpecial acknowledgment of (c) his M.
S. *Paul*, (d) alledging often throughout his
writinges, his authority.

The *laſt* obiection, fcarce worthy of recytal
or anfweare, is frô M. *Raynoldes*, (e) obiec-
ting that *Dionifius* faith concerning the bap-
tifme of infants, (f) *hereof we fay thofe thinges*
which our diuine maiſters being inſtructed by the
auncient Traditiô haue deliured vnto vs: wheras
faith M. (g) *Raynoldes Chriſt inſtructed the*
⁀ *Apoſtles*

</td></tr>
</table>

(d) Throughout his bookes ⁀ frequent allegations of S. *Paules* fayinges, onely to conuince the Centuries of vntruthes: let the reader but
obferue the feueral teſtimonies of S. *Paul* alledged in that booke *de*
Ecclef. Hierarch. c. 3. & c. 12. (e) M. *Raynoldes* in his conference
pag. 486. *fine.* (f) *Dionif, de Ecclef. Hierach.* c. 7. (g) M. *Ray-*
noldes

Apostles in Baptisme, they had it not from ould Tradition. whereto I answeare that Christes instruction, was this auncient (or first) traditio, which also
he might aptly cal auncient, not as though it were
long before the Apostles times (for who can
thinke him so insensible) but in reguard aswel of
the the first institutio therof by christ which was
auncient, as hauingnone firster, as also of the o-
ther there confuted nouel doctrine, of some who
(h) deryded the baptisme of Infants, in respect al
so of which said Nouel doctrine, he might wel
tearme this other, first, or auncient.

Hitherto concerning the writinges of Dionisius Areopagita mentioned in the (i) Actes to
be converred by S. Paul: In behalf of which
his writinges I haue the more willingly laboured, in respect of the frequent and abounding testimonies therin found of our Catholicke faith, as confessedly of (2) Apostolicke
vnwritten traditions: of (3) Chrisme, (4) Conse-
eration of Monkes: (5) diuers orders of Angels,
(6) Trinal immersion in Baptisme, (*) Interrogatories ministred vnto Infants in Baptisme; (7) prayer for the deade: and (8) sixe (of our) Sacraments
also of (9) Chancels seuered with sanctification
from the rest of the Church, into which laye persons
might not enter; of (10) the tonsure and rasure of

noldes vbi supra, pag.
487. initio.

(h)
Dionis. de Eccles. Hie-
rarch. a litle there af-
terwardes prope finem
libri. where he saith,
illi prouidentes dicunt, ali-
um pro alio diuinis sacris
initiet &c.

(i)
Act. 17. 34.

(2).
Hamelmanus de Apo-
stolicis Traditionibus col.
707. line 27. saith,
multa sine Scriptis tradi-
disse Apostolos ait Dio-
nisius. & vide ibid. col.
736. l. 56. & Whita-
ker de sacra Scriptura
pag. 655. ante med.

(3)
Hamelmannus de trad.
Apost. Col. 707. line 4.
& col. 732. line 51.

(4)
Preistes Hamelmannus vbi supra

col. 707. line 49. saith, Consecratio Monachi apud Dionisium pro traditione refertur. & vide col. 743. line 4. (5) Hamelmannus Ibid. col.
707. line 13. & col. 734. line 23. (6) Ibid. col. 741. line 24. (*)
See heretofore sect. 5. in the margen at q. (7) M. Fulke in his confutation of Purgatory pag. 353. (8) Humfred in Iesuitismi part 2. pag.
519. circa med. and Luther Tom. 2. Witenberg. An. 1562. de cap. bab.
fol. 82. b. ante med. saith, scio hunc (Dionisium) solum authorem haberi
ex antiquis, qui pro septenario Sacramentorum, licet Matrimonio omisso,
senarium tantum dederit. (9) M. Raynoldes in his coference &c. pag
488. post med. (10) Abraham Scultetus in his medulla Patrum pag. 484
circ

circa med. faith, *in libro de Ecclefiaftica Hierarchia multa fcribit (Dioni-fius) de Altaribus, de locis facris, de choro, de confecratione, Monachorum & de tonfura et rafione capitum.*

(11)
Hofpinianus in hift. fa-cram. part. 1. pag. 104. poft med. faith, *in Liturgia Dionifij incenfum in altari adoletur.*

(12)
Hamelmannus de trad. Apoftol. col. 742. line 33. and *Hofpinianus vbi fupra.* (13)
Hamelmannus de trad. A-poft. col. 741. line 41. faith, *multa refert (Dionifius) de templis, Altaribus, locis fanctis, quomodo extra Templi ambitum collocentur Catechumini, &c. ac de varijs ceremonijs.*

Preiftes heades: of (11) perfuming or burning Incenfe at the Altar, of (12) mutual falutation vpon the Pax pronounced, of (13) Altars places fanctified, and diuers Ceremonies. wherto I adde that he further mentioneth fundry Ceremonies of Baptifme, as namely (14) Exorcifme, Abrenuntiation, figne of the Croffe, Vnction, confecration of the water of Baptifme, Godfathers, the white garment: and then as next after in order enfuing the Bifhop annoynting with Chrifme the party Baptized: alfo he yet further mentioneth (15) Preifts, Alters, confecration of them with infufion of facred Oyle, (16) offering of the healthful facrifice which Chrift commaunded (17) the Preiftes wafhing his fingers, and the (18) remoual of Catechumines, penitents, and parties poffeffed before facrifice, as vnworthy to behould, the fame, the (19) Preiftes vncouering of the
^ Sacrament

(14) *Dionif. de Eccles. Hierarch. c. 2.* faith, *infufflare illum ter fatanam ac praeterea abrenuntiationem profiteri &c.* at vero Pontifex trino Crucis fancta fignaculo, vnctionem inchoans inungendum iam Sacerdotibus toto corpore hominem tradit, ipfe ad adoptionis matrem proficifcitur, eiufq; aquas fancta prece ac inuocatione fanctificans &c. Iubet adferri hominem, et cum illum eiufq; fufceptorem quifpiam facerdotum ex defcriptione celfa voce praedicauerit, &c. ter illum Pontifex mergit &c. et illum veftem Baptizati munditia congruam induunt, ficq; indutum rurfum ad Pontificem ducunt, ille diuino ac deifico prorfus vnguento virum fignans &c.* (15) See thefe hereafter tract 3. fect. 2. fubdiuif. 5. at s. t. (16) Ibid. at * next after t. (17) See this hereafter tract. 2. fect. 1. fubd. 1. at i. (18) Dionifius de Ecclef. Hierarch. cap. 3. faith, *ea recitata extra Templi ambitum collocantur Catechumini, Energumini atq; ij quos fuperioris vitae paenitet, manent autem ij qui diuinarum rerum afpectu digni funt,* & fomwhat afterwardes he further, faith of thefe, *ad facra autem opera quae deinceps fequuntur atq; mifteria fpectanda non eos conuocat (Pontifex) fed perfectos oculos eorum qui digni funt.* (19) De
Ecclef.

Ecclef. Hierarch. c. 3. he faith, At vero Pontifex &c. facrofancta & Augustissima misteria conficit, & que ante laudauerat venerandis operta atq, abdita fignis in confpectum agit, diuinaq, munera reuerenter oftendens. &c.

(20)
Sacrament and reuerend fhewing therof: And yet furthet tearmeth the external Symbols or fa- crament (20) *venerable fignes*, Di on o Chriftos femainetai cai metechetai ✓ *by which Chrift is both fignified and receiued* : not forbearing laftly to mention our Catholieke doctrine of (21) Freewil, and to tearme S. (22) *Peter the cheife and moft auncieut top (or height) of the Apoftles.*

(12) As concerning the *Liturgies* now ex-tant vnder the names of *S . Bafile* and *Chrifoftome*, I do alledge in proofe of them, that they haue bene alledged aboue eleuen hundred yeares fince by (k) *Proclus* Bifhop of Conftantinople, S. *Bafiles liturgie* being alfo alledged by S . *Damaf-cene*, and (*) in the *fecond Nicene councel*, and yet further efpecially mentioned and alledged about fome 1000. yeares fince by the Fathers of the fixt (1) *councel at Conftantinople*: Alfo the grecian Bifhops

De Ecclef. Hierarch. c. 3.

(21)
Dionifius de Ecclef. Hi-erarch. c. 9. faith, *neq enim coactam habemus vitam , neq, liberi arbi-trij gratia diuinitus da-ta mortalibus prouiden-tia diuina luce et fplen-dore obtunditur.* And fee him further *de di-uinis nominibus c . 4 . part . 4 .*

(22)
Dionifius de diuinis no-minibus, c 3. and fee his wordes fo engli-fhed by D . *Raynoldes*

in his conference pag. 485 . *ante med.* (k) *Proclus Conftantinop . de tradi-tione diuin. liturg .* telling how *Bafile*, and *Chrifoftome*, abridged for their feueral Churches, the more auncient Liturgie of their precedent times , faith, *magnus porro poftea Bafilius hominum focordiam, & ignauiam confpi-ciens &c. eofq, ob id longitudinis miffæ pertefos, &c. vt orantium atq, au-dientium ignauiam atq, pigritiam præcideret, propterea quod multum in ea tem-pors poneretur breuiorem recitandam dedit: &c. haud multo poft pater nofter Iohannes cui aurea lingua cognomen dedit &c. hominum naturæ focordiam atq, ignauiam profpiciens &c. multa præcidit, & vt breuior effet conftituit &c.*. And fee the like anfwearable teftimony here next after o. (*) See the wordes of S . *Bafiles liturgie* alledged by S . *Damafcene* l . 4 . c . 14 . & by *Epiphanius* in the 2 . *Nicene councel Act . 6 . Tom . 3 .* (1) *Concil . 6 . Conftantinop. in Trullo Can .* 32 . to proue the mingling of water with wine in the Chalice alledgeth *S . Bafiles liturgie* faying *Iacobus fra-ter Domini, & Bafilius Cefarienfis Archiepifcopus miftico nobis in fcripto tradito*

E

tradito facrificio, ita peragendum in facro mifterio ex aqua et vino facrum poculum ediderunt, which mixtion is yet now accordingly found in *Bafiles liturgie*.

(m)
Nicholaus Cabafila in liturgia expofit. cap. 29. fine faith, *et oratione quidem facramenta peragere tradiderunt Patres, qui ab Apoftolis & qui eis fuccefferunt, acceperunt &c. poft multos alios magnus Bafilius & Iohannes Chrifoftomus &c.*

(n)
Nicholaus Methonenfis, de corp. & fang. Chrifti.

(o)
Marchus Ephefius de corp. & fang. Chrfti faith, *his confequentes & qui poftea lyturgiam ipfam concifiorem e-*

Bifhops of later times, namely, (m) *Cabafilas* (n) *Methonenfis, Marcus* (o) *Ephefius, &* (p) *Beffarion*, do ackonwledge and receiue the faid Liturgics. And (¶) *Germanus* who fucceeded after *Chrifoftome* in the fea of *Conftantinople*, and liued 900. yeares fince, doth by a fpecial treatife, wherein he mentioneth and explicateth moft of the partes & ceremonies contained in *Chrifoftomes Liturgies*, geue fufficient or rather abounding teftimony that fuch a like Liturgie was then long before his owne time, precedent, and in being: furthermore the Liturgie of *Chrifoftome* hath bene alwaies placed among his workes, and reputed as parcel therof, and demonftrably proued to be in al cheife partes agreeable (*) & confonant

diderunt, tum magnus ille Bafilius tum poft eum Iohannes Chrifoftomus &c. (p) *Beffarion de Euchariftia facram et quibus verbis Chrifti corpus conficitur,* alledgeth S. *Bafiles* and *Chrioftomes* liturgies, faying, *magnus Doctor Bafilius. rogamus (inquit) vt veniet fpiritus fanctus tuus fuper nos & hæc propofita munera &c. Diuus autem Chrifoftomus emitte (ait) fpiritum tuum & fac hunc panem pretiofum corpus Chrifti tui &c.* And there afterwardes he exprefly nameth the feueral *Maffes* (or *Liturgies*) of *Bafile* and *Chrifoftome.* (¶) *Germanus in his rerum Ecclefiafticarum, Theoria,* mentioneth with explication (therof in many thinges) not only al the particulers concerning the *Church, Chancel, Veftrie, Alter, Veffels, thurible, &c.* and the *Preiftes Stoale, Albe, Girdle, Humeral,* and other Preiftly apparel for feruice time, but alfo al the other partes of thefe Liturgies, namely the *Antiphona,* the *Introite, Allelluia,* the *Preifts figning,* (or bleffing) *of the people,* the *Catechumines being conmaunded to bowe their heades, the Preiftes wafhing of his handes, the vaile before the Altar, the Preifts figning of the* facramental creatures &c. *praier for the deade, the kiffe of peace, eleuation of the Sacrament, with makeing of three Croffes in the aier, partition thereof after eleuation,* befides fundry other Ceremonies and whole fentences

ouer

ou er tedious to rehearse, yet accordingly found in the Liturgie of S. Chrisostome, predecessor to Germanus, in the same sea of Constantinople. (*) That this Liturgie attributed to Chrisostome is no other then wholly consonant with Chrisostoms workes, see a special treatise in profe therof, intituled, de Euchariſtiæ & Miſſa ritibus ex operibus D. Chriſoſtomi &c. authore Claudio de Sainctes. where most partes of the Maſſe are proued from Chriſoſtoms other

consonant therto: and the greeke Church doth stil to (q) this day, so esteeme both of Basiles Liturgie, and it, and doth daily sing them in their Churches according to certaine (r) distribution of times apointed seuerally for them, so as we haue no lesse proofe of these Liturgies to be theirs, then we haue for the Psalme of Quicunq; vult to be made by Athanasius. A thing so euident that Daniel (s) Chamierus a learned aduersary, doth for such alledge and acknowledge Chrisostomes Liturgie, as also the Proteſtant writer (t) Hamelmannus doth in like maner acknowledge both the said Liturgies of S. Basile and Chrisostome. and alledgeth them as proper to the times in which S. Basile and S. Chrisostome liued: wherto might be added like further acknowledgement made by other (u) Proteſtant writers

workes.

(q)
To this day, as appeareth by the booke entituled Acta theologorū Wirtembergentiũ & Patriarchæ Conſtantinop. D. Hieremia &c. printed at Wittenberg. 1584. pag. 103. where the said Patriarch saith, An propter nimiam fortaſſe prolixitatem hac a magno patre noſtro Baſilio, et deinde a Chriſoſtomo ad compendium redacta, de hoc nihil certi habetur, hoc tamen

constat ab antiquo iam duos tomos nobis traditos eſſe, et authenticos agnoſci, ex quibus liturgiam celebramus, tum ipſius magni Baſilij, tum S. patris Iohannis Chriſſoſtomi &c. (r) The same Patriarch there next after saith of these two Liturgies, ex his sacris duobus Codicibus miſtici sacrificij ritum obimus: atq; dominicis quidem per magnam quadragesimam paschatis diebus & nonnullis alijs Baſilij tomus recitatur ex eiuſq; preſcripto sancta miſſa misterium peragitur, reliquis vero diebus Chrisostomi. (s) Daniel Chamierus in his Epiſtolæ Iesuiticæ part. 1. pag. 58. ante med. answereth that the teſtimonies alledged from Theophilact and Damascene, touching the Sacrament being literally taken, cannot be true, contra dicentibus antiquioribus et maioris nominis viris. Basilius in Liturgia panē et vinũ Antitupa nominat &c. his teſtibus, quis Damascenum opponat sanus aut Theophilactum. (t) Hamelmannus l. de Traditionibus Apostolicis, Col. 741. fine. saith, circa Chriſoſtomi

E 2 &

& Basilij tempora, vt ex eorum lyturgijs & reliquis libris patet, ille mos serua-
tus est, vt ministri starent pretempli foribus &c. (u) *Sutlife de missa Pa-*
pistica l. 1. c. 29. pag. 151. *circa med.* saith, *per verba invocationis in-*
telligit Basilius verba consecrationis, vt ex Chrisostomi & Basily verbis (in
missis qua illis ascribuntur)

& gracarum liturgiarum formulis liquet. &c.

(*)

Hererfter in this preface sect. 16. in the margent at (*) next after b.

(x)

M. *Iewel* in his reply pag. 10. *prope initium.*

(y)

Mornay in his treatise against the *Masse* (after the english translation) pag. 51. *circa med.* saith thereof, *not onely Chrisostome is mentioned and prayed vnto in certaine copies, but many moe Sainctes who liued after Chrisostome &c.* And M. *Parkines* in his problem. &c. pag. 27. *fine.* saith likewise hereof, *Exemplaria multum variat: inter sanctos qui ibi comme-morantur ipsius Chrisostomi fit mentio.*

(z)

In the communion booke composed in king Edwardes time, are according

writers. And thus much of their proofe: As for the liturgie of S. *Iames* I refer to that which is (*) hereafter said therof.

(13) As concerning the obiections pretended in denial of these Liturgies of S. *Basile* and *Chrisostome.* Against S. *Chrisostomes* liturgie M. *Iewel* obiecteth that (x) *Chrisostoms Masse prayeth for Pope Nicholas, who was Pope An.* 857. *almost* 500. *yeares after Chrisostome*; (that) *it also prayeth for the Emperour Alexius, the first of that name, liuing An. Dom.* 1080. *and after the decease of Chrisostom* 700. *yeares.* Thus farre M. *Iewel,* with much further thereupon ensuing insultation of speach against this liturgy; wherto *Philippe Mornay* addeth that (y) *in some copies* (of that liturgie) *Chrisostome* (him self) *is named and prayed vnto*: whereto I answeare, (in ful discouery of these friuolouse cauiles) first that in al ould liturgies, praier is specially appointed to be made for Princes and Bishops, for the names of whom are certaine places which are subiect to alteration according to the chaunge of succeeding times, & persos, the like course wherof (for Princes) as we may discerne in the english (z) comunion booke, so also that it did likewise take place in those copies from whence the examples now obiected are taken, is made euidet by

to the chaunge of succeeding gouernemet inserted the names of Queene Elizabeth in some copies, and of his now most excellent maiesty in others, and yet both of them reigned after king Edward: No lesse then

did

by the prayer here made for Pope *Nicholas*: for otherwise if (with M. *Iewel*) we take him to be *Nicholas* Bishop of Rome who liued (saith M. *Iewel*) Anno. 857. and as he truly inferreth in a seueral age from *Alexius*, who (according to M. *Iewels* computation) liued *An.* 1080. then may we not thinke any man to haue bene so absurd a forger as to publish this liturgie vnder the name of *Chrisostome* who liued *An. Dom.* (a) 390. and withal to make shew of prayer therin, not for any vnknowen or fained persons, but for a certaine knowne Prince, and a like certaine knowne Bishop, as though they were then liuing, who indeed liued not onely sundry ages after *Chrisostome*, but also aboue 200. yeares thone after thother. On the other part if we take as the truth is, and as M. D. *Fulke* who (refyning M. *Iewels* obiections as being other-wise too absurd) doth for his greater aduantage (b) confesse the said *Nicholas* to haue bene not *Nicholas* Bishop of Rome, but *Nicholas* who in the dayes of the foresaid *Alexius* was Patriarch of the sea of Côstâtinople, which sea both before & since (c) clamed the title of vniuersal, yet thence also followeth a like incredible absurdity, as naely, to forge a liturgy in the name of *Chrisostô*, who was Bishop of Constantinople, and to make him pray therin for *Nicholas*, as being a knowen Bi-shop of the very same sea sundry hundreth yeares after: The *first answeare* therefore standeth true that the names of *Alexius* and *Nicholas* were in their times inserted into the liturgie then

did *Alexius* and *Nicholas*, enioy their dignities after *Chrisostome*.

(a)

M. *More* in his table affirmeth *Chrisostomes* deposal from his sea to haue bene *An.* 402.

(b)

M. *Fulke* against *Heskins, Saunders,* & pag. 674. *ante med.* saith, wheras M. *Saunders* v-seth many wordes & reasons to proue that this Pope *Nicholas* was not Bishop of Rome, as M. *Iewel* saith, but Patriarch of *Constantinople*, in the reigne of *Alexius*, I yeeld vnto him &c. And M. *Parkins* in his problem. &c. pag. 27. *fine.* saith, *Missa Chrisostomi habet precationem pro Alexio qui vixit longe post Chrisostomû, et pro Nicholao, siue Papa, siue Patriarcha Costantinopolitano.*

(c)

Of the claime to the formerly Title of vniuersal, made before these times by the Bishop of Constantinople, see the treatise entituled, *Sixe godly sermons &c.* printed 1608. by *Nicholas Okes* pag. 74. and *Crispinus* of the estate of the Church. pag. 179. *ante med.* of the now like late claime, see the booke entituled *Acta theologorum Wirtebergensium & Patriarcha Constantinop. D. Hieremia &c.* printed

Witebergiæ 1584. pag. 55. *initio*. where the said Patriarch calleth him selfe the *Oecumenicke Patriarch*, and pag. 381. *initio*. where the Protestant Diuines do geue to him the title of *Oecumenicke Patriarch*, and of the like claime made by the greeke Church *Anno Dom*. 1024. but 60. yeares before the time now in question, see testimonie therof in *Baronius* at *Anno* .1024. *sect*.
5.

(d)

In liturg. Chrisostomi pag. 63. *post med*. it is said, *Nicholai sanctissimi & vniuersalis Papæ, longa ~~sunt~~ ~~sint tempora~~. Eleutherij Alexandriæ, Cirilli Antiochiæ, Leontij Hierosolymorū longa sint tempora.*

(e)

The Century writers *Cent*. 11. *col*. 401. *initio*. speaking of this *Eleuenth age* in which *Alexius* and the other Patriarches liued saith, *Greci sibi peculiarem deligunt Papam et occidentalem Ecclesiam audacter excommunicant &c*. so far then were they from praying for the Bishop of Rome. and *Ibid. col*. 401. line 47. they further mētion *the schisme betweene the Bishops of Rome & Constantinople* which by *Osianders* computation in his *Epitom. Centur*. 11.

formerly composed by *Chrisostome*, as in like maner his Maiesties now happie name is also inserted in the *Communion booke* composed in king Edwardes time, which thing appeareth yet more plainly by the other three Patriarches of the east (d) *Eleutherius of Alexandria, Cirillus of Antioch, and Leontius of Hierusalem*, who al, liuing in the same time with *Alexius*, and *Nicholas*, are in like maner in that foresaid copie accordingly named, and praied for, onely therein is omitted the name of the Bishop of Rome, for that in those very times & some litle before the same, the greeke Church was (e) diuided from the Romaine, & condemned the same, which omission of the one and inserting of the other, most euidently sheweth it self to haue proceeded not from the ignorant mistaking of any forger, as M. *Iewel* most indicretly pretendeth, but onely vpon a true incerting or alteration of names framed according to the historical truth of that succeeding age or tyme, in which the said Emperour and Patriarches liued : *Secondly* the foresaid *praier made to Chrisostome* which *Philippe Mornay*, and M. *Parkins* do, as (*) before mention to be found, but in a *certaine copie* argueth further (directly against M. *Parkins* (¶) *absurde* inference) an alteration of names

pag. 156. *post med*. hapned *Anno Dom*. 1050. by that accompte but few yeares before *Alexius*, who reigned, saith M. *Iewel*, *Anno* 1080. during which interim prayer was, as is before mentioned made for *Alexius*

names according to the variable succeeding times in which *Chrisostomes* name was inserted, & he accordingly praied vnto: for otherwise to thinke that one should forge this Liturgie vnder the name of *Chrisostome*, and withal pray therein to *Chrisostome* him selfe, as being then deade and in heauen, were incredibly absurd. Thirdly, this pointe is yet more euident, in that the common greeke copies extant in S. *Chrisostomes* workes, as also the translation of *Erasmus*, haue not in them the names of *Alexius*, *Nicholas*, and the other foresaid Patriarches, the which are onely found in that one special copie, which being at *Constantinople* deliuered to *Leo Thuscus*, was by him (f) translated into latine vpon the request of a noble man, called *Raynoldus de monte Catano*, and from that one copy thus translated, is M. *Iewels* foresaid obiection taken: hitherto concerning S. *Chrisostomes Liturgie*. Now as concerning S. *Basils Liturgie*, I do not (g) finde against it so much as any one obiection in particular, but onely a general and bould denyal thereof, in regard it maketh so

Alexius and the Patriarches of the east without any mention therin of like praier for the Bishop of Rome.

(*)

Next heretofore at y.

(¶)

Absurde, for whereas this manifest varietie in seueral copies of names, and persons liuing in seueral times, argueth the same most clearely to be as is beforesaid according to the true and historical varietie & alteration of times and persons: M. *Parkins in Problem*. pag. 27. *fine*. shutting his eyes against so cleare light would most strangely thereup-

fully pon inferre to the contrary, that this liturgie was indeed forged at seuerall times and by seuerall persons saying to that end, *exemplaria multum variant inter Sanctos, qui ibi commemorantur ipsius Chrisostomi sit mentio, ergo non ab ipso conscripta sed ab alijs sub illius nomine diuersis temporibus varijs editionj consuta.* (f) *Leo Thuscus in prolog. ad sanctan Græcorum missam ab eo verbis latinis diuulgatam ad Raynaldum de monte Catano, saith, cum venisses Constantinopolin. (nobilis Raynalde de monte Catano &c.) nil tibi potius occurrit quam sancta et ineffabils Eucharistiæ consecrationis ordinem perdiscere &c. qua de re postulasti a me, vt Græcorum rituum non intellectas voces quibus sacra et cælistia dona incruentæ hostiæ significaiur in latinam verterem tibi orationem &c.* (g) M. *Parkins* in his Problem &c. vndertaking to set downe the writinges forged vnder the Fathers names, & entreating to this end amongst many others of S. *Basile*, and of the writinges extant vnder his name, reiecteth diuers of them without al touch

touch or exception a-
gainst his liturgie: Al-
so M. *Iewel* who deny-
eth as before *Chrisostoms*
liturgie, doth yet (with-
out any denyal that I can
finde) acknowledge *S.*
Basiles Masse in his reply
pag. 50. *post med.*

(i)
In the liturgies of *Basile,*
Chrisostome and others,
printed in Octauo by
Christofer Plantin at *Ant-*
werpe Anno Dom. 1560.
fol. 34. b. *Basils litur-*
gie there saith, *intrant*
Ecclesiam Presbiter & Di-

fully with vs, and against our aduersaries.

(14) And thus much concerning the
wronged Liturgies of S. *Basile,* and *Chriso-*
stome; In examination wherof I haue bene
the more seriouse in that their authors being
Sainctes and worthy witnesses of the primitiue Churches doctrine, do in these their Liturgies geue cleare and euident testimonie of
(i) *Chancels,* (k) *Alter,* (l) *holy Corporals,*
(m) *Paten,* (n) *Thurible,* (o) *Vestrie,* also of
our Preistly apparel in Masse time, as namely,
and confessedly of (p) *the Amice, the Girdle,*
the Chisible, and the fanel, In like maner concerning the more substantial partes of the
Masse, (q) *mingling water with wine in the Cha-*
lice: of (r) *the Preists praier to be made worthy,*
or to consecrate and offer sacrifice, of (s) *his pray-*
er

aconus, & stantibus ante Cancellos, dicit Presbiter inclinato capite hanc orati-
enem secrete &c. And see *Chrisostoms* liturgie *fol.* 53. a. *circa med. &*
66. a. (k) See next hereafter at r. a. (l) *Chrisostoms* liturgie *fol.* 50.
a. *ante med.* saith, *Diacono tenente Thuribulum : Sacerdos explicat super*
Thuribulum sancta Corporalia sacro Calici superponenda. (m) See next
hereafter at the second. q. (n) See next before at l. (o) *Et in his*
missa terminatur vbi regressus fuerit Sacerdos in secretarium dicit hanc ora-
tionem in Chrisost. liturg. fol. 66. b. *post med.* And *pergunt in sacrari-*
um tollere vestimenta sua : in liturg. Basilij fol. 48. b. *fine.* (p) Confessed
by M. D. *Raynoldes* in his coference *pag.* 598. *post med.* (q) In *Chrisost.*
liturg. fol. 49. b. *fine.* it is said, *deinde facit comixtionem in Calicem*
mittens vinum et aquam &c. (r) In *Basils* liturgie *fol.* 40. a *post med.*
suscipe nos appropinquantes sancto Altari tuo, vt simus digni offerre tibi ra-
tionabile istud et absq; sanguine sacrificium pro nostris peccatis & populi igno-
rantia &c. suscipe seruitutem nostram sicut suscepisti Abel munera, Noe sa-
crificium &c. And *Chrisost. liturg. fol.* 53. a *fine.* saith, *fac nos dignos*
offerendo tibi preces, et hostiam incruentam pro vniuerso populo tuo. And i-
bidem fol. 59. b. *fac me dignum Sacerdotij gratia indutum assistere sanctæ*
tuæ mensæ, ac consecrare sactum corpus tuum, & pretiosum sanguinem. And
againe *fol.* 60. b. *fac nos offerre tibi dona, & sacrificium spirituale pro nostris*
peccatis

dignos

peccatis, & ignorantijs populi. (s) *Chrisost. Liturg. fol.* 58. a. *initio.*
faith, *et pro dormientibus in Christo memento Domine, et quacunq̃, in vita*
deliquerunt ignosce &c. And *fol.* 62. b. *fine.* it faith, *memor esto om-*
nium in domino dormientium, ac requiem præsta eis: and *Basils Liturgie fol.*
44. b. *initio.* faith, *memento omnium dormientium &c. et refrigere eos.*

(t)
er for the dead, of his prayer to (t) *Sainctes*, to *Chrisost. Liturg. fol.* 57.
our bleſſed (u) *Ladie,* and to the (x) *Angel* b. *fine.* faith, *Apostoli*
Michael: and concerning ceremonies of the *Martyres &c. ad saluato-*
Preiſtes beginning to fay Maſſe, with (y) per- *rem pro nobis orate &c.*
fuming of holy incenſe, of (z) *bowing downe him* And *ibidem fol.* 51. b. *fine.*
ſelfe 3. times in his going to the Altar, of his (a) it is faid, *Deus per inter-*
kiſſing the Altar, of (b) *kiſſing the booke after* *cessionem sancti Apostoli, &*
the Goſpel ended, of the peoples (c) *standing at the* *Euangelistæ &c.*
reading of the Goſpel, of finging (d) *Alelluia,* of (u)
the Preiſts ſõtimes praying with (e) *bowing downe* *Chrisost. Liturg. fol.* 55.
him ſelfe, of his prayer at other times *standing* a. *initio.* faith, *intercessi-*
(f) *upright,* of the (g) *eleuation of his handes:* *onibus Dei genetricis salua*
of his prayer made ſomtimes *in* (h) *secret,* & *nos &c.* And *fol.* 57. *fine.*
                                    at *verum peperisti Deum, ipsi*

supplicant, nostras animas saluet. And ſee *Basils* Liturgie *fol.* 37. a. *initio.*
(x) *Chrisost. Liturg. fol.* 57. a. *ante med.* faith, *cælestis militiæ princeps*
Michael, rogamus te nunc indigni, vt tuis intercessionibus munias nos &c.
(y) In the beginning of *Basils* Liturgie *fol.* 34. b. it is faid, *Adolens*
super eas incensum dicit hanc orationem. And *Chrisost.* Liturgie *fol.* 50.
a. faith, *dum fumi odore imbuuntur dicit.* and *fol.* 50. b. it is faid, *Be-*
nedicti fumo incensi diffuso &c. (z) *Chrisost. liturg. fol.* 50. b. faith,
proficiscitur ad sanctam mensam Diaconus cum Sacerdote et tribus vicibus in-
clinans &c. (a) *Chrisost. Liturg. fol.* 52. a. *initio.* faith, *tunc vadit*
& cum inclinauerit sacto Altari atq̃ ipsũ deosculatus fuerit. And *ibidem fol.*
60. b. it is faid, *Sacerdos deosculatur sactum Altare &c.* (b) *Ib. fol.* 52. a.
it is faid, *finito Euangelio regreditur ad Altare Diaconus, osculáturq̃ in mani-*
bus Diaconi Sacerdotes sanctum Euangelium, quò finito, librum seorsum de-
ponit. And ſee there *fol.* 56. b. (c) *Basily Liturg. fol.* 37. a. *fine.*
faith, *legitur Euangelium stantitibus omnibus.* (d) *Alelluia cantatur in*
Liturg. Basily fol. 37. a. *& in Liturg. Chrisost. fol.* 51. b. *&* 52. a.
(e) *In Liturg. Chrisost.* it is faid, *Sacerdos pronus orat fol.* 61. a. *fine.*
& 62. a. circa med. and in *Liturg. Basily* it is faid, *dicit Presbiter in-*
clinato

F

clinato capite hanc orationem secrete, fol. 34. b. and *iterum inclinat se et dicit &c. fol.* 44. a. (f) *In Liturg. Chrisost.* it is said, *et erigens se &c. fol.* 62. a. *fine.* and in *Basils* Liturgie it is said, *leuante Sacerdote caput &c. fol.* 36. b. *fine.* and *modo erigit se pontifex &c. fol.* 44. a. (g) *Basil. Liturg. fol.* 38. a. saith, *tunc eleuans manus Pontifex dicit secrete.* (h) In *Basils Lyturgie, vt supra* at g. and *fol.* 41. b. *Pontifex secrete.* & the same yet further there, *fol.* 34. b. 38. a. b. 39. a. b. 41. b. 45. b. 43. b. And in *Chrisost. Liturg. fol.* 56. a. *fine. & fol.* 50. b. it is said, *et dicit Sacerdos remissa voce.* and *fol.* 59. a. it is said, *dicit orationem hanc Sacerdos sedatissima voce.* and see there *fol.* 61. *circa med.*

(i)

In *Basils Liturgie* it is said, Pontifex excelsa voce, fol. 38. b. see the like there fol. 39. a. & 41. a. & 43. a. fine. & b. 44. a. 46. a. b. 47. b. And in *Chrisostoms* Liturgie it is said, *tunc pronunciat cum voce Sacerdos*, and a

at other times (i) *on hye* of his some times (k) *turning towardes the people*, and *signing* (or blessing) *of the with the signe of the Crosse*, of the (l) *washing of his handes*, of his (m) *desiring praier to be made for him*, of his (n) *signing the Sacramēt*, of pronoūcing the *Canō* of the *Masse* (o) *in secrete*, of the Preistes (*) *standing alone at the Altar*, and *the Deacons houlding vp the venerable*

litle after towardes the end of a certaine praier, *eleuatio vocis fol.* 53. b. & see the same yet further there *fol.* 55. a. 54. b. 59. a. & is there yet further said, *hic exaltat vocem. fol.* 61. b *circa med.* and *fol.* 62. a. *ante med.* and 63. a. *circa med.* (k) *Basile Liturg.* saith, *tunc conuertit se Pontifex ad populum & facit tres cruces super eum, fol.* 38. a. *ante med.* And *Chrisost. Liturg.* saith *deinde facit Crucem super populum, fol.* 63. b. and, *et signat Presbiter populum tertio, fol.* 52. b. *ante med.* (l) *In Basil. Liturg. fol.* 39. b. *fine* it is said, *post lauationem manuum petit ministros pro se orare.* (m) as next before at l. and in *Chrisost. Liturg. fol.* 54. a. it is said, *orate pro me &c.* (n) *Liturg. Chrisost. fol.* 62. a. *fine.* saith, *et erigens se tertio consignans sancta munera dicit.* And see the like in *Liturg. Basilij fol.* 44. a. *ante med.* (o) In *Basil. Liturg. fol.* 42. *circa med.* is *actio seu Canon.* and next after and before the Canon, *Pontifex secrete*, til he come to the wordes of confecration which is appointed to be *voce altiore fol.* 43. a. *fine.* And see the like in *Chrisost. Liturg. fol.* 61. a. b. & 62. a. (*) In *Chrisost. Liturg. fol.* 61. a. *ante med.* is said, *quo dicto Sacerdos qui solus assistit diuinæ mensæ, et secus illam Diaconi contingentes venerabile peplum subleuat &c.*

venerable cloath or rayment of (p) the Eleuation of the holy Sacrament : of Preistes fraction,
or deuiding therof into certaine partes (q) laid
vpon the Paten in forme of a Crosse; and his the
dipping one of those partes into the Chalice; of his
(*) turning to the Image of Christ, with bowing his
head, of the kisse (r) of peace, of the preistes (s)
blessing of the people towardes the end of Masse,
and of sundrie other Ceremonies (ouer tedious now to recite) which are by our aduersaries condemned for stagelike : a thing so co-
fessedly euident in these Liturgies of Basile
& Chrisosto, that M. (t) Powel maketh it the
true reason of his reiecting them, and other
auncient Liturgies (herein agreeing with
them) for forged .

(15)   Hauing bene (frendly Reader) by reaso
of our aduersaries pretended obiectios, more
long and troblesome to thee then I expected
in examination of the bookes before mentioned: I shal now be more breefe in these o-
ther following, in regard they be by our aduersaries denyed only vpon their bare word
without al proofe. To proceede therefore
in course with them: As concerning the
booke of sermons de Baptismo Christi, de cana Domini, de ablutione pedum, de vnctione Chrismatis,
&c. by vs attributed to Ciprian, and reiected
without al proofe for new and counterfaited
by

(p)
Basils Liturgie, fol 47 . b
post med. saith, Pontifex
exaltans panem, dicit &c.
qui sursum patri consides
&c. And in Chrisost. Ly-
turg. fol . 65 . a. ante med.
it is said, after recital of
the very same foresaid
praier, Sacerdos se inclinas
suscipit portionem qua est in
sancta patena, & modicum
sustolles, dicit sancta sanctis.

(q)
In Chrisost. Liturg. fol 65 .
a. it is said, Partitur portionem sanctam in quatuor
partes, ponens eas in modum
Crucis super patenam, et v-
nam quidem partium mittit
in Calicem.

(*)
See this confessed by M .
Fulke against Heskins Saū-
ders &c. pag. 673 . ante
med. and by M . Parkins
in problem. &c. pag. 27.
fine. who thereupon re-
iect this liturgie for for -
ged. (r) In Basils Litur-

gie fol . 41 . a . it is said, pax omnibus , and then, et dant omnes pacem, and
in Chrisost. Liturg. fol . 61 . a . initio . it is said, post datum pacis osculum,
& vide fol . 64 . b . (s) In Chrisost. Liturg. fol . 65 . b . fine. it is said, tunc
Sacerdos populum benedicit &c. (t) Powel de Antichristo l . 1 . pag . 237.
initio. saith, producunt (Papistæ) suas Liturgias sub Iacobi Apostoli, Chrisostomi, Basily, aliorumq; sanctorum virorum nominibus editas, vt inde probent iam
Apostolorum temporibus ipsorum more Missas fuisse celebratas, quod fortassis
verum esse quis affirmare possit , nisi ipsemet (Liturgiæ) fraudem aparirent.

(u)
Chemnisius in his examen *part. 2. pag. 247. a. arte med.* saith hereof, *titulo Cipriani conantur simplices fallere cum veræ antiquitatis testimonijs destituuntur.*

(x)
See in *Vrsinus* his booke entituled, *Comonefactio cuiusdam theologi de 5. cæna et eiusdem commonefactionis consideratio pag.* 211. & 218. where they be tearmed *Notha & supposita.*

(y)
Suppresso nomine nostro, scripsi Paternitati vestræ in prolog. prope finem.

by (u) *Chemnitius,* and some other (x) aduersaries: I say in proofe of them, *first,* that the author therof writeth (as him self signifyeth) purposely (y) *suppressing his owne name:* though therefore it be thereby more incertaine who did write the same, yet doth it appeare to be certainely writen in that age, and speciallie (z) dedicated to *Cornelius Bishop of Rome,* to whom *Ciprian* him self did also (a) write: and vndoubtedly is (as *Erasmus* him self affirmeth therof) (b) *the worke of some learned man of that age:* Athing so euident that M. D. *Fulke* doubteth not to alledge testimony frō thence, withal affirming in behalfe therof that (c) *the author de cæna Domini, was not in time much inferior to Ciprian*; and sundry other of our aduersaries (d) *Diuines of great osteeme,* do cōfessedly, attribute it vnto *Ciprian* S. (e) *Augustine* (so many

(z)   *Ad Diuum Cornelium Papam, de Cardinalibus operibus Christi, vsqȝ ad eius Ascensum* (a) See *Ciprian l.* 1. *ep.* 1. *ad Cornelium, & ep.* 3. *ad Cornelium.* (b) *Erasmus in his Annotations in Diui Cipriani opera,* and after the Basile printe, of 1558 in his Annotation, after the end of al vpon fol. 287. being the beginning of this booke, he saith thereof, *Nec hoc opus esse Cipriani stilus arguit, licet hominis sit eruditi, qualis ætas illa complures habebat.*

(c) *M. Fulke* against the Rhemish Testament, in 1. cor. cap 11. *sect.* 6. *fol.* 282. *a. circa med.* (d) *Simon Goulartius* in his answear to *Pamelius* his Annotations vpon *Ciprian in* his animaduersions, *in sermonem de cæna Domini.* and after the edition of *Ciprians* workes, *Anno* 1593. *pag.* 504. *b. circa med.* saith, *cum recentiores theologi nonnulli magni nominis tractatum de cæna Domini Cipriano tribuant, tum propter stili conuenientiam, tum propter materiæ dignitatem &c.* (e) *August. contra Don.* 1. 4. c. 22. saith, *Baptismi vicem aliquando implere Passionem, de latrone illo cui non Baptizato dictum est, hodie mecum eris in Paradiso, non leue documentum idem beatus Ciprianus assumit:* According wherto both in sence and wordes *Ciprian in ser. de cæna Domini, prope finem.* saith, *ipse dominus &c. non differt beneficium sed repente indulgentiæ celeris docu-*
mentum

mentū eiusdē statuit et exemplum, latroni inquiens hodie mecum eris in Paradiso, latrocinium damnationem meruerat, & supplicium, sed cor contritum pænam mutauit in martyrium, & sanguinem in Baptismum: So knowen was this sermon of *Ciprian* to *S. Augustine.*

manie ages since) affording his answearable testimony therto : and thus much breifly of it. As concerning the bookes extant vnder the name of *S. Ambrose* entituled, the one of them *de Mysterijs*, and the other *de Sacramentis*, that the *firster* was writen by *Ambrose*, appeareth by the preface or beginning therof, wherin the author mentioneth his other next precedent treatise concerning (f) *the deedes of the Patriarches:* and so withall annexeth this, as a cōtinuance to that other, which said precedent treatise, being vndoubtedly the writing of *Ambrose*, proueth him to be in like maner the author of this : As concering now the booke *de Sacramentis*, which is but a continuance of the other booke *de mysterijs*, I say in further proofe therof, *first*, that the correspondence of stile & sentences betwene it and the other foresaid booke, *de mysterijs*, euidently argueth, that they both haue one and the same author : *Secondly*, both the said bookes haue beene by our very aduesaries reputed for writinges of antiquitie, (g) answearable to *Ambrose*: *Thirdly*, they haue beene many ages since alledged vnder the name of *Ambrose*, by (h) *Gratian, Petrus*, (i) *Cluniacensis*, (k) *Lanfranke*, (l) *Guitmundus*, (*) *Algerus*, and (m) *Paschasius*, also by the booke extant vnder (n) *Berthrams* name.

(f)
De Mysterijs initiandis cap. 1. *initio*. he beginneth saying: *memorabilibus quotidianum sermonem habuimus, cum vel Patriarcharum gesta vel prouerbiorum legerentur præcepta vt his informati &c. nunc de mysterijs dicere tempus admonet &c.*

(g)
Melanctō in epist. ad Fredericū Miconiū extant in lib. Epistolarum Oecolampadij et Suinglij. pag. 636. saith, *extant inter Ambrosij libros duo libelli, quorum alter titulum habet de mysterijs initiandis, alter de Sacramentis &c. sed vt non sint Ambrosij apparet, tamē circiter illa tempora natos esse, recencetur enim vetus, mos qui solitus est obseruari in Baptizandis &c.*

(h)
Gratiā de consecratione, dist. 2. *re vera mirabile &c.* & *omnia quæcunq̃ voluit &c.*

Lastly

(i) *Petrns Cluniacensis* l. 1. *epist*. 2. *ad quosdam Prouinciales Episcopos contra Petrobrusianos &c*. (k) *Lanfranke de Sacram. Eucharist.* (l) *Guitmundus* l. *de Sacram. Eucharist*. (*) *Algerus de Sacram. Euchrist*. almost in euery chapter. (m) *Paschasius* l. *de corp. et sang. Domini* (n)

Bertra

Berthram l. de corp. et
sang. Domini circa med.
and *paulo post med.*
(o)
Concerning the booke
de mysterijs, read D. *Fulke*
against *Heskins*, *Sauders*
&c. pag. 271. & 272.
and M. *Whitaker contra
Duraeum* l. 2. pag. 229.
& 230. and *Chemnitius*
in his examen &c. part.
2. pag. 5. b. and *M.
Bilson* his true difference
&c. part. 4. pag. 604.
& 664. & 665. And co-
cerning the booke *de Sa-
cramentis*, it is in like maner acknowledged for
the writinge of *Am-
brose* by M. *Iewel* in his
treatise of the Sacra-
ments printed 1583.
pag. 6. by M. *Whitaker
contra Duraeum* l. 2. pag.
229. & 230. by M.

Lastly, they are ordinarily alledged and acknowledged for the writinges of *Ambrose* by
sundry of our very (o) aduersaries; In so much
as *Peter Martir* declaring how some (p) haue
suspition in these bookes *de sacramentis*, and thinke
them to be none of *Ambrose* workes, geueth his
owne iudgement saying, (q) *which opinion neuerthelesse I passe not of, but willingly accept them.*
As concerning *S. Ambrose* his praiers preparatory to *Masse*, besides the resemblance of stile
betweene them, and *Ambrose* his other writinges, they be acknoledged and alledged as
the writinges of *Ambrose* by M. D. (r) *Bilson* now lord Bishop of *Winckesler*: As concerning the Masse or Liturgie extant vnder
Ambrose name, besides the like resemblance of
stile betweene it and *Ambrose* his other writinges, M. *Foxe* acknowledgeth the antiquitie therof saying (s) *Ambrose Masse was more
vsed in Italie then Gregories Masse, til Anno 780.*
hitherto of *S. Ambrose*.

16 As concerning *S. Gregories* booke of
Dialogues misdoubted by M. (*) *Parkins*,
wheras he liued *Anno Dom.* 590. expresse
(¶) mention and allegation vnder *Gregories*
name

Bilson in his true difference &c. part. 4. pag. 574. & 600. And concerning both the said bookes *de mysterijs* and *Sacramentis*, M. *Parkins*
in his Problem. pag. 20. vndertaking to set downe in particuler *Ambrosij spuria* the bookes fasly attributed to *Ambrose*, nameth and reiecteth
diuers without al mention of either of these. (p) *Peter Martir* in his
disputation of the Eucharist being in the collection annexed to his
common places in English, pag. 239. b. *ante med.* (q) *Peter Martir
vbi supra.* (r) M. *Bilson* in his true difference part. 4. pag. 622. see
him in the text and margent there (s) M. *Foxe act. mon.* printed
1576. pag. 121. b. *circa et post med.* and see the same yet further affirmed by M. *Sparke* in his answeare to M. *Iohn Albines*, pag. 160. *circa
med.* (*) Misdoubted by M. *Parkins in problem*, pag. 38. *circa med.* (¶)
S.

S. Damascen. in orat. de defunctis. alledgeth him saying, Gregorius Dialogus &c. let Gregorie that wrote the Dialogues, Bishop of the elder Rome be brought forth &c. Also Beda hist. l. 2. c. 1. paulo ante med. in reccytal of S. Gregories other bookes saith, libros etiam Dialogorum quatuor fecit, in quibus rogatu Petri Diaconi sui, virtutes sanctorum &c.

name of that very booke is made, specially by such as liued within one hundreth yeares after him, as namely by S. Damascene and Venerable Beda. As concerning also the Catecheses extant vnder the name of Ciril Bishop of Hierusalem: I say in profe of them, first, that they be expressely mentioned by (t) Theodoret, (u) Hierome, and (x) Damascene: Secondly, that they be (y) acknowledged, and (*) alledged for the writings of Ciril by sundry of our learned aduersaries.

As concerning the Homilies extant vnder the name of Eusebius Emissenus, among which in his 5. Homilie de Paschate, it is specialy alledged vnder his name by (z) Gratian, and Algerus, and alledged also sundry ages before by (a) Pascasius, and (¶) Beda; and is yet further alledged for his writing by diuers of our learned (b) aduersaries.

As concerning sundry other writinges of antiquitie

(t) Theodoret. in Polimorpho Dial. 2.

(u) Hierome in catal.

(x) Damascen l. 3. Apologetico pro imaginibus.

(y) Acknowledged by Whitaker contra Dureû l. 2. pag. 228. & 229. and M. Fulke against the Rhemish Testament in Luc. 22. fol. 129. a. sect. 4. (*) Alledged by Chemnitius

in his examen part. 2. pag. 5. b. circa med. and by M. Bilson in his suruey of Christes sufferinges pag. 653. initio. saying, Ciril of Hierusalem 360. yeares after Christ, repeating Catech. 4. and expounding tenne partes of the Creede &c. (z) Gratian de consecratione dist. 2. quia corpus est assumptum. And see it also often alledged by Algerus de sacram. Eucharist. l. 1. c. 5. fine. & cap. 12. & 15. & 16. (a) Paschasius l. de corp. et sang. Domini. (¶) Beda in librum Boetij de Trinitate, saith, transit substantia panis in corpus Christi, non forma, sed potius hæ subsistentes in aere vel sine substantia &c. sic exponunt illam authoritatē, inuisibilis Sacerdos, inuisibiles creaturas in substantiam corporis, et sanguinis sui, verbo suo secreta potestate couertit. this last sentence is the saying of Eusebius Emissen. hom 5. de pasch. (b) See M. Fulke against Heskins &c. pag. 195. & 269. post med. & Cranmer in his answeare to Steue Gardner touching the Sacrament

De Eusebio Emisseno vide Bellarm. de script. Eccles. pag. 145. Paschasius Ratbertus, hic citatus in margine lineâ octavâ à fine, floruit anno Dñi 820

ment 1. 3. pag. 204. &
205.

(*)
concerning the antiqui-
tie of the Liturgie attributed to S. Iames, it is
specialy mentioned & al-
ledged vnder his name a-
bout some thousand yea-
res since by the 6. Conn-
cel of Constantinople (alledged heretofore sect.
13. in the margent at 1.)
for to proue the mixion
of water and wine in the
Chalice, which point is
therin accordingly found
fol. 25. a. circa med. It
is also specially named a-

(marginal note: pag. 41. fine.)

antiquitie in like vnworthy maner reiected
by our aduersaries for coūterfaited, as namely the (*) Liturgie of S. Iames, the Epistle of S.
(c) Policarpe, the (d) Passion of S. Andrew,
writen by his disciples, the Preistes of Achaia:
S. (e) Clements booke of Apostolicke constitutions: also the (f) Apostles Canons, and (g) Hipolitus his booke of the end of the world. For
so much (freindly reader) as some (though
short, yet sufficiēt) proofe of euery of these is
elswhere in this treatise casually alledged, I wil
therefore (as hauing bene already ouer long)
content my selfe with that which is so said
therof, the which I referre to thy indifferent
and careful perusal: In hope whereof, I cease
committing thee to the protection of God almighty, whō I humbly besech to direct thee,
& me, in the loue & knoledge of his truth.

boue eleuen hūdreth yeares since by Proclus Bishop of Constantinople de traditione diuinæ Liturgiæ, where he saith, Multi &c. qui Apostolis successerunt-
&c. sacrorum illius diuinæ Missæ mysteriorum rattonē explicantes scriptis mandatum Ecclesiæ tradiderunt: In quibus primi et clarisimi sunt beatus Clemens
&c. & diuus Iacobus &c. And whreras M. Parkins in Problem. pag. 7.
obiecteth cheifely against it, that it containeth prayer for such as liue in Monasteries which were not (saith he) in the Apostles daies: the contrary is proued heretofore in this preface sect. 8. wherto also is but agreable the vndoubted austerity of life practised by S. Iames him self, and mentioned
there sect. 8. versus finem, in the margin at the letter b. Also as this Liturgie praieth for those that liue in Monasteries: so likewise in the o-
ther wordes there folowing, it praieth pro sanctis patribus & fratribus qui
in montibus speluncis, & foraminibus terræ exercentur. fol 20. b. post medium. therein manifestly agreable to the condition of those persecuting
times. (c) heretofore in this preface sect. 1. in the margine at i.
(d) See hereafter tract. 3. sect. 2. subdiuision 5. in the margin at n.
(e) See hereafter tract. 3. sect. 2. subdiuision 5. in the margin at x. *
(f) See hereafter tract. 1. sect. 4. subdiuision 2. in the margin at s. t. u. x
y. (g) See hereafter tract. 3. sect. 2. subdiuision 4. in the margin at y.

FINIS.

SECTION. 1.

Of the antiquitie of the word Masse.

For asmuch as according to (*) Aristo-tle, *names are vsed to signifie thinges*, & so accordingly our publick Liturgy, or Church Seruice, is with vs of the Latine Church, commonly called or knowne by the name of the word *Masse* : I wil now ther-fore in proofe of the antiquitie of the thing begin first with the antiquity of the name: cō-cerning which it is to be obserued, that direct and special mention is made therof, not only by S. (a) *Augustine*, S. (b) *Ambrose*, S. Le-o, (c) and (d) other fathers, but also by sūdrie ancient (e) councels, in al whom the word *Masse* is mentioned as signifying the Churches publicke seruice of those times : In so much as *Peter Martir* confesseth, that (f) S. *Augustine maketh mention of the worde Masse in his* 237 *sermon de tempore*, and also in the 91. sermons *de tempore*. And

(*) *Arist. de interpret. c. 1.* And *Hieron. Zanchius, in lib. de sacra scriptura, prin-ted* 1593 *pag. 388. sine* saith accordingly, *verba sūt vasa rerum, & earū quæ in animo sunt passionum no-tæ.*

(a) *August. ser. 91. de temp.* saith, *In lectione quæ nobis ad missas legenda est, audi-turi sumus &c. et vide ser-mon. 251. & 237.*

(b) *Ambr. l. 5. Ep. 33. saith. Ego mansi in munere, Missā facere cæpi, orare in oblatione*

Deū, vt subueniret, et vide Tom. 5. serm. de Feria tertia. post Dominicā primā Quadragessimæ. (c) *Leo Epist. 81. ad Dioscorum* saith, *Cum so-lennior festiuitas conuentum populi numerosioris indixerit, & ad eam tanta fide-lium multitudo conuenerit, quam recipere Basilica simul vna non possit. sacrifi-cii oblatio indubitanter iteretur &c. necesse autem est, vt quædam populi pars, sua deuotione priuetur, si vnius tantum Missæ more seruato, Sacrificium offer-re non possint, nisi qui prima diei parte conuenerint.* And see him further in *ep. 88. ad Episc. Germaniæ & Galliæ.* (d) See *Cassianus l. 2. Ca-non. orat. nocturn. c. 7. & l. 3. Canon. diurn. orat. c. 5. 6.* and *l. 11. c. 15.* & *Damasus in pont. in Alexandro 1.* & *Victor. l. 2. hist. de persecutione Vandalorum*, & S. *Gregorie l. epist. 12. & l. 4. ep. 10.*
(e) In the second Councel of Carthage, *can 3.* is mentioned *Missa publica*, & see further *Concil. Carthag. 4. c. 84.* & *Conc. Valentinū can.*

1. & Conc. 2. *Vafenfe can*. 4. & Conc. 3. *Arelatenfe can* 3. & Conc.
1. *Aurelianenfe cã*. 28. & Conc. 3. *Aurelianenfe can*. 14. & Conc. *Mileuita-
num can*. 12. & Conc. *Rom. fub Siluest*. 1. And the Councel called *Agathenfe can*. 47. faith, *Miffas die Dominica fecularibus totas tenere fpeciali ordine precipimus, ita vt ante Benedictionem Sacerdotis egredi populus non pre-
fumat*, and fee there *can*. 21.   (f) *Peter Martir* in his common pla
ces in englifh *part*. 4. *pag* 215. b. & 216. a. *initio*.

(g)   And wheras Maister Doctor Fulke, doth
So anfweareth M. Fulke in anfweare therto affirme *thofe fermons* to be
againft the Rhemifh Te- (g) counterfait: *Peter Martir* refelleth this
ftament in 1. *Cor*. 10. *fec*. anfwear faying, (h) *Some haue doubted whe-
9. *fine. fol*. 279. b. *poft* *ther thefe were Auguftines fermons ; truly they
med*. (h) *Peter Martir feeme vnto me to be the ftyle & fentences of Augu-
vbi fupra, part*. 4. *pagin*. *ftine*, with whom herein our aduerfarie *Crif-
216. a. *paulo poft initiũ*. pinus* (*) agreeth. In like maner do the *Cen-
(*) *Crifpinus in his book turie* (i) *writers* confeffe and reproue S. *Am-
of the ftate of the Church*, *brofe* his forefaid mẽtioning of *Maffe*, directly
page 141. *poft medium* faith againft the other euaforie anfwear thereto,
hereof, *many doubt whe-* which M. D. Fulke (k) would ftrongly en-
ther thefe Sermons be Au- force, contrary to the opinion herein of *An-
guftines : but Peter Mar-* dreas Chraftouius* (2). Alfo M. Fulke him
tir faith, the ftile & fenten* felfe doth acknowledge, that *Victor*, who li-
ces, feeme to be Auguftines* ued within the firft 500 yeares, doth in his hi-
I am of opinion (faith he) ftorie (3) *vfe the terme of Miffa, by which* (faih
that in the time of Auguftin* M Fulke *was ment*) *the celebration of the Com-
the word Miffa, began one-* munion and memorie of the Sacrifice of Chrift*.
ly to be vfurped*. (i) *Cen-* And if our Aduerfaries, wil here vrge that al
tur. 4. c. 4.*Col. 295. this auaileth nothing, feeing that the word
it is faid. *Ambrofius locu Maffe*,is not found in the Scriptures; let them
tionibus vtitur, quibus ante   in
eum ex patribus nemo vfus eft, vt Miffam facere, offerre Sacrificium & c*.

(k) M. Fulke *againft* the Rhemifh Teftament, *in* 1. *Cor. c*. 10.
fect. 9. *fine. fol*. 279. b. *poft med*. anfweareth, that *S. Ambrofe by his
wordes Miffam facere, did vnderftand the letting goe or geuing ouer*, of his
office. (2) *Andreas Craftouius*, in his booke *de opificio miffa*, printed 1594.
l. 1. *fect*. 12. *pag*. 5. anfweareth to the mentioning of Maffe by *S.
Auguftine, Ambrofe*, and other Fathers alledged by Bellarmine faying,
veris antiquis, & orthodoxis patribus & c. fonabat Miffa votorum, atq̃ pre-
catio-

cationū tranſmiſſionē , atǵ ſacram illam Lyturgiæ Chriſtianæ actionem, quæ præcibus myſticis illud quod ex fructibus terræ accipitur, offertur, benedicitur , & peracta pietatis celebratione, conſumitur: hoc enim ſonant ea verba quæ ex Ambroſio, & Auguſtino, Bellarminus attulit. And next afterwardes he there reciteth to this purpoſe, the foreſaid ſayinges of S. *Ambroſe , and S. Auguſtine .* (3) M. Fulke in his retentiue. &c. pag. 60. poſt med.

in ful anſweare of this 4 condēned ſophiſme , or Logomachia, remember that although both we and they profeſſe to beleue the *Trinitie of Perſons* : And that *Baptiſme* and the *Euchariſt* , be properly *Sacraments* ; yet them ſelues do not finde mentioned in the Scriptures, the word *Trinitie*, neither (according to the foreſaid ſenſe) the other wordes of *Perſon*, and *Sacrament*; & yet this notwithſtanding, it may not be denied, but that the ancient vſage in the primitiue Church of theſe vnwritten wordes, argueth greatly for the antiquitie of the doctrines therby ſignified . And thus much breifly concerning the confeſſed antiquitie of the word *Maſſe.*

Of the Deſcription of the Church , & how it was ſolemnly dedicated, & alſo conſecrated, and furniſhed with Chancel, Altare, Holy water, Reliques of Saincts, lightes & Pictures.

SECTION. 2.

A Nd for that the *Church* is the place in which this *Maſſe* or Lyturgie is publick-

(4) *Condemned by S . Auguſtine ,* who *Epiſt .* 174. reproueth *Paſcentius-the* Arian , ſaying, *What is a more contentious part, then to ſtriue about the name* (of *Homouſion* he meaneth) *where the thing it ſelf, is certainly knowne .* And by *Beza ,* who *in epiſt. theolog. ep .* 81. *pag . 367. circa med.* ſaith hereof, *Iſta vero pu tida obiectio voces illas in Scripturis non inueniri, quo ties obiecta, audita, repulſa, damnata, & omnium bonorum & doctorum iudicio &c.*

(5) See to this end Caluins booke of Epiſtles in latin, pag . 648. Ep . 350 *de voce Trinitatis, & de voce Perſonæ.* And ſee to the ſame effect *Beza in Epiſtola theolog . ep .* 81. pag . 367. *fine,* & 368. *initio.* (6) ly Of the greater number of Churches builded *towardes the eaſt,* ſee teſtimonie thereof geuen by *Walfridus Strabo, in lib . de rebus eccleſiaſt . cap .* 4. Alſo by *Paulinus epiſt.*

12. and by *Tertullian in libro contra Valentinianos non procul ab initio*, wher- to but adde as wel the knowen examples of so many Churches as are yet remaining in Christendome, builded of ancient tymes towardes the East: As also the answerable testimony from S. *Clemēt* the Apostles scholer, *in constitut. Apost.* (after the Antwerpe printe of 1564.) *l. 2. c. 6. fol. 55. a.* where he thus describeth the building of a Church;

ly celebrated. I wil therefore next beginne with the discription therof from antiquitie: first then it is euidēt, that the auncient Churches of Christendome, such as were originally builded by Christians, haue al of them (for the most part) one vniforme maner of building, and that *towardes the east* in reguard of the Christians auncient custome (l) *to pray* (or celebrate seruice, as we at this day yet do) *towardes the east*. They also had (m) *from most auncient tradition*, *Chancels* (as we Catholickes yet haue seperate from the Lay people, and peculier to the Cleargie) as appeareth sufficiently by testimony of (n) *Dionisius Areopagita*, and sundry other auncient (o) Fathers: These Churches were likewise not onely solemnely

Ac primum sit longa domus ad orientem conuersa, ex vtraq̃ parte pastophoria habens ad orientem quæ nauis habeat similitudinem &c. (l) This tradition or custome to pray *towardes the East*, is mentioned by *Basile de spiritu sancto. cap.* 27. in these wordes, *Dogmata quæ in ecclesia prædicantur, quædam habemus e doctrina scripta prodita quædam ex Apostolorum traditione.* & then afterwardes amongst the sundry Apostolicke vnwriten traditions by him there recited he mentioneth, *vt ad oriētem versi precemur:* that we should pray turned towardes the East. And the auncient *Origen. in homil. 5. numer. ante med.* saith accordingly, *in Ecclesiasticis obseruationibus sunt nonnulla huiusmodi quæ omnibus quidem facere necesse est, nec tamen ratio eorum omnibus patet: verbi gratia, genua flectimus orantes, & ex omnibus cæli plagis ad solam orientis partem conuersi orationem fundimus: &c.* And see further hereof *Epiphanius hæresi* 19. *circa med.* Gregorie *Nissen. orat. 5. de oratione dominica. Iustinus quæst.* 118. *Augustin. l. 2. de sermone Domini in monte c. 9.* This pointe of prayer towardes the east, is so euident in the Fathers, that the Centurie writers, *Centur. 4. col. 432. line. 11.* do accordingly confesse the same saying, *Vultu conuerso ad Orientem Christianos orasse author est Basilius: &c. quod et in Ecclesijs Africanis vsitatum fuisse ex Athanasio clarum est.* (m) *Concil. 6. Constantinop. Can. 69.* saith, *nulli omnium, qui sit in laicorum numero, liceat intra sacrum Altare ingredi &c. ex antiquissima traditione.* (n) *Dionisius in epist. ad Demophilum.* hereof see M. D. *Raynoldes* in his

his conference with M. *Harte. pag.* 488. *circa med.* (*.o*) *Hist. tripartit.* l 9. c. 30. *versus finem.* it is reported concerning Chancels how that: *Ambrosius non quieuit sed differentiam locorum edocuit.* And that S *Ambrose* said thereupon, *O Imperator interiora loca tantum sacerdotibus sunt collata, quæ cæteri nec ingredi, nec contingere permittuntur: egredere igitur &c.* And see further concerning Chancels, *Socrates hist.* l. 5. c. 17. *versus finem.* And *Sozomen. hist.* l. 7. c. 24. And *Concil. Laodicen. Can.* 19. And *Concil. Agathens. Can.* 66. And *Germanus Constantinopolitanus in Theoria paulo post initium.* saith, *Cancelli locum orationis designant quosq̃ extrinsecus populus accedit: intrinsecus autem sunt sancta sactorum solis Sacerdotibus peruia*

solemnely (p) *dedicated* & that some times euen in honour or memory of (q) *Sainctes,* but were also specially hallowed or (r) *cõsecrated,* and (amonge other Ceremonies) euen (s)

(p)
The Centurie writers, *Cent.* 4. *col.* 452. *line* 30. confesse hereof and with say : *Constantinus diem festum admodum solennem ad celebrandam dedicationem Templi indixit.* And of the dedication *of Churches,* see further, *Eusebius hist.* l. 10. c. 3. after Christofersons version. And *de vita Constantini* l. 4. c. 45. And *Ambrose* l. 5. *epist.* 5. and *ser.* 92. and *Gelatius epist.* 1. *ad Episcopos Lucaniæ &c.* c. 6. and *Prosper part.* 3. c. 38. *de promissionbus Dei.* And *Athanasius in Apologia ad Constantinum.* (q) The Centurie writers, *Cent.* 4. c. 6. *col.* 408. *line* 48. say of the Fathers : *Templa martyribus dedicarunt,* And *Sozomen. hist.* l. 6. c. 18. *initio.* mentioneth S. *Thomas Church at Edessa. Socrates hist.* l. 1. c. *vlt.* mentioneth *the Church of the Apostles. Gregorie Nissen. orat. in Theodorum.* mentioneth the Church dedicated to that Maryr: *Athanasius in epist. ad solitariam vitam agentes,* mentioneth the Church of Quirinus. And see further *August. de Eccles. dog.* c. 73. And *de ciuit. Dei* l. 22. c. 8. And *Ciril. Hierosol. Caeech.* 16. And *concil.* 5. *Carthag. Can.* 14. and. *Concil. Gangrens. in epist. & can.* 20. *Ambrose* l. 1. *epist.* 5. *ad Felicem.* and *Paulinus natal.* 1. S. *Falicis.* (r) The Centurie writers, *Cent.* 4. c. 6. *col.* 408. *line* 55. say hereof, *ex Athanasio videre est, qui Christianos in Templis nondum consecratis non conuenisse clare indicat in Apologia ad Constau.* And the 5. *Carthage* Councel *Can.* 6. saith, *similiter et de ecclesys (quoties supra earum consecratione hæsitatur) agendum est, id est, vt sine vlla trepidatione consecrentur.* And see further *Gelatius epist.* 1. *ad Episcopos Lucaniæ* c. 27. and *Leo epist.* 88. *ad Episcopos Germaniæ, et Galliæ.* & *concil.* 2.
Bracharens.

Bracharenſe can. 6. and *concil. 1. Bracharenſe can. 37.* and *concil. 2. Spalenſe can. 7.* And *Greg.* l. 12. *epiſt.* 32. (s) *S. Auguſt. in ſer.* 19. *de ſanctis* ſaith, *Crucis charectere Baſilicæ dedicantur Altaria conſecrantur &c.*

(t)

Confeſſed by M. *Fulke* a- with the figne of the Croſſe, and (t) ſprinckling
gainſt the Rhemiſh Te- of holy water. The water vſed or reſerued in
ſtament in 1. *Tim.* 4. the Church for Baptiſme, was likewiſe ſpe-
ſect. 13. *fol.* 378. a. *pro-* cially (u) conſecrated : And that alſo (x)
pe initium. And ſee *Bede* with the figne of the Croſſe, there was alſo in
hiſt. l. 5. c. 4. *poſt med.* the Church a table, which (in reguard of the
and *S. Gregorie apud Be-* external ſacrifice offered thereupon to God,
dam hiſt. l. 1. c. 30. *an-* and (y) the (confeſſed) relation and mutual de-
te med. pendence, in which Altar and ſacrifice are by na-
(u) ture linked together) was by the auntient Fa-
Ciprian Epiſt. 70. and l. thers

1, epiſt. 12. paulo poſt initium. ſaith, oportet ergo mundari ac ſactificari a-
quam prius a Sacerdote &c. Baſil. de ſpiritu ſancto c. 27. ſaith, conſecra-
mus aquam Baptiſmatis. This conſecration of the water of Baptiſme, is
further mentioned by S. Auguſtine l. 6. in Iulianum, c. 8. de Baptiſmo, contra Donat. l. 6. c. 25 et ex 50. homil. hom. 27. by Greg. Niſſen.
in orat. de Baptiſmo by Ambroſe l. 1. de Sacramentis c. 5. and by the
Carthage Councel (in Ciprians workes) c. 18. And further mention is
made of conſecrated water by Clement l. 8. Apoſt. conſtitut. c. 35.
by Dioniſius de Eccleſiaſt. Hierarchia in cap. de Baptiſmo. by Ciril. Hieroſol.
Catech. 3. by Theodoret in hiſt. 5. c. 21. poſt med. and by Epiphanius l.
1. tom. 2. hær. 30. ante med. (x) Ambroſe de myſteriis init. c. 3. poſt med.
ſaith, aqua cum fuerit myſterio Crucis coſecrata &c. Aug. de ſanctis ſer. 19.
ſaith, Crucis myſterio fons regenerationis conſecratur. And in Euangel. Iohannis Tract. 118. he ſaith, quod ſignum (Crucis) niſi adhibeatur &c.
ſiue ipſi aquæ regenerantur &c. ſiue ſacrificio quo aluntur, nihil eorū rite perficitur. And in tom. 9. de vtil. pænit. c. 1. is by him mentioned, aqua Chriſti nomine coſecrata, ſaying there further, Cruce ipſius, aqua ſignatur : & ſee
his 181. Sermó de tempore. (y) So ſaith M. Raynoldes in his Cóference
with M. Harte pag. 552. fine. And Gulielmus Zepperus in his Politia
Eccleſiaſtica l. 1. c. 12. pag. 134. paulo poſt med. confeſſeth, that Altaria lapidea & hiſtiæ ſacrificium Miſſæ ſtabiliunt propter Altariū & ſacrificiorū
correllatione. & ibid. pag. 136. initio, he further cófeſſeth ſaying, ſic itaq,
Silueſter tempore Conſtantini magni circa Annum Chriſti 320. Altaria non niſi
lapidea

Fathers (as *Pretorius* a learned Caluiniſt (*) confeſſeth) named (z) an Altar (*) receiuing ſo it name (as *Nazianzen* moſt plainly and pertinently affirmeth) *from the moſt pure and vnbloudie ſacrifice*: which in reſpeƈt of the foreſaid mutual relation to *Altar*, was alſo therefore called (¶) *the ſacrifice of the Altar*. A thing ſo euident in the Fathers, that *Peter Martir*, the Centurie wryters, and M. *Carthwright*,

lapidea eſſe voluit Roma.
(*)
Pretorius de Sacramentis. pag. 287. poſt med. ſaith, *Anno. 262. Sixtus ſecundus abrogauit menſas hacte-nus vſitatas, et coſtituit Al-taria quæ magis repreſentant Iudaiſmum, quam Chriſti-aniſmum, cum Chriſtus Al-*

Do

tari nunquam præfuerit. And *Beza in epiſt. Theolog. epiſt.* 8. *pag.* 83. *i-nitio.* chargeth the Fathers in like manner ſaying, *Introduƈta ſunt paulatim pro menſis Altaria &c.* (z) *Auguſt. de ciuit. Dei* l. 22. c. 10. ſaith, *erigimus Altaria in quibus ſacrificemus vni Deo &c. et vide Auguſt. epiſt.* 86. *ad Caſulanum poſt med.* And *Optatus* l. 6. *contra Parmen.* ſaith, *quid eſt Altare niſi ſedes corporis et ſanguinis Chriſti &c. cuius illic per certa mo-menta corpus, et ſanguis habitabat.* And *Gildas de excidio Britan.* c. 26. calleth the Altar, *Sacrificij cæleſtis ſedem.* And *Ambroſe* l. 5. *de ſacramen-tis* c. 2. ſaith, *quid eſt enim Altare niſi forma corporis Chriſti.* And l. 4. c. 2. *fine.* he ſaith, *forma corporis Altare eſt, et corpus Chriſti eſt in Altari.* And *Iſichius* l. 2. *in Leuit.* c. 8. ſaith, *eſt autem locus ſanƈtus Altare, ibi enim ſanƈtus ſanƈtorum requieſcit.* And *Auguſt. ſer.* 11. *de ſanƈtis.* ſaith, *ſuper Altare corpus Domini offertur.* And *contra Fauſtum Manichæ.* l. 20. c. 21. he ſaith, *ipſi Deo martyrū, quam vis in memorias martyrum, conſtituimus Altaria, quis enim Antiſtitum &c. aſſiſtens altari aliquando dixit, offerimus tibi Petre aut Paule.* Inſinuating ſo thereby *offering of ſacrifice vpon the Altar*, though *not to Martyrs*, yet to God. Before al theſe doth S. *Cipri-an* l. 1. *epiſt.* 9. *prope finem.* vſe the word *Altar*: and before him againe doth the moſt auntient *Ignatius in epiſt. ad Philadelph.* mention *Thuſi-aſterion*, which is in enliſh *Altar*, and applyeth that word to the table whereupon the Sacrament is celebrated. And in like ſence doth S. *Clement*, vſe and mention the word *Altar* in his 3. and 4. Canon of the Apoſtles, which Canons are confeſſed and proued hereafter *Traƈt.* 1. *ſeƈt.* 4. *ſubdiuiſ.* 2. at q. r. ſ. t. u. x. y. And ſee further concer-ning the word *Altar* hereafter *Traƈt.* 3. *ſeƈt.* 3. *ſubdiuiſ.* 4. *fine.* in the margent next after q. at this marke. *. (*) *Nazianzen. in Iulianum* mentioneth *Altaria a puriſſima et incruento ſacrificio nomen habentia.* And ſee him *apud Whitakerum contra Duræum* l. 4. *pag.* 317. (¶) *Auguſt. in*

Enchir. c. 110. *et de cura* do therefore (a) reproue certaine of the aun-
pro mortuis c. 18. And cient Fathers in particular : *Peter Martir* fay-
Gregorie in Luc. hom. 37. ing alfo further of thē in general, (b) *the Fa-*
　　　　(a)　　　　*thers fhould not with fo much liberty haue feemed*
Peter Martir in his com- *here and there to haue abufed the name of Altar ;*
mon places in englifh, with whom agreeth M. *Carthwright* fay-
part. 4. c. 12. *fect.* 21. ing, (¶) *the auntient writers abufe herein may*
pag. 225. b. *poft med. eafily appeare, in that, in this to great liberty of*
faith, *Petrus Alexandri- fpeach they vfed, to cal the holy fupper of the Lord*
nus in a certaine epiftle of his a facrifice, and the Communion table, an Altar.
in Theodoret, attributeth　(2) This *Altar* was then alfo (as it now
more to the outward Altar likewife is) fpecially (c) *confecrated* euen (d)
then to the liuely temples of with the *figne of the Croffe,* and (e) *with vnction*
Chrift. And *ibidem pag.*　　　　　　　　　　　　　　　　　　　*of*
226. a. *initio*. he further faith, *Optatus* l. 6. againft *Permenianus* faith,
what is the Altar? euen the feate of the body and bloud of Chrift: fuch fayinges
as thefe edified not the people, but rather droue them to Heathnifh, and Iewifh
rytes. And the Centurie writers, *Cent*. 4. c. 6. *col.* 409. *line* 25. fay,
Optatus Mileuitanus l. 6. *cōtra Parmen. inquit, quid eft Altare, nifi fedes cor-*
poris et fanguinis Chrifti? verum hæc confuetudo a Iudaica in Ecclefiam Chrifti
permanauit. And M. *Carthwright* in his 2. reply, the 1. parte, *pag.* 517.
prope finem. faith of Ignatius, *Ignatius calleth the Communion table vnpro-*
perly an Altar, placing in his margent there, *Thufiafterion*. And fee the
like mention of this word in *Ignatius*, confeffed by M. *Iacob* in his defence taken out of Gods word &c. *pag*. 58. *poft med*. And fee the fame
word accordingly vfed by *Ignatius* in his epiftle *ad Philadelph*. (b) *Pe-*
ter Martir in his common places in englifh, *part*. 4. *pag*. 225. b. *ante*
med. (¶) M. *Carthwright* in his fecond reply the laft part *pag*. 264.
circa med. (c) *Greg. Niffen. de fancto Baptifmo, & conc*. 2. *Spalenfe*
can. 7. and *conc*. 1. *Bracharenfe can*. 37. and *conc*. 1. *Hipponenfe can*. 5.
ditft. 1. c. *Altaria*. and *Auguft. de tempore fer*. 255. *conc*. 3. *Aurelia-*
nenfe canon. 15. (d) *Auguft. de fanctis fer*. 19. faith, *Crucis charactere*
Altaria confecrantur. (e) *Conc. Agathenfe can*. 14. faith, *Altaria pla-*
cuit non folum vnctione Chrifmatis, fed etiam facerdotali benedictione facrari.
And *Auguft. de tempore. fer*. 255. faith, *Benedictus, vel vnctus eft lapis in*
quo nobis diuina facrificia confecrantur. And a litle there before he faith,
confecrationem Altaris hodie celebramus. and *Dionifius Areopagita de Eccle-*
fiaftica Hierarchia c. 4. faith, *Diuini Altaris confecrationem fanctiffimorum*
　　　　　　　　　　　　　　　　　　　　　　　　　　　myfteriorum

of Crisme. There were yet further in the chur-ch, not onely (*) *Chalices*, and a veffel for the Sacrament called *Patena*, and the potte or cru-et called *vrceolum*, for water to the Preiftes vfe in feruice time. Al which are mentioned in the 4. (f) *Carthage Coûcel*, whereat *S. Au-guftine* was prefent and (g) *fubfcribed*, but al-fo, *fancta* (h) *velamina, holy coueringes*, or (¶) *Corporals*, the which were (according to *S. Hierome*) houlden to be fanctified and (i) *ve-nerable by reafon of their accôpanying* (or touch-ing) *the body and bloud of our Lord :* fo as (by the

myfteriorum lex, fanctiffimi vnguenti, caftiffimis infufim nibus perficit.

(*)

Concerning *Chalices, Op-tatus* l. 6. *contra Parmen .* faith, *hoc tamen immane facinus geminatum eft, dum fregiftis etiã Calices Chrifti fanguinis portatores .* And *Chrifoftome in* 1. Cor. *hom.* 24. faith *that which is in the Chalice, is the fame*

which flowed from Chrifts fide. And fee the like further in *Ambrofe* l. 4. de Sacramentis c. 5. And Leo, *fer* . 11. *de paffione :* and *Prudentius in Periftephamon. him* . 2. fee thefe alledged more particulerly hereafter, *tract* . 3. *fect* . 3. *fubdiuif.* . 3. *fine.* in the margent at b. c. d. e. (f) *Conc.* 4. *Carthag . Can.* 5. decreeth faying : *Subdiaconus cum ordina-tur. &c . Patenam de Epifcopi manu accipiat vacuam et Calicem vacuum , de manu vero Archideaconi, vrceolum cum aqua, et mantile, et manutergium .* (g) In the end of the laft Canon of that councel, it is faid, *Auguft . Hippone regien. fubfcrip.* (h) *Hierom, in epift. ad Theophilum Alexandri-num ante libros pafchales .* And *S. Ambrofe* l. *de virginibus,* faith hereof, *plus talis decet flammeus, in quo caput omnium Chriftus quotidie confecratur .* (¶) *S. Greg.* mentioneth the confecration of *Altar, Chalice, and Corporal,* for which the Centurifts *Cent* . 6. *col* . 371. *fine* . do reprehend him faying, *confecrarunt Pontifices Altare, Chalicem, corporale, vt Gregorius meminit,* l. 12. *epift* . 32. & *Theodorus Cantuarienfis* who liued *An* . *Dom* 650. l. *penitetiali.* c. 13. faith, *Corporale mudiffimu fit.* And fee *Amalarius de Ecclefiaft. offic.* l. 3. c. 19. Alfo the french Proteftant diuine in his fix godly treatifes englifhed, printed 1608. *pag.* 65. *initio* faith, that *Sixtus Bifhop of Rome in the yeare of Chrift* 121. *did trauaile to inftitute Cor-poraffes of fine linnen cloath to lay vpon the confecrated hoaftes .* (i) *Hierome in epift* . *ad Theophilum Alexandrinum ante* l. *Pafch.* faith, *vt difcant &c. qua debeat veneratione fancta fufcipere, et Altaris Chrifti minifterio deferuire, facrofq, Calices, et fancta velamina &c .' non quafi inania, et fenfu carentia factimoniam non habere, fed ex confortio corporis, et fanguinis Domini, eadem qua corpus eius et fanguis maieftate veneranda .*

(k)
*Luc. Ofiander Cent.*4.1.
3. c. 38. *pag.* 391. *initio.* faith of the Canon
made by the Fathers of
the Laodicen Councel,
hic Canon fuperftitionem o-
let, quafi vero vafa facro
minifterio deftinata, tam fint
fancta, vt ea nemo nifi Pref-
biter, aut Epifcopus at-
tingere debeat &c.

the confeffió of our owne (k) aduerfaries) it
was by the Fathers houlden vnlawful for laye
perfons, or any of the inferior orders of the
Cleargie (1) *contingere vafa dominica, to touch*
them. The Church was alfo furnifhed, not
onely oftentimes with (m) *reliques of Samctes*
tranflated thither., fometimes by fpecial (n)
reuelation, and placed commonly with great
reuerence (o) *vnder the Altar,* and repaired
vnto with frequent and religioufe (p) *pilgri-*
mage

(1) *Conc. Laodicen. can.* 21. decreeth faying,
non oportet Subdiaconos licentiam habere in facrarium & c. ingredi, et continge-
re vafa Dominica. And the very fame Canon is decreed in the Councel of
Agatha, can. 66, And fee further here of *Concil.* 1 *Bracharenfe can.* 28 .
et ex cap. Grac. finod. canon. 41. And *Gregor. Niffen. in orat. de Bap-*
tifmo, who faith, *Altare hoc fanctum cui affiftimus, &c. quoniam Dei cultui*
confecratum, atq; dedicatum eft, ac benedictionem accepit &c. non amplius ab
omnibus, fed a folis Sacerdotibus eifq; venerantibus contrectatur. And fee
Nazianzen. in orat. de feipfo contra Arianos in initio. (m) *Hieron. cotra Vi-*
gilantium ante med. faith, *Conftantinus Imperator Sanctas reliquias Andrea,*
Luc. et Timoth. tranftulit Conftantinopol. apud quas Damones rugiunt. And
fee *Auguftine de ciuit. Dei* l. 22. c. 8. (n) Of the deade bodies of
Geruafius and *Prothafius,* tranflated by diuine reualation. *Auguft,* l. 9.
confef. c. 7. faith, *memorato Antiftiti tuo per vifum aperuifti, quo loco laterent*
Martyrum Corpora Prothafy, et Geruafy, per tot Annos incorrupta &c.
cum enim propalata, et effoffa, digno cum honore transferentur ad Ambrofianam
Bafilicam &c. And fee him further *de ciuit. Dei.* l. 22. c. 8. *paulo poft*
initium. and *Ambrofe epift.* 85. *ad Sororem.* And of other like examples
reade *S. Auguftine fer.* 91. *de tempore.* and *Sozomen,* l. 5. c. 8. and l.
7. c. *vlt.* and l. 9. c. 2. (o) *Sozomen, hift.* l. 5. c. 8. *circa med.*
faith of a holy Bifhop, *extra vrbem extruxit Ecclefiam, et Altare in ea erexit,*
Martyrumq; reliquias ibi repofuit. And concerning other like examples,
fee *Ambrofe epift.* 85. *ad Sororem.* and in *exhortat. ad virgines.* and *S.*
Gregorie l. 1. *epift.* 52. *et* l. 2. *epift.* 58. *&* l. 5. *epift.* 50. and *Hierom e*
l. *contra Vigilant.* c. 3. and *Auguft. de ciuit. Dei* l. 8. c. 27. and *fer.*
11. *de fanctis.* and the fift. Carthage Councel, *can.* 14. and *conc. Aphri-*
canum can. 50. (p) This point is fo euident in the aunticnt Fathers,
that *Chamnitius* therefore reproueth them in his *examen, part.* 4. *pag.* 10.

b. *ante med.* saying, *suscipiebant etiam Peregrinationes ad loca ubi reliquias miraculis celebres et claras audiebant, ita ad terram sanctā, ad limina Petri, et Pauli Romam peregrinabantur.* And the Centurie writers *Cent. 4. c. 6. col. 457. line 58. and col. 458. initio.* affirme: *Pilgrimages to holie places to haue bene vsed in the age vnder Constantine* our first Christian Emperour, calling therefore S. *Helene the Emperours mother* (who vsed the same)

mage, and amongst other euen of diseased persons, who were oftentimes thereupon (q) miraculously cured (the miracles thereof being so certainely true that M. (r) *Whitaker* him self dare not contemne them) but was also further furnished with pictures or (s) *Images* confessed, and disliked by our (*) aduersaries,

a superstitious woman.

(q)
August. de ciuit. Dei l. 22. c. 8. paulo post initium. miraculum quod me-diolani factum est, cum illic essemus, quando illuminatus est caecus ad multorum no-
and *titiam potuit peruenire, quia*

et grandis est ciuitas &c. et immenso populo teste, res gesta est concurrente ad corpora martyrum Prothasy, et Geruasy, quæ cum laterent et penitus nesciren-tur Episcopo Ambrosio per somnum reuelata reperta sunt &c. & see there afterwardes in the same chapter, sundry other examples of like miraculous cures. And see *Basile orat. in Mamantem.* and *Nazianzen orat. in Cipri-anum.* and *Chrisostome 1. contra Gentiles fine.* and *Ambrose in ser. de sanctis Geruasio et Prothasio.* and *Hierom contra Vigilant.* and *in vita Hillarionis.* (r) *Whitaker contra Duræum l. 10. pag. 866. ante med.* answearing to *Duræus* herein acknowledgeth and saith, *nec illa miracula vana fuisse puto, quæ in martyrum monumentis facta narrantur.* (s) *Gregor. Nissen. in vi-tam Theodori,* maketh mention of the Image of *Theodorus* the Martyr : and of the painted Image of our Sauiour set vp in the Church. And *Paulinus in decimo natali Felicis,* mentioneth painted Images set vp in the Church, as namely of *Tobie* &c. And in *Chrisostoms* Liturgie, translated by *Erasmus,* mention is made of *the Preists turning to the Image of Christ, & bowing his head before it.* And *Sozomen hist. l. 5. c. 28.* maketh mentiō of Christs Image placed in the Church. (*) M. *Fulke* against *Heskins Sanders &c. pag. 672. initio.* saith, that *Paulinus caused Images to be pain-ted on the Church wales, as it is confessed to be done, so it is denyed to be wel done.* And this is yet further confessed with sundry auntient examples thereof, geuen by the Centurie writers *Cent. 4. c. 6. col. 409. post med.* saying, *Sacrary Ambrosius meminit, l. 1. offic. c. 50. et ornamenti imaginum, Sozom. l. 5. c. 21. & l. 6. c. 16. qui effigiem mulieris Ha-*

20.

morousa et Christi saluatoris apud Cæsaream Philippi a Iuliano deiectam , a Christianis in Ecclesiam rursus collocatam fuisse scripsit &c. indicat et Pru-*dentius Imagines represẽtantes martyrum passiones in Templis collocari solitas.*

(t)

The fourth Carthage Councel, *Can. 6.* saith, *Accolitus cum ordinetur &c. accipiat cereferarium cum cereo, vt sciat se ad ac= cendenda Ecclesiæ lumina mancipari.* And *Eusebius hist.* l. 6. c. 8. *ante med.* mentioneth the Churches Lightes, and a miracle done concerning them: And see *Eusebius de vita Constantini* l. 4. c. 66. *S. Greg.* l.1. *Dialog.* c. 5. mentioneth a like mi-racle in behalfe of the Churches lightes. And *Paulinus in natali* 3. *Fælicis* saith, *claré coronantur densis Altaria Lichnis &c. nocte diég̃ micant .* And

and in the day seruice time with (t) *Lightes* made euen *of waxe,* confessed in like maner, & reproued by our (u) aduersaries, & those not prophand or common, but specially (x) *confe-crated.* And thus much breifly touching the description of the Church, and the auntient outward Ceremonies, and ornamentes con-cerning the same.

Of the Preist, and that he was appointed to offer sacrifice.

SECTION. 3.

AS concerning the Cleargie by whom seruice was celebrated, there were then (as

S. Hierome contra Vigilant. c. 3. saith, *per totas orientis Ecclesias quando legendum est Euangelium accenduntur Luminaria iam sole rutilante, non vtiq̃ ad fugandas tenebras, sed ad signum lætitiæ.* And see *Hierom epist.* 27. *ad Eustachium, in epitaphio Paulæ,* c. 13. And the Centurie writers *Cent.* 4. c. 7. *col .* 497. *line* 48. say, *Accensiones candelarum interdiu in templis Constantinus instituit.* And *Isidor.* l. 7. *Etimolog.* c. 12. saith, *Accolithi Græce, latine ceraferarij dicuntur , a deportandis cereis, quando Euangelium legendum est, aut sacrificium offerendum, tunc enim accenduntur luminaria ab ijs, et deportantur, non ad fugiendas tenebras, dum sol eo tempore rutilet, sed ad signũ lætitiæ.* Further mentiõ is made of the Church lightes in the Apostls Canõs, c. 4. And in *Athanasius in epist. ad omnes orthodoxos de persecutione Arianorum, non procul ab initio.* and in *Ciril. Hierosol. in orat. de occursu Domini.* and by *Nazianzen monodia in laud. Basilij . et orat. in laudem Cæsarij.* by *Chrisost. ad populum hom .* 7. *paulo post initium.* by *August. in Psal.* 65. and see *Concil. Tarraconense* c. 7. (u) The Centurie writers *Cent.*

Cent. 4. c. 7. col. 497. line. 46. say of the Fathers of that age, *quas ceremonias non necessarias &c. excogitauerint, vt accensiones candelaru interdiu in templis, quas Constantinus instituit &c. et vide col. 410. line 7.* (x) Hereof see *Euuodius Ticinensis in benedictione cerei.* and *concil. 4. Toletanum, can. 8.* and *Prudentius in benedictione cerei Pascalis.* and *Greg. l. 9. epist. 28.*

(y)
Ignatius the Apostles scholer *in epist. ad Antiochenos fine.* saith, *saluto Subdiaconos, Lectores, Cantores, Exorcistas, Custodes, Sanctarum portarum &c.* And see further herof the Canons of the Apostles. *can. 42. & 43. Epiphan. l. 3. hær. vlt. versus finē.* And the Emperors, *Valentinianus, Valens, & Gratianus apud Iustinianum l. 1. tit. 3. l. 6.* and *Clement. l. 3. constitut. Apostolic. c. 11, and l. 8. c. 24. 25. 26. 27. 28. 32.* And *Concil, Antiochenum can. 10.*

(as now) the seueral degrees of, *Dore-keeper*, *Reader, Exorcist, Accolyte, Subdeacō, Deacon, Preist*: And that al these were in the primatiue Church, appeareth by most euident testimonie of the most auntient Fathers, (y) *Greeke* and (z) *Latine*; in so much as our aduersaries the *Centurie writers*, do (*) acknowledge the same for true. And for so much as the *Preist* was the onely man of al these, appointed to celbrate the publique Lyturgie, for the (a) *Deacon* (who is in degree next vnto him) *had not* (then more then now) *power to offer the body of Christ*, but onely authority (especially in the Preistes absence) *to* (b) *deliuer it* to the laye cōmunicantes. (so distincte then

(z) *Cornelius*, who liued almost 1400. yeares since in his epistle extant in *Eusebius hist. l. 6. c. 35.* and after M. *Hanmers* english translation *c. 42.* saith, *In qua Ecclesia non ignorabat Presbiteros esse quadraginta sex, Diaconos septem, Subdiaconos septem, Accoluthos quadraginta duos, Exorcistas, et Lectores, vna cum Ostiarijs quinquaginta duos.* And see further hereof *Concil. Romanum sub Siluestro can. 7.* and *Ciprian. l. 1. epist. 3. initio.* and *l. 3. epist. 22.* and *l. 4. epist. 7. post med.* and *Siritius epist. 1. c. 8. et 9.* and *Sozimus epist. ad Hesichium.* and *Hierom epist. 2. c. 6. et ep 91. & in c. 2. ad Titum fine.* And see *Concil. Laodicenum, can. 21, and 23. and 24.* and the 4. Carthage Councel, *can. 5. 6. 7. 8. 9.* and *Isidor. l. 7. Etimolog. c. 12.*   (*) See the Centurie writers *Cent. 3. col. 149. and 150.*   (a) *Concil. 1. Nicen. can. 14.* saith of Deacons, *hi offerendi sacrificij non habent potestatem &c.* and *Concil. 1. Arelatense can. 15.* saith, *de Diaconibus quos cognouimus multis locis offerre, placuit minime fieri debere.* Hereof see the Centurie writers *Cent. 4.*

col

col. 703. line 35. and see hereafter tract. 3. sect. 1. subdiuis. 2. at q. 1. in the margent. (b) That the Deacon might deliuer the Sacrament, see conc. 2. Arelatense can · 15. cyted by the Centuristes, cent. 4. col. 705. line. 30. And Epiphanius hæres. 79. ante med. and Cent. 4. col. 491. line 7. and Ciprian in ser. de Lapsis post med. mentioneth first the Preistes sacrificing, and the Deacons distribution afterwardes to the people saying, sacrificantibus nobis &c. vbi vero solennibus adimpletis Calicem Diaconus offerre presentibus cæpit &c. And see further hereof the Centuristes, Cent. 4. col. 426. line 60. and col. 427. line 3. and 491. line 53. and Iustinus martyr Apol. 2. fine. And see the Superintendent of Canturburie in his defence &c. pag. 585. fine. where he affirmeth, that Deacons might distribute but not minister (or celebrate) the Lordes supper. And see further to the same purpose S. Clement in his booke of Apostolicke constitutions after the edition of Antwerpe of 1564.

(c) Act. 15. 1. certaine from Iudæa taught the brethren, except you be circuncised after the maner of Moyses you cã not be saued.

(d) Galat. 5. 2. If you be circumcised Christ shal profit you nothing.

(e) So the Greeke word Iereus which signifyeth Sacerdos is referred to christian Preistes by Dionisius Areopagita de Ecclesiastica Hierarch.

then was the distributiõ of it frõ the oblation thereof to God) I wil therefore speake more peculierly of the name Preist. In discourse whereof it is specially to be obserued, that like as in the Apostles times, many being ouer much addicted to the Iewish Ceremonies, were misperswaded of the continuance of (c) Circumcision, whom the (d) Apostle specially confuteth. So likewise the Apostles in like care, lest that the Aaronical Temple and Preisthood being then but fresh in memory, should be mistakē likewise stil to continue, did therfore (in better distinction of our Church, and Preistes, from the Temple & sacrificers of Aarons order, who as yet in the Apostles time stil executed their ould fũctiõs in the Temple) purposely abstaine, as from the word Templũ, vsing insteede thereof the word Ecclesia, so in like maner frõ the word Iereus, or Sacerdos, vsing also in lik steed therof the word Presbiteros or Presbiter, wheras immediatly afterwardes (whē the difference betweene the Christiã & the Iewish law was fully vnderstoode, & al former scruple of danger herein auoided) the said wordes were with al liberty promiscuously & indiffe̅ctly vsed by the (e) auncient

auntient Fathers, *Ecclesia* and *Presbiter*, being
so the same to them in the new law, which
Templum & *Sacerdos*, were to the Iewes in the
ould. And seeing therefore it is cleare and
(*) *confessed* as wel that the auntient Fathers
confounded or vsed the wordes *Sacerdos* and
Presbiter, as signifying now in the new Testament one and the same thing; as also that the
word *Iereus*, or *Sacerdos*, for which we haue
no (f) other English thē *Preist*, (g) signifyeth
~~ificeʳ a sainctifyer~~, and that the word *Preist* (h) signifyeth (likewise) *a sacrificer by custome of our
english speach*, in so much as sundry of our aduersaries, do therefore professe their (i) dislike of that name, to be referred to their now
ministers : how much the rather then is the
word *Presbyteros*, which the Apostls vsed to be
taken likewise for *a sacrifycer*, especially considering further that the name of *Preist*, which
is properly (k) deryued from *Presbiteros*, not
onely in English, but also in other languages,
as *Latine, French*, & *Italiane &c.* is by common vnderstanding in al those nations taken
for a sacrifycing Preist. Adde but now hereunto

Hierarch. *c*. 5. *et epist*. 8.
ad Demophilū Mōnachum.
And by *Ignatius epist*. *ad
Smyrnenses*. in so much as
S. *Chrisostome* did write
a special booke of his
Preisthood.

(*)
The Fathers are so plaine
herein, that M. *Fulke* a-
gainst the Rhemish Te-
stament in *Act*. 14. *sect*.
4. and *fol*. 210. *a*. *sine*.
cōfesseth saying, *Indeede
manie of the auntiēt Fathers
confound the name of Sacerdos, and Presbiter, wherein
they are not to be cōmended*.
And M. *Whitguift* in his
defence of the answeare
to the admonition, *pag*.
722. *ante med*. saith, *I
reade in the ould Fathers
that these two names Sa-
cerdos and Presbiter be con-
founded. And M. *Whitaker cotra Dureum* l. 9. pag. 813. *initio*. saith
hereof vnto *Dureus, nos ad Patres græcos ac latinos remittis, a quibus Presbiteri* Iereis, *et Sacerdotes nominantur, quis id negat? verum id sit, vt dixi,
non propriè sed* Catachresticos: As *Peter Martir* in like maner chargeth
the Fathers with *abusing the name of Altar*, whereof see heretofore *pag*.
4. at the letter b. (f) See M. *Carthwright* in M. *Whitguiftes* defence
pag. 722. *initio*. (g) M. *Carthwright ibidem*. (h) D. *Raynoldes* in
his cōference with M. *Harte* pag. 540. *post med*. & M. *Carth*. *vbi sup*. &
M. *Whitg*. him self *Ibid*. pag. 722. *ante med*. (i) Hereof see *Carthwright*
in M. *Whitguiftes* defence *pag*. 721. *post*. *med*. and 722. *initio*. (k) *Presbiter, Prebstre, Prete, Preist*. and M. *Hutton* in his second part of the
answeare to the reasons for refusal of subscription &c. *pag*. 173. *circa
med*. saith, *the holy Ghost geuing the name* Presbyteros *to our Minister*,
which

I

which is the original whence Preist is deriued &c. And see him further there *pag. 39. initio. & 40. circa med. & M. D. Downeham,* in his two Sermons printed 1608. the second sermō being at *Lambith* of the honorable fūction of Bi-shops *pag. 8. ante med.* affirmeth, that *in the wri-tinges of the Apostles, in the auntient Fathers, & Coun-cels the word* Presbyteros *or Presbyter (noting an Ec-clesiasticall persō) doth euer-more signify a Minister or Preist, which word* (saith he there further) *is the proper english of Presbyter, and from thence deryued.*
(l) *Esay* 61.6.
(m)
Esay 66. 21.
(n) D: *Raynoldes* in his

unto the Prophecie of *Esay,* who foretelleth concerning the Ecclesiasticall function of the new Testamēt (l) *you shal be called the Preistes of the Lord, &* (m) *of thē wil I take to be Preistes* In which latter as D. *Raynoldes,* and our other aduersaries professe (n) *to graunt the name of Preist is geuen to Pastors* of the new Testament: in so much as *S.* (o) *Augustine* doubted not to say, *de Episcopis et Presbyteris &c. that now in the Chucrh they are properly called Preistes,* directly against M. *Whitaker* who saith to the con-trary (p) *Presbyteri* Iereos, *nominantur Sacer-dotes, verum id sit non proprie, sed* Catachresti-cos. As also the most aūtiēt father *Ireneus* affir-meth besides the spirituall (¶) *Preistly order of al the iust,* an other peculier *Preisthood of the Apostles, who* are, in reguard thereof, by him said *to attend daylie vpon God and the Altar.*

(2) And thus much breifely concerning the name *Preist,* whereunto I also adde the thing thereby sigmfied, which is the action of sacrificing: in respect whereof *Ignatius* (q) *who was S. Iohns scholer, and lived in Christēs time,* in his (r) vndoubted Epistle *ad Smirnen-*
ses

conference with *Harte,* pag. 544. *paulo post med.* And see the margi-nall Annotations of the english Bible of *Anno* 1576. in *Esay* 66. *verf.* 21. And see the same is graunted also by M. *Hooker* in his Ecclesiasticall pollicie, l. 5. *pag.* 236. *post med.* and by M. *Hutton* in the second part of his answeare to the reasons for refusall of subscription *pag.* 39. *circa med.* (o) *Aug. de ciuit. Dei* l. 20. c. 10. saith, *non de solis Episcopis et Presbyteris dictum est, qui proprie iam vocantur in Ecclesia Sacerdotes.* (p) *Whitaker contra Duraum* l. 9. *pag.* 813. *prope initium.* (¶) *Ireneus* l. 4. c. 20. saith, *omnes iusti Sacerdotalem habent ordinem, Sacerdotes au-tem sunt omnes Domini Apostoli, qui neq̃ agros neq̃ domos hereditant hic, sed semper Altari et Deo seruiunt, de quibus et Moyses in Deuteronomio in be-nedictione Leui ait, &c.* (q) So saith M. *Whitguift* in his defence of the answeare to the admonitiō &c. *pag.* 408. *circa med.* & see *Eusebius hist*

l. 3.

1. 3.   (r) *Ignatius* his Epiſtle *ad Smyrnenſes*, is mentioned, and diuers ſentences thereof, yet found in the Epiſtle now extant, are alledged *verbatim* vnder *Ignatius* his name and the title of his Epiſtle by *Hierome* l. *de viris illuſtribus.* and by *Euſeb.* l. 3. c. 32. as is more at large proued by M. *Whitguift vbi ſupra* and not ſo much as he gaineſaid therein by *Carthwright Ibidem.*

ſes, affirmeth the Biſhop to be *Os archierea as the high Preiſt,* and *Chriſtes Image* Cata to ierateuein, in reſpect of his *Preiſthood:* ſaying alſo there further that, *in the Church noibing is greater then the Biſhop who ſacrificeth to God for the ſaifty of the world.* & (s) *Nazianze* likewiſe hereupon affirmeth *Ton Ierea the Preiſt* to be *the mediator betweene God and man, and ſacrificing together with Chriſt.* As alſo the other auntient Fathers tearme him in like maner (t) *the Preiſt that ſacrificeth to God vpon the Altar:* that (u) *ſacrificeth the body and bloud of Chriſt vpon the Altar.* And which the Centurie (x) writers do ſpecially mention and diſlike, (y) *the Preiſt that offereth in the Church a true and ful ſacrifice to God the Father,* (z) *vnder Chriſt the* (high) *Preiſt, and in his* (a) *ſteede* or (b) *place:* for from his precedent example and warrant, do they vndertake to *offer* (¶) *ſacrifice for the people.* And ſo accordingly the Fathers affirme that our Sauiour at the time

(s)
Nazianzen. epiſt. 8. *ad Simplicium Hereticum.*

(t)
Avg. l. 22. *de ciuit. Dei* c. 10. *circa med.* ſaith, *erigimus Altaria in quibus ſacrificemus vni Deo.*

(u)
Concil. 12. *Toletanus can.* 5. decreeth ſaying, *ſacrificans corpus et ſanguinem Domini noſtri Ieſu Chriſti in Altaria immolat &c.*

(x)
Cent. 3. c. 4. *col.* 83. line 34. vnder the title of the Fathers errors, which title beginneth there *col.* 71. *circa med.* the Centuriſts do with diſlike alledge *Ciprian* ſaying,

of *vice Chriſti fungi et Deo patri ſacrificium offerri.* In ſo much as the Centuriſtes in their Alphabetical table of that 3. Centurie, vnder the letter s. do ſet downe ſaying, *Sacerdotem vice Chriſti fungi in cæna Domini ſuperſtitioſe aſſerit Ciprianus* 83. 34. (y) *Ciprianus* l. 2. *epiſt.* 3. *poſt med.* (z) *Avg. de ciuii. Dei* l. 17. c. 17. *circa medium* ſaith, *vbig; offertur ſub Sacerdote Chriſto quod protulit Melchiſedech.* (a) *Ciprian,* l. 2. *epiſt.* 3. *poſt med.* ſaith, *Sacerdos vice Chriſti vere fungitur.* (b) *Ambroſ. in* 1 *Tim. c.* 4. *verſ.* 14: ſaith of the party who is ordained Preiſt ; *vt audeat vice Domini Sacrificium Deo offerre, he may be bould to offer ſacrifice to Godin* our Lordes

place

place . (¶) *Ambros. in Pſal . 38 .* ſaith, *vidimus principem Sacerdotum ad nos venientem, vidimus et audiuimus offerentem pro nobis ſanguinem ſuum, ſequamur vt poſſimus Sacerdotes, vt offeramus pro populo ſacrificium, nam etſi infirmi merito, tamen honorabiles ſacrificio, quia et ſi Chriſtus nunc non videtur offerre , tamen ipſe offertur in terris quando Chriſti corpus offertur &c .*

(c) *Ciprian . l . 2 . epiſt . 3 . poſt med .* (d) *Heſechius in Leuit . l . 1 . c . 4 .* (e) *Heſechius ibid .* ſaith , *ſemetipſum in cæna Apoſtoloru immolauit . & vide l . 6 . c . 23 .* (*) *Heſechius in Leuit . l . 1 . c . 4 .* And *Germanus Conſtantinop . in rerum Eccleſiaſt . Theoria poſt med .* ſaith accordingly, *non enim ſemel cum ſe obtulerit*

of his laſt ſupper (c) *being the high Preiſt of God the Father* , offered firſt (as then) *ſacrifice to God the Father* , and commaunded the ſame to be done in memory of him, that (d) *he offered his owne ſacrifice* , and (e) *ſacrificed him ſelfe in the ſupper of the Apoſtles* : and did (*) *take vpon him the dignitie of Preiſthood* (prius in miſtica cæna, deinde per Crucem) *firſt in the myſtical ſupper, and afterwardes vpon the Croſſe* ; that (f) *firſt with his proper handes he offered him ſelfe to God the Father* , that (g) *he him ſelfe of his body and bloud inſtituted a ſacrifice according to the order of Melchiſedech* , that (h) *he offered him ſelf,*

& ſacrificarit Sacerdotio defunctus eſt, ſed hoc perpetuo noſtrum miniſterij munus obijt, quo et aduocatus eſt pro nobis apud Deum per æuum . (f) *Rupertus*, l . 2 . *in Exod . c . 6 .* (g) *Aug . in Pſal . 33 . Conc . 2 .* alluding to the hiſtorie of *Dauid,* chaunging his countenance in the ſight of king *Achis*, 1 . Reg . 21 . 13 . mentioneth our Sauiours chaunging the ſacrifice of the ould Teſtament ſaying of him, *coram regno Patris ſui mutauit (Chriſtus) vultum ſuum, et dimiſit eum et abijt, quia erat ibi ſacrificium ſecundum ordinem Aaron, et poſtea ipſe de corpore et ſanguine ſuo inſtituit ſacrificium ſecundum ordinem Melchiſedech, mutauit ergo vultum ſuum in Sacerdotio, et dimiſit gentem Iudæorum .* And in his booke *de ciuit. Dei* l . 17 . c . 20 . *circa med.* he ſaith further, *Agnoſcimus Dei ſapientiam &c .* menſam in vino et panibus preparaſſe, vbi apparet etiam ſacerdotium ſecundum ordinem Melchiſedech &c . quam (menſam) Sacerdos ipſe Mediator Teſtamenti noui exhibet ſecundum ordinē Melchiſedech, de corpore et ſanguine ſuo, id enim ſacrificium ſucceſſit omnibus illis ſacrificijs veteris Teſtamenti &c . quia pro omnibus illis Sacrificijs corpus eius offertur et participantibus miniſtratur . So plainely doth S . *Auguſtine* hereby affirme the ſacrifice of Chriſtes body according to the order of *Melchiſedech,* not as it was once offered on the Croſſe, but as it is dayly offered in the Sacrament . (h) *Chriſoſtom . ad Pop . hom . 60 . circa med .* ſaith, *ſanctis carnibus ſuis nos dedit impleri , ſeipſum*

and (i) *insteede of the slaughter of brute beastes, commaunded him selfe to be offered*, that (k) *he offered him selfe a sacrifice for vs &c. when he gaue to his Disciples his body to be eaten, and his bloud to be drunken*, that (l) *his body was then already offered by an inuisible and vnspeakeable meanes*. And lastly that in his last supper, (m) *he taught the new oblation of the new Testament*: Adde but now hereunto in further explication of this point, that which is said aswel (n) *heretofore* cōcerning the Churches, *Altar*, as also here after cōcerning (o) *sacrifice*, & the Preistes remayning (in reguard thereof) (p) *vnmaried*.

That the Preist might not be such a one as before
his orders taken, was Bigamus, and that
after his orders taken, he might not
marie.

SECTION. 4.

TO proceede further with the *Preist*, he might not, as is gathered from (q) *S. Paules*

opposuit immolatum,

(i)

Chrisost. in 1. *Cor*. hom. 24. and see hereafter *Tract* 3. *sect*. 1. *subd*. 1. in the margent at n. concerning the change of sacrifice.

(k)

Nissen. orat. 1. *de resurrectione paulo ante med*. saith, *Arcano sacrificij genere quod ab hominibus cerni non poterat, seipsum pro nobis hostiam offert, et victimam immolat &c. quando id prestitit cum corpus suum Discipulis congregatis edendum, et sanguinem bibendum prebuit, tunc aperte declarauit agni sacrificium iam esse peractū &c. quare cū corpus edendū et sanguinem bibendum Dicipulis exhibuit, iam*

arcana et nō aspectabili ratione corpus erat immolatū &c. (l) *Nissen. vt supra*. (m) *Ireneus* (who liued presētly after the Apostles age) l. 4. c. 32. *fine*. saith hereof, *accepit et gratias egit dicens, hoc est corpus meum, et Calicem similiter &c. sanguinem suum confessus est, et noui Testamenti nouam docuit oblationem, quam Ecclesia ab Apostolis accipiens, in vniuerso mundo offert Deo &c.* (n) See heretofore *Tract*. 1. *sect*. 2. *subd*. 1. at z. in the margent. (o) See hereafter *Tract*. 3. *sect*. 1. throughout. (p) See hereafter *Tract*. 1. *sect*. 4. *subd*. 1. at 1. & *subd*. 2. at z. a. b. c. (q) Whereas *S. Paul* 1. *Tim*. 3. 2. and *Tit*. 1. 6. mentioneth *a Bishop the husband of one wife*, that this is to be vnderstoode of the time past before his being made Bishop, is fully explained by *S. Paules* like saying more plainly of professed Widowes. 1. *Tim*. 5. 9. *let a widowe be chosen &c. who haith bene the wife of one husband*: in which place, as by the iudgement of *Caluin in omnes epistolas Pauli* (m) 1. *Tim*. 5. 9. pag. 778. 2. *circa med*. and

I 3   alledged

alledged by M. *Bancroft* in his suruey &c. pag. 218. And like iudgement of *Augustine Marlorct* in 1. Tim. c. 5. verf. 9. pag. 374. poft med.) there is forbidden precedent bigamy, in fuch widowes as were to be chofen or profeffed, fo alfo in the other like fayinges of S. Paul concerning Bifhops, is their precedēt bigamy much the rather to be thought to be forbidden. (*)

Can. Apoft. c. 17. faith, fi quis poft Baptifma fecundis nuptijs fuerit copulatus, aut corcubinam habuerit, non poteft effe Epifcopus, nec Prefbyter, aut Diaconus. et vide can. 18. of the authoritie & credit of thefe Canons, fee more hereafter *Tract. 1. fect. 4. fubd. 2.* at q. r. And in the margent there at the letters u. x.

(¶)

M. *Fulke* in his Retentiue againft *Briftow*, and difcouerie of *Saunders Rocke*, pag. 164. initio.

Paules wordes and the *Apoftles* (*) Canons be, fuch a one as before his orders receiued was Bigamus, or twife maried. This doctrine was fo general in the dayes of S. Hierome, that M. *Fulke* acknowledgeth accordidgly that (¶) *he which haith had two wiues could not be Preift in Hieromes time*. And this point is yet more fo euidently confirmed with the anfwerable practife and teftimony of the auntient Fathers (r) *Greeke* and (s) *Latine*, that (t) *Beza* doth for this their opinion, namely reproue *Origen, Leo, Innocentius, Auguftine, Ambrofe*, and *Epiphanius*, and the *Centurie writers* do in like maner reprehend for the fame opinion (u) *Chrifoftome*, (x) *Siritius*, (y) *Tertullian*, (z) *Origen*, and the Councel called (a) *Valentinianum*.

This

(r) *Origen. hom. 7. in Luc.* faith, *nec Prefbyter, nec Diaconus, nec Vidua, poffunt effe bigami.* And *Bafil. ad Amphilochiū* c. 12. faith, *Bigamos canō a minifterio omnino exclufit.* alfo *Epiphan. hær.* 59. ante med. faith, *non fufcipit fancta Dei predicatio poft Chrifti aduentū eos qui mortua ipforum vxore fecundis nuptijs coniuncti funt, propter excellentem Sacerdotij honorem.* And fee further hereof, *Chrifoft. hom. 2. in epift. ad Tit.* and *Clemens, in conftitut. Apuftol. l. 2. c. 2.* and *l. 6. c. 17.* and *Canones Apoftolorum c. 17.* and *Concil. Trallan. can. 3.* and *ex Capitulis Grac. finod. c. 43. 44.* (s) The fourth Carthage Councel (whereat S. *Auguftine* was prefent and fubfcribed) faith *Can. 69. fimili fententiæ fubiacebit Epifcopus, fi fciens ordinauerit Clcricum eum qui viduam, aut repudiatam vxorem habuit, aut fecundum.* And fee further *Auguftine de bono coniugali c. 18.* and *Innocentius, epift. 2. ad Victoricum c. 6.* and *Zozimus, epift. 1. ad Hefchium.* & *Leo, epift. 89. ad Epifcopos Peruien.* & *epift. 87. ad Epifcopos Aphricanos. et epift. 48. ad Anaftafium Theffalon.*

And

And *Ambrose*, l. 1. *offic*. c. 50. *et epist*. 82. *post med*. and *Hieron*. *epist*.
2. c. 18. *et epist*. 11. c. 2. *et epist*. 83. *ad Oceanum* c. 2. *et* l. 1. *adu*.
Iouin. c. 8. and *concil. Valentinum*. c. 1. *et vide concil*. 4. *Toletan*. c. 18.
and *concil*. 1. *Toletan*. c. 4. *& conc*. 3. *Arelatense*. c. 2. *& conc*. *Aga-*
thense. c. 1. *et conc*. *Talense*. c. 4. *et* 5. *& conc. Spalense*. c. 4. *& conc. Ge-*
rundense, c. 7. (t) *Beza de Poligamia* pag. 212. 213. & 214. (u) *Cent*. 5.
c. 4. *col*. 508. *line*. 23. (x) *Cent*. 4. *col*. 1293. *lin*. 25. (y) *Cent*. 3.
c. 4. *col*. 85. *lin*. 60. (z) *Cent*. 3. c. 4. *col*. 86. *line*. 7. (a) *Cent*. 4.
col. 847. *line*. 47.

(b) 1. *Tim*. 5. 11. 12.

(c)
This Preist also might not marrie after his   See *Caluin*. *institut*. l. 4.
orders receiued: thus much the Apostle him   c. 13. *sect*. 18. and see
selfe more then insinuateth in the example   him further *in omnes Pauli*
of professed widowes, concerning whom it   *epistolas*, in 1. *Tim*. 5.
is said, that *if* (b) *they wil marrie they haue dam-*   *vers*. 11. pag. 778. b.
nation, because they haue (thereby) *made voide*   *circa et post med. et ibidem*
their first faith, or vow to the cótrary. A place   *in vers*. 12. pag. 779. a.
so euident that *Caluin* confesseth of these wi-   and b.
dowes, that they in regard of their necessary
attendance (c) *had vndertaken the law of a per-*   (d)
petual vnmaried life, and that *if they married they*   *Chemnitius, examen. part.*
did cast of the vocation of God &c. and sinned.   3. pag. 23. a. et 38. a.
As also *Chemnitius*, and other Protestantes do   b. and see the confession
(d) acknowledge, that the said widowes   of *Bohemia* in the harmó-
make publique profession to liue vnmarried, in so   ny of confessions in eng-
much as *Augustine Marloret*, and sundry other   lish, pag. 544. *initio*.
Protestant writers, do hereupon most plainly
affirme (e) *that they might not marrie*. Onely   (e)
I wil alledge further one english Protestant   *Marloret in* 1. *Tim*. c. 5.
writer, who telling how some of these (f)   *vers*. 11. pag. 375. a. *si*
yonger widowes, through the lust of youth do betake   *ne* saith, *nabere volunt et*
them   *sane nubere &c. they wil*
marrie, and truely tamarrie
is of it selfe without fault &c. but because *they did once geue their faith to*
Christ the spouse, and to the Church, and willingly barred them selues from ma-
riage, hence it is &c. that their mariage doth decline to the ignominie of Christ.
And the Protestant author of the booke entituled *Antichristus, siue Progn*
nostica finis mundi. pag. 148. *fine*. and 149. saith, *quod Lutherus hanc*
primam fidem de fide iustificante intelligit, et non de fide pudicitiæ, id plane coac-
tum est, quam sententiam vt ipse primus habet, ita siue aliquius docti suffragio
et inuito paulo &c. Loquitur Apostolus de fide seu voto officij &c. quia autem

Paulus illis vitio uertit, quod nubere postea voluerint, clarissimum est hanc condi-
tionem in voto intercessisse &c. (f) M. *Alison* in his confutation of Brow-
nisme, *pag.* 71. And so likewise *Bullinger in* 1. Tim. *c.* 5. *in vers.* 11.
12. & 13. saith of professed widowes, euen those that were of yonger
yeares and fitte for mariage; *quæ recipiuntur viduæ quasi carni, et mundo*
iam mortuæ veluti Christo nubunt, & spem de se præbent nunquam se ad con-
iugia mundi aspiraturas &c. et sane nubere per se quidem vitio caret, honora-
bile enim est connubium apud omnes, quia vero fidem et Christo sponso et Eccle-
sia dederunt semel, et sese sua sponte abdicarunt connubio, hinc lasciuia, et nuptiæ
earum in ignominiam ver-
gunt Christi.

(g)
The Fathers like exposi-
tion hereof is confessed
by M. *Fulke* who against
the Rhemish Testament
in 1. *Tim.* 5. *fol.* 381. b.
sect. 10. *initio.* saith, *most*
of the auntient Fathers do
expound this first faith of the
vow or promise of continen-
cie. And see the like cō-

them selues to mariage againe, saith further of
them, *which though it be a matter lawful in it self*
yet is it vnlawful to those that before God and his
Church haue vowed the contrary : and *thus* (saith
he) *is this place of Paul* (concerning widowes)
expounded by Theophilact, Ambrose, Bullinger,
Claudius, Guilliand, and others; whereunto
might be added the like (g) cōfessed iudgemēt
& exposition of al the auntiēt Fathers that in-
terprete this place: if now thē this charge of
cōtinencie be incident to professed widowes,
how

fession or ackonweledgement made by *Danæus contra Bellarmin. primæ*
partis altera parte, pag. 1011. where he reproueth the Carthage Councels like exposition of this place saying, *Concilium Carthaginens.* 4. *can.*
104. *verbo Dei manifesté abutitur :* the wordes of thē said Councel wherat
S. *Augustine* was present and subscribed, *can.* 104. are, *Si quæ viduæ quan-*
tumlibet adhuc in minoribus Annis positæ, et matura ætate a viro relictæ se de-
uouerunt Domino, et veste laicali abiecta sub testimonio Episcopi, et Ecclesiæ
religioso habitu apparuerint, postea vero ad nuptias seculares transierint secun-
dum Apostolum damnationem habebunt, quia primam fidem irritam fecerunt
&c. nam si adulteræ coniuges reatu suo sunt vris suis obnoxia, quanto magis
viduæ, quæ religiositatem mutauerunt crimine adulteriy notabuntur. Si &c.
ad secundas nuptias transitum fecerint. And see the like exposition geuen
hereof for the greeke Fathers by *Epiphanius, hær.* 48. *Basil. de virgini-*
tate parum vltra med. Theodoret, Chrisostome, Theophilact, and *Oecumeni-*
us in their seueral cōmentaries, *in* 1. *Tim. c.* 5. And for the latine Fathers by S. *Augustine de sancta virginitate c.* 23. *& de bono viduitatis*

c. 8.

c. 8. *& 9. & in Pſal*. 75. by *Innocentius, epiſt*. 2. *ad Victoricum*. c. 13. *Gelaſius, epiſt*. 1. c. 23. *Tertulian*. *de Monogamia*. *Hierome*, l. 1. *contra Iouin*. c. 7. *& in Ezech*. c. 24. *prope finem*. *Fulgentius, epiſt*. 3. And by *Ambroſe, Sedulius,* and *Beda* in their Comentaries in 1. *Tim*. c. 5.

how much the rather to Preiſtes? And if the Apoſtle did not forbeare to aduiſe laye maried perſons to abſtaine from the acte of marriage (h) *by conſent for a time, that they might geue them ſelues to faſting and praier,* then as *S. Hierome* concludeth hereupon, (i) *the Preiſt that muſt alwaies offer ſacrifice and alwaies pray, muſt therefore be alwaies free from matrimonie*. And if likewiſe the Apoſtle doubted not to aduiſe further concerning laye perſons; (k) *I would haue you to be without care: he that is without a wife, careth for the thinges that pertaine to our Lord, how he may pleaſe God; but he that haith a wife, is careful of the thinges that are of the world, how he may pleaſe his wife &c.* admoniſhing yet further, (l) *I ſay to the vnmaried and to widowes, it is good for them if they ſo abide:* Affirming withal, euen of the maried, that (m) *ſuch ſhal haue tribulation of the fleſh,* how much the rather then are we to expect that the *Preiſt* ſhould not intangle himſelfe with this foreſaid *worldly care and tribulation of the fleſh*.

(2) Adde but now hereunto the Apoſtles (n) foreſaid prohibition of *bigamy* in a Preiſt, which by neceſſary implication includeth euidently

(h) 1. Cor. 7. 5.
(i)
Hierome, l. 1. c. 19. *adu*. *Iouin*. ſaith, *certe confiteris nonpoſſe eſſe Epiſcopum, qui in Epiſcopatu filios faciat alioquin ſi deprehenſus fuerit non quaſi vir tenebitur, ſed quaſi adulter damnabitur: ſed et hoc inferendum, ſi laicus et quicunq̃ fidelis orare non poteſt niſi careat officio cõgugali, Sacerdoti cui ſemper pro populo offerenda ſunt ſacrificia ſemper orandũ eſt, ſi ſemper orandum, ergo ſemper carendũ matrimonio*. And *S. Hierome, in epiſt. ad Titum. c. 1. poſt med.* yet further ſaith, *ſi laicis imperatur, vt propter orationem abſtineant ſe ab vxorũ coitu, quid de Epiſcopo ſentiendum qui quotidie pro ſuis populiq̃, peccatis, illibatus Deo oblaturus eſt victimas?* And *S. Ambroſe in* 1. *Tim*.

c. 3. geueth the very like reaſon ſaying, *ſi enim plebis hominibus orationis cauſa ad tempus abſtinere ſe pręcepit, vt vacent orationi: quanto magis Leuitis aut Sacerdotibus, quos die noctuq̃ pro plebe ſibi commiſſa oporteret orare, mundiores ergo debent eſſe cęteris, quia actores Dei ſunt*. (k) 1. Cor. 7. 32. 33. (l) 1. Cor. 7. 8. & 26. (m) 1. Cor. 7. 28. (n) See heretofore *Tract*. 1. *ſect,* 4. *ſubdiuiſion* 1. *prope initium*.

K   (*)

(o) *Epist. l. 7. 8.*
and Hierome
vpon this
place. See

(*) *1. Tim. 5. 22.* uidently his vndertaking not to marrie after
See *Conc. 5. Carthag.* his orders taken. Adde also that the Apostle
can. 3. and conc. 3. can. conioyning (*) *Chastitie* and (o) *Continencie* to
19. & conc. Anciranum, Bishops, secludeth them thereby from marri-
can. 10. age, for (according to the auntient councels)
by the word *containe,* is (*) vnderstoode an ab-

(p) staining from the acte of marriage, as appea-
If they do not containe reth yet more plainely by the (p) opposition
let them marrie, 1. Cor. which the same Apostle elswhere maketh be-
7. 9. (¶) tweene *Continencie* and *Marriage.* Adde lastly
Concil. 2. Carthag. can. that as the Fathers of the *Carthage Councel,* do
2. decreeth saying, *pla-* in plaine tearmes referre this vnmarried life of
cuit et condecet sacros sanc- Preistes to (¶) *the Apostles teaching.* So like-
tos antistites, & Dei sacer- wise the doctrine thereof is yet further accor-
dotes &c. continentes esse dingly set downe in the 50. (q) *Canons of the*
in omnibus, quo possint sim- *Apostles,* writen by *S. Clement* their (r) *scho-*
pliciter quod a Deo postulat *ler* and (s) published in latine so many ages
impetrare, vt quod Apostoli since by *Isidore,* and before him by *Dionisius.*
docuerunt, et ipsa seruauit The answearable antiquitie of the said Ca-
antiquitas, nos quoq, custo- nons, being yet further acknowledged, not
diamus: ab vniuersis Epis- only by sundrie other auntient (t) Fathers
copis dictum est, omnibus but
placet, vt Episcopi Præsby-

teri, et Diaconi, et qui Sacramenta contrectant pudicitia custodes etiam ab vxo-
ribus se abstineant. (q) *In canonibus Apost. c. 27. it is decreed in nup-*
tis autē qui ad clerum prouecti sunt, præcipimus, vt si voluerint vxores accipiant,
sed Lectores Cantoresq, solos. And see the translation thereof in *Isidore,*
with the word *tantummodo.* And see *Concil. Constantinop. in Trullo. can.*
6. recyting & expounding this very Canon of the Apostles accordingly. (r) Of *Clement* mention is made, *Philp. 4. 3.* (s) *Isidore in præ-*
fat. in 1. tom. conc. saith, *deniq, propter eorum authoritatem cæteris concilijs*
preposuimus canones, qui dicuntur Apostolorum &c. And concerning *Dioni-*
sius, liuing eleuen hundreth yeares since, and his translating them into latine, see the same at large in *Baronius tom. 2. col. 19. at Anno Christi*
102. *Num.* 10. (t) See *Iustinian. in constitut. 6. ad Epiphanium Con-*
stantinop. and *concil. Ephes. can. 8. in summa conciliorum per Barthol. Ca-*
ranzam, fol. 132. a. And *Concil. Trullan. can. 6. & 12. in Caranza.*
And *Ismarus de varijs quæst. c. 27.* And the auntient father *Epiphanius*
(*hær, 48. post. med.*) of whom M. *Parkins* in his problem, *pag. 7.*
ante

ante med. confesseth saying, *Canonum Apostolorum primus mentionem facit Epiphanius, hær . 30.* And yet such is their further confessed antiquitie, that the Centurie writers, who disable them al they can, thinke them to haue bene no lesse auntient then the time of the *Nicene Councel . Cent . 3 . c . 7 . col . 160 . line 4 .* whereas yet in euident proofe of their further antiquitie, the *Councel of Antioch* (celebrated within twentie yeares after the *Nicene Councel*) doth ,*can . 9 .* make a special decree (*secundum antiquum Canonem Patru*) *according to the auntient Canon of their Fathers .* The matter whereof is to be found, not in any then precedent Canon, which those Fathers might tearme *the auntient Canon of their Fathers*, other then the 35 . Canon of the Apostles : in which 35 . Canon the same matter is so euidently decreed that the Protestant writer *Frigeuilleus Gauuius*, in his *Palma Christiana pag . 112 . fine .* saith of the said 9 . Canon of *Antioch: Hic Canon manifeste desumptus est ex* 35 *. Canon. Apostolorum .* And in like plaine maner is the 21 . Canon of Antioch (which relateth likewise to an other then auntient precedent Canon) taken in like sorte from the 14 . *Canon* of the Apostles : So plainely were these Apostolicke Canons receiued & acknowledged for auntient in the very time of the *Councel of Antioch .* A thing in it selfe so certaine & euident, that M . D . *Downeham* in his two sermons *printed* 1608 . in the 2 . sermon at Lambith, of the honourable function of Bishops, *pag . 26 .* alledgeth (to vse his owne worde) *one of the auntient Canons called the Apostles &c. which* (said) *Canon* (saith he) *the Councel of Antioch,* c . 9 . recyteth, calling it the aunti-
but also by learned (u) Protestantes them ent Canon of their Fathers .
selues , of both whom some doubt not to (u)

(x) *M. Iewel* in his defence
of the Apologie, *pag. 512.* & after the latter editió of *Anno* 1571 .*pag .* 539 . *circa med.* alledgeth their authority calling thē *the ould Canōs of the Apostles.* And *Beza de Polygamia* pag . 193 . *fine .* speaking of the Apostles Canons saith, *mihi vero probabilis videtur eorum opinio, qui coniiciunt aliquanto post Apostolorum tempora siue a Clemente, siue ab alio quopiam eius, quæ tunc vigerit Ecclesiasticæ policiæ regulas aliquot colligi cæpisse &c .* And *Gregorius Holloander* did translate thē out of greeke, & *in epist . ad reipub .* *Norreburgensis moderatores in initio primi voluminis Concil .* calleth them *the Apostolicke Canons published by holy Clement successor of Peter :* alledging further in their proofe, *an auntient edition of them in time of Pope Stephanus,* *who liued with Ciprian .* And *Frigeuillus Gauuius* an other Protestant wri-.

ter in his booke entituled *Palma Christiana*, dedicated to her late Ma-
ieftie, writeth a fpecial treatife in their behalfe, alledging there *pag*.
44. *fine*. the forefaid teftimonie of *Gregorie Holoander*, and fundry other
proofes (*pag*. 29. 43. 44. *&c*. and *pag*. 91. 96. 112. 121.) that
they were vndoubtedly the doctrine of the Apoftles.

(x)

See this anfweare in *Ig-*
marus l. *de varijs quaft*.
and *Frigeuilleus Gauuius*
(a proteftant writer) in
his *Palma Chriftiana ad*
fereniffimā Reginam Angliæ
&c. pag. 49. *poft*. *med*.
faith in defence and an-
fweare for thefe Canons,
Synodi cōprobarunt hos Ca-
nones ante Gelafium, & a-
liæ etiam poft ipfum Gelati-

(x) anfweare the now (y) *mistaken common*
obiection vrged from *Gelafius* out of (*) *Gra-*
tian by our other aduerfaries againft the faid
Canons.

To come now to the Fathers, *Origen* expreffeth (almoft 1400. yeares fince) the doctrine of the *Greeke Church* faying, not doubtfully but refolutely, (z) *it is certaine that*
the daily facrifice is hindred in them who ferue the
neceffities of marriage, therefore it feemeth to me
that it appertaineth only to him to offer the daily fa-
crifice

um, libenter tamen audirem rationes Gelatij, at ipfe nullas propofuit, nudum de-
cretum protulit his verbis, liber Canonum Apoftolorum Apocriphus. Imo poti-
us decreta Gelatij Apocripha. (y) *Miftaken*, for the words commonly
obiected from *Gelatius* (which are, *liber Apoftolorum Apocriphus*) do not
concerne thefe Canons affirmed to be publifhed by *Clement* , for he
doth not here fo much as name *Clement*, as in the fame place he nameth
and condemneth, *itinerarium quod appellatur fancti Clementis:* But fome
other Apocriphal booke forged by fome other perfō vnder the Apoftles
names, fuch (or the fame perhaps) as is mentioned by *Leo epift*. 93. *ad*
Turbium, c. 15. for the Canons now extant are fuch fhort decrees, as
cā not be anfwearable to the title of the booke which *Gelatius* reiecteth:
Secondly, though *Gelatius* fhould hereby meane the Canons now extant,
yet may it be that he reiected them, not as they were compofed by *Cle-*
mēt & are now choifely publifhed by *Ifodore*, but as they the were, & yet
according to fome copies, are depraued with additions or corruptions.
As alfo the other forefaid Treatife of *Clement* entituled (*itinerarium Cle-*
mentis) writen (as *Epiphanius hær*. 30. *paulo ante med*. witneffeth) by *Cle-*
ment, but greatly corrupted by the *Ebionites*, whereof *Clement* him felfe
complaineth (*tefte Epiphanio hær*. 30.) is there in like manner reiected
by *Gelatius*. And fo *Igmarus* (l. *de varijs quaft*.) aboue 800. yeares
fince

since resolueth this obiection from *Gelatius,* concluding that *(nos tamen illa* 50. *capitula &c.* we notwithstanding are to receiue without scruple those 50. chapters (or Canons) which we reade, translated out of Greeke. (*)

Gratian dist. 16. c. *Canones.*
(z)

crifice who haith vowed himselfe to daily and per-petual *Chastity:* with whom agree many other greeke (a) *Fathers.* S. *Hierome* also expresseth in like maner the like doctrine of the *Latine Church* saying, (b) *if married mē like not of this, let them not be angrie with me, but with the holy Scriptures, with al Bishops, Preistes Deacons &c. who know they cannot offer sacrifice if they vse the acte of marriage.* And the like reason ot Preists abstinence from marriage, in reguard of their daily celebratiō of this Sacrament, is yet further affirmed by sundry other (c) Fathers of the Latine Church: whereunto might be added many plaine (d) testimonies of the other Fathers (and for such by our aduersaries (e) confessed) making against Preistes marriage.

Origen. in numer, hom. 23. *& vide* l. 8. *cōtra Celsum.* that *Origen* hereby ment to restraine Preists from marriage is confessed by *Chemnitius* in his *examen, part.* 3. pag. 50. a. *initio.* & 58. b. *post. med.*
(a)
See *Clement,* l. 6. *constit. Apostolicarum* c. 17. *et cōcil. Anciran. can.* 10. *& concil. Mocesariense.* c. 1. *et concil. Nicen. can.* 34. and *Eusebius de demonst.*

A

Euangelica l. 1. c. 9. *Epiphanius hær.* 59. *ante med.* And *Basil. epist.* 1. *ad Amphilochium can.* 6. *et epist.* 17. *ad Paregorium Presbyterum,* and *Ciril. Hierosol. Catech.* 12. (b) *Hieronimus in Apologia ad Pamachium* c. 3. and the same reason of Preistes abstinence from mariage in reguard of their sacrifice, he maketh in c. 1. *ad Titum paulo post med.* (c) *Innocentius epist.* 1. *ad Victoricū.* c. 9. *et epist. ad Exuperium* c. 1. and *Sirisius in epist. ad Hunericum Tarraconensem Episcopum,* c. 7. and *Beda in* c. 1. *Lucæ.* and *Leo, epist.* 82. *ad Anastasium Thessal.* c. 4. *et epist.* 90. *ad Rusticum,* c. 3. and *Gregorie* l. 1. *epist.* 42. *et* l. 3. *epist.* 34. and *Ambrose,* in 1. *Tim.* c. 3. (d) See *Concil. Arausican.* 1. *can.* 22. and 23. and *Concil.* 1. *Turonense.* c. 1. *& 2. et concil. Agathense.* c. 9. *et concil.* 2. *Arelatense. can.* 2. *et concil. Aurelianense.* 4. *can.* 17. *et concil.* 5. *Aurelianense,* c. 4. *et concil.* 3. *Toletan.* c. 4. *et concil. Matisconense,* c. 11. *et concil.* 2. *Turonense,* c. 10. 11. 13. *et concil.* 5. *Carthaginense, can.* 3. *& concil.* 3. *Carthag. can.* 17. *et* 19. (e) M. *Iewel* in his defence of the Apologie pag. 164. and after his latter edition pag. 195. *fine.* saith hereof, *here I graunt* M. *Harding is like to finde some good aduantage*

as

as hauing vndoubtedly agreat nūber of holy Fathers on his ſide. In like manner *Chemnitius* in his examen, part. 3. pag. 50. a. and 52. a. and 62. a. And the Centurie writers, *Cent.* 3. col. 148. poſt med. and *Cent.* 4. c. 7. col. 486. and 487. & *Danæus primæ partis altera parte contra Bellarm. controu.* 5. pag. 863. fine. and *Hoſpinianus in hiſtoria Sacramentaria.* l. 2. pag. 132. do reproue for their doctrine againſt Preiſtes marriage, *Baſile, Chriſoſtome, Origen, Ambroſe, Hierome, Siritius, Innocentius, Epiphanius.* and the *Councels of Arles, Carthage,* and *Noeceſaria,* and ſundry other Fathers. (f)

See next hereafter at the letter h.

(g)

See *Hierome* l. contra Iouin. where he ſaith, *certè confiteris non poſſe eſſe Epiſcopum qui in Epiſcopatu filios faciat, alioquin ſi deprehenſus fuerit, nō quaſi vir tenebitur, ſed quaſi adulter damnabitur.* And ſee him further there, c. 19. & 14. *et ad Pamachium Apol.* c. 8. (*)

Epiphanius hær. 59. *ante med.* ſaith, *at dices mihi omnino in quibuſdam locis adhuc liberos gignere, et Preſbyteros, et Diaconos &c.* whereto he anſwereth ſaying, *at hoc non eſt*

A doctrine ſo euident and general in the Primitiue Church, that (f) *Vigilantius,* (g) *Iouinian,* and (*) *others,* were by the Fathers ſpecially condemned for their mantaining of Preiſtes marriage: S. *Hierome* alledging thereupon againſt *Vigilantius,* the examples & general practiſe to the contrary of (h) *the Churches of the eaſt, of Ægipt, and the Sea Apoſtolicke.*

Of the Preiſtes ordaining, his vnction, tonſure, & apparrel vſed in the holye Maſſe.

SECTION. 5.

THis Preiſt alſo was ordained or enabled to celebrate our foreſaid publique Lyturgie, not (i) by vertue of populer election, as the (k) *Puritanes,* would enforce, but (which

areth ſaying, *at hoc non eſt iuxta Canones, ſed iuxta hominū mentem, quæ per tempus elanguit.* And See *Siritius in epiſt. ad Himericum Tarraçenſem Epiſcopum,* c. 6. & 7. (h) *Hieron. contra Vigilantium* c. 1. condemneth *Vigilantius* for this matter ſaying therefore againſt him, *quid faciunt orientis Eccleſiæ, quid Ægipti, et ſedis Apoſtolicæ, quæ aut virgines clericos accipiunt aut continentes, aut ſi vxores habuerint, mariti eſſe deſinunt.* (i) *Concil. Laodicen. can.* 13. decreed *quod non ſit populis concedendum electionem facere eorū, qui altaris miniſterio ſunt applicandi:* for which the Centurie writers, *Cent.* 4. col 435. *initio.* reprehend this councel. And ſee further

Auguſtine

Augustine de adult. *Coniug.* l. 2. c. 20. and 24. & *epist.* 110. and *Possid.* in vita Aug. c. 8. (k) See *Carthwright* hereof in *M. Whitguiftes* defence pag. 192. *post med.* and fee *the vse of the Kirke of Scotland*, printed at *Rochel Anno* 1596.

(which the *Puritanes* vtterly (1) denie) by the only right of ordaining from, & by *a Bifhop*, as appeareth by teftimony both of (m) Scripture, and (n) *Fathers*: the fame alfo being geuen (o) *fafting* euen with the external figne of (p) *impofition of handes* conferring inward (q) *grace*, In fo much as the auntient Fathers did acknowledge it for *a* (r) *Sacramente*, withal (s) comparing it (left they fhould

(1)
See *Carthwrightes* wordes hereof in *M. Whitguiftes* defence, pag. 225. *ante med. &* 196. *ante med.* (m)
See 1. *Tim.* 5. 22. and *Tit.* 1. 5. and 2. *Tim.* 6. & *Act.* 14. 22.
(n)

Hereof (to omit the other Fathers) fee euen *Hierome,* whom the Puritanes alledge moft againft Bifhops *in epift.* 85. *ad Euagrium.* *et in Tit.* c. 1. *verf.* 5. *et in epift. ad Nepotianum.* And the Centurie writers, *cent.* 4. c. 7. *col.* 489. *line* 60. confeffe hereof faying, *ordinatio minifrorum propria erat Epifcopi &c.* (o) Act. 14. 22. and fee *Leo epift.* 87. *ad Epifcopos Africanos ante med. et epift.* 81. *ad Diofcorum Alexandrinum.* (p) 1. *Tim.* 5. 22. *et* 2. *Tim.* 1. 6. *et Tit.* 1. 5. *& 1. Tim.* 4. 14. (& to omit the Fathers plentiful teftimonies hereof) the Centurie writers *cent.* 4. c. 6. *col.* 435. *line* 36. fay of this hand-impofing, *qui ritus inde vfq, ab Apoftolis ipfis in omnium locorum Ecclefys diutiffime hæfit.* (q) 1. *Tim.* 4. 14. fee this *Grace* geuen in orders, acknowledged by *M. Hooker* in his Ecclefiaftical policie, l. 5. *fect.* 77. pag. 230. *prope finem.* and by *M. Bilfon* in his perpetual gouernement of Chriftes Church, pag. 109. And *Anaftafius* the fecond in *epift. ad Anaftafium Imperatorem,* c. 7. *& 8.* affirmeth that there is in orders, and Baptifme, *Sactamenti firma gratia.* (r) *Anaftafius vt fupra.* and *Leo epift.* 81. and 87. and *Auguftin. tom.* 7. *contra epift. Parmen.* l. 2. c. 13. faith of Baptifme and orders: *Si enim vtrumq̃, Sacramentum eft, quod nemo dubitat &c. neutri Sacramento iniuria facienda eft.* And againe, *vtrumq̃, enim Sacramentum eft et quadam confecratione vtrumq̃, homini datur, illud cum Baptizatur, iftud cum ordinatur.* And fee him *de Baptifmo contra Donat.* l. 1. c. 1. (s) *Anaftafius,* and *Auguftine, vt fupra.* and *S. Ciprian in ferm. de ablut. pedum, initio.* making mention, *Baptifmi, et aliorum Sacramentorum,* of Baptifme and other Sacramentes, reckoneth vp withal in that accompt

accompt *Sacros ordines.*   should be thought to vse the word *Sacrament*
(t)   improperly) euen with Baptisme: mentio-
Pacianus in epist. 3. *ad*   ning also the Preistes (t) *vnction,* and (u) *sha-*
Simpronianum, of his vnc-   *uen crowne,* or *tonsure,* for which our aduer-
tion see further *Dionisius*   saries yet blush not contemptuously to cal our
Areopagita, de Ecclesiasti-   now Preistes, *greased* (*) *shauelinges.* This
ca Hierarchia. c. 4. And   Preist did also celebrate the *Masse* or pub-
Eusebius hist. l. 10. c. 4.   lique Lyturgie religiously (¶) *fasting,* and in
initio. after Chrisoftofer-   apparel or vestimentes, not common, but pe-
sons version. And *Gre-*   culiar and distinct for that vse: which kind
gorie l. 4. *in lib. regum* c.   of distinct vestimentes, as they are not pecul-
5. And *Ciprian. ser. de*   ar

Chrismate initio. saith, *Sacrum Chrisma conficitur, in quo mixtum oleo Balsa-*
mum, regiæ et sacerdotalis gloriæ exprimit vnitatem, quibus dignitatibus ini-
tiandis diuinitus est vnctio instituta. A saying so euident that *Chemnitius*
therefore contemneth it in his examen, *part.* 2. *pag.* 247. a. *ante med.*
(u) *Bed. hist.* l. 5. c. 21. *post med.* mentioneth the Preistes *tonsure on*
the toppe of his head in maner of a Crowne. And the Epistle extant vnder
Anicetus name (published about some 1000. yeares since by *Isodore)*
saith hereof, *desuper caput in modum sphæræ radunt.* of this Crowne further mention is made by *S. Hierome in epist. ad August. quæ est epist.* 26.
inter epist. August. and by *S. August. epist.* 147. *ad Proculianum Epis-*
copum. and *S. Isodore.* l. 2. *de offic. diuin.* c. 4. deryueth this Preistly
Crowne from the Apostles. *et vide concil.* 4. *Toletan.* can. 40. *et Dio-*
nisius Areopag. de Ecclesiastica Hierarchia. c. 6. & *Germanus Constantino-*
politanus, in Theoria paulo post initium. saith, *Tonsura capitis Sacerdotis, et*
rotunda eius pilorum media sectio, vice Coronæ est spinea quam Christus ge-
stauit. And the Protestant writer *D. Philippus Nicholay, de regno Christi,*
l. 1. pag. 46. *fine.* saith of the remote Indianes conuerted at first by *S.*
Thomas: *Sacerdotes (eorum) in capite ita sunt attonsi, vt Crucis imaginem*
in vertice summo contineant. (*) See *M. Fulke* in his retentiue &c.
pag. 69. *post. med.* (¶) The third Councel of Carthage c. 29.
decreed, *Sacramenta altaris non nisi a ieiunis hominibus celebrentur.* And
Gregor. Turonen. l. *de gloria Martyrum* c. 86. reporteth a strange
punishment which God afflicted vpon a Preist that presumed to celebrate Masse not fasting. And see further *Concil. Carthag.* 35. *can.* 48.
fine. et concil. African. can. 8. and *concil.* 1. *Bracarense. can.* 16. and
the 7. *Toletane* Councel. *can.* 2. *fine.* And see hereafter, *Tract.* 2.
sect.

ar onely toys of the Romane Church, but
are yet to this day vsed euen in thofe remo-
ter contries of *Asia*, and *Aphricke*, as namely in (2) *Armenia*, and (3) *Ethiopia*, which
(4) argueth *sufficiently* the antiquitie of them.
So are they likewife for former times purposely and specially mentioned for the latine
Church by (x) *Innocentius*, and (y) *Bonauen-*
ture who liued aboue 300. yeares since, by (z)
Rupertus and (a) *Hugo de S. Victor*, who liued 500. yeares since, by (b) *Walfridus*, *Stra-*
bo, (c) *Rabanus* and (d) *Amalarius*, who liued about 700. yeares since, and by (e) *Al-*
cuinus, and (f) others, who liued 850. yeares
since.

　　(2) And for the *greeke Church*, they be
　　　　　　　mentioned
de ricles vestementes et cappes faunnees a leur mode.
for our aduersaries can not say that thefe cotries were lately therein corrupted by the latine Church. (x) *Innocentius*, 3. l. 1. de *mysterijs*
Missæ. (y) *Bonauenture, in expositione Missæ* saith : *Sacerdos primo capiti*
Amictum superponit, quod humerale dicitur &c. postea Albam, et Cingulo se
cingit, postea Manupulum in leua manu sumit, Stolam longam collo superponit,
et eam cancellatam in pectore ad modum Crucis iuxta vtrumq̃ latus cingulo te-
nus ligamentis applicat, postea Casulam induit, et sic ad Altare procedit. (z)
Rupertus Tuitiensis l. 1. *de diuinis officijs.* (a) *Hugo de S. Victor*. l. 2.
de Sacramentis, part. 4. (b) *Walfridus Strabo, in lib. de rebus Ecclesi-*
asticis c. 24. (c) *Rabanus Maurus de institutione Clericorum,* l. 1. c. 15.
saith, *primum indumentum est &c. Superhumerale lineum &c. secundum est*
linea tunica, quæ græce Poderes, *latine Talaris dicitur &c. Tertium Cingulum*
est &c. Quartum vero Mappula siue Mantile &c. quod vulgo phanonem vo-
cant &c. Quintum est quod Orarium dicitur, licet hoc quidam Stolam vocant
&c. Sextum est Dalmatica &c. Septimum est quod Casulam vocant, hæc su-
premum est omnium indumentorum &c. (d) *Amalarius de officijs Ecclesi-*
asticis, l. 2. c. 17. mentioneth *Amictum*, and c. 18. *Albam,* and c. 19.
Casulam, et c. 20. *Stolam,* et c. 21. *Dalmaticam &c.* (e) *Alcuinus in* l.
de diuinis officijs, c. *de vestibus sacris*. maketh like particular mention of
them. (f) *Concil. Rhemense apud Burchardum,* l. 3. c. 20. saith, *nul-*
　　　　　　　　　　　　　L.　　　　　　　　　　　　　　　　　　　　*lus.*

---

(2)
Pierre Belon in his obseruations, *de Plusieurs singu-*
larites &c. prited en Anuers
1555. l. 3. c. 12. fol.
319. a. saith, *les Prestres*
des armenieus &c. (ont re-
uestuz. de Mesmes orname-
tes de Cappes et Chasubles
&c. come les latines.

(3)
Aluarez. in his historial
description *de* l. *Ethiopie*
c. 101. *fol.* 233. a. ante
med. saith, *stoyent de vestes*

lus Presbyter absq̃ Amictu,
Alba, Stola, Fanone, et
Causula vllatenus presumat
Missas celebrare.

(g)

Germanus in Theoria post.
initium. mentioneth the
Preistes girdle, and the
foresaid seueral vestiměts
calledTalaris, Alba, Hu-
merale, Mantile, and o-
thers.　　　(h)

Chrisost. in Lyturg. et ad
populum hom. 60. et in
Math. hom. 83. et concil.
4. Carthag. c. 41. & cō-
cil. 3. Bracharense c. 5. et
Hierome, l. 1. adu, Pelagian. c. 9.

(i)

Basile, and Chrisostome in
Lyturgijs.

(k)

Basil. and Chrisostom. in
Lyturgijs.　　(l) Basil.
and Chrisostome, in Lytur-

mentioned (to omitte others) by (g) Germanus Bishop of Constantinople, who liued about
900. yeares since: in so much as the other
more auntiēt Fathers, who writ not purposly
of these Church vestiments, do yet neuerthelesse in their writing of other matters casually
touch sundry of them, as namely the (h) Albe,
the (i) Girlde, the foresaid Amictus or Amice,
which S. Basile, and S. Chrisostome, cal Omi-
phorion, the (m) Stoale called Orarium, & the
vestiment called (n) Dalmatica. D. Raynolds
him selfe also confessing that (o) in the Lyturgies which beare the names of Basile, and Chrisostome, are mentioned the Amice, the Girdle, the
Chisible, and the Fanel. And other auntient authors further mentioning some of these foresaid holy vesture to be made of (p) Golden
threades: whereto might be added that mention is also made euen of the Bishopes myter,
which is named in (q) Tertulian by the name
of Insula Polucrates. Also aboue 1400. yeares
since making ansfwearable mention that S.
Iohn (r) being a Preist wore Petalon, a thinne
plate (or myter) or (as Peter Martir translateth it) (2) a pontificall plate: an (s) apparel (sath

D.

gijs. (m) Conc. 3. Bracha. c. 3. et conc. 4. Tolet. c. 39. et conc.
Laodicen. c. 23. et conc. Aurelianens. c. 16. et Ambros. in oratione Funebri de obitu fratris satiri. (n) This Dalmatica is mentioned by the
author quæstionum veteris et noui Testamenti quæst. 46. extant in the 4.
tome of Augustines workes. that this author liued before S. Augustine,
see there quæst. 44. and thereupon so affirmed by M. Hutton in the 2.
part of his ansfweare &c. pag. 194. of this vestiment, see further Damasus in vita Siluestri. (o) D. Raynoldes in his conference &c. pag.
598. post. med. (p) Theodoret, l. 2. c. 27. post initium. mentioneth,
Sacram Stolam ex aureis filis contextam &c. (q) Tertul. de monogam.
(r) Polucrates apud Euseb. hist. l. 5. c. 24. after Christofersons transl-
lation c. 23. see the place translated by Hierome, de Scriptoribus Ecclesiasticis

afticis. *verbo Policrates.* (d) *Peter Martir* in his Epiftles annexed to his cômon places in englifh. *pag.* 119. *a . prope finem.* (s) *M. Whitguift* in his defence of the admonition &c. *pag.* 269. *paulo poft med. et vide ibidem pag.* 270. *circa med.* and fee there alfo *pag.* 269. the *Birrus* or thinne plate, mentioned to be worne by *Ciprian :* whereof fee alfo *Peter Martir vbi fupra .*

D. Whitguift) *peculiar to S. Iohn, in refpect he was a Preift.* A teftimony fo plaine, chat for want of better anfweare (3) *Hofpinianus* anfwearing thereto faith, *that S. Iohn wore the fame (ob infirmitatem Iudæorum) for the weaknes of the Iewes ;* whereby is conuinced the other euation of *M. D.* (4) *Raynoldes* contending the word *Petalon,* to be taken myftically, or by way of *allufion.* To omit the lik further abouding (5) teftimonie in this kind of *M. Hutto* & others ; lik as our learned aduerfaries do acknowlege that church (t) *apparel ferueth to edification,* carying with it (u) *a fit and profitable fignification ;* in fo much as they doubt not thereupon to teach the (x) auntient vfage thereof

(3)
Hofpinianus in hiftor . Sacrament. l. 3. pag. 201. *ante med.* (4)
M. D. Raynoldes in his conference with *M. Harte, pag.* 599 . *poft med.*
(5)
M. Hutton in his fecond part of the anfweare to the reafons for refufal of fubfcriptiô, *pag.* 194. 195. & 196. faith, that *about foe* 300. *yeares after Chrift the author of the queftions vpon the old and new Teftament (alledged* next heretofore vnder n.) affirmeth *that Bifhops and Deacons, in his time did weare the Dalmatifh garments that is a kind of Ecclefiaftical attyre before his time :* and that *Conftantine* (good Emperor) *gaue a diftinct holy garment to Macharius to weare in adminiftring Baptifme, and (that) Theodoret recording the fame, reportes an example of a ftage plaier, who for bringing this Baptizing garment vpon a ftage to daunce in, fel fodainely downe and dyed.* That alfo *Eufebius* mentioneth l. 10. c. 4. *Ecclefiaftical perfons affembled in their ornamentes, and facred attyre reaching downe to their feete :* that likewife *we finde that* 60. *yeares before the dayes of Conftantine, a peculiar veftiment was appointed for celebrating of the communion* Hereto he addeth the forefaid example of *Policrates* teftimony concerning *S. Iohn.* & *that alfo of Ciprian who being to be beheaded deliueredhis Dalmatifh vefture to the Deacôs &c.* (t) *M. Whitguift* in his defence &c. pag. 286. 289. 287. & 288. (u) *M. Whitguift ibidem* pag. 270. *ante med.* & fee *Peter Martir* in his Epiftles annexed to his common places in englifh pag. 119. *b . prope finem.* (x) See the wordes of *Bullinger* and *Gualter,*

L 2 alledged

alledged *by M. Whitguift* in his defence &c. *pag.* 268. *cerca med.* where they vndertake to proue *that in the auntient Church there was a peculiar fashion of apparel for Preistes.*

(y)
thereof, with al (y) mentioning and allow-

See *M. Whitguift ibidem,* ing fundry of the fore named veftures: So al-

pag. 270. *circà med.* & fo the feueral fignifications of the forenamed

268. *circa med.* veftures, in particular are fpecially mentio-

(z)
ned & explicated by the auntiët writers both

By *Germanus Conftanti-* of the (z) *Greeke* and (a) *Latine* Church.

noplitanus in Theoria poft

initium. (a) By *Alcuinus* l. *de offic. Ecclefiaft.* c. 38. *quid*

fignificent veftimenta. By *Rabanus* l. 1. *de inftitutione Cleri-*

corum, c. 15. *etfequentibus.* By *Amalarius de Ec-*

clefiaft. offic. c. 15. 17. 18. 19. 20. 21. *et* l.

3. c. 19. And by *Walfridus Strabo,* l. *de*

rebus Ecclefiaft.

c. 24.

TRACT. 2.

*Of the Preiftes beginning to fay Maffe, and the fundrie Ceremo-
nies vfed before confecration, and of his confecration
of the Sacrament.*

SECTION. 1.

Hauing difcourfed hitherto côcerning the antiquitie of the word *Maffe*, the defcription of the auntient Church in which *Maffe* was faid, and of the *Preift* that did celebrate the fame, and his *Preiftly* apparel then vfed: next now fucceedeth to be entreated of *the forme* of this *Maffe*, or publ.que Lyturgie. Wherein to vndertake proofe of of al our particular praiers therein prefcribed, weare a labour both tedious, and improper, efpecially confidering that moft of them are by our aduerfaries acknowledged, and by their needie imitation from vs borowed or receiued into their now Cômunion booke, onely therefore (as coueting to be breife and pertinent) I wil difcourfe of that forme, and thofe Ceremonies which are by our aduerfaries moft impugned.

To beginne then with fome of the Ceremonies that are before facrifice : firft, the people are (b) *fprinckled with holie water*, wher of I forbeare further profe, for that enough haith bene

(b)
Hereof fee *Micrologus* l. *de obferuationibus Ecclefiaft*. c. 46. and the Epiftle publifhed by *Ifidore* about 1000. yeares fince vnder the name of *Pope Alexander* the firft, who was Bifhop of Rome next after the Apoftles age, in refpect whereof the French Proteftant writer in his fix godly Treatifes &c. tranflated (for their fuppofed worth) into englifh, and printed by *Nicholas Oakes Anno* 1608. pag. 92. *circa med.* faith, *Alexander the firft of that name next fucceffor of the Apoftles of Iefus Chrift , and one of the firft corrupters of the holy Sacra-*

ments, *followed the inftitution of Pompilius, continuing this Idolatrie of coniuring, and confecrating holy water to chafe away deuils &c.* And the Proteftant writer *Doctor Philippus Nicholai de regno Chrifti,* l. 1. pag. 46: *circa med.* reporteth of the remote oriental Indians conuerted as firft by *S. Thomas* faying, *in ingreffu Templi luftralibus aquis perinde vt Pontificij afperguntur* asperguntur. And see Damasus in Pontificum vitis, where he faith, Alexander constituit aquam aspersionis cum sale benedici.

(c)
See heretofore Tract. 1. sect. 2. subdivis. 1. in the margent there at u. & x.

(d)
Dionisius Areopagita de Ecclesiast. Hierarchia c. 3. faith hereof, Pontifex vbi

bene (c) heretofore said concerning the great antiquity of holy water. The Church also is perfumed with (d) sacred incense, and (e) the Preist goeth to the holy table (tribus vicibus inclinans) bowing himself three times; afterwardes (f) he boweth himself and kisseth the holy Altar: at (g) the reading of the Gospel a waxen candle is lighted, and (*) the people stand vp, and (h) after the Gospel is ended he kisseth the booke and setteth it aside &c. The bread and wine being made ready, and the Preist preparing to sacrifice, he (i) washeth his fingers; (k) signeth the bread

orationem sanctam super Altare diuinum peregit, ex ipso incensum adolere inchoans omnem Fani ambitum circuit. and Ambrose in c. 1. Luc. faith, vtinam nobis quoq, adolentibus Altaria Sacrificium deferentibus assistat Angelus. Of this incense vsed in the Church further mention is made by the Canons of the Apostles, c. 4. by Hipolitus orat. de Antechristo, by Basilius orat. in Gordium Martirem. by Euagrius hist. l. 4. c. 7. and l. 5. c. 21. by Isidore in epist. ad Ludifredum. by Damasus in pontificali in vit. Soteris, et Siluestri. by Germanus Constantinoplitanus in Theoria. and by Chrisostome in Lyturgia paulo post initium, who mentioneth there this vsage of incense, and the halowing thereof. (e) Chrisost. in Lyturg. paulo post initium. (f) Chrisost. in Lyturg. post initium. (g) Hereof see Hierome, contra Vigilant. c. 3. and Isidore, l. 7. Etimol. c. 12. alledged heretofore at large. Tract. 1. sect. 2. subdivis. 3. in the margent vnder the letter t. (*) Of the people standing when the Gospel is read, see Lyturgiam Basily, fol. 37. a. and Anastasius in epist. 1. prope initium. in 1. tom. concil. and see Clement, l. 2. constit. Apostol. c. 57. alias 61. where it is said, cum Euangelium legitur omnes Presbiteri, et Diaaconi, & Laici assurgant &c. (h) Chrisost. in Lyturgia post initium. (i) Ciril. Hierosol. Catech. 5. faith hereof, vidisti Diaconum aquam lauandis manibus porrigentem Sacerdoti. and S. August. in quast. vet. et nou. Testam. quast. 101. faith of Deacons and their office, nam vtiq, et Altare portarent et vasa eius, et aquam in manus funderent Sacerdoti sicut videmus per omnes Ecclesias. that the author of this treatise was more auntient then S. Augustine, see heretofore Tract. 1. sect. 5. subdivis. 2. in the margent at n. & 5. And Dionisius de Ecclesiast. Hierarchia, c. 3. faith vbi vero

manus

manus tùm Antistes tum Sacerdotes aqua lauerunt &c. And *in Theoria sacræ Sinaxeos*, he further saith, *illa autem Pontificis Sacerdotumq́ lauatio, quæ summis siue extremis digitis adhibetur coram sanctissimis signis &c.* of this lotion see further mention is made in the Lyturgie of *Basile*, and by *Clement costitut. Apost* after the *Antwerpe* print of 1564. l. 8. c. 15. *fol* 167. b. *initio.* And by *Isidore in epist. ad Ludifredum apud Gratian. distinct.* 25. c. *perlectis.* And by the 4. Carthage Councel *can.* 5. and by *Germanus in Theoria circa med.* (k) In the Lyturgie of *S. Iames* it is said, *Sacerdos signacula Crucis faciens super dona dicit &c.* And *S. August. serm.* 181. *de tempore* saith, *hoc enim signo Crucis consecratur corpus Dominicum &c.* and *serm.* 19. *de Sanctis* he further saith, *eiusdem Crucis charactere &c. Altaris Sacramenta cum interpositione dominicorum verborum conficiuntur.* And *in Euang. Ioannis Tract.* 118. he saith, *quod signum (Crucis) nisi adhibeatur, siue frontibus credentium, siue ipsi aquæ qua regenerantur, siue oleo quo Chrismate vnguntur, siue sacrificio quo aluntur, nihil eorum rite perficitur.* and *Chrisost. hom. quod Christus sit Deus, circa med.* saith, *In precibus Crux, in armis Crux, in sacra mensa Crux.* and a litle there afterwardes, *in fronte nostra quasi in columna figuratur Crux, sic in sacra mensa, sic in Sacerdotum ordinationibus &c. fulget.* and the same he affirmeth *in Math. hom.* 55. *circa med.* and *Germanus in Theoria.* saith, *quod in Calice faciat (Sacerdos) Crucis signum idq́ tertium sanctificatum indicat &c.* (l)

breade and wine with the signe of the Crosse, (l) *mingling water with wine in the Chalice,* as an Apostolicke tradition, thought by the Fathers to be not a matter indifferent, but (as is

This mixture of water with wine in the Chalice, is mentioned by *S. Iames* in his Lyturgie: which Lyturgie of *S. Iames* is alledged in proofe of this mixture about 1000 yeares since, by the 6. Councel of Constantinople, *can.* 32. in reguard of this mixture *Ireneus* aboue 1400. yeares since *l.* 5. *c.* 2. calleth the cup *mixtus Calix*, l. 5. c. 2. mentioning elswere, *temperamentum Calicis*, l. 4. c. 57. and *Iustinus Martir*, who liued before him saith hereof, *affertur precipuo fratri panis et Calix aqua dilutus.* and the French protestant in his six godlie treatises &c. translated into english *pag.* 52. *post med.* saith, *Alexander the first of that name, superintendent of the Romame Church the, first of the successors of the Apostles, and also the first of the corrupters of the holy Sacraments of the supper, ordained to mixe water with wine &c.* also *S. Ciprian*, l. 2. *epist.* 3. saith hereof, *quando in Calice vino aqua miscetur &c.*

And

And further, *sic in sanctificando Calice Domini, offerri aqua sola non potest quomodo nec vinum solum*. And againe in the same epistle, *Calix Domini non est aqua sola aut vinum solum*. And the third Councel of Carthage, whereat *S. Augustine* was present and subscribed, saith, *can. 24. in Sacramentis corporis et saguinis Domini nihil amplius offeratur quam Dominus ipse tradidit, hoc est panis et vinum aqua mixtum*. This mixture is further mentioned by *Hierom. in Marc. c. 14.* by *Augustine in Tract. 120. in Ioan.* and *de Eccles. dog. c. 75. et de doctrina Cristiana. l. 4. c. 21.* by *Chrisost. in Lyturg. et in Ioan. hom. 84.* And to conclude by testimony of euery age referring the same to the Apostles tradition.

(m)

The late Bishop of *Canturburie* in his defence of the answeare to the Admonition &c. *pag. 473. prope initium.* confesseth saying *Ciprian was greatly ouerseene in making it a matter so necessary in celebration of the Lords supper,* is of them by our aduersaries confessed (m) *necessary,* and (in our opinion) by the holie Scriptures not (*) *vnforetold*: In so much as *M. D. Couel* (o the force of truth) thinketh it (¶) *probable that the auntient Church receiued it from the Apostles as to signify a mysterie.* The bread also vsed for that purpose was, as *Epiphanius* witnesseth, (n) *round in figure,* or as *M.*

to haue water mingled with wine, which was at that time (no doubt) common to moe then him. And *M. Carthwright* alledged *ibidem pag. 522. fine.* confesseth likewise saying, *in the mingling of water with wine a necessitie, & great mystery was placed, as may appeare both by Iustine, and Ciprian.* And *M. Iewel.* in his reply *pag. 34. paulo ante med* speaking of this mixture saith thereof, *indeede S. Ciprian and certaine ould Fathers speake of it & force it much.* (*) *Prouerb. 9. 1.* it is prophecied thus of Christes Church, *Wisdome haith built her a house hewen out her seuen pillers, killed her hostes, she haith mingled her wine in the cuppe and prepared her table* : which prophecy is applyed to this mixture aboue 1300. yeares since by *S. Ciprian, l. 2. epist. 3.* and see *August. de ciuit. Dei l. 17. c. 20.* and *Hierom, in Prouerb. 9.* In so much that whereas our aduersaries, in preuention hereof, do in their english translations in steede of *mingled,* say *drawne* : *M. Fulke* in his defence of the english translations &c. c. 17. *pag. 458. paulo post med.* confesseth their error herein saying, *I confesse our translators should more simplie according to the word haue said mingled her wine.* (¶) *M. D. Couel* in his answere vnto *Iohn Burges,* printed 1606. *pag. 122. fine.* affirmeth that which is alledged here in the text, adding

there

M. *Carthwright* confesseth, (o) *a round wafer cake brought in by Pope Alexander*, who liued about 1500. yeares since. An vsage so further auntient that (as our aduersaries acknowledge) (p) *the beginning thereof cannot be shewed*. In like maner was prepared a cleane syndon or linnen cloath for the B. Sacrament of Chriſtes body to be laid vpon : of this Corporal or Syndon thus vsed, mentiō (*) is made by *Siluester, Hierome*, & other Fathers. The Preiſt being thus forward and there further (*in his margen of pag. 123. initio.*) in explication of the miſtery so ſignified theſe wordes viz. *Bloud and water out of the ſide of Chriſt.* (n)
Epiphanius in Anchoratu. & ſo is *Epiphanius* there tranſlated by *Bilſon* in his true differēce &c. part. the 4. pag. 566. And by *Pe-*

ter Marter in his diſputation of the Euchariſt, annexed to his common places in engliſh pag. 185. and by *Hospinian*. next here after at p. And by M. *Whitaker contra Duræum* l. 2. pag. 231. (o) So ſaith M. *Carthwright* alledged in M. *Whitguifies* defence pag. 593. And *Prætorius de Sacramentis* pag. 287. ſpeaking of this Alexander, and his time ſaith, *postea ſtatim inuentæ ſunt rotundæ, et parua illa hoſtiæ quas Greg. magnus* l. 4. *Dial. vocat nummularios panes &c.* And ſee further there pag. 281. Alſo *Zepperus* in his *politia Eccleſiaſtica*, l. 1 c. 12. pag. 136. ſaith, *hoſtias primum introduxiſſe fertur Alexander primus circa Annum Chriſti* 119. &c. *Gregorius ſane magnus qui circa Annum Chriſti* 590. *vixit, primus panum nummulariorum in regiſtro ſuo meminit*. (p) *Hospinianus in hiſtoria Sacramentaria &c.* l. 4. pag. 370. ſaith, *quando primum cæperint, vel domi, vel in templis parare ex farina ſpuma vel panes minutas et rotundas inſtar denariorum hoſtiolas et Buccellas, certe ſcire non poteſt &c. mentionem facit Epiphanius panis rotundi in cæna*. (*) *Siluester in* 1. *tom. Concil.* ſaith, *conſtituit ſinodus vt ſacrificium Altaris non in ſerico panno, aut tincto quiſq̃ celebrare preſumeret, ſed in puro lineo ab Epiſcopo conſecrato &c.* This is extant in *Iſidors* collection of the councels. And *ex libro Pontificali Damaſi extant in* 1. *tom. concil.* printed 1606. pag. 269. And S. *Bede in Marc.* 15. ſaith, *hinc Eccleſiæ mos obtinuit, vt ſacrificium Altaris &c. in lineo terreno celebratur, ſicut corpus eſt Domini in Syndone munda ſepultum*. And ſee S. *Hierom in Math.* 27. *prope finem*. And S. *Ambroſe*, l. 1. *de virginibus*, ſpeaking of the Corporal ſaith, *plus talis decet flammeus in quo caput omnium Chriſtus quotidie conſecratur*. And S. *Hierome in Epiſtola ad Theophilum Alexandrinum* mentioneth *ſancta velamina ex conſortio corporis et ſanguinis Domini veneranda*. ſee this

M   and

and further testimonies herein of *S. Gregorie* & *Theodorus Cantuarieusis* alledged heretofore *Tract. 1. sect. 2. subd. 2. at* h ¶. and. i.

the *cathecumines and penitents being (2) removed* from being present at the dreadful mysteries, and the *Energumini* or the persons possessed with vncleane spirits being also for their deliuery (3) *brought vnto the Altar* (whereof *notable* (4) *miracles* are knowen and testified)

(2)   *Chrisostom. ad Pop. hom. 61. circa med.* saith, *quid stas si es in pænitentia? sumere non debes &c. propterea qui sunt in peccatis eiciuntur: sicut enim ad mensam veniente Domino seruos, qui Dominũ offenderunt adesse non oportet, sed procul arcentur, ita scilicet et hic dum profertur Sacrificium, dum Christus immolatur &c. indigni sunt, et oculi peccatorum hisce spectaculis indigni sunt, et aures &c. non tibi magis adstare licet quã Catechumeno.* And see the like in *Chrisostome in hom. 3. ad Ephes. et hom. 24, in Math. et hom. 18. in 2. ad Corinth.* and *Dionisius de Ecclesiastica Hierarchia, c. 3.* saith, *post hæc extra delubrum Catechumini fiunt, et hi quoq, qui in penitentia sunt, manent autem intus soli, qui diuina spectare merentur atq, percipere.* And see further hereof *M. Iewels* reply pag. 94.   (3)   *Chrisost. hom. 3. de Dei natura* saith, *Energumenos tempore mysteriorum adducit, et iubet caput inclinare &c.* and *hom. 4.* he further saith, *docere vos volo cur homines demone agitatos mysteriorum primo tempore capita inclinare iubeat Diaconus; vt itaq, tempore instante quo iudex prodire et pro tribunali sedere solitus est, custodes carceris homines quos in vinculis tenent omnes carcere educunt &c. Sic Patres statuerunt, vt cum breui Christum velut pro tribunali sedere, in ipsisq, Sacramentis apparere futurum esset, homines Demone agitati, illi tanquam vinculis quibusdam detenti adducerentur &c. vt populo vniuersaq, ciuitate presente &c. omnes iugi concordia Dominum communem orarent pro his &c.*   (4)   *Guilielmus Abbas vitæ S. Bernardi l. 2. c. 3.* reporteth saying, *inter eos qui vexabantur, mulier grandæua ciuis Mediolanensis et honorata quondam Matrona vsq, ad Ecclesiam B. Ambrosy post B. Bernardum a multis tracta est, in cuius pectore pluribus annis Diabolus federat, et iam ita suffocauerat eam, vt visu, et auditu, et verbo, priuata frendens dentibus &c. monstrum non fæmina videretur &c. hanc cum aspexisset vir Dei &c. conuersus ad populum, cuius innumera erat multitudo, orare iubet attentius, et Clericis ac Minachis secum iuxta Altare consistentibus, mulierem ibidem iubet constitui et teneri, illa vero reluctans &c. expleta autem oratione dominica, efficacius hostem eggreditur vir beatus, Patenæ siquidem Calicis sacrum Domini corpus imponens talia loquebatur; adest inique spiritus, tuus iudex, adest summa*

potestas

poteftas, refifte iam fi potes &c. hic illud corpus de corpore Virginis fumptum
eft &c. in huius ergo maieftatis terribili poteftate tibi fpiritus maligne precipio,
vt ab hac ancilla eius egrediens, contingere eam deinceps non prefumas &c.
and then afterwardes it is there reported, *et confeftim pax, et falus in-*
tegra reddita eft mulieri, et iniquus illa viuifica myfteria quanta fint efficacia,
et virtutis, non confeffionis, fed fuga coactus oftendit. See this concerning
S. Bernard reported in like manner by the Centurifts, *Cent. 12. c.*
10. *col.* 1639. And *Profper de promiffionibus et predictionibus Dei, lib.*
4. *c.* 6. reporteth a like miracle saying, *noftris quoq; temporibus &c.*
Puellam quandam Demoniacam prepofitus ad Altare perduxit &c. peracto
itaq; facrificio cum eadem inter cateras breuem particulam corporis Domini
tinctam a Sacerdote perciperet &c. ftatim locum illum quem Diabolus ob-
federat, Saluatoris imperio reliquit &c. And *S. Ciprian in ferm. de Lapfis*
poft med. maketh report of an other like example whereat him felfe
was prefent.

the Preift (q) *requefteth the people to pray for*
him, saying, (r) *orate pro me &c.* he alfo
requefteth (s) *the interceffion of the bleffed Vir-*
gin Marie & al Sainctes, and to that end prayeth (t) *to her and* (u) *them,* & to (x) *the An-*
gel Michael. He likewife prayeth, *that the*
(y) *bread may be made the body of Chrift, and*
the wine his bloud.

(2) This done there followeth his con-
fecration of the Sacrament: and whereas by
our 2. *fine.*

(q)
In Lyturgia Bafilij.
(r)
In Lyturgia Chrifoftomi.
(s)
In Lyturgia Iacobi. and in
Lyturgia Bafilij & Chri-
foftomi. (t)
In Liturg. Chrifoft. et
Ambrof. in orat. praparat.
(u) *Ibidem.*

et in Lyturgia Bafil. et Ambrof. orat. 2. praparat. and *S. Ciril of Hie-*
rufalem Catech. 5. miftagog. faith hereof, *when we offer this facrifice, we*
make mention of thofe who are dead before vs. Firft of the Patriarches, Pro-
phets, Apoftles, & Martyrs, that God through their praiers wil receiue ours
&c. (x) *In Lyturgia Chrifoftomi.* (y) *Ambrof. in orat. 1. prapa-*
rat. poft med. and in *Liturgijs Bafilij et Chrifoftomi.* and in *Lyturgia Ia-*
cobi. and *Proclus in tract. de traditione diu. Lyturg.* faith hereof *per has*
igitur preces, fpiritus fancti aduentum exp ectabant, vt eius diuina prefentia pro-
pofitum facrificium panem et vinum aqua permiftum, ipfum illud corpus et
fanguinem feruatoris noftri Iefu Chrifti efficiat, qui quidem religiofus ritus ob-
feruatur ad hoc vfq; tempus &c. and *Germanus Conftant. in Theoria,* faith
likewife hereof, *et rurfus obfecrat vt conficiatur myfterium filij eius, et fiat*

fiue

ſine tranſmutetur ipſe panis et vinum in corpus et ſanguinem Chriſti. And
Cirillus Hieroſol. Catech. 5. faith, *Deum benigniſſmum oramus, vt ſuper
illa propoſita ſanctum ſpiritum emittat, vt panem quidem faciat corpus Chriſti,
vinum vero ſarguinem Chriſti.* and *Vadian de Euchariſtia,* l. 6. *fol.* 221.
acknowledgeth the antiquitie of this praier ſaying thereof, *quod enim
ante conſecrationem dicit Sacerdos petere ſe vt panis et Calix, corpus et ſanguis
Domini fiant, veteri more et recto dictum eſt.*

(z)

M. Fulke againſt the
Rhemiſh Teſtament
Math. 26. *ſect.* 7. *fol.*
53. b. *paulo ante med.*
and in 1. *Cor.* 10. *ſect.*
4. *fol.* 277. b. *paulo poſt
med.* and *M. Willet* in
his *Sinopſis* pag. 464.

(a)
*Greg. Niſſen. in ſer. Ca-
tech. de diuin. Sacram.*

(b)
Cent. 4. c. 4 col. 287.
lin. 18. in the title being, *inclinatio doctrinæ co-
plectens peculiares et incommodas opiniones, ſtipulas,
et errores Doctorum.*

(c)
Cent. 4. c. 4. col. 295.
lin. 27. it is ſaid, *Gregorius Niſſenus in oratione*

our aduerſaries doctrine, (z) *conſecration doth
conſiſt not in the wordes* (pronounced) *but in
the whole action according to Chriſtes inſtitution,
whereunto are required the taking, eating, drin-
ing &c.* The Fathers to the contrary do, with
vs, refer this conſecration not to our foreſaid taking, eating, drinking, &c. but to
the wordes of Chriſt : To which end *S. Gregorie Niſſen* faith moſt directly and pertinently, (a) *bread by the word of God and praier is
ſanctified, not becauſe it is eaten, doth it become
the body of the word, but forthwith by the word it
is changed into the body, as it is ſaid by the word,
this is my body.* A teſtimony ſo plaine with
vs and againſt our aduerſaries, that *the Centurie writers* vndertaking to mention *the* (b)
hurtful opinions and errors of the Doctors, do
withal to that end amongſt other ſpecially
(c) recyte and diſlike this foreſaid teſtimony :
whereuntomight be added ſundry other like
plaine (d) ſayinges of the auntient Fathers.
                                                                In ſo

Catechiſtica (ait) *recte nunc etiam Dei verbo ſanctificatum panem in Dei verbi
corpus credimus immutari &c. non quia commeditur eo progrediens vt verbi
corpus euadat, ſed ſtatim per verbum in corpus mutatur, vt dictum eſt a verbo
quoniam hoc eſt corpus meum.* (d) *Chriſoſt. in hom. de proditione Iudæ.
verſus finem,* ſaith hereof *Sacerdotis ore verba proferuntur et Dei virtute
conſecrantur, hoc eſt ait corpus meum, hoc verbo propoſita conſecrantur.* and
ad Pop. hom. 60. *poſt med.* he ſaith, *qui namq́ dixit hoc eſt corpus meum,
et verbum facto confirmauit &c.* And *S. Ciprian. in ſerm. de cæna Domini,
paulo*

paulo post initium saith, *ex quo a Domino dictum est, hoc facite &c. hæc est caro mea. hic est sanguis meus, quotiescunq́, his verbis et hac fide actum est, panis iste substantialis, et Calix solenni benedictione sacratus ad totius hominis vitam salutemq́, proficit &c.* And afterwardes in the same sermon he saith, *Panis &c. omnipotentia verbi factus est caro.* And that our Sauiour: *vsq́ bodie hoc veracissimum et sanctissimum corpus suum creat, et sanctificat et benedicit.* And *Iræneus* l. 5. c. 1. *post initium* saith, *quando mixtus Calix, et fractus panis percepit verbum Dei fit Eucharistia &c.* And *Ambros. de sacram.* l. 4. c. 4. saith, *quomodo potest qui panis est, corpus esse Christi consecratione? consecratio igitur quibus verbis fit? Domini Iesu &c. ergo sermo Christi hoc conficit Sacramentum. quis sermo Christi? nempe is quo facta sunt omnia: Iussit Dominus et factum est Cælum &c. vides ergo quam operatorius fit sermo Christi &c.* And againe *l.* 4. *c.* 5. he saith, *ante verba Christi Calix est vini et aqua plenus, vbi verba Christi operata fuerint, ibi sanguis efficitur qui redemit plebem.* See him also no lesse plaine *de mysterijs initiand. c. 9. paulo ante med.* and S. *Ciril. in Ioan. l.* 11. *c.* 22. *in* 17. *Ioannis,* saith, *ipsum Domini corpus coniunctum virtute verbi sanctificatur, et ad benedictionem mysticam adeo actiuum fit &c.* and *Eusebius Emissen. hom.* 5. *Pasch.* saith, *Inuisibilis Sacerdos visibiles creaturas in substantiam corporis et sanguinis sui verbo suo secreta potestate conuertit.* and againe *ibidem versus finem.* he saith, *antequam inuocatione summi nominis consecrentur, substantia illic est panis et vini; post verba autem Christi, corpus et sanguis est Christi; quid mirum, si ea qua potuit verbo creare, possit creata conuertere.* And *Remigius in* 1. *Cor.* 10. saith, *Caro quam verbum Dei Patris assumpsit in vtero virginali in vnitate suæ personæ, et panis qui consecratur in Ecclesia vnum corpus Christi sunt, sicut enim illa caro corpus Christi est, ita iste panis transit in corpus Christi, nec duo sunt corpora, sed vnum corpus &c.* and S. *August. contra Faust. Manich. l.* 20. *c.* 13. saith, *noster autem panis et Calix &c. certa consecratione mysticus fit nobis non nascitur &c.* And S. *Augvst. in lib. sententiarum Prosperi ex Augusti.* (alledged often by *Algerus de sacram. Euchar. l.* 1. *c.* 5. *&* 16. *&* 7.) saith, *cum fideliter fateamur ante consecrationem panem esse et vinum quod natura formauit, post consecrationem vero Christi carnem et sanguinem esse quod benedictio consecrauit.* And he is further alledged (*de can sacr. dist.* 2. *can.* 71. *et l.* 4. *sent. dist.* 10.) to say, *quia Christum orari dentibus fas nō est voluit Dominus hunc panē et vinū in mysterio vere carnē suā, et sanguinē suū consecratione spiritus sancti potentialiter creari, et quotidie pro mundi vita mystice immolari.* See this saying also alleged by *Algerus* vnder S. *Augustines*

name.

name *de Sacram . Euchar.* In ſo much as the Fathers after this conſecra-
l .ʼ1 . c. 16. tiō of the Sacrament did (as is (e) cōfeſſed)

(e) vſually vpon ſome occaſions (f) *reſerue it vn-*
.The Fathers are confeſ- *receiued,* as being ſo in it ſelfe before the re-
ſed to haue taught and ceiuing thereof, a complet Sacrament; wher-
practized this *Reſeruatiō* as by our aduerſaries doctrine (g) *it is no Sa-*
by *M. Fulke* againſt *He-* *crament*
ſkins, Saunders, &c. pag. 77. who there anſweareth to obiections geuen
hereof ſaying, *that the Sacrament (of ſome) was reſerued in the elder dayes
of the Church, is not ſo great a controuerſie aſ whether it ought to be reſerued
&c.* In ſo much as *M. Hutton* in his ſecond part of the anſweare to
the reaſons for refuſal of ſubſcription &c. *pag.* 71. affirmeth the re-
ſeruing of the Eucharift for them *that were abſent* by example (ſaith he)
of *Iuſtine martyr, who was in the firſt age after the Apoſtles, & in the ſecond age,
example thereof* (ſaith he) *may be taken from Dioniſe of Alexandria in his E-
piſtle to Fabius &c.* writing *the hiſtorie of Serapion, to whom, being mortally ſicke, a boy brought the Sacrament:* apud *Euſcb . hiſt. l. 6. c. 36.* And
Caluin inſtitut . l. 4. c. 17. ſect. 39. ſaith, *His rationibus clare patet
repoſitionem Sacramenti quam nonnulli vrgent, vt ægrotis extra ordinem di-
ſtribuatur, inutilem eſſe &c. ſed enim qui ſic faciunt habent veteris Eccleſiæ
exemplum fateor &c.* And *Chemnitius* in his examen &c. *part. 2 pag.*
101. ſaith, *huius conſuetudinis de priuata reſeruatione Euchariſtiæ, teſtes
ſunt Tertulianus l. 2. ad vxorem, Ciprianus ſerm. 5. de Lapſis, Ambroſius de obitu fratris Satiri, Hieronimus in Apolog. aduerſus Iouinianum,
Baſilius ad Cæſariam Patriciam, &c. notum eſt etiam quantum ex veteribus
quidam priuatam hanc reſeruationem commendarint, vt Nazianzenus in e-
pitaphio ſororis, Ambroſius de obitu fratris Satiri: et profecto ſi antiquitas
conſuetudinis late patentis, et diu propagatæ poſſet, vel neceſſitatem imponere,
vel veritati præſcribere, nulla ratione debuiſſet priuata illa reſeruatio vel mutari vel abrogari.* And *Hoſpinianus* in his *hiſtoria ſacramentaria, part.*
pag. 62. reiecteth herein the foreſaid Fathers, namely, *Baſil, Ciprian,
Ambroſe, Nazianzen, Hierom, Tertulian* and ſee further hereof *Peter
Martir l. contra Gardinerum obiect. 88. col 532. & 533.* (f) Examples
of this *reſeruation* are in the moſt auntient Fathers, as in *Iuſtinus martyr in Apol. 2. fine.* who mentioneth *the ſending of the Sacrament by Deacons, to ſuch as were abſent.* and in *Iræncus* apud *Euſeb . hiſt. l. 5. c. 24.
in Dioniſ. Alexand.* apud *Euſeb . hiſt. l. 6. c. 36. in Ciprian. in ſerm.
de Lapſis. in Greg. Nazian. in Gorgonian. in Ambroſ. in orat. in obitum*
fratris

fratris sui Satiri, c . 7 . in Hierom . epist . ad Rusticum. and in Chrisost. epist . 1 . ad Innocent . (g) *M . Willet* in his *Sinopsis* pag . 460. *ante med .*

(h)

crament *vnlesse it be receiued .* An opinion specially condemned for error by the auntient
Fathers . To which end *S . Ciril* chargeth the
Heretickes of his time saying , (h) *I heare
they say that the mystical blessing, if any remanets
therof remaine til the next day following, is vnpro-
fitable to sanctificaton, but they are madde in so saying, for Christ is not made an other, neither shal
his body be chaunged , but the vertue of blessing
and liuely grace do alwayes remaine in it .* A saying so plaine and pertinent that (*) Peter
Martir doth therefore signify his special dislike thereof . And hence it is that the Fathers
affirme Christes foresaid wordes of institutio
to be (i) *working* or powerful, saying also in
respect thereof, further concerning Preistes,
that (k) *corpus Christi sacro ore conficiunt, they
make* (present) *the body of Christ with a sacred
mouth .* Onely I wil hereto breefely adde
that which the Scriptures afford concerning
our Sauiours *blessing* of the bread and wine ;
for the Euangelistes report that (l) *he blessed,* and so doth the (*) *Greeke word* signify,

Ciril . ad Calosirium .

(*)

*Peter Martir in defensione
aduersus Stephan . Gardi-
ner . lib . de Eucharistia
printed Basileæ,* 1581. *obiect .* 213 . *col .* 838 .*saith*
of this saying of *S . Ciril ,
quod autem subijcitur, Eucharistiæ reliquias asserua-
tas in crastinum diem a sanc-
tificatione non cessare, spec-
tat opinor ad receptã quandam consuetudinem &c .
ea consuetudo etsi saperet
non nihil superstitionis, tamen illi Cirillus alijq́, sub-
scribebant , statim enim a
temporibus Apostoloru̅ paulatim cæptum est degenerari
ab illa veteri simplicitate.
diuini cultus .*

(i)

and See *Ambrose* alledged
heretofore *tract . 2 . sect . 1 . subdiuis . 2 .* in the margent vnder the letter d . where he saith, *vides ergo quam operatorius sit sermo Christi ;* and
vbi verba Christi operata fuerint . And see *Euseb . Emissen .* alledged
there . and *Ciprian de cœna Domini, post initium . saith, Panis iste &c . omnipotentia verbi factus est caro .* and see *S . Ciril* alledged there next heretofore in the margent vnder d . (k) So saith *S . Hierom . epist . 1 ,
ad Heliodorum . c . 7 .* and in *epist .* 85 . *ad Euagrium,* he saith of Preistes,
ad quorum preces Christi corpus sanguisq́, conficitur . And see the Centurie
writers, *cent . 3 . c . 7 . col .* 184 . where *Pontianus* is by them reproued
for his like saying . And *S . Ambrose, de myster . initiand . c . 9 . circa med .*
saith, *hoc quod conficimus corpus ex virgine est .* and *Chrisostom . hom . de
prod .*

prod. *Inde. verſus finem.* ſaith, *non eſt homo qui corpus Chriſti facit et ſan-guinem, ſed ille qui crucifixus eſt pro nobis Chriſtus ; Sacerdotis ore verba proferũ-tur, et Dei virtute conſecrantur.* (1) *Math. 26. 26 . Marc. 14. 22.* (*) Eulogeſas.

(m)
See the tranſlation of
M. *Fulke* of *Mar.* 14.
22. in his treatiſe againſt
the Rhemiſh Teſtament.
and *Beza in Non. Teſt.*
printed *Londini.* 1587.

(n)
So tranſlate the engliſh
Bible printed 1576. *in
Marc.* 14. 22, And ſee
the engliſh Bibles of
1562. and 1577.

(2)
Although, as ſome ob-
iect, S. *Math.* 26. 27.
and *Marc.* 14. 22. vſe
the word *Euchariſteſas* o-
uer the Cup, which ſig-
nifyeth properly *geuing
thankes,* yet is that action
of thankeſ-geuing ouer

and ſo certaine of our aduerſaries (m) *tranſlate*
the ſame. And whereas others more wil-
ful, doe inſtead of *bleſſed,* ſay (n) *he gaue
thankes,* reſtrayning ſo that action from the
creatures as directed onely to God : the Fathers (2) explaine to the contrary, that
euen by thankeſ-geuing, here cannot be
ment the action of onely thankeſ-geuing to
God, but ſpecially of bleſſing the creatures.
And ſo the Apoſtle accordingly explaineth,
calling it therefore (o) *the Cuppe of bleſſing.
which Cuppe we bleſſe:* in which place as the
Greeke word being vſed by the Apoſtle (*)
tranſitiuely, that is with a caſe following, *cannot* (by M. *Fulkes* (p) confeſſion) *ſignify geuing thankes,* as (q) *Caluin* alſo confeſſeth expreſly of this place reprouing therefore his
bretherens foreſaid other (r) contrary expoſition. So likewiſe it is thereby euident,
that our Sauiour, and alſo the Apoſtles did, as
Geſnerus, a learned (*) *Lutheran* affirmeth, refer

the creature, and importeth ſo in ſence *bleſſing,* and ſo the auntient
Greeke Fathers next after the Apoſtles age refer this action of thankeſ-
geuing to be ouer the creatures. *Iuſtinus Martyr Apol. 2. fine.* calling
it therefore Ton Arton Euchariſtetheita, *panem Euchariſtiſatum.* Alſo
Irenæus, l. 4. c. 34. poſt. med. calleth it, *panem in quo gratia actæ ſunt.*
And though to the contrary it ſhould imply thankes-geuing to God,
yet cannot that take away thother foreſaid bleſſing of the creatures,
which thother word *Eulogeſas* expreſſeth, for both bleſſing and thankeſ-
geuing may ſtand together. (o) 1. *Cor.* 10. 16. (*) O *Eulo-
goumen.* (p) So ſaith M. *Fulke* in his defence of the engliſh tranſlations, *pag.* 431. (q) *Caluin in omnes Pauli Epiſt. in* 1. *Cor. c.* 10.
v. 16. *pag.* 305. ſaith, *Calicem benedictionis vocat &c. neq́, enim ips
aſſentior*

affentior qui per benedictionem gratiarum actionem intelligunt, et benedicere exponunt, gratias agere. (r) *Beza in Annot. in 1. Cor.* 10. 16. And the marginal Annotations of the englifh Bible of 1576. *in* 1. *Cor.* 10. *v.* 16. at the letter m. fay, *which with praife and thankef-geuing we prepare.* (*) *Gefnerus in difput. profanctif. libro concord. difput.* 9. *pag.* 203. *paulo poft med.* faith, *deinde cum Marcus, itidem vt Mathaus verbum Euchariftefas, interpretetur per alterum* Eulogefas, *hoc ipfo indicant Chriftum non folum Deum Patrem laudaffe, et celebraffe, neq, Difcipulorum folummodo falutem Deo commendaffe, qua alioquin uerbi* Eulogein *fignificationes funt, fed fingulari benedictione fuper hunc panem vfum effe, qua tam fuerit efficax, vt panis iam non amplius vulgaris panis maneret, fed cum corpore Chrifti facramentaliter vniretur; quemadmodum omnipotenti fua benedictione, quinq, panes et paucos pifciculos vfq, adeo multiplicauit, vt quinq, millibus hominum faturandis fufficerent. Marc.* 6. 41. *ac proinde vt efficaciffima illa benedictio in prima creatione fuper homines, aliaq, animalia pronuntiata, crefcite et multiplicamini, hodie quoq, fuam vim retinet, ita hac Domini benedictio, ordinatio, et fanctio in hodiernum vfq, diem efficit, vt corpus Chrifti, et fanguis Chrifti in facra cana adfit &c. quapropter fanguinem Domini ore corporis biberunt &c.*

referre this benediction to the creatures: which *bleffing* as it is more then we find that Chrift vfed or prefcribed vpon the water of Baptifme; fo alfo it is (in our opinion) an argument of a more powerful and wonderful worke, wrought vpon the forefaid creatures aboue al courfe of nature, as apeareth by like example of *the fiue loaues and two fifhes which* (s) *he bleffed*, and therewith multiplied. And fo accordingly did the auncient Fathers thinke of this forefaid *bleffing* of the Sacrament, to which end it is in *Ciprian* called (t) *Calix folenni benedictione facratus, the cuppe confecrated by folemne bleffing.* and *S.* (u) *Bafile* and *S.* (x) *Chrifoftome* fay accordingly; *Bleffe o Lord the facred bread,* (and) *& bleffe o Lord the facred cup,* & to what effect it there followeth, *changing it by thy holy fpirit*: which forefaid premifes are fo plaine and euident, that *M. Fulke* being therewith wel preffed, and held in chafe, maketh thereupon

(s)
Luc. 9. 16.

(t)
Ciprian. in fer. de cana Domini paulo poft initium. and *Remigius in* 1. *Cor. c.* 10. faith, *it is called the Cuppe of bleffing which is bleffed of Preiftes on the Altar.*

(u)
Bafil. in Liturg.

(x)
Chrifoft. in Liturg.

(y)

(y)
For thus he thereupon faith, *the creatures or elementes are bleſſed and conſecrated, that by the working of Gods ſpirit, they ſhould be chaunged into the body and bloud of Chriſt, after a diuine and ſpiritual manner vnto the worthy receiuer :* in his defence of the engliſh tranſlations, *pag.435.* ſo plainly doth he acknowledge aſwel a real change and preſence of Chriſtes body, not to faith ouely, but in the creatures . As alſo that this preſence of Chriſtes body is not wrought by our onely faith, but by *bleſſing* and *conſecration,* & *the working* thereupon of Gods ſpirit.

(z)
Hereoffee *M.D.Couel* in his defence of *M. Hooker &c. pag.* 118.

(a)
Euſeb..Emiſſen. hom. 5. Paſch. faith, *antequam inuocatione ſummi nominis conſecrentur ; ſubſtantia illic eſt panis et vini, poſt verba autem Chriſti, corpus et ſanguis eſt Chriſti, quid mirum, ſi ea que potuit verbo creare, poſſit creata conuertere ?* (b) See heretofore, *traƈt. 2. ſeƈt. 1. ſubd. 2. at a .c . d.*
(*) *Phillippus Nicholai, l. 1. de regno Chriſti, pag. 22.* faith, *hoc teneant Chriſtiani*

pag. 100.

great ſtep towardes conformity, and (y) acknowledgement of our Catholicke doctrine . As alſo the Lutherans do acknowledge the truth of the Sacrament, euen (z) *before participation* or receiuing thereof; ſo fully do they rely herein vpon bleſſing & conſecration .

That after conſecration, the real preſence was acknowledged : with a continued courſe of confeſſed teſtimonies in that behalfe, from this age vp to the Apoſtles.

SECTION. 2.

COnſecration being ended, the real preſence of Chriſtes body in the Sacrament, was thereupon beliued . To which purpoſe *Euſebius Emiſſen.* faith, *before* (a) *they be conſecrated by inuocation of the higheſt name, there is the ſubſtance of bread and wine, but after the wordes of Chriſt, it is the body and bloud of Chriſt.* whereto might be added ſundry other like teſtimonies of the Fathers (b) *heretofore* in part alledged : Onely I wil now breefely touch, how generally for former ages, this doctrine of the real preſence haith bene profeſſed . To omit the laſt 500 . yeares as vnworthy of queſtion, and ſufficiently confeſſed by the Proteſtant writer *D.* (*) *Phillippus Nicholai,* it was ſo vniuerſally profeſſed in the former time of *Berengarius,* who did then a lone begin to impugne the fame, againſt the (c) general receiued doctrine

Christiani Lectores non modo Græcorum Ecclesias, verum et Rutenòs, et Georgianos, et Armenios, et Iudos, et Ethiopes, qui Christo sua nomina dederunt, veram et realem corporis et sanguinis Domini præsentiam statuere &c. (c) *Papir Masson, Annal. Francorum. l. 3. in Henrico Rege.* saith, *Berengario illius temporis Theologi bellum omnes indixere.* And *Oecolampadius, in lib. epistolarum Suingly et Oecolampadij, l. 3. pag. 712.* saith, *viuo Berengario multi cõtra eum scripserunt.*

trine of that age, that *M. Fox* confesseth hereof saying, (d) *about the yeare of our Lord 1060. the denying of transubstantiation, began to be accompted heresie: and in that number was first one Berengarius, who liued about Anno. 1060.* So generally in that age was the doctrine euen of *transubstantiation* receiued: as appeareth yet more plainely and effectually by further testimony of (e) *Lanfrancus* and others, in so much as *Lanfrancus,* who then wrote against *Berengarius,* testifyeth the generality (at that time) of the real presence, euen in those nations that were more remote, saying to that end: (*) *Interroga vniuersos &c.* aske al that vnderstand the latine tongue, aske the Gretianes, Armenians, or al the Christians of euerie nation, and they wil testify with one mouth that they hould this faith.

(2) *Paschasius* a latin writer liued about *Anno Domini* 800. and is so ful for the real presence, that he writ a (f) special booke in behalfe thereof, (2) wherein as he is so plaine that

(d)

In the actes and monuments printed, 1576. pag. 1121. And *Ioachim Camerarius* in his *historica narratio de Ecclesijs Fratrũ in Bohemia, et Morauia,* pag. 161. saith accordingly *Transubstantiationis dogma &c.* the doctrine of transubstantiation, concerning the vanishing away of bread, remained in quiet possession after the yeare of Christ 850. vntil the times of Berengarius, and the yeare of Christ about 850. for although the matter was before noted in the primitiue writinges of some, yet the first publicke conflict did spring from Berengarius.

(e) *Lanfrancus, in lib. de veritate corporis et sanguinis Domini in Eucharist. aduersus Berengarium* saith, *confitetur Ecclesia toto terrarum orbe diffusa panem, et vinum ad sacrandum proponi in altari, sed inter sacrandum incomprehensibiliter, et ineffabiliter in substantiam carnis et sanguinis commutari &c. hanc fidem tenuit a priscis temporibus, et nunc tenet Ecclesia, quæ per totum diffusa orbem Catholica nominatur.* And the like generality of this doctrine is affirmed by *Hugo Lingonensis in epist. ad Berengarium.* (*) *Lanfrancus vbi supra.* (f) Entituled *de corpore et sanguine Dom.* (2) *Paschasias*

N 2

thasas

chasius in l. de corp. et sang. Dom. c. 1. saith, *omnia quacunq; voluit Dominus fecit, in calo, et in terra, et quia voluit, licet figura panis et vini hic sit, tamen omnino nihil aliud quam caro Christi, et sanguis Christi post consecrationem credenda sunt.* and *in epist. ad Frudegardum,* he doth purposely at large proue the same doctrine, and in his litle booke of institution of the sacrament he saith, *nec ita dixit (Christus) cum fregit et dedit eis panem, hac est, vel in hoc mysterio est quadam virtus, vel figura corporis mei, sed ait non ficte, hoc est corpus meum, et ideo hoc est quod dixit, non quod quisq; fingit.*

(g).	
Fulke, against *Heskins*, Saunders &c. *pag.* 250. saith, *Paschasius alledgeth, Hillarie, Augustine, Ambrose, Ciril, and the councel of Ephesus, and doth but wraist their sayinges as the Papistes now do to vphould the error &c.* (h) *Oecolampad. in lib. epistolarum Oecolampadij. et Suingly, pag.* 711. saith,	that he is therfore charged and reiected by M. (g) *Fulke,* (h) *Oecolampadius,* the (i) *Centurie writers* (3) and *others.* So likewise he expresseth therein the generality of this doctrine for his time, saying therof: (k) *quamuis &c. although certaine may erre of ignorance in this point, yet there is no man who doth openly contradict this which the whole world beleueth and professeth.* S. *Damascen* liued *Anno Dom.* 720. and a litle after him was *Theophilact,* both of them Greeke writers, and their testimonies hereof so exceeding plaine, that M. *Carlile,* & *Oecolampadius* do ackonwledge

Paschasius magis implicabat quam explicabat legentis mentem, multa sane pia dicta ita concinnans, vt crasse opinioni quadrare putentur. (i) The Centuristes *cent.* 9. *c.* 4. *col.* 215. charge *Pascasius* with *transubstantiation.* (3) *Crispinus* in his booke o' the estate of the Church chargeth *Paschasius* with *the opinion of transubstatiation, pag.* 288. and 289. And see there *pag.* 286. and 323. and *Pratorius de sacramentis, pag.* 288. chargeth *Paschasius* with *Real presence and oral eating,* saying of him, *Docuit corporalem prasentiam, & oralem esum carnis et sanguinis Christi.* (k) *Paschasius, l. de corpore et sanguine Domini.* (l) *Damascen. l. 4. orthod. fid. c.* 14. saith, *quemadmodum naturaliter panis per cibum et vinum, et aqu. per potum in comedentis, et bibentis corpus et sanguinem immutatur, corpusq; alterum fiunt, atq; a priore ipsius corpore diuersum, sic propositionis panis, et vinum, et aqua per sancti spiritus inuocationem et aduentum, mirabili modo in Christi corpus, et sanguinem conuertuntur, nec sunt duo sed vnum, et idem &c. Dominus ipse dixerit, hoc non est corporis signum, sed corpus, nec sanguinis gumus signum, sed sanguis*. And *Theophilact* in *Math*. 26. *ante med*. faith, *non enim dixit, hoc est figura, sed hoc est corpus meum ; ineffabili enim operatione transformatur &c. panis quidem apparet, sed reuera caro est.*

(m)

ledge that (m) *Damascen taught transubstanti-* M. *Carlile* in his booke
ation. And M. *Fulke* faith that, (n) *Theophi-* that Chrift defcended
lact lived in a corrupt time, and writeth suspitiously not into hel (printed
of the carnal presence and transubstantiation. In 1582. and greatly com-
fo much as other Proteftant writers do ac- meded by *Sir Iohn Cheeke*
knowledge that both (o) *Damascen,* and *The-* and others, before the
ophilact do euidently incline to transubstantiation. beginning thereof) faith,
Gregorius magnus, liued *Anno Dom.* 590. he *fol.* 58. a. *Doe not defend*
is alfo fo (*) euident for the real prefence, *Damascene for &c. he firſt*
that made Metapoiefin, *the*

transmutation, transfaction, or transubstantiation of the bread into Chriſtes na-
tural body, and the wine into his bloud; neither (faith he) *may any queſtion be*
asked how it commeth to passe, but anſweare, hoc eſt corpus meum, this is my
body. Alfo *Oecolampadius in lib. epiſtolarum Oecolampadij, et Suingly,* printed at Bafile, 1592. l. 3. *pag.* 661. faith of *Damaſcene, Beſſarion,* and
others: *Papiſticam illam tranſubſtantiationem aſſerunt,* reiecting fo likewife
next after *Anſelmus, Guitmundus, Lanfrancus, Paſchaſius, Algerus &c.*
In like manner *Prætorius de Sacramentis* (printed 1602.) *pag.* 288. faith,
ficta eſt miraculoſa tranſubſtantiatio per Iohannem Damaſcenum Presbiterum.
(n) M. *Fulke* againſt *Henſkings, Sannders &c.* pag. 217. *& vide pag.*
204. and 296. And fee *Theophilact* plainly alledged, confeſſed, and
reiected by *Prætorius de Sacramentis,* pag. 221. where he faith, *Somni-*
ant metuſiaſta panem cænæ plane mutari, et aliud quid quam ante fuit fieri, a-
liam inquam & nouam eſſentiam & naturam (vt verbum tranſubſtantiari &
verbale nomen tranſubſtantiatio per ſe docet) induere adeoq, non manere pa-
nem, ſed fieri verum corpus Chriſti, ſpeciem tantum panis manere in oculis
hominum, ne a crudæ carnis manducatione abhorreant : ſic enim expreſſe ſcribit
Theophilactus in commentario ſuo ſuper Math. 26. in proofe whereof
he recyteth *Theophilactes* plaine faying in the wordes there next following. (o) *Vrſinus,* in his booke entituled *Commonefactio cuiuſdam The-*
ologi de ſacra Domini cæna, printed 1583. pag. 211. faith, *Theophilac-*
tus, & Damaſcenus, plane inclinant ad tranſubſtantiationem. and fee the
like in M. *Whitaker contra Duræum,* pag. 238. and in *Chemnitius* examen, *part.* 2. *pag.* 83. and *ibidem pag.* 90. (*) *Greg. hom.* 22.

N 3   *in in Euang.* affirmeth plainely our receiuing of Chriftes bloud both with our heart and bodily month faying; *quid fit fanguis agni iam non audiendo, fed bibendo didiciftis, qui fanguis fuper virem.q̃; potem ponitur, quando non folum ore corporis, fed etiam ore cordis hauritur.* and *Paulus Diaconus in vita Gregory,* about 800. yeares fince, not onely reporteth a miracle wrought by *S. Gregories* miniftery, in proofe of the real prefence, (which miracle is mentioned heareafter *tract. 2. fect. 3. fubd. 1.* in the margent at the letter h.) but alfo further alledgeth *Gregories* wordes thereupon vttered, which were, *Præfcius conditor noftræ infirmitatis ea poteftate qua cunéta fecit ex nikilo, et corpus fibi ex carne femper virginis operante fpiritu fanéto fabricauit, panem et vinum aqua mifium, manente propria fpecie, in carnem et fanguinem fuum ad Catholicam precem ob reparationem noftam fpiritus fui fanétificatione conuertit.*

(p) *Humfredus in Iefuitifmi, part. 2. contra Campian. rat. 5. pag. 626.* faith, *in Ecclefiam vero quid inuexerunt Gregorius et Auguftinus? &c. tranfulftantiationem &c.* (q) See heretofore *tract. 2. fect. 1. fubd. 2.* in the margent there vnder the letter d. *fine.* (r) *Cent. 4. c. 10. col. 985. lin. 30.* the Centuriftes fay of *Eufelius Emiffenus: De cana Domini parum commodè de tranfubftantiatione dixit &c.* (s) *Chrifoftom. in Math. 26. hom. 83. poft*	that *D. Humfrey,* doth therefore charge him and *Auguftine,* with (p) *tranfubftantiation. Eufebius Emiffen.* liued *Anno 520.* & his teftimonies (q) heretofore alledged, are fo plaine, that the *Centurie writers* affirme and fay of him that (r) he did fpeake improfitably of tranfubftantiation. *S. Chrifoftome* liued *Anno 390.* & his many (s) fayinges are fo ftrong for the real prefence

med. fpeaking of the Sacrament faith, *non fufficit ipfi (Chrifto) hominem fieri, flagellis interim cedi, fed nos fecum in vnam vt ita dicam Maffam reducit, neq̃; id fide folum, fed re ipfa, nos corpus fuum efficit. et vide ad Pop. hom. 60.* and *hom. 46. in Ioan. initio.* he affirmeth that our Sauiour faid, *caro mea vere eft efca, fanguis meus vere eft potus &c. vt eos in prædictis confirmet ne obfcure locutum in parabilis arbitrarentur.* and in *1. Cor. hom. 24.* and in *1. Cor. 10. hom. 24.* expoundeth thefe wordes, *the Cup of bleffing which we bleffe, is it not the communion of the bloud of Chrift.* he faith, *the meaning of them is, that which is in the cup, is the fame which flowed out of his fide, and thereof we are pertakers.* And fee his fayinges alledged heretofore, *tract. 2. fect. 1. fubd. 2.* in the margent vnder the letter d. and hereafter *tract. 2. fect. 8. fubd. 2.* at o. p. q. and alfo

hereafter

presence that the *Centurie writers* vndertaking to set downe (t) *the errors of the Doctors of that age,* do therein specially amongst others charge *S. Chrisostome* by name and recite his perticuler sayinges, wherein (say they) (u) *he seemeth to confirme transubstantiation.* And in like manner do they immediately next after in the same place charge (x) *Theodoret,* who liued *Anno Dom.* 370. affirming also further elswhere of *Theodoret,* that (y) *concerning the supper, he affirmeth dangerously the simbolles of the body and bloud of Christ, to be, after the Preistes inuocation, chaunged.*

(3) §. *Chrisostomus transubstanti-*

hereafter in this present section in the margent at the letter u.

(t)
Cent. 5. *c.* 4. *col.* 496. the title of the discourse there subsequent is *inclinatio doctrinæ complectens peculiares, et incommodas opiniones, stipulas, et errores Doctorum huius seculi.*

(u)
Ibidem, col. 517. they say,

ationem videtur confirmare, nam ita scribit in sermone de Eucharistia, num vides panem, num vinum, num sicut reliqui cibi in secessum vadunt? absit ne sic cogites; quemadmodum enim si cera igni adhibita illi assimilatur, nihil substantiæ remanet, nihil superfluit, sic et hic puta mysteria consumi corporis presentia &c. And *Musculus in Loc. comun. de cæna Domini,* pag. 336. saith, *quare quod Chrisostomus super Mat. hom.* 83. *dicit, non sunt humanæ virtutis opera præstita &c.* nos *ministeriorum tenemus ordinem, qui vero sanctificat ea, et immutat ipse est: Rhetorica magis est amplificatione, quam pro cause ipsius simplicitate dictum; etenim quod dicit non esse humanæ virtutis opera proposita,* etnunc quo*q; facere Dominum ea, quæ in illa vltima sua cæna sanctificando et mutando fecit, si ad id referatur quod nos facere iussit, dicens, hoc facite in mei rememorationem, prorsus a simplici dominici mandati veritate dissidet, neq; enim mandauit nobis, vt panem et vinum sanctificemus et mutemus &c.* (x) *Cent.* 5. *c.* 4. *col.* 517. the Centuristes hauing in the wordes before alledged at u. reprehended and charged *Chrisostome* with Transubstantiation, do immediatly next afterwardes say, *idem videtur sapere quod Theodoretus scribit, sicut ergo simbola Domini corporis et sanguinis alia quidem sunt ante inuocationem Sacerdotis, sed post inuocationem mutantur, et alia fiunt, ita etiam post assumptionem, corpus Domini mutatur in diuinam naturam, in dialogo secundo inconfuso.* (y) *Ibidem* col. 1008. The Centuristes say of *Theodoret de cæna periculose dicit, simbola corporis et sanguinis Domini post inuocationem Sacerdotis mutari, et alia fieri, Dial.* 2. *in confuso.* And see *Theodorets* further saying alledged, *Tract.* 2. *sect.* 8. *subdiuision* 2. at m.

(z)

(z)

See heretofore *tract. 2 .*
sect. 1 . subd. 2. in the
margent vnder the letter
d.

(a)

Antonie de Adamo, in his
Anatomy of the Masse,
fol. 221.

(b)

In lib . Epistolarum Oeco-
lampadij et Suinglij, l. 3.
pag. 756 . and the Cen-
turie writers, *cent. 4 .*
c. 4. col. 295. charge
the other writinges now
extant vnder his name,
with *transubstantiation .*

(*)

See this testified in *Cran-*
ners answeare, to *Steuen*

(3) *S. Ambrose* also liued *Anno Domini* 38
. & his sundry sayinges, (z) *heretofore in*
part alledged out of his booke of Sacramētes,
are so euident that a certaine Protestant writer confesseth that, (a) *the booke of Sacramentes*
ascribed to Ambrose, putteth this opinion of Christs
bodily presence in the Sacrament ; also *Oecolam-*
padius mentioneth sundry sayinges contained
in that booke, and (b) reiecteth them as making for the real presence : In so much as (*)
Melancton writeth to *Oecolampadius,* that *Am-*
brose would neuer haue trauailed to accumulate
so many miracles as he doth, speaking of this
matter to declare Gods omnipotency, had he not
thought the nature of bread to be chaunged. And
in like plaine manner is the foresaid iudgement of *Ambrose,* confessed and reiected by
(m) *Ioachim Vadian* the Suinglian, and by (n)
Martin Luther. S . Gregory Nissen, liued An- 34
no

Gardiner, of the Sacrament, *pag. 209 .* and *211 .* and *Oecolampadius in*
lib. epist. Oecolampadij et Suinglij, pag. 636. alledgeth *Melancton* saying ; *extant inter Ambrosij libros duo libelli, quorum alter titulum habet de*
mysterijs initiandis, alter de Sacramentis ; in his palam affirmatur, quod non
tantum significet panis corpus Domini, sed reipsa corpus Christi, detur in cæna
&c. ibi sic legitur &c. quantis igitur (ait *Ambrosius*) *vtimur exemplis vt*
probemus non hoc esse quod natura formauit, sed quod benedictio consecrauit ,
maioremq́ vim esse benedictionis, quam naturæ, quia benedictione etiam natu-
ra ipsa mutatur? Virgam tenebat Moyses, proiecit eam et facta est serpens
&c. And then after many other like miracles alledged by *Ambrose* to
the same purpose, *Melancton* concludeth saying there, *pag. 637. hæc*
tam longa recitatio exemplorum, clare ostendit authorem sensisse panem non
esse tantum signum, sed naturam panis mutari. (m) Ioachim Vadian de
Eucharistia Aphorismi, l. 5 . pag. 150. hauing alledged against the
real presence, certaine sainges in the other writinges of *Ambrose,* and
comming to speake of his booke of Sacramentes, confesseth saying ,
nec me fugit quid libri illi de Sacramentis, qui Ambrosio tribuuntur, doceant,
sed Ambrosij non esse illud magno argumento est, quod in his libris quos eius

esse-

esse non dubitatur nihil tale vnquam docuit, nec est dubium, quin vel Augusti-
nus praeceptoris sui consilium excusaturus fuisset, et declaraturus, cur ab eo
dissentiret, si adhuc modum libri illi de sacramentis ab eo script et editi fuis-
sent. Imo ne ipsum Ambrosium tantopere a seipso discedere commendando
docuisset &c. (n) *Luther, in lib. contra Henricum Regem Angliae circa*
med. intreating of transubstantiation saith, *Ambrosium inducit (Tho-*
mista Rex) asserentem nihil remanere nisi corpus et sanguinem post consecra-
tionem, quid ergo respondeam &c. Ambrosium hic errasse palam palpemus &c.

(c)

no Domini 340. and his (c) testimony of the
Sacrament doth so manifestly affirme the real
presence, that our aduersarie *Crastonius* in his
booke against *Bellarmine* doth therefore affirme (d) *the iudgement of Gregory Nissen to be*
absurd. And the *Centurie writers* vndertaking
to mention the (2) *hurtful opinions and errors*
of the Doctors, do withal specially (3) recite
and dislike an other of his plaine testimonies
as making for *transubstantiation. Ciril. Alex-*
andrinus, liued about the latter end of the same
age, and him doth *Peter Marter* reproue for
his (e) affirming of the real presence saying

See this testimony alled-
ged in part heretofore
tract. 1. sect. 3. subd. 2.
fine. at k. in the margent.

(d)

Andreas Crastonius de offi-
ficio Missae, contra Bellar-
minum, l. 1. sect. 164.
pag. 81.

(2)

Cent. 4. *c.* 4. *col.* 287.

(3)

Cent. 4. *c.* 4. *col.* 295.

saith, *Gregorius Nissenus*
in oratione Catechistica ait; recte nunc etiam Dei verbo sanctificatum panem
in Dei verbi corpus credimus immutari &c. And to proue that this change
is no lesse real, then was the chaunge of that bread which was by our
Sauiours eating and digestion turned into his flesh. *Nissen* there further saith, *itaq, qua ex causa panis in eo corpore mutatus in diuinam virtutem*
transyt, eadem de causa nunc etiam fit &c. non quia comeditur eo progredi-
ens, vt verbi corpus euadat, sed statim per verbum in corpus mutatur, vt dictum
est a verbo, hoc est corpus meum. Thus farre S. *Gregorie Nissen,* alledged
by the Centuristes, and a litle afterwardes in the same tract *Gregory Nis-*
sen further saith, *Haec autem tribuit virtute benedictionis in illud (corpus*
suum) rerum quae videntur naturam mutans. And see his other wordes
in this tract of Christes body being in respect hereof in many places at
once, alledged here after *tract. 2. sect. 4. subd.* 1. at 3. next before d.
(e) *Cirillus Alexandrin. ad Calosirium,* saith, *ne enim horreremus carnem*
et sanguinem apposita sacris Altaribus condescendens Deus nostris fragilitatibus
influit

influit oblatis vim vitæ, co̅uertens ea in veritatem propriæ carnis. and *in Ioan. l. 10. c. 13.* he further saith of the Sacrament, *A̅ fortaſſe putat ignotam nobis myſticæ benedictionis virtutem eſſe? quæ cum in nobis fiat, nonne corporaliter quoq̃ facit communicatione carnis Chriſti, Chriſtum in nobis habitare.* and afterwardes, *vnde conſiderandum eſt, non habitudine ſolum, quæ per charitatem intelligitur Chriſtum in nobis eſſe, verumetiam participatione naturali.* and *in Ioan. l. 11. c. 27.* he saith, *corporaliter enim ſilius per benedictionem myſticam nobis vnitur vt homo, ſpiritualiter autem, vt Deus.*

(f)

Peter Marter, in his e-pistles annexed to his common places in english in his epistle there to Beza, pag. 106. In so much as in his second Alphabetical table there of the additions vnder the letter h. at the word *hereſy,* is set downe there, *hereſie of Ciril touching our co̅munion with Chriſt* 106.
(g) See *Peter Martir vbi ſupra* in his epistle there to *Caluin, pag. 98.* and see him in *defenſ. ad obiect. Gardiner. part. 4. pag. 724.*

ing, (f) therefore *I wil not ſo eaſily ſubſcribe to Ciril, who affirmed ſuch a com̅union, as thereby euen the ſubſtance of the fleſh and bloud of Chriſt firſt is ioyned to the bleſſing, for ſo he calleth the holy bread &c.* And in like manner doth he in sundry other (g) places reiect *Cirilles* iudgement of the Sacrament. S. *Hillarie* li-ued about *Anno Domini,* 370. and he is likewise ſo plaine (2) in affirming with *Ciril,* our real and corporal vnion with Chriſt vpon our receiuing of the Sacrament, that *Caluin,* as enforced, doth therfore specially reproue both him

(2) *Hillarie l. 8. de Trinitate multo ante med.* affirmeth our corporal vnion with Chriſt, teaching that we are corporally vnited to him, by his taking vpon him our humane nature, and he corporally vnited to vs by our receiuing him in the Sacrament, to which end he saith, *ſi enim vere verbum caro factum eſt, et nos vere verbum carnem cibo dominico ſumimus ; quomodo non naturaliter manere in nobis exiſtimandus eſt, qui et naturam carnis noſtræ iam inſeperabilem ſibi homo natus aſſumpſit, et naturam carnis ſuæ ad naturam æternitatis ſub Sacramento nobis communicandæ carnis admiſcuit? &c. Si vere igitur carnem corporis noſtri Chriſtus aſſumpſit &c. noſq̃ vere ſub myſterio carnem corporis ſui ſumimus &c.* And a litle afterwardes *ipſe enim ait, caro mea vere eſt eſca, et ſanguis meus vere eſt potus, qui edit carnem meam, et bibit ſanguinem meum, in me manet, et ego in eo, de veritate carnis et ſanguinis non eſt relictus ambigendi locus &c. hæc accepta atq̃ hauſta id efficiunt, vt et nos in Chriſto, et Chriſtus in nobis ſit.* And a litle after, *cum ille in patre per naturam diuinitatis*

diuinitatis esset, nos contra in eo per corporalem eius natiuitatem, et ille rursum in nobis per Sacramentorum inesse mysterium crederetur &c. perfectè autem huius vnitatis Sacramentum superius iam docuerat, dicens, sicut me misit viuens Pater, et ego viuo per Patrem, et qui manducat meam carnem, ipse viuat per me ; viuit ergo per Patrem, et quomodo per Patrem viuit, eodem modo nos per carnem eius viuemus &c. Hæc vero vitæ nostræ causa est quod in nobis carnalibus manentem per carnem Christum habemus &c. And some what after that *cum et per honorem nobis datum Dei filij, et per manentem in nobis carnaliter filium, et in eo nobis corporaliter et inseparabiliter vnitis mysterium vera ac naturalis vnitatis sit predicandum.*

(3)

him and *Ciril,* to gether with other auncient Fathers, affirming that, (3) *the auncient Fathers especially Hillarie and Ciril, went further* (in this matter) *then was conuenient.* with much (4) *more* in their like further reprehension. 350. *Optatus* liued about *Anno Domini* 350. and he also (complaining vehemently against the barbarous sacrilege of the *Donatists*) saith, (5) what is so sacrilegious as to breake, scrape or shaue, & remoue the *Altars of God,* (in quibus) on which (Altars) you also some time haue offered &c. For what is the *Altar* but the seat of the body & bloud of *Christ ? &c.* What had *Christ* offended you, whose body and bloud dwelleth there at certaine momentes? &c. this so greeuous wickednes is doubled, whilest you also breake (*Calices Christi sanguinis portatores*) the *Chalices* (which are) the cariers of *Christes* bloud. A saying so plaine & euident, that it is for such specially condemned (6) by *Peter Martir* and the *Centurie writers .*

Caluin in lib. epistolarum et respons. epist . 208. pag. 392. saith, *quanquam autem veteres ac Hillarium præsertim et Cirillum, longius quam par sit prouectos fuisse video &c.*

(4)

Caluin, ibidem saith there further of those Fathers, *illi in sua inscitia deprehensi ad miseram latebram suffugiunt, nos quoq, eiusdem cum Christo esse essentia: Hoc autem confesso, multis absurdis inuolui necesse fuit ; sed modò ne eorum authoritatem nobis obtendant noui isti fusores, mihi satis erit non subscribere &c.*

(5)

(4) *Optatus l. 6. contra Parmen. prope initium.* saith, *quid enim est tam sacrilegum, quam Altaria Dei* (in quibus et vos aliquando obtulistis) frangere, radere, remouere ? &c. quid est enim Altare, nisi sedes, et corporis, et sanguinis Christi ? Hæc omnia furor vester aut rasit, aut fregit &c. quid vos offenderat Chtistus, cuius illic per certa momenta corpus et sanguis habitabat &c. (and afterwardes) hoc immane facinus geminatum est, dum f egistis etiam Calices Christi saguinis portatores .*

O 2

(6) Se

(6) See the wordes of *Peter Martir* and the Centurie writers, alledged heretofore, *tract.* 1. *sect.* 2. *subdiuis.* 1. in the margent vnder a. *p. 66.*

(2)
Ciril · Hierosol. catech. 4. saith, *Hoc sciens &c. knowing this, and houlding it for most certaine that this bread which is seene of vs, is not bread (although our taist iudge it to be bread) but the body of Chrift, and that the wine which is seene of vs (although to the sence of taist it seeme wine) yet is not wine, but the bloud of Chrift.*

(3)
Ciril. catech. 4. saith further, aquam aliqvando &c. he sometimes in Cana of Galilee by his onely wil chaunged water into wine, which is neare to bloud, and shal he not be worthy whom ne may beleeue that he chaunged wine into bloud : wherefore with al assurance let vs receiue the body and bloud of Chrift, for vnder the forme of bread his body is geuen to thee, and vnder the forme of wine his bloud is geuen. Can any Catholicke of this age, write more plainely?*

(4) By which foresaid, not doubtful, but confessed testimonies of *Chrisoftome, Theodoret, Ambrose, Gregorie, Niffen, Ciril, Alexandrinus, Optatus,* and *Hillarie,* who al liued within the compasse of that one age in which *Conftantine* himfelfe liued, it appeareth moft plainely that our doctrine of the real presence, was vndoubtedly the receiued doctrine of those very auncient times : which point is made, as yet vnanfwerably, more euident by *Ciril* Bifhop of *Hierusalem,* who liuing *An. 320.* no 320. which was fomewhat before thefe Fathers, doth not onely fet downe in moft plaine woirdes the doctrine of (2) *tranfubftantiation,* but doth alfo yet further alledge other like miraculous (3) *changes* wherby to explaine his meaning; in fo much as he is therefore (*) *difliked* and (4) *reiected* further euen in the point of *Maffe.* Before al thefe forefaid Fathers liued S. *Cipriã an. Dom. 24.* 240. who doth very plainely affirme that (h) *the bread which our Lord gaue to his Difciples (was) chaunged, not in fhew, but in nature,* and which is more, *by the omnipotency of the word made flefh:* explaning himfelfe yet further by comparifon

(*) *M. Iewel* in his reply, *Art.* 10. *pag.* 432. anfweareth *M. Hardinges* obiection of thefe forefaid places of *Ciril,* faying thereto, *many of Cirilles confiderations be verie like to M. Hardinges iudgment in this article, that is to fay, like, accidens fine fubiecto, a fhew of wordes without fubftance.* So euidently did S. *Ciril* make againft him. (4) See this hereafter tract. 3. *fect.* 2 *fubdiuif.* 3. at the letter f. (h) *Ciprian in ferm. de cœna Domini poft initium* faith, panis ifte quem *Domiuus Difcipulis porrigebat*

rigebat, non effigie, sed natura mutatus, omnipotentia verbis factus est caro et sicut in persona Christi humanitas videbatur, et latebat diuinitas, ita sacramento visibili diuina se infudit essentia.

comparison that (i) *as in the person of Christ his humanity was seene, and his diuinity lay hid, so in the visible Sacrament, the diuine essence hath vnspeakably infused it selfe:* and that wheras (k) the law did forbid the eating of bloud, the Gospel doth commaund that it be drunke. that also (2) *we are annointed with this bloud, not onely outwardly* (in body, which conuinceth our bodily receiuing thereof) *but also inwardly in soule.* and that in this Sacrament our Lord (l) *doth yet to this day, creat, sanctify, and blesse his most true and holy body, and distribute it to the godly receiuers; requiring lastly euen our* (m) *teares in the presence of this body.* In which and sundry his other sayinges, he is so plaine, that a certaine Protestant writer, doth therefore confesse and say, that in this foresaid sermon or treatise, (n) *are many hard sayinges which seeme to establish transubstantiation;* affirming (for his last refuge) in steede of better answeare thereto, that the said sermon or treatise (o) *is counterfeate:* which miserable shift is (p) heretofore fully auoided. Hereunto might be added in more ful explication of the auncient Churches iudgement in behalfe of real presence, the knowen (q) practise of those times

(i)
Ibidem paulo post vt supra.

(k)
Cyprian, ibidem ante med. saith, *noua est huius Sacramenti doctrina, & scholæ Euangelicæ hoc primum magisterium protulerunt, & doctore Christo primum hæc mundo innotuit disciplina, vt biberent sanguinem Christiani, cuius esum legis antiquæ authoritas districtissime interdicit: lex quippe esum sanguinis prohibet, Euangelium præcipit vt bibatur &c.*

(2)
Cyprian, ibidem paulo ante med. saith, *ipse Christus pincerna porrexit hoc poculum, & docuit vt non tantum exterius hoc sanguine liniremur, sed et interius aspersione omnipotenti anima muniremur.* (l) *Cyprian ibidem post med.* saith, *Do-*

minus vsq, hodie hoc veracissimum et sanctissimum corpus suum creat, et sanctificat, et benedicit, et piè sumentibus diuidit, in huius (corporis) presentia non superuacua mendicant lachrimæ veniam. (m) *Cyprian. ibidem vt supra.* (n) See *Zacharius Vrsinus* his booke, entituled, *commonefactio cuiusdam Theologi de sacra cæna Domini, et eiusdem commonefact. consideratio.* pag. 211. where it is said, *a Cipriano multa sunt dicta quæ transubstantiationem tueri videntur.* (o) *Ibidem* it is said, *sed sunt notha et supposititia.* (p) See heretofore in the preface to the reader sect. 15. initio. (q) See pag. 51.

this practise confessed by *M. Fulke*, in his answeare to a counterfeate Catholicke, *pag. 87.* and in the *Tower disput.* the 2. dayes conference, and by him obiected against *S. Augustine*, and the Church in his time as an error.

(r)
Impertinent, for whereas *M. Fulke* in his foresaid answeare &c. *pag. 87.* saith, *S. Augustine was in this error, that he thought Infants must receiue the Sacrament vnder paine of damnatiou, and was deceiued by false interpretation of this scripture, except you eate the flesh of the sonne of man and drinke his bloud &c. this error he affirmeth to be common to al the westerne Church, & to Pope Inocent &c.* thus farre *M. Fulke*. This error, though for the time admitted, is so farre from helping our aduersaries, that it argueth strongly to the contrary, that in the opinion of those Fathers *Christes flesh & bloud*, was by those Infantes really *eaten and drunken*, as being so present to their bodily mouth, and so by them receiued. (s) *Wrongfully charged*, for first it is euident by *S. Augustine contra duas epist. Pelag. l. 3. c. 3. & l. 1. c. 13. & de Simb. ad Catechum. l. 3. c. 10*, that *Baptisme* doth geue al remission of sinne: in so much as *de pec. mer. & rem. l. 1. c. 20.* he teacheth that *if a child, hauing receiued Baptisme, depart out of this life (soluto reatu cui originaliter obnoxius &c.) seeing the guilt is loosed to which he was bound by birth, he shal be perfect &c.* (and saued) *for nothing but sinne maketh seperation betweene God and men. Secondly* as neither *S. Augustine* nor any other father of those times, do directly to the point, affirme in any of their writinges, that a child being baptised, and dying before he receiue the other Sacrament, is damned. So *S. Augustine* to the contrary, and directly to the point yet further saith, *nulli ambigendum &c. no man may doubt but that euery one of the faithful is then made pertaker (of the grace and efficacy) of the body and bloud of Christ, when in Baptisme he is made a member of Christ, and that he is not alienated from the felonshippe of that cup and bread, although before he eate that bread and drinke of that cup he depart out of this world in the vnity of Christes body, viz.* the Church, *August. in ser. ad Infantes ad Altare : ci-*
tatur

times in ministring the Eucharist some times vnto litle Infants, whereof testimony is geuen by *S. Augustine, Inocentius*, & *S. Ciprian*, and the same so done to them, not as though they could not be otherwise saued, with which mistaken opinion (r) *(impertinent* also to helpe our aduersaries in the point now questionable)* S. Augustine* is by them *wrongfully* (s) *charged*, neither in respect of our aduersaries

uersaries pretended (t) real presence of Chistes body in the Sacrament, exhibited to the mouth of faith, which (u) *commeth by hearing*, whereof yong Infantes are not capable, but do confessedly (x) *want* the same, and therefore the said Fathers could not vpon such intention minister the holy Sacrament to thē; but onely in regard of Christes blessed body really present, & exhibited to their bodily mouth, so thereby to worke in them the good effectes of his gratious pleasure, whereof memorable example confirmed euen with miracle, is not wanting, and the same reported, not from any Apocriphal legend, but from *S. Ciprian* himselfe, and the thing done (saith he) present, *ac teste meipso*, (y) *him selfe being present and witnesse* thereof. In the

tatur apud Bedam, in 1. Cor. c. 10.

(t) Of this real presence so taught by our aduersaries, see hereafter *tract. 2. sect. 5. subdiuis. 2.* throughout.

(u) *Rom. 10. 17.*

(x) That Infants *want* faith, is affirmed by *M. Carthwright* in *M. Whitguiftes* defence &c. *pag. 611.* & by the *diuines of Geneua*, in their *Propositions & principles &c.* englished *pag. 178. sect. 4.* and by *M. Whitaker contra Dureum, l. 8. pag. 682.* (y)

Ciprian serm. 5. de Lapsis circa med. reporteth saying, *presente ac teste meipso, accipite quid euenerit &c.* heare what came to passe my selfe being present and witnes, the parentes of a child fleeing away while for feare (of persecution) they tooke no good aduisement, left their yong daughter vnder the cherishing of a nurse, the nurse brought her so left, vnto the magistrates, who before an Idol, where the people were gathered, because for her age she could yet eate no flesh, gaue vnto her bread mixed with wine which remained of the (wicked) sacrifice of them that perish; afterwardes the mother receiued her daughter who could not speake and declare the offence committed, any more then she could vnderstand & before prohibit it: Through ignorance therefore it fel out that her mother brought her in with her (*sacrificantibus nobis*) whiles we were sacrificyng, whenas the Infant girle being among the holy ones, and impatient of our praier and supplication, was constrained sometimes to cry out, and sometimes with vehement greefe of minde was tossed here and there as though a tormentor compelled her &c. But after the solemnities (of the Preistes foresaid sacrifice) being accomplished, the Deacon beganne to deliuer the Chalice to them that were present (so distinct then was this distribution to the Communicantes from the Preistes act of sacrificyng) when the rest had receiued, & the girles place was next, the litle one, by instinct of diuine maiesty, turned away her face, pres-

sed

sed (together) her mouth with her lippes clofed, and (fo) refufed the Chalice; yet the Deacon perfifted, and to her, though it were againft her wil, powred in fomewhat of the Sacrament which was in the Chalice, then followed belking and vomit; in a body and mouth defyled (fo with participation of former meates offered to Idols) the Eucharift could not remaine: the drinke fanctified in the bloud of our Lord, brake out of her polluted bowels, fo great is the power of God, fo great his maiefty, the fecrets of darkenes are vnder his light difcouered.

(z)
See *Origens* plaine faying next hereafter in the margent vnder the figne 4.

(4)
Scultetus in his *medulla Theologiæ Patrum*, pag. 169. faith, *Centuriatores Magdeburgenfes*, c. 10. cent. 3. *confubftantiationis erroneum dogma* *Origini tribuunt*. And fee *Origens* fayinges alledged hereafter, tract. 2. fect. 3. in *pag. 230.* the margent vnder the letter h, and tract. 2. fect. 6. prope finem, at the letter q. and *Origen hom.* 5. in diuerfa loca Euangelij, faith, *quando vitæ pane et poculo frueris, manducas et bibis corpus et fanguinem Domini, tunc Do-*

fame time or fomewhat before *Ciprian*, liued *Origen*, who is fo (z) plaine for the real prefence that (as *Abraham Scultetus* confeffeth and difliketh) his brethren (4) *the Centurie writers do attribute to him confubftantiation*. Before thefe times liued *Irenæus, Anno Domini* 170; who to proue that Chrift was not onely the fonne of God creator of the world, but alfo the Creator thereof himfelf, vrgeth his argument from the Churches then common receiued doctrine of the real prefence in the Sacrament, faying, (5) *but how fhal it be knowen vnto them that the bread on which thankes are geuen, is the body of their Lord, and the cup of his bloud, if they fay not that he is the fonne of the maker of the world, that is to fay his word, by which* (word) *the wood doth beare fruict, the fountaines do fpring &c.* And to proue the refurrection of our bodies, he vrgeth the fame argument of the real prefence further faying, and (6) *how do they affirme that our flefh fhal fal to corruption and not receiue life, which is norifhed of the bo-* dy

minus fub tectum tuum ingreditur, et tu ergo humilians temetipfum imitare hunc Centurionem, et dicito, Domine non fum dignus vt intres fub tectum meum, vbi enim indigne ingreditur, ibi ad iudicium accipitur ingredienti. thefe wordes *indigne ingreditur*, fhew that he vnderftandeth this entrie to be by meanes of our bodily mouth, and not of faith, becaufe that to him that receiueth by faith, Chriftes body entreth not *vnworthely* (and) *to iudgement*. (5) *Irenæus, l. 4. c. 34. poft med.* (6) *Ibidem paulo* poft.

post. And a litle after in the same place he further saith, *corpora nostra percipientia Euchariſtiam iam non ſunt corruptibilia ſpem reſurrectionis habentia.* and ſee his like ſaying *l. 5. poſt initium*.

dy and bloud of Chriſt. So clearely doth *Iræneus* affirme the preſence and nutriment of Chriſtes body and bloud in the Sacrament, not onely to our faith, but alſo to our bodies. A thing ſo euident in him, that *(7) Melancton* writing in proofe of the real preſence, wherein he aduiſedly proteſteth to *(8)* diſſent from *Oecolampadius,* and vndertaking in his cyting of the Fathers, to alledge *(9) none but ſuch as ſpeake plainely,* (10) alledgeth yet withal amongſt others the foreſaid ſayinges of *Iræneus.*

(5) Before *Iræneus* liued *Iuſtinus martyr, Anno Domini,* 130. in the age next after the Apoſtles: wheras in his time Chriſtiãs were by the heathen generally ſlandered, *humanis veſci carnibus,* (2) *with the eating of mannes fleſh ;* which

(7)
Melancton in epiſt. ad Fredericum Miconium, extant *in libro epiſtolarum Oecolampadij et Suinglij,* printed *Baſilea,* 1592. *pag.* 618.

(8)
Ibidem, pag. 603. *in epiſt. ad Oecolampad. Melancton* ſaith, *non cogitaui modo ipſe quid in vtramq̃ partem dici poſſit, ſed inquiſiui et iam veterum ea de re ſententias &c. cum omnia quæ in vtraq̃ parte firmiſſima videntur expendi, dicam pace tua, non tamen eo in ſententiam*

tuam, nullam enim firmam rationem inuenio, quæ conſcientiæ diſcedenti a proprietate verborum ſatisfaciat &c. (9) *Ibidem in epiſt. ad Fred. Micon. pag.* 619. he ſaith, *nonnulli ſine delectu maximum numerum teſtimoniorum congeſſerunt, in quibus pleraq̃ ſunt ambigua & obſcura, nos tantum ea recitauimus, quæ videbantur eſſe quàm maxime perſpicua* (10) He alledgeth the foreſaid wordes of *Iræneus, Ibid. pag.* 635. (2) *Iuſtin. in colloqu̇ cum Triphon. poſt initium.* ſaith hereof, *num et vobis perſuaſum eſt, nos humanis veſci carnibus.* And in his firſt Apologie, *verſus finem.* he alledgeth the conſtancy of Chriſtian martyres, in refelling of this ſlander ſaying, *quis enim voluptati deditus, aut intemperans, aut ſuauiter veſcens, humanis viſceribus poſſet morte gaudere.* in thoſe times alſo *Attalus* the martyr, ſaid at the time of his being tormented in a fyrie chaire, *ecce, ecce, hoc eſt homines vorare, quod vos facitis ; nos quidem neq̃, voramus homines &c.* *Apud Euſeb. hiſt. l. 5. c. 1. verſus finem.* and ſee *cent. 2. c. 3. col.* 30. And the Centurie writers in their Alphabetical table of their 2. Centurie, at b. do ſet downe, *Biblidis reſponſum ad obiectionem, quod Chriſtiani humanis viſceribus veſcerentur.* ſee it there at large, *col.* 223. and

P

col

col. 27. and in *Euseb. hist. l. 5. c. 1.* In like manner doth *Tertuli-* *an* make mention of this slander in his *Apologetico. c. 7.* and after the *Paris* print of 1566. *pag.* 593. *prope finem.* saying, *dicimur scelera-* *tissimi de Sacramento infanticidij & pabulo cruda &c.* And *Origen* expres-seth the Iewes misconceiued opinion of Christians in respect of real presence, and sacrifice saying, *(l. 6. contra Celsum ante med.) et sane apparet nil secus egisse ac Iudai in ipsis Christiana religionis, & vera disciplina primordijs factitabant, qui ad nostra doctrina notam ẽ[t] infamiam illud dissemi-narent, quod Christianis puerum aliquem immolandi mos esset, cuius et carnem singuli degustarent.* so euidently doth this slander, thus geuen forth by the Iewes, *ad nostra doctrina notum ac infamiam,* argue sufficiently the Christian doctrine in those firster times, both of real presence & sacrifice. Also this foresaid slander against Christians in those times, is yet further mentioned by *Minutius Felix, in octauio,* and by *Atha-nagoras, in Apol. ad Antoninum.* And yet the same notwithstanding *S. Ciprian,* who liued in the same time with *Origen* (who as before geueth testimony of this slander) saith, in respect of our Christian doctrine had of the Sacrament, (in his booke *de cæna Domini ante med.*) *noua est huius Sacramenti doctrina &c. Doctore Christo, primum hæc mundo innotuit. disciplina, vt biberent sanguinem Christiani &c. Lex quippe esum sanguinis prohibet, Euangelium præcipit vt libatur.*

(*)

For so much as this slan-der went of al Christians in generall, and was also by so many of the heathē so generally diuulged & obiected, it is thereby probable, that it did not begin or arise, vpon the which said slander, is by *Athanagoras* mentio-ned and refelled, in his Apologie to *Antoni-nus* the heathen Emperour : *Iustinus* writing as then, his like Apologie to the very same Em-perour, and being thereby in his discourse of the Sacrament (the reported doctrine wher-of cōcerning the real presence was the (*) *true,* and immagined fact, of some one or other Christian in perticuler, but as *O-rigen* next before saith, *ad doctrina notam,* in respect of their mistaken doctrine, practise, and profession in generall ; which thing is made as yet more euident, aswel by the testimonie of the auncient Father *Pruden-tius,* who in *Peristephanion. himn. 2.* iuduceth the *Tyrant,* thus insulting and saying to the blessed martyr *S. Lawrence, Hunc esse vestris orgijs morémq́, et artem productum est, hanc disciplinam fæderis libent, vt auro An-tistites argenteis scyphis ferunt fumare sacrum sanguinem.* As also by like testimonia

restimony of the French Christians of those firster times, who in their e-
pistle recyted by *Euseb. hist. l. 5. c. 1.* and by the Centurie writers,
cent. 2. col. 26. lin. 2. saith of the heathen, *commenti sunt aduersum
nos thyestea conuiuia et incestus Oedipodis,* they haue slandered vs with bankets,
made of dead children, and incestious meetinges, deuised so in respect of the
Sacrament then celebrated by Christian assemblies, not in the day time,
but (in reguard of persecution then raging) before day in the morning,
whereof the Centuristes *cent. 3. col. 132.* say, *Eucharistia Sacramentum, inquit Tertulianus, etiam antelucanis catibus sumimus.* So that in respect of those assemblies to the Sacrament, and the real presence therein
the acknowleged, they were charged with the foresaid *banquets* made of
mannes flesh. And in respect of their foresaid nightly assembling therto, they were likewise, as witnesse the Centuristes, *cent. 3. col. 143.*
further charged with *incestuouse* & promiscuous wantonnes in the darke.

and (3) *confessed cause* of the foresaid slander)
occasioned to explaine the same to the refelling of that slander, and al suspicion thereof,
so farre as truth would permit, saith yet neuerthelesse thus of the Sacrament, (4) *we receiue not these as common bread, and common
drinke, but euen as by the word of God. Iesus
Christ our Sauiour being incarnate, had both flesh
and bloud for our saluation, so we are taught that
the foode, which by the praier of the word of God,
is by him consecrated with thankesgeuing, (or made
the Eucharist) of which foode our flesh & bloud
by transmutation are (*) nourished, is the flesh
and bloud of that Iesus Christ which was incarnate:*
alledging in further proofe or declaration
thereof, the wordes of our Sauiour, *this is my
body, this is my bloud.* In which saying his meaning

(3)
So confessedly the cause, that
euen *Vadian* the *Suinglian,
de Eucharist. l. 6. fol.*
198. confesseth & sayeth
therof, *inter foeda et nefaria
multa, et illud Christianis
obijciebatur, quod Infanti-
bus trucidatis cruenta conuiuia celebrarent, sanguine
crudum humanum dicerent,
in eo panem intingerent, et
sic vescerentur, Deinde sacu-
ri promiscuos concubitus a-
gerent, foedoq; incestu pollu-
erentur, id genus criminati-
ones amarulentissimas, natus
apud illos de cana nostra ru-*

peyerat
mor preparat : *discere quidem ex his potuerunt, quos quotidié ad tormenta ra-
piebant, hoc sentire Christianos, quod in catu, et in cana illa sua carne Domini
vescerentur, et sanguinem eius biberent &c.* (4) *Iustin. Apol. 2. versus
finem.* (*) Wheras *M. Fulke* against *Hoskines &c. pag. 238.* inferreth hereupon, how that *Iustine* affirmeth the Eucharist to be nourishing

and foode to our bodies, and that therefore it is not Chrisles body, but onely bread and wine : This is manie waies auoided. (1) *First,* in that *Iustine* onely meaneth, that the same foode in kinde, wherwith our bodies are nourished, being once confecrated, is therby made the body of Chrift, this vnderstanding of *Iustines* wordes is so euident, that the learned Caluenist *Gasper Laurentius,* in his *Catholicus & orthodoxus consensus,* printed 1595. & by him dedicated to the *Connte Palatine of Rhene,* pag. 368. obserueth this fence in his tranflation of *Iustines* wordes out of Greeke, thus tranflating that part : *Sumimus ante hunc panem, et hunc potum, non vt communem, sed eo modo quo edocti sumus Iesum Christum Seruatorem*

ning in our behalfe, is made many waies euident : As (1) *first* by the comparison which he vseth betweene the Eucharist & our Sauiours incarnation, in respect of one and the same powerable manner, whereby one and the same truth is a like in both of them effected, affirming as before to that end of the Eucharist, that *by the praier of the word of God it is made* (not a figne or figure but) *the flesh and blood of Chrift, euen as by the* (like powerable) *word of God Iesus Chrift had flesh and blood for our saluation.* (2) *Secondly,* in that *Iustine* writing this to a heathen Emperour, ignorant of our Sacramentes, was occasioned thereby to explaine the same in proper and plaine wordes, and not by figuratiue speaches, to make the mysteries of our religion (in them felues otherwife more eafie) to feeme to the fame Emperour straunge, and incredible. *Thirdly,* the fufpicion or flander before mentioned, whereby Christians were charged with eating mannes flesh (how foeuer it was begun or grounded) did altogether prouoke *Iustine* in preuention of further fufpition to haue explained our Sauiours forefaid wordes, as being figuratiue, wheras he not onely recyteth them without fuch explanation, but alfo affirmeth thereupon the Eucharist to be *the flesh of Chrift,* thereby not fo much excufing, as greatly

nostrum habuiffe pro falute nostra carnem et fanguinem : fic etiam cibum illum ex quo nostra caro et fanguis aluntur, post benedictionem ipfius, effe carnem et fanguinem Domini. (2) *Secondly,* admit he fpoke here of that foode after it were confecrated, yet his meaning is not that it is foode to our bodies in refpect of the bellie, (for neither is the Sacrament by vs to that end receiued, neither would *Iustine* trouble himfelfe with fo vnneceffarie a point) but onely that it is foode to our bodies in refpect it *nourisheth them to refurrection and immortality.* In which fpecial fence *Irenæus neus* and many other Fathers do affirme that it nourisheth our bodies, whereof see *Iraneus* next heretofore in this section, *subdiuis*. 4. at 6. both in the margent and text.) and see *Ignatius* hereafter, *tract*. 2. *sect*. 11. *subdiuis*. 1. in the margent at 1. And see S. *Iohns* Gospel, *c*. 6. *vers*. 54. (3) *Thirdly*, admit *Iustine* meant that the Sacrament were *cibus ventris*, yet doth not that make so against the assertion of vs, who acknowledge that the external Sacrament, reteyneth stil the former properties of colour, taist, nourishment, &c. whereof see S. *Thom.* part. 3. *quest*. 77. *art*. 6.

(5)

M. *Willet* in his Synopsis, pag. 460.

(6)

greatly rather increasing the suspicion aforesaid, which doubtlesse he would neuer haue done, if he might with truth so easily haue auoided the same by his contrary explanation.

(6) *Sixtly*, wheras our aduersaries sacramental presence dependeth vpon receiuing, to which end they affirme that *(5) it is no sacrament vnlesse it be receiued*: *Iustine martyr* in the place before mentioned, teacheth to the contrary euen the Sacraments *reseruation*, affirming to that end, that after *(6) he who is cheife* (in that action, meaning the Preist) *hath praied and geuen thankes* (or consecrated the Sacrament) *then are the thinges consecrated distributed, to al* (present) *and sent to those that are absent by Deacons* who, as D. *Whitguift* & others affirme, might (7) *distribute, but not minister* (or consecrate) *the Lords supper*. In so much that M. *Cartwright* speaking of this very *sending* of the Sacrament thus mentioned by *Iustine*, saith, it (8) *was a corruption then* (vsed) *in the Church and* (9) *contrary to the institution*. Al which premisses alledged from *Iustine*, are in themselues so plaine, that the Centurie writers, *whose writinges are* (by our aduersaries houlden (10) *worthy of immortal*

Iustine martyr Apol. 2. *fine.* which point of *reseruation* is so euident in *Iustine*, that it is specially confessed by M. *Hutton* in his second part of the answeare to the reasons for refusal of subscription &c. pag. 71. And M. *Sutliue de Missa Papistica, l*. 4. *c*. 15. *fol*. 54. saith of *Iustine, mos erat, vt vtraq; species ad absentes pariter deferetur per Diaconos, vt ex Apologia Iustini secunda colligere licet &c. illi deniq; qui Sacramentum in Ecclesia sumebant eius particulas ex praua superstitione asseruare solebant.*

(7) M. *Whitguift* in his defence, pag. 585. and see heretofore tract.

1. *sect*. 3. *subdiuis*. 1. at a. b. (8) M. *Cartwright*, in M. *Whitguistes* defence, pag. 585. (9) M. *Cartwright* in his second reply.

part.

part. 1. *pag.* 77. (10)
Christ descended into hel,
fol. 23.

(11)

Cent. 2. *col.* 48. saith,
nec senserunt panem et vini
figuras duntaxat nudas corpo-
ris et sanguinis Christi esse.

(12)

Docuerunt cum pane et vino
iuxta verbum et institutio-
nem Christi ipsiusmet, in-
carnati Christi carnem et
sanguinem distribui, quem-
admodum aperte Iustini lo-
cus in apol. 2. testatur.
(*cent.* 2. *col.* 48.) And
againe, *qua perspicuitate e-*
tiam Iræneus de Eucharistia
loquitur &c. Ibid. col. 48.

(s)

So saith D. *Whitguift,* in
his defence &c. *pag.*
408. and see *Euseb. hist.*
l. 3.

(t)

See the Protestant trea-
tise entituled, *Recitatio-*
nes de consilio scripti libri
concordiæ. printed *Lipsiæ.*

M. D. *Hil,* in his defence of the article,

mortal memory) do affirme of *Iustine,* as also of
Iræneus, that they (11) *did not thinke that bread*
and wine, were onely naked figures of the body and
bloud of Christ, but were both of them (12)
plaine in this question of the real presence,
hitherto concerning *Iustine.*

(7) Before him was *Ignatius* (s) *who was*
S. *Iohns scholer, and liued in Christes time:* he,
in his vndoubted testimonie, alledged specially by *Theodoret* aboue 1200. yeares since,
reproueth (as the *Lutheranes* thereupon doe
obserue) (t) *certaine Sacramentaries or Caper-*
naytes, who did presently after the Apostles times
(no lesse then as (2) apeareth by the 6. of
Iohn, they did before in Christes time) *deny*
the real presence, saying of them, (u) *they do*
not admit Eucharistes and oblations, because they
do not confesse the Eucharist to be the flesh of our
Sauiour Iesus Christ, which flesh suffered for our
sinnes. could he speake more plainely?

This current of testimonies thus continued vp to the Apostles age, is so euident, that
our aduersaries do confesse that (x) *transub-*
stantiation entred early into the Church: In so
much as in respect of this confessed successiue
and not interrupted antiquitie, an other Protestant writer confesseth likewise and saith,

I(y)

1581. *nona recitat. pag.* 177. (2) See this hereafter *tract.* 2. *sect.* 3.
subdiuis. 1. *prope et post initium.* (u) These wordes of *Ignatius* are
alledged vnder the name of *Ignatius,* by *Theodoret, dial.* 3. and *Hamel-*
manus (a Protestant writer) *de tradit. Apost. &c. col.* 746. alledgeth
not onely *Theodoret,* but also one *Widefortus* alledging, *Anno* 1396. this
saying of *Ignatius,* out of *Ignatius* his epistle extant with this saying
found in it, in an auncient copie of that time. And so likewise doth
Chemnitius in his examen, *part,* 1. *pag,* 94. And see *Ignatius* his other
saynges

faying alledged hereafter, *tract. 2. sect. 11. subdiuis. 1.* in the margent at l. (x) *Adimus Francisci, margarita Theologica, pag. 256.* saith, *commentum Papistarum de transubstantiatione mature in Ecclesiam irrepsit.*

I (y) haue not beene hitherto able to know when this opinion of the real and bodily being of Christ in the Sacrament did beginne. By al which is abundantly discouered, the measurelesse and exceeding bouldnes of those our aduersaries (namely, *M. Willet, M. Whitaker, M. Sutliue,* and others) who (without al forehead) haue not bene abashed to abuse their reeders, with pretending and serious affirming to thé, that our doctrine of real presence is but (3) *new* : that also (4) *transubstantiation was first inuented by Innocent the third, in the Lateran Councel* (which was but *Anno Domini* 1215.) and that (5) *neither the matter nor name of transubstantiation were knowen before the* (said) *time of the Lateran Council, and Innocent the third* : then which what more vntrue, bould, & outfacing.

That the Scriptures are agreeable to that sence, fully prouing the Real Presence of Christes body and blaud in the Eucharist.

SECTION. 3.

ONely now I wil hereunto adde, a breefe touch of such correspondence as the Scriptures yeelde to our foresaid doctrine of the real presence. As (1) *first,* in that our Sauiour (his wordes being literally taken) seemeth to promise the same, as where

(y)
Antonie de Adamo, in his Anatomie of the Masse, pag. 236.

(3)
Anthonie de Adamo in his Anatomy of the Masse, fol. 221. tearmeth it, *this new opinion of Christes bodily presence in the Sacrament.* And *M. D. Willet* in his Sinopsis, printed *Anno* 1592. *pag.* 451. saith, *this their deuised and forged opinion of the real presence of Christ, is of no antiquitie in the Church, neither was there any question about it, for a thousand yeares after Christ, til the time of Berengarius, who liued Anno* 1060. *this grosse opinion sauoreth not a whitte of antiquitie.*

(4)
M. Whitaker contra Dureum, l. 7. pag. 480. saith, *qui transubstantiationem primus excogitauit, is fuit Innocentius tertius in Lateranensi concilio.* (5) *M. D. Sutliue, de* be *Missa Papistica l. 2. c. 5.*

fol. 196. saith, *nullum transubstantiationis vestigium reperire possunt ante tempora Lateranensis concilij sub Innocentio tertio, aut seculum illud in quo ille Concilium*

Concilium illud congregauit &c. ante illud tempus notum fu-isse constat.

(z)
Ioan. 6. 51.
(a)
Peter Martir, l. cōtra Gar-dinerum, obiect. 34. *pag.* 359. faith, *in eodem erro-re Papiste versantur cum Capernaitis, dicunt enim se manducare Christum car-naliter et corporaliter &c.* & *M. Sutline* in his suruey of Poperie printed 1606. *c.* 8. *pag.* 55. *sect.* 8. faith, *the Capernaites beleeued that Christes flesh was to be eaten, and his bloud to be drunken really, and that both were to be receiued into the mouth.* (2) Io. 6. 42. *Is not this Iesus the sonne of Ioseph, whose fa-ther and mother we knew.* (b) *How can this man gene vs his flesh to eate.* Ioan. 6. 52. *this is a hard saying, who can heare it.* Ioan. 6. 60.

he said, (z) *the bread which I wil geue is my flesh &c.* and wheras the Iewes and his Disciples hereupon (a) did (as *Peter Martir* confesseth) vnderstand that *Christes flesh should be eaten cor-porally as the Papistes thinke.* And thereupon the Iewes taking him to be but (2) *the sonne of Ioseph,* made (b) question of his ablenes to accomplish the same, as (c) *thinking that he spoke aboue his power*; to such purpose demaun-ding and saying, (3) *how can this man gene vs his flesh to eate,* most euidently thereby (as *Peter Martir* heretofore confesseth) vnder-standing our Sauiours wordes of *eating his flesh,* to be meant of eating, not by onely faith, but by the bodily mouth. The point now here-upon worthy of al special obseruation, is, that our Sauiour (this their coufessed vnder-standing of his wordes, notwithstanding) doth

(c) *Chrisostom. in Ioan. hom.* 46. *ante med.* faith, *putabant enim eum supra vires suas loqui.* And S. *Augustine, tract.* 26. *in Ioan.* faith, *Hoc quando caperet caro (id est homo carnalis) quod dixit panem carnem, voca-tur caro, quod non capit caro, et ideo magis non capit caro, quia vocatur caro, hoc enim exhorruerunt, hoc ad se multum esse dixerunt, hoc enim non posse fieri putauerunt.* (3) *Ioan.* 6. 52. *Ciril. in Ioan. l.* 4. *c.* 13. hereupon faith, *Si verò tu o Iudea, quomodo etiam minus clamas, hanc tuam imperitiam ego quoq, secutus, libenter quomodo ex Ægipto exiuisti rogabo? quomodo in serpen-tem Moysaica fuit virga conuersa? Quomodo lepra manus affecta vno momento temporis in pristinum statum iterum restituta fuit? Quomodo in naturam san-guinis aqua transierunt? Quomodo Patres tui per maria et per aridam effuge-runt?* with sundry other moe like examples implying more then a Sa-cramental change, saying yet further a litle there before, *nec in men-tem venit &c. it came not to their minde, that nothing was impossible with*

God

God, who wickedly said, how can this man geue vs his flesh: but we may make profit of their sinne, beleeuing the mysteries, and taking a lesson neuer to say or once to thinke how, for it is a Iewish word. And *Theophilact in Ioan. 6. 52.* saith, *Iudæi cum audissent de esu carnis illius, discredunt, ideo et verbum incredulitatis dicunt, quomodo &c. et propterea ipse volens hoc ostendere, quod non sit impossibile, sed etiam valdé necessarium, ait &c.*

doth yet reproue them, not for mistaking the meaning of his wordes (a strong reason that they vnderstood them rightly,) but for not (d) beleeuing of his said wordes; for their better preparing in which behalfe, he purposely before (*) wrought the the late strang precedent miracle, requiring them withal often, both in the beginning and further passage of this discourse, for to (4) *beleeue.* In so much as he alledgeth for that purpose to them the (e) argument of his diuinity, and answeareth their incredulous demand, not with a qualified explication or correction of speach, but to the cōtrary aggrauating his former sayings with most frequent & most pregnant (5) distinguished

(d) Their offence here in not beleeuing, is specially noted, *Ioan. 6. 64.*

(*) He purposely wrought the great miracle of *the fiue barlie loaues and two fishes. Ioan. 6. 9. 10. 11. 12. 13.* wherof *S. Chrisostome in Ioan. hom. 45.* saith, *propterea id prius fecit miraculum, vt per illud non essent amplius increduli his quæ post modum diceret.*

(4) *Ioan. 6. 29. 35. 40. 47.*

(e) *Iesus knowing that his Disciples murmured at this, said to them, doth this offend you? what if you shal see the sonne of man ascend where he was before. Ioan. 6. 61. 62.* these wordes where he was before, shew, that he hereby vrgeth the argument of his diuinity. (5) This distinct mention of *eating* and *drinking* of *flesh* and *bloud,* and of *eating* the one, and *drinking* the other, argueth our answearble receiuing thereof vnder the seueral Sacramental formes, and not spiritually by faith; for that to faith, *eating* and *drinking* is al one, neither doth our receiuing by faith, make any such distinction of *flesh* and *bloud:* for although *Prætonius de sacramentis, pag. 193. and 195.* answeareth thereto, that in the sence of eating spiritually by faith, *eating may be vsed for drinking, or drinking vsed for eating,* as being al one; yet seeing that our Sauiour doth not here mencion the one for the other, as not eating onely, neither drinking onely, but both of them at once, and as being *diuers,* proportioning *eating,* to his *flesh,* and *drinking,* to his *bloud,* it argueth sufficiently that

he

he spoke here of *eating* and *drinking*, as being not one and the same supposed action of faith, but as being the real seueral actions of the bodily mouth, and in respect of the seueral outward Sacramental formes or elementes, which hauing vnder them realy present Christes body and bloud, are accordingly receiued by our *eating* and *drinking*.

(f)

Ioan. 6. 53. 54. 56. in distinguished repetition of (f) *eating his flesh,* so much as *S. Leo in ser.* *and drinking his bloud,* withal, telling them *6. de Ieiun. 7. mensis.* most plainly that (g) *his flesh is truely meate,* repeating the 53. vearse, *his bloud is truly drinke: speaking* (obserue good saith thereupon, (most reader) so plainely saith *S. Chrisostome,* (h) directly against our ad- *least they should thinke he spoke obscurely in para-* uersaries denyal of oral *bles:* for our Sauiour vsing, and so often re- receiuing, vnder pretece   peating of spiritual receiuing) *hoc ore sumitur, quod fide creditur &c. that is re-* *ceiued with the mouth, which is beleeued with the heart, and they do answeare* *Amen in vaine that dispute against that which they receiue.* (g) *Ioan.* 6. 55. (h) *Chrisostom. in Ioan. hom. 46. prope initium.* saith, *quid autem signat,* *caro mea vere est cibus, sanguis meus vere est potus? aut quod is est verus ci-* *bus qui saluat animam, aut vt eos in prædictis confirmet ne obscuré locutum in* *parabolis arbitrarentur.* And *Origen, hom. 7. in numer. ante med.* saith in like sorte, *Manna was meate in a darke manner, but now the flesh of the* *word of God is meate in a plaine manner, as him selfe saith, my flesh is truly* *meate, my bloud is truely drinke.* And a litle afterwardes in the same place he saith of our Sauiour; *he spoke not in a darke speach, but in a plaine manner.* And *Euseb. Emissen. hom. 5. Pasch.* saith, *merito cælistis confirmat au-* *thoritas, quia caro mea vere est esca, et sanguis meus vere est potus, recedat ergo* *omne infidelitatis ambiguum, quandoquidem qui author est muneris, testis est* *veritatis, nam inuisibilis Sacerdos visibiles creaturas in substantiam corporis et* *sanguinis sui verbo suo secreta potestate conuertit.* And *Paulus Diaconus in vi-* *ta Sancti Gregorij,* doth report that when *S. Gregorie,* to perswade an in- credulous woman in the real presence, had, *after praier made, found the* *litle portion of the* (Sacramental) *bread which he had placed on the Altar to* *be made flesh, he said to the woman, learne and now beleeue him witnessing &c.* *my bloud is truly drinke.* And see hereof *Ioannes Diaconus in vita S. Gre-* *gorij, l. 2. c. 41.* Also *S. Hierome in epist. ad Ephesios, c. 1.* distingui- shing our Sauiours flesh in the Eucharist, from that which was crucified, in reguard of accidental properties, saith, *dupliciter caro Christi et san-*
                                                                                    guis

A mira= cle. 1.

the truth

guis intelligitur, vel spiritalis illa atq; diuina de qua ipse dixit, caro mea vere est cibus, et sanguis meus vere est potus &c. vel caro et sanguis quæ crucifixa est, et qui militis effusus est Lancea. adding imme diatly next after (which preuenteth al euasion) a like difference of our mortal flesh, from our other immortal flesh after our resurrection, saying, *Iuxta hanc diuisionem et in sanctis eius diuersitas sanguinis et carnis accipitur, vt alia sit caro quæ visura est salutare Dei, alia caro et sanguis, quæ regnum Dei non queant possidere.* accordingly as the Apostle maketh also like distinction saying, *it is sowen a natural body, it shal rise a spiritual body.* 1. *Cor.* 15.44. And *S. Hillarie* (*de Trinit. l.* 8. *ante med.* speaking of the Sacrament, as *Beza epist.* 5. *pag.* 60. vnderstandeth and alledgeth him) saith, *ipse enim ait, caro mea est &c.* him selfe saith *my flesh is verily meat, my bloud is verily drinke &c.* there is no place now left to doubt of the truth of his flesh and bloud, for now by the confession of our Lord him selfe, it is verily flesh and verily bloud, and these being taken and drunken bring to passe that Christ is in vs, and we in Christ &c. we are in Christ by his corporal natiuity, and he againe in vs by the mystery of the Sacramentes of his body and bloud, in reguard of which latter, he affirmeth that we haue *manentem in nobis carnaliter filium,* and that *verè verbum carnem cibo Dominico sumimus.*

peating these his former & so earnest sayinges of *eating his flesh,* and *drinking his bloud,* by way of answeare to the Iewes vpon their doubt-ful demaund, must needes be thought to an-sweare them with speach vttered not darkly, but according to their owne fosesaid sence and vnderstanding of his wordes, or els that he answeared to harden and perswade them directly in their error, which were wicked to imagine : which point of his so plaine speaking, is yet also further argued by his vehe - ment protesting to them; (i) *Amen, Amen, I say to you &c.* also by his so euident (k) requiring them to *beleeue,* which was altogether improper if they had not before vnderstoode his wordes; for how could they beleeue that which they did not vnderstand. And where it is said (as our aduersaries do obiect) (l) *it is the spirit that quickneth, the flesh profiteth nothing, the wordes that I speake are spirit and life.* To forbeare what both *Beza* and *Caluin* do (6) answeare in ful dis—

(i)
1. *Ioan.* 6. 53.
(k)
Ioan. 6. 64.
(l)
Ioan. 6. 53.
(6)
Whereas *Alemanus,* and certaine other Prote - stants, did impugne, as in clining to Poperie, the doctrine of *Caluin* & Be-za

charge

za concerning Chriſtes body really receiued, and preſent to the mouth
of faith, acknowledging onely no other preſence then Sacramental or
of ſignification; in proofe whereof they alledged againſt *Caluin* and
Beza, theſe wordes of Chriſt now vrged. *Beza in epiſt. Theologicis, epiſt.*
5. *pag.* 59. anſweareth with vs thereto ſaying, *Secundo loco profers inſignem illum locum Ioan. verba quæ loquor ſpiritus et vita ſunt, caro nihil proderſt ſpiritus eſt qui viuificat: quæ verba dum ſic torquens quaſi omnem ſubſtantiæ, ſiue ipſiuſmet Chriſti communionem tollant, tu videris quo fundamento, nitaris; certe, ſi ſimpliciter, et ſine diſtinctione exiſtimas carnem Chriſti, nihil prodeſſe, conuelleris ipſius Chriſti teſtimonio, qui carnis ſuæ et ſanguinis ſui perceptionem toties eodem loco inculcat &c.* Alſo *Caluin in Ioan.* 6. *verſ.* 63.
expounding the wordes now obiected, reprehendeth thoſe who hereupon impugne the eating of Chriſtes fleſh, ſaying: *nec recte etiam illi (intelligunt) qui Chriſti carnem prodeſſe dicunt quatenus crucifixa eſt, comeſam vero nihil nobis afferre, quia potius comedere eam neceſſe eſt, vt crucifixa poſſit profit, &c. tenemus nunc quomodo caro vere ſit cibus, et tamen nihil profit &c. nihil prodeſt, ſi ex ſua origine & natura æſtimetur &c.*

(m)

Chriſoſtom. in Ioan. hom. 46. *paulo ante med.* ſaith, *vides quod ea particula, caro non prodeſt quicquam, non de ipſa carne, ſed de carnali auditione dictum eſt.* (and a litle there before) *quid igitur caro non prodeſt quicqam, non de ipſa carne dicit, abſit, ſed de his qui carnaliter accipiunt quæ dicuntur.* And *Martin Bucer* in his *enarrat. in ſacra.*	charge hereof, I anſweare further, that this mencion here made of *fleſh* and *ſpirit*, was made (not (m) as is pretended) to ſeclude the preſence of Chriſtes fleſh, or to qualify his former ſayinges, but (directly to the contrary) as an earneſt admonition to ſtir them vp to beleeue, and not to meaſure his power herein by *fleſh*, that is (n) *by wiſdome of the fleſh*, or carnal ſence, which (o) *diſcerneth not the thinges that be of God*; whereof it is ſaid elſwhere (*) *you iudge according to the fleſh*; (¶) *fleſh and bloud haith not reuealed this to thee.* And

4. *Euangelia*, printed *Baſileæ* 1536. in *Ioan. c.* 6. *pag.* 685. ſaith, *Ad quod ſil ycit, caro non prodeſt quicqam, varie accipitur, D. Chriſoſtomus intelligit de carne noſtra quæ nequit percipere quæ ſunt ſpiritus &c. de carnali auditione, qui ſenſus admodum quadrat.* (n) *Fleſh* is vſually taken in the Scriptures for carnal wiſdome or iudgement, as *Rom.* 8. 6. 7. and *Ioan.* 8. 15. where it is ſaid, *you iudge acdorcing to the fleſh.* (o) 1. *Cor.* 2. 14. & *Rom.* 8. 7. (*) *Ioan.* 8. 15. (¶) *Math.* 16. 17.

(P)

And so do certaine Protestants (p) expound;
but *by spirit, that is, (7) by wisdome of the spirit,*
consisting in faith, & opposite to carnal iudgement, as apeareth yet more euidently by these
wordes next after following in the very same
place, (q) *but there be certaine of you that beleeue*
not. he said not, saith S. *Augustine,* (r) *there*
be some among you who vnderstand not. So plainly did he hereby instruct them, not how to
vnderstand, but to beleeue: for had he for
their better vnderstanding intended hereby
to haue qualified or corrected his former sayinges as to be meant of eating spiritually by
faith, (which kind of onely eating, him selfe
yet further there impugneth, aswel in the example of (8) *Manna* as (9) otherwise) he
would yet then (as he (s) did vpon other like
occasion or demaund) haue explained him self
in plaine tearmes, and to be vnderstoode, &
so withal therby haue satisfyed the Iewes and
his doubtful Disciples, whereas it is most euident to the contrary, that euen after these
wordes

(p)
Wygandus in Syntagm. ex
Nouo Test. col. 263.
saith, *addit, spiritus est qui*
viuificat, caro non prodest
quicquam, quo iudicat ista
spiritus sancti auxilio intel
ligi oportere, carnem enim,
hoc est, humanam rationem
in hisce diuinis rebus nihil
prodesse &c. est enim vsita
tum in Scriptura, vt caro
hominem non renatum seu
naturales vires significet, et
presertim si spiritui oppona
tur &c.

(7)
That by *spirit* is meant
wisdome of the spirit, see
the like opposition made
betweene *flesh,* and *spirit,*
and so explained, *Rom.*
8. 6. and see the said

wordes in the 6. of *Iohn,* so as yet further expounded by *Wygandus vbi su*
pra col. 263. and by *Iacobus Andreas in confutat. disput. Ioan. Iacobi*
Grinæi de cæna Domini, pag. 258. (q) *Ioan.* 6. 64. (r) *Aug. in*
Ioannem, tract. 27. saith hereof, *sed sunt quidam (inquit) in vobis qui non*
credunt, non dixit, sunt quidam in vobis qui non intelligunt. and to shew
that the very misbeleeuing of his wordes was a misunderstanding of
them, S. *Augustine* there next addeth; *sed causam dixit quare non intelli*
gant, sunt enim quidam in vobis qui non credunt, et ideo non intelligunt,
quia non credunt. (8.) For wheras M. *Fulke* against the Rhemish
Testament, *in* 1. *Cor.* 10. *v.* 3. *fol.* 277. *a. sect.* 2. saith, *Manna was*
not onely the figure of the Lords supper, but the Sacramental communication of
the body and blond of Christ indeede &c. the Iewes receiued no lesse the truth
and substance of Christ, and his benefites in their Sacramentes, then we do in ours.
our Sauiour yet saith exclusiuely to this, *not as your Fathers did eate*
Manna &c. Ioan. 6. 58. the eating therefore whereof, our Sauiour

hcie

here entreateth, implyeth more then onely eating by faith. (9) See next hereafter *subdiuis*. 2. *initio*. in the margent at the figure 3. (s) He did explaine him selfe elswhere, as *Ioan*. 3 . 3 . 4 . 5 . and concerning matters of much smaler importance, as *Math*. 16. 6 .11 .12. *Ioan*. 4 . 32 . 34. *Math*. 13 . 36 . 37. *Marc*. 4. 10. 14. and 4 . 34. *Luc*. 8 . 9. 12. and *Ioan*. 16 . 17. 19. 20.

(t)
Ioan. 6 . 66 .

(u)
Math. 16. 12.

(x)
Ioan. 16 . 29 .

(y)
Ioan. 6. 68. 69. vpon which wordes S. *Augustine (in Ioan. tract .27.)* faith, *verba vitæ æternæ habes, videte quemadmodū Petrus dante Deo, recreante spiritu sancto, intellexit, vnde, nisi quia credidit? verba vitæ æternæ habes, vitam enim æternam habes in ministratione corporis et sanguinis tui, et nos credidimus et cognouimus*. In so much as some litle afterwardes there, he doubteth not to tearme *manducatores*, *the eaters* of his Sacrament, *portatores carnis et sanguinis sui*. adding further, *hoc ergo totum ad hoc nobis valeat delectissimi, vt carnem Christi et sanguinem Christi non edamus tantum in Sacramento, quod et multi mali, sed vsq̃; ad spiritus*

wordes were vttered, they murmured and doubted, & were no lesse vnsatisfied then before: in so much as after these wordes *(t) manie of his Disciples went backe, and walked not with him* : which they neuer did before time for any figuratiue speaches, especially if (as our aduersaries do here pretend) the same was then before explained to them. And as touching *Peter*, and the rest that did not depart, but staied behind with him and were satisfied, the reason thereof is set downe to be, not for that vpon the forefaid obiected saying they vnderstoode him otherwise then before, but for that after so manie his earnest exhortations, they yeelded to beleeue that he was the sonne of God, and able to performe what he had said, and therefore the text faith not of them, as it is said elswhere vpon his explanation of his other doubtful sayinges, (u) *then they vnderstoode what he said,* or (x) *behould now thou speakest plainely*, but to the contrary, (y) *thou hast the wordes of eternal life and we beleeue*. Hitherto I only adde, that admitting our Saujours supposed strange forbearing to explaine his forefaid sayinges, to the satisfaction & vnderstanding of his vnsatisfied hearers, it is not yet vnlike, but that some one or other of the Euangelistes should haue explained them in case they had beene obscure and not rightly vnderstoode, as to (omitte the others) S. *Iohn* onely (the very writer

of

of this now in queſtió) is obſerued to haue (*) expoûded ſundry other of our Sauiours doubt ful ſayings, though being in the ſelues of much ſmaler importance. Vpon al which premiſſes I do conclude, that ſeeing neither our Sauiour, nor any of his Euangeliſtes, did expound his foreſaid promiſſe *of geuing his fleſh to be eaten*, but that our Sauiour to the contrary did argue his ſcrupulous hearers, not for wantof vnderſtanding, but for want of beleefe; it doth from thence & other the premiſſes, abundantly follow, that his foreſaid promiſe was not obſcure and figuratiue, but plaine and litteral for our receiuing of him with our bodily mouth. And thus much concerning his promiſe.

(2) *Secondly,* as our Sauiour promiſed (¶) ſaying, as before moſt pregnantly in the future tenſe twiſe repeated, (z) *the bread which I wil geue is my fleſh, which I wil geue for the life of the world.* So likewiſe, which maketh the true meaning of this ſaid promiſe as yet more euident, he made (as *Caluin* and others (*) cófeſſe) a moſt anſweareable accompliſh-ment

tus participationem manducemus et bibamus.

(*)

So *S. Iohn* expoundeth, *the raiſing vp of the temple in three daies.* c. 2. 19. 21. *Chriſtes exaltation frō the earth.* c. 12. 32. 33. *the ſleeping of Lazarus,* c. 11. 11. 13. *the waters flowing out of the bellie of the beleeuer.* c. 7. 38. 39. *the girding of Peter & ſtretching forth his handes.* c. 21. 18. 19.

(¶)

He ſaid not (faith Enthimius in cap. 6. *Ioan.) quem do, ſed quem dabo, which I do geue, but which I wil geue, for he minded to geue it in his laſt ſupper.* The bread therefore which our Sauiour promiſed that he would geue in time to come, and which he calleth his *fleſh,* cannot in our aduerſaries opinion ſignify Chriſt as he is receiued onely by faith, for this eating of him by faith, is houlden common to al times, paſt, preſent, and to come; and in this ſorte is he ſaid to haue beene eaten by the Fathers of the old Teſtament, (whereof ſee *M. Whitaker contra Duraum, l.* 2. *pag.* 170. and 171. And ſee *acta diſputationis de S. cœna in Accademia Heilderburgenſi, habit. Anno,* 1584. *fol.* 73. & 74. and *fol.* 6. and 77. and 78. therefore the eating of this *fleſh,* whereof our Sauiour there intreateth, was peculiar onely to the time then to come, and not to eating by faith onely: which point is made yet more manifeſt by the difference which our Sauiour maketh betweene *his* Fathers guiſt, & his owne guiſt, ſaying in the preſent tenſe of his Fathers guiſt, (which was his owne incarnation then preſent) *my Father geueth you the true bread from heauen.*

Ioan.

Ioan. 6. 32. but of his owne guift (concerning his flesh to be eaten in time to come) he saith, *the bread which I wil geue is my flesh.* (z) *Ioan*. 6. 51. (*) *Caluin, l. 4. institut. c. 17. sect.* 14. saith, *cum cæna nihil aliud sit quam conspicua eius promissionis testificatio, quæ Ioannis sexto habetur &c.* And *M. Bilson* in his true difference &c. *part.* 4. *pag.* 579. confesseth that, *the promise was made by Christ in the* 6. *of Iohn,* (saying) *the bread which I wil geue is my flesh,* and pag. 580. he likewise acknowledgeth, *the wordes of the supper, this is my body, performing the same* promise

(a)
Math. 26. 26. *Marc.* ment of that promised guift, when accor-
14. 22. *Luc*. 22. 19. & dingly at his last supper (a) *he tooke bread &*
1. *Cor*. 11. 24. *blessed and brake, and* (as he promised) *gaue to*
(*) *his Disciples, and said, take ye and eate: this is my*
Prætorius, de Sacramen- *body, which is geuen for you, that is* (saith (*)
tis, pag. 152. saith, *pro* *Prætorius* in the wordes of *Iohn,* 6. 51 :) *geuen*
vobis, id est pro mundi vita. *for the life of the world;* euery word whereof is
(7) not onely answearable to Christes foresaid
Final relation, for where promise, but doth also otherwise proclaime
our aduersaries do vsual- yet further the truth of our Catholicke doc-
ly obiect, that if *hoc* doe trine; for the demonstratiue *this* which doth
relate to *corpus,* then so point to the substance there meant, & should
soone as the Preist haith so (if our aduersaries opinion be true) relate
pronounced *hoc,* the *body* to *bread,* doth yet to the contrary (in regard
should so thereupon be of the (7) *final relation* which vpon the wordes
present, though the o pro-
ther wordes vsually following, were not atal pronounced : I say thereto, that the pronowne *hoc,* may of it selfe be referred as wel to any o-
ther thing as to *body,* and therefore not euery *hoc* relateth as here it
doth to *corpus,* but that which is parcel of Christes foresaid wordes, *hoc*
est corpus meum. Therefore, supposing no more to be for the time pronounced then *hoc,* the word *hoc,* is so no more the word of *Christ,* then of
Terence, but ioine the other wordes of Christ to it, then doth it (as being
Christes word) finally demonstrate and relate to *corpus* : As in like example of Gods other *operatorie* speaches, when he said, *let there be light,*
& there was light. againe God said, *let there be a firmament in the midest of the*
waters. Gen. 1. 3. 6. *take vp thy bed and walke. Ioan*. 5. 8. *thy sonne li-*
ueth. Ioan. 4. 50. in these and such like, the first word onely without
the other, did not worke the effect; as neither in the example of *Bap-*
tisme

tisme vpon the pronouncing of the first word without the other, is the Sacrament of Baptisme accomplished, but in al these and other like, the first word alwaies suspendeth it determination, til the other wordes following be conioyned thereto.

(b)

The word *bread* is in latin *panis*, in greeke *Artos*, being both of them in the *Masculine gender*, and the word *body* is in latin *corpus*, in greeke *Soma*, being both of them of the *Neuter gender*, and the Pronowne demonstratiue *this*, is in latine *hoc*, in greeke *Touto*, being both of them of the *neuter gender*, whereby it is euident that the said pronowne *this* which poin-teth to the substance there meant, pointeth not to *bread*, but finally to

pronounced it haith to *body*) differ in gender from *bread*, & agree therein with *body*: which difference from the one, and agreement with the other, (b) appeareth both in the *Greeke* and *Latine* copies. To the *iust* (*) reproofe of the Puritanes who (in fauour of their sacra-mentarie error) are not ashamed to mistrans-late *this bread is my body*. As for the weake e-uasion which our aduersaries would make in affirming that the Pronowne *hoc* standeth here neutrally or substantiuely, signifying *this thing* and so by implication *bread*, it is altogether (c) vnprobable; In so much as *Carolastadius* and

the word *body*. (*) *Iust reproofe,* made by M. Hutton, in his answeare to the second and last part of reasons for refusal of subscription. pag. 259. & 260. where hauing recited their mistranslating, he addeth saying, *had it beene in our Communion booke, we should haue beene chalenged for adding these wordes (this bread) more then is in the Euangelistes, or S. Paul* &c. (c) *Altogether improbable,* for the Pronowne *hoc*, is taken sub-stantiuely, onely when the substantiue is not expressed in the speach then present, whereas here the substantiue *bread*, is expressed, for the wordes are. *accepit panem* &c. *et dixit, hoc est* &c. Secondly, though the substan-tiue had not bene expressed, yet being then present in his hand, and pointed vnto, the word *hoc* cannot be therefore taken substantiuely, for who seeing his father present would say, *hoc est Pater meus. Thirdly,* if the word *hoc* were to be taken here substantiuely, then the *Latine* Fa-thers (to omitte the *Greeke*, as not so perspicuouse in this point, because the word *blood*, is with them of the *neuter gender*) would in like manner haue said of the other kind not *hic*, but onely *hoc est sanguis meus* (for so purposely to auoide this daunger) doth *Beza in Nou. Test.* printed Londi-ni, Anno 1587. in *Marc.* 14. and *Math.* 26. very strangely and singu-

R

larly

larly tranſlate the text directly againſt *Caluin, in Harm. in Math.* 26. 28. & *Marc.* 14. 24. and his other brethren, who to the contrary read, *hic eſt ſanguis meus.* and ſo likewiſe do the latin Fathers read: In ſo much as *Ciprian de cæna Domini, prope initium.* and *Paſchaſius lib. de corpore et ſanguine Chriſti. c.* 1. ſay concerning the body, *hæc eſt caro mea.* And *Gaudentius tract.* 2. *in Exodum,* ſaith, *hæc agni caro, hic ſanguis eſt:* ſo plaine it is that the pronowne *hoc* ſtandeth not ſubſtantiuely.

(d)

Carolaſtadius alledged by *Suinglius in l. epiſt. Suinglij et Eocolampadij. pag.* 543. ſaith, *Chriſtus iſtud pronomen hoc non in panem direxerit, ſed in ſeipſum &c.* and ſee *Sleiden* in engliſh, *hiſt. l.* 5. *fol.* 65. and *Muſculus in loc. commun. c. de cæna Domini. pag.* 324. ſaith of others, *ſcio quoſdam Fratres voculam hanc* Touto *id eſt (hoc) non ad panem retuliſſe, ſed ad ipſum Domini corpus, quaſi verſo ad ſe digito dixerit, hoc corpus meum quod hic coram cernitis dabitur pro vobis.* (2) *Andraas Carolaſtadius in dial. de cæna.* ſaith, touto

and *others* who deny the real preſence, do yet in reguard of ſo manifeſt premiſſes (d) *refer the particle (this)* not to *bread,* but to *the very body of Chriſt; Carolaſtadius* confeſſing that he is (2) enforced thereto: Hereby then alſo is abundantly confuted the error of them, who placing their pretended *trope* in the word *body,* would thereby vnderſtand *the figure of his body;* for ſeeing they do affirme *the bread* and not *his body* to be the figure of his body; this ſo euident relation made by the Euangeliſtes of the particle *hoc,* not to *panis* but to *corpus,* doth euidētly cóuince againſt our aduerſariſe, that by the word *body* cānot be vnderſtood *the figure of his body.* which point as it is (*) acknowledged for plaine, and confeſſed by the learned Caluenteſtes them ſelues; ſo alſo is it yet further inuinſibly proued by theſe other there next enſuing wordes of the text, (8) *which is geuen for you;* for to ſay that the figure of

eſt Græcum pronomen indicans nomen neutrū, iam vero vocabulū Artos *latine panis eſt Maſculinum, ideoq; pronomen* Touto *ei adiungi non poteſt &c. ideo neceſſe habeo fateri Chriſtum dicendo, hoc eſt corpus meum, corpus ſuum non panem demonſtraſſe.* (*) *Acknowledged* by *M.* Whitaker, and *M.* Hooker next here after at f. h. (8) *Luc.* 22. 20. the holy Ghoſt inſpiring *S. Luke* to ad theſe wordes, which are omitted by *S. Mathew,* and *S. Marke,* affordeth a ſtrong argument againſt our aduerſaries vnderſtanding by the word *body, the figure of his body:* for if we interpret the nowne *corpus,* by *figura corporis,* then what place *corpus* did occupy, the verie ſame

same must *figura corporis* retaine: from whence it would follow that but *the figure of his body was geuen for vs*; neither wil it suffice to say that the relatiue *quod* in english *which* doth relate not to the nowne *figura* but to the Genetiue case *corporis* and so the sence to be *this is the figure of my body, which body is geuen for you*, becaufe that so the nowne *body* though but there once named, should yet therby haue a double acceptió, the first improper when it standeth for the *figure of his body*, the second proper, when it is said to be *geuen for vs*, which weare strange and against al example; therefore the nowne *corpus* being here but once named in the whol sentence, looke how it is taken as being after the verbe *est*; in the same sence also is it to be taken as relating to, or going before *datur*, so as if most clearly it cannot signify *the figure of his body* in respect of *datur*, neither then can it so signify in respect of *est*. A thing made yet more euident by the relatiue *quod* in english *which*, for if by the word *body* be vnderstood *the figure of his body*, then cannot the said relatiue take halfe of that signification, and lay a side the other halfe, but howsoeuer the nowne *corpus* is taken, so must the pronowne relatiue *quod* repeate it againe.

of his body was geuen for vs, either then in the Sacramēt, or afterwardes vpó the Crosse, is more then absurd. Also concerning the word *blessed*, what efficacy it importeth, haith (e) *heretofore* bene in part declared. In like manner the word *is* being in the *present tense*, and before their receiuing, argueth aginst our aduersaries and with vs, that it was a perfect Sacrament, before their receiuing thereof: In so much also as *Suinglius* and his scholers (in remedy hereof) thought it best to offer force to the text (in like bould manner as did the (*) *Puritains*) & falsifying the same, to translate, not onely by way of (3) recital, but also

(e)
See *heretofore tract*. 2. *sect*. 1. *subd*. 2. at k .l. *. &c.

(*)
Of the *Puritaines* mistranslating, see next heretofore after b. at *

(3)
Conradus Schlusselburg. in Theologia Caluenistarum, l. 2. *art*. 6. *fol*. 43. saith hereof, *Sacramentarios ipsius Dei verbum falsare et mutare certissimum est*, *et*

quidem insigne et euidentissimum huius rei, exemplum est apud Suinglium in lib. de vera et falsa relig. pag. 262. *vbi in recitatione verborum institutionis filij Dei pro verbo* (*est*) *ponit significat: ita enim textum recitat Suinglius, sic ergo habet Lucas quo ex Euangelistis contenti erimus, et accepto pane gratias egit, fregit, et dedit eis, dicens, hoc significat corpus meum, quod pro vobis*

his datur, Hactenus Suinglius &c. nec potest hoc scelus Suingly vllo colore excu-
sari, res est manifestissima &c.

(4)
Of the *Dutch* tranflations
fet forth by the *Suingli-*
ans, the fame Proteftant
author *Conradus Schluf-*
felburg. faith *vbi fupra*.
fol. 44. *Ego in Saxoniæ*
opido Mundera, Anno.
Dom. 60. *apud fcholæ*
Rectorem Humbertum vidi
exemplar Germanicorū Bi-

alfo euen in their printed (4) *Bibles*, infteed
of this is my body, this fignifyeth my body; & wheras *M. Whitaker*, and fome other englifh Caluiniftes not daring fo to miftranflate, would
yet by their expofition enforce a figure or
trope, affirming withal that (f) *the trope is not*
in the body or bloud of Chrift, nor in bread or wine,
but *in the word is,* which doth in their opinion
import, (g) *fignify*; befides that this is *moft* (*)
demonftrably confuted, afwel by example from

S.

bliorum quæ Tiguri erant impreffa, vbi non fine infigni admiratione et animi per-
turbatione, verba filij Dei ad imitationem Suingly fomniatoris deprauata effe de-
prehendi: nam in omnibus illis quatuor locis. Math. 26. Marc. 14. Luc.
22. et 1. Cor. 11. vbi verba inftitutionis teftamenti filij Dei recenfentur,
Hoc eft corpus meum, hic eft fanguis meus, Textus erat falfatus, hoc fignificat
corpus meum, hoc fignificat fanguinem meum. (f) *Whitaker contra Duræum*
l. 2. pag. 180. and *Pratorius de Sacramentis. pag.* 256. (g) *M. Wil-*
let in his finopfis *pag.* 448. and *Suinglius tom. 2.* affirmeth in many
places that *eft* is here placed for *fignificat*, as *fol.* 250. and 210. and 209.
and 423. and 424. in fo much as *Hofpinianus in hiftor. facram. part. 2.*
fol. 34. faith, *Suinglius euidentiffime probat in verbis inftitutionis, eft pro*
fignificat oportere accipi. And fee alfo *M. Fulke* in his reioynder to *Bri-*
ftowes reply and anfweare to *Saunders* &c. *pag.* 587. (*) *Moft demon-*
ftrably, for *Luke* 22. 20. faith according to the original greeke *Touto*
to poterion ecainæ diathecæ en to aimatai mou. *Hic Calix nouum Teftamentum*
in fanguine meo, *this cup the new Teftament in my bloud*. the fentence ftanding thus imperfect for want of *a verbe* to knit the partes together, our
aduerfaries cannot here fupply the fame with the verbe *fignificat*, becaufe that the nowne *Diathece*, *Teftament*, is here put in the nominatiue
cafe, whereas if *S. Luke* had meant to vnderftand the verbe *fignificat*, he
would then moft clearely haue put it in the accufatiue cafe: Therefore
that the verbe *fignificat* cannot be here vnderftood, is in it felfe fo certainely euident, that al our learned aduerfaries in their tranflations of
this place, do forbeare to make perfect the fentence, with putting in
of that verbe, fupplying it otherwife with the verbe fubftantiue *eft*. And

so accordingly *M. Fulke* against the Rhemish testament, & our *English Bibles* do tranflate saying, *this cup is the new Testament in my bloud*; which word *is*, being so euidently by *S. Luke* not expressed in the original text but onely vnderstood, most conuincingly secludeth our aduersaries tropical sence of *significat*, for is it in any sort probable, or but so much as colourable, that the verbe substantiue *est*, being so euidently not expressed, but onely vnderstood, and thereupon accordingly supplied or placed to make vp the sence of the text, should so soone, as it is so of necessity placed, be immediately cast out and changed into the verbe *significat*? that the vse of speaking doth often make it left out, or not expressed, as being easy to be supplied or vnderstood, I willingly graunt; but that euer any vse of speach should in such case, cause it to be (as here in the now example of *S. Luke*) brought in and placed, and yet withal to lose it proper signification, is no lesse strange, then is our aduersaries doctrine thereupon grounded: So euidently doth *S. Lukes* omission in this place of the verbe substantiue *est*, which our aduersaries are compelled of mere necessity, onely by supplying, to expresse, abundantly suffice (in explanation of alte the Euangelistes) to conuince and proue, that in our Sauiours wordes of institution, the word *is*, can not import to *signify*; which point is in like sort made yet more euident by the foresaid euident relating of *hoc*, not to *panis*, but to *corpus*, for to say that *his body* should *signify* his *body* were more then idle.

(h

S . Luke, who in his speaking of the *cup* quite omitteth & leaueth out the verbe *substantiue*, so as thereby cannot be vnderstood the verbe *significat*, as alfo by that which haith bene next heretofore said concerning the vndoubted relating of the particle *hoc*, not to *panis*, but most euidently to *corpus*. *Bartholomæus Keckremanus* (a prime man among the Caluenists) and alfo *Oecolampadius* and *M. Hooker* do al of them (h) affirme likewise to the contrary, that the figure cannot be in the word *is*, and so from them selues there is no trope in any

Keckremanus in System. theolog. pag. 444. saith, *Alij volunt tropum esse in copula, quod et ipsum non potest probari, nam &c. et vide* pag. 445. and *Hospinian. in histor . Sacram. part. 2. fol. 35.* saith, *Oecolampadius tropum ostendit in nomine corpus &c. cessit igitur his Oecolampadius, qui contendunt verbum est, non esse figura cc signi-*

ficationis, sed veritatis &c. And *M. Hooker* in his ecclesiastical pollicy, *l. 5. sect. 67. pag. 177.* faith, *we do not interpret the wordes of Christ, as if the name of his body did import but the figure of his body, and to be, were onely to signify &c .*

(i)
Of our Sauiour, see heretofore *tract . 2 . sect . 3 . subdiuis.* 1 . in the margent at the letters. and for the Euangelistes, see onely *S . Iohn,* 2 . 19 . 21 . and 7 . 38 . 39 . and 11 . 11 . 13 . & 12 . 32 . 33 . and 21 . 18 . 19 .

(k)
Melancton in epist . ad Fredericum Miconium in lib .

of our Sauiours foresaid wordes. Which point is yet more euident, aswel in that the Euangelistes do recite the foresaid wordes without expofition or mention of any *trope,* whereas elswhere in matters of much lesser waight, our Sauiour himselfe and they likewise do (i) explaine his figuratiue sayinges : As also (which (k) *Melancton* specially obserueth) in that our Sauiour vttered his foresaid wordes in promulgation and institusion of a Sacrament, and (which is more) with a (5) commaundement thereto annexed saying , *take*

epistolarū Oecolampadij et Suingly, pag. 645. faith, *non enim inuenio firmā rationem, cur nomine corporis in verbis cœnæ, oporteat tantum abfentis corporis fignum intelligi, quanquam enim fermo in facris litteris plenus fit figurarum omnis generis, plurimum inter narrationes rerum geftarum intereft, et ordinationes diuinas. feu dogmata de natura, feu voluntate Dei &c, neceſſe eft enim certam eſſe fententiam illorum locorum vnde dogmata feu articuli fumuntur : quod fi nobis licet hos quoquomodo interpretari, deprauari poterunt omnia &c . A- brahæ mandatum eft vt circumcideret præputium, quis non irrifit inter Ethni- cos, neq̃ tamen licuit illi cum inftitueretur ritus aliud fufpicari quam quod verba fonant ; homo aftutus poterat difputare rem tam ridiculam nullo modo precipi a Deo, fed fignificari libidines eſſe coercendas ac frenandas.* And *Iaco- bus Andræas* alledged *in Collat . cath . et orthod . Chriftianorum fidei &c . pag.* 321 . *numer .* 39 . faith hereof, *funt enim verba Chrifti verba tefta- menti in quibus diferte et perfpicue locutus eft, vt ab omnibus quid velit intel- ligi poſſit.* And *Prætorius* a learned Caluinift (*in lib . de Sacramentis, pag .* 158 .) faith likewife hereof, *quicquid igitur vel citra vel contra expreſſa Chrifti et Apoftolorum verba, vel Simboli alicuius articuli genuinum fenfum, cum in alijs tum vero in hac re facramentàli fiue a nobis fiue ab alijs, id totum licet pulchre oculis niteat, eleganterq̃, auribus fonare videatur, tamen tanquam fententia male in deliberatione dicta fine vllo perfonæ refpectu reiectum difpere- at . Imo Anathema efto &c .* So plainely doth manifeft truth enforce his teftimony euen againft him felfe . (5) The Apoftles being hereby thus fpecially commaunded to *take* and *eate,* were alfo therein comaun- *ded*

ded to *take* and *eate* it, after this or that certaine manner, as either *figuratiuely, spiritually,* or *really,* and if onely either of the first, then is this commandement instituted in obscure and figuratiue wordes; whereas it is euident by example of al other like commaundementes published in the old Testament, that the wordes of such commaundementes so at first published or instituted, are, and ought to be plaine and perspicuouse, lest otherwise through obscurity, occasion be geuen of transgresing the same: for albeit that our Sauiour in his ordinary exhortation or preaching to the people, did somtimes, to stir them vp vnto greater attention, remember them in figuratiue wordes of some general duty or commaundement not then first prescribed, but formerly knowen and commaunded, as where he saith, *beware of false Prophets who come vnto you in sheepes cloathing. Math. 7. 15. Beware of the leauen of the Pharasies Math. 16. 6.* and such like; yet the first promulgation of euery peculier commaundement, is euermore deliuered in plaine wordes. And hence it is, that not onely the *ten Commaundementes,* but also al other like commaundementes wherein certaine rytes are instituted, are accordingly instituted, and at first deliuered in plaine and proper speach, which argueth euidently that these wordes of the institution *take eate this is my body,* are in like manner to be taken accoding to common and ordinarie vnderstanding.

take eate &c. do this &c. making also as then his wil or (1) *testament;* euery of which argueth his sayinges not to be figuratiue, or obscure, but plaine (6) *manifest,* and according to ordinarie vnderstanding: And so accordingly in other matters both *Fathers,* and *Protestantes* do hereupon (*) infer. Furthermore

(1)
My bloud of the new Testament. Math. 26. 28. & *Marc. 14. 24. & Luc. 22. 20.* and *Musculus in loc. commun. c. de cana Dom. num. 2. pag. 332. post med.* accknowledgeth, *that Christ at his last supper made his Testament,*

which argueth that he did it in wordes plaine to be vnderstood. for as the Apostle saith, according to *Bezas* translation, *if it be but a mans testament &c. no man addeth thereto. Gal. 3. 15.* much lesse then to our Sauiours Testament may our aduersaries adde so many of their owne glosses. (6) *Ciril. ad Calofyrium* saith, *non dubites an hoc verum sit, eo manifeste dicente, hoc est corpus meum.* (*) Concerning the Fathers *Tertulian contra Marcionem.* saith, *non est verisimile, vt ea species sacramenti &c. it is not like that that kind of Sacrament, into which al faith is committed,*

should

should be doubtfully vttered or obscurely propounded, Also *S. Hillarie, l. 8. de Trinitate post initium.* faith, *aut forte qui verbum est &c. doth he which is the word not know the signification of the word &c. and he that is vertue, was he in that infirmity that he could not vtter what he would haue to be vnderstood?* he vttered plainely the true and sincere Sacramentes of Euangelical faith. and afterwardes *prope finem*, he further faith, *consulens itaq, &c. God therefore reguarding humaine infirmity taught vs faith with no vncertaine nakednes of wordes.* and see the like in *Iraeneus l. 2. c. 47.* whom our learned aduersary *Chemnitius* in his examen, *part. 1. fol. 74.* alledgeth, concluding from his seueral sayinges, *sanum sensum (Scripturae) et qui sine periculo est, illum esse, qui aperté & sine ambiguo, ipsis dictionibus in Scripturis ponitur.* and *ibidem. pag. 48. b. ante et circa med.* he agreeth with *Andradius, Scripturam vbi dogmata seu praecepta tradit, esse certam et minime ambiguam.* (and) *regulam ipsam veritatis in Scripturis sacris in aperto positam esse.* in so much as *M. Bilson* in his true difference &c. *pag. 568.* vpon the point of Christes ordaining Sacramentes, acknowledgeth it for right, *that in Scripture, so long as the letter may possibly be true, we may not flee to figures.* and *M. Hooker, l. 5. Eccles. pol. sect. 59. pag. 130.* holdeth it for a most infallible rule in expofition of Scripture, *that where a literal construction wil stand, the furthest from the letter is commonly the worst.* and the very same faith *M. Couel* against the plea of the innocent. *pag. 194.* Also *Carion* in his Cronicle publifhed by *Melancton & Peucerus,* printed *Bernae*, 1601. *pag. 237.* faith, *in articulis fidei, in lege morali, et in promissione gratiae, necesse est retineri natiua verborum significatione.* Also *Vrsinus in commentar. catech. fol. 42.* affirmeth that, *quae enim ad fundamentu pertinent, vt sunt articuli fidei, praecepta decalogi perspicue recitata, saepe inculcata, et copiose exposita sunt in Scripturis.* and see further there *pag. 416.* and see *M. Bilsons* suruey of Christes sufferinges. *pag. 417. & pag. 555.* against these like figuratiue euafions. And see *M. Fulke* alledged hereafter *tract. 2. sect. 5. subdiuif. 4.* in the margent at the second f.

(m)   more these other wordes, *is geuen for you*, be-
Is geuen for you, is shed for ing likewife in the *prefent. (m) tenfe*, and be-
you, so readeth the *greeke*   fore
in al the three Euangelistes., and in *S. Paul,* and therefore when our aduersaries do anfweare that here, by *is geuen*, is meant which *shalbe geuen*, it is violence to the text, for though it be true that his body was afterwardes geuen vpon the Crosse, yet vnder collour thereof to deny
this

this other geuing at his laſt ſupper expreſſed in the *preſent tenſe* by al the three Euangeliſtes, and *S. Paul*, is ouer violent. See more hereof hereafter *tract. 3. ſect. 3. ſubdiuiſ. 1.* in the margent at n.o. q. & ſubd. 2. at y. z.

fore his paſſion, can not agree to *bread* and *wine*, for they may not be ſaid to haue bene then *geuen* for vs; neither to his geuing vpõ the Croſſe, for that guiſt was not then preſent, onely therfore they relate *to his body*, & *bloud*: which according to the foreſaid (n) teſtimony of the Fathers, he then gaue or offered for vs in his laſt ſupper: which thing is made yet much more plaine by *S. Luke*, who ſaith, (which can not agree to the Croſſe that euen the (o) *cup was ſhed for vs*, of which point more is ſaid (p) *hereafter*.

(3) *Thirdly, S. Paul* vndertaking to explaine our Sauiours foreſaid doctrine (*M. Hooker* therefore calling him (q) *the Lordes interpreter*) ſaith by way of expoſition and demaunde, & therefore not obſcurely (for who expoundeth or demaundeth ſo conſtantly, as *S. Paul* here doth, a thing in figuratiue and darke ſpeach?) (r) *the cup of bleſſing which we bleſſe, is it not the communion of the bloud of Chriſt?* in ſo much that *S. Chriſoſtome* expounding thoſe wordes ſaith, (s) *the meaning of them is, that which is in the cup, is the ſame which flowed from Chriſtes ſide*. In likemaner doth the ſame Apoſtle affirme of vnworthy receiuers, that (t) *they are guilty* (not ſaith he, of Chriſt or of the violating of his inſtitution, but) *of the body and of the bloud of our Lord*, which they vnworthily receiued, (u) not *diſcerning* (the ſame to be) *the body of our Lord*: for which cauſe he affirmeth that (x) *many were mira-* culouſly *re fluxit, et illius ſumus participes.*

(n)
See heretofore *tract. 1. ſect. 3. ſubd. 2.* at e. f. g. h. k. l.

(o)
Luc. 22. 20.

(p)
See hereafter *tract. 3. ſect. 3. ſubd. 2.* from y. throughout the reſidue of that ſubdiuiſion. and ſee further *tract. 3. ſect. 3. ſubdiuiſ. 3.* throughout.

(q)
M. Hooker in his Eccleſiaſtical pollicy, *l. 5. ſect.* 67. *pag.* 176. and *M. Whitaker contra Duræum, l. 2. pag.* 188. and *Caluin. in epiſt.* 353. *pag.* 662. do (both of them) ſay, *Chriſti optimus interpres eſt Paulus &c.*

(r)
1. *Cor.* 10. 16.

(s)
Chriſoſt. in 1. *Cor. hom.* 24. ſaith, *maxime ſibi his verbis et fidem facit, et horrorem, eorum autem eiuſmodi eſt ſententia: quod eſt in Calice, id eſt, quod e Late-*

(t) 1. *Cor.* 11. 27. (u) 1. *Cor.* 11.

S

29. (x) *Therefore are there among you, many weake and feeble, and many sleepe.* 1. Cor. 11. 30.

(y)
D. *Raynoldes* in his conference with *M. Harte*, pag. 68. and *Beza de cæna, contra Westphalum* extant in his *tract. theolog.* printed *Anno* 1570. pag. 216. saith, *hoc quidem sæpe diximus quod nunc quoq, repetam non posse retineri,* To reton *in his verbis, hoc est corpus meum, quin transubstantiatio Papistica statuatur.* see this also alledged by *Daniel Chamierus* in his *epistola Iesuitica, part.* 1. *pag.* 49. and allowed by him there *pag.* 61. repeating the same and saying thereof, *Agnosco verissimam præceptoris mei vocem &c.*

(z)
Beza contra Brentium.

(a)
Ridley in the actes and monumentes, pag. 964.

(b)
M. Whitaker in his answeare to *M. Raynoldes* refutation 179. and 180.

culoufly stroken or punished, some with siknes, others with death, which is more then we finde written concerning Baptisme.

That the real presence is not impossible, nor to faith absurd.

SECTION. 4.

ANd whereas our aduersaries are vpon these so plaine premisses enforced to acknowledge and say to vs, (y) *I graunt the wordes of Christ, this is my body, are plainer in shew &c. for your real presence, then for our sacramental:* And yet neuerthelesse do in the end of al, finally betake them selues to tropes and figures, onely for that they thinke it impossible that Christes body should at once be in heauen, & in the Sacrament, and in the Sacrament also, not according to the natural manner of bodily quantity and circumscription: In respect whereof *Beza* bouldly said, (z) *I deny that God is able to make Christes body present i.. the Sacrament*; and M. *Ridley Raynoldes* likewise said, (a) *I do affirme that it is impossible Chris to be both in heauen and earth at one time*; M. *Whitaker* also affirmeth the real presence to be a (b) *contradiction and therefore impossible.* To forbeare aswel M. *Whitakers* (7) *mistaking of*

(7) *Mistaken for contradiction,* doth consist of two sayinges, whereof thone is *affirmatiue,* thother *negatiue,* as for example, to say that Christes body is present in this place, and Christes body is not present in this place, is *contradiction,* but the presence of Christes body in this place, and that place at one time, is not of this kind, for it denyeth not the
being

being of his body in either place, but onely affirmeth it in both; in like manner to say Christes body is in heauen visible and circumscribed, and it is not in heauen visible and circumscribed, is a like *contradiction*, but to say it is in heauen visible and circumscribed, and it is in the Sacrament inuisible and incircumscribed, is no conrradiction, by reaso of the diuersity of respect, according to which diuersity both those
sayinges may be true.

of contradiction, and his, and thothers to much   (c)
temerity, in so restraining Gods infinit po- See heretofore *tract*. 2.
wer to the narrow compasse of their weake *sect*. 3 . *subdiuis*. 1 . in the
vnderstanding, (for which very offence the margent there at the let-
Capernaites were as (c) *before* reproued) as ters, c. e. q.
also the examples that might be alledged of   (8)
sundry sortes of bodies , from which God *Suspended,* for so was the
haith *miraculosly* (8) *suspended* certaine of waight downwardes of
their a heauy body suspended
in the Iron falne into the water which Elizeus caused to swim. 4. *Reg*. 6. 5 .
in so much as the French Caluinistes in the coference at *Paris* englished, and printed 1602. *pag*. 99. & 100. do confesse that, *a body may be exempted from al waight* ; so was the action of burning suspended from *fier,* aswel in the *bush* which *Moyses* saw. *Exod*. 3. 2 . as in the *exceeding hot fornace,* when the *three children walking in the middest of the fyer* had no hurt, and not so much as *a haire of their head was burned. Daniel .* 3. 22. 25. 27. So was the fluxility of water suspended in the red sea, *Exod*. 14. 22. and *the waters of Iordane. Iosue* . 3 . 13. 16. So was stayed or suspended the natural course or motion of the *Sunne* & *Moone,* at *Iosuas* commaundement. *Iosue.* 10. 12. 13. the light of the Sunne at our Sauiours passion. *Luc*. 23. 44. 45. the *wasting* or *diminishment,* aswel of the *meale* and *oyle* of the widow in *Sareptha* though dayly eaten by *Elias,* her selfe, and her sonne. 3. *Reg*. 17. 9. 14. 15, 16. as also of *the apparel of the Israelites* worne by them in the wildernes 40. *yeares* together without any consuming thereof; in so much as *Coclenius* a learned Caluinist confesseth saying, *non nego propria essentialia, omnipotentia Dei absoluta remoueri, seu tolli posse citra rei destructionem . apud Buscherum,* in his *fasciculus quæstionum,* printed *Witebergæ.* 1598. *pag*. 92. To come now to our Sauiours body, *he walked vpon the Sea. Math*. 14. 26. *Marc*. 6. 49. *Ioan*. 5, 19. against the natural property of his bodies waight or els of the waters deuiding . *He was transfi :*

        gured

gured vpon the mountaine. *Math.* 17. 2. *Luc.* 9. 29. *Marc.* 9. 3. & appeared to two of his disciples in an other shape. *Marc.* 16. 12. *Came & stoode (euen) in the midest of his Disciples the doares being shut.* (whereof see hereafter in this present section, and subdiuision, at the figure 6. in the margent) and *sitting at the table* with two of his Disciples sodainely *became vnseene of them:* whereof see hereafter in this present section at the figure 4. in the margent.

(9) *Luther, who was so learned as to discerne of contradiction saith, in tom. 7. Witemberg. An. 1557. defens. verborum canæ fol. 388. what Scriptures haue they to proue that these two propositions be directly contrary, Christ sitteth in heauen, and Christ is in the supper, the contradiction is in their carnal imagination, and not in faith or the word of God.*

their natural qualities, the truth and nature of the said bodies yet stil preserued. And to omitte also further discourse to be had of this matter (whereof this short treatise is not capable) it shal suffice (for the present) to refel this conceipt with the only testimoy of their more learned and sober writers: Amongst which to passe ouer *Martin* (9) *Luthers* iudgment of the possibility of Christes body being in many places at once, & sudry other (2) examples

(2) The example of the *Trinity* is perspicuoufe and pertinent; In respect whereof, both our aduersaries and we, do confesse to beleeue one and the same substance in number, to be at once in three seueral and distinct persons: a matter no lesse wonderful then is the being of one body in many places at once, for as there is in this a distinction *of places,* so in the other a like distinction *of persons;* in which different persons, as there is a most simple vnity of essence or nature, notwithstanding the said distinction of persons, so likewise there may be (without al daunger of contradiction) a like vnity of body in seueral places notwithstanding the said diuersity of places. To this like purpose also is not impertinent the mysterie of our Sauiours incarnation, wherein we acknowledge one and the same hipostacy or person in two perfect, but yet most different, natures, of God and man: And for so much as the vnion betweene hipostasy and nature, is more true and real then is the vnion betweene the body and the place circumscribing it, in that the firster is intrinsecal and substantial, wheras this other is but external and accidentary; it herof followeth that it is more wonderful for one and the same hipostasy to be in two so far different natures, then for one body to be in two places. In like manner the

soule

foule being not proportionable to the extention of the body (for so it were material, depending of the body, and mortal with it) but an indiuisible vnity and immortal is , as philosophy and truth teacheth , wholly in the whol body, and wholly in euery part thereof, and we may easily imagine , and that God by his power is able to concerue it at once in seueral members cut of and deuided from the said body, euen as it was before in the said members, when they were vnited to the same body. The difficulty whereof may be better conceiued (rather then directly proued) by example of one and the same word, the which being once vttered, is therevpon at one instant in the seueral hearing of sundry persons, and that, not as an indistinct noyse confusedly multiplied in the aier, but as one and the same peculier word, distinguished with the selfe same sillables wherein it was vttered. Also it is of no more difficulty for one body to be at once in seueral places, then it is for seueral bodies to be at once by penetration, in one place, the examples whereof are alledged next hereafter in this present subdiuision at the figures 5 . and 6. in the margent, in our Sauiours confessed rising out of his graue, it being then *shut vp*, and his entring to his Disciples *the doares being* fast *shut &c*. Adde but now hereto our Sauiours appearing to *S . Paul*, mentioned hereafter *tract . 2 . sect . 10. subdiuis. 2 . fine*. in the margent vnder b.

(3)
Chrisost . in epist . ad Hæb .

examples and (3) testimonies of the Fathers *hom . 17.* saith hereof;
confir- *This is one sacrifice, other-*
wise by this reason, because it is offered in many places, there should be many
Christes, not so, but one Christ in euery place, here whol, and there whol, one
body. so plainely doth he acknowledge *one Christ* and *one body to be in*
many places . and the same wordes are vsed by *S . Ambrose in hæb . c .*
10. and see *Chrisostoms* further plaine testimonies concerning this point
alledged hereafter *tract. 2 . sect. 10. subdiuis. 2 . fine*. in the margent
at b. and *tract . 3 . sect . 5 . subdiuis. 4 .* in the margent at e. & *tract .*
2. *sect. 8 . subdiuis. 2 .* in the margent vnder the letter, o. also *S . Gregory Nissen, in orat . Catech . c .* 37. saith, *considerandum est, quomodo fieri*
queat, vt cum vnum illud corpus assidue per totū orbem terrarū tot fidelium mil-
libus impertiatur, totū cuiusq̀ per partem euadat , & in seipso totum permaneat
&c. And *S . Augustin . in Psalm . 33. con . 2. fine*. saith, *accepit &c*.
he tooke into his handes that which the faithful know (& ipse se portabat quo-
damodo) and after a certaine (wonderful) manner he carried him selfe in his
cwne

owne handes, when he said, this is my body, expressing yet more plainely this *manner of carying him selfe in his owne handes,* to be, not figuratiue but *according to the letter* and aboue *conceiuing :* for, writing a litle there before in *Psal. 33. con.* 1. vpon these wordes, *ferebatur in manibus suis* he saith hereupon; *Hoc vero Fratres quomodo posset fieri in homine quis intelligat ? quis enim portatur in manibus suis ? manibus aliorum potest portari homo, manibus suis nemo portatur: quomodo intelligatur in ipso Dauid secundum litteram non inuenimus ; in Christo autem inuenimus, ferebatur enim Christus in manibus suis, quando commendans ipsum corpus suum, ait, hoc est corpus meum, ferebat enim illud corpus in manibus suis,* so plainely doth he affirme that our Sauiour at his last supper *caried him selfe in his owne handes,* which though it were done not visibly but *(quodamodo) after a certaine* (wonderful) *manner,* yet (as appeareth by the firster place in which he also leaueth out the word *(quodamodo)* it was done *(secundum literam)* truly, and *according to the letter,* and so as *(quis intelligat ?) was a boue conceiuing,* and to *Dauid* impossible to be applied .

      (d)

Act. mon. pag. 998. to the 18. argument.   (*) *Caluin, institut. l. 4. c. 17. sect.* 10. saith, *etsi autem incredibile videtur in tanta locorum distantia penetrare ad nos Christi carnem, vt nobis sit in cibum meminerimus quantum supra sensus omnes nostros emineat arcana spiritus sancti virtus, et quam stultum sit eius immensitatem modo nostro velle metiri.* and *Ibibem sect.* 24. he further saith, *vnde hæc carni virtus vt animas viuificet? naturaliter non fieri omnes dicent ; humanæ rationi nihilo magis placebit penetrare ad nos Christi carnem, vt nobis sit alimentum &c.* And see *Caluin* further hereafter *tract.* 2. *sect.* 10. *subdiuis.* 2. *fine·* in the margent vnder b. (e) *M. Iewel* in his reply against *M. Harding,* pag. 352.

confirming the same. *M. Foxe* saith, (d) *Chrifts abyding in heauen, is no let, but that he may be in the Sacrament if he list .* And *Caluin* doth accordingly teach, that by the (*) *secret power of the holy Ghost,* and *aboue al sence, the flesh of Christ doth penetrate to vs, to be our meate in* (or notwithstanding) *so great a distance of places ,* as of heauen and earth, which argueth the so being thereof to be inuisible incircumscript, and in many places at once : also *M . Iewel* saith, (e) *God is able by his omnipotent power to make Christes body present without place & quantity . M. Cramner* likewise saith, (f) t·e *controuersy in this matter, is not what may be, but what is, Christs body may be aswel in the bread as in the doare* (which was shut) *and stone* of his se- pulchre

(f) *Cramner*

(f) *Cramner* in his aſweare to *Steuen Gardiner* , pag. 454.

(g)

pulchre ; And to omit the plaine further con- *Caluin inſtitut* . printed
feſſion of (g) *Caluin* and (h) *others*, and the *Argentorat* . 1539. de ca-
ſundry examples and demonſtratiue reaſons *na Domini* , *c* . 12. *pag* .
that may be alledged in confutation of the 336. ſpeaking herof ſaith
difficulty conceiued and vrged from the (4) of vs : *hic vt nobis inuidi-*
viſibility   *am faciant de omnipotentis*

Dei potentia, maligne nos loqui criminantur ; ſed aut ſtulte errant aut maliti-
oſe mentiuntur : non enim hic queritur quid Deus potuerit, ſed quid voluerit,
ſo plainely doth he diſclaime in the queſtion of contradiction and impoſſibility. And ſee *Caluines* other edition, *l* . 4. *c* . 17. *ſect* . 24.   (h)
The Diuines of *Wittenberg*, in the Engliſh Harmony of confeſſions, pag .
454. ſay, *we beleeue that the omnipotency of God is ſo great, that in the Eu-*
chariſt he may either annihilate the ſubſtance of bread, or els chaunge them in-
to his body, but that God doth exerciſe this his abſolute omnipotency in the
Euchariſt, we haue no certaine word of God for it . and *Vadian de Euchariſt* .
l . 4. *pag* . 111 . b . ſaith of tranſubſtantiation, *primum probent, ac doceant*
hoc Chriſtum voluiſſe &c . quod vbi oſtenderint & probarint, haud grauate
recipiemus poſſibilem fuiſſe, et eſſe &c . and *Ibidem pag* . 112 . he ſaith,
quam facile eſſet recipere Papæ de Euchariſtia ſententiam, ſi vlla eſſent in Scrip -
turis teſtimonia, quæ panem in Chriſtum mutari conſecratione affirmarent ? pro-
fecto tam facile hoc crederemus canonicis Scripturis edocti, quam facile et in-
dubitanter illa credimus .   (4)   When our Sauiour *ſate at the table* with
two of his Diſciples, ſodainly he vaniſhed out of their ſight . *Luc* . 24.
31. which was not by his remoual away *in inſtanti* for the text ſaith not ſo
& if it were ſo, thē is the miracle therof as ſtupendiouſe as the other, becauſe that *omnis motus fit ſucceſſine* : In like manner, whē *alin the ſinagogue*
&c . *caſt him out of the city, and brought him to the edge of the hil &c* . *that*
they might throw him downe headlong, he paſſing through the mideſt of them,
went his way Luc . 4. 29. 30. and of his like eſcape read, *Ioan* . 10 .
39. and 8 . 59. In this former example they ſee him, catch faſt hould
of him, and ſo leade him to the top of the hil, and being then ſo
ſeene, and as yet led and houlden, he ſodainly *paſſed through the mid-*
deſt of them and ſo eſcaped ; whereupon *Buſcherus* a learned Prote -
ſtant writer in *excercitat* . *Theolog* . *pag* . 264. and 265. inferreth &
mantaineth againſt *Piſcator*, that our Sauiours body was then to the
Iewes both *inuiſible*, and alſo *intangible* .

(5) It is

(5)   *visibility*, (5) *quantity*, and (6) *circumscripti-*
It is no more impossible *on* of our Saviours body; *M. Whitaker* his
(in respect of *quantitie*) other former assertiō, notwithstanding saith,
for Christes body to be   (vpon
present in the Sacrament, then it was *for a Camel to passe trough the eye
of a nedle. Math. 19. 24.* and *Marc. 10. 25. 27.* whereof our Sauiour
saith, *with men this is impossible, but with God al thinges are possible. Math.*
19. 26. and the like possibility thereof is affirmed, not onely by *S.
Augustine de spiritu et litera c. 1.* by *Nazianzen, l. 4. de Theologia.* by
Origen. incap. 19. Math. but also by *M. Willet* in his sinopsis, printed
1600. *pag. 526.* where he saith, that *God by his absolute power can
drawe the huge body of a Camel, remaning stil of that bignes, trough a nedles
eye*; onely he denyeth that God wil do it, *because* (saith he) *it is contrary to the law of nature.* And it is no lesse strange that the God-head being infinit, should yet be wholly in the limited nature of his humanity, and before his natiuity wholly also in his mothers wombe, she being therfore called *the mother of our Lord, Luc. 1. 43*, and *the mother
of God:* whereof see *Vincent. Lyrinensis l. aduers. hær. paulo ante med:*
And *Ambros. l. 2. de virginibus et Concil. Ephes. in epist. ad Nestorium.*
This difficulty is made as yet more intelligible by the examples of nature, amongst which we see how that a faire *Diamond*, or litle *looking glas*,
comprehend in them in ful proportion of outward shew (incompara -
bly aboue the bignes of them selues) the external figure of great cham-
bers, with a distinguished and answearable proportion, of wales, tables,
beddes, formes, and stooles therein contained, and al this in such due
resemblance, as that who so behouldeth but in the said *Diamond* or *glas*
the said figures so therein represented, shal withal behould therein a
shew of proportion and largnes, far exceeding the said glasse or Diamond, and so large as if he had seene the thinges them selues.   (6)
As concerning circumscription, the difficulty hence conceiued, aryseth by
reason of *quantity*, which is heretofore auoided in the example of *the
Camels passing through a nedles eye.* Also, concerning both *circumscription*, and *quantity*, see further *Luther* and *M. Iewel* alledged hereafter
tract. 2. sect. 5. subdiuis. 4. in the margent at a. *.* next before x.
And in further demonstration, that a true body may be without *circumscription*, the Euangelist witnesseth, that when *the Disciples were gathered
together for feare of the Iewes*, our Sauiour entred in amongst them *clausis
Ianuis, the doares being shut. Ioan. 20. 19. 26.* And we finde no men-
                                                              tion

tion that the doare was then miraculoufly opened, as elſwhere it is mentioned how *the Angel opened the gate of the prifon*. *Act*. 5. 19. and 12. 5. 10. but the miracle here, is in our Sauiours fodaine *ftanding euen in the middeft of the Apoftles when the doares were fhut*. *Ioan*. 20. 26. for which caufe *S. Iohn* very carefully obferueth, and *twife* ouer *Ioan*. 20. 19. and 26. recyteth *the doares being fhut*: In fo much as the Apoftles at this his apperance, fo much againſt the property of a natural body being troubled and frighted, imagined that they faw a fpirit. *Luc*. 24. 37. as they were in like manner affraid vpon an other like occafion elſwhere fignified. *Math*. 14. 26. *S. Ambrof*. *in cap. vlt. Luc*. fpeaking of this matter faith, *It was a wonder how the corporal nature paffed trough the impenetrable body*. And *S. Hillarie, l. 3. de Trint. poft med*. faith hereof, *nothing of that which is folid, geueth place, neither doth the wood or ftone, by their nature loofe any thing &c*. *our Lords body doth not depart from it felfe, that it fhould refume it felfe of nothing &c. fence and fpeach geueth place, and the truth of the fact is without mans reafon*. Hereunto might be added the like example vrged by *Bufcherus in exercitat. theolog. &c*. *pag*. 666. of our Sauiours refurrection from the graue, the fame being then before clofed or *fealed vp with a ftone*. *Math*. 27. 66. for as *Bufcherus* collecteth from the text, the fepulchre remained fo *fealed vp* til the Angel defcended and rouled backe the ftone. *Math*. 28. 2. before which time our Sauiour was rifen, for the angel defcended and rouled backe the ftone, not as a minifter of helpe of his refurrection, but onely as a witnes thereof. And fo accordingly *M. Cranmer* next hertofore at the letter f. vnderftandeth; as alfo *M. D. Doue* in his confutation of *Atheifme, pag*. 90. vrgeth to this end, by the authorities and examples of Scripture, *how Chrift arofe out of his graue, the graue being fhut vp, and the ftone not rouled away, how after his refurrection he went into the houfe where his Difciples were, the doares being locked, how at his afcention he pearced the heauens &c*. And *S. Auguftine de ciuit. Dei, l. 22 c. 8.* reporteth a like miracle of *the ring which fel from Petronas girdle being then tyed faft about her*, without breach of either.

vpon a fecond and better confideration) (i) *M. Whitaker* in his anthat *Chrift can make the bread his body we graunt*, fweare to *M. Raynoldes onely fhew that Chrift wil make* of real bread his refutation, *pag*. 192. real And the fame is affirmed in the very fame wordes by *M. Robert Bruis* in his fermons vpon the Sacrament

crament. the 3. sermon, fol. 85.

(7)
See this their answeare in *Bulengers decades* in english, *ser. 8. pag. 971*. and (to omit many others) see *Angelus Politianus* in his *philosophica Eucharist*. printed 1604. in a whol special Tract thereof, entituled *de voluntate Dei*, beginning there at page 134. and continued til page 186.

(8)
M. Whitaker in his answeare to *M. William Raynoldes* refutation, *pag. 179*. saith hereof to his aduersary, *your schoolemen teaching, & that truly, that God cannot do any thing wherin is included a cōtradiction, because he cannot lye, haue in deede ground to*

real flesh, and then this controuersy is brought to an end. And here by the way it is not amisse, if we breefly but obserue the manner of our aduersaries dealing with vs in their disputes of this matter: for the question of the real presence being but propoūded, they quickly (7) tel vs that Christ neuer intended or willed it: And when to declare his wil we alledge his word, they make then new question of his power, as denying such to be his wil or sence of wordes, vnder pretence that it is (8) contradictorie to the truth and nature of his humane body now (*) in heauen, & is so therby (9) impossible, and when in reply thereto we proue to them directly, that it is not impossible, then returning (per circuitum) to their said firster euasion, they answeare that, the (10) question is not of his power, but onely of his wil; and dancing so in a round they trifle and delude vs of, with subtil escape of endlesse circulation: wherein to close vp their mouthes with eternal silence, onely from that which is in it selfe euident, and for such by them selues confessed. First it is vndoubted that these wordes of our Sauiour (11) this is

pouder your conceipt of real presence, which without most cleare contradiction can neuer be mantained. And see the like *in Apolog. modest. ad acta Conuentus quindecim Theologorum Torgæ &c. pag. 51*. (*) *M. Willet* in his sinopsis, *pag. 450*. argueth saying, *Christ in his flesh is ascended vp to heauen, and there must remaine til his comming againe. Act. 3. 21*. ergo he cannot be present in the Sacrament vpon earth. and againe *ibidem. pag. 451*. he further saith, *a natural body haith a natural presence, but so haith not Christes body in the Sacrament &c*. (9) See this their assertion of impossibility heretofore *tract. 2. sect. 4. subdiuis. 1. at z. x. b*. in *Beza, M. Ridley* and *M. Whitaker*. (10) See this heretofore *tract. 2. sect. 4. subdiuis. 1. at g. h. i.* in *Caluin, the diuines of Witeberge, M. Whitaker*, and *M. Brúice*. and *Vadian de Eucharistia, fol. 111*. saith;

my
primum

primum doceant hoc Christum voluisse &c. (11) *Math. 26. 26. Marc.*
14. 22. Luc. 22. 19. & 1. Cor, 11. 24.

(12)

my body, were by him vttered to institute a
Sacrament, with a commaundement thereto
annexed of our *taking and eating,* and do so
thereby concerne a principal article of our
faith. *Secondly,* it is no lesse vndoubted that
in the first institution or publishing of any such
commaundement & article of faith, the scriptures are confessedly alwaies to be (12) taken
according to the plaine and vsual signification
of the words, if so the same may possibly stand
with the other Scriptures and articles of our
faith. *Thirdly,* it is also euident and confessed,
that the visual or litteral sence of these words,
this is my body, doth make most directly for (13)
the real presence. *Fourthly,* it is no lesse euident & confessed, that the same sence is not so
repugnant to any other Scripture or article of
faith

M. Bilson in his true difference &c. *pag.* 568.
vpon the question of
Christes *ordaining Sacra-*
mentes, acknowledgeth it
for *right, that in Scripture,*
so long as the letter may
possibly be true, we may not
flee to figures. and *Vrsinus*
in his *commentar. catech.*
printed 1586. *pag.* 416.
holdeth it for a true rule,
that *Articuli fidei debent*
proprie intelligi, si nō pugnet
aliquis articulus proprie ac-
ceptus cum alijs Scripturæ
locis. Also *M. Hooker, l.*
5. *Eccles. pol. sect.* 59.
pag. 130. *holdeth it for a*

most infallible rule in exposition of Scripture, that where a litteral construction
wil stand, the furthest from the letter is commonly the worst. and the very same
reaffirmed by *M. D. Couel* against the plea of the Innocent, *pag.* 194.
And *Carion* in his Cronicle printed *Bernæ,* 1601. *pag.* 237. saith, *in ar-*
ticulis sidei, in lege morali, & in promissione gratiæ, necesse est retineri inatiua ver-
borum significatione, thus far the Caluinistes. And the reason hereof is
in it self euident, for if those textes of Scripture which expresse the articles of our faith, and being litterally taken, are not directly against
any other Scripture or article of faith; if those (I say) may be peruer-
ted and turned into tropes and figures, then as *Melanllon* (heretofore
tract. 2. sect. 3. subdiuis. 2. in the magent at k.) rightly obserueth &
saith to this very point: *deprauari potuerunt omnia &c. al other pointes*
of faith may in like sort be deprauced. (13) *M. Raynoldes* in his conference
pag. 68. saith, *I graunt the wordes of Christ, this is my body, are plainer in*
shew &c. for your real presence, then for our Sacramental. and *Beza in tract.*
theol. printed 1570. *tract. de cæna contra Westphalum. pag.* 215. saith, *non*
potest vrgeri To reton, *in his verbis Christi &c. quin Papistica transubstan-*

tiatio

tiatio constituatur. and see him, and *Daniel Chamierus* further alledged to this purpose heretofore *tract. 2. sect. 4. subdiuis. 1. initio*. in
the margent at y.

(14)
May al of them possibly be
true. for to repeate breefly somwhat that hath
bene alledged hereto-
fore; his being in heauen
is not gainsaid by his real
presence in the Sacramēt,
but may both of the stand
together: Whereof M.
Foxe Act. mon. pag. 998.
to the 18. argument)
saith, *Christes abiding in
heauen, is no let but he may
be in the Sacrament if he
list*. In like manner concerning *circumscription*, &
being in place, M. *Iewel*
in his reply, *pag. 352*. saith, *God is able by his omnipotent power to make
Christes body present without place and quantity*. And in like sort also concerning the other natural properties of Christes body being *suspended*,
the truth of the said body yet stil remaining. *Coclenius* a learned Caluinist (*apud Buscherum* in his *fasciculus quaestionum* printed *Witebergiae* 1589.
pag. 92.) saith, *non nego propria essentialia, omnipotentia Dei absoluta remoueri seu tolli posse, citra rei destructionem*. and see the sundry examples
thereof alledged.heretofore *tract. 2. sect. 4. subdiuis. 1.* in the margent
after c. vnder the figure 8. (15) *Possible*, so expresly confessed next
heretofore by M. *Cranmer. Caluin, Whitaker, Bruice, the diuines of Witeberge,* and *Vadian,* at f. g. h. i. (16) See this next heretofore at i.
(k) *Caluin institut. l. 4. c. 17. sect. 32.* saith, *absurda reytio, quae aut
caelesti Christi maiestate indigna, aut ab humanae eius natura veritate aliena
esse apparet &c.* also M. *Willet* in his *sinopsis, pag. 454.* saith,
*It is an ingloriouse, vnworthy, and vnseemely thing, that the glorious and im-
patible body of Christ, should be inclosed in the formes of bread and wine, deuou-
red, and chewed, eaten, and gnawed of myse, be spitle on the ground, burne*
in the

faith, but that confessedly al *of them* (14) *may
possibly be true*, and that so accordingly the real
presenc is vndoubtedly (15) *possible*: Al which
so necessary coherence of wordes and matter
conioyned together, being in it selfe euident,
and for such confessed, euen by those who do
impugne the real presence, what now remaineth to infer therupon, but only to cóclude in
M. *Whitakers* last recited woordes, that hereby (16) *this controuersy is brought to an end*.
(2) The possibility and truth of the real
presence being thus confessedly proued, the
carnal man is not for al this yet satisfied, but
seemeth stil offended at sundry pretended absurd, and indecent (k) indignities hence (as
he thinketh) ensuing against the honour of
Christes body; as for example that he should
indecently

in the fyre &c. And *Algerus* (almoſt 600 . yeares ſince) *l . 2 . de Sacrament . Euchar . c . 1 .* mentioneth the like obiections of the heritikes of his time ſaying , *ſed iterum opponunt hæretici ad tanti ſacramenti indignitatem , quod panis et vinum in Sacramento mucidum vel putridum fiat, panis a muribus corrodatur, & in ventre eorum inueniatur, ignibus comburatur &c.*

indecently paſſe into the ſtomacke of man . That likewiſe he ſhould be ſubiect to the eating of myſſe, to the burning of fyer , and ſhould alſo, vpon the dayly corruptions of the formes of breade and wine, be as it were in continual voyage of aſcending vp againe to heauen, as alſo vpon the Preiſtes dayly conſecration , in like continual motion of deſcending from heauen : Againſt which ſcruples ariſing from infidelity, I muſt anſwere (as doth *S . Auguſtine* againſt the other like côceiued indignities pretended likewiſe by Iewes, Paganes, and Heretickes, againſt the other confeſſed myſteries of our Chriſtian religion) that (l) *we ſhould not beleeue in Chriſt him ſelfe, if our Chriſtian faith did but reguard the ſcornes of the heathen*; for ſo the *Saducees* propounded to our Sauiour , a ridiculous (m) queſtion, as charging thereby with abſurdity (in their opinion) the doctrine of *the Reſurrection of the dead*; againſt which, both the *Marcioniſtes* and *Origeniſtes*, did alſo (n) argue with like reaſon pretended from the conceiued abſurdity thereof, whereto our Sauiour aſweareth ſaying, (o) *you do erre not knowing the Scriptures , nor the power of God ; for in the reſurrection, neither ſhal they marrie nor be married*. So likewiſe did the *Marcioniſtes* argue againſt the incarnation of Chriſt (p) vrging

And ſee the like obiections yet further mentioned in that time by *Guitmundus l . 2 . de Sacram .*

(l)
In ipſum Chriſtum non crederemus , ſi fides Chriſtiana cachinnum metueret Paganorum . Auguſt . epiſt . 49 . ad deogratias quæſt . 6 .

(m)
Math . 22 . 24 . 28 .

(n)
Witneſſe hereof *Tertulian in lib . de reſurrect . carnis .* and *Hierome in epiſt . ad Pamachium contra errores Ioannis Hieroſol .* who mention their arguments to be, that if in the reſurrection there be a diſtinction of ſexe, male , and female, then alſo in their opinion followeth procreation, Nurſes &c . and that if alſo in the reſurrection there be palat, bellie &c . then alſo muſt follow meate, egeſtion &c
(o)
Math . 22 . 29 .

(p) *Tertul . de carne Chriſti, paulo poſt initium .* ſaith hereof to *Marcion, Igitur ſi non q̃, vt impoſſibilem, nec̃ vt perculoſam Deo repudias corporatione*,

ging

ſupereſt

fupereſt vt quaſi indignam reijcias & accuſas ; ab ipſa quidem exorſus odio ha-
bita natiuitate, perora age iam ſpurcitias genitalium in vtero elementorum, hu-
mores et ſanguinis fæda coagula, carnis ex eod. m cano alendæ per nouem men-
ſes ; deſcribe vterum de die in diem inſoleſcentem, grauem, anxium, nexum,
totum incertum libidinibus faſtidij et gulæ : Inuehere iam et in ipſum mulieris
enitentis pudorem &c. horres vtiǵ, et oblitum, et infantē cū ſuis impedimentis
profuſū vtiǵ dedigna beris, quod pannis dirigitur, quod vinctionibus formatur,
quod blanditijs deridetur &c. & a litlethere before : *hoc tu potentiori Deo*
aufers quaſi non valuerit Chriſtus vere hominem indutus Deus perſeuerare. And
againe afterwardes ; *Turpe hocDeo, et indignū hoc Dei filio, et ſtultū propter*
ea qui ita credat. whereto he there anſweareth, *ſit plane ſtultum , ſi de noſtro*
ſenſu iudicemus Deum : ſed circumſpice Marcion, ſi tamen non delecta, ſtulta
mundi elegit Deus, vt confundat ſapientiā &c. non eris ſapiens niſi ſtultus ſeculo
fueris, Dei ſtulta credendo &c. quodcunǵ Deo indignum eſt mihi expedit.

(q)

Euagrius, hiſt. l. 1. c. 2. ging how abſurd and diſhonourable to God
fine. reporteh that (*Ne-* it was to be encloaſed in a womans wombe
ſtorius hanc impiam ſenten- &c. In like manner did *Neſtorius* (q) thinke
tiam proferre non dubitarit, it vnworthy that God ſhould or might be ter-
nimirum) *Neſtorius* doub- med, *bimeſtris* or *bicubitus*, which yet in re-
ted not to vtter this ſpect of Chriſt being God and withal an in-
wicked ſaying, *ego eum* fant in his mothers wombe, might truly be
qui ſpacijs meſtruis, hoc eſt affirmed : according to which ſence the aun-
bimeſtri & trimeſtri, et ita cient Fathers doubted not to tearme our bleſ-
deinceps, adoleuerit, Deum ſed Lady (r) *the mother of God* ; (s) a title in
certe non appellauero. And reguard of like pretended indignity, by ſome
ſee like further teſtimony of
geuen of *Neſtorius* by *Theodoret l. 4. hæret. fab.* (r) How this title
was by the auncient Fathers attributed to the moſt ſacred Virgin, &
the impugners thereof ſpecially cenſured for heretickes. See *Socrates*
hiſt. l. 7. c. 32. and *Ciril in epiſt. ad Neſtor. in 2. tom. Concil.* alſo
the Fathers of the *Calcedon* councel. *Act. 5.* (in the 2. *tome* of
Councels printed 1606. *pag. 93.* ſay, *iſta fides Patrum, definitio Deo pla-*
cuit, iſta fides orthodoxorum, fides fraudem non patitur, ſancta Maria the-
otocos ſcribatur. And ſee further there *epiſt. 3. Ioan. Papa. pag. 408. a.*
ante med. And ſee alſo *Vincentius Lir. aduer. hær, ante med.* where he
reproueth *Neſtorius* for that, *aſſerit ſanctam Mariam non* Theotocon *ſed*
Chriſtotocon *eſſe dicendam.* See alſo moſt of this confeſſed and reported

ted by the *Centuristes cent*. 5. *col*. 802. *& col*. 608. *& col*. 124.
(s) *The holy thing which shal be borne of thee, shal be called the sonne of God*.
Luc. 1. 35. *whence commeth this to me, that the mother of my Lord should*
come to me. *Luc*. 1. 43.

of our aduersaries no lesse bouldly then shame
fully (*) denyed. In like sorte did the Iewes and Paganes deride and (t) charge
our Christian religion with absurdity of beleeuing in Christ who was condemned and
hanged among theeues; in respect whereof
the Apostle tearmeth, *Christ crucified* (u) *a*
scandal to the Iewes, and to the Gentiles foolish-
nesse. Hereunto might be added the like further example, as wel of the (x) *Arians* old
and new impugning the diuinity of Christ,
as being (in their conceipt) ful of indignity
and against the honour of God the Father,
and of the (y) *Nouatians* and *Caluinistes* denying vnder like pretence of dishonour thereby to God, the power of remitting sinne geuen by Christ vnto his Church, as also of the
hereticke (z) *Valentius* who vnder like pretended

(*)
Denyed by *M. Charke*,
whereof see the defence
of the Censure.

(t)
Witnesse whereof *Iusti-*
nus Martyr in dialogo cum
Triphone. and *Minutius*
Felix in Octauio. And see
further testimony hereof
alledged by the Centurie
writers, *Cent*. 5. *col*.
1510.

(u)
1. *Cor*. 1. 23.

(x)
For the old *Arians*, see S.
Hillary de Trinitate, l. 9.
11. *et* 12. *& in libro con-*

tra Constantium. concerning the *Arians* in the reformed Churches in
Poland (so *M. Hooker in Eccles. pol. l*. 4. *sect*. 8. *pag*. 183. tearmeth them, in reguard that at first they were, and yet in other pointes
stil continue, Caluinist Protestantes) they as appeareth by their pu-
blisheddoctrine defended by *Gratianus, Prosper* extant in *Iunius* his answeare thereto entituled, *examen enuntiationun &c. quas Gratianus, Pro-*
sper &c. printed *Lugduni Batauorum* 1596.) do thus argue, *omnes dij*
extra Patrem Domini Iesu Christi, sunt fugiendi &c. (*ibidem pag*. 33.)
againe, *omnes dij extra Patrem, sunt dij commentitij et fugiendi*; *Trinitas, &*
quodcunq, aliud Idolum, est Deus extra Patrem, ergo est nomen commentitium
et fugiendum. *ibidem pag*. 61. *circa med*. also *Iesus Christus est creator*
cæli et terræ, hæc Propositio falsa est, quia creare cælum et terram est proprium
Dei Patris. Ibidem, pag. 88. yet futthermore, *Filius æqualis Patri nul-*
lo pacto potest &c. ibidem, pag. 171. (y) See this concerning the
Nouatianes alledgedmore at large hereafter *tract*. 3. *sect*. 5. *subdinis*. 1.
initio

initio. in the margent vnder the figure 7. and concerning the *Caluinistes*, see there at the figure 8. their argument in this kinde recited &
confuted by other Proteſtantes. (z) *Tertulian*. *de carne Chriſti paulo
poſt med*. ſaith, *licuit Valentino ex priuilegio, hæretico, carnem Chriſti ſpiritalem comminiſci &c*. *nam vt penes quendam ex Valentini factione legi, primo
non putant terrenam & humanam Chriſto ſubſtantiam informatam, ne deterior Angelis Dominus deprehendatur &c*.

(a)

*M. Whitaker contra Du-
ræum, l. 2. pag. 169.
ſaith to Duræus, nec vero
de corpores preſentia dubitamus, ſed tantum de huius
preſentia moda quærimus,
quem vos carnalem et Ca-
pernaiticum, nos celeſtem,
et ſpiritualem, et vere diui-
nū eſſe dicimus &c. Chriſti
corpore pro nobis in ſacrificium oblato, paſcimur, deni-
q̃, Chriſti carnem edimus,
et ſanguinem bibimus.* ſee
more hereafter tract. 2.
ſect. 5. ſubdiuiſ. 2. at a.
b. c. d. f. And *M. Fulke*
againſt *Heſkins, Sanders
&c. pag. 265.* tearmeth
it, the ſpirituall fleſh of Chriſt which is in the Sacrament.

tended vnworthines of Chriſtes humanitie,
(as being in his opinion ouer groſſe) affirmed, that the fleſh of Chriſt was (onely) ſpiritual,
as our aduerſaries recyting now in like manner our doctrine of real and bodily preſence,
for ouer carnal and groſſe, do in like ſorte
faigne to them ſelues (a) a real, but yet ſpiritual preſence of Chriſtes body. This kinde
of curioſity haith extended it ſelfe ſo far, that
euen the Caluiniſtes foreſaid laſt mentioned
opinion of real and ſubſtantial (though yet
but ſpiritual) communion of Chriſtes body,
is now alſo by certaine of their Suinglian
brethrē diſliked, as being *ipſi Chriſto indecora,*
(b) diſhonourable to Chriſt him ſelfe: In reſpect
whereof they do recite it, acknowledging
thereupon (c) *no other preſence then that which
is of ſigniuication.*

The

(b) Hereof *Beza
on epiſt. theolog. epiſt. 5. pag. 61.* ſaith to *Alemanus* the Suinglian,
*poſtnemo ſpiritalis iſta corponis et ſanguinis Chriſti communio, quam ſubſtan-
tialem eſſe dicimus, videtur tibi, et quod ad nos attinet, ſuperflua et ipſi Chriſto
indecora &c.* whereto he anſweareth ſaying theee next after, *non eſt autem Chriſto indecora hac noſtri cumipſa coalitio, quoniam nullis membrorum
ſordibus caput illud inquinatur &c.* (c) *Peter Martir* in his epiſtles annexed to his common places in engliſh, pag. 107. ſaith, *I marnaile that in
the ſecond article it is ſaid, that ſignes haue alwaies ioyned with them the
thing it ſelfe that is ſignified, and that in the third article is declared, the manner of that coniunction which is ſaid not to be called onely figuratiue, or ſha-
dowing*

Therefore, as to the forefaid obiections of *indecency and abfurdity* formerly pretended againft our Catholicke doctrine of real pre-fence, I do anfweare (referring neuerthelefle the reader to that which was almoft 600. yeares fince more at large fpecially (d) an-fweared thereto by *Algerus*, and *Guitmun-dus*) firft, concerning the forefaid obiection of Chriftes fuppofed continual voyage in a-fcending to heauen vpon the dayly corrupti-ons of the formes of bread and wine; I ex-plaine the fame (in fome meafure to the ca-pacity of the vulgar) by example of the foule, which confeffedly is wholly in euery part of mannes body, that when as an arme or legge is cut of, the foule that informed that mem-ber before it was cut of, doth not perifh with it (for then he that lofeth his arme fhould withal lofe or want his foule) neither doth it hange in the aier, becaufe the aier is not organized to receiue the information proceeding from the foule, but ceafing to in-forme the member fo cut of, it doth without any motion to place, onely become abfent and lofe that fubiect and place, keeping ftil the place and refidence in the boby where it was before: Euen fo the body of Chrift when the formes of bread and wine are cor-rupted in the ftomake, or otherwife (doth without any local motió from place to place) onely become abfent & leaueth that aboade, keeping the place which then, and before it had in heauen. As in like manner *the holy Ghoft appearing* (as is (e) confeffed) (f) *in the forme*

dowing: *verily for my part I know no other coniunction of flefh & bloud with the fignes, then that which is of fignifi-cation:* And fee the fame doctrine yet furher alled-ged from the faid *Alema-nus*, and others hereafter *tract. 2. fect. 5.*

(d)

See this at large in *Al-gerus de Sacram. Euchar. l. 2. c. 1.* and in *Guit-mundus l. 2.* (e) *Tertulian. l. de carne Chrifti, paulo poft initium,* faith hereof, *tam vere erat et columba, quá et fpiritus.* and *Caluin. de cæna Dom.* extant in his *tractat. the-ologic.* printed *Geneuæ. 1597. pag. 3.* faith here-of, *cum vellet Dominus fpi-ritum fuum in Baptifmo Chrifti apparere, eum fub Columbæ figura reprefenta-uit, Ioannes Baptifta illam hiftoriam recitans, fpiritum fanctum defcendentem fe ui-diffe ait; fi propius attenda-mus, comperiemus ipfum ni-hil præter columbam vidiffe, ñ fancti fpiritus effentia in-uifibilis eft, cum tamé fciret vifionem illam inanem figu-*

ram non effe, fed fpiritus fancti præfentia fignum certiffimum, affirmare non du-bitat fe illum vidiffe &c. ita in communione quam in Chrifti corpore et fan-guine habemus dicendum eft &c. merito igitur panis appellatur corpus, cum id non

V

id non modo representat, verũ etiã nobis offerat . And in his *Harmonie in Math* . 3 . *verf* . 16 . he faith, *vidit (Ioannes) fpecie columbæ fub qua Deus fpiritus fui præfentiam monftrauit* . (f) *And the holy Ghoft defcended in corporal fhape as a doue vpon him* . *Luc* . 3 . 22 . *&* *Math* . 3 . 16 . *et Marc* . 1 . 10 .

(g)

Tertulian de carne Chrfti, vbi fupra . faith , *fed quaris columbæ corpus vbi fit refumpto fpiritu in cælum &c* . *eadem ratione interceptum eft, qua et editum fuerat , fi vidiffes cum de nihilo proferebatur , fciffes cum in nihilum fubducebatur* . & *S* . *Thomas part* . 3 . *quæft* . 39 . *art* . 6 . *ad* 2 . faith hereof, *repente extitit et poftea ceffauit, ficut flamma quæ in rubo apparuit Moyfi* .

(h)

For as the holy Ghoft defcending in forme of a doue, was not by local

forme *of a doue*, did (without al motion from, or to any place) ceafe vpon the doues vanifhing or (g) returne to nothing , to be in fuch fort there, retayning the aboade which then, and before, it had in heauen, & by this alfo is no leffe (h) explained the other like vnworthy conceiued fcruple of our Sauiours fuppofed continual local motiõ in defcending from heauen vpon the Preiftes dayly confecration ; fo as further explicatiõ thereto here needeth not .

Now as concerning the other pretended abfurdities of the bleffed Sacramentes paffing into the ftomake of man, and it being fubiect to be eaten of myfe, and to be throwne into the fyer &c . Al which are conceiued as vnworthy and difhonourable to the body of Chrift; I do explaine as before: *Firft*, concerning

motion from, or leauing of his former aboade in heauen, fo neither is Chriftes prefence vpon the Preiftes confecration by leauing his former aboade in heauen, no more then he may be faid to haue left his aboade in heauen when (as is confeffed abiding yet there) he was by the way *feene to Paul,* and fo neare to him as he not onely *faw* him, but alfo heard the voice of his mouth (*Act* . 9 . 27 . *& 22* . 15 . *& 26* . 15 . 16 *.*) And at an other time afterwardes *in the Caftle our Lord ftanding by Paul* faid, *be conftant &c* . *Act* . 23 . 11 . (whereof fee more hereafter *tract* . 2 . *fect* . 10 . *fubdiuif* . 2 . *fine* . in the margent vnder b .) And in like manner did he appeare vpon earth to *S* . *Peter* (as is witneffed by *S* . *Ambrofe in orat* . *contra Auxentium* .) and by *Egefippus, l* . 3 . *de exidio vrbis Hierofol* . *c* . 2 . And to *S* . *Antonie* (as witneffeth *Athanafius in vita Antonij*) and to fundry others, whereof the Fathers geue teftimony, among al which I fpecially refer the reader to that which *Paulinus* more

at large

at large and most pertinently to this purpose reporteth *in epist. ad Macharium.*

cerniug the obiection of burning with fyer, or other like violence, that the same can no more endaunger, nor is any more dishonou-rable to our Sauiours body, being now im-mortal & impatible, then was the fyer to his immortal God-head, or but to *the vnconsumed bush* it selfe wherein he (i) *appeared to Moyses.* And if (k) *the three children walking* (with their corruptible bodies) *in the midest of the fyer,* were yet so preserued as *not a haire of their head was burned:* may we then become doubtful or scrupulouse (against that which God haith in this like case reueiled to vs by special (*) miracle) left that our Sauiours body being now immortal and incorruptible, should be subiect to dager of any whatsoeuer violence? *Secondly* as to the supposed indecency of mans stomake receiuing the blessed Sacrament: I explaine that euen as our Sauiours diuinity fil leth al places how vndecent or vncleane so-euer; the sunne beames also reflecting vpon a dunghil, and not defyled therewith, so like-wise our Sauiours body cannot be defyled with the touch or impression of any infec-tiouse or vncleane creature. The stinke of sinne when he conuersed on earth among sinners, did more dislike the smel of his soule, then this other could molest his body: And as it was not vndecent, but a signe of great mercy & loue that he would suffer that,

(i)
Our Lord appeared to him in a flame of fyer out of the middest of a bush; and he saw that the bush was on fyer and was not burnt: Moy-ses therfore said, I wil goe and see this great vision, why the bush is not burnt: And our Lord seeing that he went forward to see, he cal-led him out of the midest of the bush, & said &c. (Exo. 3. 2. 3. 4.) and see the marginal notes of the en-glish Bible of *An.* 1576. *in Act.* 3. 32. testifying *the presence of Christ the mediator in this fyrie bush.*

(k)
See *Daniel.* 3. 22. 25. 27. (*)
Nicephorus Calixt. hist. l. 17. *c.* 25. telling (ac-cording to the decree of *Concil.* 2. *Matisconense. can.* 6.) how the remai-nes of the Eucharist were in some places vsually geuen to be receiued by *innocent children,* amongst

so is whom at one time was the sonne of a Iew, to whom casually among others the same were deliuered, reporteth of the Childes father being angry thereat, *Pater &c. The father hearing therof, tooke the boy & threw him into a burning furnace: and the mother missing her child lamenting greatly, did the third day al sighing neare to the said furnace (name or) cal for her child, who hearing his mothers voice answeared from thence, whereupon the mother breaking open the mouth of the furnace, saw her child standing in midest of the fyer al safe, not so much as a haire of his head being hurt &c.* And see further *Rupertus Tuitiensis in lib. de incendio opidi Tuitiensis. cap. 3.* reporting of certaine knowledge, a very strange miracle, how the holy *Corporal* (wherewith the blessed Sacrament was couered) was by God miraculously *preserued saife in the midest of the flame.* And *ibidem, c. 4. & 5.* he further reporteth of like knowledge concerning *the Pixe and the sacred Hoste reserued therein:* how in that general combustion *al aboute the Altar being burned vp*, *sola Pixis illa cum corpore Dominico incolumis & intacta permansit, the pixe together with the Lordes body remained vntoucked,* affirming there further that this Pix was *lignea, made of wood* most subiect to fyer.

(†) so it is no more vnseemely that he should admit the other, seeing he thereby suffereth nothing, but onely his remaning there, to testify and worke (as the auncient Fathers do affirme) admirable effectes both of (1) loue and grace

Admirable effectes of loue, whereof S. Chrisostome in Math. hom. 83. post med. saith, multæ matres post partum alijs nutricibus infantes dederunt, quod ipse (Christus) faeere noluit, sed proprio corpore nos alit et sibi coniungit atq; conglutinat, And a litle there before, *ipse vero seipsum tibi tradit, non vt videas solum, verumetiam, vt tangas et in te habeas &c. non enim sufficit ipsi, hominem fieri, flagellis interim cædi, sed nos secum in vnam, vt ita dicam, Massam reducit, neq; id fide solum, sed reipsa nos corpus suum efficit.* And in *Ioan. hom. 45. circa med.* he yet further saith, *quam admiranda mysteria &c? Cur data sint, et quænam eorum vtilitas &c. vt autem non solum per dilectionem, sed reipsa in illam carnem conuertamur, per cibum id efficitur quem nobis largitus est, cum enim suum in nos amorem indicare vellet, per corpus suum se nobis commiscuit, et in vnum nobiscum redegit, vt corpus cum capite vniretur, hoc enim amantium maxime est: Hoc Iob significabat de seruis a quibus maxime amabatur, qui suum amorem, præ se ferentes dicebant, quis daret nobis vt eius carnibus impleremur? quod Christus fecit vt maiori nos charitate adstringeret, et vt suum in nobis ostenderet desiderium, non se tantum videri permittens, sed et tangi et manducari, et dentes carni suæ infigi, et desiderio sui omnes impleri &c. Parentes sepenumero liberos suos alijs alendos dederunt, ego autem meo carne alo &c. vester ego frater esse volui, et communicaui carnem propter vos et sanguinē, et per qua vobis coniunctus sum, ea rursus vobis exhibui &c.* See *Chrisostomes* like further saying *ad Pop. hom.*

(m) grace. *Thirdly*, as to the foresaid obiection of fyer, eating by beastes, or any other
indecent violence; I do further answeare o-
uer and besides that which haith bene said
concerning his body, being now immortal,
impatible, and not subiect to violence. That
when as the blessed Sacrament is so pro-
phanely vsed that it cannot conueniently be
of vs at fitting time religiously receiued, it
is not incredible that our Sauiour should in
such special cases of vnworthines or propha-
nation, withdraw at his good pleasure, his
presence from the outward formes, restoring
them to their firster substance, euen as *Aarons
rodde* though (n) *turned into a serpent,* was in
like manner (o) restored vntil (p) the appointed time that such miraculous chaunge
thereof was to be had in vse: which withdrawing in such cases of our Sauiours presence, is made more probable by sundry examples (testified by the auntient (q) Fathers)
of his like withdrawing him selfe (in case
of vnworthines) made knowen and apparent
miraculously to sence euen by sensible change
of the

hom. 61. *prope initium.*
(m)
Admirable effectes of grace,
hereof *S. Chrisostome* in
his other wordes there
next following saith, *hic
mysticus sanguis Demones
procul pellit &c. Demones
enim cum Dominicum san-
guinem in nobis vident in
fugam vertuntur.* and
*Tertulian. l. de. resurrect.
carnis* saith, *caro corpore
et sanguine Christi vescitur.
vt anima de Deo saginetur.*
Also *Ireneus l. 4. c. 34.*
saith, *quomodo autem rursus dicunt carnem in corrup-
tionem deuenire et non percipere vitam qua a corpore
Domini et sanguine alitur
&c. Corpora nostra perci-
pientia Eucharistiam iam
non sunt corruptibilia, spe
resurrectionis habentia.* &

lib. 5. paulo post initium. he saith, *quomodo negant carnem capacem esse do-
nationis Dei qui est vita aterna, qua sanguine et corpore Christi nutritur.* Also
Ciprian. de cana Domini arte med. saith, *noua est huius Sacramenti
doctrina &c. Lex quippe esum sanguinis prohibet, Euangelium pracipit vt
bibatur &c. bibamus autem de sanguine Christi ipso iubente, vita aterna cum
ipso et per ipsum particeps &c. ipse Christus pincerna porrexit hoc poculum et
docuit vt non tantum exterius hoc sanguine liniremur, sed et interius aspertio-
ne omnipotenti anima muniremur &c. esus igitur carnis, huius quadam aui-
ditas est, et quoddam desiderium manendi in ipso.* And see the other like
plaine sayinges of *Cirillus Alexandrinus,* and *Hillarie,* alledged heretofore *tract. 2. sect. 2. subdiuis. 3.* in the margent at the letter e. and
the figure 2. next after g. (n) *Exod. 4. 3.* (o) *Exod. 4. 4.* (p)
Exod. 7. 10. (q) *Ciprian. in sermone de lapsis.* alledged hereafter *tract.*

2: *sect. 6. subd.* 2. at n. o. reporteth two pregnant examples here-of, him selfe concluding thereupon, *documento vnius ostensum est Dominum recedere cum negatur.* and see there also in the margent vnder n. *Gregorius Turonensis, l. 1. c.* 86. reporting a like miracle.

(r)
1. Cor. 2. 14. *& Rom.* 8. 7.

(*)
Forewarned scruples, in respect whereof *Epiphanius* going about to proue that man is the image of God though he seeme not so, because man is corporal, finite, and mortal; whereas God is *spiritual,* infinit, & eternal, laboureth to demostrate by other example that

of the outward elementes them selues. And thus much concerning the foresaid pretended absurdities conceiued by flesh and bloud. Against al which, or any other like *forewarned* (*) *scruples,* whether concerning the vnlike of lesser quantity of the external Sacrament; or our other discerning thereof by our *eye or taist,* which in them selues are no other then as onely proceeding from (r) *the carnal man* (who) *discerneth not the thinges that be of God:* I do conclude admonishing the Christian reader with S. *Chrisostome,* saying of this verie matter, (s) *let vs beleeue although that which he
saith*

a thing may be that which it seemeth not to be, and to that end produceth the example of the Eucharist, not as being onely the appointed memorial or figure of Christes body, though vnlike to it, for neither are his wordes thereof such, neither yet were that so strange, as appeareth by many memorials or figures, whereto resemblance or likelihood of the thing figured, was not needeful, but as being indeede (which is to sence and reason most strange) Christes very body, though it seeme not so, whereof he saith, *videmus &c. we see what our Sauiour did take into his handes &c. and we see that it is not semblable or like, not to his image in the flesh, not to the inuisible Deity, not to the lineamentes of his members, for this is rounde in forme,* and (in respect of such outward appearing forme, is also to looke vnto, deade or *insensible in power: and yet our Lord by grace would say, this is my body &c. and euery man beleeueth him, for* (which auoideth al tropes) *who so beleeueth not, that the same is true according as he spoke it, that man is falne from grace and saluation.* Thus farre *Epiphanius in Anchorat. circa med.* In like manner S. *Ciril* of Hierusalem *Catech. mistagog:* 4. saith, *Cum igitur Christus dicat de pane, hoc est corpus meum, quis deinceps audeat dubitare? &c. quare cum omni certitudine corpus et sanguinem Christi sumamus, nam sub specie panis datur
tibi*

tibi corpus &c. hoc sciens et pro certissimo habens panem hunc qui videtur á nobis non esse panem, etiamsi gustus panem esse sentiat. And *ibidem catech.*
5. he further saith, *nam hoc corporeo palato vt istud diiudicetis vobis precipitur nequaqnam, sed potius fide certa et omnis dubitationis experti: gustantes enim, non panem aut vinum vt gustent iubentur, sed quod sub specie est (videlicet panis et vini) corpus et sanguinem Christi.* (s) *Chrisostom. in Math, hom.* 83. saith, *credamus itaq; vbiq; Deo nec repugnemus ei, etiamsi sensui et cogitationi nostrae absurdum esse videatur quod dicit &c. nam verbis eius defraudare non possumus, sensus vero noster deceptu facilimus est, illa falsa esse non possunt, hic saepius atq; saepius fallitur: quoniam ergo ille dixit, hoc est corpus meum, nulla teneamur ambiguitate, sed credamus &c.*

saith may seeme absurd, both to sence and thought &c. his wordes cannot deceiue vs, but our sence is easily deceiued &c. For so much therefore as he haith said, this is my body, let vs in no sort doubt but beleeue.

(t)
Suinglius tom. 2. de vera et falsa relig. fol. 210. faith, *probatum erit quod etiam hoc loco, est, pro significat accepi oporteat.* and *ibidem fol. 209. ponitur ergo nostro iudicio hoc verbum, est, hic pro significat.*

Of the contradiction and absurdity of the Protestantes real presence.

SECTION. 5.

(u)
See this heretofore *tract. 2. sect. 3. subdiuis. 2.* in the margent at the figure 3. next after e.

(x)
Suinglius. tom. 2. de vera et

AN d for so much as our learned aduersaries haue not forborne to charge (as before) our doctrine of real presence with absurdity, impossibility, and contradiction; it wil not be here altogether vnfitting to make some litle examination in this behalfe of theirs, that the indifferent reader may so thereby discerne which doctrine it is that vpon due consideration falleth out to be in very deede absurd, contradictory, & impossible. *Suinglius* (whom *Oecolampadius* imitated) & who in this last age began at *Tigure*, to impunge the the general receiued doctrine of real presence, (t) affirmed that the particle *is* in our Sauiours words, did import only to *signify*, & that accordingly in his saying, *this is my body*, he yet only meant, *this signifyeth my body*, in so much as *Suinglius* doubted not so to (u) translate the text it self: which admitted, together with his further (x) affirming that our Sauiours wordes in the sixt of
Iohn

et falsa relig. entreating Iohn, did not concerne the Eucharist, there're
of the sixt of Iohn saith, maineth no (y) further proofe from the Scrip-
est ergo hæc secunda nota, tures of any presence of Christes body in the
quod Christus hoc capite per Eucharist, other then onely that which consi-
panem, et edere, nihil aliud steth solie in signification: And so according-
quam Euangelium et cre- ly Suinglius taught saying, (z) the Eucharist
dere intelligit &c. et quod or Communion, or Lordes supper, is nothing els
prorsus non loquitur de Sa- but a commemoration &c. (a) The Sacramental
cramentali vsu &c. a litle presence of Christes body in the supper, is as Charles
after est ergo hæc tertia in- the Emperour, or the King (of France) is said to
dubitata nota, quod Chri- be in the kingdome of Naples, because their Ban-
stus hic non loquitur de Sa- ners or Scutchions are there &c. so Christ also is
cramentali vsu. fol. 204. here present in the heartes and mindes of the faithful,
And againe, atq; hæc est as for bread and wine they are wont to be called
quinta et disertissima nota Christes body and bloud, but they are no more the
quia deprehendimus Chri- same with Christes body and bloud, then those ban-
stum hic nullo pacto de Eu- ners or scutchions are the kinges them selues: for
charistiæ Sacramento loqui (b) this bread, this bread I say, is nothing els but
&c. affirmeing yet there bread

further, that caro Christi comesa, penitus nihil prodest. ibidem fol. 205. (y)
If in our Sauiours saying the word is, doth but import to signify, then in
Suinglius his opinion, why not so likewise, 1. Cor. 10. 16. and if also
the sixt of Iohn do not concerne the Eucharist, what other text can then
be alledged to proue any further presence then onely of signification.
(z) Suinglius, ibidem fol. 212. saith, est ergo Eucharistia, siue Synaxis,
siue cæna Dominica, nihil aliud quam commemoratio &c. And tom. 1. resp.
ad Valent. fol. 237. he saith, non aliud est quam commemoratio et gratiarum actio mortis Dominicæ. and tom. 2. de cæna Dom. fol. 293. he saith,
non aliud est quam signum vel figura, quæ corporis Christi pro nobis traditi memoriam refricaret &c. Hoc est, id est, significat corpus meum, quod perinde est
ac si quæ matrona coniugis sui Anulum ab hoc ipsi relictum mostrans: en Coniux
hic meus est, dicat. (a) Suinglius tom. 2. ad Lutheri confessionem respons.
duæ fol. 477. and ibidem tom. 2. de Baptismo, fol. 60. he further
saith, Sacramentum ergo &c. the Sacrament is an external marke whereby
we shew what we be, and what our duty is, as one that beareth a white
Crosse declareth him selfe therby to be a Suitzer. (b) Hunc panem qui
præter panem, non est quicquam amplius. (Suinglius ibidem fol. 435.

(c) Suinglius

bread: denying elſwhere (c) *Sacramentes to be ſuch ſignes, as when we vſe them, that is inwardly done in our heartes, which is outwardly ſignified by the Sacrament:* nay he doth not acknowledge the Sacrament to be ſo much as but (d) *a ſigne aſſuriug vs (rei intus iam peractæ) of the grace formerly wrought in vs:* nor ſo much as but (e) *a ſigne to confirme or ſeale our inward faith*; concluding that they are (as he before haith ſaid) matters onely of ſignification, as (f) being (but) *ſignes or ceremonies by which a man doth ſhew him ſelfe to be the ſouldier of Chriſt,* making rather the whol congregation aſſured of his faith then him ſelfe. Thus farre *Suinglius,* recyted herin by (g) *Melancton,* wherto aſſented (*) *Oecolampadius.* This then being the firſt beginning doctrine which in this laſt age oppoſed it ſelfe againſt the then vniuerſal profeſſed beleefe of real preſence: *Iohn Caluin* (a man neither vnwitty nor vnlearned) diſcerning vpon his peruſal of the Fathers writinges (who euery where ingeminated the true preſence of Chriſtes body in the Euchariſt) that the foreſaid doctrine of *Suinglius* was euen in the very tearmes of ſpeaking wholly diſagreeing from al antiquity, did therefore profeſſe his ſpecial (g) diſlike therof

(c)
Suinglius tom. 2. fol. 198. ſaith, friget ergo iſta opinia quæ putat Sacramenta talia eſſe ſigna, vt cum exerceantur in homine ſimul intus fiat quod Sacramentis ſignificetur &c.

(d)
Ibidem fol. 198. adding there further in the margent, *Sacramenta non reddunt nos certos de gratia.*

(e)
Suinglius, tom. 2. l. de Baptiſmo, fol. 63. ſaith, *quoſdam in ea opinione fuiſſe cernimus, vt docuerint ſigna in hunc finem data eſſe, vt fidem internam confirment, et id quod edocti ſumus, aut quod nobis promiſſum eſt ceu ſigillo quodam infallibili obſignent; qui hæc tradidere, a vero longiſſime aberrarunt.*

(f) *Suinglius tom. 2. fol. 198.* ſaith *ſunt ergo Sacramenta ſigna vel cæremoniæ &c. quibus ſe homo Eccleſiæ probat, aut candidatum aut militem eſſe Chriſti, reddumq̃ Eccleſiam tantum potius certioremde tua fide quam te &c.* (g) *Melancton in c. 4. ad Rom.* (alledged alſo by *Schluſſlburg. in theolog. Caluiniſt. l. 1. fol. 55.*) ſaith, *repudienda eſt Suingly et ſimilium Sacramentariorum opinio, qui tantum ciuili more indicant de ſignis, ſcilicet ſigna et Sacramenta tantum eſſe notas profeſſions inter homines.* (*) Concerning *Oecolampadius* his like doctrine with *Suinglius,* ſee *Oecolampadius in lib. de verbis Domini. Hoc eſt corpus meum.* And ſee further teſtimony thereof in *Lauatherus* his *hiſtoria Sacramentaria, pag. 4.* (g) *Caluin. in libello de cæna Domini, prope finem,* extant in his *tractat. theologic.*

theologic. omnes. printed *Geneua.* 1597. *pag.* 12. faith of *Suinglius* and
*Oecolampadius, quam præsentiam Christi in cæna credere debeamus, qualis illic
communicatio corporis et sanguinis ipsius recipiatur, dicere omittebant : adeo vt
Lutherus eos nihil præter signa nuda et spiritualis substantiæ vacua relinquere
velle existimaret &c. habemus igitur qua in re impegerit Lutherus, in qua
etiam Oecolampadius et Suinglius.* And concerning *Caluins* diſſent herein after *Suinglius* his death from the Tigurines, ſcholers to *Suinglius* :
ſee *Caluines* epiſtle to
them, in *Oſianders cent.*   of (directly againſt that which (h) *Beza* oueꝛ
16. *pag.* 521. And *M.*   bouldly affirmeth to the contrary.) And for
Hooker in his Eccleſiaſti -   ſo much as being in the curioſity of his iudge-
cal pollicy *l.* 5. *ſect.* 67.   ment enclined to follow the inundation of
pag. 174. faith, *ſome did*   noueliſme, which the ouerflowed, & therupó
exceedingly feare leſt Suin- reſolued to caſt of the Catholicke doctrine of
glius and Oecolampadius, real preſence, wherein he was formerly
would bring to paſſe, that brought vp, and yet withal foreſeeing & care-
men ſhould accompt of this ful to refine and make more plauſible that
Sacrament but onely as of wich in *Suinglius* and *Oecolampadius* ſeemed
a ſhadow deſtitute, empty, as yet more horrid and prophaine, he
and voide of Chriſt &c.   therfore did, in the conceipted ſubtilty of his
(h)   owne apprehenſion, deuiſe and publiſh (as
Beza, in epiſt. theolog. being in ſhew of wordes, though nothing at
epiſt. 1. *pag.* 7. faith,   al in meaning, ſomewhat more agreeable to
dico impudentes eſſe calum- the Fathers ſayinges) his nouel doctrine of
niatores, qui inter Suinglij, true and real preſence of Chriſtes body in
Oecolampadij, Caluini, the Sacrament, verily eaten and receiued by
maximorum virorum doc - the mouth of faith : which his doctrine be -
trinam de Sacramentis vl- ing that which *M. D. Whitaker, M. D .*
lam vnquam fuiſſe repug- *Fulke* and other Engliſh, and forraine diuines,
nantiam comminiſcuntur. haue profeſſed to follow; I wil but ſparingly
what a bould aſſertion and modeſtly examine whether it be free from
was this?   that note of abſurdity, impoſſibility, and con-
(*)   tradiction, wherwith they indeuour to charge
Caluin, inſtitut. l. 4. *c.* our Catholicke doctrine.
17. *ſect.* 21. faith, *ad-*   (2) In which courſe, I wil firſt but recite
iunctam ſecum habent ve- the doctrine as it is by *Caluin* & his followers
ritatem   deliuered : To which purpoſe *Caluin* teacheth
that the Sacramental ſigne haith the thing ſignified adioyned (*) therewith,

with, and that therefore *in* (i) *the myſtery of* | ritatem *&c. ſimbolum eſt*
the ſupper by the ſignes of bread and wine, is truly | *quo veram corporis ſui man-*
deliuered to vs Chriſtes body and bloud : that alſo | *ducationem nobis offert Do-*
(k) *in his holy ſupper he commaundeth me to take,* | *minus.* And in his *Harmo-*
eate, and drinke, vnder the ſymboles of bread and | *nie in Math. 26. verſ. 26.*
wine, his body and bloud. and (ſaith he) *I nothing* | he ſaith, *viſibili ſigno res*
doubt but he truly geueth it, and I receiue it, ma- | *ſignata coniunᵭa eſt, qua eſt*
king it no (l) leſſe truly preſent there, then | *eius veritas.* And ſome-
was the holy Ghoſt truly preſent vnder the | thing after, *effeᵭus vere*
forme of a doue. Affirming alſo of the Sacra- | *ad figuram accedit &c. ve-*
ment *that* (m) *it not onely figureth, but truly* | *re igitur, non ſigno tantum*
exhibiteth Chriſtes body: In ſo much that where | *monſtratur, ſed reipſa quoᵭ*
as the *Swinglianes,* to auoid the real preſence, | *exhibetur carnis Chriſti*
do vſually vrge that our Sauiours wordes *are* | *manducatio.*
figuratiue, and that ſo the Sacrament is but a | (i)
figure: Caluin doth in defence of his real pre- | *Caluin inſtitut. l. 4. c.*
ſence particularly confute and (n) anſwere | 17. ſeᵭ. 10.
the obieᵭion therof; concluding that (o) *the* | (k)
ſubſtance of Chriſtes true body and bloud as he once | *Ibidem ſeᵭ. 32.* he ſaith, *in*
receiued it of the Virgin, is preſent in the ſupper | *ſacra cæna iubet me ſub ſim-*
as wel to the faithful as vnfaithful &c. Martin | *bolis panis ac vini, corpus et*
Bucer affirming yet further, that vnworthy | *ſanguinē ſuum ſumere, man-*
beleeuers (*) *who haue not true and liuely faith* | *ducare, ac bibere, nihil du-*
doe | *bito quin et ipſe vere porri-*

gat, et ego recipiam. (l) See this plainly heretofore *traᵭ. 2. ſeᵭ. 4. ſubdiuiſ.*
2. in the margent at e. and hereafter *traᵭ. 2. ſeᵭ. 10. ſubdiuiſ. 1.*
in the margent at k. (m) *Non figurat tantum, ſed vere etiam exhibet.*
l. 4. inſtut. c. 17. ſeᵭ. 21. with much more to the ſame effeᵭ there,
and *l. 4. c. 17. ſeᵭ. 10.* (n) See this hereafter *traᵭ. 2. ſeᵭ. 10.*
ſubdiuiſ. 1. in the margent vnder e. and ſee *M. Hooker* there at m.
and *M. Bruce* there in the margent at l. (o) *Caluin, in epiſt. et reſponſ.*
epiſt. 372. pag. 725. ſaith. *in articulo de cæna ſic reponatis, ſubſtantiam*
veri corporis et ſanguinis Ieſu Chriſti vti ex virginis vtero illam ſemel accepit,
preſentem eſſe in cæna tam fidelibus quam Infidelibus. (*) *Martin Bucer*
in his *ſcripta Anglicana* printed at *Baſil. Anno. 1577. pag. 654.* affirmeth, *eos qui verba et inſtitutionem retinent et fidem Sacramento huic adhibe-*
ant, et ſi veram & viuificam fidem non exerant, atᵭ ita indigne Sacramen-
tum hoc ſumant, adeoᵭ rei idcirco fiant corporis Domini ; cō tamen nihilomi-

nus

nus non solum panem et vinum, sed etiam verum corpus et sanguinem Domini accipere prout et credunt sibi illud corpus iuxta Domini verba exhiberi. And see there further *pag.* 679. where he reneweth the said assertion, denying yet there a litle afterwardes that, *Impij corpus Christi corporaliter manducant & in os stomachi transmittunt.* and *Ibidem pag.* 680. he signifieth the Lutheranes dissent from him, so plainely was he a Caluinist at his writing of the premisses, as appeareth yet further, *ibidem pag.* 652. *et* 653. and s e also there *pag.* 611. *Prop.* 8. & 544. *numer.* 49. concerning the like presence of Christ to the vnworthy receiuer.

(4)
Hospinian . histor . facram . part . 2 . fol. 251. thus recyteth it, *fatemur in cæna Domini non omnia modo Christi beneficia, sed ipsam filij hominis substantiam, ipsam inquam veram carnem &c . non significari duntaxat &c. sed vere ac certe represntari , exhiberi, &c. adiunctis simbolis minime nudis, sed quæ &c. semper rem ipsam vere ac certo coniunctam habeant, siue fidelibus siue infidelibus proponantur .* a litle after it is said, *Huic confessioni, Farellus. Beza. Carmelus, & Budæus subscripserunt . &c.*

doe receiue not onely breade and wine, but also Christes very body and bloud. And the French confession (whereto subscribed *Farelus, Beza, Carmelus, and Budæus*) teacheth with *Caluin* a like (4) presence of Christes very flesh to the worthy and vnworthy: In respect of which so plaine and confessed doctrine, *M. Whitaker* saith to vs, *nec vero de corporis presentia &c.* (p) we make no question of the presence of Christ s body, but only we dispute of the maner of this presence &c. As also *M. Hooker* saith, (q) *al sides at length are growne to a general greement concerning the real participation of Christ &c.* neither may any thinke that hereby is meant the onely presence of the spiritual effectes and grace of Christes body: For, saith Caluin, (r) *we reiect the doctrine of those who affirme that we receiue but the spirit of Christ, his flesh and bloud excluded.* Also *Amandus Polanus,* professor at *Basile*

&c. (p) *Whitaker contra Duræum pag.* 169. and see *Whitaker* further in his answeare to *M. Raynoldes c. 9. pag.* 194. and *M. Parkins* in his reformed Catholicke, *pag.* 187. saith accordingly: *we differ not (from the Papistes) touching the presence it selfe, but onely in the manner of presence.* and *ibidem pag.* 183. *we beleeue and hould a presence of Christes body in the Sacrament, and that not fained, but a true and real presence.* And *M. D. Couel* in his defence of *M. Hooker pag.* 116. saith of vs and them selues, *al agree in the real presence.* (q) *Hooker* in his *Ecclef. pol. l. 5. sect. 67. pag.* 174. (r) *Caluin in epist. et responf.*

Basile saith, (s) *not onely bread and wine, nei-*
ther onely the Deity, neither onely the vertue and
efficacy of Christ is present in the supper, but the
very body and very bloud of Christ, are in very
deede present in the sacred supper. And the very same is yet further affirmed by (t) *M. Whi-*
taker, the publique (u) *confession* of *Belgia, M.*
(x) *Parkins,* (y) *M. Hooker,* & (z) diuers o-
thers; in so much as they doubt not yet further to explaine the selues, that by the word
spiritual, somtimes by the vsed, they intend no
thing lesse then as therby to seclude their real
presence of Christs body formerly metioned.
To this end the diuines of *Geneua* say (a) *spi-*
ritalis perceptionis nomine &c. By the name of
spiritual receiuing we do not meane that whereby is
receiued the onely spritual grace of Christ, (b) *but*
such a communion with the Apostle do we affirme
whereby

(s)
epist. 372. pag. 725.

Amandus Polanus in sillo-
gethesium &c. de cæna
Dom. pag. 307. and in
his other treatise entituled, partitiones theologicæ.
pag. 279. he againe saith,
non igitur tantum panis et
vinum, nec tantum Deitas
Christi, nec tantū Christi
virtus et efficacia in cæna
præsens est, sed etiam ipsum
corpus, et ipse sanguis Christi
renera adsunt in sacra cæna.

(t)
M. Whitaker contra Du-
raum l. 2. pag. 169. saith

a Christo ad vim et beneficium corporis dilabi, valde ieiunum est, quasi vim et
beneficium ab ipso corpore seiunxerim, aut quando corporis communionem ex-
cludi negauerim, non palam ipsum corpus sumi defenderim. (u) The confession of *Belgia* in the english harmonie, pag. 431. saith, *that which is*
eaten, is the very natural body of Christ, and that which is drunke, is the very
bloud of Christ &c. we are pertakers aswel of him selfe, as of the merites of
his death and passion. (x) *M. Parkines* in his reformed Catholicke pag.
184. & 185. doth to this purpose acknowledge a threefould presence
in the supper, *one sacramental,* an other *effectual,* and besides these a third
which he calleth *real. & vide ibidem* pag. 182. (y) *M. Hooker* in
his *Eccles. pol. l. 5. sect. 67. pag. 177.* saith, *this sacrament is a true and*
real participation of Christ: the Eucharist is not a bare signe or figure onely, and
the efficacy of his body and bloud is not al we receiue in this sacrament; these
mysteries do instrumentally both make vs pertakers of the grace of that body, and
besides also do impart to vs euen in true and real, though mystical, manner, the
very person of our Lord him selfe. (z) See this point further thus explained by *M. Smith* in his sermons, *serm. 1. pag. 103.* and *Iohn Bale*
in his *examen recitationum Selneceri. pag. 379.* and *M. Bruce* in his
sermons pag. 16. & 17 and by the author of the obseruations vpon

W 3   the

the harmony of confeſſions in engliſh, in his obſeruation vpon *pag.* 426. and by *Grinæus apud Iacobum Andræam in confut. diſput. Grinai*, printed 1584. *pag.* 88. *numer.* 4. *et* 5. and by *Beza in epiſt. theol. epiſt.* 5. *pag.* 56. (a) *In Apol. modeſt. ad Acta Conuentus quind cim theologorum torgæ nuper habit. pag.* 49. (b) In the Proteſtant treatiſe entituled, *Collatio Catholica et orthodoxæ Chriſtianorum fidei de perſona Chriſti et ſacra eius cæna.* printed *in quarto. Anno Dom.* 1582. *pag.* 349. it is ſaid; *ad vocabulum ſpiritualiter quod attinet, nequaquam per hoc intelligimus ſpiritum ſanctum tantum adeſſe, aut ſolam Chriſti corporis virtutem, hoc eſt merita nobis communicari, ſed talem* Coinonian *cum Apoſtolo prædicamus, qua corpus Chriſti, ſubſtantia, merito et efficacia nobis communicetur.*

(c)
Beza in epiſt. theol. epiſt. 5. *pag.* 56. ſaith, *nec enim ſpiritualis appellatur ratione eius rei quam participamus, ſed quoniam ſpirituali modo participamus.*

(d)
The French confeſſion in the engliſh harmony, *pag.* 426. ſaith, *we ſay this is done ſpritualy, not that we may con terſe ate an imagination or thought, inſteed of the efficacy & truth, but rather becauſe this myſtery of our vnion with Chriſt, is ſo high a thing,*

whereby *the body of Chriſt is in ſubſtance, merit, and efficacy, communicated to vs,* and no leſſe careful explication is made thereof by (c) *Beza* and other French (d) Proteſtantes; nay they forbeare not to proceede yet further in ſetting forth the omnipotency of God acted herein vpon the very Sacrament, ſaying therof that (*) *it haith vertue infuſed into it, not only to repreſent his body, but to conuey his body & him ſelfe to vs:* that alſo, (e) *the cooperation of his omnipotent power, maketh it his body and blood to vs:* and againe that, (f) *the creatures or elementes are bleſſed & conſecrated, that by the working of Gods ſpirit they ſhould be chaunged into the body and bloud of Chriſt, after a diuine and ſpirituall manner vnto the worthy receiuer.*

(3) And that it ſurmounteth al our ſences, yea and the whol order of nature &c. and becauſe it being diuine and heauenly, cannot be perceiued nor apprehended but by faith. And *Caluin in epiſt. & reſponſ. epiſt.* 372. *pag.* 726. ſaith, *et quamuis illa perceptio ſpiritualis ſit, non ideo minus tamen fit re ipſa.* (*) *M. Smith* in his ſermons printed 1592. *pag.* 102. & 103. (e) *M. Hooker* in his eccleſiaſtical poſlicy, *l.* 5. *ſect.* 67. *pag.* 177. and ſee the very ſame affirmed of the Sacrament by *M. D. Couel* in his defence of *M. Hooker, pag.* 116. (f) So ſaith *M. Fulke* in his defence of the engliſh tranſlation againſt *M. Martin, pag.* 435. and *M. Sutliue*

de miſſa

(3) And hence it is that they enter into a kind of extasy of admiring the omnipoten-cy of God shewed herein. To this end saith *Caluin, nihil restat &c.* (g) *nothing remaineth but that I should burst forth into admiration of that mystery, to which neither the minde in thinking, nor tongue in speaking can be equal:* wherto his other followers agree affirming, that (h) *this mystery of our communion with Christ is so high a thing, that it surmounteth al our senses, yea and the whol order of nature:* and (i) *being far aboue the reach of our capacity, cannot be compre-hended of any:* for (k) *it is a secret more high then can be comprehended by wit, or declared by wordes:* And which (saith Caluin) *I rather feele by experience, then can vnderstand:* for say they yet further, *nihilominus fatemur &c.* (l) *neuerthelesse we confesse the mystery of God to be incomprehensible,* whercby it commeth to passe, *that the thing which is in heauen and no where els, should be truly communicated to vs who are on earth and no where els.* whereto the diuines of *Geneua* do in like tearmes (m) assent: *Cauin* himselfe saying yet further thereof, *etsi autem incredi-bile videtur &c.* (n) *although it may seeme in-credible, that in so great a distance of places (as of heauen and earth) the flesh of Christ should pene-trate to vs that it may be meate for vs, we must yet remember how much aboue al our sences the secret power of the holy Ghost can shew it selfe.* The like whereof is affirmed by (o) *Bucanus: Cal-uin* *terris positi quamuis spiritualiter, vere tamen per fidem participemus &c. hoc inquam captum nostrum superat, et mysterium illud est quod Apostolus mag-num esse pronunciat.* and *ibidem pag. 23.* they further say of the very same point, *omnem ipsorum etiam Angelorum captum superat.* (n) *Caluin instit. l. 4. c. 17. sect. 10.* and see further the like *penetration of Christes flesh to vs,* affirmed there *sect. 24.* and see the further saying of

de Missa Papistica, l. 1. c. 29. fol. 173. saith, *mutatur panis in carnem non realiter, sed spirituali-ter.* (g) *Caluin instit. l. 4. c. 17. sect. 7.*

(h) The French confession in the english harmony, *pag. 426.*

(i) The *Confession of Belgia* in the english harmonie, *pag. 431.*

(k) *Caluin, l. 4. institut. c. 17. sect. 32.*

(l) So saith *Beza de re sacra-ment. quest. 9.* extant in his *tract. theolog.* printed *Geneuæ 1570. pag. 209.*

(m) The diuines of *Geneua* in *Apolog. modest. ad acta Conuentus quindecim theo-logorum torgæ nuper habit. &c.* printed *1575. pag. 47.* saith, *At quinam sie-ri possit, vt Christi carnem in cælis nunc positam, nos in*

of *Caluin* and *Bucer* alledged hereafter *tract*. 2. *sect*. 10. *sul diuis*. 2. in the margent vnder b. (o) *In loc. commun. de cana Dom. loc. 48. pag. 709.* saith, *Deus est omnipotens, ergo potest efficere, vt nos in terris existentes participemus verum corpus Christi in calis existentis.*

(p)
Caluin institut. l. 4. c. 17. sect. 10. saith hereof, *quod ergo mens nostra non comprehendit, concipiat fides spiritum vere vnire qua locis disiuncta sunt. Caluin l. 4. institut. c. 17. sect. 24.* saith herof, *nihil magis incredibile qua res toto cali et terra spatio dissitas ac remotas in tanta locorum distantia, non solum coniungi sed vniri.*

...uin affirming further hereof that, (p) *the spirit doth truly ioyne together thinges locally seuered.* A thing by his owne confession so strange, as (saith he) (*) *nothing is more incredible.* *Bastingius* affirming yet further thereof that, *it* (q) *dependeth of the onely almighty power of the holy Ghost, which being not to be comprehended by vs, maketh thinges absent to be present:* neither haue they contented them selues herewith, but haue vpon other sequel vrged from their foresaid doctrine proceeded yet further to more strange assertions, as namely that (r) our Sauiours said body (and not the onely figure

(q)
Bastingius, in his exposition vpon the Catechisme &c. *fol. 150.* (r) *Whitaker contra Duraum l. 2. pag. 170.* saith in defence hereof, *Si enim Christus fuit a principio mundi occisus, tum fuit priscis patribus corpore et morte sua presens &c.* and *pag. 171.* he further saith, *Apostoli in hanc sententiam Clarissima verba sunt, omnes Patres eandem escam spiritualem edisse et eundem potum spiritualem bibisse, nempe Christum, quod si autem Christum ederunt et biberunt, Christum illis presentem fuisse sequitur.* And in the booke entituled *Acta disputationis de sancta cana in accademia Heidelbergensi habit. Anno 1584.* *Grinaus* the Caluinist answeareth herein to the Lutheran opponent thus, *duplex igitur est petitio principij, primo quod in veteri Testamento omnino non extiterit corpus Christi. fol. 73.* and againe: *Iam quia fateris Patres (veteris Testamenti) per fidem viuifica corporis Christi* Energeias *perticipes factos esse, necessario et iam hoc fateri necesse est, eosdem quoq; participes factos esse corporis Christi. fol. 74.* yet more. *Aut tibi negandum est Patres veteris Testamenti* Energeias *corporis Christi participes factos esse, aut concedendum est eos non minus atq; nos participes corporis Christi factos esse &c. nec differo de beneficijs Christi tantum, ac si solius gratia bonorum seu beneficiorum Christi Patres participes facti sint, neq; de* Energeia *ago, fol. 74. & 75.* yet further perspicue dico
corporis

corporis et sanguinis Christi Oulian reuera sed non nisi spiritualiter ab vtrisq́,
tum ijs qui vixerunt in veteri Testamento, et qui in nouo Testamento fuerunt, et
adhuc sunt, percipi &c. fol. 76. with much more there at large in pretended defence of this opinion .

figure or efficacy thereof) was no lesse truly
and really present (long before it was in being) to the Fathers also of the old Testament,
and that they likewise no lesse really & truly
receiued the same ; in so much as in reguard
of their like real eating thereof before it was
borne and in being (which manducation or
eating is but an accident thereto) our aduersaries doubt not to affirme and defend that
(s) *non ens* may haue *accidentia,* a thing in it
selfe more strange, then is their common obiection against vs of (t) *accidens sine subiecto*:
which their foresaid doctrine pretending in
it so (u) *many miracles* is in our aduersaries
owne opinion so exceedingly more repugnāt
and hard to be conceiued or explicated then
ours, that Caluin confesseth him selfe (x) vnable to declare the maner thereof ; and *Beza*
with other the diuines of *Geneua,* do therefore, not in couert, but plaine tearmes, openly affirme, that (y) *their maner of presence is a*
more admirable and euident testimonie of the di-
uine omnipotēcy, then is (the) *real & oral eating* ;
professing yet further that by such their foresaid

(s)
Whereas the Lutheran
opponent argueth (there
fol. 73.) saying, *non entis*
nulla sunt accidentia, at
Christi caro in veteri Testa-
mēto nō fuit, nec itaq́, potuit
manducari, manducatio e-
nim actio est atq́, accidens.
Grineus doth there *fol.*
73. answeare thereto
saying : *maiorem argu-*
menti tui negamus esse
vniuersalem, in qua dicis
non entis nulla esse acciden-
tia &c. in so much as
this very point is yet at
this present a principall
question among the re-
formed Churches in Ger-
manie.

(t.)
See this obiected by *M.*
Iewel in his reply *art. 10.*
pag. 421. 422. &c. (u)
Caluin institut. l. 4. c.
17. sect. 24. saith here-
of, *qui non sentit multa subesse miracula, plus quam stupidus est.* (x) *Cal-*
uin ibidem. sect. 32. saith, *porro de modo si quis me interroget, fateri non*
pudebit, sublimius esse arcanam, quam vt vel meo ingenio comprehendi, vel ver-
bis declarari queat. (y) *Beza* with other the diuines of *Geneua* in their
foresaid *Apologia modesta ad acta Conuentus. 15. theol. &c.* printed
Geneua 1575. *pag. 52.* say, *deinde et illud dicimus spiritualem illum pre-*
sentia & communicationis modum, longe euidentius et admirabilius esse diuinæ
omnipotentiæ Tecmerion *quam realem illam &c. et oralem manducationem.*

X   (z) The

(z)

The fame Diuines there pag. 23. fpeaking of *our partaking here vpon earth, Chriftes flefh abyding in heauen*, fay thereof: *An non fatis oftendit plura etiam nos Chrifti omnipotentia tribuere, quam eos qui Chrifti Coinonian aboleri putant, nifi realis illa præfentia cum pane in terris, & oralis illa ipfiufmet corporis manducatio ftatuatur*   (a)

The fame diuines *pag.* 52. fay of real prefence to the bodily mouth, *quamuis vt ipfi volunt inuifibilis, tamen naturalis eft, nec fane eo mirifica. quid enim eft magis legibus naturæ confentaneum, quam vt corporis inftrumentis percipi res proximæ et contiguæ feu inuifibiles poffint?*

(b)   See this alledged from *Vadian* heretofore *tract.* 2. *fect.* 4. *fubd.* 1. in the margét at h.   (b) See this heretofore *tract.* 2. *fect.* 5. *fubdiuif.* 3. *fine.* at y. z. and *fubdiuif.* 2. at e. f.

(c)

Ibidem. at u. and *Caluin (apud Hofpinianum in hift. Sacrament. part.* 2. *fol.* 279.) further faith, *ergo in facra cæna miraculum agnofcimus, quod et natura fines et fenfus noftri modum*

faid doctrine they (z) *do attribute more to the omnipotency of Chrift, then thofe who (hould) the real prefence and receiuing of Chriftes body with the mouth:* cócerning which real prefence to the bodily mouth they yet further fay that, (a) *thouh it be inuifible, it is yet (but) natural, nor truly fo wonderful* (as theirs but) *more agreeable to the lawes of nature &c.* and (b) *very eafily beleeued.* And thus much in declaration of our aduerfaries doctrine.

(4)   Now as concerning the repugnancy thereof, our aduerfaries in their forefaid doctrine of real prefence to the mouth of faith, do not thereby meane the ordinary action of our beleeuing, or that our Sauiours body is prefent to vs by faith, in fuch fort onely as are prefent therto the other thinges which our faith apprehendeth, for fo we fhould be no more pertakers of his body, then we are of his glory, which alfo is the obiect of our faith, and by vs vndoubtedly beleeued. But the real prefence by them affirmed is (as appeareth by the premiffes of their doctrine) of an other nature, as whereto is required (b) *the omnipotency of God to accomplifh* (c) *the many miracles* therein acknowledged whereby it is (in their opinion) (d) *more wonderful* in it felfe, then is our other Catholicke doctrine of real prefence: which their affertion of it, being *more wonderful* then ours, I eafily acknowledge; for that *Chriftes body* (e) *being in heauen and no where els, we on earth and no where els*; his very faid body (and not the onely figne or efficacy thereof) *fhould yet be truely prefent in the facred fupper vpon earth*, euen

modum exuperat. (d) Heretofore *tra&ct. 2. se&ct. 5. subdiuis. 3. fine.* in the margent at a. (e) *Ibidem.* at l. m. n. (f) *Ibidem. subdiuis. 2. at* r. s. t. u. x. y. z.

euen (*) *to the vnfaithful* . And should also as *Caluin* further saith, (g) *penetrate to vs & enter into vs* ; so as it should be (i) *truely ioyned to vs,* and yet (k) *locally seuered from vs* ; and also truly (l) *present to vs,* being yet in very deede at the same time (m) *absent* : of this I must confesse and say (as our learned aduersaries haue heretofore said) that (n) *neither minde in thinking, nor tongue in speaking, can equal it* ; and that it (o) *exceedeth the conceiuing both of men and Angels* ; for being in it selfe so feeling, repugnant, and contradictory, how can it be so much as but conceiuable ? *Secondly,* wheras our aduersaries do further hold, concerning their said real presence, that Christes very body is really and truely present, and yet not (p) *bodily and corporally,* but onely (q) *spiritually* present, by which word *spiritualy* they

(*)
Ibidem. subdiuis. 2. at o. in which wordes of *Cal-uin* affirming Christes body in the supper preset to the vnfaithful who refuse him, whereof he saith yet further, *non figurat malis filij sui corpus, sed reipsa exhibet, offert, et porrigit* (*in* 1. *Cor.* 11. *vers.* 27. *& pag.* 325.) he euidently signifyeth Christsbody to be so present to them, not as it is in heauen, for they want true faith wherewith to ascend thither, but as being present to them with the

also sent to them with the Sacrament in the supper, where they refuse him being there present, & so exhibited to & offered thē ; which thing appeareth more euidētly by *Bucers* forealledged wordes, which testify that such as haue *faith,* being otherwise *vnworthy,* do yet *truly receiue his body* . See *Bucers* wordes next heretofore *se&ct.* 2. at * : next after o. (g) *Ibidem. subdiuis.* 3. in the margent at n. (h) *Caluin,* in his institutions in French . *l.* 4. *c.* 17. *se&ct.* 24. saith hereof, *la chaire entire iusq̃ a nous.* (i) Heretofore *tra&ct.* 2. *se&ct.* 5. *subdiuis.* 3. in the margent at p. (k) *Ibidem.* at p. and further there also at o. (l) Heretofore, *tra&ct.* 2. *se&ct.* 5. *subdiuis.* 3. at q. (m) *Ibidem.* at q. (n) *Ibidem.* at g. (o) *Ibidem.* at l. and in the margent there at m. (p) *M. Parkins* in his reformed Catholicke *pag.* 187. saith hereof, *though we hould a real presence of Christes body in the Sacrament, yet do we not take it to be bodily, but spiritual* . Also it is further said (*apud Hospinianum in hist. Sacram. part.* 2. *fol.* 168.) *In Sacramentis profitemur Christum esse, non personaliter aut corporaliter &c. sed solum essendi modo iam dicto spirituali* .

And

And see the like in *M.* *Fulke* against the Rhemish Testament, *in* 1. Cor. 15. *sect.* 5. of the marginal notes *fol.* 300. And *M. Sutliue de Missa Papistica, l.* 1. *c.* 29. *fol* 173. saith, *mutatur panis in carnem non realiter, sed spiritualiter.* And see *M.* *Whitaker,* and *M.* *Fulke,* alledged heretofore, *tract.* 2. *sect.* 4. *subdiuis.* 2. in the margent at a. (q) As next before at p.

(r)
Heretofore, *tract.* 2. *sect.* 5. *subdiuis.* 2. at a. b. c. d.

(s)
Ibidem, at r. b.

(t)
Suinglius, tom. 2. *de vera et falsa Religione. fol.* 206. saith, *nec eos audiendos esse putamus qui sic decernunt; edimus quidem veram corpoream̃q́; Christi carnem, sed spiritaliter, non dum enim vident simul stare non posse, corpus esse, et spiritaliter edi: sic enim diuersa sunt corpus et spiritus, vt vtrumcunq́; accipias, non possit alterum esse &c. vnde corpoream carnem spiritualiter edere nihil aliud est, quam quod corpus sit, spiritum esse adserere &c. Age nunc, quid fælicitatis hinc nascatur intellige, si credas te corpoream sensibilem̃q́; Christi carnem edere, aut vt alij dicunt, cor-*

also yet professe to meane no (r) thing lesse then the onely presence of the spiritual effectes of that body, or as thereby to (s) seclude the true and real presence of his body. How this also should be free from repugnancy, I cannot discerne; for, to forbeare what might be inferred by shewing how that our vnderstanding in which faith is seated, receiueth into it, according to the nature & capacity of it selfe, but the abstracted formes and notions of thinges and not the very thinges them selues, as also that the proper obiect of our faith, is no other then *prima veritas, or truth reuealed*: I do as now onely say, that to affirme, that Christes very body, and not the onely figure or efficacy thereof, should be truely and really present, and yet not bodily, but spiritually present, is in it selfe inexplicable, and, as (t) *Suinglus* in confutation thereof rightly obserueth, is vpon the matter no other then to turne his body into a spirit; for as the true substance of Christes spirit cannot be said to be present to vs onely corporally or bodily and not spiritually, because it is a spirit and no body, so neither, may the substance it selfe of Christes very body be said to be present to vs, not bodily, but onely spiritually (nor at al spiritually

poream carnem spiritualiter edere, fateberis indubie nihil aliud quam perplexitatem, stuporem &c. quis quæso similia ludibria vnquam commentus est? &c. tearming it there next afterwardes, *Commentum argutum quod solis verbis*

tually vnleſſe we do, which is impertinent to the matter now in hand, vnderſtand the word *ſpiritual* (as the (u) Apoſtle doth) becauſe it is a true and real body, and no ſpirit. The difficulty, or rather contradiction hereof, far exceedeth our aduerſaries common obiection againſt vs of the *viſibility and circumſcription* of our Sauiours body, for theſe being not eſſential to a body (*) may therefore be (and in our Sauiours body were) (x) ſuſpended, the truth of the ſaid body yet ſtil preſerued, whereas to haue it being bodily, is eſſential to a body, and cannot be ſuſpended or ſeuered: Which point *M. Iewel* ful wel diſcerned, and therefore, as herein exceeding his other brethren at the leaſt ſo far as concerned truth and probability of ſpeaking, he doubted not to affirme that (y) *Chriſtes body dwelleth* (not in our faith but) *in our bodies, and that not by way of imagination, or by figure, or fantaſy, but really, naturally, ſubſtantially, fleſhly, and in deede.*

(5) As concerning the abſurdity of *Caluin, Beza,* and others in their foreſaid doctrine (to forbeare that it (*) *excludeth* the Apoſtles

bis conſtat: a meere floriſh *of wordes* without ſubſtance of matter.

(u)

1. *Cor.* 15. 44. in which place the word *ſpiritual, doth not impugno the ſence of bodily or corporal,* but onely ſignifyeth that after the reſurrection our bodies ſhal be free from the neceſſities of meate, drinke, & other like earthly & mortal condition, as *Caluin* vpon this ſaid place vnderſtandeth the ſame.

(*)

Of ſundry other like properties *ſuſpended* from other bodies, ſee heretofore, *tract.* 2. *ſect.* 4. *ſubdiuiſ.* 1. in the margent at the figure 8. next after c. and that theſe alſo may in poſſibility be

ſuſpended. *Luther* cyted by *Peter Martir* in his *diſput.* annexed to his common places in engliſh, *pag.* 221. ſaith, *a body of a quantity may be without a quantitatiue meaſure.* Alſo *M. Iewel* in his reply, *pag.* 352. ſaith, *God is able by his omnipotent power, to make Chriſtes body preſent without place and quantity.* and *M. Willet* affirmeth that by like poſſibility *the huge body of a Camel remaning of that bignes, may be drawen through a needles eye. Sinopſis* printed 1600. *pag.* 526. (x) Of theſe properties *ſuſpended* in our Sauiours body, ſee the confeſſed examples thereof alledged heretofore *tract.* 2. *ſect.* 4. *ſubdiuiſ.* 1. at f. and ſome litle after there in the margent vnder the figures 4. 5. (y) *M. Iewel* in his reply *art.* 5. *pag.* 341. (*) *Excludeth* the Apoſtles, for whereas *Caluin* and his followers do altogether require to the receiuing of

Chriſtes

Chriftes body in the Sacrament, our beleeuing of his body offered
for vs vpon the Croffe, and rifen againe &c. it appeareth, *Marc*. 16.
14. and *Luc*. 24. 20. 21. 25. 26. that they did not know that he
fhould dye and rife againe. *S*. *Iohn*, 20. 29. faying exprefly yet further, that *as yet they knew not the Scripture that he fhould rife againe*. So
as by *Caluines* doctrine, the Apoftles them felues did not receiue
Chriftes body.

(z)
M. D. Raynoldes in his
conference &c. *pag*. 68.
faith, *I graunt that the
wordes of Chrift, this is my
body, are plainer in fhew for
your real prefence, then for
our Sacramental.*

(a)
M. Bilfon in his true difference &c. *part*. 4. *pag*.
568. confeffeth, that *in
Scripture, fo long as the letter may poffibly be true,
we may not flee to figures
(but faith he) the litteral
acception of thefe wordes,
this is my body, is firft impoffible &c.*

(b)
See this heretofore *tract*.
2. *fect*. 5. *fubdiuif*. 3.

Apoftles them felues fró receiuing of Chriftes
body) it appeareth yet further in this, that
hauing confeffed our Sauiours wordes to be
(z) *more plaine for our real prefence, then for their*
other doctrine, and profeffing alfo to reiect
ours in regard (a) of pretended repugnancy which it haith with the natural properties
of Chriftes humane body, they would now
yet in lewe thereof, obtrude vpon vs their
other deuifed forefaid real prefence, which,
in refpect of it, farre greater difficulty and
repugnancy, doth in their owne opinion (b)
attribute more to Gods omnipotency then ours, as
being in it felfe (c) *more wonderful*, and (d)
leffe agreeable to the lawes (or condition) *of
nature*. *Secondly*, whereas our faid aduerfaries
do (e) teach that we are to beleeue nothing
for neceffary but what may be proued from
the Scriptures, and the fame fo thereby proued, not by voluntary collection, but by (f)
neceffary fequel thence inferred. And where alfo
fine. at y. z. (c) *Ibidem*. at a. (d) *Ibidem*. at a. (e) *M.
Willet* in his finopfis. *pag*. 37. faith hereof, *we conclude that nothing neceffary to faluation, either concerning faith or manners, is elfwhere to be founde,
but in the holy Scriptures* : This is with our aduerfaries *an axiome* fo general as needeth no further proofe. (f) *M. D. Fulke* in his treatife againft the defence of the Cenfure, *pag*. 319. faith, *in matters neceffary to faluation, we admit no gueffes*, but *either manifeft wordes of Scripture,
or els that which is neceffarily concluded out of manifeft wordes*. And in his
confutation of Purgatory, *pag*. 189. he faith, *al articles of our beleefe*
are

are plainely taught in the Scripture, either by manifest wordes, or by necessary *conclusion.* And *Ibidem . pag .* 364. he saith, *not standing vpon voluntary* *collection, but either in plaine wordes, or necessary conclusion, for there is no-* *thing that we are bound to know or do, but either in expresse wordes, or necessa-* *ry collection, it is set forth in the Scriptures.* And see further to this purpose *Vrsinus in commentar . Catech . fol.* 42 . and *Chemnitius* in his examen
part . 1 . *fol.* 48 . & . 74 . & *part . 2 . fol .* 162 .   (g)

D . *Goad* in the Tower
so they further teach, that our Sauiours wor-   dispute , the 3 . dayes
des of institution, *this it my body, are* (g) *figu-*   conference, x . iii. and
                                      ratiue,   M . *Bilson* in his true dif-
ference *part.* 4 . *pag.* 571 . & *pag.* 579 . & . 560. endeuoreth by long
discourse to make good the title of that leafe, which is, *the wordes of*
Christ to be figuratiue. also see M . *Willet* in his sinopsis, *pag.* 448 . and
pag. 449. where he compareth our Sauiours wordes with his other
figuratiue sayinges, saying thereof ; *when Christ said I am the dore. Ioan.*
10 . 9 . *I am the vine. Ioan.* 15 . 1 . *he spake* by a figure as he doth here,
for neither was he a vine, or a dore, as the bread was not his body. And *Vr-*
sinus in commentar . catech . pag . 613 . saith of our Sauiours wordes, *Lo-*
cutio est sacramentalis seu metonomica, qua simbolo tribuitur nomen rei signi-
ficata. Also M . *Whitaker contra Camp . rat.* 2 . *pag .* 36 . affirmeth our
Sauiours wordes to be *tropical.* to that end comparing thē to *Gen.* 17.
10 . *et Exod.* 12 . 11 . And *contra Duræum, l.* 2 . *pag .* 172 . he saith,
tribus exemplis demonstraui verba illa, hoc est corpus meum, Tropicos *in-*
telligenda esse. and hauing spent two leaues afterwardes in further proofe
thereof, he concludeth concerning our Sauiours wordes, that *necesse*
est vt ea verba ex perpetuo scripturæ more metonumicos *interpretemur.*
saying yet furher there, *pag,* 180 *hæc verba, hoc est corpus meum figu-*
rate ac Metonumicos *interpretanda sunt.* And *Beza de cæna Dom.*
contra Westphalum extant in his *tract . theologic . pag .* 213 . vnder the
title *ad caput tertium de tropo in verbis cænæ Domini,* maketh a long dif-
course in proofe thereof, to that end comparing our Sauiours wordes
with the other figuratiue sayinges before mentioned. And *Caluin in*
confes . de re sacramentaria, extant in his *tractat . theologic . pag .* 874 .
num . 22 . saith, *extra controuersiam ponimus (solennia cænæ verba, hoc est*
corpus meum) figuraté *accipienda esse &c. neq, vero nouum hoc aut insolens*
videri debet, vt per Metonomiam ad signum transferetur rei figuratæ nomen ,
cum passim in Scripturis eiusmodi locutiones occurrant. & vide ibidem pag
885 . and *pag.* 895 . & 896 . and see further the like in *Caluin . insti-*

l. 4. *c.* 17. *sect.* 22. And see *M.* Iewel in his defence printed 1571. *pag.* 509. labouring to proue our Sauiours wordes to be figuratiue,.

(h)

Whitaker contra Duraeum. *l.* 2. *pag.* 180. saith, *figura non est in corpore, aut in sanguine Christi, nec quidem in pane aut vino, sed in copula est.* And *Praetorius de Sacramentis,* *pag.* 256. saith, *restat igitur vt tropus sit in verbo est.* and see further *Caluin,* & *Vrsinus,* next heretofore in the margent vnder g.

(i)

That figuratiue sayinges afford no certaine proofe or argument in matters of faith, see *Chemnitius* in his examen, *part.* 3. *pag.* 127. *Aretius in loc.*

ratiue the sence of them being, (h) *this signifyeth,* or is the signe of *my body;* wherto they ad, that a *figuratiue saying proueth* (i) *nothing,* and admitting here it should proue, yet according to their owne foresaid exposition, it *cannot* (k) *necessarily* infer and conuince further then that the Sacrament is a *figure* whereby Christes body is signifyed. Hence it ineuitably followeth, that their said other opinion of *real presence so wonderfully exhibited,* is but their owne voluntary collection without al necessary sequel from the Scriptures: for if our Sauiours foresaid wordes of *institution* do not proue the same (as being figuratiue they cannot) much lesse then can (l) other textes of Scripture, lesse plaine, so confirme and proue it, but that the same or like answeare, which auoided our Sauiours forerecyted wordes, wil much more suffice to

commun. loc. 52. *pag.* 162. & *loc.* 81. *pag.* 262. *M.* Willet in his Sinopsis, printed 1592. *pag.* 27. *Oecolampadius in libro Epistolarum Oecolampadij et Suinglij. l.* 1. *pag.* 223. *Lubbertus, de principijs &c. pag.* 409. and *M. D.* Downham in his booke of Antichrist. *c.* 15. *pag.* 169. saying, *it is a rule in diuinity that, Theologia Simbolica non est argumentatiua.* (k) *Not necessarily,* no more then their other alledged examples of, *I am a dore, I am a vine, the rocke was Christ,* and such like, can proue Christ to haue beene after a like wonderful manner, and no lesse really and truely *a rocke, a dore, a vine &c.* (l) For as concerning the 6. of Iohn, *M.* Bilson in his true difference, *part.* 4. *pag.* 582. affirmeth that, *the wordes of Christ in the sixt of Iohn, are Allegorical, mystical, and figuratiue.* and see the same further there, *pag.* 579. & 583. the title of his diuers leaues together there being, *in S. Iohn the maner of speaking is Allegorical.* And as for 1. *Cor.* 10. 16. it lyeth no lesse open to be thought figuratiue, when do our Sauiours wordes

of the

of the institution, in so much as *Caluin in* 1. *Cor.* 10. *vers.* 16. though thence inferring his wonderful presence, confesseth yet saying thereof, *figuratam locutionem esse fateor.* And see further *Caluin. instieut. l.* 4. *c.* 17. *sect.* 22.

to auoide the other, so as our aduersaries haue no proofe of their opinion from the scriptures. Thirdly, the premises here alledged in examination of our aduersaries foresaid doctrine of real presence, are so plaine and euident, that *Celius secundus Curio*, though a learned Caluinist, is by our very aduersaries reported to haue (m) stumbled thereat, and others (not of vulgar note) haue vpon a second consideration reiected the same, choosing rather to imbrace the other doctrine formerly taught as beforsaid by *Suinglius and Oecolampadius*. To this end *Peter Martir* expresseth his iudgment saying directly against *Caluins* foresaid doctrine, (n) *I maruaile at this, that in the second article it is said, that signes haue alwaies ioyned with them the thing it selfe that is signifyed, & that in the third is declared, the maner of that coniunction, which is said not to be called only figuratiue or shadowing; verily for my part I know no other coniunctiõ of the flesh & bloud with the signes, then that which is of signification*. And againe most directly against (o) *Caluin*, (p) *wherefore I do not thinke that the maner of this presence is to be accompted obscure or doubtful*. In like sorte *Lodouicus Alemannus* reiected *Caluines* doctrine saying, (q) *neither also by faith, or by*

(m)
Conradus Schlusselburg (a learned Lutheran) in his *Theologia Caluinist. l.* 2. *fol.* 73. allegeth his wordes saying of him, *Celius secundus Curio in Pasquillo suo ecclatico. fol.* 74. *&* 75. *conscientia dubitante haud obscure fatetur Caluinistas nihil certi habere in hac controuersia cui insistere possint; verba eius hac sint: harea ita me Deus amet, et Lupum auribus teneo, nam si discopa nent &c.*

(n)
Peter Martir in his epistles annexed to his common places in english, *epist.* 25. *pag.* 107.

(o)
Caluins doctrine mentioned next heretofore *sub. diuis.* 3. in the margent at. x.

(p)
Peter Martir, vbi supra.

pag. 108. an opinion so euident in *Peter Martir*, that *Bucer* at his being in England with *Peter Martir*, wrote purposly vnto him thereof, as perswading him to professe the other opinion, *si fieri omnino possit tua conscientia salua.* See this in *Buceri script. Anglican. pag.* 549. (q) *Alemannus in positionibus apud Lugdunenses editis Anno.* 1566. saith hereof, *neq; etiam per fidem seu incomprehensibili modo, vt vocant, quia hoc totum imagina*

Y

imaginarium, et apertissime repugnat Dei verbo. And see further *Bezaes* epistle to the same *Alemannus* to perswade him from *Suinglianisme* to the other opinion extant in his *epist. Theolog. epist. 5. Alemanno.*

(r)

Vrsinus in his *commonefact. cuiusdam theologi de cæna, et eiusdem commonefactionis consideratio.* printed **1583. pag. 10.** faith, *non alia communio contigit nobis in cana &c. nisi qua etiam alijs temporibus quandocunq, in Christum credimus.*

(s)

Next heretofore *subdiuis.* 2. at e.

(t)

In the Christian letter to that reuerend man. M. R. Hoo. pag. 35.

(*)

Others likewise, for *Hospinianus in hist. Sacram. part. 2. fol. 344.* geueth testimony of the *Heluetian* Churches dissenting herein from the French,

or by any *vncomprehensible maner as they tearme it, for al this is but imaginary, and most directly against the word of God.* As also *Vrsinus* acknowledgeth (r) *no other communion of Christ in the supper, then that which hapneth* at other times, whensoeuer we beleeue in Christ. And the Puritaines reprehend M. *Hookers* (s) forsaid doctrine saying to him, *(t) instruct vs vpon what ground of scripture it may be proued that the cooperation of his omnipotent power, doth make it his body and bloud to vs, and in what sence, whether such phrases do not helpe the Popish &c.* Thus did they (and (*) others likewise) vpon dislike of Caluines doctrine, as being absurd and contradictory, euidently incline to *Suinglianisme,* which our other aduersaries reiect for naked & (u) prophane: both of these opinions being indeede so grosly repugnant to faith and the wordes of Christ, that (x) *Martin Luther,* hauing vpon deliberate consideration long consulted & striuen with himselfe, how to abandon the doctrine of real and corporal presence, as discerning the same to be

saying, *hoc ipso Anno* (1571.) *præcipui Gallicarum Ecclesiarum ministri Rupellæ magno numero sinodum habuerunt,* affirming there afterwardes that this Sinode did condemne, *quosdam Gallos qui pro re per panem et vinum significata, (solam euergiam, id est, effectum pro re ipsa statuentes, imperitos turbarint.* And it appeareth there *fol.* 344. that the *Heluetian Churches would not receiue the word substantial* prescribed by that *Sinod:* in so much as *Bullinger* (alledged there *fol.* 344.) reproueth against *Beza* this decree of the Sinod, *damnamus eos qui non recipiunt substantiæ vocabulum,* tearming there *decretum verbis paulo inconsideratius conceptum et pronuntiatum.* saying withal there next after, *quis enim ignoret nos ex*

corum

eorum numero eſſe qui hoc non recipimus, nec vnquam recipere voluimus.
So euidently were the *Suinglians* and *Caluiniſtes* diuided herein among
them ſelues. (u) *M. Rogers* in his doĉtrine of the Church of England, *pag.* 176. reieĉteth and condemneth them by the names of
Simboliſtes, Figuriſtes, and *Significatiſtes.* (x) See *Luthers* owne ful
teſtimony herof alledged
to *be more in preiudice of the Papacie,* which he next hereafter *traĉt.* 2.
greedily thirſted after, did yet in the end geue *ſeĉt.* 6. *ſubdiuiſ.* 1. in
ouer ſuch his endeuour, retaining ſtil his for- the margent at the fi-
mer opinion of real preſence, and confeſſed gure 6. next after k.
him ſelfe to be *houlden captiue, and no way left* (i)
him to eſcape, the text of the Goſpel being ſo plaine *Traĉt.* 2. *ſeĉt.* 4. *ſubdiuiſ.*
and ſtrong &c. 1. *et* 2. throughout.
(2)
D. Raynoldes, in his con-
Of the miracles ſhewed by God in teſtimonie ference with *Harte. pag.*
of the real preſence. 68. alledged next here-
after, *ſeĉt.* 4. *ſubdiuiſ.* 1.
initio. at y. *pag.* 146.
SECTION. 6. (3)
See heretofore, *traĉt.* 2.
S Ince then, the ſtumbling blocke of pre- *ſeĉt.* 3. *ſubdiuiſ.* 1. *initio.*
tended impoſſibility and abſurdity con- from z. throughout that
ceiued againſt our doĉtrine, and whereat fleſh ſubdiuiſion.
and bloud haith taken ſuch ſcruple & offence, (4) See
is by that which haith beene (i) heretofore
alledged ſo clearely remoued, and that this matter is now at laſt confeſſed to be poſſible, as depending onely vpon Gods holy wil : Since
likewiſe his wil, which cannot be better knowen to vs then by his word
is herein made ſo plaine to vs euen by his written word, that if our aduerſaries would but for the time ſuppoſe that the holy Ghoſt were
mindful to decree by Scripture the realpreſence, them ſelues can hardly imagine wordes more euident to that purpoſe then are theſe wordes :
this is my body which is geuen for you : which wordes as our learned aduerſaries (2) *graunt are plainer in ſhew for our real preſence, then for their*
Sacramental. Since alſo the anſweareable ſence of the ſame wordes is
accordingly côfirmed to vs, not only by our Sauiours foreſaid (3) pro-

misse, S. *Paules* agreeable (4) *explication*, and the (5) confessed testimonies of *the Primatiue Church,* which (as our learned aduersaries do acknowledge) (k) *is the true and best mistris of posterity, and going before, leadeth vs the way;* but also by open (6) cofession, which euident truth enforced from *Martin Luther,* euen when the more to displeasure the Pope, he stroue with himselfe to become a *Suinglian.* I wil now therefore without further a do conclude this point, with onely adding thereto in further testimony and confirmation to vs of Gods holy wil in this behalfe, the vndoubted miracles which haue beene wrought, not by false Prophets, but imediatly by God himselfe: and those not reported onely by vs Catholickes, but (for sundry of them) by the auncient Fathers or learned Protestantes them selues. As for (l) example, *in February, Anno.* 1510. *in a towne called Knobloch, one Paul, a sacrilegiouse person, went secretly into the Church by night, broake the Pix where the Sacrament was reserued, and stole from thence*

(4)
See heretofore *tract.* 2. *sect.* 3. *subdiuis.* 3. at q. r. s.

(5)
See these confessed testimonies heretofore *tract.* 2. *sect.* 2. throughout.

(k)
So saith the *Confession of Bohemia* in the English harmony &c. *pag.* 400.

(6)
Luther in epistola ad Argentinenses, saith hereof, *Hoc diffiteri nec possum, nec volo, si Carolastadius &c.* this I cannot nor wil deny, that if *Carolastadius,* or any other, could for these last fiue yeares haue perswaded me that there had bene nothing in the Sacrament but bread and wine, he

should haue bound me vnto him by a great good turne; for I haue taken great care in discussion of this matter, & haue endeuored with al my power & screwes stretched out, to be ridde thereof, for I did wel see that thereby I might very greatly hurt the Papacy &c. but I do see my selfe captiue, no way being left to escape, for the text of the Gospel is so plaine and so strong &c. And immediatly after to signify his yet further endeuoring him selfe to the Suinglian opinion, he further saith thereof: *Sum enim, proh dolor, plus aequo in hanc partem propensus.* See also this saying of *Luther* cyted by *M. Fulke* at large in the treatise against the defence of the Censure. *pag.* 99. and 100. and partly *in Lutheri loc. commun. clas.* 2. *pag.* 145. and 146. and wholly in *Luthers* workes set forth by *Melancton, tom.* 7. *Wittenberg. fol.* 502. printed at *Witebergie.* 1558. (l) *Surius in Cronics.* And *Nicolaus Basilius in additione ad Cronicon Naucleri.* and *Pontanus, l.* 5. *rerum memorabilium.*

(m) *Ioanne s*

thence two confecrated Hoftes, one of which he
fould to a Iewe; afterward the Iewe blinded with
malice faid: if thou be the God of Criftianes manifeft thy felfe; and that faid he pearced the Sacrament with his dagger, whereupon bloud did miraculoufly iffue forth &c. This miracle was
not priuate, but fo knowen and difcouered,
that thirty eight Iewes, affenting thereto, were
therefore apprehended and publiquely burned the
19. of Iuly. 1510. in the marchie of Braudi-
burge: and al (other) Iewes were alfo thereupon
by publique decree banifhed out of the faid Terri-
tories. This hiftory being reported more at
large by our Catholicke writers, was a matter fo knowen in the country, where it was
done that *Melancton, Ioannes Manlius, Michael, Beuther,* and *Luke Ofiander,* al of them proteftant writers, do not forbeare to geue fpecial (m) teftimonie therof. Hereunto might
be added fundry other miraculous apparitions of *bloud* iffuing from the Sacrament v-
pon the *Iewes* like misbeleefe or violence
thereto offered: As about *Anno Dom.* 360.
when (n) *S. Bafile* was miniftring the Sacrament. Alfo *Anno Dom.* (o) 1290. when
by a certaine *Iewe at Paris,* the bleffed Sacrament

(m)
*Ioannes Manlius in loc.
commun.* pag. 87. faith
hereof, *Anno poft natum
Chriftum* 1510. *die* 19.
*Iuly combufti funt in Mar-
chia Braudeburgenfi.* 38.
*Iudai, qui facramentalem
hoftiam a facrilego quodam
emptam pugionibus et cul-
tellis in ipfius Chrifti et Ecclefiæ Chriftianæ ignominiã
impie confoderant, adiectis
blafphemys, quod Chriftianorum Deus nullum haberet
fanguinem, qui tamen mira-
culofe promanauit, adeo vt
celari nullo modo potuerit:
quare comprehenfi fcelerati
omnes viui funt exufti, ex-
ceptis paucis qui facro Bap-
tifmate conferfi, poftridie
capitis fupplicio funt affecti.
Sacrilegus vero ifte qui ven-
diderat, candentibus primã
forcipibus dilaceratus, vi-
uus etiam combuftus eft.*

that *Manlius* who publifhed this treatife, is but the collector of *Melanctons* report, appeareth by *the verfes* in the beginning of the booke:
And *ibidem.* pag. 89. the reporters mentioneth his being at *Katisbone,*
and difputing there with *Ecchius,* which was meant of *Melancton.* and
Beuther in his *Ephemerefis hiftorica.* pag. 226. maketh the very fame report of this forefaid miracle. and fo alfo doth *Luc. Ofiander in epitom.
hift. Ecclefiaft.* cent. 16. c. 14. and pag. 28. 29. (n) *Cirus Theodorus Prodromus* who liued *Anno Dom.* 440. *in Epigrammate in D. Bafi-
leum,* thus faith of this miracle; *Inruicus pauem, et nigrum in cratere Lieum
riferat hæbræus facra myftica Chrifticolarum, hæc vbi Bafilius perfenferat v-
traq, edenda porrigit, illa ftatim cruor et caro verfa refultant.* And fee the
Centurie

Y 3

Century writers *cent*. 4. *col*. 431.   (o) *Fulgosus l. 1. c. 6.* and
Nauclerus in generatione 44.

(*)
It is thereof said by the
said author, *hostiam gla-*
dio pupugit, ex qua confe-
stim sanguis manauit. and
a litle after, *Iudæi domus*
in Templū conuersa est, quæ
etiam Saluatoris Bullientis
nomine compellatur, vbi
hostia, gladiusq̃ etiam nunc
ostenduntur.

(p)
Suffridus Misnensis, l. 3.
de Anno. 1299.

(q)
Albertus Crantzius hist.
Vandorum. l. 8. *c*. 8.
(r) *Iacobus Meterus An-*

ment was transfixed, whereof vndoubted
monumentes (*) *are yet remaining*. Also vpon
like violence offered thereto by the Iewes,
Annis. Dom. (p) 1299. *at Rutligen in Fran-*
conia, and (q) 1323. *in Vandalia*. and (r)
1368. at *Bruxelles*, and againe most notably
(s) at *Bruxelles Anno*. 1369. In so much as
the (t) *Iewes confessing the same, were thereupon*
publiquely condemned and burned vpon the assen-
tion eue. *Anno*. 1370. In memory whereof,
the very same sacred host is yet to this day
religiously (and most miraculously *without cor-*
ruption) (u) reserued in the Church of *S. Gu-*
dula in *Bruxelles* where it is yet to be seene
transfixed and *bloudy*, God hauing sithence
shewed sundry miracles thereat, as publickly
of late vpon (x) *Margaret Iesope* a lame wo-
                                                        man

nalium Flandriæ. l. 33. and *Theodoricus Loer a Syratis de miraculis Brux-*
ellis, æditis circa venerabilem Eucharistiam. prosecuteth by witnesses the
history at large.   (s)   See *Theodoricus Loer de miraculis Bruxellis,*
æditis circa venerabilem Eucharistiam &c. And *Tilman Breudebachius in*
collationum sacrarum l. 9. *c*. 25.   (t) *Vide vbi supra*. (u) Hereof see
Thedoricus Loer de miraculis Bruxellis æditis &c. (x) *Margaret Iesope,*
borne at Longwicke in Risborow parish in Buckinghamshire, serued *Anno*.
1568. one *Samuel Rogers* a Duchman in the old Baly in London,
went to *Bruxelles, Anno*. 1569. there to seeke for *Iohn Masten* a Duchman, her affianced husband : at what time being brought in Childbed,
she became vpon her trauaile and deliuery so *lame*, as that she kept her
bed for a quarter of a yeare, a deepe hole remaning in her right side,
as if some of her ribbes had bene sunke far within her body, the skin
yet continuing whol, and the sinewes in her hamme of her *right legge*,
were so contracted and shrunke, that from the hippe downeward
it was shorter then the other legge by more then halfe a foote, in which
estate shee was knowen there to continue *three yeares and foure monethes* :
at the end of which time she went with the helpe of her crutch to the
                                                        Church

Church of *S. Gudulaes* to heare the solemne Masse of the foresaid blessed *miraculouse Sacrament,* whereat in the presence of hundrethes of eye witnesses she left her Crutch, being miraculously restored to perfect health : Which miracle by reason of her former knowen long continued lamenesse, was proclaimed in Pulpittes of the Cities round about, and in memory thereof her *Crutch* was then left, and is yet to this day remaining in the place nere to the said blessed Sacrament. See this reported more at large by *D. Bristow* in his Motiues. *Motiue* 5. *pag.*

man of our owne nation, whereof many hundreth were eye witnesses, and of them sundry yet liuing, able to testify the same. Also the like miraculouse apparition of bloud vpon the Iewes like violent offer hapned (y) the 22. of *October Anno.* 1492. (*) at *Sterneburge thirty Iewes being thereupon burned.* And (z) *Anno.* 1556. in *Polonia, whereupon the offenders, one Bishem a Iew, and Dorathy his woman seruant, were vpon fryday after the assention day publidkly burned.* And lastly (a) *Anno* 1591. at *Presburge* in *Hungary, where three Iewes that offended were publickely executed.* Hitherto concerning such examples wherein Preistes were no agentes, the same being also done not priuately, but so far from al suspition of fiction, that the very time in which they hapned is specially described, the place particulerly named, the numbers of the offenders noted, and their publicke condemnation and execution euen to death, certainly set downe, and the offence in al these discouered vpon occasion of astonishment at the miracle shewed : vnto which might be added other testimonies of like example reported by (b) *M. Willet,* and the (c) *Century* writers.

(y)
Hermannus Schedelius in Chronicis de hoc Anno. Nauclerus generatione .5.

(*)
Sub dominio Principum Magnopolentium.

(z)
Rouerus Pontanus rerum memorabilium, l. 5. et Laurentius Surius in commentario rerum in orbe gestarum.

(a)
Ianfonius Doccomensis frisius Mercurij Gallobelgici, l. 4. de Anno. 1591.

(b)
Willet de vniuersali et nouissima Iudaeorum vocatione. fol. 30.

(c)
Centur. 13. *c.* 10.

(d)
D. Humfrey haith no other answeare thereto but derydeth it in his *Iesuitismi*

(2) And like as God haith thus miraculously confirmed this truth against the Iewes, so haith he done in like manner against other misbeleeuers, whereof most graue and credible testimony is not wanting:

A5

suitismi. part. 2. ratione. 5. pag. 626. saying, in Ecclesiam (Anglicanam) quid inuexerunt Gregorius et Augustinus &c. transubstantiationem, quando Matrona quadam audiente, panem quem manibus suis fecerat, a Gregorio corpus Domini appellari, et subridente, mox ad coarguendam, et depellendam mulieris incredulitatem, particulam panis instar digiti carnem ille effecit.

(*)

See heretofore; tract. 2. sect. 3. subdiuis. 1. in the margent at the letter h. (e) Pascasius l. de corpore et sanguine Christi. cap. 14. (f) Paschasius ubi supra saith, nemo qui sanctorum vitas et exempla legerit, potest ignorare quod sæpe hac mystica corporis et sanguinis Domini Sacramenta, aut propter dubios, aut certe propter ardentius amantes Christum, visibili specie in Agni forma, aut in carnis & sanguinis colore monstrata sint &c. aut quod latebat in mysterio, patesceret adhuc dubitantibus in miraculo. (g) Petrus Damianus epist. 13. (h) Petrus Damianus ibidem saith, vester ille finitimus piæ recordationis Amolphitanus Episcopus, Stephano Romano Pontifici, me presente, sub iureiurando testatus est, quia cum aliquando ad mensam Domini sacrificaturus accederet, sed super Sacramenta Domini corporis incredulus hæsitaret, in ipsa confractione salutaris hostiæ, rubra prorsus ac perfecta caro inter eius manus apparuit, ita ut etiam digitos illius cruentaret. (i) Elizabeth Schonaugiensis l. 1. visum Dei saith, introspexi &c. et apparuit species vera carnis in ea &c. testis autem est mihi Deus quia nihil in his omnibus fingo. (i) Petrus Cluniacensis de miraculis sui temporis. l. 1. c. 1. reporteth this at large as done in his time, and so credible that he saith thereof, ego quoq; omnibus istud diligentibus scribendo intimare curaui.

As for example, aboue 1000. yeares since in the like apparition of flesh, which by D. (d) Humfreys confession was shewed to an incredulous woman vpon the praiers of S. Gregorie (*) heretofore alledged. Also about 800. yeares since in the (e) apparition of a child to a religious Preist named Plegils: which kind of like apparition was often before (f) those times manifested, as is affirmed by the reporter hereof Paschasius a graue and credible author, who liued in the same age. Also about 550. yeares since, in the like apparition of flesh to a wicked (g) woman, and at another time to a certaine (h) Bishop of holy memory, who (as the reporter hereof Petrus Damianus a graue author affirmeth) did testify the same vpon oath in his presence to Steuen Bishop of Rome. and aboue 400. yeares since to a holy professed woman called Elizabeth, who reporteth

pag 250.

(k) Mathew

reporteth the same, and faith thereof, (*) *I draw God to witnes, that herein I faine nothing*: to which might be further added sundry other like apparitions testifyed by credible reporters as aboue 400. yeares since by (i) *Petrus Cluniacensis*, aboue 300. yeares since: by *Mathew* (k) *Paris* an author of confessed credit with (*) Protestantes: And (to omit others (l) in the same age) by *Thomas* (m) *Cantipratensis*, who is the reporter, and was also one of those many witnesses to whom that apparition was publickely manifested in the open Church at *Doway*. And as Christ haith vouchsaifed thus to manifest his presence by miracle, so at some other times haith he in like maner miraculously withdrawen his presence from the vnworthy person: To this end is memorable, that which S. Ciprian aboue 1300. yeares since reporteth concerning

(k)
Mathew Paris, in hist. Anglicana. de Anno 1154. after the Tigurin print of *Anno.* 1606. *pag.* 90.

(*)
The Protestant diuines in their beginning of their preface to the reader, set before the beginning of that booke, do tearme *Mathew Paris* his said booke, *opus laudatissimū*, affirming there further of him, *Author vero ipse singularis fidei testimonium reliquit, quod temporibus illis iniquis, cum omnia mendacijs & fabulis deprauata essent, tam equa-*bile tamen, & temperatum iudicium seruauerit &c. apud hunc causa & veritati omnia deferuntur, personis, affectui, tempori, omnia denegantur &c.*

(l)   Other like apparitions are testifyed by *Carolus Sigonius de regno Italiæ. l.* 19. *de Anno.* 1264. by *Onuphrius Pauinius in Platina vrbanum quartum.* By *Guilielmus Brito Armoricus de Gestis Philippi Francorum Regis. l.* 1. by *Robertus Abbas de monte, de Anno.* 1181. *in appendice ad cronographiam Sigeberti.* by *Vincentius Belnatensis speculi historialis. l.* 29. *c.* 24. by *Helmoldus l.* 4. *Cronicorum. c.* 14. by *Alexander Halesius, quarto parte summa, quast.* 11. *memb.* 2. *art.* 4. *parag.* 3. by *Iacobus Vitriacus. l.* 2. *c.* 4. *vitæ Mariæ Oeginacensis.* by *Lanfrancus de corpore et sanguine Domini.* and by *Guitmundus de corpore et sanguine Domini l.* 2. (m) *Thomas Cantipratensis. l.* 2, *miraculorum. c.* 40. reporting how that this hapned at *Doway*, saith further, *clamans, ergo Presbiter, Canonicus vocat, occurrunt illi, spectant in panno corpus viuificum &c. et mox connocato populo ad spectaculum, presentatur, et indifferenter nulli tamc cælitus visio denegatur, hac cum audissem fama vulgante, veni in opidum &c. petij videre miraculum &c. Ecce vidi faciem in mensuram ætatis plenitudinis Christi, spineam habentem coronam in capite, et duas guttas*

Z   *sanguinis*

sanguinis de fronte ex vtra- concerning (n) a certaine woman, who, when she
q̨ parte naſi deſcendentes . would with vnworthy handes haue opened her Co-
(n) fer wherein was (reſerued) the holy thing of our
Ciprian. in ſerm. de lapſis . Lord, there ſprang vp fyer from thence, whereby
multo poſt med. And wher- ſhe was ſo terrifyed that ſhe durſt not touch it.
as this Sacrament, being And (o) when (ſaith he) a certaine other defiled
then reſerued, is ſo vn- perſon preſumed after that the Preiſt had celebra-
like to the Proteſtantes ted ſacrifice, to receiue with others, he could not
Sacrament, which is with eate nor touch the holy thing of God, for in his
them no Sacrament, but opened handes he found (onely) aſhes: (*) by do-
when it is receiued : cumentes whereof (ſaith *Ciprian*) it is ſhewed
That *M . Fulke* againſt that the Lord doth depart when he is denyed. In
Heſkins, *Sanders* &c . like manner are vndoubted examples extant
pag . 523. anſweareth, of miraculouſe helpe, ſhewed to thoſe who
that *this was a iuſt puniſh-* with deuotion reſpected the bleſſed Sacra-
ment for her reſeruing of ment, euen when it was reſerued and vnre-
that which ſhould haue ceiued. To this end doth *S . Ambroſe* report
beene receiued. S. *Cipri-* how that (p) *his brother Satirus being by ſhip-*
ans wordes are quite to *wracke throwen into the ſea, and hauing tyed the*
the contrary, affirming *diuine Sacrament in a ſtole, and faſtned the ſtole*
this puniſhment to haue *about his necke, ſought no board whereby ſuppor-*
hapned, for that *ſhe would* ted he might be holpen , but thinking him ſelfe
haue touched it , indignis therewith ſufficiently defended required no other
manibus , with vnworthy helpe

handes. and *Greg. Turonenſ. l . 1 . de gloria Martyrum. c . 86.* reporteth a like miracle ſaying, *Lecta igitur paſſione cum reliquis lectionibus quas*
Sacerdotalis Canon inuexit, tempus ad ſacrificium offerendum aduenit, accep-
taq̨ turre Diaconus in qua myſterium Dominici corporis habebatur &c .
elapſa de manu eius ferebatur in aera &c . quod non de alia cauſa credimus
actum, niſi quia polutus erat in conſcientia . he affirmeth there that his
mother and others were preſent and ſaw the ſame . (o) *Ciprian . i-*
bidem. (*) *Documento vnius oſtenſum eſt, Dominum recedere cum nega-*
tur. (p) *Ambroſe , orat . funebri de obitu fratris Satiri . c . 7.* this
place is ſo euident, that *Peter Martir, l . contra Gardinerum, obiect . 88.*
acknowledgeth the matter of fact, and inſteede of better anſweare reproueth both *S . Ambroſe,* and his brother *Satirus.* As alſo in like maner *M . Whitaker l . 10. contra Duraum. pag . 872 .* dare not deny the
matter of fact, but onely reproueth *Satirus* for ſo putting hope in the
Sacrament

Sacrament, and referuing it, saying thereof that, *sine omni Scripturæ authoritate factum est.* (q)

helpe, neither did his hope leaue him, nor his opi-
nion deceiue him ; but being the first that was fa-
ued from the water, he was set safe on shore &c.
and went to the Church, that being deliuered he
might geue thankes, and acknowledge the eternal
mysteries. Thus far *S. Ambrose*, whereunto
might be added a most memorable and vndoubted miracle shewed by God publickly a-
gainst a (q) *cleargie man in Lesmore* vpon his
denyal of the real presence, wrought aboue
400. yeres since, by the ministery of holy *Ma-*
lachias, who was (r) *one of the Monckrs of Ben-*
char and afterwardes *Bishop* and legate to the
Pope : it is reported by *S.* (s) *Bernard*, who
as he liued in that time, and was most (2)
familiar and conuersant with *Malachias,* and

Bernardus in vita Malachiæ
saith, *fuit quidam Clericus*
in Lesmor &c .is sciolus in
oculis suis presumsit dicere
in Encharistia esse tantumo-
do Sacramentum et non rem
Sacramenti, id est solam
sanctificationem, non corpo-
ris veritatem &c. Domi-
nus (inquit Malachias) ve-
ritatem te fateri faciat
vel ex necessitate, quo respon-
dente Amen, soluitur Con-
uentus, tali ille inustus cau-
terio, fugam meditatur &c.
cum ecce subita correptus
infirmitate sistit gradum,

deficiens

(3) present

viribusq́, ~~efficiens~~*, eodem loco iactat se super solum, anhelus et fessus, forte in-*
cidens in id loci vagabundus infantis offendit hominem, quidnam vbi agat per-
contatur, respondit graui se infirmitate teneri &c . et ille, infirmitas ista haud
alia inquit quam ipsa mors est, hoc autem non dixit a seipso, sed pulchre Do-
minus per insanum corripuit eum qui sanis acquiescere noluit &c. et addit
reuertere Domum, ego te iuuabo, deniq́ ipso duce reuertitur in ciuitatem,
edit reddit *ad cor, et ad misericordiam Domini, eadem hora accitur Episcopus, ag-*
noscitur veritas, abycitur error, confessus reatum, absoluitur, petit Viaticum,
datur reconciliatio, et vno pane momento, perfidia ore abdicatur, et morte dilu-
itur : ita mirantibus cunctis sub omni celeritate completus est sermo Malachiæ.
(r) See *Hollinshead Cronicle* of Ireland after the edition of *An.* 1577.
in the historie thereof next after the discription. pag. 13. ' (s)
Bernardus, in vita Malachiæ. (2) See *Hollinshead vbi supra.* and *S.*
Bernard in his preface *in vitam Malachiæ.* saith, *deinde sepultus apud nos*
est, nobis specialiter hoc opus incumbit, quid quod me inter speciales amicos
sanctus ille habebat &c. nec mercede mihi vacat tanta familiaritas sanctita-
tis. in so much as *Osiander in epitom. hist. Ecclef. Cent .*12. pag. 315.
confesseth saying of *Malachias, S. Bernardo admodum familiaris fuit,*
eius Monachatum admiratus et imitatus est &c. mortuus est in Claraualle.

the

the place of *S*. *Bernardes* then aboade, and where-ofhe was then Abbot.

(3)

S. *Bernard* in his said preface saith, *Accucurri ego vt benedictio morituri super me veniret, at ille cum iam membra alia mouere non posset, fortis ad dandam benedictione eleuatis sanctis manibus super caput meum benedixit mihi, et benedictionem hareditate possideo, quomodo ergo illum silere queam?* And afterwardes towardes the end of his tract, he describeth at large the maner of his blessed death and his owne presence thereat.

(4)

So credible that in the end of his foresaid preface

(3) *present at his death,* so is he likewise an author so graue and (4) *credible* that our aduersaries do acknowledge him for (t) *a Saint,* (u) *a godly writer,* (x) *a good Father; and one of the Lampes of the Church of God.* And another miracle no lesse, if not more wonderful, shewed specially in confutation of the foresaid error by the ministery of *S*. *Anthony*, is in like maner (y) reported by *Surius and Antoninus:* Hitherto concerning the real presence of Christes body in the Sacrament vpon the Preistes consecration, and before the receiuing thereof.

That after consecration, the Sacrament was shewed to the people, with eleuation thereof.

SECTION. 7.

C Onsecration being ended, and the real presence as before acknowledged, the Sacrament is shewed to the people: In the Greeke Church the Preist was, in reguard of the

he saith, *sane narrationis veritas apud me secura est &c.* (t) *M. Whitaker* against *M. William Raynoldes,* pag. 125. and 126. and also *l. de Ecclesia contra Bellarmin.* pag. 369. (u) *Caluin institut. c. 10. sect.* 17. (x) *Pasquils* returne into England printed, 1589. pag. 8. and 13. (y) *Surius tom. 3. et Antoninus in summa historiali. pag. 3. tit.* 24. *c. 3. parag. 2.* report, how that *S*. *Antony of Padua* disputing against one of the Albigenses who denying the real presence, the heretickes hearing of the wonders then formerly wrought by *S*. *Antony* said, *habes iumentum cui per integrum triduum cibum non dabo, exacto triduo, adsis tu cum Sacramento, ego adero cum iumento, atq̃ ante illum hordeum effundam, si iumentum hordeo derelicto ad Sacramenti venerationem accesserit, credam.* which was afterwardes put in execution with miraculous and answearable successe to the heretickes confutation.

(z) *Chrisostom.*

the greater reuerence and maiesty of this dreadful mystery, copassed with *a veale til consecration* was ended, which done, (z) *the veale (saith Chrisostome) was withdrawen, the sacrifice brought forth, and Christ offered.* Of this shewing of the Sacramēt to the people, further mention is made by *Dionisius* (a) *Areopagita,* and also by *S.* (b) *Basile,* whose wordes do import a *shewing* made euen with *lifting vp:* sundry Fathers mentioning also *eleuation,* whereof *S. Basile,* and *Chrisostome* say, (c) *the Preist bowing downe him selfe, taketh the portion which is in the holy Paten, and holding it a litle vp saith, Sancta Sanctis:* And the auncient writer of the scholies vpon *Dionisius* doth in his fore alledged place meane *the eleuation of the diuine breade which the Bishop lifteth vp.* As also *Germanus* Bishop of *Constantinople,* mentioneth *the* (*) *eleuation of* (Christes) *venerable body,* and how that *the Preist subleuateth the diuine bread: and with the venerable and quickning bread, maketh three times the signe of the Crosse in the aier.* Of this eleuation further answearable mention is made by (4) *Pelagius* the second, and sundry

(z)
Chrisostom. ad Pop. hom. 61. *circa med.* saith, *dum hic profertur sacrificium, et Christus immolatur, et ouis Dominica, cum audieris, oremus omnes communiter, cùm vela videris retrahi, tunc superne cælum appetiri; cogita et Angelos descendere* &c.

(a)
Dionisius, de Eccles. Hierarch. c. 3. saith, *Pontifex* &c. *sacrosancta et augustissima mysteria conficit, et quâ ante laudauerat venerandis operta átq; abdita signis, in conspectum agit, diuinaq; munera renerenter ostendens* &c.

(b)
Basil. de spiritu, Sanct. c. 27. see next hereafter at the letter f.

(c) *Chrisostom. in Liturg.* saith, *Pontifex exaltans panem dicit* &c. *Sancta Sanctis.* and see *Basil. in Liturgia.* A thing so euident that the Protestant writer *Eusebius Altkircherus de mystico et incruento sacrificio,* printed 1584. *Neustady Palatinorum.* pag. 348. alledgeth *S. Basils Liturgie* in these wordes; *Deinde Sacerdos extendit manus, et tangit sanctum panem, ad hoc vt faciat sanctam eleuationem, et Diaconus dicit, attendamus; tunc Sacerdos exaltans sanctum panem exclamat, Sancta Sanctis.* And see him there *pag.* 105. alledging the very same forme of wordes from *Chrisostomes Lyturgie.* (*) *Germanus Constantinopolitanus,* who liued *Anno.* 720. *in Theoria.* saith, *elatio in altum venerandi corporis representat Crucis elationem* &c. *quod autem subleuat Sacerdos diuinum panem et signum Crucis ter facit inaere cum venerabili et viuifico pane, id innuit* &c.

(4) The Centuristes, *cent.* 6. *col.* 675. sayth of *Pelagius* the second

(who liued within the firſt 600. yeares) *vt memoria defunctorum fieret in omni Myſſa poſt eleuationem hoſtiæ ſalutaris conſtituit Pelagius.*

(d)

Georgius Presbiter, who liued *Anno.* 620. *in vita Theodori Archimandritæ.* ſaith, *cum beatus Theodorus ſacrificaret, dum, vt regionis eſt mos, diſcum in ſublime tolleret, vt ſanctum panem oſtenderet &c.* And *Damaſcen,* who liued *Anno.* 730. *in Triſagio.* ſaith, *in eleuatione panis Euchariſtiæ nos non dicimus triſagios &c. ſed vnus ſanctus &c.* Rabanus *Maurus,* who liued *Anno.* 850. *de inſtitut. Clericorum, l.* 1. *c.* 34. ſaith, *eleuatio* Sacerdotis *et Diaconi corporis et ſanguinis Chriſti eleuationem eius ad Crucem inſinuat &c.* And *Amalarius Treuerenſis de officijs Ecclesiaſt. l.* 3. *c.* 24. ſaith, *quod actitatur a Sacerdote quando ſuſcipit oblatam in ſecreta Myſſæ, aut quando hic eam eleuat,* he liued *Anno.* 820. (e) *Hoſpinianus in hiſt. Sacramentaria, l.* 4. *pag.* 285. and *l.* 3. *pag.* 187. ſaith, *panem et calicem conſecratum eleuarunt, vt a populo conſpici poſſent.* To which purpoſe he there alledgeth *Damaſcen* and *Rabanus.* (f) *Baſil. de ſpiritu ſancto. c.* 27. reckning vp certaine vnwriten Traditions ſaith, *Inuocationis verba, dum oſtenditur panis Euchariſtiæ et poculum benedictionis, quis ſcripto reliquit?* That this praier was made at the *eleuation* is confeſſed by the Proteſtant writer *Euſebius Altkircherus de myſtico et incruento ſacrificio &c. pag.* 79. where, hauing recyted this very place, and ſaying of *S. Baſile,* he ſetteth downe in the margent thereof the performance of this prayer to be *in eleuatione, videlicet, cum dicitur attendamus.* ſee alſo next heretofore in the margent at c.

ſundry other (d) Fathers who liued in the ages following, in ſo much as (e) *Hoſpinianus* a Caluiniſt writer acknowledgeth the ſame.

That the Sacrament was adored, with a continued courſe of teſtimonies thereof vp to the Apoſtles age.

SECTION. 8,

AFter this next followeth *Adoration of the Sacrament,* our anſwearable practiſe whereof S. *Baſile* ſignifyeth mentioning expreſly that there was vſed a preſcript forme of prayer or (f) *wordes of inuocation whiles the bread of the Euchariſt, and cup of bleſſing were ſhewed:* but to proceede with the anſwearable obſeruation hereof throughout al ages. Firſt

(g) the

First concerning the age present, the practise thereof is euident in the Churches of (g) Æthiopia, and the (2) *oriental India,* also in the *Greeke Churches,* at (h) *Venice,* and at (i) *Constantinople* ; and in the publicke (k) *Lyturgie* of the Greeke Church : And as for the Latine Church of this age *Erasmus* (whom our aduersaries do greatly esteeme) saith hereof, (l) *hitherto with al Christians haue I adored Christ in the Eucharist, neither do I yet see any cause why I ought to depart from that opinion, I can by no humane reason be withdrawen from the agreeable indgment of the whole world.* Martin

(g) The reuerence of the *Aethiopianes* was so much aboue ordinary, that *Zaga* Zabo, the Æthiopian Embassador in *confessione fidei Aethiopica. Anno.* 1576. saith, *nec Sacerdoti, nec Laico &c.* *Assumpta venerabili Eucharistia, licet expuere a tempore matutino vsq, ad occasum solis.* See this yet further testifyed in the history of *Africke*

in english. printed, *Anno.* 1600. *pag.* 400. where it is said of the Aethiopians *the Sacramentes being receiued, they may not vnder paine of greauous punishment,* so much as once *spit til the going downe of the Sunne* . And see *Aluarez* &c. in the French treatise entituled, *Histoire de le Aethiopie descript . per Dom. Francis. Aluerez. &c.* printed, *Anno.* 1558. *c.* 80. *fol.* 194. (2) *Ioannes Petrus Maffeius in hist . India. l. 2. circa med.* saith of the now Christians in the remote nations of the Oriental *India* conuerted by S . *Thomas* the Apostle : *Altaris mysteria religiose venerantur, eoq; viatico decedentes e vita se muniunt.* (h) *Graci Venetijs habitantes.* *Ad quast.* 6. *Gardinalis Guisiam, num Sacerdos aliquando rem sacram peragit, populo non presente, sed tantum homine vno, et an Laici Eucharistiam congeniculando venerantur.* the answeare of the Gretians hereto is, *Sacerdos rem sacram populo non presente peragit, saltem cum puero, qui &c. ei respondere possit: cui quidem actioni cum Laici adsunt, ad terram vsq, coram Eucharistia religiose cum reuerentia procedunt .* (i) *Hieremias Constant . resp . 2. c. 4.* saith, *qua propter cū omni reuerentia &c. accedamus ad Eucharistiā &c. honoremus vero illam omni munditia tum nimi tum corporis.* this is extant in the booke published by the diuines of *Witenberge,* entituled *Acta. &c. Theologorum Wittenbergentium et Patriacha Constantinopolitani D. Hieremia &c.* pag 241 . (k) *Ecclesia Grecorū nostro tempore in Lyturgia mysteriorum ante consecrationem .* it is said, *tunc capit sacrum panem Sacerdos cum accomodata veneratione &c. statim ingreditur Sacerdos ad sanctam mensam, et deponit, sancta adorans, et Thure adolens omni cum reuerentia &c.* (l) *Erasmus, l. 9. epist. epist. ad Pellicanum.*

Pellicanum, cuius initium | in *Luther* did write a special (m) booke of
est, Euangelij vigor. | this argument, and he and his followers, do
(m) | so manifestly (n) teach this adoration, that
Entituled *de adoratione* | the Sacramentaries did therefore (o) repre-
Sacramenti ad Fratres. | hend him; of which their reprehension *Lu-*
(n) | *ther* him selfe taketh notice saying (p) *they*
Georgius Princeps Anhal- | *mocke vs at their pleasure, calling vs shamefull*
dinus præposit. Magdeburg. | *eaters*

Conc. 4. *de Sacramento Altaris. fol.* 188. affirmeth that *Anno.* 1541.
*he conferred with Luther vpon this point, whereupon it was resolued that Christ is
to be adored in the Sacrament no lesse then was the holy Ghost descending in
the forme of a doue.* And *Timotheus Kirchmerus in thesauro &c. fol.* 586.
ex Genesi. tom. 4. *fol.* 182. *c.* 47. teacheth out of *Luther* and saith,
*cum in ea credamus adesse verum corpus et sanguinem cum verbo &c. sic bo-
num est quod Sacramentum Altaris colitur inflexis genibus, quia ibi est verum corpus Domini &c.* And *Martin Chemnitius* in his examen, *part.* 2.
pag. 91. affirmeth this point of adoration to be *(extra controuersiam)*
out of controuersie betweene him and vs Catholickes. and *vide ibidem
pag.* 92. and *ibidem. pag.* 94. he saith, *quando vero interior et spiritualis
hæc deuotio, veneratio et adoratio in corde exitata est, tunc externæ significati-
ones in reuerentia et veneratione huius Sacramenti recte et sponte sequentur
&c. tali externa confessione seiungimus nos a Sacramentarijs &c.* This
point of adoring the Sacrament, is so euident and confessed in *the
Lutherans,* that they are therefore specially reprehended by *Melancton*:
See his seuerall epistles hereof extant in *Caluins* booke of Epistles in
Latine. *epist.* 187. *pag.* 341. and *epist.* 214. *pag.* 400. (o) *Vide
Apolog. modest. ad acta Conuentus quindecim theologorum torgæ nuper habit.
pag.* 40. and *Caluin in epist. et respons. epist.* 93. *pag.* 209. saith, *quor-
sum enim illud Lutheri adorabile Sacramentum, nisi vt Idolum in templo Dei
erigatur.* And Suiuglius (*tom.* 2. *ad Lutheri librum de Sacramento responso.
fol.* 384.) saith to Luther, *præterea vt panem & vinum non adorari debere intelligant, vt tu extra omnem diuina veritatis consensum, in libro de ado-
ratione Sacramenti, docere non es veritus &c.* (p) Luther, *tom.* 7.
Wittenberg. de Euchristia. fol. 235. *et vide loc. com. Lutheri. quin.
clas. c.* 15. *pag.* 48. *et vide Conradum Schlusselburg. in catal. hæreticorum. l.* 13. *et ultimo. pag.* 867. in so much as the Caluinistes of
Geneua in their *Apologia modesta ad acta Conuentus quindecim theologorum
torgæ nuper habit.* printed *Geneua.* 1575. *pag.* 40. hauing recyted certaine

taine sayinges of Luther, testifying his adoration of the Sacrament, do conclude and say of *Luther*, that *ipsum nec panem adorabilem et sensit et scripsit*. And *Zepperus* the Caluinist, *in his politia Ecclesiastica &c*. printed *Herbonæ* 1607. *pag*. 9. chargeth his Lutheran brethren saying, *adhuc visuntur et defenduntur &c. Altaria, hostia, seu panes numularij, corporalia, et Calices consecrati, sacrorum simbolorum in ora communicantium ingestio, verborum sacræ cænæ institutionis, quoties sacra simbola deficiunt, repetitio, eleuatio, et adoratio Christi impanati &c. hisq; similia quorum colluuies et sordes in plurimis Euangelicorum Ecclesijs secundum magis et minus etiam nunc hodie inueniuntur*.

eaters of flesh, and drinkers of bloud, and that we worship a god made of bread. Before this time the denyal of the Sacrameures adoration was (3) *Anno. Dom*. 1384. impugned as new & singuler in *Ioannes Muntziger*. And before this againe did *Lyra*, who liued *Anno*. 1300. and whom D. *Whitgaift* tearmeth (q) a reuerend Father of singuler vertue and learning, affirme and defend this adoration saying, (r) the visible formes are not adored as God, but Christ him selfe being inuisible under those formes: And it was as then so vniuersal that *Vrbane the fourth*, who liued about *Anno*. 1260. did in regaurd thereof, and of the then late priuate contradiction of heretickes, (7) institute the festiual day of corpus Christi. *Honorius the third*, liued about *Anno*. 1220. his (4) institution, which our aduersaries do so wilfully misaply, was not a general beginning of adoration then before not vsed (for no aduersary (5) writer

(3) *In Catalog. testium veritatis*, printed. *Anno*. 1597. *tom*. 2. *pag*. 794.

(q) M. *Whitguift* in his defence &c. *pag*. 434.

(r) *Lyra aduersus Iudæum impugnatorem Euangelij secundum Mathæum*. and he explaneth it there by a like similitude saying, *similiter habetur quodammodo Exod*. 3. *vbi dicitur, quod Dominus apparuit Moysi in flamma ignis de medio rubi, et non est dubium, quin Moyses adoraret eum quando Dominus dixit ipsi, solue calceamentum de pedibus tuis, locus in quo stas terra sancta est &c. Deum &c. sed adorauit Deum inuisibilem sub similitudine inuisibili apparentem.* (7) This institution is cófessed by *Chemnitius, examen. part*. 2. *pag*. 95. (4) *Honorius tertius, l*. 3. *decretalium, tit*. 41. *de celebr. Missa*. saith, *Sacerdos frequenter doceat plebem suam, vt cum in celebratione Missarum eleuatur hostia salutaris, se reuerenter inclinat &c*. (5) No aduersarie writer, for there were

nec adorauit illum ignem seu flammam tanquam

ter

A 2
in that

in that age many aduersaries to the Romane Church as appeareth by *Ofiander, in epift. hift. Ecclefiaft. cent.* 9. 10. 11. 12. 13. *&c.* as namely the Albigenfes. *pag.* 329. the *Georgians. pag.* 340. *Raymundus Lullus. pag.* 341. *Arnoldus de noua villa. pag.* 344. the heretickes called *Athoci. pag.* 348. the *Maronites. pag.* 350. the *Armenians. pag.* 352. the *Flagellantes. pag.* 372. *Ioannes de Poliaco. pag.* 384. and the *Begardi. pag.* 347. of which fome were condemned for denying the real prefence, and fome alfo, as namely *the Begardi,* for their then finguler *denyal of adoration to the Sacrament in time of eleuation,* whereof fee *Ofiander, ibidem. pag.* 413. And *Crifpinus* in his booke of the eftate of the Church. *pag.* 397. and yet of al thefe no one is found to haue charged either *Vrbane the fourth, or Honorius the third,* with any innouation or chaunge in doctrine, in either of their forefaid decrees.

(6)

The Greeke Church con- *ter* of that time, no not the (6) *Gretians* *tinued at variance and* (though then, and afterwardes deuided from *diuided from the Roman,* the Roman Church) do fo charge him. *M.* *both before and after the* *D. Sparke* affirming that not fo much as *knee-* *forfaid decree of Honorius.* *ling at Communion* was firft (7) *brought* in by *As Anno. Dom.* 1138. *Honorius*

(*Ofiander, cent.* 12. *pag.* 261. & 262.) And *Anno.* 1245. *ibidem. pag.* 361. which was about 80. *yeares* before *Honorius* his faid decree, and 25. yeares after the fame. And the like variance or diuifion, was at fundry other times afterwardes, and is fuch likewife at this prefent day ; and therefore *the Gretians* being fo at variance with the *Roman Church,* would neuer haue beene fo fparing as to conceale an innouation of this importance, but (if fo that truly they might haue done it) would in al probability haue charged the Roman Church with innouation herein ꞓ whereas they not onely lay no fuch imputation to the *Roman Church,* but (moft directly to the contrary) do yet to this day (though being at variance with the Roman Church) profeffe them felues to teach and practife this adoration. whereof fee the *Greekes* at *Venice. Ad quaft.* 6. *Cardinalis Guifiani.* And alfo *Hieremias Conftantinopolitanus, refponf.* 2. *c.* 4. alledgeth heretofore in this prefent fection in the margent at h. i. In fo much as the faid *Hieremias* in his booke publifhed and printed by the Proteftant diuines of *Wittenberge. Anno.* 1584. affirmeth moft plainely in feueral places thereof, their vndoubted doctrine of *tranfubftantiation.* As *pag.* 96. and 100. and 240. againft which opi-,
nion.

nion of the Greekes so signifyed, the said Protestantes do there professe to write, *pag.* 318. (7) See this in *M. Sparkes* brotherly perswasion to vnity, printed. 1607. *pag.* 16. (8)

Honorius, but was cleane to the contrary a particuler (8) ordinance for Preistes to admonish the Laye people against their late former negligence in that behalfe: In so much as *Cesarius Heisterbachius*, who was as auncient as (s) *Honorius* mentioneth an other like precedent decree of *Cardinal Wido* for the peoples adoration vpon hearing of *the sacring bel.* Before these times liued *Odo Parisiensis, Anno.* 1170. who admonished (in like maner as did *Honorius*) saying, *let the* (t) *laye people be often admonished, that wheresoeuer they see the body of Chrift to be caried, they ftraight way bowe their knees as to their Lord and creator, praying with ioyned handes &c.* Before this liued the heathē Philosopher *Auerroes* (9) *Anno.* 1142. in whose time the doctrine of the real presece, and of adoring Chrift in the Sacrament, was so knowen and receiued, that he therefore in contempt of Chriftians said, (10) *I haue trauailed ouer the world, I haue found diuers sectes, but none so foolifh as is the fect of Chriftians, for they deuoure with their teeth their God whom they do adore:* In so much that *M. Fulke* inferreth hereupon, that in those times (11) *the Popifh idolatry gaue great offence to the heathen.* so fully doth he ioyne with *Auerroes* in charging and reiecting that age with our foresaid Catholicke adoration of Chrift in the Sacrament. Before this time liued S. *Bernard, An.* 1130. who also admonisheth saying (u) *adore with*

A peculiar ordinance, for had it bene an innouation of doctrine then before not beleeued, it would then haue bene general both to *Preistes* and *laye men,* but being as it is a particuler admonition onely for Preistes to inftruct the *laye people,* it agueth sufficiently the Preistes former beleefe thereof, and the *laye* peoples latter negligence.

(s)

Cesarius Heisterbachius l. 9. *c.* 51. saith, *Wido Cardinalis prœcepit, vt ad eleuationem hostiœ, omnis populus in Ecclesia, ad sonitum nolœ veniam peteret &c. prœcepit etiam idem Cardinalis, vt quoties deferendum esset ad infirmum scholaris siue campanarius Sacerdotem precedens, per nolam illud proderet, sicq̃ omnis populus, tam in ftratis, quam in domibus, Chriftū adoret.*

(t)

Odo Parisiensis in finodicis constitutionibus . cap. 5. *de Sacramento Altaris.*

(9) See *M. Coupers Chronicle, fol.* 208. *Fulke* against *Hefkins, Sanders &c.* *pag.* 235.

(10) Alledged by *M. Fulke ibidem.*

(11) *M. Fulke ibidem.*

A a 2 and

and *M. D. Sutliue*, in his abridgement or suruey of Popery. *c. 47. pag. 295.* faith accordingly, *Auerroes, of al religions accompteth Poperie to be most absurde, for that Papistes worship a peece of a Masse cake for their God, and yet presently deuoure him into their bellies.* (u) *Bernard de cæna Domini ad Petrum Presbiterum.*

(5)
Suriani Sacramentis nostris nullam exhibent reuerentiam, nec assurgere volunt quando corpus Domini ad Visitandos infirmos nostri deferūt Sacerdotes. so faith *Iacobus Vitriacus, historiæ Orientalis. c. 75.*

(x)
Algerus de Sacramento Altaris. l. 2. c. 3. fine.

(y)
Simeon Metaphrastes, in vita Stephani Iunioris. faith, *quid an tu quoq, corporis et sanguinis Christi Antytypa ab Ecclesia proscribes? vt qua imaginem et veram illorum figuram teneant, qua et adoramus et osculamur, et eorum preceptione sanctitatem consequamur.* And *Damascen. l. 4. c. 13.* faith, *ipsum porro omni puritate cola-*

with more deuotion, and worship more often in the Sacrament of the Alter, the saluation of the world that suffereth for thee.

(2) Before him, the adoration of the Sacrament was so general, that the heretickes called *Suriani*, were *Anno. Dom. 1100.* specially condemned for their then singuler impugning of this adoration, as is most plainly testifyed by *Iacobus* (5) *Vitriacus*, who was liuing at the time of *Honorius* his foresaid decree. Before this againe liued *Algerus, An. 1060.* who faith hereof (x) *with this faith do we adore (ipsum Sacramentum) the Sacrament it selfe as being a diuine thing, and to it, as being liuing and reasonable we speake and pray, Lambe of God that taketh away the sinnes of the world, haue mercy vpon vs, because (not which is seene but which truly is) we beleeue Christ to be there.* I omit purposly the more (y) auncient testimonies of *Simeon Metaphrastes, Paschasius, Damascen, Beda &c.* who liued in the seuerall ages next before, and are (z) confessed clearly to haue taught the real presence, whereof adoration is (as our aduersaries confesse) (z) a necessary sequele: in so much as our aduersarie

mus, hoc est spirituali ac corporea, siquidem duplex ipse est ardenti cupiditate, ad eum adeamus, manibusq, in Crucis formam compositis crucifixi corpus suscipiamus. And *Ioannes Climachus,* who liued *Anno. 580. gard. 23.* faith hereof, *quid est quod domum cæleste suscipiens adoro.* and *Iustinianus Imperator,* who liued *Anno. 530.* (in *Authentica de priuilegij dotis hæreticis mulieribus non præstandis*) tearmeth it *sacrosanctam et adorabilem Communionem.* (z) See heretofore *tract. 2. sect. 2. subdiuis. 2.* at g. h.

i. me.

i . m . n . o . (2) See hereafter, *sect* . 9 . *subdiuis* . 2. in the margent at *. next after b.

sary *Pratorius*, speaking namely of (a) *Dama cen*, and charging him with *transubstantiation*, doth (to the further clearing of *Honorius the third*) confesse that there was vsed in (b) the yeare 735. the *adoration of bread as though it were Christ himselfe*: So confessedly for many seuerall ages before *Honorius the third*, was this adoration of the Sacrament publickly professed and in vse.

To make entry now within the first 400 . yeares after Christ, S. *Basile* mencioneth (as (3) before) a prescript forme of prayer or wordes of inuocation, *whiles the bread of the Euchariſt, and cup of bleſſing were ſhewed*. S . *Auguſtine* also writing vpon these wordes of the psalme (c) *worſhip ye the foote-ſtoole of his feete*: doth by the foote-ſtoole vnderſtand *earth*, and by *earth Chriſtes fleſh*, which he there (d) affirmeth *we are to adore*. And where D . *Bilſon* in his anſweare thereto, would confound eating with adoring, affirming that (e) *the very eating of it* (by faith) *is the adoring of it*, his afweare is *maladicta gloſſa*, as being ouer violent and againſt the very

(a)
Pratorius, *in l . de Sacramentis . pag*. 288.
(b)
Pratorius , *ibidem* . ſaith , Anno. 735. *ſubſecuta eſt panis adoratio ac ſi ipſo Chriſtus eſſet*. and *Carion in Chronic. pag* . 451. doth not onely charge *Damaſcen* moſt expreſſly with *tranſubſtantiation*, but doth alſo there (pag . 476 . & 477.) place *Artolatria*, *that is to ſay* (ſaith he) *the adoration of the reſerued and eleuated bread*, *(ſequentibus annis quingentis) within the ſecond* 500. *yeares after Chriſt*.

(3)
See heretofore in this ſection *ſubdiuiſ* . 1. ini - *tio* . in the margent at the letter f.

(c) *Pſal* . 98. (d) *Auguſtin. in Pſal* . 98 . ſaith, *alio loco Scripturæ dicit, Calum mihi ſedes eſt, terra autem ſcabellum pedum meorum ; Anceps factus ſum, timeo adorare terram, ne damnet me qui fecit cælum et terram, rurſum timeo non adorare ſcabellum pedum Domini mei, quia Pſalmus mihi dicit, adorate ſcabellum pedum eius: quæro quid ſit ſcabellum pedum eius? et dicit mihi Scriptura, terra ſcabellum pedum meorum : fluctuans conuerto me ad Chriſtum, quia ipſum quæro hic, et inuenio quomodo ſine impietate a- doretur terra, ſine impietate adoretur ſcabellum pedum eius, ſuſcepit enim de terra terram, quia caro de terra eſt, et de carne Mariæ carnem accepit, et quia in ipſa carne hic ambulauit, et ipſam carnem nobis manducandam ad ſalutem dedit, nemo autem illam carnem manducat niſi prius adorauerit, &c. ideo ad* pag. 251.

A a 3   *terram*

terram quamlibet cum te inclinas atq̃, prosternis, non quasi terram intuearis &c. (e) *M. Bilson* in his true difference, betwene Christian subiection, and vnchristian rebellion, *part.* 4. *pag.* 536.

(f)
August. vt supra.

(4)
This word *before* argu-eth that in *S. Augustines* iudgment it is Christes flesh, and present before *we eate it.*

(g)
Augustin. vt supra.

(h)
Ambros. de spiritu sancto l. 3. *c.* 12. saith, *per scabellum, terra intelligitur, per terram autem, caro Christi, quam hodie quoq̃, in mysterijs adoramus, et quam Apostoli in Domino Iesu, vt supra diximus, ado-rarunt.* so plainly hereby doth he compaire our a-doring of Chistes flesh in the Sacrament with the Apostles adoring of it in his visible humanity.

(i)
August. ex lib. sentent. Prosperi. cyted also by *Gratian. dist.* 2. *nos au-tem.* this saying is ac-knowledged to be *Au-gustines* by *Hospinianus in historia Sacramentaria. l.* 5. *pag.* 533. where with miserable terguiersation
he

very letter of S. *Augustines* wordes, who ex-pressly there distinguisheth *eating from adoring,* making, as we do, *adoring* in priority to *eating,* affirming to that end most directly in the very same place there, that *we are* (f) *to adore Christs flesh, before* (4) *we eate it:* in so much as he proceedeth yet further saying, (g) *when thou doest bowe downe and prostrate thy selfe to euery earth, behould it not as earth:* So plainly do his wordes expresse our external *bowing & prostra-ting of our selues, ad terram quamlibet,* euen to *euery earth* (or Sacrament) *which we behold*; for these wordes cannot be said to concerne that adoration which is due to his body as it re-maineth alwaies present to vs, after one and the same maner in *heauen,* because the wor-des *euery earth,* are improper and repugnant to that sence; therefore they must needes concerne that special kind of external reue-rence and *prosternation,* which in our often & renewed celebration of the publicke Lytur-gie, is by vs diuersly (according to the diuer-sity of time and place) exhibited *ad terram quamlibet,* to euery consecrated *host* which we behold. And so S. *Ambrose* in like maner re-ferreth this adoration to the Sacrament say-ing (h) *by the foote-stoole is vnderstoode the earth, and by earth, the flesh of Christ, which we also do at this day adore* (not mystically or in a myste-ry, but *in mysterijs*) in the mysteries of the ex-ternal elementes of the Sacrament: As S. *Au-gustine* in like maner saith, (i) *we do truly ho-nor in forme of bread and wine which we see, thin-ges inuisible, that is to say, flesh and bloud.* To
omit

omit aswel S . (k) *Augustines* sundry other
plaine sayinges, and S . *Ambrose* his contes-
sed, and by our aduersaries (l) reiected iudgement of adoration, as also the vnworthy *scan-*
dals or opinions thereat in this age conceiued
by (*) *the heathen* not vnlike to that which

he laboureth in vaine to
answear it.

is
table and receiue of his body and bloud, but they adore onely (saith he *) and*
are not filled . And *in Psal . 21 . con . 1 .* he further saith of them, *the*
rich haue eaten the body of their Lord, and are not filled as the poore are, yet
notwithstanding they haue adored . That these places cannot be meant
of adoring and eating spiritually is euident, in that al sides do agree
that the wicked (of whom S . *Augustine* here speaketh) do not adore and
eate spiritually : onely therefore they are to be vnderstoode of Christes
body in the Sacrament, which the wicked comming to the Lordes
table, did vnworthily eate and externally onely adore . see also further
S . *Augustine epist . 118 . ad Ianuarium . c . 3 . (*l*) Ambros . in orat .*
præparat . ad Myssam . is so plaine herein, that *the Century writers, cent .*
4 . *col . 430 .* do therefore reproue those prayers saying, *continent ado-*
rationem panis in Sacramento . And M . *Parkins* in his *Problema de Roma-*
næ fidei ementito Catholicismo . pag . 21 . doth therefore likewise reiect
them saying, *preces preparatrices ad Missam, non sunt Ambrosij .* whereof
he geueth this onely reason saying, *ibi adoratio Sacramenti .* And *Cri-*
spinus in his booke of the estate of the Church, *pag . 87 .* saith, *the two*
preparatiue praiers shuffled into the workes of Ambrose, containe errors, as the
adoration of the Sacrament, inuocation of Sainctes &c . And yet are these
praiers acknowledged and alledged by the late superintendent of
Winchester, as the writing of S . *Ambrose,* in his true difference &c .
part . 4 . pag . 622 . (*) Scandals of the heathen, for S . *Augustine, l .*
20 . *contra Faustum Manich . c . 13 .* saith of the heathen ; *nos propter pa-*
nem ac Calicem , Cererem, et librum, colore existimant . whereto he answeareth saying , *a cerere et libro, Paganorum Dijs, longe absumus, quamuis pa-*
nis et Calicis Sacramentum, nostro ritu amplectamur . why were Christians
thus charged to worship *Baccus* & *ceres* for the Sacramental *bread* & *cup,*
rather then *Neptune* for the water in Baptisme, were it not in respect
of the honour then peculiarly exhibited by Christians to this holy Sa-
crameut ? In like further manifestation whereof, *Maximus Madau-*
rensis)a heathen writer) in his epistle to S . *Augustine,* extant in S .
August.

Augustin. tom. 2. epist. 43. post. med. demaundeth of S. *Augustine* sayiug, *illud quaso vir sapientissime &c. ipsa re approbes, quis sit iste Deus quem vobis Christiani quasi proprium vendicatis, et in locis abditis præsentem vos videre componitis? &c.* how did this opinion of the heathen, conceipting that Christians worshiped and *saw their God present in secret places,* arise otherwise, then from the blessed Sacrament, in which they honoured Christ really *present,* celebrating the same in their Churches which were kept *secret* or priuate from the *vnworthy eyes of Cathecumines and vnbeleeuers,* as appeareth heretofore in the preface to the reader, *sect.* 11. *fine.* at 18. *& tract.* 2. *sect.* 1. *subd.* 1. after p. at the figure 2. and *tract.* 2. *sect.* 8. *subdiuis.* 3. at k. 1.

(4)

Next heretofore, *subduis.* 1. at the figures 10. 11. next before u.

(m)

Theodoret. dial. 2. wheras the *Eutichian* hereticke affirming (as heretofore *tract.* 2. *sect.* 2. *subdiuis.* 2. *fine.* at x.) *Christes body to be after his assumption changed into his diuinity,* doth in colorable example thereof, alledge the Churches knowen doctrine of *trasubstantiation,* which his argument *Theodoret* setteth downe by induction of the heretickes person, and is reproued by the *Centuristes* heretofore. *tract.* 2. *sect.* 2. *subdiuis.* 2. *fine.* at x. y. for his so setting downe of the same. *Theodoret* vndertaking there to impugne the hererickes foresaid opinion of Christes body being so changed into the diuinity, and being thereupon occasioned to deny the real presence, for that but denyed, had quite ouerthrowne the heretickes foresaid argument, he not onely not denyeth the same, but answeareth further the heretickes said obiection, and saith of *the mystical signes, that though they did* (vnto sence, otherwise then the heretickes taught of Christs body being changed) *abide in their former substance, figure, and forme, and may be seene and felt,* as before consecration: *intelliguntur autem ea esse quæ facta sunt &c.* yet (faith he as enforced) *to vnderstanding and faith, they are the thinges which they are made, (& adorantur vt quæ illa sunt quæ creduntur) and they are adored as being the*

is heretofore reported of (4) *Aueroes.* And to proceede with the precedent times, like as we say, according to vsual speach, that *we adore the Sacrament,* not meaning thereby that we adore the outward formes, but onely Christ, whom we beleeue to be there present: So that auncient Father *Theodoret,* with like wordes and meaning faith, (m) *the mystical Symbols are adored as being the same thinges they*

thinges

thinges which they are beleeued. And whereas *M. Bilson* (in his true difference, *part. 4. pag. 557.*) and *M. Abbot* (against *Paul Spence* Preist, *pag.* 107.) wil not hereby vnderstand diuine honour, it is to be obserued (to the contrary) that *Theodoret* referreth here the same word of *worshipping* to the holy mysteries, which within few lines next after in the very same place he referreth to Christes *immortal body sitting on the right hand of God.* And the said word so by him vsed alike in both places being *Pros cuneo,* which (as *M. Fulke* against *M. Martin, c.* 19. *pag.* 479. confesseth) signifyeth that worship which is made with *bowing* or genuflection of the body, and being so euidently as here referred by *Theodoret,* not as from man to man, which might make it *Ciuile,* but to the Sacrament, argueth the said adoring to be more then *Ciuil,* and no lesse then *religiouse, expresly forbidden* (saith *M. Fulke, vbi supra*) *to any creature.* To the denyal of which said adoration, and of the real presence, if truth had permitted, *Theodoret* was altogether compelled by the heretickes foresaid alledged argument so euidently taken from the Churches the knowen doctrine of transubstantiation, which *Theodoret* setteth downe, & is therfore therein reprehendded as beforesaid by *Virp: iii* the *Centurie writers.* see further hereof at large *tract. 2. sect. 11. subdiuis. 3.* at a. b. c. &c.

they are beleeued. To omit *S.* (n) *Ciril, S. Chrisostome* also testifyeth this adoration saying, (o) *I wil shew thee vpon earth (and not in heauen onely) that which is worthy of great honor &c.* euen *the kingly body in heauen which is now set before thee on earth to be seene.* And againe he saith most plainly (p) *this body did*

(n)
Ciril. mistagog. catech. 5. faith, *accedens ad Communionem non expansis manum vobis accede, neq; cum disiunctis digitis, sed sinistram veluti sedem quanda the subijcias dextra qua tantum regem susceptura est, & concaua manu suscipe corpus Christi, dicens Amen & c. tum vero post Communionem corporis Christi, accede ad Calicem sanguinis illius, non extendens manus, sed pronus adorationis in modum et venerationis dicens. Amen.* (o) *Chrisost. in 1. Cor. hom. 24. quod summo honore dignum est, id tibi in terra ostendam, nam quemadmodum in regia non parietes, non tectum aureum, sed regium corpus in throno sedens, omnium præstantissimum est, ita quoq; in cælis regium corpus, quod nunc in terra tibi videndum proponitur, non Angelos neq; Archangelos, non cælos, non cælos cælorum, sed ipsum horum omnium tibi Dominum ostendo. Animaduertis quonam pacto quod omnium maximum est atq; præcipuum, in terra non conspicaris tantum, sed tangis,*

B b   neq;

neq̑ folum tangis fed comedis &c. (p) *Chrifoft. ibidem.* faith, *hoc corpus in præcepi reueriti funt magi, et viri impij, & Barbari, longe itinere confecti, cum timore et tremore plurimo adorauerunt : Imitemur igitur faltē Barbaros nos qui cælorum ciues fumus &c. tu vero non in præfepi id, fed in Altari, non mulierem quæ vlnis teneat, fed Sacerdotem præfentem et fpiritum perabunde fuper propofito diffufum facrificio vides.*

(5)

This matching of *Altar* with the *manger*, argueth *Chrifoftomes* meaning to be that he is now prefent and to be adored on *the Altar* no leffe truly then he was prefent and

the *wife men worfhip in the manger &c. Let vs therefore imitate thofe ftrangers &c. thou feeft it not in the manger but* (5) *on the Altar, not a woman which houldeth it in her armes, but a Preift prefent:* which his meaning of adoring Chrift vpon the Altar is fo plaine in thefe and (6) other his fayinges, that he alfo admonifheth vs to (7) *pray to him* (as he is) *lying thereon,* affirming

adored in *the manger.* And fo accordingly doth S. *Chrifoftom. in orat. de S. Perhilogonio,* explaine him felfe faying, *truly this table fulfilleth the place of the manger, for here alfo is our Lordes body laid.* (6) In the *Lyturgy of Chrifoftome* it is prefcribed and faid, *thou that fitteft aboue with the Father, and art here prefent with vs inuifible, vouchfaife to geue vnto vs thy vndefyled body, and thy precious bloud, and by vs to al the people, then the Preift adoreth, and the Deacon in the place where he is, thrife fayeth fecretly : God be merciful to me a finner, and al the people likewife with godlines and reuerence do adore.* And fee the Proteftant writer *Eufebius Altkircherus, de myftico et incruento facrificio.* printed, *Neuftadij Palatinorum.* 1584. pag. 349. cyted from the Lyturgies of S. *Bafile* and S. *Chrifoftome,* as followeth, *poftea fimiliter Sacerdos fumit fanctum panem inclinato capite ante facram menfam orans &c. tenens autem Sacerdos fanctum Calicem, vocat Diaconum dicens, Diacone accede, et Diaconus veniens adorat femel, dicens, ecce venio ad immortalem Regem, credo, et confiteor ; tunc Sacerdos, accipe ferue Dei Diacon,e preciofum corpus et fanguinem Domini &c. tunc Diaconus fumit fanctum Calicem cum veneratione, eumq̑ extollens ad populum dicit, cum timore Dei et fide, accedite.* (7) To this end doth *Chrifoftome in* 1. *Cor. hom.* 41. fay, *nec fruftra memoriam mortuorum inter Sacra myfteria celebramus, aut accedimus deprecantis pro illis agnum illum iacentem &c.* As alfo the *firft Nicene Councel* faid in like maner, *let vs by faith vnderftand to lye vpon that facred table the lambe of God &c.* this *Canon* is acknowledged by *Grinæus apud Iacobum Andræam, in confut. difput. Ioannis Iacobo Grinai de nei de cæna Domini pag.* 88. by *Oecolampadius in lib. epistolarum Oecolampadij et Suingly. pag.* 663. and 667. and by *M. Bilson* in his true difference &c. part. 4. pag. 555.

affirming further (as we do) in reguard of his body thus honoured vpon the Altar, (q) *that the Angels are present with the Preist, and that the place round about the Altar is filled for the honor of him that lyeth thereon, and that the Angels are present at this wonderfull table, and do compasse it about with reuerence.* In which opinion he is so serious that he confirmeth the same with report of a vision thereof (r) *tould by an old man to whō many reuelations were shewed:* which said attendance of Angels and vision thereof, as it is confirmed with other graue (s) testimonies: So also it is so pregnant for our Catholicke opinion, that *D. Humfrey* tearmeth it

(q)
Chrisost. de Sacerdotio. l. 6. c. 4. et hom. 1. de verbis Isaiæ. see these places weakely shuffled of, rather then answeared, by *M. Fulke* against the Rhemish Testament, *in reuelat. c. 4. fol.* 468.

(r)
Chrisost. de Sacerdotio, l. 6. c. 4. saith, *ego vero et commemorantem olim quendam audiui, cum diceret senem quendam virum*

admirabilē, et cui reuelationū mysteria multa diuinitus fuissent detecta, sibi narrasse se tantū olim visione dignum habitum a Deo esse: ac per illud quidem tempus Angelorum multitudinem conspexisse &c. fulgentibus vestibus indutorum Altare ipsum circundantium: deniq, sic capite inclinatorum, vt si quis milites presente rege stantes videat. Alius quidam mihi narrauit &c. dignus habitus qui id et vidisset, ipse, et andisset quod qui de hac vita emigraturi sunt, si mysteriorum huiusmodi cum munda et pura conscientia fuerint participes, spiritum efflaturi, ab Angelis eorum animæ satellitum more stipantibus, propter assumptum illud sacrum recta in cælum abducuntur. (s) *Ambros. in c. 1. Luc.* saith, *non dubites adsistere Angelum quando Christus adsistit, Christus immolatur.* and *Chrisost. hom. 3. in Ephes.* saith, *adsunt Angeli mensæ huius ministri.* and see him in *Act. hom.* 22. *et hom. in Encenijs.* And *S. Gregory, l. 4. dial. c.* 58. saith, *quis enim fidelium habere dubium possit in ipsa immolationis hora ad Sacerdotis vocem cælos aperiri, in illo Iesu Christi mysterio, Angelorum choros adesse.* And sundry miraculous *visions of Angels* seene in celebration of the *Sacrament*, are perticulerly reported by *Palladius in hist. Sanctorum Patrum c.* 20. *et* 72. and *Sozomen, hist. l.* 6. *c.* 29. and by *Cirillus Eremita in vita Sancti Euthimy*.

(t) *Hum-*

(t)
Humfred. in Iesuitismi.
part. 1. pag. 134.

(u)
Nazianzen. orat. 11.
quæ est de Gorgonia sorore.

(*)
Ibidem.

(*)
Fulke in respons. ad Sta-
pletonum, de successione Ecclesiastica. pag. 230. saith,
Eucharistia in Altari non
fuit ab ea adorata, quam-
uis in magna reuerentia,
et fortasse non sine superstitione habita.

(x)
Ioannes Bechtoldus in his
assertions *theologica de*
Sacreamento cænæ Domini
quas præside D. Philippo
Merbachio in accademia
Argentinensi professore &c.
proposuit assert. 47. saith,
consuetudinem antiquissi-
mam quod attinet quæ Ec-
clesia populo in Missa exhibere adorandam Euchari-
stiam consueuit, quam D.
Basilius in aurea columba

it (t) *dotage to beleeue that Augels be there*
present.

(3) In like maner doth S. *Gregorie Nazi-*
anzen report how his sister *Gorgonia* being
diseased, (u) *prostrated her selfe before the Al-*
tar, and (*) *calling vpon him who is worshiped*
on it &c. O miracle, (saith he) *she departed*
presently receiuing health: A place so euident
that *M. Fulke*, who wil not yeeld therto, but
endeauoreth to colour the same by al meanes
he can, is enforced yet to affirme thereof
that, (*) *Gorgonia had the Eucharist being on*
the Altar, in great reuerence, and perhaps not
without superstition: as though *Nazianzen*
would haue conmended his sister for superstition, or as though God him selfe would
by the *miracle* here reported haue so confirmed such her superstition.

Hitherto of the Fathers within the first
400. yeares, whose alledged testimonies of
adoration are against our aduersaries cauel-
ling and euasory answeares, made as yet further plaine on our behalfe, aswel by further
(x) acknowledgment of other our learned
aduersaries, as also by sundry answearable
external obseruations by those Fathers prescribed, & by vs yet reteined in respect of theho-
nor and reuerence by them and vs mutually
exhibited to this blessed Sacrament. As for
example (to omit sundry other like confessed euen

reseruauit, et argenteæ turris, aureorum Calicum fit mentio apud Gregorium
Turonens. August. Ambros. Chrisost. Hieronim. et quod Prudentius sic lo-
quentem Tyrannum Beato Laurentio introducit &c. et quæcunq, alia propria intentione vel præter vel contra institutionem Christi fuere obseruata, il·
lis omnibus et singulis cultibus electitys rectissime opponitur &c. ex Cipriano consuetudo sine veritate, vetustas erroris est &c.

(7) *Beza*

Sed euen by (7) *Beza* (i) *first the* (z) *Chalices &*
holy coueringes (or corporals) were holden to
be *venerable by reason of their accompanying* (or
touching) *the body and bloud of our Lord:* In
so much as the inferior orders of the Cleargy
(a) *might not touch them*; as in some like resemblance *S. Iohn Baptist* in like maner
thought him selfe (2) *vnworthy to touch the*
lachet of our Sauiours shooes. and *Moyses* was
in like (3) *signe of reuerence* restrayned in like
sort when he was commaunded to (4) *put of*
his shooes from his feete, because the place where
he did stand was made holy by the (5) *presence*
of God: And thereupon it came to passe that
it was in some places vnsual for a lay person to (b) *take the Communion with his owne*
hand, except it were *by necessity of times and*
persecution, when the Preist was not present. An
auncient vsage so euidently begunne, practised, and retained in honor of the Sacrament,
that (6) *Beza* doth accordingly confesse

ter l. (2) *Marc.* 1. 8. *Luc.* 3. 16. *Ioan.* 1. 27. (3) See the
marginal notes of the english Bible of *Anno.* 1576. *in act. c.* 7. *vers.*
33. (4) *Exod.* 3. 5. and *Act.* 7. 33. (5) See the marginal
notes of the said Bible in *Exod. c.* 3. *vers.* 5. (b) *Basil. in epist.*
ad Cæsariam Patritiam. And *Prætorius de Sacramentis &c.* pag. 287.
saith, *Anno* 615. *in Concil. Rhotomagensi. est prohibitum ne Sacerdotes*
Laicis panem et poculum darent in manus, sed in os ingererent, ne res illæ
sanctæ prophanarentur contactu inaspersarum manuum. And the 6. *Councel*
of *Constantinople, can.* 101. signifyeth how that in some places of the
greeke Church, they vsed *insteed of the hand, to make litle vessels of gold for*
receiuing of the diuine guift: Against which, though the Councel doth
decree, reprehending them for so *preferring a dead mettel before* (a man)
the image of God; and prescribing insteed thereof a reuerent composed gesture, as namely *to frame their handes in forme of a Crosse,* and so
(saith *Damascen. l.* 4. *orthodox. fid. c.* 14.) *to receiue the body of him*
that was crucifyed. yet doth this sufficiently argue, that the true ground

B b 3

of these

(7)

Beza in epist. theolog. epist.
8. *pag.* 83. saith, *non pla-*
cuit simplex et communis
apparatus, idcirco conquiri
marmora, inaurari parietes,
vasa aurea et argentea com-
parari pretiosa etiam et pon-
tificales, atq; adeo Impera-
toriæ vestes, quibus mini-
stri circundari cæperunt ho-
norandi, scilicet Sacramenti
causa &c.

(z)

See heretofore *tract.* 1.
sect. 2. *subdiuis.* 2. in
the margent there at the
letter i.

(a)

See heretofore *tract.* 1.
sect. 2. *subdiuis.* 2. in the
the margent there at the let-

of these premises was the Churches the general receiued doctrine concerning the *honoring* of Chrifts bleſſed body in the Sacrament. (6) *Beza
epiſt . theolog. epiſt. 8. pag. 84.* ſaith hereof, *buccellam in os ingerere
maluerunt reuerentiæ nimirum cauſa.* and *epiſt. 2. pag. 25. et 26.* he
further affirmeth thoſe *rectius facere qui manu, qnam qui ore, Sacramenta
ſumunt.* becauſe, ſaith he, *probabile eſt iſtam oris ſumptionem non aliunde
initio quam a ſuperſtitioſa ſignorum veneratione profectam.* So plainly doth
this auncient vſage proue the then honouring of the Sacrament.

(c)
See *Hierom . in Apol. ad-
uerſ. Iouin.* And ſee this
confeſſed by *M . Fulke*
againſt *Heſkins, Sanders
&c. pag. 458.*

(d)
*M. Fulke , ibidem . pag.
458.*

(e)
*Hoſpinianus in hiſtoria Sa-
cramentaria. l. 2. pag.
46.* ſaith, *in Primitiua
Eccleſia Euchariſtia ſumpta
fuerat caſte.* And he doth
demonſtrate this perti-
culerly in ſundry aunciēt
Fathers. (f) *Auguſt.*

the ſame. (2) *Secondly,* vpon this ground
alſo (c) *admonition was geuen to married perſons to abſtaine from their wiues* certaine dayes
before their communion; which thing *M.
Fulke* confeſſerh and tearmeth, (d) *Popiſh diuinity:* So plainly alſo were thoſe Fathers
Papiſtes with vs in this point, as is yet further acknowledged by (e) *Hoſpinianus.* (3)
Thirdly, it was (f) *vniuerſally obſerued,* and as
S. *Auguſtine* ſaith, *it pleaſed the holy Ghoſt, that
our Lords body ſhould enter into the mouth of a
Chriſtian firſter then other meates: as Tertulian*
ſaith, *ante omnem cibum* (g) *before al meate ,*
the reaſon whereof S. *Auguſtine* affirmeth
with vs to be, *in honorem tanti Sacramenti,* (h)
in honor of ſo great a Sacrament: In ſo much
as

in epiſt . 118. c. 6. (g) *Tertulian. l. 2. ad vxorem.* (h) *Auguſt.
epiſt. 118. c. 6.* ſaith, *placuit ſpiritui ſancto, vt in honorem tanti Sacramenti in os Chriſtiani, prius Dominicum corpus intraret, quam cæteri cibi &c.*
And the ſame reaſon is geuen by *Iſidore, l. 1. de diuin. offic. c. 18.*
by *Amalarius, l. 3. de offic. Eccleſiaſt. c. 34.* and by *Walfridus Strabo.
l. de rebus Eccleſiaſt. c. 19.* this receiuing of the Sacrament *faſting* is
further taught *concil. 3. Carthag. c. 29.* and *concil. Hipponenſi. c. 30.*
and *concil. 2. Brachar. c. 10.* & *concil. 2. Mathiſconeſ. c. 6.* & *concil.
Anticiodorenſ. c. 19.* and *concil. Trullan. c. 29.* and by *Sedulius in*
1. *Cor. 11.* And by *Chriſoſto. in* 1. *Cor. hom. 27.* & *in epiſt. 125. ad
Ciriacum exulem,* he ſaith moſt earneſtly againſt the imputation hereof laid to his charge: *multa aduerſum me ſtruxerunt, aiuntq́, me poſt epulas*
quibuſdam

quibufdam Communionem impertijſe, hcc ſi feci, de Epiſcoporum libro nom̨ⁿ meum expungatur, nec in orthodoxæ ſidei volumine ſcribatur, neq̢ enim quic⁻ quam eiuſmodi perpetraui, ac Chriſtus a regno ſuo me abijciat.

as the receiuing there of not faſting is repor-
tedto haue beene miraculouſly (i) puniſhed.
(4) *Fourtly*, in reguard of the *Cathecumines*,
or vnbaptiſed nouices in faith who were preſent at Church ſeruice, it was vſual in the
greeke Church to conſecrate with (k) *Vayles*
or curtaines (l) *drawen to* withhould the Sacrament *from their vnworthy eyes*, and til the
Cathecumines were more prepaired & worthy
for the receiuing thereof, it was likewiſe v-
ſual to geue them in the meane time (m) *holy bread*, which *M. Fulke* tearmeth (n) *a ſu-
perſtitiouſe bread, geuen in S. Auguſtines time
to thoſe that were Catechumines in ſteed of the Sacrament.* (5) *Fifthly*, and laſtly (o) S. *Auguſtine*, and S. (p) *Ciril*, do witnes the great
care then had, left any part of the Sacrament
ſhould fal to the groũd, which their like care to be
had of the water of Baptiſme we do not find.
And thus much concerning the Fathers *Greeke*
and *Latine*, that liued in the *fourth hundreth
yeares* after Chriſt.

(i)
See this miracle repor-
ted by *Gregorius Turonen-
ſis, l. 1. de gloria Martyrum 6. 87.*

(k)
hereof ſee hertofore *ſect.
7. initio.* at z.

(l)
*Chriſtomus ad pop. hom.
61. paulo poſt med.* ſee
this confeſſed:and repro-
ued in the Fathers by *Beza in epiſt. theolog. epiſt.
8. pag. 80.*

(m)
*Auguſt. de peccat. merit.
et rem. l. 2. c. 26.* ſaith
hereof, *quod accipiunt Catechumini, quamuis non ſit
corpus Chriſti, eſt tamen
ſanctius quam cibi quibus
alimur.* And that the *Catechumines* might not re-

(4) To
ceiue the Sacrament which S. *Auguſtine here* calleth *corpus Chriſti*, appeareth by S. *Auguſtine, l. de pec. mer. et rem. c. 2.* and *in Ioan.
tract. 11. et 96.* (n) *Fulke* againſt *Heſkins, Sanders &c. l. 3. c. 23.
pag. 277.* (o) *Aug. l. 50. homiliarum. hom. 26.* ſaith, *quanta ſo-
licitudine obſeruamus quando nobis corpus miniſtratur, vt nihil de ipſo in terram
cadat. et vide Auguſt. in ſerm. ad Infantes, apud Craſtouium,* in his praxis de cæremonijs, ſect. 13. (p) *Cirillus Hieroſol. Catech. 5. prope
finem.* ſaith hereof, *take heede left any thing of it ſal from thee &c. wilt
thou not prouide more diligently for this which is more pretiouſe then gold,
that no crum of it ſal downe.*

(q) *Origen.*

(q)
Origen. hom. 13. in Exo.
faith, noftis qui diuinis my-
fterijs intereffe confuestis,
quomodo cum fufcipitis cor-
pus Domini, cum omni
cautela et veneratione fer-
uatis, ne ex eo parum quid
decidat, ne confecrati mu-
neris aliquid dilabatur;
Reos enim vos creditis, &
recte creditis, fi quid inde
per negligentiam decidat.

(r)
Origen. hom. 5. in diuer-
fa loca.

(s)
Tertul. in libro de corona
militis faith, *Calicis aut*
panis etiam noftri aliquid
decuti in terram anxie pa-
timur. fee *Vadians* confeffion and ridiculoufe eua-
fion concerning this teftimony of *Tertul.* here-
after *tract. 2. fect. 9.*
fubdiuif. 2. in the margent at *. next before z.

(t)
Ciprian. ferm. de cæna
Domini multa poft med.
faith, *qui vfq, hodie hoc ve-*
raciffimum et fanctiffimum

(4) To come now to the more auncient
Fathers before thofe times, *Origen* liued a-
bout *Anno.* 230. in the age next but one to
the Apoftles fcholers, he in his earneft ad-
monifhment to Chriftians, not to reiect nor
caft away from their minde the word of God
which they had once receiued and *beleeued*,
doth thereupon take occafion to expreffe the
forefaid external reuerend cuftome of the
greeke Church in his time concerning the
Sacrament faying: (q) *you that are accuftomed*
to be prefent at the diuine myfteries do know, that
when you receiue the body of our Lord, you do with
al warines and reuerence take heed that no litle
thereof fal downe; affirming it further to be
offence if any thing thereof fal to the ground,
though but *by negligence.* In like maner doth
he mention our now Catholicke cuftome faying (r) *when &c.* thou doeft eate and drinke the
body and bloud of our Lord &c. follow the Cen-
turion and fay, Lord I am not worthy that thou
enter vnder my roofe. *Tertulian* liued in the
fame age and (s) expreffeth for the *Latine*
Church, the like former careful warines, left
any of the Sacrament fhould fal downe to the
ground. *S. Ciprian* alfo who liued in that age,
requireth (t) *our teares in prefence of this body.*
Pius, who liued about *Anno.* 150. in the
age next after the Apoftles, decreed that (u)
if by negligence any of the bloud fel vpon the earth,
it fhould be licked with the tongue, and the table
fcraped &c. And laftly *Dionifius Aropagita* (x)
mentioned

corpus fuum creat, et fanctificat, et benedicit, et pie fumentibus diuidit, in
huius prefentia, non fuperuacuæ mendicant lachrimæ veniam &c. (u) *Si per*
negligentiam aliquid de fa ruine ftillauerit in terram, lingua lambatur, tabula
radatur, fi non fuerit tabula, vt non conculcetur, locus corrodatur, et igne
confumatur, et cinis intra Altare recondatur et Sacerdos 40. diebus pæniteat.

this

mentioned in the actes doth (in thofe writinges whofe anfwearable antiquity is (y)
heretofore proued and by our aduerfaries confeffed) before he enter into difcourfe of the
Sacrament, make *a folemne inuocation*, or prayer to it faying, (z) *but o moft diuine and holy
myftery reuealing the ænigmatical coueringes
which are fimbolically* (*) *circumiacent to thee,
be opened clearly vnto vs, and fil our fpiritual
eyes with the finguler and open brightnes of thy
light*. So plainly doth he direct his prayer
to Chrift, not as he is in heauen, but as being prefent vnder the external fymboles:
whereto might be added like teftimony from
S. *Clement* the Apoftles (2) *coadiutor*, who
admonifheth *communicantes to* (3) *receiue
the prettioufe body and bloud with feare and trem-
bling, coming thereto as to the body of a Prince;
women with their heades vealed in decency*; and
that *the doares be kept that no Infidel or Cate-
cumen may enter:* fo great external reuerence
and obferuation was euen in thofe firft times
prefcribed and teftifyed.

this decree of *Pius* is men
tioned by *Gratian. dift.*
2. *fi per negligentiam.*
And by *Iuo. l. 1. decret.*
and by *Burchard. l. 5.*
in fo much as *Hofpinianus
in hift. Sacramentaria. l.
2. pag. 123.* and *l. 5.
pag. 516.* pretendeth
anfweare thereto, with-
out denying of *Pius* to be
the author thereof. And
D. *Barnes* in his booke
entituled, *vitæ Romanorū
Pontificum*, printed at *Bafile, pag. 11.* chargeth
Pius as author of this decree faying hereof, *Pius
ftatuit &c.* And the
French proteftant in his
difcourfe tranflated for
the fuppofed worth there
of, into englifh, & prin-
ted 1608. vnder the title

That

of *fixe godly treatifes neceffary for Chriftian inftruction &c. pag. 65.* chargeth *Pius Bifhop of Rome. Anno. 144.* with *ordaining that the confecrated
bread and wine falling on the ground, fhould be left to the facrificer, and the
reft remaning fhould be burned with fyer, and the afhes fhould be laid vp.*
And fee further there *pag. 96.* In fo much as certaine Lutheran
Proteftantes haue imitated the fame. To this end doth *Ofiander* in
his *centur. 16. pag. 687.* fay of *Sarcerius* a learned Lutheran, *Sarcerius iubet delapfas particulas colligi, & erafa terra comburi.* and *ibidem.
pag. 688. Sarcerius de comburendis particulis cænæ Dominicæ fcripfit.* And
Melanteton, l. 2. Epiftolarum printed, 1570. *pag. 107.* reporteth of
Weftphalus (a learned Lutheran) that he condemned thofe who taught,
nihil habere rationem Sacramenti extra vfum inftitutum. (2) *Philip. 4.*
3. (3) *Clement*, in his booke of Apoftolicke conftitutions after the
edition at *Antwerpe, Anno. 1564. l. 2. c. 61. fol. 56.* fee this booke

C c   proued

proued hereafter, *tract.*
3. *sect.* 2. *subdiuis.* 5.
in the margent at x.
and *.

(a)

See heretofore, *tract.*
2. *sect.* 8. *subdiuis.* 1.
at t. u. *et ibidem.* *sub-diuis.* 2. at x.

(b)

See heretofore, *tract.*
2. *sect.* 8. *subdiuis.* 1.
in the margent there at
the figures 4. & 8.

(c)

See heretofore *tract.* 2.
sect. 8. *subdiuis.* 2. in
the margent at b.

(d)

*M. Foxe, Act. mon.
pag.* 896. to this end
faith, *the eleuation and
adoration of the Sacrament
we cannot finde to come
in by any other then by Honorius the third, Anno.*
1222.

(e)

M. Whitguift, in his defence of the anſweare
to the admonition, *pag.*
351.

(f)

*That no firſt beginning of adoration of the Sacra-
ment can be found, and how forcibly that argueth, and of certaine miracles in proofe of
adoration.*

SECTION. 9.

HItherto in proofe of our adoration of
the Sacrament; concerning which I
do further ad theſe few breefe obſeruations.
(1) *Firſt,* that as it is made vndoubted by
ſundry plaine teſtimonies (a) *heretofore* alledged from *Algerus, Odo pariſienſis,* & others
who liued ſundry ages before *Honorius* the 3.
and alſo by the very (b) wordes of *Honorius* his foreſaid decree, and by the (c) confeſſion of our aduerſaries them ſelues, that
this adoration was not firſt begunne by *Honorius,* but practiſed long before his time:
ſo likewiſe it is made no leſſe euident by the
foreſaid ſucceſſiue continued gradation of
teſtimonies deduced from this preſent age vp
to the Apoſtles, and by like confeſſion & acknowledgement of our very aduerſaries, that
as this adoration was not firſt brought in by
Honorius ; ſo they (d) *cannot finde it to come in
by any other:* So cleare and free it is from al
noted and knowen beginning ſince the A-
poſtles times. (2) *Secondly,* I further infer,
that like as *D. Whitguift,* argueth truly and
learnedly againſt the Puritaines, in profe of
Metropolitaines, Archbiſhops &c. that (e)
*for ſo much as the original and being of theſe names Metropolitaines, Archbi-
ſhops &c. cannot be found,* it is therefore (ſaith he) to be *ſuppoſed that
they had their original from the Apoſtles.* So likewiſe the ſame reaſon
doth ſo much the rather proue adoration of the Sacrament to be A-
poſtolical, by how much it is euident, that it is a point of far greater
consequence

consequence, and no lesse free from al original and knowen beginning since the Apostles
times, then is the other: And therefore the-
probability of *D. Whitguiftes* argument, de-
monstrateth it selfe much more probable in
this, & that by most euident and necessary sequele from the Scriptures: for seeing it is witnessed by Scriptures, that Christ haith placed
in his Church *Pastors* (f) and *Doctors* (to continue) *to the consummation of Sainctes, til we al
meete in vnity of faith,* (as our aduersaries do
hereupon expound) euen (g) *for euer.* And
as *M. Fulke* hereupon confesseth (h) *from
Christes time to Luthers age.* Since also the
same Scripture telleth of these (i) *watchmen* or
(k)*Pastors,* that they (l) *shal not be silēt,* but shal
as *M. Fulke* confesseth (m) *almaies resist* al
false opinion, euen *with open reprehension:* and
that (n) the religion *being of God, no feare of
man shal keepe them backe:* because, as the A-
postle saith, (o) *with the heart a man beleeueth
vnto iustice, and with the mouth confesseth to saluation.* Since likewise the office and nature
of the true Church argueth this most inuincibly, for how can she be the true Church
and suffer an error of such importance, (as
is our adoration of the Sacrament, supposing
it for an error) to infect her children (and
that so vniuersally) without some knowen
resistance vpon her part in some one or other
nation. Since also this point is yet further
cōfirmed with the aswearable experience had
of al former times, in which aswel other
herefies

*shal haue to the end, successiuely in al ages, in one place or other, such as haue
shewed the truth faithfully vnto others, as haue shyned as lightes in their dayes
set vpon a Candlesticke.* (n) *M. Beering,* in his readinges vpon the
Epistle to the Hebrewes. *c. 3. lecture* 15. (o) *Rom.* 10. 10.

C c 2 (p) This

(f)
Ephes. 4. 11. 12. 13.

(g)
D. *Fulke,* against the
Rhemish Testament in
Ephes. sect. 4. fol. 335.
Caluin. institut. printed
Geneua. Anno. 1550. *c.*
8. *de fide. sect.* 37. 38.
pag. 233. *et* 234. *Melancton in loc. commun.
(adit.* 1561.) *cap. de Ecclesia.*

(h)
M. Fulke, against *He-
skins, Sanders &c. pag.*
569.

(i)
Esay. 62. 6.

(k)
See the marginal notes
of the english Bible of
Anno. 1576. in Esay 62.
6. (l)
Esay. 62. 6.
(m)
M. Fulke, in his an-
sweare to a counterfeate
Catholicke &c. *pag.* 100.
And *M. Sparke* in his
answeare to *M. Iohn
Albines, pag.* 11. saith
accordingly, *the Church of
Christ haith almaies had &*

(p)

This is made plaine by the publique contradiction made in euery age againſt the hereticks the aryſing, exemplifyed in particuler *by the Centurie writers* in their 5. *chapter* of euery feueral Century or hundreth yeares, from Chriſtes time to this preſent age.

(*)

Ioachim Vadian, a learned Suinglian *de Euchariſt. Aphoriſ. l. 1. pag. 2. 3. 4.* maketh mention of theſe feueral errors contradicted in the more ancient Church, as namely of *the Artotyritæ,* who in their aſſemblies *vſed cheeſe and bread.* of the *Aquarij,* who inſteede of wine *vſed water.* of the *Anthropomorphites,* denying reſeruation. of the *Meſſalians,* affirming *the*

(p) hereſies, though but in other matters of much leſſer importance, and not ſo generally diſperſed. As alſo (which is very pertinent) the confeſſed dayly ariſing (*) *errors* concerning euen this very Sacrament, are yet to vs at this day knowen and teſtifyed to haue beene directly and perticulerly contradicted in the teachers thereof, at or before their far diſperſing or enlarging of the ſame in many nations : In ſo much as our aduerſaries (which point onely is ſufficient to conuince them) are not in matters out of controuerſie, able to alledge other example, ſo much as of any one error ſo important and diſperſed, which is not yet at this day knowen to haue bene directly as beforeſaid, withſtoode and contradicted in the teachers thereof. *Berengarius* him ſelfe, (2) *who about the yeare of our Lord* 1060. *denyed tranſubſtantiation,* being therefore (as is by our learned aduerſaries confeſſed) accordingly (3) *accompted an hereticke,* and generally *withſtoode* (4) *by al the diuines of that time,* as being thought to teach doctrine ſtrange and ſinguler, and contrary *to* (5) *that faith which al that vnderſtoode the Latine tongue, the Grecians, Armenians, and al the Chriſtians of euery nation, did with*

Sacrament neither to hurt nor profit, to which alſo he there addeth *the Neſtorians,* and *Eutichians &c.* If now theſe leſſer errors concerning this Sacrament, were at their firſt apearing ſo noted and contradicted, could then the other much more important doctrines of real preſence and adoration (ſuppoſing them errors) preuaile newly to begin, and ſo generally to diſperſe them ſelues without al note and contradiction. (2) See heretofore, *tract. 2. ſect. 2. ſubdiuiſ. 1.* at d. (3) *Ibidem.* at d. (4) See there alſo in the margent at c. & d. (5) See there at *. next after e. and concerning the like teſtifyed further generality thereof in the time of *Paſchaſius* who was aboue

300. yeares

with one mouth (then) testify and hould. Could now then the *greeke* & *latine* Churches, the Christians of *Asia*, *Africke*, and *Enrope*, be so vniuersally perswaded, not only to beleeue, but also to put in publicke practise, an innouation of adoring bread and wine for God, and the same not then directly contradicted in the teachers thereof, so much as by any one approued Father or writer of the Church? Or could the great contradiction or alteration, which vpon the beginning or dispersing of so strange a doctrine and practise, (as the Superintendent of *Winchester* (confesseth in the like case) be thought of necessity to haue ensued, and is in al other like examples yet to this day remembred, be in this onely quite forgotten, buried in silence, and not once remembred in any one nation of the earth, so much as by any one approued writer, Ecclesiastical or Prophane? May this be thought to be either (7) *Probable*, or (r) *possible*, or can our aduersaries expect

300. yeares before this time. see there *subdinis.* 2. at. k.

(q)

See heretofore *tract.* 2. *sect.* 8. *subdinis.* 1. at g. h. i. k. l. and see in this present subdiuision next heretofore at the figure 5. (6)

M. Bilson, in his *suruey* of Chrifts sufferings &c. *pag.* 660. mentioneth *Eusebius* his report of *Thadeus* his teaching Chriftes descending into hel, which *M. Iacob* denyeth, saith thereupon, *were there no more but the recordes of Edessa then remaining, and the report of Eusebius translating the same, they fairely proue this clause*

of Chriftes descending to Hades, to haue beene aunciently and openly receiued, and professed in the Primitiue Church, otherwise the religious of those ages that lined with, and after Eusebius, if he had vnder this pretence broached any new point of faith, as in duty they were bounde, so no doubt they would haue resisted and refuted it. If now *M. Bilson* may truly thinke that in a point of doctrine, so smale, in comparison, no innouation could be without some open knowen and testifyed contradiction, what is then to be in the like case thought of this other so far more waighty point, of *adoring the Sacrament:* And if, according to his opinion, the onely want of such knowen testifyed contradiction against any point of faith supposed to be innouated, be proofe sufficient, that no such innouation was or could be, why then should not the like confessed want of al knowen contradiction vpon any first supposed new teaching or practise of adoring the Sacrament, behould likewise for proofe sufficient that it neuer came in by way of innouation. (7) *Improbable* in re-

C c 3 guard

guard that the experience of al former times is to the contrary.
(r) *Impossible*, in reguard of the Scriptures foretelling the contrary, whereof see next heretofore, *subdiuis*. 1. at f.
g. h. i. k. l.

(8)

So much the more *strong*, becaufe that the more abfurd any doctrine was; fo much the more like it was to be contradicted at the firft teaching thereof.

(s)

Pretorius in lib. de Sacra-mentis. pag. 288. faith, Anno. 735. subsecuta est panis adoratio ac si ipse Christus esset. And fee *Carions* like further con-feffion herof, heretofore *tract. 2. sect. 8. subdiuis.* 2. in the margent at b.

p. 206.

(t)

Chemnitius in his examen. *conc. Trident. part. 2. pag. 91.* faith, *si ergo credimus Christum Deum et hominem in actione coe-na sua peculiari modo pre-sentiae et gratia adesse, ita quod tibi vere & substantiali-*

expect or require at our handes matter of proofe for vs or againft them more plaine, more fenfible, more demonstratiue? for by how much the more abfurd that our now pro-feffed doctrine and practife of adoring the Sacrament, is in our aduerfaries opinion thought to be, fo much the (8) *more strong* is the probability of that which is now in-ferred, and doth in al reafon fo much the more conuince.

(2) *Thirdly*, I obferue that as our aduer-faries are not able to fhew any firft begin-ning fince the Apoftles times of this adora-tion; fo we on the contrary (as appeareth by the premifes) haue fhewed a gradation or courfe of probable teftimonies fuccefliue-ly continued, from this prefent vp to thofe *purer* times which fucceeded after the Apo-ftles: fundry of which faid teftimonies are fo confeffed, plaine, and euident, that *Pre-torius*, though a learned Caluinift, and enemy to this adoration, doth yet confeffe that *An-no* (s) 735. *bread was adored as though it had beene Christ.* And as to the other before alled-ged teftimonies of thofe more auncient Fa-thers who liued in the *fourth hundreth yeares* after Chrift, their like meaning herin is many waies made manifeft vuto vs, as *firft* by their
forealledged

ter exhibeat vescentibus corpus et sanguinem suum &c. fieri nec potest nec debet, quin fides Christum in illa actione presentem veneretur et adoret. Ita Iacob. Gen. 28. Moyses, Exod. 34. Elias. 3. Reg. 19. non habebant sane peculiare mandatum, vt in illis locis Deum adorarent, sed quia habebant generale mandatum vt Deum vbiq, adorarent, et certierant, Deum sub exter-nis et visibilibus illis simbolis vere adesse &c. Certe Deum ipsum, quem ibi presentem

præsentem credebant, adorabant &c. nec vero Deum illi procul in cælo empineo a se remotum et absentem, sed vere præsentem &c. adorarunt, recte igitur Augustinus in Psal. 98. &c. ita Ambrosius &c. Nazianzenus in epitaphio sororis suæ &c. et sententia Eusebij Emisseni &c. Lutherus etiam contra Louanienses, art. 16. vocat Euchariftiam Sacramentum venerabile et adorabile
And *Ibidem. pag. 91.* he maketh this adoration during the time of celebration to be (*extra contrauersiam*) out of *controuersy* betweene him and the Trident Councel, affirming further (*Ibidem. pag. 94.*) that thereby saith he, *seiungimus nos a Sacramentarys, we seperate our selues from the Sacramentaries.*

forealledged very wordes, being so plaine, and direct, that (t) *Chemnitius* a most learned Protestant, doth accordingly for such alledge them, and vrge them also by the (u) *confessed iudgement* in many of them, of *real presence* and *transubstantiation*, whereof adoration is but a confessed nece ssary (*) *sequele*: furthermore by the like (x) confessed current & practise of adoration, from this present age til the foresaid time of *Anno. 735.* According vnto which, the plaine seeming testimonies of those other more auncient and precedent Fathers, are in al probability to be vnderstoode; for seeing that the Fathers both before *Anno. 735.* and after it, do agree so fully together in shew of wordes, and no first beginning of this adoration in the meane time noted, how may we vpon mere supposal, presume them to differ in truth of meaning. Lastly by those (y) *forealledged answearable* external obseruations which those more auncient Fathers them selues prescribed, as namely concerning *lay peoples* forbearing in some places to *touch* the Sacrament, or the sacred vessels containing it; also the receiuing of it *fasting*, obserued, saith *S. Augustine,* and

z. a. b. c. e. f. k. n. o. p.

(u)
See this heretofore *tract.* 2. *sect.* 2. *subdiuis.* 2. *pag* at g. m. n. o. p. r. u. 108. 109. confessed in *Paschasius, Damascen, Theophilact, Gregory Emissen,* and *Chrisostome.* and see there *subdiuis.* 3. at a. b. *. d. f. 3. 4.* the same yet further cofessed in *Ambrose, Gregory Niscen, Ciril Alexand.* and *Hillary.*

(*)
See hereafter in this present 9. section *subdiuis.* 2. in the margent at *. next after b.

(x)
See this at large in *tract.* 2. *sect.* 8. from the beginning of subdiuision 1. vntil the letter b. in subdiuision 2.

(y)
See heretofore *tract.* 2. *sect.* 8. *subdiuis.* 3. at

(*) See

(*)
See there at f. and in the margent there at the letter h.

(*)
Ioacbim Vadian a learned Suinglian *de Eucharistia, l. 6. pag.* 230. saith hereof, *testatur autem Tertulianus, veteres ægre passos de pane aut Calice etiam cibario, nedum sacro aliquid in terram decussum, qui mos iam inde ab Apostolorum temporibus adusǵ proxima secula, magna cura retentus est.* Obserue here this mannes fraude, who seeing it plaine by *Tertulian* and others, that this custome was vndoubtedly from the Apostles times, would in euation extend it to *common bread*

and others in (*) honour of so great a Sacrament. In like maner the careful reguard left any of it should fal to the ground, continued as is (*) confessed from the Apostles times, (which care was more then was had of the water of Baptisme.) And (to omit other) they enioyned abstinence from the act of mariage certaine dayes before their receiuing of the Sacrament: Al which being obserued onely of an honourable and reuerend reguard had to this Sacrament, are most sure interpreters, that as those said Fathers other sayinges, do found plainly for *adoration*, so their sence and meaning is vndoubtedly agreeable thereto. *Fourthly*, I do obserue that like as this foresaid adoration, was the vniuersal (z) *practise* of the Christian world at *Luthers* first appearing, and by him then stil (a) *reteined*, & from his time as before continued and deduced so neare vp to the Apostles age: So like wise (which is most worthy of obseruation) the sacred Scriptures them selues are (as I haue before shewed) confessed by

and *drinke not yet consecrated*, for which as he haith not any testimony in *Tertulian* or any other, so is it improbable to thinke, that with religious Christians in the Apostles times such great care should be, left any part of such common bread or drinke should fal to the groud. In which respect *M. Sutliue* (as disliking of this answeare) in his booke *de Missa Papistica.* printed 1603. *l.1. c.29. fol.* 140. vndertaketh (as enforced and contrary to his brethrens doctrine and practise) a religious care saying, *respondeo, Sacramentum Eucharistiæ esse sancte tractandum, et diligenter esse cauendum, ne vel panis sanctificatus, ad terram cadat, vel vinum sanctum effundatur.* And see heretofore *tract. 2. sect. 8. subdiuis. 3.* at o. p. and *subdiuis.* 4. at q. u. the testimonies of *Augustine, Ciril, Origen,* and *Pius,* who refer this circumspection and care onely to the Sacrament. (z) See heretofore *tract. 2. sect. 8. subdiuis.* 1. at g. h. i. k. l. (a) See there at p. and in the margent there at n.

(b) *M.*

by our aduersaries (b) *to be plainer in shew for
our real presence* (whereof adoration is but
a confessed (*) necessary sequele) *then for their
Sacramental*: which plainenes of the Scripture in this behalfe is also heretofore more
particulerly exemplifyed in our Sauiours (c)
promise, his answearable (d) *performance*, and
the Apostles foresaid (e) *explication*: this exceeding plainenes of the Scriptures in this
behalfe, being then thus euident and
confessed, can there be any more sure & saife
interpreter of those so plaine Scriptures, then
is the foresaid answearable and vncontrow-
led, both beleefe and practise of adoring the
Sacrament for so many succeeding ages.

(3) *Fifthly*, & lastly I do further obserue,
that it haith pleased God to make this special point as yet more plaine, with his owne
immediate testimony of vndoubted *miracles*
peculiar to this purpose, as in the former
vision of Angels attending vpon the Altar,
reported

(b)
M. Raynoldes, in his conference with *M. Harte*.
pag. 68. and the diuines
of *Geneua* in *Apologia modesta ad acta conuentus
quindecim theologorū &c:
pag.* 18. *ante med.* saith,
*si simpliciter accipiantur
verba Christi, consequi necessario transubstantiationis
delirium necesse est &c.*

(*)
The *Tigurine* Caluinistes
say, *quid vero panis verum
et naturale Christi corpus
est? &c. cur ergo illic Dominus adorari non debet,
vbi illum presentem esse di-
citis? &c. quod si Domini
panem naturale Christi corpus reuera esse doceremus,*

cum *Papistis certe fideliter quoq; essemus adoraturi.* see this saying of the
Tigurine diuines in *Gropperus, de Eucharistia.* printed 1560. *pag.* 461.
and in the Protestant treatise entituled, *Collatio Catholica et orthodoxæ
Christianorum fidei, de persona Christi et sacra eius cæna &c. pag.* 355. it
is said, *certum est eqdem ex consubstantiatione quos ex transubstantiatione
errores sequi, nimirum adorationem, circumgestationem, inclusionem, oblationem &c.* And *Osiander. in cent.* 16. *part.* 2. *pag.* 752. alledgeth *the
diuines of Wittenberge,* saying, *si dicatur panem in cæna Domini esse substanti-
ale corpus Christi, facile sacrificium Missæ, et Sacramenti adorationem defer-
di posse.* And also the diuines of *Geneua,* in their *Apologia modesta ad
acta connentus quindecim theologorum torgæ nuper habit.* printed *Geneuæ.*
1575. *pag.* 29. say to the Lutheranes, *num vero Curiosorum est quærere,
an in pane illo & vino illo adorandus sit, vere realiter ac substantialiter præsens Christus, hoc quidem nostri iudices negant, sed illa posita consubstantiatione non minus quam transubstantione concessa, necessario sequitur.* And see
hereafter, *tract.* 3. *sect.* 4. *subdiuis.* 1. *fine.* in the margent at 's. r.

D d (c) here-

(c) Heretofore *tract.* 2. *sect.* 3. *subdiuis.* 1. *initio.* from z. throughout that fubdiuifion.   (d) Heretofore *tract.* 2. *sect.* 3. *subdiuif.* 2.
at z. a. b. &c.   (e) Heretofore *tract.* 2. *sect.* 3. *subdiui*. 3. at
q. r. s.

(f)
Heretofore *tract.* 2. *sect.*
8. *subdiuif.* 2. at q . r.

(*)
Heretofore, *tract.* 2.
sect. 8. *subdiuif.* 3.
at u.

(*)
Num. 22. 28.

(g)
Heretofore, *tract.* 2. *sect.*
6. *subdiuif.* 2. at the let-
pag.196. ter y. in the margent.

(h)
Thomas Waldensis, tom.
2. *de Sacrmento Eucha-*
ristiæ c. 63. faith of this
Taylor , *Cumq́; flecti ad*
fidem omnino non posset ,
nec aliud quam benedictum
panem sacratissimam hosti-
am volebat apellare vel cre-
dere, tandem iussus facere
reuerentiam hostiæ, respon-
dit blasphemus, vere (in-
quit) dignior est aranea re-
uereri: at statim de Alto
eulmine tecti descendes ingens
& horribilis visu aranea,
ad os blasphemi directo filo
peruenit, et dum loquere-
tur, vt intraret per poluta
vix potuit prohiberi.   (i)

reported by *S.* (f) *Chrisostome.* Alfo in the
example of *Gorgonia* miraculoufly reftored to
health, teftifyed, as before of certaine knowledge, by (*) *Gregory Nazianzen.* Likewife in
the former example of *Antoninus,* when (not
vnlike to the reproofe which God miraculoufly gaue to *Balaam,* by the (*) *speach of his*
asse on which he then rode) the brute bealt
did for our inftruction (g) *prostrate* himfelfe
in reuerence before the blessed Sacrament:
Furthermore in that memorable example of
(h) *the Taylor* who being conuented publicke-
ly in Paules Church, before the Archbishop of
Canturburie, the Bishop of Norwich and others,
and commaunded to do reuerence to the (facred)
host, anfweared, truly a spider is more worthy of
reuerence: whereupon faith the reporter, *pre-*
fently from the high roofe of the building there came
downe a spider, great, and horrible to be feene, &
came with direct threede to the mouth of the blaf-
phemer, labouring bufily to enter as he spoke fo as
hardly it could be ftayed by the handes of the by-
ftanders. The reporter hereof *Thomas Walden-*
sis, being an author of credit, faith that he was
prefent and (i) *faw it with his owne eyes;* that
alfo (k) *the noble Prince Thomas Duke of Ox-*
ford then Chancellor of the kingdome, (was likewife prefent and *faw the wonder: that the Arch-*
bishop (thereupon) *spok: thereof to the whole*
multitude there assembled &c. I am not ignorant
labia solicite procurauit, & multorum manibus
Waldensis, vbi fupra. beginneth his report
hereof faying, *Historiam refero quam ego præsens vidi oculis carnis meæ in*
Cathedrali

Cathedrali Ecclesia S. Pauli Londini, vbi venerandus Cantuariensis antistes, fælicis recordationis Thomas Arundel &c. (k) *Astitit illustris Princeps Thomas Oxoniensis dux tunc Cancellarius regni, & vidit prodigium, ac prædictus Archiepiscopus statim surgens cum alijs exponit omni populo ibi collecto*

rant how that *M. Sutliue* for want of better answeare, reiecteth this report for (*) fabulous and lying. But is it probable that any man (especially an author so graue as *Waldensis*) should without al shame be so desperatly resolued to lye, as in his owne countrie to publish to the world for sooth, a matter of this importance to be done in his owne time, euen in his owne presence and knowledge, neither obscurely, but in a place no lesse publicke and frequented then Paules Church, vpon occasion so perticuler, and before so many great Personages then liuing as are here specially named, with further speciality also of the Archbishops oration therupon made to the people, & al this at the same time *knowen* vnto euery man, to be but false and deuised, and yet now sithence continued as true and vncontrouled? Could any matter of this consequence being fained and vntrue, be pretended to be now done so publickly in Paules Church? and might or durst any author of accompt in his now publishing thereof, so expose him selfe to the certaine daunger of al mennes knowledge to the contrary.

quod vltrix manus Domini fuerat in blasphemum &c. Waldensis vbi supra.

(*)

Sutliue de Mysa Papistica &c. l. 1. c. 17. fol. 99. without al proofe or reason geuen for his answeare saith, *quod narrat Bellarminus Iumentum hæreticum confutasse, & genibus curuatis Sacramentum adorasse, ostendit ipsum & sodales ipsius similes esse asinis & iumentis qui Deum non norunt, sed derelicto Deo vero coram Idolis procumbunt: similis est narratio Thomæ Waldensis de araneo et Tilmanni Brebendachij de adolescente quem oua paschalia suffocasse dicuntur, quia male sensit de Eucharistia, nihil enim aliud continet illa narratio quam fabulas & mendacia &c.* and againe there, *Bellarmini miracula ex*

Obiections

mendacissimis legendis deprompta sunt. So he without al reason or proofe other then his bould and bare denyal.

 (l) See

(1)
See heretofore *tract*. 2. *sect*. 3. *subdiuis*. 1. *initio*. from z. throughout that subdiuision.

(m)
See heretofore *tract*. 2. *sect*. 3. *subdiuis*. 3. at q. r. s.

(n)
Which is geuen for you, in the present tense, whereof see heretofore *tract*. 2. *sect*. 3. *subdiuis*. 2. next after e. at 3. 4. & see there at m. n. o. & see hereafter *tract*. 3. *sect*. 3. *subdiuis*. 1. in the margent at n. In so much as it is said in Luke (according to the greeke) that *the cup was shed for vs*. whereof see hereafter *tract*. 3. *sect*. 3. *subdiuis*. 2. at y. and so on forward from thence to the end of that 2. & thother next ensuing *third subdiuision*.

Obiections against the real presence, taken from the Scirptures, answeared.

SECTION. 10.

FOr so much now as it appeareth sufficiently by the premises, that the wordes of our Sauiour, *this is my body*, are not only accompanied with our Sauiours answearable (1) *promise*, the Apostles (m) agreeable explication, and other probable (n) *circumstance* of the text it selfe, and not (o) *expounded* by any Euangelist for figuratiue, but are further also confirmed with the Fathers confessed doctrines of the (p) *real presence*, and (q) *adoration*, grounded vpon those wordes for so many succeding ages: of both which said doctrines, as is yet further confessed by our aduersaries, no beginning (r) can be found, whose beginning and contradiction is yet to this day (s) knowen and testifyed: There is I hope hereby sufficiently discouered aswel the contrary and parcial exposition of our aduersaries of whose like, *S. Augustine* not vnaptly saith,

(o) Whereas many of our Sauiours figuratiue sayinges in matters of lesser importance, were explained, whereof see heretofore *tract*. 2. *sect*. 3. *subdiuis*. 1. in the margent there at the letter s. and *tract*. 2. *sect*. 3. *subdiuis*. 2. in the margent at the letter i. (p) See this heretofore throughout, *tract*. 2. *sect*. 2. *subdiuis*. 2. 3. 4. 5. 6. (q) Heretofore *tract*. 2. *sect*. 8. *subdiuis*. 2. at b. and see the other testimonies there afterwardes following. (r) That real presence is proued to be without any knowen beginning after the Apostles times: see heretofore *tract*. 2. *sect*. 2. throughout and so confessed, *tract*. 2. *sect*. 2. *fine*. at the letter y. And for adoration, see the like proofe heretofore, *tract*. 2.

sect.

sect. 8. throughout, and like confession of no first beginning thereof found *tract. 2. sect. 9. subdiuis. 1.* at d. (s) Hereof see heretofore *tract. 2. sect. 9. subdiuis. 1.* in the margent there at the letter p. and at *.

ly saith, (*) *if the preiudice of any erroneous perswasion preoccupate the minde, whatsoeuer the Scripture haith to the contrary, men take it to be a figuratiue speach.* As also their vnfit and weake application of those other common obiected places, where our Sauiour is called (t) *a rocke,* (u) *a dore,* (x) *a vine,* which being not onely voide of al like *promise,* other answearable *explication* of Scripture, and further confessed testimonie of Fathers, to be taken litterally, are also otherwise, inreguard of their *indefinite* (y) *generality,* and sundry other *material* (*) *differences* altogether vnequal & vncomparable to our Sauiours pointing

(*)
August. de doctrin. Christian. l. 3. c. 10.
(t)
1. *Cor.* 10. 4.
(u)
Ioan. 10. 19.
(x)
Ioan. 15. 1.
(y)

For whereas in the example of the Sacrament our Sauiour did take a certaine portion of bread into his hand and pointing

to that determinate substance said, *this is my body,* in the other examples he spoke not to any like determinate substance so much as then present or in being, into which he might be channged, but vseth onely a general name of a kind of substance: as *I am a vine &c.* which haith in it selfe no determinate and proper being, and therefore must needes be *figuratiue.* (*) Sundry *other material differences* as (1) *first,* in that in these and such other like alledged examples to vse the tearmes of Logicke, *di paratum predicatur de di parato,* that is one different nature is affirmed of an other, and seeing that two such different natures cannot be truly & properly said to be one, wholy whiles they be so diuers, the rule of true and common vnderstanding therefore enforceth, that in this kind of affirming thone to be the other, should be signifyed not *identitie* of substance, but likenes of condition or property, wheras in Christes other wordes *this is my body,* one different nature is not affirmed of an other, for the Pronoune *this* pointeth not at al *to bread,* but finally *to body,* as is fully shewed heretofore *tract. 2. sect. 3. subdiuis. 2.* at b. c. d. (2) *Secondly,* these examples and others vulgarly alledged, as where it is said, *the seauen kine are seauen yeares.* Gen. 41. 26, *the seauen heades are seauen mountaines.*

D d 3 *Apoc.*

Apoc. 17 . 9 . *the seede is the word of God.* *Math.* 13 . and such like,
are al of them spoken vpon occasion of explication, and to explaine
an other truth or saying then formerly in being or precedent, whereas these other wordes, *this is my body*, are not spoken vpon occasion,
or by way of explication of any other saying or truth then precedent,
but are originally vttered as by way of *institution*, and to ordaine and
make a thing (no lesse then a Sacrament) then before not precedent
or in being. What licentious bouldnes then is it to affirme, that those
wordes be improper and figuratiue, becaufe the other sayinges, from
which these so much differ, are figuratiue or improper? By which
kinde of vsurped liberty, a man might, in behalfe of the ould heretickes,
defend afwel that this saying, *the word was made flesh*. *Ioan.* 1 . 14 .
15 . is likewise improper and figuratiue .

(*)

What great difference is betweene our Sauiours sayinges, vttered in his *institution* of a Sacrament, & his other sayinges, such as are these obiected, appeareth further by *Melanctons* testimony alledged heretofore, *tract* . 2 . *sect*. 3 . *subdiuis*. 2 . in the margent at the letter k - and the figure 5 . ting in his (*) institution of a Sacrament, & great *commaundement* to a determinate sub-stance in particuler, and saying thereof, *this is my body:* whereunto may be also further added the very *circumstances* of the other forefaid obiected places directly (z) explaining them selues to be figuratiue. In like manner where it is obiected that circumcision is called the (a) *couenant*, and that *the lambe* is called (b) *the pasouer*, suppofing the obiection for true, the circumstances of the same places do yet sufficiently (c) *explaine* them.

(z)
Where our Sauiour is called a Rocke. 1.*Cor.* 10 . 4 . the same place in the wordes there next precedent explaineth this rocke, *to be the spiritual Rocke*. Also where he is called *a dore, Ioan.* 10 . 7 . in the very same place there *verf*. 1 . 2 : and 6 . it is explained that the word *doare*, was vsed by way of *prouerbe*. and where he is called *a vine. Ioan.* 15 . 1 . in the same place he explaineth him selfe, *verf*. 5 . and 6 . saying, *I am the vine you are the brauches &c. If any man abide not in me he is cast forth (sicut Palmes) as a branch.* so plainly doth he there explaine him selfe to speake by way of comparifon. (a) *Gen.* 17 . 10 . (b) *Exod.* 12 . 11 . (c) For in *Gen.*

Gen. 17. 11. Circumcision is called *the signe of the couenant.* And in Exod. 12. the Lambe is called *the sacrifice of the Lords pasouer. vers.* 27. and the bloud thereof is called *a token for you vpon the houses. vers.* 13. this interpretation is by them selues acknowledged, namely by *Bullinger,* in his sermons diuided into Decades in english, *Decad.* 5. *serm.* 6. *pag.* 988. and see *Vrsinus* his booke entituled, *Commonefactio cuiusdam theolog. et eiusdem Commonefact. considerat. pag.* 102. and *Io. sias Nichol.* in his treatise entituled, *Abrahams faith, pag.* 111. saith, *God openeth his minde when he calleth the same Circumcision by the name of a signe.* And see *Praetorius de Sacramentis, pag.* 258.

that those wordes *this is my body,* are explained in like sort by our Sauiour saying, (d) *do this in remembrance of me:* their assertion herein is of no force, for he hereby calleth not the Sacrament *a remembrance,* but onely (as S. *Paul* explaineth) directing vs how *to shew* (*) *his death til he come,* saith to his Apostles and their successors, *do this in remembrance of me &c.* which said *doing* or celebration hereof in memory of him, is obserued by vs Catholickes, otherwise to vrge hereupon that the Sacrament is onely a remembrance, impugneth no lesse our aduersaries real presence of Christes body to faith, then our real presence thereof to the bodily mouth: In so much as *Caluin* him selfe disliketh and specially (e) answeareth this very obiection. Also we further answeare that though the Sacrament had beene called *a remembrance,* as it is not, yet may it (the diuersity of respect onely admitted) be his body, & also a Sacrament or remembrance thereof. So our Sauiours body

(d)
Luc. 22. 19. and see *Praetorius de Sacramentis, pag.* 258.

(*)
1. *Cor.* 11. 26.

(e)
Caluin. in omnes Pauli epist. in 1. *Cor.* 11. *pag.* 323. saith, *cana* Mnemosune *est &c. quod autem hinc nonnulli colligunt, absesse igitur a cana Christum, quoniam memoria non nisi rei absentis sit, prompta est responsio &c.* and *in l. instit. de cana Domini. c.* 12. *pag.* 331. he further saith of the Sacrament, *non figurat tantum, sed vere etiam exhibet &c.* and

Ibidem. pag. 326. and in his institution after the other edition *l.* 4. *c.* 17. *sect.* 10. he saith, *nec est quod obyciat quispiam figuratam esse locutionem, qua signata rei uomen signo deferatur &c.* And in the Protestant discourse entituled, *Collatio Catholica et orthodox. Christianorum fidei, de persona Christi, et sacra eius cana. pag.* 358. *numer.* 19. Protestantes do disclaime

disclaime in affirming, *quod in verbis Testamenti Christi, per vocabulum corpus, nil aliud quam figuram corporis Christi intelligant, vera corporis Christi presentia negata*, affirming there *pag.* 375. of this and other like opinions, obiected against them by the *Lutheranes*, that they be *dogmata conficta, perq; calumniam et inuidiam orthodoxis obiecta, quorum conuinci nunquam poterunt*.

(f)
Math. 17. 2. *Luc.* 9. 29. *Marc.* 9. 3.

(g)
Hebr. 1. 3.

(h)
2. *Cor.* 4. 4.

(i)
Philip. 2. 6.

(k)
Caluin. in omnes Pauli epist. in 1. *Cor.* 11. 24. *pag.* 321. saith, *Cur ergo appellatio corporis pani tribuitur? omnes puto concedent eadem ratione qua spiritum sanctum. Ioan.* 1. 32 *Columbam uocat &c.*

body (f) *transfigured vpon the mountaine*, was a figure or resemblance of his glorifyed body in heauen. In like manner is our Sauiour called the (g) *figure of his Fathers substance*, (h) *the image of God*, and the (i) *forme of God*; and is yet neuer the lesse the same substance with the Father and also very God: And to this like effect is this difficulty explained by (k) *Caluin*, and (l) *M. Bruce*, in so much as *M. Hooker*, doubted not to deliuer the answearable doctrine of the Church of england saying, (m) *we do not interpret the wordes of Christ, as if the name of his body did but import the figure of his body, and to be, were onely to signify his bloud*.

(2) And where it is further vrged, that the *Columba autem spiritus sanctus vocatur, quia certa sit tessera inuisibilis spiritus presentia*. and in his booke *de cæna Domini inter opuscula*, he affirmeth that *the bread and wine are rightly called the body and bloud of Christ*, and such a figure as was *the doue which was* (saith he) *a most certaine signe of the presence of the holy Ghost*: in so much as he there calleth this, *a very apt example*. (l) *M. Bruce* in his sermons vpon the Sacrament, *pag.* 10. saith *I cal them signes because they haue the body and bloud of Christ conioyned with them, yea truly is the body and bloud of Christ conioyned with that bread &c. and not in respect only of their representation are they called signes*. And see further the said example of the *holy Ghost apearing in forme of a doue*, alledged and applyed in like maner by *Martin Bucer*, in his *scripta Anglicana*, printed at *Basile*. 1577. *pag.* 652. And see further *Caluin. in Harm. in Math.* 3. *vers* 16. (m) *M. Hooker* in his Ecclesiastical pollicy, *l.* 5. *sect.* 67. *pag.* 174.

(n) 1. *Cor.*

the Apostle calleth the Sacrament, (n) *bread*; howsoeuer this may be alledged against *tran-substantiation*, yet against consubstantiation or the real presence, it maketh nothing : but in answeare for *transubstantiation* I say. *First*, that the Sacrament may be called *bread*, in reguard of the firster forme, the like whereof is vsed in other real chaunges, as for example : *Aarons rod* being (o) *turned into a serpent*, was yet after called (p) *a rod*; *water turned into wine*, was yet afterwardes called (q) *water*, notwithstanding that the chaunge in them both, was apparent euen to sence ; And Angels appearing in the shape of men, were therefore called (r) *men* : much the rather therefore may the Sacrament be in like respect called *bread*, considering not onely that it was *bread*, but also (which was wanting in the two firster examples) reteineth yet stil the forme of bread. *Secondly*, (to omit that the *Apostle* (*) explaineth himselfe sufficiently not to speake of material *bread*; I answeare, that the learned Caluinistes them selues do affirme that

(n)

1. Cor . 10. 16.

(o)

Exo . 17. 10.

(p)

Exod . 17. 12.

(q)

Ioan . 2. 9.

(r)

Gen . 18. 2. et 19. 5. Marc . 16. 5. Luc . 24. 4. Act . 1. 10.

(*)

The Apostles words are, *the bread which we breake is it not the participation of the body of Christ, for we that are many are one bread, one body, in as much as we al are partakers of one bread.* 1. Cor . 10. 16. 17. if the Apostle speake here of material bread which is broken into seueral

partes, and receiued by *vs that are many*, at seueral times and in seueral places, then is not this *bread one*, but diuers or many, whereas the Apostle saith plainly to the contrary, that the bread whereof he speaketh is *but one bread*, by our pertaking whereof we (also) *are one bread, one body*, so plainly doth he explaine him selfe not to speake of material bread which we in no sence can be said to be, (no more then we can be tearmed the cup or the wine) but of that *one immaterial bread*, which is *Christes one body*, which also we are said to be, *in as much as we are partakers of* that one immaterial bread mentioned in *Ioan.* 6. 35. 48. 51. see the answearable exposition hereto of *Remigius in* 1. *Cor.* 10. where he saith, *licet panis videatur, in veritate corpus Christi est, ex quo pane quicunq, communicant, corpus Christi edunt, quoniam vnus panis, subaudis Christi, et vnum corpus Christi, multi sumus qui conedimus illum panem : caro quam verbum Dei in vtero virginali in vnitate*

E e

sua

ſua perſonæ, et panis qui conſecratur in Eccleſia vnum corpus Chriſti ſunt, ſi-cut enim illa caro corpus Chriſti eſt, ita iſte panis tranſit in corpus Chriſti, nec ſunt duo corpora, ſed vnum corpus. And the very ſame ſentence is affir-med in the ſame wordes

by *Haymo in* 1. *Cor.* 10.
As alſo *Primaſius in cap.*
10. *ad Hæbræos.* ſaith in
like maner, *eſt vnum cor-*
pus Chriſti cum illo quod
ſuſcepit de vtero virginali,
non multa corpora.

(s)
Aretius, in loc. commun.
pag. 260. and 40. and
ſee *Marloret* in his En-
chiridion at the word
panis.

(t)
Ioan. 6. 35. 48. 51.

(u)
Math. 26. 29. *et Marc.*
14. 25.

(*)
For whereas it may
ſeeme by the Euange-
liſtes, that our Sauiour
did firſt deliuer the Sacrament, and afterwardes
ſaid the wordes, *Math.*
26. 26. in ſo much as
S. *Marke.* 14. 23. 24.
ſaith, *and taking the Cup*
&c. he gaue to them, and

that (s) *vnder the name of bread, the Scripture*
doth (ſometimes) *vnderſtand not naked bread,*
but al kinde of foode which concernẽth this pre-
ſent life, or the eternal: according to which
acceptance, the Sacrament may alſo be called
bread, and ſo accordingly is our Sauiour him
ſelfe in like ſort called (t) *bread.*

And where our aduerſaries do further vrge
that our Sauiour affirmed the Sacrament to
be wine ſaying, (u) *I wil not drinke from hence*
forth of this fruiƈe of the vine; I do anſweare
hereto. *Firſt,* that if this obieƈtion were true
and not miſtaken, yet wete it fully auoided
by that which haith bene already ſaid concerning the Sacrament being called *bread.*
Secondly, I ſay that this obieƈtion is miſtaken,
for theſe wordes were not ſpoken of the Sacrament, but of the wine of the paſchal *lambe,*
and though *Mathew,* and *Marke,* place theſe
wordes after the inſtitution of the Sacrament, yet this forceth not, conſidering that
the Scriptures do often times admit (*) *a*
Hiſteron Proteron, not recyting alwaies thinges in that due order, wherein they were
done: which to be true in this, appeareth by
conference with *Luke,* who writing after
Mathew, and *Marke,* and profeſſing to write
al thinges in (x) *order,* ſetteth downe before
the

they al drunke of it, and he ſaid to them, this is my bloud &c. Peter Martir
in his diſputation of the Euchariſt in the colleƈtion annexed to his common places in engliſh *pag.* 213. ſaith hereof, *where it is written that*
Chriſt firſt gaue before he ſaid, this is my body, it is the vſual figure called
Hiſteron Proteron, that is to wit, when a thing is ſet forth by a contrary
order.

order. And see him there againe *paulo ante med*. (x) *Luc*. 1. 3. and *M. Fenner* in his *sacra theologia. fol*. 167. saith, *Lucæ proprium studium erat, vt historiam exactam et plenam, ex rerum ordine, et serie, con-texeret. &c.*

the institution of the Sacrament these wordes now vrged, and not onely referreth them to the Cup of the old Testament, but also (which maketh the same relatiō as yet more euident) vseth the (z) *same phrase*, euen of the Paschal Lambe. In so much as our aduersary *Hutte- rus, Doctor*, and publicke professor in the vni- uersity of *Wittenberge*, doth (*) acknowledge that these wordes were spoken of the wine of *the Pascal Lambe*, whereupon I now re- tort this obiection as strong against our ad- uersaries: for if our Sauiour drinking the wine of the Paschal Lambe, tould his Disci- ples that *he would not from thenceforth drinke of the fruite of the vine &c.* the liquor then which was contained in the cup of the new Testament, and whereof he so presently af- ter drunke to them, was not of the fruicte of the vine, and so by consequent was not wine. And thus much brefely concerning our aduersaries most principal obiectiōs from the Scriptures. As for these other sayings, (a) *the poore you haue alwaies with you, but me you haue not*

(y)
Luc. 22. 18.
(z)
Luc. 22. 16. *hence forth I wil not eate of it &c.*
(*)
Hutterus de sacrificio Mis- satico. pag. 393. saith, *il- la verba, non bibam de hoc genimine vitis &c. serua- tor prolocutus est in tractan- do Sacramento veteris Te- stamenti, Agno nimirum Paschali*.
(a)
Math. 26. 11. this place, as appeareth by circum- stance of the text concer- neth onely his visible presence amongst them, needing their releefe and so according to this like respect he may be said to be absent, when

otherwise he is truly present, as him selfe insinuateth saying after his resurrection, *these are the wordes I spake to you when I was yet with you. Luc*. 24. 44. as though he had not beene then present with them; as for the sence which our aduersaries would enforce, it doth no lesse seclude their real presence of his body to faith, then it doth our real presence thereof to the bodily mouth, for the letter being so precisely vrged maketh against both a like. In so much as *Martin Bucer*, euen after his reuoult from Lutheranisme, as appeareth by his preface there to the Bishop of Herforde saith hereof, *(in his enarrat. in sacra quatuor Euang. &c.* printed *Basilea*. 1536. *in Euang. Math. c.* 26. *pag*. 490.

E e 2

and

and 491. *ex his liquet credendam et confitendam eſſe veram in ſacra cæna, preſentiam & exhibitionem corporis et ſanguinis Domini &c. nec pugnat cum hac confeſſione vel quæ de veritate humanæ naturæ in Chriſto, vel de glorifi- catione eius cæleſti Scripturæ habent &c. proinde nihil iſta præſentia et ex- hibitio Domini ſacra cæna, vel humanæ in Chriſto naturæ derogat, nec locis il- lis qui teſtificantur eum relicto mundo, conceſciſſe in gloriam Patris.* (and then next after moſt direɛtly with vs) *his namꝗ locis nihil poteſt inferri quam Dominum iam non hic agere patibili ratione & vita ſenſibus perceptibi- li: ita teſtificatione de abitione ſua eundo ad Patrem, certum eſt Dominum nihil docere amplius voluiſſe, quam ſe ex ratione viuendi huius ſeculi erumno- ſa & ſenſibus expoſita, in glorioſam ac cæleſtem viuendi rationem concedere.* So euidently and plainly is this obieɛtion anſweared and refelled by *Martin Bucer.*

(b)   *not alwaies:* (b) *the heauens muſt receiue him,* **Aɛt. 3. 21.** That *the* and ſuch like, I paſſe them ouer as being mere *heauens receiue him* we ſted cauils vnworthy of al further anſweare; re- faſtly beleeue, & ſo like -   ferring wiſe that he is really preſent in the Sacrament, for theſe be both of them ſeueral truthes, commended to our beleefe by the Scriptures. And whereas our aduerſaries ſay as before, *traɛt. 2. ſeɛt. 4. ſubdiuiſ.* 1. *p. 14* at 1. *that it is impoſſible for Chriſt to be both in heauen and earth* at one time, they hereby fal into a new queſtion, which maketh aſmuch a- *p. 170* gainſt their real preſence mentioned, *traɛt. 2. ſeɛt. 5. ſubdiuiſ.* 2. and teſtifyed by *M. Bruce* next heretofore, *traɛt. 2. ſeɛt. 10. ſubdiuiſ.* 1. *p. 23* *fine.* in the margent there at the letter l. and by *Caluin* there at the letter k. and by *M. Fulke traɛt. 2. ſeɛt. 1. ſubdiuiſ.* 2. in the margent at the letter y. and by *M. Hooker,* next heretofore at m. and *hereafter traɛt. 2. ſeɛt. 11. ſubdiuiſ.* 1. at the letter p. in ſo much as *Caluin* inſtitut. *l. 4. c. 17. ſeɛt.* 10. doth therefore purpoſly pre- uent the ſame, ſaying, *although it may ſeeme incredible that in ſo great a diſtance of places* (as of heauen and earth) *the fleſh of Chriſt ſhould pene- trate to vs, that it may be meate for vs, we muſt yet remember how much aboue al ſences the ſecret power of the holy Ghoſt can ſhew it ſelfe &c.* and in his *epiſt. et reſponſ.* (printed, 1597.) *epiſt. 272. pag. 726.* he further ſaith, *confitemur Chriſtum ita eſſe in cælo ſecundum humanam ſuam naturam vnde & illum expectamus, vt tamen pro infinita ſua virtute quæ ſeſe vbiꝗ porigit, ex quo ad dextram Patris concedit, poſſit nos incomprehenſibili modo vere paſce- re corpore et ſanguine ſuo ſine vlla mutatione loci.* And *Bucer* in his fore- ſaid *enarrat. &c. in Math. c. 26. pag.* 491. ſaith, *vt ſol vere in vno* *loco cæli visibilis circumscriptus est, radys tamen suis præsens vere et substantialiter exhibetur vbilibet vrbis, ita Dominus etiamß circumscribatur vno loco cæli arcaniet diuini, id est gloria patris verbo, tamen suo & sacrß simbolis vere, et totus ipse Deus et homo presens exhibetur in sacra cæna, eoq̃ substantialiter.* Ad hereunto that *Caluin, Bucer, Beza, Farellus,* and others, alledged *heretofore tract. 2. sect. 5. subdiuis. 2. at o. *.* do teach the *real presence in the supper of Christes very flesh present there, and offered to the very vnfaithful,* which cannot be in respect of his onely presence in heauen, for vnbeleeuers want faith, wherewith to ascend thither : therefore his being so present to them in the supper, cannot stand with his onely being present in heauen . In like maner (to forbeare our Sauiours other apparitions testifyed *heretofore tract. 2. sect. 4. subdiuis. 2.* at h.) the Scriptures witnes that our Sauiour (his foresaid remaning in heauen notwithstanding) was seene to *S. Paul Act. 9. 27.* and *22. 15.* and *26. 16.* and *1. Cor. 9. 1.* and *1. Cor. 15. 5. 6. 7. 8.* not far of as when *S. Steuen* saw him *the heauens being opened, Act. 7. 55. 56.* for no such thing is mentioned in *S. Paules* seeing of him, but at one time, *Epistas auto, he stoode by him. Act. 23. 11.* euen neare to him with *light* (at another time) *aboue the brightnes of the Sunne shyning round* about *Paul,* and those that were with him, *Act. 26. 13.* and *22. 7.* and *9. 3.* in so much as *S. Paul,* did there not onely see him, but also *heare the voice of his mouth. Act. 22. 15.* in like sort doth *S. Chrisostome* refel this doubt saying *de Sacerdotio l. 3. c. 4. O miracle, he that sitteth aboue on the right hand of God the Father, is notwithstanding in the time of sacrifice conteyned in the handes of men.* And in *hom. 2. ad Populum, fine.* he maketh not a comparison (as our aduersaries answearing hereto would pretend) but an opposition betweene our *Sauiour,* and *Helias ,* our *Sauiours flesh ,* and *Helias his mantle ,* affirming that whereas *Helias ascended being depriued of his mantle,* our Sauiour *did much more, for he left both vs his flesh & ascended hauing the same .*

Lastly, this point is hereferring neuerthelesse the vnsatisfyed or doub-
tofore, *tract. 2. sect. 4.*
ful reader, to that which is breefly said of *subdiuis. 1. at d. e. f.*
them in the margent hereto annexed . And
yet further answeared by
thus much breefly of obiections had from
the learned Caluinistes
the Scriptures.
them selues, who *disclame*

Obiections in al pretended *impossibi-
lity* of Christes being at once both in heauen and in the Sacrament.

Objections against the real presence, taken from the Fathers, answeared.

SECTION. 11.

AS concerning the objections pretended from the Fathers, whereas certaine
of their sayinges are more obscure and
perplexed in their discourse of this Sacrament, then they are in other ordinary pointes
of faith, the reason thereof in general is to
be obserued as proceeding from the height
of so sacred a mystery, the which as they did
in such respect debarre (2) *from the sight of*
Cathecumines reputed *vnwortly* to behould
the same; so also did they of a like religious
care oftentimes forbeare to write so plainly
and openly of it, as they did of other matters, as being fearefull to expose the doctrine
thereof, to the not sufficiently instructed conceiuing of *Catechumines*, or the prophane
contempt and contumelies of the vnfaithful.
Hence it is that so frequently in this, aboue
other pointes of faith, they professe to write
with a respectiue kinde of reseruation, wherby they signify somwhat to be vnderstoode or
kept secret, which they durst not so plainly vtter. So the Apostle beginning to discourse
thereof saith, *vt prudentibus loquor &c. I speake*
as to wisemen, your selues iudge what I say &c.
And againe entring into discourse of *Melchi-*
sedech, whose sacrifice & Preisthood, (*) prefigured the Preisthood and sacrifice of Christ,
he likewise saith, (4) *of whom we haue many*
thinges to say, inexplicable to vtter, because you
are become weake to heare. So also *Theodorets*
dispute set downe Dialogue-wise with the

Eutichian

---

(2)
See this heretofore pre-
fat: reader. sect. 11. fine.
at 18. & tract. 2. sect.
1. subdiuis. 1. after p.
at the figure 2. & tract.
2. sect. 8. subdiuis. 3.
at k. I.

(3)
1. Cor. 10. 15.

(*)
See this hereafter tract.
3. sect. 4. subdiuis. 1.
initio. at 2. 3.) s. t. u.
and so forwardes there.

(4)
Habr. 5. 11. where-
upon S. Hierome, epist.
126. saith, *he spoke to*
the Hebrewes, that is to the
Iewes, and not to the faith-
ful, to whom he might
haue beene bould to vtter
the Sacrament.

(5)
Heretofore, tract. 2.
sect. 2. subdiuis. 3. in
the margent at x.) and
tract. 2. sect. 8. subdi-
uis. 2. in the margent

(6)
Theodoret dial. 2.

(7)
Theodoret, Ibidem.

(8)
August. in Psal. 33.
saith, *nondum enim erat*
sacrificium

Eutichian heretik, when (immediatly before the wordes (5) *heretofore* alledged) the hereticke beginneth to make his argument from the Sacrament saying, (6) *quid appellas &c* . *what dost thou cal the guift (which is offered) before the Preistes inuocation? the Catholicke orthodoxus,* answeareth thereto saying, (7) *I may not speake openly, for it is like that some are present not admitted to the mysteries,* whereto *Eranstes* there replyeth saying, *respondeatur ænigmatice,* then answeare darkly . To this like purpose also doth *S . Augustine* often speake of this Sacrament with like retyred circumspection, as saying thereof somtimes (8) *norunt fideles &c . norunt qui initiati sunt &c .* And the like is yet further (9) vsedby *Origen, Chrisostō,* & other Fathers, al whichcircumspection was in it selfe causeles, had the Fathers thought our Sauiours wordes to be figuratiue, and was also no more necessary in this Sacrament then in Baptisme, had the said Fathers acknowledged no otherpresence in this then they did in Baptisme : Hereby then it is euident

sacrificium corporis et sanguinis Domini quod fideles norunt &c . & in *Psal .* 39 . he termeth it, *sacrificium verum quod fideles norunt* and *l .* 50 . *homil . hom .* 42 . he saith, *norunt fideles quid accipiant .* And *de ciuit . Dei, l .* 10 . *c .* 6 . *fine .* he saith, *quod etiam Sacramento Altaris fidelibus noto frequentat Ecclesia .* And in *Psal .* 109 . he saith, *Tu es Sacerdos in æternum secundum ordinem Melchisedech, fidelibus loquor si quod non intelligunt. Cathecumini, auferant pigritiam &c .* and in *Psal .* 33 . *con .* 2 . he saith, *accepit (Christus) in manus suas quod norunt fideles .* And *de verbis Domini, ser .* 46 . he saith, *quid enim dixt*

Dominus Iesus iam fideles nouerunt, tu autem Catecumenus diceris audiens et surdus es . And *apud Bedam in* 1 . *Cor .* 10 . he saith, *norunt fideles quemadmodum manducent carnem Christi .* and in *Ioan . tract .* 26 . he saith, *norunt fideles corpus Christi .* and *epist .* 162 . he saith, *Tollerat ipse Dominus Iudam &c . sinit accipere inter innocentes Discipulos quod fideles nouerunt precium nostrum .* thus far onely *S . Augustine .* (9) *Origen in Leuiticum hom .* 9 . *prope finem* saith, *nouit qui mysterijs imbutus est & carnem et sanguinem verbi Dei, non ergo immoremur in his quæ et scientibus nota sunt, & ignorantibus patere nonpossunt .* In like maner *S . Chrisostome in hom . de S . Philogino .* saith, *qui mysterijs initiati sunt, intelligunt quæ dicuntur .* And in *Gen . hom .* 27 . *prope finem .* he saith, *si hoc fecerimus poterimus pura conscientia ad sanctam terribilemq̃ hanc mensam accedere &c . sciunt initiati illi quid dicatur &c .* And the like kinde of couert speaking doth he vse elswhere, as namely *ad Pop . Antioch . hom .* 51 . *&* 58 . *&* 61 .

& 61. & *in* 1. *Tim*. *hom*. 5. and fee the like in *Sozomen*. *hift*. *l*. 8. *c*. 5. *poft*. *med*. where it is faid, *intelligunt autem qui Chrifto funt initiati quid dicam*.

(c)
pag 106. See heretofore, *tract*. 2. *fect*. 2. throughout.

(d)
pag 199. See heretofore, *tract*. 2. *pag* 201. *fect*. 8. *fubdiuif*. 1. 2. 3. throughout, for the vfage of adoration, & fee there *pag*. also *fubdiuif*. 3. through- 212 out, and *fubdiuif*. 4. at *p*. 216. q. 5. for the fundry other like external obferuations of *forbearing the acte of mariage*, & *to touch the facred Chalices*, of receiuing it fasting, of holy bread. and concerning the *care had that no part of the Sacrament fel downe*. and *tract*. 2. *fect*. 1. *fubdiuif*. 2. at e. f. h. *.

dent that the Fathers forbearing fomtimes for the reafons beforefaid, to fpeake fo plainly of this Sacrament as they did of other matters, haue thereby left to fuch as conceiue not the true reafon, certaine of their faid fayinges more fubiect to doubt and difficulty of being miftaken; from whence arifeth pretence of obiection. And thus much being but faid ingeneral; I further ad, that to anfwere al obiections in particuler, is more then the intended breuity or methode of this fhort difcourfe can admit. And although the Fathers doctrine of real prefence, be *heretofore* fufficiently made manifeft by their euident (c) *fayings* like (d) *practife*, and confeffed (e) iudgment, fo as our aduerfaries reft bound in al reafon, and likewife by their (10) *owne rules*, to vnderftand the Fathers doubtful fayinges, as agreeable to thofe other which are more plaine, for otherwife,

for referuing the Sacrament vnreceiued, and *hereafter tract*. 2. *fect*. 1. *fubdiuif*. 3. at r. s. 4. 5. t. u. x. *for offering it to God for the finnes of the liuing and deade*. (e) See heretofore *tract*. 2. *fect*. 2. through- out. (10) Whereas *Iulianus* the hereticke, to proue that children *An obiecti-* are without original finne, obiected this faying of S. *Chrifoftome*, we *on anfwered* Baptife children although they haue not finne. S. *Auguft. contra Iulian. Pelag*. *l*. 1. *c*. 2. teacheth how to vnderftand this doubtful fentence faying, *intellige propria, et nulla eft contentio*: *vnderftand* (by finne) proper (or their owne actual finne) *and there is no difagreement*: *but thou wilt fay* (faith S. *Auguftine* to *Iulianus*) *why did not* (*Chrifoftome*) *him felfe ad* (the word) *propria*, whereto S. *Auguftine* anfweareth faying, *becaufe that difputing in the Catholik Church, he did thinke he fhould not be otherwife vnderftoode*. This point, and very example thereof, is obferued by *Peter Martir* in his common places in englifh *part*. 2. *pag*. 228. and by *Chem-*

nifius

nitius in his examen, *part. 1. fol. 80.* in so much as *Chemnitius* doth there further infer and obserue saying, *hoc modo &c. in this sort did Augustine by a commodious interpretation make agreeable vnto the anallogy of faith the* (more obscure) *sayinges of Hillary, Ambrose, Chrisostome,* and *Hierome, which Pelagius* (the hereticke) *alledged in confirmation of his error:* affirming further a litle there before, that it was vsual with *the Fathers to mitigate and excuse by a profitable exposition (incommode dicta veterum) such sayinges of the Fathers as were vttered inconueniently.* In this sort also doth *Gellius Snecanus* in his *methodica descriptio. pag. 429. 430. & 432.* excuse the more obscure obiected sayings of *Caluin,* and *Beza,* saying, *non de singulis huius, aut illius doctoris scriptis, de Ecclesiarum fide et doctrina mutuandnm est iudicium. pag. 429.* & againe, *necesse est vt obscuriores nostrorum phrases, aut sicubi minus commode videntur loqui &c. referas ad primaria inter reliqua paulo posita fundamenta, atq́, ex ipsis principiis et fontibus aliorumq́, locorum collatione, vbi apertius sese exponunt &c. tantum abest vt nostros quasi sibimet ipsis repugnantes asseras pag. 430.* yet more, *si obscuriores quidam loci vbi minus plane nostri sese exponunt, ex aliorum collatione explicarentur; quemadmodum Beza hic facit in Caluino commode intelligendo &c. pag. 432.* and *Beza* him selfe *in epist. theolog. epist. 82. pag. 382.* excuseth thus the obiected saying of *Caluin,* saying in answeare thereto, *comparanda sunt inter se sepenumero vnius eiusdemq́, scriptoris loca, vt quæ fuerit eius sententia liquido perspiciatur, cum omnia omnibus locis, etiam de re vna quapiam, dici nec possint nec debeant: Hoc qui non faciunt, dici non potest quam iniuriam sæpe bonis doctisq́, scriptoribus faciant &c. sic etiam intelligatur quod Caluinus eo loco scripsit &c.* And *M. Carthwright* in his 2. reply *part. 1. pag. 627.* saith, *if it be a simple answeare to set one author against an other, it is much more simple to set one authority at variance with it selfe, without shewing any way of reconciliation:* whereby it is plaine and conuincing, that seeng the Fathers sayings and practise, are heretofore made plaine & confessed, both for *real presence,* and *adora-*

otherwise, if a naked resemblance of wordes may suffice wherewith to perplexe the doubtful reader; I bouldly affirme that many moe, & more plaine seeming sayinges (*hertofore*(11) in part recyted) may be alledged from *Caluin, Beza,* and other their followers in pretended proofe of our Catholicke doctrine of real presence of Christes body in the Sacrament, then

tion, that therefore their other obscure & lesse plaine sayinges should be

commodi-

commodiously qualifyed or expoûded as to be made confonant and agreable thereto.

(11)

Heretofore, *tract. 2. fect. 5. fubdiuif. 2. & 3.* throughout.

(*)

Confeffed for a neceffary fequel hereafter, tract. 3. fect. 4. fubdiuif. 1. at r. s. t. pag. 339.

(f)

See heretofore, *tract. 2. fect. 10. fubdiuif. 2.* from the beginning of that 2. fubdiuifion til u.

(g)

Obtulit hoc idem quod Melchifedech, obtulerat, id eft, panem et vinum, fuum fcilicet corpus et fanguinem. Ciprian. l. 2. epift. 3. paulo poft initium.

(h)

Hierom. in c. 1. Malachia. faith, *poluimus panem, id eft, corpus Chrifti, quando indigni accedimus ad Altare.*

(i)

See *D. Fulke* againft *Heskins, Saunders &c.* pag. 136.

(k)

Primafius, in c. 5. ad Habr.

then our aduerfaries can alledge againft it from al the Fathers. And though likewife the circumftances of the places obiected by our aduerfaries from the Fathers, would afford to euery of them in perticular, a plaine and fufficient anfweare, the aduantage wherof I muft (for the reafon aforefaid) purpofly forbeare: I wil now yet, to auoide al fcruple, admit for the time their matterial obiections had from the Fathers, to be fo ftrong in fhew of wordes as they pretend, and that done wil yet difcouer them to be of no force at al: for the better conceiuing wherof, I wil breefly reduce their obiections had from the Fathers to thefe fiue fpecial ranckes or heades. *Five obiect.* *The firft* is cocerning the Sacrament being *answe* fomtimes by them called *bread. The fecond* is *et.* concerning their like affirming it to be *a figure* or *myftery. The third* is of fuch Fathers as affirme our *fpiritual* receiuing by faith. The *forth* is of fuch as feeme to difclaime in our eating or deuouring of mans flefh. *The fiueth* and laft is concerning fuch teftimonies as feeme to affirme that the nature of bread remaineth in the Sacrament. For *the firft,* although being admitted, it maketh onely againft tranfubftantiation, but nothing at al againft the real prefence, which is the principal controuerfy, and whereof tranfubftantiation is confeffedly *a neceffary* (*) *fequel.* And though likewife it may receiue it fufficient anfweare in that wich haith bene (f) *heretofore* faid in this like behalfe, yet I further anfweare, that *the Fathers,* in calling the Sacrament *bread,* do it fomtimes with fuch a *correction* of fpeach as fufficiently explaineth their meaning in other places. Thus doth *S. Ciprian* correct and expaine him felfe faying (g) *he offered* be offered bread and wine, that is to say, his body and bloud. S. *Hierome* also saith in like maner, (h) *we polute the bread, that is to say, the body of Christ, when we come vnworthely to the Altar.* and againe, (i) *our mystery is signifyed in offering bread and wine, that is the body & bloud of our Lord Iesus Christ.* *Primasius,* saith accordingly, *instar illius &c.* (k) *in resemblance of Melchisadech he offered bread and wine, that is to say, his body and bloud.* S. *Gregory Nissen,* vrging our worthy preparation to the Eucharist which he there compareth with *Manna,* saith there, (2) *it is bread (prouided for vs) without seede, without plowing, and without any other worke of man:* affirming there further that *corpus omnino est,* and *corporis cibus,* it is (Christes) *body* and *food* (euen) to (our) *bodies,* which argueth that he speaketh here of Christes body as it is receiued in the Sacrament by our bodily mouth, and not as it is eaten by faith. And *lastly,* (to omit (3) others) *Ignatius* saith, *I* (1) *desire the bread of God, which is the flesh of Christ &c.* so fully doth the Fathers explaine what they intend in ther sometimes calling the Sacrament *bread.* Whereto I onely ad, that where they in reguard of the external forme, do cal it but somtimes *bread,* they do in reguard of the internal substance, much more often cal it his *body,* both which pointes, to the more ful solution of this obiection S. *Ciril* doth accordingly expresse saying, (m) *vnder the figure of bread, his body is geuen to thee, vnder the figure of wine his bloud is*

Chrift him selfe gaue bread, the which bread was to be betrayed. (l) *Ignatius, in epistola ad Rom. post med.* saith, *panem Dei volo, panem cælestem, panem vitæ, qui est caro Iesu Christi &c. et potum volo sanguinem eius.* This difference of *flesh* and *bloud,* to be eaten and drunken, is not in re-

Habr.

(2)
Nissen. in lib. de vita Moys.

(3)
Ambros. l. 5. de Sacramentis c. 4. circa med. saith, *Dixi vobis &c.* I tould you that before the wordes of Christ (pronouced) that which is offered, is called bread, but whe the wordes of Christ are come, it is not then called bread, but body. Why therefore in the Lordes prayer, which doth follow after (consecration) doth the Preist mention our bread? truly he mentioneth bread, but withal calleth it Epiousion, that is to say, supersubstantial; it is not that bread which entreth into the body, but that bread of eternal life which strengthneth the substance of our soule. And *Sedulius in opere Paschali,* speaking of the *bread* which Christ at his last supper gaue to *Iudas,* saith thereof, *panem cui tradidit ipse, qui panis tradendus erat:* To whom

(l) *Ig-*

spect of spiritual eating; for that to faith *eating and drinking is at one*, neither doth it make such distinction of *flesh* and *bloud*. And *in e-pist. ad Ephes*. he further saith, *frangentes panem qui est medicamentum immortalitatis &c.*

(m)
Ciril. Hierosol. Catech.
4.　(n)
Caro eius est quam forma panis opertam in Sacramento accipimus, et sanguis eius quem sub vini specie et sapore potamus. And againe *nos autem in specie panis et vini quam videmus, res inuisibiles, id est carnem et sanguinem, honoramus. August. in lib. sentent. Prosperi*. these are acknowledged to be the sayinges of *S. Augustine*, by *M. Iewel* in his reply, *pag.* 471.
(o) *Ciril. Hierosol. Ca-*

is *geuen to thee*. whereunto might be added sundry (n) other like sayinges of the Fathers, as also their other testimonies, wherin they do most directly affirme of the Sacrament, that (o) *it is not bread*. As concerning the second, I say, *first*, that it is (*) *heretofore* sufficiently answeared. *Secondly* I say in further answeare, that our aduersaries do know, how that we affirme (aswel as they) that the external Sacrament is *a figure*, or representation of Christ, and that we do accordingly celebrate it in memory of him. And therefore the Fathers affirming it to be a figure, do but affirme that which we graunt, making no more therin against vs, then against our aduersaries, for though our aduersaries affirme it to be *a figure*, yet say they aswel as we, (p) not *onely a figure*, but do admit together

tech. 4. saith, *hoc sciens et pro certissimo habens, panem hunc qui videtur a nobis, non esse panem, etiamsi gustus panem esse sentiat, sed esse corpus Christi: et vinum quod a nobis conspicitur, tametsi sensui gustus vinum esse videatur, non tamen vinum, sed sanguinem Christi esse*. And *Ambros. de Sacrament. l. 4. c. 4.* saith, *de pane, fit corpus Christi*. and *de mysterys init. c. 9*. he saith, *non est quod natura formauit &c.* alledging there in example thereof *Moyses rod* turned into a serpent, and other like real chaunges. And see his other wordes alledged next heretofore in this pisent subdiuision in the margent at 3. next before l. Also *S. Bernardus in serm. de cæna Domini*. saith, *hostia quam vides iam non est panis, sed caro &c. similiter liquor iste quam vides, iam non est vinum, sed sanguis &c.* And *Chrisostom. in serm. de Eucharistia in encænys*. saith, *num vides panem, num vinum &c. absit ne sic cogites*. see this plaine saying at large alledged and reiected by the Century writers *heretofore, tract. 2. sect. 2. subdiuis. 3.* in the margent at u. (*) See heretofore *tract. 2.*

sect.

pag. *sect.* 10. *subdiuis.* 1. at. e. f. g. h. i. k. l. m. (p) In the discourse
231 entituled, *Collatio Cathol. et orthod. Christianorum fidei &c.* pag. 348.
the Caluinist Protestantes do say of them selues, *nec quisquam inter or-*
thodoxos vnquam repertus est, qui corpus Christi in cæna Domini, figurari aut
significari tantum dixerit &c. And the same is yet further affirmed there
pag. 355. And *M. Bilson* in his true difference betweene Christian
subiection, and vnchristian rebellion. *part. 4. pag.* 592. speaketh *against*
them who defend the Sacrament doth onely figure, not offer, grace. And see
M. Hooker alledged heretofore, *tract. 2. sect.* 10. *subdiuis.* 1. at the
letter m. And see him also in his Ecclesiastical pollicy *l. 5. sect. 67.* pag.
177. where he affirmeth that, *the Eucharist is not a figure onely, and that*
the efficacy of Christes body and bloud, is not al we receiue in this Sacrament.
affirming there further that *these mysteries do make vs pertakers both of the*
grace of that body, and besides also do impart to vs, euen in true and real,
though mystical, manner, the very person of our Lord him selfe. And
see *Caluin* and others alledged heretofore, *tract. 2. sect.* 10. *subdiuis.*
1. in the margent at the letters e. and k. And see *M. D. Couel* in
his defence of *M. Hooker,* pag. 116. And *M. Iewel* in his reply to
M. Harding, pag. 341.

ther with the *figure* a real presence of Christes
body (q) annexed spiritually to the creatures & so offered present to their faith, against
which this their obiection, maketh as much
as it doth against our opinion; In so much
as *Caluin* doth therefore signify his (r) special dislike of it. *Thirdly,* I say, that the Fathers do sufficiently explaine their doctrine,
and ours, declaiming in what (s) sorte the
Eucharist is a figure, Sacrament, or mystery
and

(q)
See *Caluin* and *M. Bruce,*
heretofore, *tract.* 2. *sect.*
10. *subdiuis.* 1. in the
margent at the letters k.
and l. And *M. Fulke* in
his defence of the english
tranflations, against *M.*
Martin, c. 17. *sect.* 4.
pag. 435. saith, *the crea-*
tures or elementes, are bles-

fed and confecrated, that by the working of Gods spirit they should be chaunged
into the body and bloud of Christ, after a diuine and spiritual manner vnto the
worthy receiuers. And *M. Sutliue de Missa Papistica.* printed *Londini.*
1603. *l.* 1. *c.* 29. *fol.* 173. saith, *mutatur panis in carnem spiritualiter.*
Caluin *institut. l.* 4. *c.* 17. *sect.* 10. saith hereof, *nec est quod obyciat*
quispiam figuratam esse locutionem, qua signatæ rei nomen signo d feratur &c.
(s) S. *Augustine in sententys Prosperi.* saith, *hoc est quod dicimus, quod*
omnibus modis approbare contendimus, Sacramentum Eucharistiæ duobus con-
fici,

fici, duobus conftare, vifibili elementorum fpecie, et inuifibili Domini noftri Iefu Chrifti carne et fanguine, Sacramento, id eft, externo facro figno, et re ſacramenti, id eft corpore Chrifti. this faying is acknowledged by *M. Iewel* in his reply, *pag.* 448. end fee *S . Auguftines* other fayinges alledged next heretofore in the margent at the letter n. and *Dionifius Areopagita de Ecclefiaft . Hierarch . c. 3 .* tearmeth the external fimbols *venerable fignes, by which Chrift is (both) fignifyed and receiued .*

(t)
Hierofol. catech . 4 .

(u)
note. This fentence is alledged vnder the name of *Auguftine* by *Profper* in his collections, and fpecially cyted by *Algerus, l . 1 . c . 5.* And by *Gratian. dift . 2 . hoc eft .*

(x)
Hillary, l . 8 . de trinit .

(4)
Ciprian. de cæna Domini ante med .

(5)
Chemnitius in his examen. *part . 2 . pag . 91 .* faith, *veteres fæpe de elementis Euchariftiæ difputantes, de fignis, figuris, et fimbolis loquuntur: Sacramentarij autem non recte faciunt, qui propter has veterum fententias fubftantiam corporis et fanguinis Chrifti, ex cæna Domini proturbant .*

(y)
See *M. Hookers* wordes alledged next heretofore in the margent at the letter

and how alſo it is the truth : Which ſaid figure and truth, they do at once yet further expreffe, as where they fay (t) *vnder the figure of bread his body is geuen to thee ; vnder the figure of wine his bloud, is geuen to thee .* (u) *It is his flefh which we receiue in the Sacrament, coueredin the forme of bread, and it is his bloud which we drincke vnder the figure and taift of wine .* (x) *nos vere ſub myfterio &c .* we receiue the flefh of his body truly vnder a myftery ; and (4) we eate vpon earth the bread of Angels vnder a Sacrament .

So wel doth figure and myftery agree with the truth and prefence of Chriftes body vnder the fame . A thing ſo euident that the learned (5) *Chemnitius,* doth therefore condemne this very obiection in his brethren the Sacramentaries .

(2) As concerning *the third,* I anſweare, firft, that it is manifeft that we do acknowledge *a fpiritual* receiuing by faith, of the effectes and benefites of this holy Sacrament ; and therefore the Fathers in affirming but thus much, do therein make nothing againft vs : but where our aduerſaries vrge this to feclude the real prefence of Chriftes body in the Sacrament, it is not onely a deceiptful labouring ſo to refel one truth by an other, but is alſo vpon the matter directly aſmuch againft their opinion as ours ; for them ſelues are now at laft brought to (y) graunt, that

ter   they

3

ter p. and in the diuines of *Geneua* in their *Apologia modesta ad act. conuentus quindecim theologorum torga nuper habit*. pag. 49. fay, *spiritalis perceptionis nomine non eam intelligimus qua percipiatur sola Christi virtus spiritualis &c. itaq̃, corporalem, id est ipsiusmet Christi corporis perceptionem ac* Coinonian *minime tollimus ex cana*. And in the Caluinistes difcourfe entituled, *Collatio Catholicæ et orthodoxæ Christianorum fidei, de persona Christi, et sacra eius cana&c*. pag. 349. it is accordingly faid, *ad vocabulum, spiritualiter, quod attinet, nequaquam per hoc intelligimus spiritum sanctum tantum adesse, aut solam corporis Christi virtutem, hoc est, merita nobis communicari, sed talem* Coinonian *cum Apostolo prædicamus, qua corpus Christi substantia, merito, et efficacia, nobis communicetur &c. & vide ibidem*. pag. 324. *numer*. 66. and 67. And fee the like affirmed by *M. Whitaker contra Duræum. l. 2. pag*. 169. and by the *confeffion of Belgia* in the harmony of confeffions in englifh. *pag*. 431. and fee the *French confeffion* in the fame harmony, *pag*. 426. and the obferuations vpon that place, annexed by the tranflator to the faid harmony. and fee *M. Smithes* fermons, *ferm*. 1. *pag*. 103.

(z)

they receiue, not *onely figuratiuely, neither onely the efficacy of his body spiritually by faith, but also the very body it selfe*: (z) *not onely bread* (faith *Amandus Polanus* profeffor at *Bafile*) *neither onely the Deity, neither onely the vertue & efficacy of Christ, is prefent in the supper, but the very body and very bloud of Christ, are in very deede prefent in the sacred supper*. Secondly, I further fay, that the Fathers do fufficiently explaine them felues in this point, affirming moft directly with vs that we are vnited to Chrift by this bleffed Sacramēt, not only by (a) vniō of wil

Amandus Polanus in filoge-thefium &c. de cana Domini, pag. 307. And fee him alfo in *partit. theolog. l. 1. pag.* 279. where he faith, *non igitur tantum panis et vinum, nec tantum Deitas Christi, nec tantum Christi virtus et efficacia, in cæna presens est, sed etiam ipsum corpus et ipse sanguis Christi, reuera adsunt in sacra cæna*. And fee the like in *M*. (a) *Hillary, l. 8*. faith,

Hookers ecclefiafticall pollicy *l. 5. pag*. 177. *voluntatis tantum inter Patrem et Filium vnitatem hæretici mentientes vnitatis nostræ ad Deum vtebantur exemplo, tanquam nobis ad filium, et per filium ad Patrem; obfequio tantum et voluntate religionis vnitis nulla, per Sacramentum carnis et fanguinis naturalis communionis proprietas indulgeretur, cum &c. permanentem in nobis carnaliter filium &c. mysterium vera ac naturalis vnitatis fit predicandum*. and a litle before in the fame place he faith, *si voluntatis*

Si voluntatis tantum vnitatem intelligi vellet, (Chriſtus) cur gradum quendam atḡ, ordinem conſummandæ vnitatis expoſuit, niſi vt cum ille in Patre per naturā diuinitatis eſſet, nos contra in eo per corporalem eius natiuitatem, et ille rurſum in nobis per Sacramentorum ineſſe myſterium crederetur.

(b)

Ciril. Alexand. l. 10. wil neither *onely* (b) *ſpiritually,* neither (e) *in Ioan. c. 13.* faith, onely by faith, but (f) *carnally,* (g) *corporally,* *non negamus recta nos fide* and in (h) *very deede.* And that we receiue *charitateḡ, ſincera, Chriſto* Chriſtes body (*) *not onely with the mouth of* *ſpiritaliter coniungi, ſed* the heart, but alſo *with the mouth of the body:* *nullam nobis coniunctionis* And *rationem ſecundum carnem, cum illo eſſe, id profecto pernegamus &c.* An for- *taſſis putat ignotam nobis myſtica benedictionis virtutem eſſe, quæ cum in nobis fiat, nonne corporaliter quoḡ, facit communicatione corporis Chriſti, Chriſtum in nobis habitare?* and *lib. 11. in Ioan. c. 27.* he faith, *corporaliter e- nim filius per myſticam benedictionem nobis vnitur vt homo, ſpiritualiter autem vt Deus.* (e) *Chriſoſtomus in Math. hom. 83. poſt med.* faith, *non enim ſufficit ipſe hominem fieri, flagellis interim cædi, ſed nos ſecum in vnam, vt ita dicam, maſſam reducit, neḡ, id fide ſolum ſed reipſa nos corpus ſuum efficit &c. veniat tibi in mentem quo ſis honore honoratus, qua menſa fruaris &c.* (f) See *Hillaries* wordes alledged next before at the letter a. (g) See *Cirils* wordes next heretofore alledged at the letter b. (h) See *Chriſoſtomes* foreſaid wordes here at the letter e. and ſee him *ad Pop. hom. 61. initig.* (*) S. *Gregory, hom. 22. Paſch.* faith, *quid namḡ, ſit ſanguis agni &c.* for what the bloud of the Lambe is, you haue now lear ned, not by hearing, but by drinking, which bloud is put vpon either poaſt, when it is dunke, not onely with the mouth of the body, but alſo with the mouth of the heart. And S. *Auguſtine l. 2. contra aduerſar. leg. et proph. c. 9.* faith, *mediatorem Dei et hominum, hominem Chriſtum Ieſum, carnem ſuam nobis manducandam bibendumḡ ſanguinem dantem, fideli corde et ore ſuſcipi- mus.* And S. *Leo in ſerm. 6. de Ieiunio ſept. menſis.* faith, *ſic ſacræ menſæ communicare debetis, vt nihil prorſus de veritate corporis Chriſti et ſanguinis ambigatis, hoc enim ore ſumitur quod fid creditur.* And S. *Ciprian in ſerm. de cæna Domini ante med.* faith, *Chriſtus pincerna porrexit hoc poculum, et docuit vt non tantum exterius hoc ſanguine liniremur, ſed et interius aſper- ſione omnipotenti anima muniremur,* and a litle afterwardes *quo ſanguine interius exteriuſḡ, rubricati, a ſapientibus huius ſæculi iudicamur amentes.* And ſee *Ireneus* alledged heretofore, *tract. 2. ſect. 2. ſubdiuiſ. 4.* at r.

with

with whom agreeth *Tertulian in lib . de resurrectione carnis*, saying, *caro ablutur vt anima emaculetur &c. caro corpore et sanguine Christi vescitur, vt anima de Deo saginetur.* And see *Gregory Nissen,* alledged next heretofore *tract . 2. sect . 11. subdiuis. 1.* next after k. at the figure 2. *p. 243.*

And thus much of the thirde obiection.

As concerning *the fourth,* S . *Ciril* is (*) obiected saying, *what, (i) doest thou pronounce this our Sacrament to be, a deuouring of man &c.* In answeare whereof I say, that *Nestorius* against whom S . *Ciril* doth here write, affirmed, as is were confessed by *Peter Martir,* that (*) *Euchariftia,* was *comestio nudi et puri hominis :* And that so in the Sacrament we receiued Chrift, as being onely man, which S . *Ciril* tearmeth *grosse.* This appeareth yet more plainly by the Fathers of the coūcel of *Ephesus,* who in the *eleauenth Anathematisme,* expoūded by S. *Ciril,* say he rof. (k) *the Eucharist is not the body of any cōmō person, (for the flesh of a common man, should not quicken) but of the word it selfe: But the hereticke Nestorius dissolueth the vertue of this mystery, holding mans flesh, onely to be in the Eucharist:* against which his error, the Fathers of the said Councel do directly write saying, (l) *comming to the mystical blessinges, we are sanctifyed, being made partakers of the holy body & pretious bloud of Chrift the redeemer of vs al, not taking it (as) common flesh, but as the true quickning flesh, and proper to the word it selfe. And againe, we ought not to esteeme it as the flesh of a man, one of vs &c.* By which said error of *Nstorius,* thus plainly affirmed , and by the said Fathers thus impugned, it is more then manifest that the corporal presence of Chrift in the Sacrament, was the common knowen doctrine of the Church in those times. A thing so euident, that euen S . *Ciril* him selfe,

who

G g

(*)
Obiected by *M . Iewel* in his defence of the apologie, printed, 1571. pag. 319.

(i)
Ciril. Alexand. Anethematis. 11.

(*)
Peter Martir , l . contra Gardinerum, obiect . 211 .

(k)
Ciril. vbi supra.

(l)
In Epist . concilij Ephesii ad Nestorium .

(m)
Peter Martir in defens. ad obiect . Gardineri. part . 4. pag. 724. saith a gainst Ciril , the flesh of Chrift so to dwel in vs corporally &c. as this man interpreteth &c. is not in any case to be graunted, no, not if a thousand Angels , much lesse if one Ciril said it. And see his further re prehension of *Ciril* heretofore *tract. 2. sect. 2. subdiuis. 3 ,* at f. g . *pag. 114.*

(n) *Aug.*

(n)
August. in Psalm. 98. saith, *non hoc corpus quod videtis, mandicaturi estis, et bibituri illum sanguinem quem fusuri sunt qui me crucifigent, Sacramentum aliquod vobis commendaui, spiritualiter intellectum viuificabit vos, et si oportet visibiliter celebrari, oportet tamen inuisibiliter intelligi.*

(2)
Pretorius de sacrasanctis Sacramentis, pag. 245.

(3)
August. in Psal. 98. in the wordes precedent to these other before alledged saith, *durum illis visum est quod ait, nisi quis manducauerit carnem meã, non habebit vitam aternam: acceperunt illud stulte, carnaliter illud cogitauerunt, et putauerunt, quod praecisurus esset Dominus particulas quasdam de corpore suo et daturus illis, et dixerunt, durus est hic sermo.*

who was one of those Fathers (and here specially obiected) is yet neuertheleffe specially charged and reproued by (m) *Peter Martir,* for his confessed doctrine of the real prefence.

In like manner where our aduersaries do obiect S. *Augustine* saying, (n) *you shal not eate this body which you see, nor drinke the bloud which they that crucify me shal sheede: I haue commended a Sacramēt to you, the which spiritually vnderstoode shal quicken you:* which saying of S. *Augustine* together with an other testimony of *Luthers* to the like effect, (2) *Pretorius* the Caluinist, is not abashed to vrge no lesse bouldly against S. *Augustines* true meaning, then most ridiculously against *Luthers* confessed and knowen doctrine to the contrary. The answeare thereto is, that the *Capernaites,* to whom S. *Augustine* there speaketh, (3) *carnaliter illud cogitauerunt &c.* considered that thing carnally, and thought that our Lord would cut of certaine peeces from his body and geue to them: against which grosnes following the saying now obiected, wherein he instructeth that they should not eate his flesh (4) *(sicut illi intellexerunt carnem &c.)* so carnally as they conceiued, but should eate it, though truly, yet but *inuisibly,* and in a *Scrament,* after a heauenly and *spiritual* manner, tearming it therefore in the very same place, *Sacra-*

And then somwhat after follow the other forefaid wordes obiected, by comparing whereof together, it appeareth that *the spiritual vnderstanding,* required in the wordes formerly obiected, was but as onely to seclude this other carnal grosse imagination, that he would *cut peeces from his flesh, and so geue it them to eate,* which thing appeareth yet more plainly by his other sayinges elswhere, as *tom.* 9. *in Euang. Ioan. tract.* 27. where he faith of the same matter and persons, *Caro*

non

non prodeſt quicquam, ſed quomodo illi intellexerunt : carnem quippe ſic intel-
lexerunt, quomodo in cadauere dilaniatur , aut in macello venditur, non quo-
modo ſpiritu vegetatur. And *tom.* 10. *de verbis Apoſt. ſerm.* 11. he
further faith, *putaſtis quia de hoc corpore quod videtis partes faſturus ſum*,
et membra mea conciſurus, et vobis daturus. and *in Euang. Ioan. traſt.* 27.
he moſt effectually explaineth, and concludeth ſaying, *ſpiritus eſt qui*
viuificat, caro non prodeſt quicquam, ſicut illi intellexerunt carnem , non ſicut
ㅤㅤㅤㅤㅤㅤㅤㅤㅤㅤ*ego do ad manducandum*
Sacramentum latens, the which (as he there ㅤ*carnem meam.*
further ſaith) *oportet inuiſibiliter intelligi.* af-ㅤㅤ(4)
firming there withal but ſome litle before ㅤ*Auguſtine,* in his wordes
the wordes now in queſtion moſt plainly ㅤlaſt of al next before re-
the real preſence, and our eating of his fleſh, ㅤcyted vnder 3. frō *traſt.*
and adoration in reſpect thereof, by our *(o)* ㅤ27. *in Ioan. pag.* 250. *fin.*
proſternation (ad quamlibet terram) euen to eue-ㅤㅤ(o)
ry *Sacrament* which we *behould. Secondly,* I ㅤSee theſe wordes alled-
further ſay that our aduerſaries further vr-ㅤ ged at large heretofore
ging of this ſaying, according to the letter ㅤ*traſt.* 2. *ſeſt.* 8. *ſubdi-*
ſeclude their owne foreſaid *(p)* real eating ㅤ*uiſ.* 2. in the margent
of Chriſtes body no leſſe then ours, and ma-ㅤ at the letter d. *pag.* 206.
keth ſo no leſſe againſt them, then againſt vs.ㅤㅤ(p)
A thing ſo euident that *Alemannus,* denying ㅤSee hereof heretofore,
{with *Peter Martir* and other Proteſtant wri-ㅤ*traſt.* 2. *ſeſt.* 10. *ſub* p. 232.
ters) our aduerſaries foreſaid real *(5)* pre-ㅤ*diuiſ.* 1. *fine.* at m. and
ſence of Chriſtes body ſpiritually, and to ㅤin the margent there at p. 232
faith, as *a mere imaginary fiction, and contrary* ㅤ(k. l. and *traſt.* 2. *ſeſt.*
to Scripture; and acknowledging inſteede ㅤ11. *ſubdiuiſ.* 1. in the p. 245.
thereof no other preſence, *(6) then that which* ㅤmargent at p. and ſee
is Sacramental, or of ſignification, doth therefore ㅤfurther *ſubdiuiſ.* 2. in the
earneſtly *(7)* obiect & vrge againſt our now ㅤmargent at y. and z. p. 246 247.
aduerſaries foreſaid other doctrine, this very ㅤㅤ(5)
ſaying of *Auguſtine,* inſiſting vpon the bare ㅤSee heretofore *traſt.* 2.
letter thereof now againſt them, as they do ㅤ*ſeſt.* 5. *ſubdiuiſ.* 5. *prope*
moſt ridiculouſly againſt vs : In ſo much as ㅤ*finem.* at n. o. p. q.]
(8) Beza is thereupon enforced to make ſpe-ㅤㅤ(6)
cial anſweare thereto ; vnto which I refer ㅤSee heretofore *traſt.* 2.
ㅤㅤㅤㅤㅤㅤㅤㅤ the ㅤ*ſeſt.* 5. *ſubdiuiſ.* 5. *fine.*
at n. **(7)** Hereof ſee in *Beza, in epiſt. theolog.* *epiſt.* 5. *Aleman. pag.* 59.

(8) *Beza, Ibidem.* faith, to *Alemannus, Itaq, locum illum Augustini in Psal.* 98. *non hoc corpus quod videtis commesturi estis &c. non est quod sic accipias quasi sententiæ tuæ faueat, neq, enim omnem veri corporis manducationem sic excludit August. &c.*

(*)
Imitating, for so the aun-
cient Father *Vincentius Lyrinensis, l. aduers. hær. post initium.* faith of the innouations of his time, *captant plerunq, veteris cuiuspiam viri scripta pau-lo inuolutius ædita, quæ pro sui obscuritate dogmati suo quasi congruant, vt il-lud nescio quid quodcunq, proferunt, neq, primi neq, soli sentire videantur.*

(q)
Obiected by *M. Fulke* against *Heskins &c. pag.* 514. & 515. & 516.

(r)
Chemnitius in his examen part. 1. *fol.* 80. faith, *Patres igitur quando con-tra hæreticos aliquos dispu-tant, hoc tantum sibi propo-nunt, vt istorum opiniones euertant, de alijs interim articulis, non sunt admodum soliciti, et inde multa non sa-tis circumspecta de alijs dog-matibus dicta Patribus sæ-pe exciderunt.*

(s) *Humfred. in Iesuitis.* part. 2. rat. 5. pag. 501. faith of the Fathers, *videndum est quando loquuntur dogmatice, quando* Eristicos *seu agonistice vbi contentionis feruor caliginem*

the vnsatisfyed reader. And thus much bref-
ly in answere to the obiections had from the
Fathers, whose *obscure sayinges* our aduersares
(*) (*immitating* therein the elder nouelistes)
are not abashed to alledge against the said
Fathers most certaine and knowen meaning,
thinking it enough, if they can but so procra-
stinate time, and entertaine or perplex their
doubtful reader with new colours or surmi-
ses, though in them selues otherwise neuer
so vntrue.

(3) As concerning *the fift, Theodoret* is (q)
obiected to say, *the mystical signes after consecration do not depart from their nature, for they remaine in their former substance, figure, and shape,
they may be seene and handled as before*: In answeare whereto I must first put the reader in
minde of this general and confessed *rule*, that
we are to make great difference betwene
those sayinges which the Fathers vttered
Dogmaticos, that is by way of instruction, &
those other which they deliuer *Agonisticos,*
that is in heate of disputation and prosecution of argument, for that in these latter,
their meaning may easily be mistaken. This
rule together with the euident reason thereof, is prescribed & agreed vpon, by (r) *Chemnitius,* Doctor (s) *Humfrey,* and sundry (t) o-
ther learned Protestantes, and also by the
auncient Fathers them selues: for whereas
the Sabellianes, who denied the distinction
of per-

5:
vid. fol.
missio

caliginem alioqui acutis offundit &c. and *Ibidem.* pag. 129. he so excuseth *Luther.* (t) *Gellius Snecanus* (a learned Caluinist) in his *methodica descriptio.* pag. 490. doth so likewise excuse *Beza,* saying, *respondeo eum partem esse commode interpretandum pro ratione sui instituti, & ex hipothesi aduersariorum contra quos disserit &c.*

of persons, vsed the aduantage of a saying so vttered by *S. Gregory Neocesarien.* who being in argument with *Alianus an Ethnicke,* and declaring to him the mysteries of the Trinity, affirmed the Father and the Sonne to be one *in hypostacy,* which may signify one in person (the vsual signification of the word being vrged) wherby yet he onely meant one in essence, vsing so the word *Vpostasis* insteed of *Ousia.* S. *Basile* excuseth in this sort S. *Gregory,* affirming, that this was by him vttered, not (u) *as from one that prescribed or set downe doctrine, but as from one contending and excercysed in argument:* whereupon he further saith, that *S. Gregory* (x) *did not vse exact and absolute diligence in choosing of his wordes,* but did rather fauour the weakenes of the Ethnicke whom he thought to conuert. In like manner doth S. (y) *Basile* excuse with like moderatió certaine writings of *Dionisius Alexandrinus:* And (z) *Chemnitius* alledgeth further to this purpose, sundry other like examples thereof in the auncient Fathers, whereto I refer the reader. This point being thus declared, I now further say in answeare of this obiection; that *Theodoret* there writeth against the *Eutichian* hereticke, who taught that the humane nature of Christ was after his assumption, turned into the God-head, which error *Theodoret* there confuteth in a special

And *D. Bancroft,* in his suruey of the pretended holy discipline, *pag.* 336. doth so likwise insinuate *Hieromes* excuse, reprouing therein the Puritaines, saying, *it wil not be admitted of in this case, which in some other, the best of them are forced to admit. viz. that such his wordes were vttered in heat of disputation, & not dogmatice.*

(u)
Basile, epist. 64.
(x)
Ibidem.
(y)
Basil. epist. 41.
(z)
Chemnitius in his examen. part. 1.

(a)
In *Theodoret, dial.* 2. the interloquutors do thus argue. *Orthodoxus. Dic ergo &c. Say the the mystical simbols which are offered to God, by the Preistes of God, of what thinges sayest thou are those simbols. Erranistes. of the body & bloud of our Lord. Orthod. of that body which truly is; or of such a body as truly is not? Erranist. which truly*

G g 3

truly is. Orthod. &c. therefore our Lordes body is now also a body, and not chaunged into the diuine nature, but filled with diuine glory.

(b)

Imediatly next after it followeth. Erranistes. it came wel to passe, that thou shouldest speake of the diuine mysteries, for euen out of the same, wil I shew to thee that our Lordes body is chaunged into an other nature; therefore an weare vnto my question. Orthodox. I wil answeare. Eranistes. What doest thou cal the guift which is offered before the inuocation of the Preist? Orthod. I may not speake opely for it is like that some not admitted to the mysteries are present. Eranist. then answeare darkely. Orthod. It is that meate which is made of such kind of seedes. Eranist. And how do we cal the other signe. Orthod. That is also a comon name which signifyeth a kinde of drinke. Eranist. But after sanctification how doest thou cal them? Orthod. The body and bloud of Christ. E-

cial Dialogue by him penned vnder the persons of Orthodoxus the Catholicke, and Erranistes the Eutichian, in which he laboureth to proue that Christes body is not chaunged into the Godhead, but doth yet stil remaine in it former nature, forme, and figure, and whereas to that end he maketh his (a) argument from the Eucharist, which, saith he, could not be the Sacrament of Christes body, if so his body were chaunged into the Godhead: The Eutichian hereticke, as thinking the example of the Eucharist to make for him in reguard of the Churches then knowen doctrine of transubstantiation, laboureth to illustrate his supposed chaunge of Christes body after his assumption, into his diuinity, by (b) vrging the like chaunge made of the bread and wine after the Preistes consecration: wherto Orthodoxus the Catholicke, as wholly occupyed in heate and prosecution of argument, replyeth with that which is now obiected saying there next afterwatdes, (c) thou art taken with thy owne nettes which thou hast made, for the mystical simbols do not after consecration depart (viz. to sence, as thou teachest of Christs body) frō their nature, for they abide (vnto sence) in their former substance, figure, and forme, and may be seene and felt as before, but they are vnderstoode to be those things which they are made to be, and are beleeued, and adored, as being the same things which they are beleeued: whereupon he presently afterwardes concludeth with application thereof to his aduantage, that in like maner our (d) Sauiours body haith the former shape, and figure, and circumscription, and to say al at once, the bodies

ranist. And doest thou beleue that thou art made partaker of the body & bloud of Christ. Orthod. So I beleeue. Eranist. therefore euen as the simbols of the body

dies *substance*. The passage of *Theodorets* discourse being thus opened, I now answeare, first, that *Theodoret*, as al attentiue to the prosecution of his argument, (as S. *Gregory* Neocessarien. against the *Sabellians*) is to be excused with like moderatió, in his vsing the wordes(nature, & substance)as was (e) *Neocessarien*, in his foresaid vsing the word *hipostasis*,and the more easily *Theodoret* in that labouring to proue the yet continuing *former shape, figure, and circumscription*, of our Sauiours body, by example of the Sacrament, which yet likewise retaineth it *former figure, and forme, and may be seene, and felt as before:* he so thereby explaineth him selfe to vse the word *substance*, according to common capacity, and not as it is distinguished against the accidentes thereof, but as intending thereby the onely nature and essence of the external simbols, that is, of the sensible accidentes which he affirmeth, not to be chaunged, but to remaine stil subiect to sence, as they did before consecration. *Secondly*, I say, that answearable to the other *rule* (f) heretofore proued and confessed, the Fathers obscure and doubtful sayinges, are to be vnderstoode according to the more common receiued opinion of the auncient Church, which is so (g) *abounding for transubstantiation* as affordeth

& bloud of our Lord, are one thing beforethe Preists inuocation, & after his inuocation, are chaunged and made other thinges: euen so the Lords body after his assumption, is chaunged into the diuine substance.

(c)
Theodoret dial. 2.

(d)
Ibidem.

(e)
Next heretofore at u.x.

(f)
Heretofore *tract*. 2. *sect*. 11. *subdiuis*. 1. in the margent before f. at the figure 10. *pag*. 240 ll. *lineâ a sino*.

(g)
Abounding for transubstantiation, for S. *Cipri-* an saith, *the bread is chanǵed, not in shew but in nature &c.* heretofore, *tract*. 2. *sect*. 2. *subdiuis*. 4. 116·117· at h. n. *Gregory Nissen*. saith, *we beleeue the consecrated bread to be chaunged into the body of Christ,* 113·

{heretofore *tract*. 2. *sect*. 2. *subdiuis*. 3. after d. at 2. 3. in the margent) *Ciril of Hierusalem* saith, *he chaunged somtimes water into wine, and shal he not be worthy whom we may beleeue, that he chaunged wine into bloud &c.* (heretofore *tract*. 2. *sect*. 2. *subdiuis*. 3. in the margent before 116·112· h. at z.) S. *Ambrose* saith, *by what examples may we proue this not to be that which nature framed, but which blessing consecrated, and that by blessing nature it selfe is chaunged. Moyses held a rodde, cast it from him, and it became a serpent.* (heretofore *tract*. 2. *sect*. 2. *subdiuis*. 3. in the margent
after

after b . at *.) *Cirillus Alexandrinus* faith of the bread and wine, that *our Sauiour doth chaunge them into the truth of his proper flesh.* (heretofore *tract . 2 . sect . 2 . subdiuis . 3 .* in the margent vnder e) *S. Chrisostome* faith hereof, *the bread and wine are consumed &c. he who doth sanctify and chaunge them, is Christ him selfe.* (*Ibidem.* in the margent at u.) *Eusebius Emissen.* faith, *the inuisible Preist doth chaunge the visible creatures into the substance of his body and bloud.* (*tract . 2 . sect . 1 . subdiuis . 2 .* in the margent vnder d . fine. and *tract . 2 . sect . 2 . subdiuis . 2 . at r*). Al which said sayinges of these alledged Fathers are in them selues cleare, and by our learned aduersaries confessed, as making for *transubstantiation,* in the seueral places here cyted; whereto might be added the Fathers further expresse denyal, *that the Sacrament is bread,* alledged heretofore *tract . 2 . sect . 11 . subdiuis .* 1 . in the margent at n . o . which so euident testimonies but considered together with that which (heretofore *tract . 2 . sect . 2 . subdiuis .2 . at* h. i. l. m. n. o. p.) is further acknowledged by our aduersaries concerning *Paschasius*, *Damascen, Theophilact,* and *Gregory* the great, al of them confessedly affirming *transubstantiation,* and also (heretofore *tract . 2 . sect . 2 . subdiuis . 6 . fine . at x.*) from our learned aduersaries them selues confessing, that *transubstantiation entred early into the Church,* do sufficiently explaine, that *Theodoret* saying (though more doubtful then appeareth) is (yet) to be vnderstoode and reduced to a senee, not dissenting, but agreeable, to the confessed iudgment and doctrine of so many foresaid Fathers .

(*)

Euident vrging of transubstantiation, as appeareth by his foresaid inference of the real chaunge of *the mystical simbols,* as thereby to illustrate his other conceipted *real chaunge of Christes humane nature into the God-head,* which his inference

deth thereby a ful explication of *Theodoret.* Thirdly I say, that the heretickes foresaid so euident (*) *vrging* of transubstantiation in the Sacrament to proue his pretended transubstantiation of Christes humane nature into the God-head; maketh strongly for our now Catholicke doctrine of *transubstantiation;* for it is absurd and vnlike, that the hereticke should so vrge against the Catholicke his argument from *transubstantiation,* as from a point of

had bene languishing and wholly improper, had he by this chaunge in the Sacrament but meant , that whereas before it was common bread, it was now *after the Preistes* inuocation made Sacramental: for

of faith then knowen, and not to be denyed, if the said doctrine of transubstantiation
had bene then either vnknowen or condemn-
ned for false: As also it is like that *Theodoret* (to his manifest aduantage against the hereticke) would haue directly and plainly *denyed* the same if truth would haue permitted
him; which thing (h) *he doth not*, but answeareth with al warines, that the Sacrament
doth yet stil retaine it external forme and
figure, contrary to that which the hereticke
taught of our Sauiours body, and in pretended proofe whereof he so alledged the example of *transubstantiation*, made in the Sacrament. In more cleare manifestation whereof, it is to be noted, that the foresaid assertion of *transubstantiation* in the Sacrament,
vttered by *Eranistes*, is the saying & penning
of *Theodoret* him selfe, set downe by inductio
of the heretickes person. And therefore
Theodoret being an *orthodoxal* Father, neither
would nor could haue so propounded the
heretickes argument, as grounded vpon the
Churches then receiued doctrine of transubstantiation, had the same bene then vnknowen or reputed false: Al which premises
do so euidently proue that *Theodoret* allowed of *transubstantiation*, although he disalow-
ed the disparity and inconsequence of the inference thence vrged, to proue the other pretended, and vnlike chaunge of our Sauiours
humane body, that our learned aduersaries
the Century writers (great (i) *enemies to transubstantiation*) do therefore reproue and charge
Theodoret him selfe (as being the endyter
hereof) with the very foresaid wordes deliuered in the person of *Eranistes*, as making
(k) *dangerously* in their oponion for *transub-*

for this had but rather
hindred then holpen to
illustrate his other pre-
tended chaunge of Chri-
stes humane nature into
the God-head.

(h)

He doth not deny the vrged chaunge, but warily
forbearing the point of
chaunge, onely saith they
do not depart from their
nature &c.

(i)

Great enemies, for *cent.*
11. *c.* 5. *col.* 238. they
place *transubstantiatores*,
vnder the chapter *de hæ-
resibus*, affirming there
lin. 44. of transubstantiation, that it is *grauissi-
mus error. &c.*

(k)

*The Centuristes vnderta-
king centur.* 5. *c.* 4. *col.*
496. to make a special
Tract, the title whereof
there, is, *inclinatio doctrina complectens peculiares &
incommodas opiniones, stipulas, & errores doctorum huius seculi.* and hauing
vnder that title at *col.*
517. charged *S. Chriso-
stome* saying, *Chrisostomus
videtur transubstantiationem confirmare, nam ita
scribit &c.* they do next
after

H h   *stantiation*

after ad saying, *idem videtur sapere quod Theodo-
retus scribit (aiens) sicut
ergo simbola Domini corporis et sanguinis, alia quidem sunt ante inuocationem
Sacerdotis, sed post inuocationem mutantur & alia
fiunt, ita etiam corpus Domini post assumptionem mutatur in diuinam naturam.
In dial. 2. in confuso.*
And *ibidem. col.* 1008.
they yet further say of
*Theodoret, de cæna pericu-
lose dicit, simbola corporis
et sanguinis Domini post inuocationem Sacerdotis mu-
tari et alia fieri, in dialog.
2. in confuso.* so far in
their opinion was *Theo-
doret* from impugning
transubstantiation.

(*)

Some late *scholemen,* euen
after the Church had de-
clared expresly for tran-
substantiatiõ of the bread
though notwithstanding
that they mighthold som
part of the breades sub-
stance to remaine, either
the matter (as it doth in
al substantial trãsmutati-
ons of nature) or els the
substantial forme, vatil

stantiation. *Fourtkly* I yet further say, that
though *Theodoret,* or some one or other auncient Father, had spoken against *transubstantiation,* yet this forceth not so much, considering that the special maner of Christes presence in the Sacrament by transubstantiation
of the creatures, being but *de modo,* is such
a matter as some auneient Fathers (al of them
yet agreeing vniuersally in the *conclusion* it
selfe of the real presence) might be ignorant
of, as of latter times certaine (*) *scholemen,*
in some sort were, til the Church had declared her publicke iudgment therein. *Fyfthly,*
and lastly I say, that this passage of *Theodoret* proueth most inuincibly against our aduersaries that (howsoeuer transubstantiation
was then houlden questionable, yet) the doctrine of real presence was in *Theodorets* time,
general and confessed both by *Catholickes* and *heretickes;* otherwise how could
the hetericke haue so vrged his argument e-
uen from *transubstantiation?* And why also
did not *Theodoret,* being thus prouoked, so
much as but deny the real presence, and affirme the chaunge made in the Eucharist to
be but (as our aduersaries now hold) sacramental, for this but done, *Theodoret* had quite
dissolued and disioynted the very frame of
the heretickes whol argument, from which
Theodoret was so far, that he affirmeth as
before most plainly to the contrary, both
real (1) *presence,* and (m) *adoration* of the Sacrament. And thus much concerning the
obiection so much insisted vpon from *Theodoret.*

As

the last *Council of Trent* determined the same, as yet more specially.
Sef. 13. *c.* 4. (1) Saying as before in respect of *real presence.* (1) *that he
might*

might not speake openly, in reguard of some not admitted to the mysteries, which his circumspection was needlesse, had he intended no other presence then that which our aduersaries tearme sacramental. (2) Also he affirmeth that vpon our receiuing of the Sacrament, we are made *partakers of the body and bloud of Christ.* (3) That also though not vnto sence, yet to *vnderstanding and beleefe they be those thinges, (viz.* his body and bloud) *which* (vpon the Preistes inuocation) *they are made.* (4) That lastly *they are adoared as being the thinges which they are beleeued.* (m) Concerning adoration see, *vt supra.* at 1. and see *pag.* further heretofore, *tract. 2. sect. 8. subdiuis.* 2. in the margent at ˌm. 208.

(n)

As concerning the like obiection from *Gela-sius,* affirming that *the substance and nature of bread and wine ceaseth not to be:* for so much as this is greatly vrged by our aduersaries, and by *M.* (n) *Fulke,* so specially & at large recyted and obiected, I answeare thereto. As *first* I (o) deny that this *Gelasius* was Bishop of Rome, as *M. Fulke,* and others do pretend but not proue. *Secondly* I say, that whosoeuer he were, he most euidently writeth against the same *Eutichian* heresie, that did *Thedoret,* and therupon vseth accordingly to his

M. Fulke against *Heskins, Sanders, &c.* pag. 530. saith, *I wil produce testimony of Gelasius an auncient Bishop of Rome, thus he writeth contra Eutich. certe Sacramenta &c. certainly the Sacramentes of the body and bloud of Christ which we receiue,* are a di-*uine thing, and therefore by them we are made partakers of the diuine nature,*

and yet the substance and nature of bread and wine ceaseth not to be. And surely an Image or similitude of the body and bloud of Christ, is celebrated in the action of the mysteries, therefore it is shewed to vs euidently inough, that we must iudge the same thing euen in our Lord Christ him selfe, which we professe, celebrate, and receiue, in the which is an image of him, that as by working of the holy Ghost they do passe into a diuine substance, and yet abide stil in the property of their nature; euen so the same principal mystery doth shew that one Christ abideth whol and truly, whose efficiency and truth it doth truly represent to vs, those thinges of which he consisteth properly, stil remayning. Thus far *M. Fulke* out of *Gelasius,* concluding and saying thereupon, *thou seest gentle Reader that this auncient Bishop of Rome, doth vtterly ouerthrow transubstantiation.* (o) That he was not Bishop of Rome appeareth, *first,* in that vndertaking to alledge the testimonies of al the Fathers, he yet maketh no mencion of S. *Hierome, Augustine, Leo,* and such like *Amost pregnant proofe.*

like as *Pope Gelasius* would not haue omitted. *Secondly* he alledgeth sundry teſtimonies frō *Eusebius Cesariensis*, whoſe writings *Pope Gelasius* reproueth, *in decret. Gelasy de Apocriphis ſcripturis*. *Thirdly*, I therfore take him to be that *elder Gelasius Biſhop of Ceſarea*, whom *Theodoret* cyteth, *dial*. 3. and *Hierome* mencioneth *in catal. de ſcriptor Eccleſ.* and who in deede was liuing long before the time of *Pope Gelasius*.

(p)
Cranmer, in his anſware to *Steuen Gardiner &c.* printed 1551. *l*.2.*pag*. 351. and *Chemnitius* in his examen, *part*. 2. *pag*. 88.

(2)
As next before in the margent vnder n.

(3)
As next before in the margent vnder n. *p. 259*.

(4)
See theſe wordes engliſhed next before in the mergent at n. *pag. 259*.

(5)
Chemnitius, examen *part*. 2. *pag*. 88. ſaith of *Gelasius*, *dicit panem et vinum Euchariſtiæ in diuinā tranſire ſanɗo ſpiritu perficiente ſubſtantiam, corporis ſcilicet et ſanguinis Chriſti: et certe hæc verba videntur fortiter ſonare pro ſtabiliendā tranſubſtantiatione, quod enim tranſit in aliam ſubſtantiam, et quidem ſpiritu ſanɗe operante, certe videtur non manere in priore ſua ſubſtantia.*

(6) See

his like aduantage, the wordes *ſubſtance* and *nature*, in the ſame ſence as did *Theodoret*, not ſaying as *M. Fulke* vntruly reporteth, *ſubſtantia, & natura, &c.* the *ſubſtance and nature of bread ceaſeth not*, but in the diſiunɗiue (as *M.* (p) *Cramner* & others do alledge) *eſſe non deſinit ſubſtantia vel natura panis et vini*. the *ſubſtance or nature ceaſeth not*: extenuating ſo, and reſoluing the word *ſubſtance*, by the word *nature*, and not contented ſo, but explaineth him ſelfe yet further ſaying, *permanent in ſua proprietate natura*, they (2) *remaine in property of their nature*, moſt plainly ſo declairing him ſelfe to meane, by the word *ſubſtance the properties of nature*, namely as did *Theodoret*, *fi-gure, forme*, and ſuch like. *Thirdly* I ſay, that this author (though greatly prouoked to the contrary by the exigence of this argument againſt the ſaid hereſie) acknowledgeth in this very place, real preſence: In reſpeɗ wherof he tearmeth the Sacrament (3) *a diuine thing by which we are made partakers of the diuine nature*. affirming yet further euen *tranſubſtantiation*, ſaying of the bread and wine that (4) *in diuinam tranſeunt ſpiritu ſanɗo perficiente ſubſtantiam*: moſt euidently ſo by theſe wordes *tranſeunt in ſubſtantiam*, pointing to the very tearme of *tranſubſtantiation*. In ſo much as *Chemnitius*, though he wil not aſſent to the truth thereof, is yet enforced to confeſſe that this (5) *ſoundeth ſtrongly for tranſubſtantiation*. *M. Cramner*, hauing no other euaſion, left in anſweare thereto but (direɗly against the very wordes (6) of *Gelasius*, & the answearable confession of (7) *Chemnitius*) to affirme that this (8) *transition* is not meant of bread and wine, but also of the persons receiuing the same. And thus much concerning *Gelasius*.

As concerning the obiection commonly (9) vrged from *Origen*, as affirming of the Sacrament, that (10) *according to that which it haith material,* (it) *goeth downe into the belly and is cast forth into the draught,* whereupon is inferred that the matter and substance of bread remaineth. To admit this booke for *Origens* (which thing (11) *Erasmus* doubteth) and that also he spoke not here of *holy bread,* confessedly (12) vsual for *Catechumines* in S. *Augustines* time, but directly of the Eucharist; I answeare therto: *First* that *Origen* saith not absolutly of the Sacrament, that *it is cast forth into the draught, but with limitation, as namely, iuxta id quod habet materiale, according to that which it haith material,* namely the magnitude and other sensible accidentes, which in reguard of their signification and otherwise are material, and (as it is (13) confessed) do nourish, and so by digestion *are cast into the draught. Secondly* I say, this maketh for the Catholicke opinion, for what occasion or colour had *Origen,* and so many other Fathers, to touch this point, so much as but to make any question or speach therof, otherwise the only in reguard of real presence in the Sacrament. A thing so euident that S. *Bernard, Damascene, Chrisostome*

secrationem, iuxta id quod habet materiale, abit, et insecessum eiicitur.
Erasmus. in his preface before that booke saith, *neq, enim Hieronimus agnoscit hoc opus.* (12) See heretofore, *tract. 2. sect. 8. subdiuis. 3.*

(6)
See *Gelasius* his wordes translated by *M. Fulke,* next before in the margent at n.

(7)
Chemnitius, vt supra. at 5.

(8)
Cramner, in his foresaid answeare, pag. 358. saith, *the transition which Gelasius meant is in the persons that receiue the Sacramentes which be transformed into the diuine nature; but the transition is not in the bread and wine.* most extreame bouldly & vntruly against the very expresse wordes and meaning of *Gelasius.*

(9)
Vrged by *M. Fulke* against *Heskines, Sanders, &c.* pag. 41. and by *Peter Martyr* in his common places in english. part. 4. pag. 182.

(10)
Origen. in Math. c. 15. saith, *quod si quicquid ingreditur in os in ventrem abit, & insecessum eiicitur, et ille cibus qui sanctificatur per verbum Dei, perq, ob-*

(11)

at m. n.

(14)

S. Bernard, in serm. de caena. faith, *Hostia quam vides iam non est panis, sed caro mea quae pependit in Cruce pro mundi vita, sa-ne mutatio ista benedictionis opus est non Originis &c. iste est panis Angelorum qui nescit putrescere, non vadit in secessum.* And *S. Damascene, l. 4. Orthodox. fid. c. 14.* tel-ling how *Melchisadechs* bread and wine, prefigu-red the Sacrament, faith, *illa mensa hanc mysticam praefigurauit mensam &c. hunc panem panes figurabāt Propositionis haec est pura scilicet hostia et incruenta &c. corpus videlicet et san-*

sostome, and *Ciril of Hierusalem,* from whom it is vnlike that *Origen* should dissent, do al of them also touch this point, expresly with-al (14) affirming concerning the Sacrament, and in respect of the inward substance there-of, that *it doth not passe into the draught.*

(4) Wherein further to make good what I say, to the further discouery of their foresaid indirect dealing herein whith the Fathers: I wil alledge sundry examples of their like knowen practise in this kinde. *Paschasius* liued about 700. yeares since, and did write a special treatise of *Christes body & bloud* in the Sacrament, wherein he doth so plainly & of purpose affirme & (q) proue our Catholicke doctrine of the real presence, that *M. Fulke,* and sundry other Protestantes confessing the same, do therfore specially (r) reiect him, yet al this notwithstanding, whereas this author in the same booke doth but

guis Christi in stabilimentum animae nostra, et corporis inconsumptum & in-corruptum, non in secessum iens, absit enim &c. A saying so euident that *Peter Martir* in his common places, *part. 4. c. 10. sect. 57. pag. 182.* doth therefore reproue *S. Damascene,* saying of him, *he addeth more ouer that this Sacrament is not cast into the draught, and surely it cannot o-therwise be spoken of the transubstantiators.* And *S. Chrisostome, in hom. de Eucharist. in encaenijs.* faith of the Sacramēt, *num vides panem? num vinum? num sicut reliqui cibi in secessum vadunt? absit ne sic cogites &c.* And *Ci-rillus Hierosol. in catech. mistagog. 5. paulo post med.* faith, *panis hic non in ventrem discendit et in secessum emittitur, sed per te totum ad corporis et a-nimae vtilitatem distribuitur.* (q) Of *Paschasius* his plaine assertion of the real presence, see heretofore, *tract. 2. sect. 2. subdiuis. 2.* at k. and also *tract. 2. sect. 6. subdiuis. 2.* at the letter f. in the mar-gent where he alledgeth miracles in special proofe thereof. (r) *D. Fulke,* against *Heskins Sanders &c.* pag. 250. faith, *Paschasius alled-*

ging

ging *Hillary, Ambrose, Augustine, Ciril &c.* doth but wrest their sayinges as the Papistes do now to vphould that error &c. In like maner is he reiected by *Oecolampadius,* and *the Century writers,* and others, wherof see heretofore, *tract. 2. sect. 2. subdiuis. 2.* in the margent at the letters h. and i.

but speake of our *spiritual* (s) *receiuing* by faith, which no Catholicke denyeth. D. *Bilson* forbeareth not therefore to alledge (t) *Paschasius,* placing him expresly among those his pretended (u) Catholicke *Fathers, who teach a spiritual kind of eating, not a corporal,* as *the Papistes do.* And in like bould maner is the very same Father at large alledged against the real presence, by (9) *M. Sutliue,* and also by (x) *Hospinianus,* because he mentioneth *spiritual* receiuing, and calleth the Sacrament a *figure.* In like sort do they pretend testimony euen from (10) *Bernard,* who liued about 400. yeares since, & professed his (11) *obedience to the Pope,* at that time when the real presence was most (y) *vniuersal,* and S. Ber-

(s)
Paschasius de corpore et sanguine Domini, c. 11. 12. 14. and *29.*

(t)
M. Bilson, in his true difference betwene Christian subiection, and vnchristian rebellion, *part. 4. pag. 624,* and *. 625.*

(u)
M. Bilson, ibidem. pag. 625.

(9)
Sutliue de missa Papistica. fol. 32. 173. and *208.*

(x)

Hospinianus in historia Sacramentaria. pag. 318. 319. 320. 321. 322. 323. and *324.* alledgeth *Paschasius* at large, pretending that he was a Protestant in opinion against the real presence. (10) By *Peter Martir, l. contra Gardin. obiect. 252. 253.* and *254.* and in like maner is *Bernard* alledged as a good Protestant, and making against the real presence *by Hospinianus, in historia Sacramentaria. pag. 341. 342.* nd *343.* (11) See *S. Bearnard, l. 2. de considerat. ad Eugenium. et vide epist. 125. 131.* and *190. ad Innocent. Papam.* in so much as D. *Fulke,* against the Rhemish Testament, *fol. 133.* and D. *Whitaker, contra Duraum. l. 2. pag. 154.* do in plaine tearmes charge him with acknowledging *the Popes Primacy.* And *the Century writers, cent. 12. c. 10. col. 1639.* do reprehend him, saying of him; *Ad comitem aquitaniae apud perteniacum dixit: quicquid extra Ecclesiam, eamq, Romanam est, illud necessario iudicio Dei interire, sicut ea quae extra Arcam fuerunt, in diluuio absorpta sunt: Item qui Papam Romanum (Antichristum) persequitur, hunc ipsum Dei Filium persequi &c.* (y) *S. Bernard* liued, *Anno. Dom.*

Dom. 1120. in the very ſame time with *Hugo de ſanĉto Victore*, and *Petrus Cluniacenſis*, who did then purpoſely write againſt *Berengarius* his error herein, and when the Pope had condemned the ſame by Councels, and how vniuerſal at that time was the real preſence, ſee heretofore, *tract*. 2. *ſect*. 2. *ſubdiuiſ*. 2. at d. e. k. And *Ioannes Angelus Politianus*, in his *Philoſophia Euchariſtica contra Bellarminum*. part. 2. c. 8. pag. 164. ſaith, *vixit Bernardus quando iam in Latinis Eccleſys, deiecto de ſua ſententia Berengario, vbiq̄ fere dominaretur tranſubſtantiatio*.

(z)

Bernard in ſerm. de cœna Domini. ſaith, *hoſtia quam vides iam non eſt panis, ſed caro &c. ſimiliter liquor iſte quem vides non iam eſt vinum, ſed ſaguis &c. Odor, ſpecies, ſapor, pondus remanet &c. vt horror penitus tollatur et meritum ſortiatur, etinim ne humana infirmitas eſum carnis, et potum ſanguinis inſumptione horreret, Chriſtus velari et palliari, illa duo voluit ſpecibus, panis et vini &c.*

S. *Bernards* doĉtrine thereof, (z) euident, and (12) confeſſed. And like pretence of teſtimony they alledge and make from (a) S. *Ambroſe*, his booke of Sacramentes, which (as is by them ſelues confeſſed) (b) *putteth the bodily being of Chriſt in the Sacrament*, from his prayers (c) *preparatory to Maſſe*, which are ſo plaine for real preſence, that others of them do therefore reieĉt them, as (d) *contayning adoration of the Sacrament*. from *Euſebius* (e) *Emiſſenus*, whom *the Centurie writers,*

charge

And in his treatiſe *de vita Malachiæ*. he reporteth a great *miracle*, ſhewed by God in ſpecial proofe of this doĉtrine; which miracle mentioned heretofore, *tract*. 2. *ſect*. 6. *ſubdiuiſ*. 2. in the margent at the letter q. (12) Confeſſed by *Peter Martir, l. contra Gardin. obieĉt.* 252. ſaying, *ſi diceremus Bernardum de hoc negotio non recte ſenſiſſe, quod omnia illa tempora ſuperſtitionibus & tenebris eſſent mirabiliter obfuſcata, quis merito poſſet de nobis conqueri?* And the *Centuriſtes, cent.* 12. c. 10. col. 1628. ſay of S. *Bernard, Acerimus propugnator ſedis Antichriſti fuit: hoſtiam ſuo Deo Maozim obtulit*. and ſee there yet more plaine wordes *ibidem. col.* 1639. (a) *Ambroſe*, alledged againſt the real preſence by *Hoſpinianus, in hiſtoria Sacramentaria, pag.* 78. (b) See this heretofore, *tract*. 2. *ſect*. 2. *ſubdiuiſ*. 3. at the letter a. (c) So doth *M. Bilſon*, in his true difference &c. part. 4. pag. 622. (d) Hereof ſee heretofore, *tract*. 2. *ſect*. 8. *ſubdiuiſ*. 2. in the magent at the letter l. (e) *M. Bilſon*, in his true difference &c. part. 4. pag. 623. and *Hoſpinianus, in hiſtoria Sacramentaria. l. 5. pag.* 542. & 543.

(f) See

charge with (f) *transubstantiation.* from (g) Gregory *the great,* whom D. *Humfrey,* and others, charge with (h) *transubstantiation.* from *Theophilacte,* and (i) *Damascene,* whom, D. *Fulke,* & many others, do likewise charge. with (k) *transubstantiation,* & most exceeding bouldly euen from (13) *Lanfrancus,* (14) *who wrote against Berengarius,* in the very question of *transubstantiatiō:* wherunto I could easily ad other like examples of testimony pretended by our aduersaries against the real presence: from *Beda, Alcuinus, Rabanus, Fulbertus,* and many others, whose contrary doctrine is as plaine, certaine, and confessed, for the real presence, as are the writinges of *Bellarmine,* or any other Catholicke writer of this age: onely I wil in this discourse recreate the reader with the further example in this kinde of *Clictoueus,* a knowen Catholicke writer of this time who did purposly write (15) against *Oecolampadius* in this very question of the Sacrament. And for so much yet as he vndertaking to supply (l) certaine bookes of *S.Ciril,* vpon *Iohn,* which are lost, doth in the sixt

(f) See *Eusebius* his plaine sayinges heretofore *tract. 2. sect. 2. subdiuis. 1. p.106.* initio. at a. and *tract. 2. p. 100 sect. 1. subdiuis. 2.* in the mergent vnder the letter d. *fine.* and see him therfore reiected by the *Centurie writers, heretofore, tract. 2. sect. 2. subdiuis. 2.* at the letter r. *pag. 110.*

(g) *Hospinianus, in historia Sacramentaria. l. 3. pag.* 253. and *l. 5. pag.* 543. and M. *Iewel.* in his publique chalenge nameth this *Gregory* as one of those Fathers, by whō to be tryed in this controuersy.

(h) See *Gregory* so reiected heretofore, *tract. 2. sect. 2. subdiuis. 2.* in the margent at the letter p. and hereafter, *tract. 3. sect. 2. subdiuis. 2.* at.l. (i) *Theophilact* is so alledged by *Hospinianus in hist. Sacrament. l. 4. pag.* 325. and 326. and 227. and so is *Damascen.* also *ibidem. pag.* 256. and 294. (k) See them thus reiected heretofore, *tract. 2. sect. 2. subdiuis. 2.* at m. n. o. (13) M. *Sutline de missa Papistica. fol.* 208. (14) That *Lanfrancus* wrote against *Berengarius,* is confessed by M. *Fulke,* against *Heskines, Sanders &c.* pag. 297. and by *Chrispinus,* in his booke of the estate of the Church. pag. 285. and 286. and by *Hospinianus in hist. Sacrament. pag.* 338. (15) *Hospinian. in hist. Sacram. part. 2. fol.* 46. saith, *circa hoc tempus Iodocus Clictoueus, duos libros, & Ioannes Fisherus Rophensis, libros quinq, contra Oecolampadium, de venerabili Sacramento Eucharistiæ conscripserunt.* (l) Whereas of the twelue bookes of *Ciril*

I i

of *Ciril,* vpon *Iohn* heretofore extant, foure of the midle bookes are periſhed: *Cliƈtoueus* did ſupply them, as appeareth by the inſcription or title of the ſaid bookes.

(m)
Lib. 6. c. 14.
(n)
Peter Martir, in libro contra Gardinerum. col. 151. *&* 152. after the edition at *Baſile,* 1581. alledgeth and vrgeth againſt the real preſence many places out of *Ciril,* and amongſt thoſe, this ſaying of *Cliƈtoueus.*
(o)
See this heretofore *traƈt.* 2. *ſeƈt.* 2. *ſubdiuiſ.* 3. at the letter f. and alſo next heretofore, *ſubdiuiſ.* 2. in the margent at m.
(p)
Hereof ſee *M. D. Couel,* in his defence of *M. Hooker &c. pag.* 118.
(q)
Affirmed by the 15. *Lu-*

(m) *ſixt* booke ſo by him added or ſupplyed, mention Chriſtes withdrawing his bodily preſence from hence, and his being preſent with vs according to his God-head, this teſtimony is in great ſadnes (n) alledged, and vrged by *Peter Martir,* as making directly againſt the real preſence, notwithſtanding alſo that *Peter Martir* him ſelfe doth elſwhere (o) *reieƈt* euen the fame *S. Cirils* vndobted writinges for affirming our Catholicke doctrine *of the real preſence;* ſo ridiculoufly do our aduerſaries aduenture, to obieƈt the obſcure or doubtful ſaying of any author againſt his moſt certaine and knowen meaning.

(5) And to difcouer this their praƈtiſe more fully, as with the Fathers, ſo alſo with like bouldnes in this neede do they entreate their owne brethren *the Lutheraines,* who are knowen and confeſſed to defend the *real being of Chriſtes body in the Sacrament* (p) *before participation,* and preſent alſo (q) *to the bodily mouth,* euen (r) *of the vnworthy receiuers,* in ſo much as they (s) adore it: and yet *M. D.*

theran diuines, as appeareth by their wordes in the anſweare made to them, entituled, *Apolog. modeſt. ad aƈta conuentus quindecim theologorum Torgæ, nuper habit. pag.* 35. and 48. and ſee *Luther* there alledged affirming the ſame *pag.* 36. (r) That the wicked receiue truly Chriſtes body, is affirmed by *Iacobus Andraas, in confut. diſput. Ioan. Iacobi Grinæi. pag.* 110. & 115. & 244. And by *Chemnitius* in his Enchiridion. *pag.* 345. and by *Adamus Francifci, in margarita theolog. pag.* 260. & 261. and by *Marpachius, in Peter Martirs* epiſtles, annexed to his common places in engliſh. *pag.* 96. and ſee *Luther* alledged by *Peter Martir* in his collections annexed to his common places in engliſh and his treatiſe there *of the Lordes ſupper. pag.* 138. (s) See this heretofore, *traƈt-*

D. *Fulke* is not abashed most bouldly & vntruly to affirme, that (t) *the Lutheranes, and Suin-*
glians, do both consent in this, that the body of
Christ is receiued spiritually, not corporally, with
the heart, not with the mouth. And *Peter Mar-*
tir affirmeth seriously vpon report of (2) credit that *Luther iudged not so grosly of this mat-*
ter. And that (3) *Luther in very deede put no*
other coniunction but Sacramental, betweene the
body of Christ and the signes; as though the hot
and (u) tragical contentions had, and yet
to this day, continued about the Sacrament,
betweene the *Lutherans,* and the *Suinglians,*
were to the world vnknowen or but only a
dreame or imaginary fiction : And hence it is
that *the Lutherās* do greuously cōplain against
our aduersaries, (x) *because* (saith he) *that you*
alledge Luthers words against his minde; which
thing as *Luther* did in his life time perceiue
by experience, & thereof greauosly (y) com-
plaine, so also did he specialy foresee, & a litle
before his   death

(t)
M. Fulke in his answe-
are to a counterfeate Ca-
tholicke, *art.* 17. *pag.*
61.   (2)
Peter Martir, in his common places in english
part. 4. *pag.* 188.

(3)
Peter   Martir, *ibidem.*
pag. 195.

(u)
Of the hot contentions
concerning the real pre-
sence, had betweene the
Lutherans, and *Suingli-*
ans, see *Luke Osiander in*
epitom. cent. Ecclesi.cent.
16. see *l.* 2. *c.* 10. *pag.*

133. 134. 135. *&c.* and *M. Couper,* in his Cronicle, *fol.* 284.
290. and 270. and *M. Whitaker de Ecclesia,* pag. 322, and they are [570]
yet further notifyed by the very many writinges by them published to
the world, one against an other. (x)   *Gerhardus Giesekenius* a Lutheran, in his booke *de veritate corporis Christi in cæna, contra Pezelium,*
pag. 93. so chargeth the Caluinistes. And the *Lutheran diuines in*
colloquio Alteburgensi impres. Iena, ad salam. 1570. *fol.* 166. com-
plaine further saying, *Sacramentarij Lutherum prose citantes faciunt eum*
Sacramentarium &c. quid igitur tandem futurum est cum tanta audacia et
temeritate, Lutherus contra sua ipsius scripta torqueatur, crucifigatur, lani-
etur? and *ibidem fol.* 575. the Lutheran diuines say further of the
Caluinistes, *debebant igitur eiusmodi falsatores librorum Lutheri publica*
censura tanquam Ecclesia latrones, fures, et sacrilegi notari. &c. And see
further there, *fol.* 227. *& fol.* 285. and see the like in *Conradus Sclus-*
selburge, in theolog. Caluinist. l. 2. *fol.* 56. (y)   *Luther in præfat.*
in Smalcadicos articulos, extant in Luke Osiander, epitom. centur. Ecclef.

cent. 16, *saith there pag.* 253. *pag.* 254. *quid dica, quomodo quæreba instituā, adhus sæpe stes sum, scribo concines habeo, et prelego publice, et quotidie, et tamen virulenti homines non tantum ex aduersarys, sed,etiam falsi fratres, qui nobis cum se sentiri aiunt, mea scripta, et doctrinam meam simpliciter contra me adferre, et allegare audent, me viuente vidente, et audiente, etiamsi sciant me aliter dicere, et volunt virus suum meo labore exornare &c. quid ergo bone Deus post obitum meum fiet.*

(z)
Ibidem. next after he saith, *deberem quidem ad omnia respondere dum ad-huc viuo &c.* and the *Ti-gurine diuines in confessione orthod. Eccles. Tigur. tract.* 3. *fol.* 108. al-ledge *Luthers* confession made a little before his death, wherein *Luther* saith, *ego quidem sepulchro vicinus &c.* I that now

death (z) *forewarne* against the same. In like maner do *the Lutheranes,* charge our aduer-saries for that, with like extreame bouldnes (a) they *endeauored to make the confession of Augusta* (which teacheth the real presence) *to be Suinglian,* that is, against the real presence, exclaming thereat, and saying thereof, *si hæc res &c.* (b) if *this, thing had bene done in Ara-bia, America, Sardinia, or such like remote coun-tries, and of former times this vsurpation of fraud, and historical falshood, were more tollerable, but* seeing (say they) *the question is of such things as be*

walke nigh to my graue, wil carrie this testimony and glory to the tribunal seate of Christ my Sauiour, that I haue with al carefulnes condemned and a-uoided those fantastical men, and, enemies of the Sacrament : Suinglius, Oecolampadius, Swinkfeldius, and their scholers, whether they be at Zu-rich, or in what other place soeuer vnder the sunne. (a) Gerherdus Giese-kenius, l. de veritate corporis Christi in cæna. pag. 76. saith, *Suinglianam Augustanam confessionem reddere conantur, sed tam manifestis mendacijs et conspicua falsitate &c.* And see there further, *pag.* 118. and see in *Luke Osiander in cent.* 16. *pag.* 146. the like or worse complaint against the *Suinglians,* concerning *the confession of Augusta.* and as much also in *Colloquio Alteburgensi.* printed *Ienæ, ad Salam.* 1570. *fol.* 521. and 522. In like maner whereas the *confession of Auspurg,* was exhibited by the same diuines, and in the same yeare, and to the same *Emperour Charles the* 5. as was the *confession of Augusta,* as appeareth by com-paring of *Luke Osiander, cent.* 16. *pag.* 144. and. 145. with the Ca-tolog of confessions *initio.* set before the *Harmony of confessions* in en-glish, and their doctrine of the real presence, is deliuered in the very same wordes, as in *the confession of Augusta.* Yet *M. Chaterton* (or, who

as *be done in our time, and in the sight of al men, who with a quiet minde can endure such lyes?* Hitherto gentle reader of our aduersaries bouldnes in alledging in this queſtion of the real preſence, the doutful ſayinges of the ancient Fathers, and later writers, againſt their moſt certaine & knowē mening; which like courſe S. (c) *Auguſtine* noteth for vſual in the noueliſtes of his time. And though this their fraud thus diſcouered in this one queſtion of ſo great importance, be ouer ſparingly touched by me, as not being ſet forth with ſuch an ſweareable vehemency and proportion of wordes, as the waight and conſequence of the cauſe requireth, yet ſhal this my ſobriety I hope ſuffice to ſerue as a iuſt motiue for thy ſtayed conſideration and due examination hereafter to be had of their like fraudulent practiſe (no leſſe plainly diſcouerable) in other controuerſies.

who els ſo euer was the author of *the obſeruations vpon the harmony of conſeſſions in engliſh*) is not abaſhed in his obſeruations vpon the *confeſſion of Auſpurg*, to endeauour by this explication to make it agreeable in ſence to Caluiniſme. And ſo likewiſe as is there teſtifyed did the *Neuſtadianes in their late admonition c. 5.*

(b)

Gerherdus Gieſekenius vbi ſupra. pag. 77.

(c)

Auguſtin. tom. 7. *de nuptijs et concupiſcentia. l. 2. c.* 91. ſaith, *non eſt mirum ſi Pelagiam dicta noſtra in ſenſus quos volunt detorquere conantur, quandoquidem de ſacris Scripturis non vbi obſcure aliquid dictum eſt, ſed vbi clara et aperta ſunt teſtimonia id facere conſueuerunt, more quidem hæreticorum etiam cæterorum.*

Ii 3

That the

*That the wordes concerning Sacrifice in the now Missal, are
agreeable with the forme vsed in the auncient Lyturgies, and with the practise of the auncient
Fathers .*

TRACT. 3.

SECTION. 1.

(2)
Hereof see *Primasius,* and
Eusebius Emissen. alledged hereafter *tract.* 3 .
sect. 5. subdiuis. 4 . in the
margent vnder the letter
e. (*)
See this testifyed by *Isidore l. 7. Etimol. c.* 12 .
alledged hertofore *tract.*
1. *sect.* 2. *subdiuis.* 2 .
in the margent vnder
the letter t.
(3)
See heretofore, *tract.* 2 .
sect. 1, *subdiuis.* 1 .
at y.
(a)
The whol Canon of the
Masse is set forth by *M.
Foxe, act. mon. pag .* 891 .
& see these orders there .
and see in *Misal. Rom.*
printed at *Antwerpe, An-
no.* 1594 . *pag.* 255 .
(b)
Ambros. l. 4. *de Sacrament. c.* 5. *initio.* saith,
accipe

AFter *consecration* and *adoration,* followeth the Preistes *Sacrifycing,* wherein
he doth before his owne communion of the
blessed Sacrament and distribution thereof
to the people, offer it vp to God the Father
as an external sacrifice, (2) *prescribed* by our
Sauiour to continue, and apply to vs the memory and efficacy of his bloudy sacrifice offered vpon the Crosse. Imediatly before
this offering of Sacrifice by the Preist (*) *the
Acolyte lighteth a waxe candle :* which point,
gentle reader, of *offering sacrifice,* for so much
as it is the very touch or essence of the Masse .
A thing at this day houlden so hateful and
scandalouse, I must therefore craue thy patience, more specially and at large to entreate
thereof. *First* then, to the better iustification
hereof, of our publicke Lyturgy. I wil alledge
that very *forme of wordes* therein contained,
wherein is expressed the Preistes sacrifycing,
and wil thereupon see if the same be any o-
ther then such as was vsed in the auncient
Lyturgies of the Primitiue Church ; to the
end that euen by the very agreement in wordes betwene the foresaid ancient Lyturgies,
and our now Masse, their like agreement in
meaning may thence more easily be discer-
ned ; for seeing that wordes are but the significations

∎ifications of thinges, it were ſtrange to imagin that the auncient Fathers ſhould conſent with vs in forme of ſpeaking, and yet diſcent from vs, to agree euen with our very aduerſaries in contrary ſence and meaning.

To begin therefore with the wordes of our Maſſe, the Preiſt before conſecration, prayeth in our *Liturgy* as he did (?) *before,* for the bread to be made Chriſtes body: So likewiſe now that it may be made an acceptable ſacrifice ſaying, (a) *which oblation we beſech thee o almighty God in al thinges to make bleſſed, apointed, ratifyed, reaſonable, and acceptable &c.* which very forme is accordingly mencioned by (b) *S. Ambroſe,* and (c) reiected, as making moſt euidently for ſacrifice, by our learned aduerſaries *Hutterus,* and *Baldwinus.* after conſecration he offereth the ſame ſaying; (d) *wherefore o Lord we alſo thy ſeruantes and thy holy people, being mindful aſwel of the bleſſed paſſion and reſurrection, as of the glorious aſcention of the ſame Chriſt thy ſonne our Lord God, do offer vnto thy excelent maiſtey, of thy owne rewardes and guiftes, a pure hoſt, a holy hoſt, an vndefyled hoſt, the holy bread of eternal life, and Cup of eternal ſaluation: vouchſaue thou alſo with a merciful & pleaſant countenance to haue reſpect hereunto, and to accept the ſame as thou dideſt vouchſaife to accept the guiftes of thy rigteouſe ſerſeruant Abel, and the ſacrifice of our Patriarch Abraham, and the holy ſacrifice, the vndefyled hoſt which thy high Preiſt Melchiſadech did offer vnto thee: wee hubly beſech thee o almighty God, commaunde theſe to be brought vp by the handes of of thy holy Angel vnto thy high Altar &c.*

Hitherto concerning the forme of Sacrifice vſed in our Lyturgies: al which is accordingly

accipe quæ ſunt verba, dicit Sacerdos, fac nobis (inquit) oblationem aſcriptam, rationabilem, acceptabilem &c.

(c)

Hutterus, de ſacrificio, pag. 691. ſaith of theſe wordes being there by him recyted, *Exhorreſcat cælum, contremiſcat terra, ſtupeſcant elementa, ad iſtæ blaſphemiarunt portenta.* And *Baldwinus,* the Lutheran *in l. de diſput. Lutheri, cum Diabolo &c. pag.* 308. ſaith hereof. *deinde magna blaſphemiarum portenta in ſinum ſuum expuit ſacrificulus dum orat, vt Deus oblationem iſtam, benedictam adſcriptam, ratam, rationabilem, acceptabilemá, facere dignetur &c.*

(d)

See this in *M. Foxe, act. mon. pag.* 892. and in *Miſſal. Rom. pag.* 257.

(e)

Ambroſ. l. 4. de Sacrament. c. 6. initio. deſcribeth the very like, or rather very ſame forme of the Church in his time ſaying, *Sacerdos dicit, ergo memores glorioſiſſimæ eius paſſionis, et ab inferis reſurrectionis* clariſſimæ

ly

rectionis, et in cælum ascen- | ly in sence, and verbatim almost in the very
sionis offerimus tibi hanc | same wordes mencioned by (e) *S. Ambrose*;
immaculatam hostiam, ra- | and no lesse if not more fully by (f) other
rationalem hostiam, incru- | auncient Fathers, so that if the celebration
entā hostiā, hunc panem sanc- | of this be offensiue in vs at this day, *S. Am-*
tum, et Calicem vitæ æter- | *brose,* and the auncient Fathers of the Primi-
na, et petimus, et precamur, | tiue Church were in their times no lesse guilty
vt hanc oblationem suscipias | thereof

in sublimi Altari tuo per manus Angelorum tuorum sicut suscipere dignatus es munera pueri tui iusti Abel, et sacrificium Patriarchæ nostri Abrahæ, et quod tibi obtulit summus Sacerdos Melchisadech &c. this and thother former saying are so plaine and directly agreeing with our now Canon of the Masse, that *the Century writers, cent. 4. c. 6. col.* 429. do therefore vtterly dislike it saying thereof; *prolixum Canonem Ambrosius recitat. l. 4. de Sacramentis.* As also *M. Sutliue* in his suruey of Popery, printed 1606. *pag.* 115. *sect.* 38. saith thereof, *they compare the sacrifice of Christes body and bloud in the Masse, with the sacrifice of Abel that offered brute beastes, which no Catholicke euer did.* And *Hutterus de sacrificio missatico. pag.* 696. mencioneth and reiecteth this foresaid forme of praier saying thereof, *quid execrandum magis, quam orare vt Deus corpus et sanguinem Christi eo saltem habeat loco et præcio, quo ouem aut vitulam Abelis, et Abrahami habuit &c.* And in like sort is the same reiected by *Andræas Chrastouius,* in his *praxis de cæremonijs,* printed 1594. *sect.* 107. *pag.* 71. in so much as he haith no other answeare to *S. Ambrose,* hauing the same then (without al proofe and forehead) to deny his foresaid booke *de Sacramentis,* in which the same is extant. in sufficient proofe of which said booke; see heretofore in the preface to the reader *sect.* 15. so confessedly in their opinion doth this forme of prayer make for sacrifice, that the same is also for such yet further reiected by *Suinglius, tom.* 1. *in epicher. de Canone Missæ, fol.* 185. where he saith thereof, *Blasphemia est &c.* and by *Martin Luther tom.* 2. *Witteberg. fol.* 72. saying, *Missa creditur passim esse sacrificium quod offertur Deo, in quam opinionem & verba Canonis sonare videntur, vbi dicitur, hæc dona, hæc munera, hæc sancta sacrificia, et infra hanc oblationem, item Charissime postulatur, vt acceptum sit sacrificium sicut sacrificium Abel &c.* (f) That our very Canon now vsed in the Masse (in which the foresaid wordes are) was aboue 1000. *yeares* since, extant in the time of *S. Gregory* the great, is confessed by *Chemnitius* in his examen

men, *part*. 2. *pag*. 177. *et ibidem*. 178. & by *Musculus, loc. com*. *de Missa Papistica*. *pag*. 368. and by *Anthony de Adamo*, in his Anotomy of the Masse, *fol*. 31. and by *Hutterus, de sacrificio missatiuo*. *pag*. 641. and by *Zegedin, in speculo Pontificum*. *pag*. 59. In so much as *Alcuinus* who liued aboue 800. *yeares* since doth in his booke *de opificijs Ecclesiasticis cap*. *de celebratione Missa*. alledge and expound our said Canon verbatim; & yet al this acknowleged antiquitity therof notwithstading, it is cōfessedly so euident for *Masse*, and *sacrifice*, that therefore *Caluin in lib*. *epist*. *et respons*. *epist*. 195. *pag*. 364. saith, *Missa est sacrificium ab hominibus institutum pro redemptione viuorum et mortuorum, vt certo loco Canon Missæ perhibet: Missa igitur execranda est blasphemia*. since therefore our aduersaries do thus condemne our now Canon, as making for sacrifice, how can they then deny, but that the very same Canon and wordes thereof imported likewise sacrifice in those other more auncient times in which it was in like maner extant.

therof: And if it was in thē reputed for sacred & honorable, how thē is the very same becōe so penal & hateful now in vs. And although this onely agreement herein of the auncient Churches *Liturgie* with our now Masse, be a sufficient iustification thereof; I wil yet in this so great plenty of testimonies (wherein I am troubled, rather what to omit, then which to vse) disceend from the forme of wordes to the further proofe of the thing it selfe, which is *sacrifice*, & the very *act of sacrifycing*. And *first*, concerning the Eucharist to be a sacrifice, the auncient Fathers are so plentiful herin, that therfore they doubt not to tearme it, not only *a sacrifice*, but do also therewith further ad therto such sūdry pregnāt *Epithets* as argue that they vsed the word sacrifice not improperly. To this end they cal it (*) the *visible sacrifice*, (g) the *true sacrifice*, (h) the daily

(*)
S. Augustin. de ciuitate Dei l. 10. *c.* 19. saith, *Sacrificantes non Alteri visibile sacrificium offerendum esse nouerimus quam illi cuius in cordibus nostris inuisibile sacrificium nos ipsi esse debemus.*

(g)
Ciprian. l. 2. *epist.* 3. *versus finem. et August. de ciuitat. Dei l.* 10. *c.* 20. *et de spiritu et litera. cap.* 11. *et concil.* 12. *Toletan. c.* 5.

(h)
It is called in *Augustine, de ciuit. Dei, l.* 10. *c.* 20. *quotidianum Ecclasiæ sacrificium*. And *in concil.* 1. *Toletan. can.* 5. *sacrificium quotidianum*. And in *Ciprian. de cæna Domini. post med. perpes sacrificium*. And in *Euseb. Emissen hom.* 5. *de Paschate*. *perennis illa victima*. and in *Origen in numer. hom.* 23. alledged heretofore, *tract.* 1.

sect. 4. *subdiuis*. 2. at 2. *sacrificium indesinens*. and *in Chrisost*. *in hom*. 17. *in* 9. *habr*. *hostia inconsumptibilis*.

(i)   *daily sacrifice*, the (i) *sacrifice according to the*
Ciprian. *l*. 2. *epist*. 3.   *order of Melchisadech, the* (k) *sacrifice of the bo-*
et Augustin. *de ciuit*. *Dei*.   *dy and bloud of Christ*; *the* (2) *sacrifice of his bo-*
l. 16. *c*. 22. *l*. 17. *c*.   *dy and bloud, instituted according to the order of*
5. *fine*. et *c*. 20. et *l*. 18.   *Melchisadech, the* (3) *sacrifice of the Altar, the*
c. 35. *circa med*. et in   (l) *sacrifice of the Church, and the* (m) *sacrifice*
Psal. 33. *conc*. 2. *Oecu-*   *of the new Testament, which* (n) *succeeded al the*
men. et Haymo in *habr*.   *sacrifices of the old Testament*.
c. 5.   (k)   (2) As

Augustin. *de ciuit*. *Dei*. *l*. 22. *c*. 8. *paulo ante med*. et *Fulgentius lib*. 2. *ad Monimum*. *c*. 2. *initio*. *et concil*. 12. *Toletan*. *c*. 5. *et Augusti. l*. 20. *contra Faustum*, *c*. 18. *et in Psal*. 33. *et Hierom*. *l*. 3. *contra Pelag*. (2) *August*. *tom*. 8. *in Psal*. 33. *con*. 2. *saith, ipse de corpore et sangui-ne suo instituit sacrificium secundum ordinem Melchisadech*. (3) *August*. *in enchirid*. *c*. 110. *et de cura pro mortuis*, *c*. 18. and *Greg*. *in Luc*. *hom*. 37. *et epist*. 59. *ad Paulinum, in solut*. 5. *quæstionis*. (l) *Augustin*. *de ciuit*. *Dei*. *l*. 10. *c*. 20. *et l*. 1. *contra*. *aduers*. *c*. 18. *et Fulgen-tius ad Monimum*. *l*. 2. *c*. 6. *et* 9. *initio*. *et Ciprian*. *de cæna Domini*, *paulo post initium*. (m) *Ireneus, l*. 4. *c*. 32. *fine*. *et Augusti*. *de gratia noui Testam*. *c*. 18. *et Euseb*. *demonst*. *Euang*. *l*. 1. *c*. vlt. (n) *August*. *de ciuit*. *Dei*. *l*. 17. *c*. 20. saith most pertinently vpon these wordes of *Ecclesiastes* : *non est bonum homini nisi quod manducabit et bibet, quid credibilius dicere intelligitur, quam quod ad participationem mensæ huius per-tinet, quam Sacerdos ipse mediator Testamenti Noui exhibet, secundum ordinem Melchisadech, de corpore et sanguine suo? Id enim sacrificium successit om-nibus illis sacrificijs veteris Testamenti quæ imolabantur in vmbra futuri &c*. *quia pro illis omnibus sacrificijs et oblationibus, corpus eius offertur, et partici-pantibus ministratur*. seemeth not this plaine enough to our learned ad-uersaries ? In like maner concerning the *chaunge* of the sacrifices of the old law, into this now sacrifice of the Eucharist, *S*. *Chrisostom*. *in* 1. *Cor*. *hom*. 24. saith of Christ, *ipsum mutauit sacrificium, et pro cæde bru-torum, seipsum iussit offerri*. And *Theophilact*. *in Math*. 26. saith, (in re-spect of the Sacrament) *sicut vetus Testamentum immolationem habebat et sanguinem, ita nouum Testamentum sanguinem habet, ac immolationem*. And *S*. *Augustin*. *epist*. 86. *ad Casulanum*. saith, *vrbicus ille in sui er-roris confirmationem inter alia ait, vetera sic transisse, vt in Christo cederet &c*.

cederet pui

pani pecus, poculo sanguis &c. dicit cecisse pani pecus, tanqam nesciens, et tunc in Domini mensa panis propositionis poni solere, et nunc se de immaculati agni corpore partem sumere; dicit cessisse poculo sanguinem, non cogitans etiam nunc se accipere in poculo sanguinem: quanto ergo melius et congruentius vetera tansisse, et noua in Christo facta esse sic diceret, vt cederet Altare Altari &c. panis pani, pecus pecori, sanguis sanguini. And S. *Clement,* the Apostles scholer, *in Apost. constitut.* (after the Antwerpe print of 1564.) *l. 6. c. 22. fol. 123. b. circa med.* saith, *Circumcisionem sustulit &c. pro sacrificio cruento, rationale, & incruentum, ac misticum sacrificium instituit, quod in mortem Domini per simbola corporis et sanguinis sui celebratur.* And see further hereof S. *Leo,* and *Hesichius,* alledged hereafter, *tract. 3. sect. 3. subdiuis. 4.* in the margent at 10. and S. *August. in Psal. 33. con. 2.* alledged hereafter, *tract. 3. sect. 4. subdiuis. 1.* in the margent vnder d. this chaunge of sacrifice vpon chaunge of the law, is in regard of the relation or the dependance betweene law and *Preisthood,* whereof the Apostle saith, *if the Preisthood be translated, of necessity also there is made a translation of the law. Habr. 7. 12.*

(2) As concerning *the act of sacrifycing,* although it be sufficienly proued by that which haith bene *heretofore* said concerning (o) *Altar,* and *Preist,* (which I wish the reader carefully to peruse, and to confer with this next ensuing) yet to ad further demonstration thereof, whereas our aduersaries would euade, affirming that (*) *the Fathers by offering of sacrifice meant onely their distribution of the Sacrament to the communicantes:* I wil now further shew that the Preistes of those times before their owne communion and distribution thereof to the people, did actually offer it vp in sacrifice to God the Father. To this end the Fathers of the *first Nicene Councel,* do in plaine tearmes mention (q) *the offering of Christes body, and the distri-bution*

(o)
See heretofore *tract. 1. sect. 2. subdiuis. 1.* and in the margent there at the letter z.

(p)
See heretofore, *tract. 1. sect. 3. subd. 1.* throughout.

(*)
Hutterus, de sacrificio missatico, pag. 310. saith, *sacrificare corpus Christi nihil aliud fuit Patribus quam illud fidelibus manducandum offerre et distribuere &c.* And the like euasion is geuen by *Vadian, de Euchavist. Aphorism.*

l. 6. pag. 209. (q) *Conc. 1. Nicen. can. 14.* saith, *peruenit ad sanctum concilium quod in locis quibusdam et ciuitatibus Presbiteris Sacra-*

meta Diaconi porrigat, hoc neq, regula, neq, consuetudo tradidit, vt hi qui offerēd *sacrificij, non habent potestatem, his qui offerant corpus Christi porrigant.* And that the Deacon was restrained from this offering of sacrifice, was *decreed* likewise, by the *first councel* called *Aretatense. c . 15.* as is witnessed by the Century writers, *Cent . 4. col. 703.* and yet the same Fathers alledged *cent . 4. col. 705.* *Deacons might in the Preistes absence deliuer the Sacra-* *ment,* hereof also see *Epiphanius har. 79. ante med·* alledged by *the* Century writers, *cent. 4. col. 491.* and see *Ruffinus, l . 1. c. 6.* cyted by the Centurists, *cent . 4. col. 426.* and 491. and see more hereof *apud Whitakerum, contra Duraum l. 8.pag. 659.* and . 660.

(r)
Concil . 1. Nicen. can . | bution thereof to the people, as being thinges
14. vt supra and see here- | in nature different, allowing (r) *the Deacon*
tofore, *tract. 1. sect. 3.* | *authority to do the one, but not the other.* In like
subdiuis.1. at a. b. | maner long before that time, doth *S . Cipri-*
(s) | *an* acknowledge the like difference affirming,
Ciprian. in serm. de Lapsis, | that (s) *when the Preist had celebrated sacrifice,*
multo post med. faith to | then afterwardes followed the Deacons di-
this end , *quidam alius* | stribution thereof to the people, and the ve-
&c. sacrificio a sacerdote | ry same difference of offering it in the sacri -
celebrato partem cum cate- | fice from the communion thereof, is yet fur-
ris ausus est latenter acci- | ther mentioned by the (2) *Apostles scholer S.*
pere. and in the same | (3) *Clement,* by (t) *Prosper, S.* (u) *Augustine,*
sermon *post med.* he sig- | and
nifyeth this further, saying, *sacrificantibus nobis &c . vbi vero solemnibus* *adimpletis Calicem Diaconus offerre presentibus cæpit &c.* (2) See menti-
on made of *Clement,* by *S . Paul. Philip. 4. 3.* (3) *Clement,* after the edition at Antwerpe of 1564. *l. 2. Apostol. conft. c. 61. fine.* faith, *his perfectis sacrificium peragatur astante omni populo atq, secreto orante ; ac* *postquam oblatum fuerit, accipiant singuli per se ordine dominicum corpus et* *pretiosum sanguinem, gradatim, cum pudore ac tremore tanquam ad regis cor-* *pus accedentes &c.* And see further there, *fol. 181. a. initio.* See this booke of *Clement,* proued hereafter, *tract. 3. sect. 2. subdiuis. 5.* in the margent at x .*. (t) *Prosper, de promissionibus et prædictionibus Dei. l.* *4. c. 6.* faith, *peracto itaq, sacrificio, cum eadem inter ceteras breuem particulā* *corporis Domini tinctam perciperet &c.* (u) *August. de ciuit. Dei lib.* *15. c. 7. paulo post initium.* faith, *vni Deo sacrificandum est, non autem* *recte diuiditur dum non discernuntur recte, vel loca, vel tempora, vel res ipsa* *quæ*

*quæ offeruntur, vel qui offert, vel cui offertur, vel hi quibus ad vescendum
distribuitur quod oblatum est*. And *contra Faustum Manichæum. l. 20. c.
18.* saith, *vnde iam Christiani peracti eius sacrificij memoriam celebrant sacrosancta oblatione et participatione corporis et sanguinis Christi*. and *de Trinitate. c. 14.* he saith, *quid tam grate offerri et suscipi posset quam caro
sacrificij nostri corpus effectum Sacerdotis nostri*. And see him *l. 2. re-
tract. 6. 11.*

& the ancient Coūcels of (x) *Neocessaria*, (y)
Brache, and (z) *Tolledo*. whereunto might be
added sundry other testimonies concerning
the Preistes ●blatió therof euen (a) *vnto God.*
diuers of the Fathers mencioning (which (2)
Hutterus so much disliketh) the Preistes
offering (3) the *sacrifice of the body and bloud of
Christ vnto God* : others of them saying also
accordingly as the Preist said in the auncient
Liturgies, (b) *offerimus tibi &c.* a forme of
wordes so pregnant for sacrifice that it is
therefore

(x)
*Concil. Neocessarienf. can.
13.* saith, *Presbiteri qui
conregionales non sunt, in
Eclesia presentibus Episcopis, vel Presbiteris ciuita-
tis, offerre non possunt, nec
dare panem sanctificatum,
nec Calicem porrigere.*

(y)
*Concil. Bracharenf. 3.
can. 3.* (after *Isidorca*

collection) saith, *cum Sacerdos ad solemnia Missarum accedit, aut ipse Deo
sacrificium oblaturus, aut Sacramentum corporis &c. sumpturus &c.* (3)
Concil. 12. Toletan. can. 5. saith, *relatum nobis est quosdam de Sacerdotibus &c. in vno die si plurima per se Deo offerant sacrificia, in omnibus
se oblationibus a Communione suspendunt &c. quasi non sit totiens illi vero et
singulari sacrificio participandum, quociens corporis et sanguinis Domini nostri
Iesu Christi immolatio facta constituerit &c. ergo modis omnibu tenendum est,
vt quotienscunq̃, sacrificans corpus et sanguinem Christi &c. in Altari immolat, tociens perceptionis corporis et sanguinis participem se prabeat.*
(1) Concerning mention of the Preistes offering sacrifice vnto God.
see *Ciprian. l. 2. epist. 3. et August. l. 1. contra aduers. leg. et Prophet. c. 20. et de sanctis serm. 11. contra Faustum Manichæum.
l. 20. c. 21. et Euseb. l. 1. demonst. Euang. c. 10. et in Liturgijs
Chrisost. et Basil. et Ambros. l. 4. de sacramentis. c. 6.* (2) *Hutterus, de sacrificio Missatico. pag. 313.* (3) See this phrase in the
Fathers of the 12. *Tolletane Councel, can. 5.* and in *Fulgentius, l. 2.
ad Monimum c. 6. initio. et l. 2. ad Monimum. c. 2. initio.* alledged
next hereafter, *subdiuif. 3.* in the margent at k. n. and see *Fulgentius
l. 1. ad Monimum. c. 2.* (b) *Ambros. l. 4. de sacramentis, c. 6.
initio.* saith, *offerimus tibi hanc immaculatam hostiam &c. et hunc panem*

sanctum et calicem vitæ æternæ. And see the like in the Liturgies of S.
Iames, printed Antwerpiæ. 1560. fol. 26. b. initio. and of Basile, after
the same edition fol. 40. a. fine. and of Chrisostome, after that edition,
fol. 53. a. fine. and see Clement l. 8. constitut. Apostol. c. 18. (4)

Hutterus de sacrificio missatico. pag. 320. saith to
Bellarmine of these very
wordes, offero tibi, as followeth nec vere, nec pie,
immo plusquam blaspheme
verbis istis ad Deum direc-
tis missifices vti, iterum atq́
iterum ingeminamus. (*)
August. contra Faustum
Manichæum. l. 20. c. 21.
(c) Aug. de ciuit. Dei, l.
22. 10. circa med.   (d)
Aug. de ciuit. Dei, l. 8. c.
27. initio. et cōtra Faust.
Manich. l. 20. c. 21. (*)
This argueth that the
Preist then standing at
the Altar said, though
not to Peter, or Paul, yet
to god, offero tibi sacrificiū.
(5) August. de ciu. Dei, l.
10. c. 19. saith, visibile
sacrificium offerendum esse
nouerimus, calling it
there c. 10. quotidianum
Ecclesiæ. sacrificium, et sū-
mum verumq́ sacrificium.

therefore specially reproued by (4) Hutterus
in his discourse hereof against Bellarmine:
which said forme of external oblation so made
to God, S. Augustine most euidently insinuateth saying, (*) although in memory of martirs yet to no martir, but to God of martirs, do we
erect Altars (c) in quibus, &c. vpon which
Alters we offer sacrifice, not to martyres,
but to the God of martyres. And yet againe
saith he more plainly, (d) for which of the faithful haith at any time heard the Preist standing
at the Altar (which in the honour of God is erected vpon the body of a martir) to say (in precibus)
in (*) seruice time: ● Peter, Paul, or Ciprian,
I offer to thee sacrifice; so fully doth he insinuate the foresaid forme of offerimus tibi, vsed
in the auncient Liturgies; and he is yet o-
therwise so ful in this point of external sacrifice offered to God, that he not onely affirmeth an external and (5) visible sacrifice to be
offered, distinguishing (6) the same yet further most expresly from the improper spiritual sacrifices of praier, and almes, calling it
also the (7) sacrifice of the Altar, (8) the sacrifice
of the mediator, (9) the sacrifice of our price, the
sacrifice of Christians, offered vpon the Altar, (11)
                                the daily sacrifice

(6) August. de cura pro mortuis, c. 14. saith, pro mortuis siue Altaris, siue o-
rationum, siue elimosinarum sacrificijs solenniter supplicamus &c. and in
Enchirid. c. 110. he saith, cum ergo sacrificia siue Altaris, siue quarūcunq́
elimozinarum pro baptizatis defunctis omnibus offeruntur, pro valde bonis sunt
grattarum actiones, pro non valde malis propitiationes sunt &c. (7) Aug-
Enchirid. c. 110. vt supra et de cura pro mortuis, c. 14. vt supra. and
                                                                tom.

tom. 2. epist. 59. ad Paulinum in solutione 5. quæstionis (8) August. Enchirid. c. 110. (9) August. l. 9. confes. c. 12. (10) August. de ciuit. Dei. l. 8. c. 27. and l. 17. c. 5. fine. (11) August. de ciuis. Dei. l. 10. c. 20.

facrifice of the Church, the (12) facrifice of the
body and bloud of Chrift, which is offered, and
moft pregnantly agreeable to our doctrine
(13) *the facrifice inftituted of his body and bloud
according to the order of Melchifadech,* (14) offered (now) *fub Sacerdote Chrifto, vnder Chrift*
the (high) Preift, (15) *in euery place as Ma-*
lachy (16) forefheweth, *from the ryfing of the
funne to the going downe thereof,* but alfo further
(e) anfwereth the obiection of the *Manichees,* made againft it, and affirmeth (f) *this
oblation of facrifice to be a kinde of worfhip,* which
is by him there tearmed *cultus latriæ, properly due to the God-head,* wherupon (faith he) *it is
called idolatry in thē* (qui hoc etiā Idolis exhibēt)
who exhibit alfo *this oblation of facrifice to Idols :*
So plainly by this comparifon did the aunci-
ent Fathers in thofe times practife and exhibit external facrifice *to God,* no leffe properly and truly then did the heathen Idolaters
to their proud ambitious (17) *emulating Idols,*
which faid courfe of the heathen *S. Auguftine,*
to the further manifeftation of this matter,
profeffeth

(12)
*August . tom . 7. de animæ
et eius orig. l. 1. c. 11.*
faith, *nulla ratione conce-
ditur vt pro non baptizatis
offeratur facrificium corporis et fanguinis Chrifti.*
and *de ciuit. Dei. l. 22.
c. 8. ante med.* he telleth
how that in helpe of a
houfe infefted with wic-
ked fpirits, *porrexit vnus
(Presbiter) obtulit ibi facrificium corporis Chrifti
&c.*

(13)
*August . in Pfal . 33. cone .
2 .* and moft plainly *de
ciuit. Dei. l. 17. c. 20.*
(14)
*August . de ciuit. Dei. l.
17. c. 17.*
(15)
August. de ciuit. Dei. l.

18 *c. 35. paulo ante med.* & moft plainly *cōtra aduerf. legis et prophetarum.
l. 1. c. 20.* (16) *Malach. 1. 11.* (e) See *August. tom. 6.
contra aduerf. leg. et Proph. l. 1 . c. 19. et contra Fauftum Manichæum.
l. 20. c. 18.* (f) *Auguft. contra Fauftum Manich. l. 20. c. 21.*
fpeaking of the facrifice which Chrift commaunded in his inftitution
of the new Teftament at his laft fupper faith, *non dixi facrificare Deo
in memoryis martyrum quod frequentiffime facimus illo duntaxat ritu quo fibi
facrificari noui Teftamenti manifeftatione præcepit, quod pertinet ad illum cultum qui latria dicitur, et vni Deo debetur.* what can be more plainly
fpoken to proue that Chrift in his inftitution of the Sacrament, ordained

ordained and commaunded ſacrifice. (17)   The Diuel affecting (in the pride of his heart) to be like *the moſt high. Eſay.* 14. 14. doth emulate God in his honour, to that end, by his Idols requiring ſacrifice. 1. *Cor.* 10. 19. 20.

(18)

Auguſt. epiſt. 49. *Deo-gratias. Preſbit. in ſolut.* 3. *quaſt.* ſaith, *quapropter qui ſacras literas vtriuſ$q,$ Teſtamenti ſciunt, non hoc culpant in ſacrilegis ritibus Paganorum quod conſtruant Templa, et inſtituant Sacerdotia, et faciant ſacrificia, ſed quod hac Idolis & demonijs exhibeant.*

(g)

See the Liturgies of *S. Iames, Baſil.* & *Chriſoſt.*

(h)

Conc. Carthag. 3. *can.* 23. (2) See next heretofore *ſubdiuiſ.* 2. in the text and margent at f.

profeſſeth to reproue, (18) *not for their offering ſacrifice* (a thing then houlden lawful) *but* (onely) *for offering the ſame to Idols.*

(2)   This point is as yet made more euident by the order obſerued in al auncient (g) Liturgies, and are mencioned by the (h) Fathers whereby it was accuſtomed for the Preiſt to direct his oblation and praier namely to *God the Father:* In ſo much as the *Arians* ſeeing the Father in time of oblation onely named iudged hereby that the foreſaid *cultus latria,* conſiſting in ſacrifice and mencioned (2) *heretofore* by *S. Auguſtine,* was (as is (3) confeſſed) properly in their opinion due and belonging, not to *the ſonne,* but to *God the Father,* whereupon they vrged (i) *the Father to be greater then the ſonne, becauſe that to him*

(3) The Proteſtant writer *Euſebius Altkircherus, l. de miſtico & incruento ſacrificio aduerſus abominandam miſſa ſuperſtitionem.* printed *Neuſtadij Palatinorum.* 1584. *pag.* 241 ſaith concerning this very point debated by *Fulgentius: Hinc enim quaſi ex totius Eccleſia concenſu, & in oblationis ſacrificio facta confeſſione &c. Filium Patre minorem eſſe, et quod ſoli Patri, non etiam Filio hoc Eccleſia ſacrificium offeretur, probare et euincere ſe poſſe putabant Ariani &c. ita quoq, ſentiebant Ariani Chriſtum in hoc ſacrificij cultu Patri non eſſe aqualem.* In ſo much as in the margent there is ſet downe, *Argumentum Arianorum pro perſonarum in Trinitate in aqualitate a ſacrificio Eccleſia.* can any thing more confeſſedly, proue the doctrine of the Church at that time to be, that the Euchariſt was a proper and external ſacrifice? otherwiſe how impertinec had this foreſaid doubt or queſtion beene? and how vainly els had the *Arians* framed their foreſaid obiection, as grounded vpon the Churches receiued doctrine? See alſo the ſaid Proteſtant writer there, *pag.* 236. abridging in the margent

margent *Ireneus* his argument, set downe there at large from the Churches receiued doctrine concerning sacrifice, which the said author thus abridgeth, *illatio argumenti quo vtitur Iræneus a sacrificio Ecclesia, contra Marcionem: si panis et vinum non sunt creatura Dei, Patris Christi, ergo in horum sacrificio & oblatione est cupidus alieni.* (i) *Vide Marcellinum, in epistola ad Salamonem Episcopum initio. in* 1. *tom. concil.*

to him alone (as they hereupon misiudged) the sacrifice was offered : which their argument *Fulgentius* tearmeth (k) *the principal obiection of the heretickes*; whereunto he and others answeare and explaine, not denying the Eucharist to be a sacrifice, but to the contrary shewing that, (l) *euen as to the Father, so like-wise to the sonne, not onely in Christian times, but also in elder times (of the old Testament) sacrifices were offered by Preistes.* And the same doth(m)*Fulgentius* (in further answere therto) proue, by sundry sacrifices of the old Testament so offered. By al which premises it appeareth that, (n) *the sacrifice of Christes body and bloud, which* (saith he) *many thought to be offred to the Father onely,* was by the Preists of those times offered to God as an external sacrifice, as wel as were before time the other sacrifyces of the old Testament: which point is yet vnanswearably more euident, in that it was offered as now by vs, so likewise then by them, (o) *for the health of the Emperour,* (p) *for the sicke vpon sea and land, and the fructes*

(k) *Fulgentius, l.* 2. *ad Monimum. c.* 2. *initio.* saith, *dicis a nonnullis te interrogatum de sacrificio corporis et sanguinis Christi, quod plerig, soli patri existimant immolari, hanc etiam asseris hæreticorum esse quasi palmarem interrogatione &c.*

(l) *Fulgentius vbi supra.*

(m) *Fulgentius, l.* 2. *ad Monimū, c.* 3. saith, *cum itag, nos dicimus sacrificium non soli Patri sed simul vnū patri filiog, offerri, illi autem soli patri existimant immolari in sacrificio Patriarcharum, vera ac Deo placita quæramus immolationis indicium ab illo, itag, nobis est documentorum series inchoanda &c. certe consentiunt non ob aliud ædificari nisi ad*

ab Abraham filio Altare constructum, Altare vero offerendum sacrificium Deo, veteris Testamenti lectio frequenter insinuat. et vide ibidem. c. 4. (n) *Fulgentius l.* 2. *ad Monimum, c.* 2. *initio.*
(o) *Tertulian. ad Scapul. c.* 2. saith, *sacrificamus pro salute imperatoris, sed Deo nostro et ipsius.* for if *Onias* the high Preist offered sacrifice for the life of *Heliodorus,* whereupon God graunted him his life. 2. *Machab.* 3. 32. 33. how much more auailable then in that behalfe

L l

may our now fo far more excellent facrifice of the new Teftament be
thought to be. (p) *Chrifoft. hom. 27. in act. Apoft.* faith, *pro infirmis et terra, et maris et vniuerfi orbis fructibus facrificamus.* And *Clement*,
l. 8. Apoft. conftit. c. 18. fol. 173. b. & 174. a. after the Antwerpe print
of 1564. faith. *offerimus tibi pro aeris falubritate, et fructuum fertilitate,*
        (q)   (& a litle there before) *pro laborantibus infirmitate.*
Auguft. de ciuit. Dei. l.
22. c. 8. faith hereof, *fructes of the earth*, for the purging (q) of
perrexit vnus, obtulit ibi houfes that were infefted with wicked fpirits
facrificium corporis Chrifti, for the finnes of (r) *the liuing*, as is confeffed, &
orans quantum potuit vt in particular proued by (s) *Craftouius*, and
ceffaret illa vexatio, Deo Szegedinus, both of them learned Caluiniftes.
protinus miferante ceffauit.   And
(r) *Bafil. in Liturgia fol. 40. a. fine. et b. initio.* prayeth, *vt digniffimus offerre tibi rationabile iftud, et incruentum facrificium pro noftris peccatis et populi ignorantia.* and S. *Chrifoftom. hom. in Encaniys.* faith, *menfa mifteryis inftructa eft, et agnus Dei pro te immolatur.* and in *Math.*
hom. 83. he further faith, *fi remiffionem hoc peccatorum facit, ficuti*
certe facit &c. And *Ciprian de cana Domini. prope intium.* faith, *quotiefcunq, bis verbis et hac fide actum eft, panis ifte fubftantialis et calix benedictione folemni facratus ad totius hominis vitam falutemq, proficit, fimul medicamentum et holocauftum exiftens ad fanandas infirmitates, et purgandas iniquitates exiftens.* and *Origen, hom. 13. in Leuit.* faith hereof, *ifta eft*
commemoratio fola qua propitium facit Deum hominibus. and *conftantine* the
Emperour, *in epift. ad Epifcopos Tiri, collectos* faith, *et vos qui eius diuinitati pro nobis fancta debetis offerre mifteria.* And *Ignatius* the Apoftles fcholer affirmeth of the Bifhop that, *he doth facrifice to God for the faifty of*
the whol world. iniepift. ad Smirnenfes. and fee further hereof S. *Hierome,*
in c. 1. epift. ad Tit. and *Auguft. l. 1. contra Crefconium, c. 25.* and
Concil. 3. Brach. can. 1. (in Ifidors collection) *initio Canonis.* (s) *Craftouius de opificio miffæ, contra Bellar. l. 1. pag. 167.* reprehedeth the Fathers,
hereafter by him named faying of them, *dicta autem Patrum non folum*
impetrationem, fed etiam intrinfecam quandam vim placandi innunt. O-
rigen, hom. 13. in Leuit. ifta eft commemoratio fola qua propitium facit
Deum hominibus. Athanafius in ferm. de defunctis, apud Damafcenum,
incruenta hoftiæ oblatio propitiatio eft. Ambrof. l. 1. de officio c. 48. offert
Chriftus feipfum quafi Sacerdos vt peccata noftra dimittat. Chrifoftomus, l.
6. de facerdotio. Sacerdos pro vniuerfo terrarum orbe legatus intercedit, deprecatorq,

precatorâ est apud Deum vt hominum omnium non viuentium modo sed etiam defunctorum peccatis propitius fiat. August. quast. 57. in Leuit. in multis sacrificiys qua pro peccatis offerebantur, vnum hoc nostrum sacrificium signification *in quo vera sit remissio peccatorum. Greg. l. 4. Dial. c. 58. hac victima singulariter ab aterno interitu animam saluat. Beda, l. 4. hist. c. 22. sacrificium hoc salutare ad redemptionem valet anima et corporis &c.* Thus far *Crastonius* recyting as thus, and reiecting the foresaid particuler sayinges of the Fathers concerning the Eucharist to be a propitiatory sacrifice. And *Szegedinus, in speculo Pontificum. pag.* 50. saith accordingly, *Alexander primus docuit missa sacrificio peccata deleri, hunc imitatus Gregorius Magnus certos instituit dies quibus in templo solemni ritu sacrificaretur et proposuit delictorum veniam ad id solemne accedentibus.*

(4)

And lastly (aboue al) euen for the sinnes of (4) *the dead,* to which end *S. Augustine* affirmeth that (5) *the sacrifice of our price was offered for his mother Monica being dead,* & (t) *that it is not to be doubted but that the soules of the deade are relived by the piety of their liuing frendes, when for them is offered the sacrifice of the mediator:* and therefore that (u) *the vniuersal Church doth obserue, as deliuered from our forefathers, that for those who are deade in the Communion of Christes body and bloud when in time of sacrifice they be remembred in their place, praier is made for them (ac pro illis id quoq, offerri commemoretur) and (besides this praier) for them also it is remembred the sacrifice be offered. in so much that (as it were in preuention of*

See *Bullingers* testimony hereof in his decades in english, pag. 1082. And M. *Fulke* against Purgatory, pag. 362. and 363. and *Hospinan.* alledged hereafter, *tract. 3. sect. 2. subdiuis. 3.* in the margent at f. and also next hereafter in the margent at b.

(5)

Aug. l. 9. cōf. c. 12. saith, *cum offerretur pro ea sacrificium pretij nostri.* And *ibidem, c. 13.* he further saith of his sicke mother,

non ista mandauit (Monica) nobis, sed tantummodo memoriam sui ad Altare tuum fieri desiderauit &c. vnde sciret dispensari victimam sanctam qua deletum est chirographum quod erat contrarium nobis. (t) *August. in Enchirid. c, 110.* saith, *neq, negandum est defunctorum animas pietate suorum viuentium releuari, cum pro illis sacrificium mediatoris offertur.* (u) *August. de verbis Apost. serm. 34.* saith, *hoc enim a Patribus traditum vniuersa obseruat Ecclesia vt pro eis qui in corporis et sanguinis Christi communione defuncti sunt, cum ad ipsum sacrificium loco suo commemorantur*

oretur

oretur, ac pro illis quoq̃ id offerri commemoretur.

(x)
Anguft. Enchirid. c. 110. et vide Auguft. de verbis Apoftol. ferm. 17. et in Ioan. tract. 84.

(y)
Ciprian. l. 1. epift. 9. faith, Anteceffores noftri &c. cenfuerunt ne quis frater excedens &c. Clericum nominaret, ac fi quis hoc feciffet, non offerretur pro eo, nec pro dormitione eius facrificium celebraretur.

(z)
Chrifoftomus hom. 69. ad populum faith, non temere ab Apoftolis hæc fuerunt fancita, vt in tremendis mifteriis defunctorum agatur commemoratio, fciunt enim illis inde multum contingere lucrum, vtilitatem multâ.

of our aduerfaries ordinary anfweare) he further affirmeth that, (x) *the facrifice of the Altar, or of almes which are offered for the deade are thankef-geuing, for thofe that be very good,* (or in heauen); *and propitiarions for thofe that be not very euil,* (or not in hel.) And the like mention of facrifice for the deade, is made by (y) *S. Ciprian,* (z) *Chrifoftome,* and (a) other Fathers, and by our learned aduerfaries in fundry of them (b) confeffed. In fo much as *M. Gyfford* affirmeth, that euen (*) *in the Churches publicke worfhip to pray for the foules of the dead, and to offer oblation for the dead, was general in the Church long before the day es of Auguftine, as appeareth in Ciprian, & Tertulian, which was before him and nearer to the Apoftles* time. And *M. D. Fulke* further acknowledgeth that (c) *Tertulian, Ciprian, Auguftine, Hierome, and a great many moe, are witnes that facrifice for the deade is referred to the tradition of the Apoftles;* for which he doth there afterwardes more fpecially reprehend (d) *Tertulian, Auguftine,* and *Chrifoftome.* The credit of whofe teftimonies herein
(though

and the very fame he affirmeth *in hom. 3. in epift. ad Philip. et vide hom. 21. in acta Apoftolorum. et hom. 41. 1. Cor.* (a) *Tertul. de corona militis.* faith, *oblationes pro defunctis, pro natalitiis Annua facimus.* And *Ciril. Hierofol. catech. 5.* faith, *maximum effe credimus animarum iuuamen pro quibus offertur obfecratio fancti illius et tremendi quod in Altari pofitum eft facrificii.* (a) See further hereof *Eufebius de vita Conftantini, l. 4. c. 17.* and *Ambrof. l. 2. epift. 8. ad Fauftinum. et Concil. 2. Cabilonenf. can. 39.* and *Concil. 1. Brach. can. 34. 35. 39.* and fee the Liturgies of *S. Iames, fol. 28. a.* of *Bafile, fol. 44. initio.* and of *Chrifoftome, fol. 62. b. fine.* and *Clemens, l. 8. Apoftol. conftitut.* after the Antwerpe print of 1564. *c. 18.* (b) See this hereafter, *tract. 3. fect. 2. fubdiuif. 2. at f. g. 1.* and *ibidem. fubdiuf. 3. at r. f. g.* (*) *M. Gyfford,* in his demonftration that our
Browniftes

Brownistes be Donatistes &c. *pag.* 38. (c) *M. Fulke,* in his confutation of Purgatory, *pag.* 362.   (d)   *M. Fulke, ibidem . pag.* 363 .

(e)

(though contemned by our aduersaries) was
yet neuerthelesse so probable to *Suinglius,*
that not daring to deny, or contemne the
same, he enclined rather to inuent a more
strange answeare, as namely that (e) *the Apostles did permit certaine persons in reguard of their
weaknes to pray for the deade .* Hitherto I now
but ad in further manifestation of the auntient Churches actual offering Christes body
in sacrifice , that further argument which
may be drawen from the misconceiued opinion of the *Iewes,* who thereupon charged
(*) *the auntient Christians with the custome of
offering a child in sacrifice .*

Suinglius, tom. 1. *Epi-
cherens. de can. Mis.
fol.* 186. saith, *perhibent
Augustinus , et Chrisostomus, morem pro defunctis
orandi ab Apostolis ꝰ̃ẽ̃ ã̃
Manasse quod ego vehemen-
ter admiror, cum nemo A-
postolorum quicquam de eo
prodiderit, at si omnino res
haberet vt Augustinus, &
Chrisostomus prodiderunt,
non puto Apostolos alia de
causa quam indulgentia infirmitatis quibusdam per-
misisse pro mortuis orare .*

(*)

*A further demonstration of sacrifice practised
in euery age vp to the Apostles .*

SECTION. 2.

Nd although this point of sacrifice
A wherein consisteth the very essence of
the *Masse,* haith bene *heretofore* sufficiently
declared from the ancient Fathers, by sundry
euident demonstrations, as by that which
haith bene heretofore said, *first,* concerning
(f) *Altar, Secondly,* concerning (g) *Preistes,
Thirdly,* concerning the agreeable, or rather
(h) same *forme* of wordes betwene our now
Masse, and the auncient Liturgies, *Fourtly,*
concerning (i) *the sacrifice* it selfe, and *fiftly,*
concerning

*Origen. l. 6 . contra Cel-
sum, ante med.* saith, *Iudæi
in ipsis Christianæ religionis et veræ disciplinæ primordijs ad nostræ doctrinæ
notam et infamiam illud
disseminarent, quod Christianis puerum aliquem im-
molandi mos esset, cuius et
carnem singuli degustarent.*

(f)

See heretofore, *tract.* 1.
sact. 2 . *subdiuis.* 1. at y.
*. z. a. b. ¶. &c.

(g)

See heretofore, *tract.* 1.

sect. 3. *subdiuis.* 1. throughout.   (h)   See heretofore, *tract.* 3.
sect. 1. *subdiuis.* 1. from the beginning to the midest of that 1. *sub-*

diuision

diuision.   (i)   See heretofore, *tract*. 1. *sect*. 3. *subdiuis*. 2. throughout. and *tract*. 3. *sect*. 1. *subdiuis*. 1. at g. h. i. k. and so forwardes
to the end of that subdiuision.

(k)
Heretofore, *tract*. 3.
sect.   1. *subdiuis*. 2.
throughout. and *subdi-
uision* 3. throughout.

(l)
Heretofore *tract*. 2. *sect*.
2. throughout.   *descend*

(m)
Heretofore, *tract*. 2. *sect*.
8. throughout.

(n)
The now Catholicke v-
sage of *pilgrimage to Hierusalem*, is very auncient.
To this end *Euseb. hist.
l. 6. c. 9*. saith of one

concerning the very actual (k) offering therof to God: yet (*vt obstruatur omne os loquen-
tium iniqua*) I wil to the further euidence of
this matter, as before in the former examples of *real* (l) *presence*, and (m) *adoration*, so
also now in this deduce, the same from the
Apostles age to this present, by a continued
diffent or succession of testimonies, & those
not doubtful, but in them selues manifest or
by our learned aduersaries confessed, and
that the same may appeare more plaine and
perspicuouse, I wil begin with this present,
and the last precedent ages and the experience had therein vpon the dayly concourse
of (n) *Pilgrimes to Hierusalem*, from so many (*) remote nations of the Christian
world

Alexander (who liued a hundred yeares before *Constantine* the great)
*Alexander Hierosolimam tum voti, tum visendorum locorum causa propera-
uit*. And see *Hierome, de viris illustribus in Alexandro*. also *Palludius
in historia Lausaica, c*. 113. *prope finem*. telleth how the holy man *Phi-
loromus* said, *voti gratia bis proprijs pedibus venirem Hierosolimam ad ho-
noranda loca sancta*. also it appeareth by *Hierome ad Rusticum, epist*.
46. that *Rusticus* vowed a pilgrimage to *Hierusalem* ; concerning
which his vow *Hierome* saith there to him, *redde quod presente Domino spospondisti*. and it was so general in auncient times, that *Zozomen
in hist. l. 2. c. 25*. saith thereof, *Ecclesia Hierosolimitana quot annis
diem festum splendide celebrat : adeo vt &c. dies octo deinceps conuentus fiant, compluresq́ ex omnibus totius orbis terra partibus vndiq́, ad loca sacra
visenda confluerent*. And the *Century* writers, *cent*. 4. *c*. 6. *col*. 458.
do for this reproue *S. Helen*, mother to *Constantine*, saying therfore
of her, *Helina mater Imperatoris, mulier superstitiosa illuc profecta adoran-
di causa*. and after in the same place they affirme that pilgrimage was
made in that age yearely to *Hierusalem, confluentibus eo ex omnibus terræ partibus Christianis*. (*) Concerning the Christians repayring yearly to

ly to *Hierusalem* in pilgrimage from so many remote nations of the
world, see *Pierre Belon*, in his observations, *de Plusieurs singularites &c.*
(printed) *en Anuers*, 1555 . *l* . 2 . *c* . 82 . *fol* . 249 . and *c* . 85 . *fol*.
253 . and see *les Voyages du seigneur de Villamonte &c* . *l* . 2 . *c* . 21 .
and 22 . 23 . and 24 . and next hereafter at a . And the Protestant
writer *Doctor Phillippus Nicholai de regno Christi*, *l* . 1 . *pag* . 59 . saith
that *Hierusalem* is, *velut perpetua sinodus omnium nationum orbis Christiani.*

(a)

world, whereby it is (a) *made euident*, that *Made euident ;* for con-
concerning the Christian *Greekes*, ~~mo~~*scouites*, cerning al the seueral na-
Georgianes, *Syrians* , and likewise euen the tions next hereafter men-
(*) *Armenians, with whom* (as *M. Fulke* con- cioned in the text, *An-*
fesseth) *al the oriental Churches do agree:* con- *drew Theuet*, chosmogra-
cerning also the Christian *Æthiopians*, or *A-* pher to the French King,
bisines, vnder their Emperour vulgarly called in his Cosingaraphy *v-*
Presbiter Iohn, and the Christians of *Iaua, Ta-* *ninerselle &c.* printed at
probane, Cephala, Quinsay, and other remote *Paris, Anno*. 1575. *fol.*
countries 173. saith vpon the ex-
perimental obseruation of his owen trauailes, *Ie vous peux asseurer &c.*
I assure you that I found at Hierusalem in the holy (passion*) weeke more then*
foure thousand Christians of seueral (remote) *nations* (hereafter mencioned)
my selfe being sole (amongst them) *with an Almang of the Romane Church* .
And a litle after he further saith, *tontes les nations chantent la Messe aues*
parelle opinion sur sa reale presence &c al those *nations do celebrate Masse*
with the like opinion of the real presence of the body and bloud of our Lord as
we (of the latine Church) *hould, notwithstanding that they do not acknow-*
ledge neither Pope, nor Cardinal, King, or Emperour of ours . And some litle
after yet he further saith, *ils neme sairent monstrer que iamais &c. none can*
shew that the Abissines, Armenians, Maronites, Georgians of Persia, Nesto-
rians, Iacobites, Sirians, Iauanes, which be of the Ilandes next the oriental
India Burians, Darians, Cephalians, the men of Guinsay, most remote of al
the oriental Iudia ; (*of al which nations I saw in Hierusulem, in the holy* (pas-
fion) *weeke) euer learned from vs* (of the latine Church) *their sacred*
misteries (or *Liturgie) which they affirme themselues to haue receiued from*
the Apostles : Thus far *Andrew Theuet* . Also the Protestant writer
Doctor Philipus Nicholai de regno Christi, l . 1 . *pag*. 22. confesseth saying, *hoc teneant Christiani lectores, non modo Græcorum Ecclesias, verum*
et rutenos, & Georgianos, & Armenios, & Indos, et Æthiopes, qui Christo
sua

*fua nomina dederunt, veram et realem corporis et fanguinis Domini prefen-
tem ftatuere &c.* and *ibidem pag.* 35. he faith, *Armenij fuis quoq̃ nauis
laborant, nam in ipforum Liturgiæ forma inuocationis, et interceffionis fanc-
torum, et oblationis Sacramenti pro alijs experffior & prolixior mentio fit &c :*
and *ibidem. pag.* 64. he reporteth of the remote *Cataians,* reparing to
Alexandria faying, *in hac vrbe Cataini, & genuenfes in monopolijs & merca-
torijs ædibus fua habent facella, in quibus pro mercatorum peregrinantium incolu-
mitate ritibus Miffifq̃ Pontificijs litatur .* (*) *M. Fulke de fucceffione
Ecclefiaftica contra Stapletonum, pag.* 466. faith, *de Armeniorum confeffi-
one in quam confentiunt orientales omnes orthodoxi &c.*

(o)

As concerning the con-
uerfion *of the Indians* in
the Apoftles times reade
*Petri Maffæi hiftor . Indic .
impref. Coloniæ, Anno Do-
mini.* 1593. *pag.* 36.
and *Hayton Armen . lib.
de Tartaris, c . 6. & Luc.
Ofiander , cent , 1. pag.*
37. and *Paulus Veneftus,
l. 3, c . 27.* and 43.
And concerning the con-
uerfion of the *Aethiopi-
ans* in the Apoftles times,
See *Eufeb . hift. l. 2. c.*
1. *fine .* And fee *Gualter* in his fermons vpon *Zephaniah .* englifhed
fol. 108. 109. concerning the Apoftolicke doctrine yet to this day
preferued ... *Aethiopia, vide ibidem . fol.* 107. As concerning the con-
uerfion of the *Armenians* in the Apoftles times, *Chemnitius examen,
part. 2. pag.* 7. faith, *Armenis Bartholomeus Euangelium prædicauit .*
And that the *Græcians* were conuerted in the Apoftles times, appeareth by *S. Paules* feueral epiftles to fundry of them, as to the *Corinthians, Ephefians, Theffolonians, &c.* And fee *reuelat.* 1. 11. and concerning the couerfion of the moft countries by the Apoftles, See *M.
Willet* in his finopfis, printed, *Anno Domini.* 1600. *pag.* 1065. (p)
M. Sutliue, de Miffa papiftica, l. 3. c. 13. fol. 273. acknowledgeth
that the Liturgies do only vary in ceremonies, agreeing neuerthelesse al
of them

country in the *oriental India (*diuers of which
as the *Aethiopians, Indians, Armenians, Gretians &c.* were (o) *conuerted* in the Apoftles
times, and are from thefe partes fo far di-
ftant, as that the *latine Church,* was for many precedent ages vnknowen to fundry of
them til the latter times, howfoeuer al thofe
or any of them haue in other matters departed from their primitiue Fathers, or els inreguard of other leffer pointes of ceremony
or doctrine, are diuided from the latine
Church, or among them felues ; yet as appeareth not onely by their feueral (p) Liturgies now in vfe, and not lately inuented

by

of them in the point of *sacrifice* saying, *at missa sacrificium multiforme est, aliter atq; aliter celebratur, et eius magna est apud omnes gentes Missæ studiosas varietas: aliter enim Græci, aliter Latini, aliter Æthiopes sacrificant &c.* And to make further examination of the Liturgies in particuler in the *Æthiopian Liturgy* attributed to *S. Mathew* the Preist saith, *transfer panem hunc in carnem tuam immaculatam, et vinum hoc in sanguinem tuum pretiosum, fiat sacrificium ardens et acceptabile, medela, et salus animæ et corpori nostro.* And in the Liturgy of the Church of *Hierusalem*, attributed to *S. Iames* the Preist saith, *Domine qui &c. concessisti vt confidentes accederemus ad sanctum Altare tuum, et offerremus tibi verendum hoc et incruentem sacrificium pro peccatis nostris et ignorantijs &c. placeat tibi Domine vt nos ministri simus noui tui Testamenti ac sacrificij immaculatorum tuorum misteriorum &c.* and againe, *rogamus vt spiritus sanctus &c. efficiat hunc panem corpus sancti Christi tui, et Calicem hunc pretiosum sanguinem Christi tui.* And in the Liturgy of the Church of *Alexandria*, attributed to *S. Marke* the Preist saith, *largire communionem sancti corporis et pretiosi sanguinis vnigeniti filij tui &c.* and againe, *offerrimus rationabilem et incruentam* Latreian, *seu oblationem hanc quam offerunt tibi Domine omnes gentes &c.* And in the Liturgy of the *Armenians*, the Preist saith, *dimitte Domine in oblationem ante nos positam spiritum sanctum, vt sanctificetur iste panis verum corpus Christi saluatoris &c.* and againe *offerrimus tibi hanc oblationem suscipe in conspectu tuo collocatum et coæqua illam corpori et sanguini Domini nostri Iesu Christi &c.* And in the Liturgie of the Church of *Constantinople*, attributed to *S. Chrisostome* the Preist saith, *fac panem hunc pretiosum corpus Christi tui et quod est in calice iste, pretiosum sanguinem Christi tui, transmutans spiritu tuo sancto.* and againe, *fac me dignum Sacerdotij gratia indutum assistere sanctæ huic tuæ mensæ et consecrare sanctum corpus tuum et pretiosum sanguinem, tu enim es offerens et oblatus.* And in the Liturgy of the of Church *Syria*, attributed to *S. Basil* the Preist saith, *ostende panē istum, ipsū honorificum corpus Domini, et quod est in calice isto ipsum sanguinem Domini* and againe *Domine &c. qui posuisti nos fieri ministros noui Testamenti tui, et ministros sanctorum misteriorum tuorum, suscipe nos appropinquantes sancto Altari tuo &c. vt simus digni offerre tibi rationabile hoc, et incruentum sacrificium pro peccatis nostris.* And concerning now the *Latine* Church in *S. Ambrose* his *orat. 1. præpar. ad Missam.* the Preist saith, *concede mihi hodie et semper missarum solemnia puro corde et pura mente celebrare &c. quanta animæ puritate istud diuinum ac celeste sacrificium est celebrandum, vbi caro tua in veritate sumitur et*

 tur et

tur, et fanguis tuus in veritate bibitur. and *l. 4. de Sacram. c. 6. initio. Sacerdos dicit &c. offerimus tibi hunc immaculatam hoftiam &c.* And the auncient *Canon* yet to this day vfed in the publicke Liturgy of the *Latine* Church, is fo pregnant for real prefence, and external facrifice, that it is therefore reiected by *Szegedine in fpeculo Pontificum, pag. 59.* of whom it is there tearmed *Canon impius,* hereof fee alfo *Caluin* alledged heretofore *tract. 3. fect. 1. fubdiuif. 1.* in the margent at f. Hitherto concerning the agreement of the publicke Liturgies of feueral nations, as namely of *Hierufalem, Alexandria, Conftantinople,* the *Æthiopians, Syrians, Armenians,* and the latine Church.

(q)

As concerning the Li- by the *Pope,* but very (q) *auncient,* as being turgies of the *Æthiopians,* in, or nere the Apoftles times ; but alfo by and *Armenians, M. D.* the general conftant (*) report of trauellers, *Fulke* in his confutation they do al of them agree with our now Catholicke of Purgatory, *pag. 357.*

anfwering the obiection of their antiquity faith, *thofe Liturgies of the Æthiopians, and Armenians, as they are more modeft then your Maffe, fo they are not of fuch antiquity that they can prefcribe by continual claime vp to the Apoftles times, nor within a hundred yeares or more of their times ; fo* cófeffedly ancient doth he infinuate thé to be. As concerning the antiquity of the Liturgies of *S. Iames, Bafile, & Chrifoftome,* fee hertofore in the preface to the reader, *fect. 12.* And concerning the confeffed antiquity of the now *Canon* of the Maffe, fee heretofore, *tract. 3. fect. 1. fubdiuif. 1.* in the margent at f. (*) Remitting to that which haith bene heretofore in this fection at *. before o. alledged from *Andrew Thevet ;* concerning al thefe nations ingeneral, I do further ad in particular, concerning the agreement herein of the *Gretianes,* it appeareth in the treatife fet forth by the Proteftant diuines of *Wittenberge,* entituled *Acta Theologorum Witebergentium et Hieremiæ Patriarchæ Conftantinop.* printed *Witebergæ. Anno. 1584.* that the *Greeke* Church yet to this day profeffeth and teacheth *tranfubftantiation* (*pag.* 86 and 96. and 100. and 240. and 318.) and *facrifice* (*pag. 102.*) euen *facrifice offered for the deade.* (*pag. 95.* and 104.) And concerning the *Syrians* their agreement herein with the Roman Church, is made euident by their Church continued in mount *Vaticane* at Rome, in which the banifhed *Syrians* do celebrate their Liturgy, according to the ryte of their owne nation, whereof fee *M. Fulkes* booke *de fucceffione*

successione Ecclesiastica &c. pag. 426. and 467. concerning the like
agreement of the now Æthiopianes with the *Roman Church*. *Aluarez.,*
in his treatise entituled, *historiale description de L. Æthiopie contenant v-
raye relacion des terres et pais du graund Roye et Empereur prete Ian. &c.*
printed *en Anuers* 1558. affirmeth that the *Æthiopians*, who by the
commaundement of *Pretzian* were present at Masse, celebrated there
by the *Portugal Embasadors Preist*, *Louans grandement &c. commended
greatly the order of our office* (or Masse) *wherein they found nothing to gainsay,
but that we gaue not the communion to al those who were present at Masse,*
c. 81. *fol.* 194. That also *Preteian* him selfe *heard our Masse which
caused him great contentment, fol.* 227. and 205. and see the Aethi-
pians allowance and liking of our Masse further testifyed there *fol.*
199. and 204. and 328. In so much that many of *the great Lordes
of Preteians court* being present at our Masse, *confessed and receiued the
Sacrament with great deuotion. Ibidem. pag.* 205. and *Aloysius Cada-
mustus*, in his *nauigatio ad terras ignotas, c.* 60. saith of the *Aethiopians*
& their Liturgy, *parum in cultu diuino a nobis differunt.* And see also *les
voyages del siegneur de villamonte &c.* printed at *Paris,* 1598. *l.* 2. *c.* 24.
fol. 185. and 186. And concerning the like agreement of the *Armenians, Georgians &c.* see the booke entituled, *les obseruations de plusieurs singularites &c. per Pierre Belon du mans.* printed *en Anuers* 1555.
l. 3. *c.* 12. *fol.* 319. where it is said, *les prestres des Armeniens &c.
celebrent le Messe en Calice come les latines et sont vesteus de mesmes ornaments
de cappes, et chasubles, ne consecrant pas en grand paine come les Grees mais en
petit ostie come les latines.* And ibidem. pag. 319. *sonuent auouns assise au
seruice des Chrestiens Armeniens qui viuent per les villes de Turquie mais a-
uouns troue que ils approchent plus des ceremonies des latines que nulle des
autres nations Chrestiens.* and *Villamonte vbi supra. l.* 2. *c.* 23. *pag.*
183. saith of the *Armenian* Preistes, *Au demeurant ils accordant fort auec
nous en L. office de la saincte Messe, ils aut des Callices et des platines en
nostre forme et la consecration faicte ils esleuant la saincte hostie qum ils met-
tent sur la platine, puis ils esleuent le calice ainsie que vous faisons.* And
Nicholas de Nicholay in his *discource et historie veritable des nauigations &c.*
printed *at Anuers, Anno.* 1586. pag. 172. saith of the *Armenians,
ils celebrent leur office quasi a la mode de L. eglice latine.* And whereas in
the Councel of *Florence* houlden about *Anno.* 1430. *transubstantiation* and sacrfice of the Masse for the liuing and deade, are specially
decreed, the *Greekes, Armenians,* and *Iacobines,* assented to this councel,

as appea-

as appeareth by the actes of the said councel: and is also confessed by *Osiander* in his *epitom. &c. cent.* 15. *pag.* 477. And see also further hereof *sum. Concil. collect. per Barthol. Carransam.* printed 1570. *fol.* 388. and 392. and 393. and 394. In like maner *Abdisu Primate* of the *Armenians,* subscribed to the Councel of *Trent.* And *Brochardus in descriptione locorum terra sancta.* extant in the booke entituled, *nouus orbis Regionum, ac Insularum &c. impres. Paris. Anno.* 1533. *pag.* 284. saith, *Armeni, vero et Georgiani, habent Prælatos quos Catholicos vocant, qui sub se habent Archiepiscopos, Episcopos &c. interfui etiam semel in die anuntiationis sacris eorum, et aduerti eos eisdem fere vti caremonijs et precationibus quibus nos in missa. et vide ibidem. pag.* 283. And see further hereof *Theodorus Bibliander de missa Papistica, l.* 3. *c.* 103. *An.* 1548. and *Belforest, in Cosmograh. vniuers. l.* 6. *c.* 23. and concerning the *Russines* or *Muscouites, Hipatius Ruthenorum legatus in sua fidei professione.* saith, *profiteor pariter in missa offerri Deo, verum, proprium, et propitiatorium sacrificium pro viuis et defunctis.*

(*) *Caluin. institut. l.* 4. *c.* 18. *sect.* 18. saith, *missa abominatio omnes reges terra, et populos a summo vsq̃ ad nouissimum in ebriauit. et ibidem. sect.* 1. he saith, *pestilentissimo errore Satan totum pene orbem obcæcauit, vt crederet missam oblationem et sacrificium esse ad impetrandam peccatorum remissionem &c. ea opinione Romanus Antichristus ac eius Prophetæ totum orbem imbuerunt.*

tholicke Roman Church in the point of offering external sacrifice to God: which their so general agreement, as it is yet further euident and confessed by (*) *Caluin, Luther,* and others, so likewise it argueth strongly against our aduersaries, that the doctrine thereof could not be any pretended corruption deriued from the latine Church to so many nations so far remote and distant each from other, sundry of which were vnknowen to the latine Church, and many of them at variance therewith, and that therefore (as D. (b) *Bilson* doth vpon this ground wel vrge

and *Luther de captiu. Babil. c.* 1. saith, *Missa creditur passim esse sacrificium quod offertur Deo, accedunt his dicta sanctorum Patrum, tot exempla, tantusq̃ vsus per orbem constanter obseruatus,* (et paulo post) *nec moueat quod totus orbis contrarium et sensum et vsum habet.* And *Hospinius in hist. sacram. in epist. dedu. fol.* 6. saith, *Missa tanquam medicato quodam poculo omnes terrarum Reges, Principes, et populi hucusq̃ ab annis proximis* 600. *fuerunt inebriati &c.* (b) *M. Bilson* in his

perpetual

perpetual gouernment of Christes Church, c. 13. pag, 285. saith in behalfe of Bishopes, *al the Churches of Christ throughout the world could not at any one time ioyne in one and the selfe same kinde of gouernment, had it not bene deliuered and setled by the Apostles.* And *M. D. Feild* of the Church, *l. 4. c. 21. pag. 242.* setteth dowen for a certaine rule, that *whatsoeuer al, or the most famous and renowmed, at the least in diuers ages haue constantly deliuered, as receiued from them that went before them, no (orthodoxal) man conrradicting or doubting of it, may be thought to be an Apostolical tradition :* in application of which rule ; *first,* concerning the vniuersality of Masse for the last whol *thousand yeares* before Luther, see confessedly hereafter *tract. 3. sect. 2. subdiuis. 2.* at. 1. n. and after q. at 4. *secondly,* as concerning supposed contradiction, it is euident that diuers (which onely would suffice) of those foresaid ages namely in, and after the times of *Gregory* the first, are without al surmise and pretended example thereof : and the ensuing contradiction which afterwardes happened but in some of the other ages, was in *Almericus, the Apostolici, Albigenses, Waldenses, Berengarius, Wiclife,* and such others onely as were al of them confessedly noted and condemned heretickes . whereof see hereafter *tract. 3. sect. 7. subdiuis. 1. & 2.* throughout , so abundantly doth *D. Feildes* rule proue the Masse to be Apostolicke .

vrge in behalfe of Bishops) it was an euident article of the Primitiue faith, first planted by the Apostles in al those nations, wherin no lesse then in sundry other like principal pointes of faith (such as is *the Trinity, the Baptisme of Infantes* and other like) the foresaid nations did, and as yet do agree, notwithstanding their diuersity in other lesser matters .

(2) And although the onely consideration hereof may be thought to be a sufficient vew and suruey of al former ages ; to proceede yet further with euery other former age in perticuler; (r) *Iohn Husse,* (whom our aduersaries would pretend to be of their Church, liued about the (s) *yeare* 1405. in which time *Masse* was so general that he acknowledged

(r)
M. Fox Act. mon. pag. 190. and 241. and *M. D. Downham* in his treatise concerning Antichrist, *pag.* 40.

(s)
Symon de Voyon, in his discourse vpon the Catalogue of the Doctors &c. *pag.* 159.

(t)
Act. mon. pag. 209.

(u)
M. Iohnson, in *M. Iacobs* defence of the Churches and ministry of England

knowledged the same, calling therefore the Eucharist, (t) *the Sacrament of the Altar,* and being him selfe a Preist (u) *said Masse euen to his dying day.* To which Masse the people, during his last restrant, resorted at his hostes house in *Constance,* as is witnessed by a citizen of *Constance* who liued in that time. In like maner did *Sir Iohn Ouldcastle, al.* the *Lord Cobham,* about that time acknowledge the Masse, and therefore calleth the Eucharist (y) *the Sacrament of the Altar,* and (z) *the sacred host,* & is no where charged with the contrary opinion, but as *M. Foxe* witnesseth (a) *his opinion as the Papistes thought at that time was perfect concerning the Sacrament.* As concerning the *thirtenth,* and *twelft* hundreth yeares after Christ, that the *Masse* was during al those times vniuersal, is in it selfe euident and so acknowledged by (b) *the Centurie writers* and others. Concerning the *eleuenth* hundreth yeares after Christ, *the Centuristes* say, (c) *the Idolatrical Masse did bewitch al the Doctors of this age:* and as much do they confesse of the *tenth* hundreth yeares after Christ charging it with (d) *the stagelike spectacle & sacrifice for the liuing and deade:* & the same do they

land &c. pag. 13. & see *M. Foxe in Apocalipsin. c. 11. pag. 290.* where he saith of *Husse, quid de trãsubstantiatione statuit fides Pontificia, quod ipse pariter cum ijsdem Pontificijs non confirmauit. quis Missas illo religiosius celebrauit. &c.*

(x) *Huldericke Reichental, hist. teutonic. de conc. Constantien.* And see *Cocleus; l. 2. histor. Hussitarum.*

(y) *Act. mon. pag.* 265. & 267.

(z) *Act. mon. pag.* 267.

(a) *Act. mon. pag.* 273.

(b) The Century writers in *cent.* 12. *c.* 6. *col.* 887. say of the twelueth age, *mansit quoq̃ theatricum Misse spectaculum in frequentissimo vsu &c.* And concerning the 13. age they say *(in centur.* 13. *c.* 4. *col.* 455.) *Inualuit hoc tempore profanatio cænæ Dominicæ, itaq̃ missam omnes defendunt.* and *cent.* 13. *c.* 6. *col.* 611. they further say of the same age, *Theatricum misse spectaculum in frequentissimo fuit vsu.* (c) *Centur.* 11. *c.* 4. *col.* 233. it is said, *Idolatria missatica omnes Doctores huius quidem secult fascinauit &c.* (d) *Centur.* 10. *c.* 6. *col.* 307. it is said, *cænam Domini in theatricum spectaculum et sacrificium pro viuis et mortuis a superiorum temporum Pontificibus transformatam, iam quoq̃ retinuerunt.* (e) *Cent.* 9. *c.* 6. *col.* 245. it is said, *cænam Domini in theatricum spectaculum transformatam, Romam Pontifices etiam hoc seculo retinuerunt.*

(*) *Cent.*

they (e) affirme of the *ninth age*, reckning vp
withal in particular, the Massing (*) *ceremo-*
nies therof yet to this day vsual. The *eight*
age or hundreth yeares after Christ, is also
by them charged (f) with *stakelike spectacle*
and sacrifice for the liuing and deade. The *sea-*
uenth age is in like maner by them and others
charged with (g) *Masse celebrated in latine,*
(and with) *number of wicked Masses for the*
deade

(*)
Cent . 9 . *c* . 6 . *col*. 245 .
and 246 .

(f)
Cent . 8 . *c* . 6 . *col* . 361 .
it is said, *canam Domini*
in Theatricum spectaculum
& sacrificium pro viuis et
mortuis Romani Pontifices
commutauerunt eamq́; alijs

Ecclesijs obtruserunt. And *Osiander* in his *epitom* . *hist* . *Ecclef* . *cent* . 8 .
pag . 52 . saith of *S* . *Beda* who liued in, or somewhat before the beginning of this eight age or Century, *omnibus Pontificijs erroribus in*
articulis in quibus nos hodie a Papa dissentimus inuolutus fuit, nam et Idolo-
rum cultum, et Missas Pontificias, et inuocationem sanctorum, & monasti-
cam vitam admiratus et sectatus est . (g) The Centuristes, (*cent* . 7 .
c . 6 . *col*. 154 . do say, *et Anno Domini* 681 . *Ioannes legatus Papæ, Constan-*
tinopoli coram Imperatore, et Patrarcha, & plebe primus in templo sophie la-
tinam missam celebrauit, approbantibus omnibus qui aderant &c . *Beda de*
ratione temporum: sic de duobus Eualdis idem tradit quod in Saxoniam mi-
grantes quotidie missas celebrarint habentes secum (as our english Preistes
now in like manner secretly likewise haue) *Altare portabile & sacra*
vasa &c. And *Luke Osiander* in *epitom*. *hist*. *Eccef*. *cent*. 7 . *pag* . 189 .
saith, *incidit in hac tempora Anglicarum Ecclesiarum deformatio verius quam*
reformatio, missi enim sunt a Pontifice Romano vitaliano in Angliam, qui ibi
a prioribus Pontificibus inceptam deformationem continuarent & instituarent;
cantica latina, Missam latinam, Sacerdotum tonsuram, Altarium cum Idolis
impositis, superstisiosam consecrationem &c . *et id genus alia &c* . And the
Centuristes, *cent* . 7 . *c* . 7 . *col*. 233 . say, *Missas latinas et ritum Pasca-*
tis Romani Pontifices Britannis obtruserunt circiter Annum Domini 666 .
and see further hereof, *col*. 143 . & *col*. 233 . also it is there further
said (*col*. 143 .) concerning the Masse of that time, *Idolomania in*
missarum pompa perpetrabatur &c. And *M*. *White* in his way to *the true*
Church, pag. 378 . acknowlegeth that there was *masse in latine where the*
people vnderstoode it not in the time of Gregory (within) *sixe hundreth yeares*
after Christ. And *Hospinian* . *hist*. *sacram*. reproueth the Fathers that
liued about this time, namely *Carolus Magnus, Tharasius, Ioannes Ele-*
mozinarius, Damascen, and *Isidore,* charging them directly *with Masse*
for the

for the deade : for which he recyteth their particular ſayinges, *l.* 3. *pag.* 281. and he doth alſo *pag.* 282. charge in like maner thoſe times. with *Maſſes for tempeſtes, for the ſikce,* and *for men in warfare* . And *Hutte-rus de ſacrificio miſſatico, pag.* 516. ſaith accordingly to *Bellarmine, non attendimus quid Rabanus, quid Iſidorus, quid concilia tua de Idolo Miſſatico dicant.* And *M. Sparke* in his anſweare to *M. Iohn de Albines pag.* 161. mencioneth latine ſeruice in England, *Anno Domini* 657.

     (h)

M. Iewel in his chalenge ſet forth by *D. Humfrey, de vita et morte Iuelli, pag.* 123. ſaith, *O Gregory, o Auguſtine, o Hierome, o Chriſoſtome, o Leo, o Dio-niſe, o Anacletus, o Calix-tus, o Paul, o Chriſt, if we be deceiued you haue decei-ued vs, thus you taught vs &c.* And continueth the ſame yet further as ap-peareth by his reply, *pag.* 1. where he ſaith, *if al the learned men a liue be able to bring any one ſufficient ſentence of any old Catholicke Doctor or Father &c. for the ſpace of ſixe hundreth yeares after Chriſt &c. I am content to yeelde.* And ſee *M. Whitak rs* like chalenge *contra Camp. ad rat.* 5. and *contra Duraeum, l.* 5. pag. 406. ſaying thereof, *rem par-uam requirimus, vnicum nobis certum, clarum enucleatum, teſtimonium ſuffi-ciet &c.* (i) *M. Iewel ibidem.* (k) Hereof ſee *S. Bede, hiſt. l.* 2. *c.* 1. *& 2.* and *Holinſheade,* in his great Cronicle after the laſt e-dition *volum.* 2. *l.* 5. *c.* 19. and *M. Fulk* in his confutation of Purgatory, *pag.* 335. (2) *S. Gregory* in his booke of Dialogues, ſpecially mentioned ſo many ages ſithence by *S. Bede, hiſt. l.* 2. *c.* 1. *ante med. l.* 4. *c.* 58. ſaith, *debemus &c. quotidiana Deo lacrima-rum ſacrificia, quotidianas caxnis et ſanguinis eius hoſtias immolare, haec nam-ꝗ ſingulariter victima ab aeterno interitu animam ſaluat &c. licet (Chriſtus) reſurgens a mortuis iam non moritur et mors ei vltra non dominabitur, tamen in ſeipſo immortaliter et incorrutibiliter viuens pro nobis iterum, in hoc mi-ſterio ſacrae oblationis inmolatur &c.* and *hom.* 27. *in Euang.* he ſaith, *quoties ei hoſtiam ſue paſſionis offerimus toties nobis ad abſolutionem noſtram ipſius*

deade. The *ſixt* age is that time whereto *M. Iewel* in his publicke (h) chalenge did (to ſpeake ſparingly) ouer bouldly appeale. In that age liued *S. Gregory,* being one of thoſe Doctors to whom alſo *M. Iewel* ſo by name (i) appealed, he it was that by *Auguſtines* meanes firſt (k) conuerted the Saxons of our nation to the Chriſtian faith, and his ſundry (2) ſayinges (*M. Iewels* foreſaid chalenge notwithſtanding) are ſo euident for ſacrifice and Maſſe, that *Melancthon* ſaith, (l) *Gregory allowed*

ipsius passionem reparamus. And see *Gregories* other sayinges alledged hereafter, *tract. 3. sect. 6. subdiuis.* 1. at q s. y. and reiected by *M. Fulbe ibidem.* at g. (l) *Melancthon. l. 4. Chronic. in Henrico,* 4. *fol.* 186, and 187. *et vide Apolog. corsef. August. de vocabulo missae fol.* 216. and *Charion* in his Cronicle enlarged by *Melancthon, l. 4. pag.* 567. saith, *opinionem de oblatione corporis et sanuginis Christi facienda pro mortuis, quae horribilem peperit prophanationem Sacramenti, Gregorius comprobauit &c.* And see the like further testimony there, *pag.* 390. and *Vadian de Eucharist. l. 6. pag.* 218. saith hereof, *Gregorius fauior Purgatory mortuis etiam illud sacrificium applicuerit.*

(3)

allowed by *publicke authority the sacrifice of Christes body and blond, not onely for the huing but also for the deade.* And in like sort doth *M. Beacon* (whom our learned aduersaries tearme (3) *a diuine of cheife note in their Church*) (m) charge and reprehend him, affirming further that in *Gregories* time (n) *the Masse was* (in reguard of the forme thereof) *by him fully finished, and reigned as a puisant Empresse in al Churches of the part of the world vnto the time of Charles the siueth,* in which Luther appeared. And *Luther* him selfe saith, *Gregorius author fuit Missae priuatae,* (o) *Gregory was author of priuate Masse.* And D. *Humfrey* and others confesse that *Gregory,* and *Augustine,* at the time of our countries foresaid conuersion taught

tosam missam ferimus acceptam. (n) *M. Becon, ibidem. fol.* 344. And *Chrispinus,* in his booke of the estate of the Church, *pag.* 180. confesseth accordinly saying, *the greatest part of the ceremonies of the masse came in by this Gregory &c. he brought al the masse into certaine lawes, and almost such as is at this day: and therefore many say he was the author thereof.* (o) *In thesauro explicationum omnium articulorum &c. ex reuerendi &c.* D. *Martini Lutheri &c. operibus collect. pag.* 879. and 461. and *Chitraeus l. de Baptismo, et Eucharistia.* chargeth Gregory with *priuate masse.* And *Luther in colloquiis Germanicis c. de missa.* saith, *priuate masse hath deceiued many Sainctes, and carried them into error from*

So is *M. Beacon* tearmed by the ministers of *Lincolne Dioces.* in their abridgement &c. pag. 65.

(m)

Se in the third part of *M. Thomas Becons* workes in the treatise entituled *the reliques of Rome, fol.* 340. And *Bullinger de origine erroris Missae.* saith, *neq mouearis huius sanctimonia, hic est ille Gregorius cui non modo infinitas superstitiones, sed et omnium suprestitionum caput portentosam*

N n

the time of Gregory for 800. _yeares, Iohn Huſſe was deceiued therewith._

(p)

Humfred. in Hieſuitiſmi, taught vs (p) _Maſſe_ and (q) _ſacrifice._ In ſo _part._ 2. _contra Camp._ much that _Robert Bellarmine,_ obiecteth the _rat._ 5. _pag._ 626. And vniuerſalty of _Maſſe_ for many ages paſt, our _Luke Oſiander in epitom._ learned aduerſary _Hutterus_ doctor and pub- _cent._ 6. _l._ 4. _c._ 17. _pag._ lique profeſſor in the vniuerſity of _Wittenberge,_ 290. And ſee _Holinſhea-_ anſweareth and acknowledgeth ſaying (4) _des_ great Cronicle, _vol._ _libenter concedo &c._ I _do willingly graunt that_ 2. after the firſt edition, _the Popiſh Idolatry, the ſinnow whereof is the ſa-_ _pag._ 148. and 149. & _crifice of the Maſſe, haith innaded almoſt the whol_ after the laſt edition _vol._ _world eſpecially for the laſt thouſand yeares._ So 2. _pag._ 100. and _pag._ euidently is that penalty, wherwith we are by 101. See alſo _Bale in ca-_ the law threatned for hearing of Maſſe, im- _talog. Scriptorum illuſtriũ_ poſed vpon vs for our adhering and continu- _maioris Britanniæ. cent._ ing in that faith & publique worſhip of God, 14. _pag._ 116. (q) _Humf._ whereto wee engliſhmen were ſo many ages _in Ieſuit. part._ 2. _pag._ 626. ſince (5) _conuerted._ (4) _Hutterus de ſacrificio_ _miſſatico, pag._ 377.

(3) To come now to the times before

(5) _Gregory,_ although the onely foreſaid confeſſed _M. Roger Aſcam,_ in his generally of the Maſſe _throughout almoſt the_ _Apol. pro cæna Dom. pag._ _whol world_ in the time of _Gregory,_ do ſuffici- 33. ſaith, _de origine miſ-_ ently argue the continued profeſſion and _ſæ apud alias gentes non_ practiſe thereof long time then before _tantum laboramus, quomo-_ (for to thinke it could be then vpon the ſo- _do vero irepſit in Angliam_ daine ſo general eſtabliſhed, is more then in- _hoc certo ſcimus : Augu-_ credible) we wil yet alſo in further manife- _ſtinus Anglorum Apoſto-_ ſtation of this point examine the ſeueral _lus qui appellatur, profliga-_ ages that were precedent to _Gregory,_ in which _tor vera religionis et fun-_ accompt we finde that _Pelagius_ predeceſſor _dator omnis papiſticæ doc-_ to _Gregory_ is charged and reprehended by _trinæ ſcribit ad Gregorium_ _Muſculus,_ for that, ſaith _Muſculus_ (r) he com-

municated

Papam quærens quomodo miſſam in Angliam conſtitueret &c. And _pag._ 34. he further ſaith of _Gregories,_ and _Auguſtines,_ proceedinges in England, _præcipites feruntur in omnem licentiam condendi & recondendi miſſarum vias_ _pro arbitratu ſuo._ (r) _Muſculus in loc. com. cap. de cæna Dom. num._ 2. _pag._ 339. ſaith, _Pelagius commemorationem mortuorum in ſecreta Cano-_

nis miſſaticæ

ris missatici retulit &c. vt mortuis virtus et efficacia missa communicaretur.
& *Crispinus* in his booke of the estate of the Church, *pag.* 170. saith that
about *Anno.* 590. *in the councel of Mascon, offering of (the Sacrament)*
is commaunded for remissi-

municated to the deade the virtue and efficacy of
the *Masse*. Also Pope *Symachus*, who succeeded *Anastasius* the second, was Bishop of Rome
(s) *Anno.* 501. he (as the Centuristes confesse) did acknowledge (t) *the Masse*, for
which they charge him (u) *to haue the notes of
Antichrist*. *Leo* the first was Pope *Anno.* 440.
of whom *Bale* saith, (x) *Leo the first allowed
the sacrifice of the Masse not without great blasphemie to God*. And in like maner is *Eucherius*
(who liued in the same time (y), charged by
the *Century* writers. S. *Augustine* liued about
Anno. 400. whose many plaine sayinges are
heretofore (*) alledged, and being by our aduersaries houlden to be the (2) *soundest* of al
the *Fathers* he is yet neuerthelesse reiected by
them in this question of *sacrifice*: for wheras
to such alledged Fathers as mencion *sacrifice
for the deade*, our aduersaries do vsually answere that the Fathers thereby meant not
sacrifice, but onely *praier for the deade*; in so
much that where also *Bellarmine* in preuention thereof replyeth, as his aduersary *Hutterus Doctor and publicke professor in the vniuersity
of Witeberge* alledgeth him, that (3) *Ciprian
affirmeth sacrifice to be offered vpon the Altar for
the*

on of sinne.

(s)
See *M. Mores* table.
pag. 128.

(t)
The Century writers,
cent. 6. *c.* 10. *col.* 664.
say, *notas Antichristi et hic
habuit, Missam enim in formam redegit.* And so likewise saith, *Iohn Bale* of
him in *Act. Rom. Pontif.
pag.* 35.

(u)
The Centurie writers, *vt
supra.*

(x)
Bale, in his pageant of
Popes, *fol.* 27. and in
*Catal. scriptorum illustri-
um maioris Britanniae, cent.*
1. *pag.* 45. and see *Szegedine in speculo Pontificum
pag.* 68.

(y)
The Centurie writers,
cent. 5. *c.* 4. *col.* 518.

say, *incommode etiam Eucherius de oblatione, imitatione veteris Testamenti
loquitur inquiens &c. oblationem panis et vini, id est corporis et sanguinis eius
Sacramentum in sacrificium offeramus, ibi quippe primum apparuit sacrificium
quod nunc a Christianis offertur Deo toto orbe terrarum Eucherius l. 2. in
Genesim.* (*) See *Augustines* plaine sayinges alleged heretofore,
tract. 3. *sect.* 1. *subdiuis.* 2. at *. *c. d. e. f.* &c. and *ibidem. subdiuis.*
3. at the figure 5. and at t. u. x. (2) *Gomarus in speculo vera Ec-
cl[i]a*

clesie, pag. 96. saith, *Augustinus Patrum omnium (communi sententia) purissimus habetur.* (3) *Hutterus de sacrificio missatico,* pag. 524.

(4)
Hutterus, ibidem. pag. 525.

(5)
See heretofore, *tract.* 3. *sect.* 1. *subdiuis.* 3. at the figure 5. and at t. u. x.

(6)
Hutterus de sacrificio missatico, pag. 525.

(7)
August. enchirid. c. 110. see heretofore, *tract.* 3. *sect.* 1. *subdiuis.* 3. at x. and *Hutterus vbi supra.*

(8)
Hutterus vbi supra pag. 525.

(9)
See this hereafter *tract.* 3. *sect.* 2. *subdiuis.* 4. in the margent at b.

(10)
M. Fulke, in his confutation of Purgatory, pag. 362. and 363.

(11)
Bucer in enarat. in sacra quatuor Euangelia. printed *Basilea,* 1536. *in Math. c.* 12. pag. 311.

the deade, and that S. *Augustine distinguisheth* three thinges offered for the deade, (namely) almes, praier, and sacrifice · *Hutterus* answearing thereto, excuseth as before *Ciprian,* affirming stil that by (4) sacrifice celebrated vpō the Alter for the deade, he onely yet meant but prayer made at the Altar for the deade: But comming there to answeare S. *Augustines* foresaid euident sayinges hertofore also in part (5) alledged, for that they do so expresly distinguish sacrifice for the deade, from praier for the deade, and are thereby more plaine then to be so auoided, he doth therefore insteede of the former answeare or excuse made concerning *Ciprian,* openly reproue S. *Augustine* saying, (6) we doubt not to affirme that S. *Augustine is not at one with him selfe in in this question* confessing immediatly afterwardes, that whereas he (7) affirmeth the sacrifice to be a propitiation for such as being deade are not very euil, or in state of damnation, it is a saying so plaine and pregnant that, saith *Hutterus, in aternum* (8) defendi non potest, it can neuer be excused. And no lesse plainly is S. *Augustine* reproued and charged by *Caluin* (9) with sacrifice of the *Masse,* and by *M. Fulke* with referring (10) sacrifice for the deade to the tradition of the *Apostles,* whereto might be added his like further (11) reprehension both by *Bucer Luther* and others. S. *Ambrose*

saith, ex eo quidem quod ab initio prope Ecclesie praces et Eleemosine fiunt pro defunctis, sensim irrepsit ea sententia quam D. *Augustinus* ponit in enchirid. c. 110. (vbi inquit) neq, negandum est defunctorum animas pietate suorum viuentium releuari, cum pro illis sacrificium mediatoris offertur &c.

and

and a litle after at *pag* . 312 . he faith, *hinc itaꝗ non dubitamus exortum hoc in defunƈtos officium pro illis orandi et facrificandi publico facrificio Ecclefiæ . &c* . And *Luther, tom* . 2 . *Wittenberg* . *fol* . 259 . faith concerning Maſſe, *noſtri Papiſtæ dicunt, S . Bernardus fic fecit, ergo fic eſt faciendum, S . Auguſtinus fic fecit, ergo fic eſt faciendum &c . hic in facrificio miſſæ illis contigit, et abſꝗ dubio bonis et eleƈtis viris contingit, vt fimplici cordis fide celebrent, arbitrantes pro errore facrificium eſſe* . and *Eufebius Altkircherus l . de miſtico.et incruento facrificio* . printed, 1584 . *pag* . 7 . although he there do very bouldly deny *S . Auguſtine* to haue beleeued the real prefence, yet doth he charge him fo fully with beleeuing the Euchariſt to be a facrifice, as that but admitting his like iudegment of the real prefence, the Catholicke or Popifh facrifice doth thereupon follow to which purpofe he there faith, (vpon his owne recytal offundry fayinges of *S . Auguſtine* as making plaine for facrifice) *Agnofcit Auguſtinus Ecclefiæ fui temporis maſſam, agnofcit quoꝗ in ea facrificium, quid igitur obſtat, quo minus, fi corporalis prefentia et manducatio ponenda fit, etiam realis in facrificium oblatio concedetur?* in fo much as there *pag* . 241 . he acknowledgeth, *totius Ecclefiæ confenfum et in oblationis facrificio faƈtam confeſſionem* . fee this more fully heretofore, *traƈt* . 3 . *feƈt* . 1 . *fubdiuif* . 3 . *initio* . in the margent at the figure 3 . next before 1 . & alfo next hereafter in this feƈtion, *fubdiuif* . 3 . in the margent at the figures 18 . next before m.

brofe liued *Anno* . 370 . whofe (z) fayinges are fo pregnant for facrifice that the *Centurie*

(z)
Ambrof . *l* . 5 . *de facram* . *c* . 6 . faith, *offerimus tibi

hanc immaculatam, rationabilem, et incruentam hoſtiam &c . et precamur vt hanc oblationem fufcipias &c . ficut fufcipere dignatus es &c . quod tibi obtulit fummus Sacerdos Melchifadech. and *in orat* . 1 . *præparat. ad Miſſam* he faith, *vt offeram tibi facrificium quod tu inſtituiſti et offerre præcepiſti in commemoratione tui pro falute noſtra: fufcipe ergo iſtud quæfo &c . defcendat etiam Domine ille fpiritus fanƈti tui &c . qui et oblationes noſtras corpus et fanguinem tuum efficiat &c . vt placide, benigne facrificium fufcipias de manibus meis ad falutem omnium tam viuorum, quam defunƈtorum* . and *in Pfal* . 38* . he deriueth *our Preiſtes now facrificing here vpon earth* of our Saiours body and bloud for the people,, from our Sauiours like facrifycing thereof *feene and heard* at his laſt fupper, faying to this end: *vidimus principem Sacerdotum ad nos venientem, vidimus, et audiuimus, offerentem pro nobis fanguinem fuum, feqnamur vt poſſumus Sacerdotes vt ofe-*

ramus

ramus pro populo facrificium, etfi infirmi merito, tamen honorabiles facrificio, quia etfi Chriftus non videtur offerre, tamen ipfe offertur in terris, quando Chrifti corpus offertur. And fee *Ambrofe* his other fayinges heretofore, *tract.* 3. *fect.* 1. *fubdiuif.* 1. in the margent at the letter e. and *tract.* 2. *fect.* 8. *fubdiuif.* 3. in the margent at the letter s. and *tract.* 3. *fect.* 1. *fubdiuif.* 2. in the margent at the letter b.

(a)
Cent. 4. *c.* 4. *col.* 294.
and *col.* 295. it is faid,
Ambrofius locutionibus de cæna vtitur quibus ante eum ex patribus nemo vfus eft, vt miffam facere, offerre fa crificium &c.

(b)
Cent. 4. *c.* 4. *col.* 295.

(12)
Cent. 5. *c.* 10. *col.* 963.

(13)
Efichius in leuit. l. 1. *c.* 4. faith, *femetipfum in cæna Apoftolorum immolauit.*

(14)
Efichius ibidem.

(15)
The *Centurie* writers profeffing to fet downe his errors. *cent.* 5. *col.* 969.

rie writers do mencion (a) fundry of them with great diflike charging (b) them with tranfubftantiation and application (of the Euchariſt) for the liuing and the deade, *Efichius* (as the Centuriſtes obferue) (12) *was Preiſt at Hieruſalem, and fcholer to Gregory Nazianzen,* who liued *Anno. Dom.* 340. he doth fo plainly affirme that our Sauiour (13) *facrificed him ſelfe in the fupper of the Apoſtles,* and that he alfo (14) *did take vpon him the dignity of Preiſthood, firſt in the miſtical fupper, and afterwardes vpon the Croſſe,* that the *Century* writers do therfore fpecialy (15) reprehend him. *Gregory Niſſen,* a doctor of the Greeke Church, liued *Anno.* 340. he faith, that our Sauiour (c) *offered himſelfe a facrifice for vs &c. when he gaue to his Diſciples his body to be eaten &c.* And that his body was *then already offered:* wherein his meaning is fo pregnant, that (d) *M. Whitaker* therefore feemeth to diflike his wordes

recite among others, faying, *ibidem. de cæna incommoda phraſi vtitur dum in ea dicit Iefum fe immolaſſe, ſic enim ſcriptura non loquitur &c.* (c) *Niſſen. in orat.* 1 *de reſurrectione.* faith, *pro ineffabili arcanoq, & qui ab hominibus cerni nequit facrificij modo ſua diſpoſitione et adminiſtratione præoccupat impetum violentum, ac ſeſe oblationem ac victimam offert pro nobis Sacerdos ſimul et agnus Dei qui tollit peccatum mundi quando hoc accidit ? cum ſuum corpus ad commedendum et ſanguinem ſuum familiaribus ad bibendum præbuit &c. aperte demonſtrat iam perfectam et abſolutam factam eſſe immolationem.* (d) *Whitaker contra Duræum pag.* 320. argueth againſt *Niſſens* wordes faying thereupon, *ſi Chriſtus in cæna perfecte atq, abſolute*
Immolatus

wordes. & *Andreas Crastouius* a learned Caluinist doth thereupon affirme (e) *the opinion of*
Gregory Nissen to be absurd. Ciril of Hierusalem an other Father of the Greeke Church
liued *Anno. Dom.* 320. he is likewise so
(16) plaine herein that *Hospinianus* doth there
fore, not onely specially reprehend him for
his (f) *affirming the sacrifice of the Altar to be*
the greatest releefe to the departed soules; but
confesseth also further, that this doctrine was
(g) *the receiued custome of that age.* A thing
so euident in the Doctors of those times, that
Iohn Caluin doth therefore charge & affirme
(h) *the auncient Fathers* (of those times) *to*
haue wrested this memorial (or Sacrament) *o-*
therwise then did agree with the Lordes instituti-
on, in that their supper did carie before it the
face of a repeated, or at least a renued sacrifice &c.
imitating more nerely the Iewish maner of sacrify-
cing then Christ ordained. And elswhere:
         I wonder

immolatus fuit, quid opus
erat postridie denuo immolari &c.

(e)
Crastouius de opificio Mis-
sa contra Bellarminum l.
1. pag. 81. saith, *An*
ignorat opinionem Nisseni
per se absurdam esse &c.
ait ille Nissenus, cum itaq;
dedit (Christus) *Discipulis*
suis corpus suum ad comme-
dendum &c. iam libenter [latenter]
&c. ineffabiliter, inuisibi-
liter corpus immolatum e-
rat &c.

(16)
Ciril. Hierosol. catech. 5.
mistag. saith, *deinde vero*
postquam confectum est, il-
lud spirituale sacrificium et

ille cultus incruentus, super ipsa propitiationis hostia obsecramus Deum pro
communi Ecclesiarum pace, pro tranquilitate mundi, pro regibus &c. postea
facimus mentionem etiam eorum qui ante nos obdormierunt &c. maximum
esse credentes animarum iuuamen pro quibus offertur obsecratio, sancti illius
& tremendi quod in Altari positum est sacrificij &c. Christum pro nostris
peccatis mactatum offerimus, vt et nobis, et illis (defunctis) *eum qui est be-*
nignissimus propuium reddamus. Can any Catholicke writer of this age
speake more plainly? (f) *Hospinianus in histor. sacram. l.* 2. pag.
167. saith, *dicit Cirillus pro sui iam temporis recepta consuetudine sacrifi-*
cium Altaris maximum iuuamen esse animarum. (g) *Hospinianus vt*
supra. (h) *Caluin. l.* 4. *institut. c.* 18. *sect.* 11. and after the e-
dition *Argentorat. Anno.* 1539. *pag.* 350. saith, *sed quia veteres quoq;*
illos video, alio hanc memoriam detorsisse quam institutioni Domini conuenie-
bat (quod nescio quam repetita aut saltem renouata Immolationis faciem eorum
cæna præ se ferebat) nihil tutius pijs pectoribus fuerit quam in pura simpliciq;
Dei ordinatione acquiescere &c. imitati sunt enim propius Iudaicum sacrifi-
candi morem quam aut ordinauerat Christus aut Euangelij ratio ferebat &c.
            (i) *Caluin*

(i)
Caluin in omnes Pauli epistolas in epist. ad Habr. c.7.9.pag.924. saith, quo magis tot veteres Ecclesiæ Doctores hac opinione occupatos fuisse miror &c.

(k)
Cum ipsi sacrificium in Christi cæna nullo eius mandato finxissent, adeoq̇ cænam adulterassent addito sacrificio &c. Caluin. vbi supra in c.7. ad Habr. pag. 924.

(l)
Caluin. in lib. de reformat. Ecclesiæ. saith, *veteres excusandi non sunt, quatenus scilicet ipsos apparet a puro et genuino Christi instituto defflexisse, nam cum in hunc finem celebranda sit cæna, vt sacrificio Christi communicaremus, eo non contenti oblationem quoq̇ addiderunt.* And *Caluin. in libel. de cæna Dom.* extant in his *tractat. theolog.* printed. 1597. pag. 7. saith, *neq̇ tamen possum veteris Ecclesiæ consuetudinem excusare,, quod gestu aut ritu suo speciem quandam sacrificy figuraret: ijsdem fere ceremonijs quæ sub veteri Testamento in vsu erant, eo excepto quod panis hostia animalis loco vtebantur.*

(i) *I wonder* (saith he) *that so many old Doctors weare possessed with this opinion:* And in the same place he chargeth them in plaine tearmes with hauing (k) *forged a sacrifice in the Lordes supper without his commaundement,* and with *hauing so adulterated the supper with adding of sacrifice.* And no lesse plainly in sundry (l) other places doth he confesse and reiect this foresaid iudgement of those auncient Fathers reprehending therefore by name (17) *Arnobius, Ambrose, Augustine,* and *Athanasius:* whereunto might be added *Eusebius Altkircherus,* and *Andræas Chrastouius,* both of them learned Caluinistes, confessing likewise and (18) acknowledging the Fathers knowen iudgement concerning sacrifice.

(4)   *S. Ciprian* liued *Anno. Dom.* 240.
and

(17) See this saying alledged next hereafter in this subdiuision, and section, in the margent at the letter b. (18) As concerning *Andræas Crastouius,* see his wordes alledged hereafter, *tract.3.sect.4.subdiuis.1.* in the margent at g. And as concerning *Eusebius Altkircherus,* he in his booke *de mistico et incruento sacrificio.* printed *Neustady Palatinorum* 1584. pag. 241. affirmeth, *totius Ecclesiæ consensum et in oblationis sacrificio factam confessionem.* and *ibidem* pag. 6. he saith, *fuit autem hæc perpetua semper omnium Ecclesiasticorum Patrum concors & vnanimis sententia, quod instituta per Christum passionis et mortis suæ in sacra cæna memoria etiam sacrificy in se contineret commendationem. Hinc Ciprianus (ait) &c.* alledging to that purpose the very same saying of *Ciprian* next hereafter in the text following, and reiected by *the Centurises,* putting also in the margent there as being

pregnant

pregnant for sacrifice these wordes of *Ciprian, Sacerdos vice Christi,* which wordes are by the *Centuristes* likewise for the same reason disliked. In like sort doth he there next after alledge diuers sayinges of S. *Augustine* as making for sacrifice, concluding thereupon *pag.* 7. that, *Augustinus agnoscit Ecclesiæ temporis sui missam, agnoscit quóq; in ea sacrificium.* And to the same purpose also doth he alledge (amongst others the *Councel of Ephesus,* and the *first Nicene councel (ibidem. pag.* 5.) concluding their sayinges for sacrifice to be so direct and plaine; that, but admitting onely the real presence (which himselfe there impugneth) our now sacrifice of the Masse is, in his opinion, by such their sayinges confirmed: To which purpose he saith of the Lutheranes, *nulla restat ipsis effugij ratio quo minùs duabus oecumenicis Nicena et Ephesina sinodis, realis oblationis, qua corpus et sanguinem Christi realiter in sacrificium offerre oporteat manifestissimè conuincantur.* See more of this authors further acknowledgement herein heretofore, *tract.* 3. *sect.* 1. *subdiuis.* 3. *initio.* in the margent at the figure 3. next before 1.

(m)

and his (m) sayinges are so ful for sacrifice, that *M. Fulke* saith, (n) *it is graunted that Ciprian thought the breade and wine brought forth by Melcisadech, to be a figure of the Sacrament, and said that herein also Melchisadech resembled the Preisthood of Christ.* And *the Centurie writers* do in like maner recite this special saying of Ciprian, (o) *our Lord Iesus Christ, saith Ciprian, l. 2. epist. 3. is the high Preist of God the Father, and first offered sacrifice to God the Father, and commaunded the same to be done in remembrance of him, and that Preist truly execeuteth Christes place, that doth imitate that which Christ did, and then he offereth in the Church a true & ful sacrifice to God the Father &c.* in which wordes *Ciprian* is so plaine for sacrifice that *the Centurie writers,* vndertaking to set dowen (p) *the errors of the Doctors in that age,* do therein specially taxe and charge *Ciprian,* for his affirming, as before, (q) *the Preist to execute truly Christes steede, and sacrifice to be offered to*

Ciprian. l. 2. epist. 3. post initium. saith, *obtulit (Christus) hoc idem quod Melchisadech, id est, panem et vinum, suum scilicet corpus et sanguinem.* and afterwardes, *in sacrificio quod Christus est, non nisi Christus sequendus est.*

(n)

M. Fulke against *Heskins,* pag. 100.

(o)

Cent. 3. *c.* 10. *col.* 247.

(p)

Cent. 3. *c.* 4. *col.* 71.

(q)

Cent. 3. *c.* 4. *col.* 83. *Sacerdotem inquit, vice Christi vere fungi, et Deo Patri sacrificium offerri.* & *Ioannes*

O o   God

Ioannes Bechtholdus, in his *assertiones theologicæ de sacram . cœn . Dom . assert.* 67. saith, *Cyprianus tibi ipse aduersatur et repugnat, quod Sacerdotem vere vice Christi fungi affirmat &c.*

(*)
The Centurie writers in their Alphabetical table of their third Centurie, vnder the letter s. do say, *Sacerdotē vice Chrsti fungi in cæna Domini, superstitiose asserit Cyprianus.* col . 83.

(r)
Cent. 3. c.6. col. 138.
(s)
Centur. 3. col. 139.
(t)
Cent. 3. c.6. col. 138. and *Osiander, cent. 3. l. 1. c. 5. pag.* 10. and *M. Fulke* in his confutation of Purgatory, *pag.* 265. chargeth *Tertulian* with mencioning *the yearly oblation offered for the deade.* (u) *M. Fulke*

God the Father, which they tearme (*) *ā superstitiouse assertion;* In so much as they do also further charge him with (r) *sacrifice in memory of Martyres,* and that (s) *l. 1. epist. 9.* he *mencioneth sacrifice for the deade. Tertulain* also liued *Anno. 220.* and him *the Centurie writers,* and *Luke Osiander* charge, for that in his booke (t) *de corona militis,* he saith, *we offer sacrifice for the deade:* and in like maner is he together with *Ciprian,* acknowledged as reprouable by *D. Fulke* for (u) *witnessing that sacrifice for the deade is the tradition of the Apostles. Hipolitus* liued in the same age, & speaking in the person of our Sauiour at the day of iudgement saith, (x) *come you Bishops who haue purely offered vnto me sacrifice day and night, and haue dayly offered my pretiouse body & bloud:* A saying so euident that some of our aduersaries in steede of better answeare therto, do (y) vndeseruedly affirme the booke to be counterfeate. In the beginning also

of

in his confutation of Purgatory, *pag.* 262. (x) *Hippolitus in libro de consummatione seculi.* (y) Whereas *M. Iewel* and some others, do, for want of better answeare, reiect this booke of *Hippolitus* for counterfeted . *M. Iewel* in his reply pag. 12. to such purpose obiecting against it that, saith he, *it is of smale credit, lately set forth, neuer before acquainted in the world;* beginneth the first sentence of his booke with (*enim*) which a veris child care would do, he saith that *Antichrist shal be the Deuil and no man &c.* thus far *M. Iewel:* whereto is answeared, first, concerning the word *Gar,* or *enim,* it is vntrue that he beginneth therewith, for his first wordes are, *Epede gar,* the word *Epede* signifying, *postquam, quum, quandoquidem,* which is not maner of beginning is vsual, the word *gar* notwithstanding in the first place, but onely added as abounding to garnish vp the phrase. And so accordingly doth *Aristotle* begin his

gin his booke *de respiratione* saying, *Peri gar anapnoes* . *Secondly*, as concerning his opinion of Antichrist, he speaketh not determinatly, but
onely deliuereth his owne priuate opinion thereof, saying, *I am of opi-*
nion dearly beloued, that the deuil shal take this phantastical substance of his
flesh in steede of an instrument to worke by: whereto I ad, that neither
this nor any other like supposed erroneouse opinion obiected by *M.*
Iewel, can any more proue the booke now in question, not to be writen
by *Hippolitus*, then the like or greater errors wherewith *M. Fulke* in
his answeare to a counterfeate Catholicke *pag.* 35. chargeth *Papias,*
Iustine, and *Ireneus*, (al of them *auncient to Hipolitus*) can proue the
confessed writinges of any of those Fathers to be none of theirs. And
whereas *M. Whitaker contra Dvraeum, l.* 5, *pag.* 367. further obiecteth
saying, *Hierome affirmeth that Hipolitus did write of Antichrist, but of this*
booke of the end of the world he was ignorant. I answeare thereto, *first* ,
though *Hierome* had beene ignorant of this booke (as most confessedly
he was of many other bookes before his time) how smally yet this
maketh against the credit of this booke appeareth heretofore in the
preface to the reader, *sect.* 6. at x. y. A thing furthermore so euident that *Eusebius, l.* 6. *c.* 16. hauing mencioned sundry writinges
of *Hipolitus* which came to his knowledge, addeth further saying, *extant*
preterea nonnulla alia eius monumenta, there remaineth besides these sundry
other writinges of his &c. Secondly I say, that *S. Hieromes* confessed testimony of *Hipolitus* booke *of Antichrist*, geueth therein ful proofe of
this booke, for as there is nothing more vsual then seueral titles to be
somtimes geuen to one, & the same boke, in regard of the seueral argu
mentes entreated of therin, so the argument of the booke now in question being both of *Antichrist*, and of *the latter end of the world*, at which
time *Antichrist* should come, the booke may in such respect passe vnder either title: whereto I ad, that if any late author had forged this
booke vnder the name of *Hipolitus*, he might easily (for more credit
thereof) haue geuen it the same title *de Antichristo*, mencioned by
Hierome, whereto if any reply that perhappes he knew not of any such
booke or title mencioned by *Hierome*, this also maketh more strongly
against al suspition of forgery, for how then could he make his forgery so colorable as to write vnder the name of *Hipolitus* of the very same
special argument of *Antichrist* which *Hierome* mencioneth and attributeth to *Hipolitus*, so plainly doth this variety of title, argue that this
booke was not forged. A thing so euident that *Germanus Bishop* of
Constantinople, who liued about 900. yeares since, in his *rerum Ecclef*.

theoria. extant with the Liturgies of *S. Iames, Basile*, and *Chrisostome*, printed, 1560 . at *Antwerpe, pag*. 96 . alledgeth vnder the name of *Hipolitus*, special matter yet to be found in this booke : In so much as *M. Sutliue de missa papistica, l . 3 . c . 14 . fol .* 294 . endeauoring to answeare the very sentence alledged here in the text out of this booke, acknowledgeth herein both the booke and saying of *Hipolitus*, seking to euade otherwise. And so likewise doth *Hutterus de sacrificio missatico, l . 1 . c . 15 . pag.* 310 . not denying the booke, but reiecting the authority of *Hipolitus* saying, *Hipolitum martirem si de immolatione proprie dicta locutus est non moramur .*

(19) See heretofore *tract . 2 . sect . 1 . subdiuis . 3 .* in the margent at the letter s.

(20) *M . Couper* in his Cronicle, *fol .* 111 .

(z) *Ireneus, l . 4 . c . 32 .* saith, *eum qui ex creatura panis est, accepit, et gratias egit dicens, hoc est corpus meum, et Calicem similiter, qui est ex ea creatura, quæ est secundum nos, suum sanguinem confessus est, & noui Testamenti nouam docuit oblationem, quam Ecclesia ab Apostolis accipiens in vniuerso mundo offert Deo &c . de quo in* 12 . *prophetis Malachias sic præsignificauit, non est mihi voluntas in vobis &c .*

(a) The Century writers, *cent . 2 . c . 4 . col .* 55 . vndertaking to set downe *the declining peculier incommodiouse opinions and errors of the doctors* of those times, do in their said tract of this matter, *col .* 63 . say, *de oblatione porro . et Ireneus, l . 4 . c .* 32 . (*si tamen locus fraude ac mendo vacat*) *satis videtur loqui incommode, cum ait noui Testamenti, nouam docuit oblationem, quam Ecclesia ab Apostolis accipiens in vniuerso mundo offert Deo.* In so much as they haue no other imagination of excuse for *Ireneus*, but to suppose that he thereby onely meant *the oblation of bread & wine by the people to the vse of the Lords supper, and afterwardes* (the remaine thereof) *to the vse of the Preistes and of the poore :* as though Christ
in his

of this age liued *Origen*, and him together with *Athanasius*, and others doth *Crastouius* reprehend, charging them euen with (19) *propitiatory sacrifice. Ireneus* liued *Anno* (20) *Dom .* 170 . in the very age next to that which succeeded the Apostles, he saith of our Sauiour, (z) *he tooke bread and gaue thankes saying, this is my body &c . and taught the new oblation of the new Testament, which the Church receiuing from the Apostles, offered to God in al the world : whereof Malachias foretould &c .* A saying soeuident with vs, that *the Century writers* mencioning the same do therefore say, that, (a) *Ireneus affirmeth it very incommodiously.*
And

in his oblation made in the inftitution of the Sacrament, whereof *Ireneus* profeffeth exprefly here to fpeake, did (to vfe *Ireneus* his wordes) *teach* (this offering to the vfe of the poore to be) *the new oblation of the new Teftament.* This being no leffe then open violence to the wordes and meaning of *Ireneus*; the *Centuriftes* do therefore *col.* 113. plainly charge him *to haue beene negligent and improper in his fpeaking,* (and) *often calling the Eucharift an oblation,* affirming therefore as before of his firft recyted faying, (*fi tamen locus fraude ac mendo vacat*) which extreameft fhift of vnwotthy fuppofal againft the general confent of al agreing copies they would neuer haue vndertaken, nor yet haue (as before) placed the fame faying in their forefaid fpecial tract or recital of *the Doctors errors of thofe times,* affirming alfo therof, (as before) that *fatis videtur loqui incomode,* had not his faid fayings bene (in their iudgemet) plain with vs, and againft them, in this queftion of facrifice; which their iudgement is herein fo euident that *M. Sutliue* doth accordingly confeffe the fame in his *fubuerfion of the three conuerfions.* pag. 32. anfwering thereto, *what the Magdeburgians do yeelde, let them yeelde for them felues, we do not in al pointes take our felues bound to allow their fayinges, nor finde any fuch inconuenience in thefe tearmes as the Fathers* (there before mentioned, whereof *Ireneus* is one) *vnderftood them, as the Magdeburgians pretend.* A bould and defperate refuge fo to charge his learnedbrethren with caufeleffe *yeelding,* and *pretending* againft them felues.

And *Caluin* doth likewife namely reprehend *Ireneus* for his fo (b) *expounding Malachie of the facrifice of the Maffe:* In defence whereof he affirmeth that *Ireneus* and other auncient Fathers by him there named, did alledge the Scriptures, to vfe his owne wordes, (21) *fo ridiculofly* (faith he) *as both reafon, and truth conftraineth me to diffent from them.* Alexander was Bifhop of Rome, (22) *Anno.* 110. as *M. Cartbwright* chargeth him with bringing

(b) *Caluin. de vera Ecclefia reformanda ratione,* faith, *folenne eft nebulonibus iftis* (meaning vs Catholicks) *qnicquid vitiofum in Patribus legitur corradere &c. cum ergo obijciunt locum Malachiæ de Miffa facrificio ab Ireneo exponi, oblationem Melchifadech fic tractari ab Athanafio, Ambrofio, Auguftino, Arnobio, breuiter refponfum fit, eodem illos fcriptores alibi quoq, panem interpretari corpus Chrifti, fed ita ridicule, vt diffentire nos cogat ratio et veritas &c.* (21) *Caluin, vbi fupra.* (22) *M. Whitguift,* in his defence &c. pag. 594. (23) In *M. Whitguifies* defence

fence, pag. 593.

(c)
Szegedin. in speculo pontificum, pag. 59. saith,
authores Canonis sunt A-
lexander primus, Siritius
Gelasius, Leo, Gregorius,
Scholasticus.

(d)
Szegdin. in speculo pontificum, pag. 50. saith, A-
lexander primus docuit missæ sacrificio peccata delere,
hunc imitatus Gregorius
magnus certos instituit dies,
quibus in templo solenni ritu sacrificaretur, et proposuit delictorum veniam ad
id solenne accedentibus.

(e)
M. Whitguift in his de-
fence &c. pag. 408.

(f)
These wordes are alled-
ged as the saying of Ig-
natius by Theodoret, di-
al. 3.

(g)
Ignatius, in epist. ad Smer-
nenses. see this more at
large heretofore, tract. 1.
sect. 3. subdivis. 2. at r.

bringing (23) in of wafer cakes, in forme, fashiō, &
substāce like the Papists God of the Altar. So likwise Szegedinus, a learned Caluinist maketh
him one (c) of the authors of our now Canon of
the Masse, affirming further that, (d) Alexander the first, taught that sinnes were forgeuen by
the sacrifice of the Masse, whom Gregory the
great imitated therein &c. Ignatius (as D. Whitguift affirmeth) (e) was S. Iohns scholer, and
liued in Christes time, he reprehending the heretickes of his time saith accordingly, as
Theodoret aboue 1200. yeares since, alledgeth
his wordes (f) they do not admit Eucharistes
and oblations, because they do not confesse the Eucharist to be the flesh of our Sauiour Iesus Christ,
which flesh suffered for our sinnes; he doth also
affirme the (g) Bishop to be as the high Preist,
and Christes image, in respect that he sacrifyceth
to God for the saifty of the world: In so much
as the Century writers do dislike his sayinges
hereof, as being (to vse their wordes) (h)
doubtful and incommodiouse. In the same time
liued holy Martialis who mencioneth (i)
sacrifice offered to God vpon the Altar, that we
offer Christes body and bloud vnto life euerlasting,
and set forth the same vpon the Altar, accordingly as our Lord conmmaundeth the same to be done
in memory of him, wherein he is disliked by
(k) the Centurie writers, and by M. (l) Fulke,
who without al proofe or reason tearmeth
him therefore a counterfeate, whose vndoubted

*. and alledged by M. Whiteguift in his defence &c. pag. 408. paulo
post med. (h) Cent. 2. c. 4. col. 63. it is said, quædam ambigua et
incommode dicta in quibusdam occurunt, vt in epist. Ignatij ad Smirnenses,
non licet, inquit Ignatius, sine Episcopo offerre, neq; sacrificium immolare, ueq;
dochen celebrare. and cent. 2. c. 10. col. 167. they affirme these wordes of Ignatius to be periculosa et quasi errorum semina. And see M. Sutline
in his

in his subuersion *of the three conuersions, pag.* 32. acknowledging *the Centuristes* reprehension of *Ignatius, Ireneus, Tertulian,* and *Martialis,* for their doctrine of *sacrifice.* (i) *Martialis, in epist. ad Burdegalenses.* (k) *Cent.* 3. *c.* 4. *col.* 83. (l) *M. Fulke,* against *Heskins, Saunders &c. pag.* 123: & 124.

ted antiquity is yet neuerthelesse so euident and confessed, that the *Century writers* who wrong him herein al they can, doubt not for (m) to place him in the third age or hundreth yeares after Christ.

(m)
Centur. 3. *c.* 4. *col.* 83.
(*)

(5) *Also the Preistes of Achaia* (being the disciples of S. *Andrew* in their booke *of his passion,* howsoeuer reiected by (*) *M. Fulke* in reguard of the plaine testimonies therein contained, yet not to be gainsaid by any probable reason but (n) *confirmed* with graue & auncient

M. Fulke, against *Heskins &c. pag.* 234. saith, *As for the legend of S. Andrewes passion, which M. Heskines saith, was writen per Presbiteros & Diaconos Achaiæ, it is of as good credit as the booke of Beuis of*

Hampton. (n) In proofe of this booke it is to be obserued: *first,* that (as *the Centuristes, cent.* 1. *l.* 2. *c.* 10. *col.* 565. and *M. Foxe, Act. mon.* printed 1595. at the history of S. *Andrew,* whereof see his table) do collect from S. *Hierome, in catalog. scriptorum Ecclesiast.* S. *Andrew* made his aboade for the time in *Achaia,* and was there put to death vpon the Crosse by the *proconsul Aegeas*; al which is accordingly found in the booke now extant. *Secondly,* S. *Andrewes* ioyful wordes of *salue sancta Crux,* there said to be spoken by him at the time of his suffering. and now accordingly celebrated in the whol Church of Christ, geue like answearable testimony of the antiquity of the booke. *Thirdly, Ciprian. in lib. de duplici martirio, ante med.* saith accordingly, *Beatus Andraeas vt habet humana quidem historia, sed satis probata fidei, gaudens, sibiq, gratulans, ibat ad Crucem:* whereupon *Ioannes Pappus* a learned Protestant of *Germany* in his *epitom. hist. Eccles.* pag. 36. saith, *extat historia martiry Andreæ scripta a Presbiteris et Diaconis Ecclesiarum Achaiæ, cuius quidem historia, liber etiam de duplici martirio Cipriano inscriptus mentionem facit.* And like further probability of this booke is had from *Remigius in Psal.* 21. from *Lanfrancus lib.* 1. *contra Berengarium.* and from *S. Bernard in serm. S. Andrea.* in so much as *Craftouius,* a learned Caluinist in his booke *de opificio missæ. l.* 1. *pag.* 116. doubteth not to alledge the very seutence here alledged
as being

as being the vndoubted faying of *S. Andrew* faying, *quomodo verum erit S. Andrea Apoftoli Apothegma quem fcribunt Prasbuteri et Diaconi Achaia in paffiove fua Agea Proconfuli dixiffe, ego immaculatum agnum in Altari offero &c.* And *Ioannes Bectholdus* (in his affertions *Theolog. de Sacram. cana Dom. Thef.* 80. although in his anfweare he there pretend the writinges of *Dionifius Areopagita* to be counterfeated, obiecting his reafons therefore, yet doth he there acknowledge this other treatife and teftimony concerning *S. Andrew,* and endeauoreth accordingly to make other anfweare thereto. *Fourtly,* there is nothing in this booke that taifteth of nouelty. *Laftly,* M. *Parkins,* who in his probleame &c. *pag.* 7. reiecteth the fame, and fundry other treatifes extant vnder the Fathers names, geueth his reafons of exceptions againft others, but none againft this, faue onely his vnworthy exception to the forefaid ioyful faying of *falue fancta Crux.* And his affirming that neither *Eufebius,* nor *Hierome.* do mencion this treatife, which is *heretofore* in the preface fufficiently an-

fweared.	auncient teftimony) do report how *S. Andrew* faid to the the *Proconful Aegeas,* (o) *I do offer vpon the Altar an immaculate lambe, whofe flefh after that al the beleeuing people haith eaten, the lambe which is offered remaineth whol and liuing.* And whereas D. *Raynoldes* affirmeth truly, that (p) *Altar and facrifice are linked in relation and mutual dependance,* fo as the one being affirmed, the other doth thereupon neceffarily follow. *Dionifius Areopagita* mencioned in the (q) *Actes,* doth in his writing (r) *heretofore* proued, and confeffed accordingly mencion, not onely (s) *Preiftes,* but alfo (t) *Altars,* and *the confecration of them with infufion of facred Oile :* faying further, (*) *the Bofhop doth reuerently and according to his Bifhop-like office after the holy praifes of Gods worker, excufe himfelfe that he taketh vpon him to offor the healthful facrifice which is aboue his degree, crying out firft to him in feemely wife ; Lord thou*
(o)	
In lib. paffionis S. Andrea.	
(p)	
M. *Raynoldes,* in his conference, *pag.* 552.	
(q)	
Act. 17. 34.	
(r)	
See *heretofore* in the preface to the reader. *fect.* 5. 6. 7. 8. *&c.*	
(s)	
Heretofore, *tract.* 1. *fect.* 3. *fubdiuif.* 1. in the margent at the letter e.	
(t)	
Heretofore, *tract.* 1. *fect.* 2. in the margent at the letter e.	(*) *Dionifius de Ecclefiaftica Hierarchia*

rarchia, cap . 3 . faith, itaq́ religiofe, et vt Pontificem decet poſt facras diui-
norum operum laudes de ſacrificio quod ipſius dignitatem ſuperat ſe purgat,
dum primo ad eum clamat tu dixiſti, hoc facite in meam commemorationem,
deinde cum rogauit vt hoc diuino ſacrificio dignus ſit &c.

thou haſt commaunded thus, ſaying, do this in re-
remembrance of me; ſo plainly doth he affirme
the bleſſed Sacrment to be the healthful ſacrifice which the Biſhop offereth to God, according to our Sauiours commaundement or
inſtitution thereof when he ſaid, *do this &c.*
In like manner *S. Clement,* who is mencioned by (u) *S. Paul,* doth in his booke *of A-*
poſtolical conſtitutions (the authority of that
booke being (x) confirmed with auncient
testimony

(u)
Phillip . 4 . 3 .

(x)
Ireneus, apud Euſeb. l. 5 .
c . 6 . affirmeth that *Cle-*
ment led his life with the
Apoſtles them ſelues, and
being inſtructed of them,
kept freſh in memory their
tradition: whereby it appeareth that he was a
man moſt like to penne a

booke of this argument. *Secondly , Photius* (who liued almoſt 800.
yeares ſince*) in Bibliotheca.* ſaith, that *he haith red two volumes of Cle-*
mens of Rome, whereof the one is entituled the conſtitutions of the Apoſtes .
Alſo the 84. Canon extant vnder the Apoſtles names, mencioneth
the conſtitutions ſet forth by Clement in 8. bookes; which Canon though
we ſhould ſuppoſe it to be of latter time, for ſo much yet as it is one
of the 85. *Canons* which *the 6. councel of Conſtantinople in trullo . can.*
2. doth mencion, it is thereby euident, that a treatiſe of that title
anſwearable in diuiſion of bookes to this now in queſtion, was extant in that time which is now about ſome 1000. *yeares* ſince . Alſo in *Athanaſius, in epiſt. ad Amnum monacum* is mencioned a booke,
which is called the doctrine of the Apoſtles. And in *Euſeb. hiſt . l . 3 . c .*
19. is likewiſe mencioned, *that which is called the doctrine of the Apoſtles .*
And he numbreth it not among ſuch bookes there mencioned as were
publiſhed by heretickes vnder the Apoſtles names, and reiected for abſurd ;
but with *Paſtor, and the Apocalips of S. Iohn,* whereof queſtion onely
was made, whether they were ſacred Scriptures or not. And in like
manner doth *Epiphanius har . 70. poſt med .* mencion the booke called
the conſtitutions of the Apolſtes, ſaying thereof, *it is not diſallowed for it haith*
nothing amiſſe touching faith, whereto might be added further teſtimony
of *Proclus de traditione diuina Liturgia,* and of *Damaſcen. l. 4 . de or-*
thod . fidei. Thirdly, it is yet more particularly teſtifyed vnto, for *Ciril*

P p   Biſhop

Bifhop of *Hierufalem*, aboue 1200. yeares fince, *in catech*. 18 . *multo ante med*. alledgeth namely out of *Clement* the example of *the Phænix* to proue the refurrection, which is accordingly found in the bookes of conftitutions after the *Antwerpe* print 1564. *l*. 5 . *c*. 8. almoft in the fame wordes. Alfo the imperfect worke vpon *S*. *Mathew* extant vnder *Chrifoftomes* name and reputed for no leffe auncient. *hom*. 53 . *multo ante med*. mencioneth the 8. booke *of the Apoftles rules* concerniug the *ordaining of Preiftes*, which matter is accordingly handled in the booke now in queftion, *l*. 8 . *c*. 1 . *poft med*. And *Epiphanius har*. 70 . *poft*. *med*. faith, *let vs heare the Apoftles fpeake in the (booke of) conftitution, he that aflicteth his foule on the Lords day is accurfed of God:* which thing is accordingly forbidden, *l*. 5 . *conft*. *c*. *vlt*. *fine*. and *har*. 45 . *prope finem*. he faith, *the Apoftles (in the booke) called the conftitution, fay; the Catholicke Church is the plainting of God and a vine,* which is accordingly to be found, *l*. 1 . *conft*. *c*. 1 . fundry other examples might be geuen of *Epiphanius* his like fpecial alledging of this booke; a thing fo euident that *Chemnitius, exam. part*. 4 . *pag*. 125 . and the *Centuriftes, cent*. 4 . *col*. 310 . do acknowledge the fame in *Epiphanius*. And that the forefaid booke was extant in his time and by him fpecially alledged, and were it not to auoide tedioufneffe (wherof this fhort treatife is not capable) it might be yet further proued that this booke was knowen alfo to *Ignatius,* and alledged fpecially by him in his vndoubted epiftles.

The cheife obiection a- (*)   teftimony, and the obiections againft it fufgainft this booke is, how ficiently (*) anfwearable) affirme that our Sauiour that in fundry partes thereof it menci oneth the death of certaine of the Apoftles and yet afterwardes bringeth them in as being liuing and geuing preceptes: whereto I anfweare with *Photius* who in *Bibliotheca*. faid hereof, whereas *the conftitutions feeme to be guilty of euil fiction, it may eafily be auoided,* the anfweare therfore is plaine and euidently true, that *Clement* did write this booke *Mimeticos,* that is, by induction *of perfon,* (much like to that which is vfed in a dialogue) and that he was geuen to this kinde of writing appeareth by an other example (teftifyed by *Eufebius, hift*. *l*. 3 . *c*. 32 . *et* 12 . and by *Hierome in catalog*.) of his *vndoubted epiftle whriten by him vnder the perfon of the Roman Church:* In which kinde of writing it is not material whether the parties fo induced, be liuing or deade; this his method being acknowledged

acknowledged, dissolueth al difficulty of the foresaid repugnancy. In further euidence whereof he doth *l. 8. constit . c . 41 .* bring in *Iames the brother of our Lord,* as being a liue, and geuing preceptes, and yet a litle before *(l . 7 . c . 46. initio .* he bringeth in the Apostles numbring vp the Bishopes made by them, and saying thereof, *de ordinatis autem a nobis Episcopis in vita nostra &c. concerning the Bishopes which were ordained by vs in our life time ;* most euidently so by these wordes *in our life time* signifying, that the method of his writing is *by induction of person* according to which he bringeth in the Apostles as speking after they were deade . As in like sort *Tullie l. 13. epist. ad Atticum . ante med .* affirmeth, that he likewise made his *fiue books* Peri telon *de finibus,* inducing therein as speakers, *L. Torquatus, M. Antonius,* and *M. Piso,* al which as he there affirmeth, were deade before . And so also *Plato* vttered what he thought concerning nature and manners vnder the person of *Socrates, Parmenides,* and *Timeus .* And thus much in answeare of the foresaid obiection . As concerning that which is further obiected from the 6 . *Councel of Constantinople,* affirming *can. 2.* that *in the constitutions of the Apostles written by Clement, certaine forged thinges and different from godlines are inserted, which do obscure the elegant and delectable forme of those diuine bookes.* I answeare thereto, *first,* that this is a strong auncient testimony that *Clement* was author of this booke. *Secondly,* as to the corruptions inserted by heretickes, I answeare, that this concerned not al, but onely certaine copies of this booke so then in those partes corrupted, for that al were not corrupted appeareth by *Epiphanius, hær . 70. post med .* who expresly saith, that *omnis regularis ordo in (constitutione Apostolorum) habetur, et nihil a fide adulteratum &c .* *Thirdly,* admit there were some one or other auncient corruption inserted in this booke (whereof it were hard to geue through out the whol booke, so much as but three probable examples) yet can such one or other said corruption but concerne that only anciēt perticular error in fauer wherof such said corruption was inserted, so as the same, notwithstanding the authority of this booke, is yet for al that indifferent and sufficient to determine the controuersies of our times, especially where it is found to be agreeable and consonant with the succeeding testi-monies of the other Fa-thers .

Sauiour *(y) hath in steede of bloudy sacrifice, instituted reasonable, vnbloudy, and mistical sacrifice, celebrated by the simbols of his body & bloud ;* After the print thereof

(y)

at *Antwerpe*. 1564. *l. 6.*
constit. Apost . c . 23. fol.
123. b.

(z)
Ibidem . l. 8. c. 3. fol.
160. b.

(a)
Ibidem . l. 2. c. 61. fine.
fol. 56. b. he faith, *his*
peractis sacrificium peraga-
tur &c. as postquam ob-
latum fuerit, accipiant sin-
guli. per se ordine domini-
cum corpus, et pretiosum
sanguinem, gradatim cum
pudore ac tremore tanquam
ad regis corpus accedentes .
et vide ibidem. l. 8. c.
20. *fol.* 17. a. *fine.*

(b)
Ibidem. vt supra .

(c)
Lib. 8. c. 52. post med.
he faith, *Christus spiritu-*
ale sacrificium offerens Deo
et Patri suo ante passionem,
solis nobis precepit hoc face-
re. & *l. 8. c.* 18. he faith ,
offerimus tibi pro populo
hoc &c. pro aeris salubri-
tate &c. (d) See here-

and that *Preistes* haith power geuen them (z)
to offer vnto God a cleane and vnbloudy sacrifice,
ordained by Christ for the mistery of the new Te-
stament. And (a) diftinguishing elswhere
moft plainly oblation of sacrifice from diftribution thereof to the people, he calleth it (b)
our Lordes body and his pretiouse bloud with
sundry other plaine (c) sayinges in behalfe
of sacrifice.

Thus euidently euen by teftimony of
our learned aduersaries is our sacrifice of the
Maffe deduced from this prefent age vp to
the Apoftles ; whereunto I do yet further
ad, that as our learned aduersaries haue *here-*
tofore confeffed concerning (d) *real presence,*
and (e) *adoration,* that they are not able to
shew any firft beginning of them since the
Apoftles times (which point how auailable it
is for vs, I haue (f) *heretofore* alfo shewed)
fo likewife they are fo vnable alfo to shew any
nouel and firft beginning since the Apoftles
times of *Maffe or sacrifice,* which is *heretofore*
plentifully mencioned in writinges of euery
age, that to the contrary *M. Afcham* (no
vulgar aduersary) confeffeth in plaine tearmes that, *verissime sciri non potest,* (g) *moft*
certainly it cannot be shewed. And *M . Beacon*
hauing as is (*) *before* affirmed, the general
vfage thereof in forme as it now is, for thefe
1000. yeares laft paft, addeth withal further
vpon

tofore, *tract . 2. sect . 2 . subdiuis. 6 . fine .* at the letter y . (e) Heretofore, *tract . 2. sect . 9. subdiuis.* 1 . at the letter d . (f) See heretofore *tract . 2. sect . 9. subdiuis.* 1 . at e . f. g . &c. (g) *Afcham*
in his *Apolog . contra Miffam,* printed 1578. *pag .* 31 . hauing set dowen
in his margent *inuentio Miffæ,* as to be entreated vpon, confeffeth saying, *quibus temporibus, et per quos homines cæna Dominica de poffeffione (ua*
per miffam deturbata sit, verissime sciri non potest &c . Diaboli aftutia pru-
dentiores

dentiores sunt quam vt a quouis percipi possint. (*) See heretofore, *tract. 3. sect. 2. subdiuis. 2.* at the letters m. and n.

vpon the credible *report* of auncient *histories* saying, not *ironice* but *seriously* (h) the *masse was begotten, conceiued, and borne* a none after the *Apostles* times, *if al be true that historiographers write. Hospinianus* also doubteth not to reproue likewise the Apostles owne age, affirming that euen in (i) *that first age when the Apostles were as yet liuing* , *the deuil was more busie to peruert this Sacrament then Baptisme, and by litle and litle brought men from the first forme or institution* thereof. And *Sebastianus Francus* an other of our aduersaries, concludeth this point most plainly saying, (k) *presently after the Apostles times al thinges were turned vpside downe &c. the supper of our Lord was turned into a sacrifice.* Hitherto concerning confessed testimonies from the Fathers of euery age in behalfe of sacrifice: To whose graue authority (gentle reader) if so thou shalt geue no further respect then did (*) *Martin Luther, Bullinger,* and *Caluin,* the collection hereof so painfully prepared , is then but lost and al in vaine. *But* (a) *with the Apostle) of you my dearest we are perswaded better thinges and such as do accompany saluation. That*

(h)
M · Beacon, in the third part of his workes in the treatise entituled *the reliques of Rome, fol.* 344.

(i)
Hospinianus in historia Sacram. l. 1. c. 6. pag. 20. saith, *iam tum primo illo seculo viuentibus adhuc Apostolis magis, huic Sacramento quam Baptismo insidiari ausus sit (Dæmon) et homines a prima illa forma sensim abduxerit, donec illis posterioribus ætatibus penitus obscurauit* .

(k)
Sebastianus Francus, in epistola *de abrogandis in vniuersum omnibus statutis Ecclesiasticis* . saith, *statim post Apostolos omnia vniuersa sunt &c. cæna Domini in sacrificium transformata est.* (*) *Luther, tom. 2. Witeberg. fol. 72.*

saith, *quid ergo dicemus ad Canonem & authoritates Patrum, primum respondeo, si nihil habetur quod dicatur, tutius est omnia negare quam Missam concedere*. and nere the beginning of the same leafe it is said, *Missa creditur passim esse sacrificium quod offertur Deo &c. accedunt his dicta sanctorum Patrum, tot exempla, tantusq̃, vsus per orbem constanter obseruatus: his omnibus quia pertinacissime insederunt, oportet constantissime opponere verba et exemplum Christi.* Also *Bullinger* in his Decades in english, *pag.* 1082. saith, *where some obiect that the auncient Fathers haue made mencion of offering for the deade, we suppose that it appertaineth not vnto vs, for &c. we*

belecue

beleeue not the Fathers further then they can proue their sayinges by the Canonical Scriptures &c. and therefore if the Fathers thinke that the supper is a sacrifice to be offered to procure rest to the soules departed ~~which~~ do not receiue that opinion &c.

And see Caluins like contempt herein of the Fathers *heretofore* in this present section, *subdiuis.* 3. at h.i.k.l. (a) *Habr.* 6. 9.

(*)
No prophecy of Scripture is made by priuate interpretation. 2. Petri. 1. 20.
(l)
Peter Martir in his commõ places in englifh, *part.* 4. *c.* 12. *pag.* 221. & *Craftonius de opificio Mif. fæ. fect.* 127. *pag.* 57. and *fect.* 139. *pag.* 65.
(m)
M. Hooker in his Ecclefiaftical pollicy, *l.* 5. *fect.* 67. *pag.* 173. and *pag.* 174. and *fect.* 57. *pag.* 128. and *Peter Martir* in his Common places in englifh. *part.* 4. *pag.* 153. faith accordingly in Baptifme, *Chrift is geuen as a regenerator, but in the Euchariſt, he is diftributed to vs as meate and nourifhment.*
(*)
Primafius, in Habr. c. 10. faith, becaufe we finne daily

That the Scriptures of the new Teftament are agreeable thereto.

SECTION. 3.

THis forefaid vfage of offering the Eucharift in facrifice to God being, as before is proued, the confeffed practife of al ages vp to the Apoftles times, it wil now I hope be proofe fufficient from the Scriptures, if the wordes thereof appeare to be but of them felues indifferent to beare that fence: for fo much only being obtained, it neceffarily followeth that the Scriptures fence and expofition muft needes be taken, not after (*) *priuate interpretation,* but according to the Churches confeffed practife in that behalfe of al fucceeding ages. In this prefent tract therfore I wil now fhew, not that the words of Scripture are indifferet to receiue the fence of facrifice (which onely would fuffice) but that they are manifeftly and neceffarily enclining thereto: And whereas fome perhaps may doubt how the Eucharift being *a Sacrament,* can alfo be *a facrifice.* Firft to explaine that point, I fay with *Peter Martir,* that in diuers refpectes (l) *one thing may be both a Sacrament and a facrifice.* And the like is acknowledged by *Andreas Craftonius,* it is therefore *a Sacrament,* in that it is deliuered to vs to be receiued into our bodies with peculiar (m) *grace, not to begin as Baptifme doth, but to continue life* ; and it is *a facrifice* in that

that it is offered to God for vs, and ordained to (*) continue the memory of Christes death and oblation vpon the Crosse, with the application of the general vertue therof to our perticular necessities.

To proue now that our Sauiour as being the *high Preist*, did institute this sacrifice at his last supper, and that before his deliuery thereof to his Disciples, he did first offer the same for them vnto his Father, the wordes are pregnant, as being, (n) *which is geuen* in

dayly, and haue dayly neede to be clensed, and because he cannot now die, he haith geuen vs this Sacrament of his body and bloud, that as his passion was the redemptiō & absolutiō of the world, so also this oblation may be redemption and cleansing to al that offer it in truth and verity. and *Euseb*. the *Emissen. hom*. 5. *de Pascate*. geueth his like reason of our now sacrifice saying ; *quia corpus assumptum &c*. *because he would take his assumted body from our eyes and bring it into heauen, it was necessary that in the day of his supper he should consecrate to vs the Sacrament of his body and bloud, that what was once offered for our price might be celebrated continually by mistery; that because the daily and vnwearied redemption did runne* (or continue) *for the saluation of al men, the oblation of that redemption might be perpetual, and that eternal sacrifice should liue in memory, and be alwaies present in grace, a true, one, & perfect sacrifice, to be esteemed by faith, and not by outward shew &c*. *for the inuisible Preist by his word with secret power conuerteth the visible creatures into the substance of his body and bloud*. And *S . Ciprian de cœna Dom . paulo post initium*. repeating our Sauiours wordes, *this is my flesh, this is my bloud*, saith thereupon, *quotiscunq; &c*. *so often as with these wordes and this faith it is acted* (or celebrated) *this bread substantial and cup, consecrated with holy blessing, profiteth to the health of the whol man, being both a medicine and a sacrifice to heale infirmities, and purge iniquities*. And *S . Bede hist . l*. 4 . *c*. 22 . *fine*. saith accordingly, *many godly men were stirred vp to offer sacrifice for the deade, for they vnderstoode that the healthful sacrifice auailed to the euerlasting redemption both of soule and body*. and *Greg . hom*. 37. *in Euang*. saith, *quoties ei hostiam suœ passionis offerimus, toties nobis ad absolutionem nostram ipsius passionem reparamus*. And see further heretofore, *tract*. 3. *sect*. 1 . *subdiuis*. 3 . in the margent at the letter s. what is in this behalfe confessed of the Fathers by the the Protestant writer *Crastouius*. (n) Didomenon *is geuen. Luc*. 22. 19. and *S. Paul* vseth the same Tense in the word Clomenon ~~is brother~~ *for you*. 1. *Cor*. 11 . 24. the word *frangitur*, signifying some-
~~(broken)~~
                                                                        time,

times the same with *datur*, and it should here signify *breaking* , yet is it so more forcible as being thereby referred to the Sacrament in reguard of the outward formes which are in time of sacrifycing *broken*, but not to the Crosse, for *when they saw he was deade they brake not his legges &c. that the Scripture might be fulfilled, you shal not breake a bone of him. Ion.* 19. 33. 36. and *S. Chrisostome* in 1. *Cor. hom.* 24. writing vpon these words of the Apostle, *the breade which we breake &c.* saith thereupon accordingly, *why doth the Apostle ad, which we breake ?* this *in the Eucharist may be seene, but on the Crosse not, but altogether the contrary, for a bone of him* (saith the text) *you shal not breake, therefore what he doth not suffer on the Crosse, that doth he* (by way of misterie and signification, in reguard of the Sacrament which is broken) *suffer in the sacrifice,* which perspicuity of referring the foresaid wordes, *is broken for you* onely vnto the Sacrament, and not to the Crosse, maketh so strongly for real presence in the Sacrament, that *Pratorius* the Caluinist, *l. de Sacramentis, pag.* 152. and 153. laboureth therefore to refer this *fraction for vs* to the Crosse, directly against the former sayinges of *Chrisostome* and *S. Iohn.*

(o)

Enchumomenon, *is shed. Math.* 26. 28. *Marc.* 14. 24. *Luc.* 22. 20.

(p)

M. Whitaker, de sacra Scriptura controu. 1. *quast.* 2. *pag.* 128. saith, *nullam nos editionem nisi Habraicam in vetere Gracam in nouo Testamento authenticam facimus &c.* and the like is affirmed by *Piscator in volum.* 1. *Thesium theolog. pag.* 34.

(q

M. Fulke against the Rhemish Testament in *Math.* 26. *sect.* 10. *fol.*

the present tense, concurring agreeably with his action then present, and not *to you, but for you,* and (o) *which is shed for many vnto remission of sinnes ;* for the Greeke being the original, and in our aduersaries iudgement the onely (p) authentical text, haith the present tense in al the three Euangelistes, as also in *S. Paul,* and so accordingly our aduersaries translate, *is geuen, is shed.* Aud wheras our aduersaries do flee from the wordes of the text, answearing, that (q) *the Apostles and Euangelistes vsed the present tense for the future, as signifying Christes passion was at hand;* & that therefore by *is geuen,* is meant *which shal be geuen vpon the Crosse.* It shal here suffice to note that the text is not onely indifferent, which would suffice, but directly against the, and is therefore to be taken according to the Churches confessed practise of al following times: And it were strange to thinke that

that in euery place where the inftitution is
mencioned, the Apoftles, and Euangeliftes,
fhould al of them vfe the prefent tenfe, and
without explication, vnleffe it had beene
moft certaine that our Sauiour him felfe had
accordingly vfed the fame as needing no explication: And where our aduerfaries do further (s) anfweare that the prefent tenfe is
fometime vfed for the future, and that the
vulgar interpreter tranflateth accordinly (t)
which fhal be fhed; we reply thereto, that
though the prefent tenfe be vfed fomtimes
for the future, yet much more often to fignify a thing prefent; and the rather here, in
that not one onely, but al the *three Euangeliftes,* and *S. Paul,* likewife do to our Sauiours forefaid action them prefent ad, and vfe
the prefent tenfe, the fence whereof doth
alfo agree with the confeffed practife of al
fucceeding ages. As for the vulgar traflation our aduerfaries are in great ftraites when
they do appeale from the original text to it,
which they affirme to be (u) *an old rotten
traflation ful of corruptions in al partes thereof,
and of al others moft corrupt.* Therefore this
point being fo clearly determined by the
Euangeliftes them felues in their owne original writinges, who al of them vfe the prefent tenfe, is not to be gainfaid by any tranflation whatfoeuer; neuertheleffe in behalfe
of the vulgar interpreter, we fay that as he
tranflateth in the future *which fhal be fhed,* fo
alfo he vfeth the prefent tenfe tranflating
(x) *which is geuen,* both which he vfeth to
fignify a certaine truth, the *prefent tenfe,* fignifying that his body was then geuen in the
Sacrament, *the future* not impugning the former fence, but fignifying withal further that
it

Q q

(s)
M. Fulke vbi fupra.
(t)
Math. 26. 28.
(u)
So faith *M. Whitaker* in
his anfweare to *M. Wil-
liam Raynoldes* refutation
againft the preface there
pag. 25. 26. and fee
there *pag.* 344. and 223.
and 218.
(x)
Luc. 22. 19.
(z)
1. *Cor. 11. 24.*
(*)
Caluin, in 1. *Cor. 11.
24. pag.* 323. faith, *his
frangi pofitum interpretor
pro immolari, improprie quidem fed non abfurde &c.
neq, enim fimpliciter et fine
adiectione Dominus corpus
fuum nobis offert, fed quatenus pro nobis immolatum
fuit.* and *Chemnitius* in
his examen, *part.* 2. *pag.*
153. faith accordingly
of the Sacrament, *ibi di-
fpenfatur, et fumitur victima quæ pro peccatis noftris
femel in cruce oblata eft.*
Alfo *M. Whitaker contra
Duræum. l. 2. pag.* 169.
faith of our receiuing
Chrift in the Sacrament,
*Chrifti corpore pro nobis in
facrificium*

sacrificium oblato pascimur, it should be then also afterwardes geuen v-
deniǭ, Christi carnem edi- pon the Crosse.
mus, et sanguinem bibimus   (2)   Which point of our Sauiours then
&c. If now Chrst was present geuing in the Sacrament, is yet fur-
at his last supper present ther, and vnanswearably made euident aswel
in the Sacrament by way by *S. Paul* who saith, (2) *is broken for you*,
of sacrifice, and before wheruopō euē (*) *Caluī* him self & others do
his sacrifice done vpon collect that our Sauiour did at his last supper
the Crosse, how can it be deliuer ᷠhis body to his Disciples as sacrifyced
but that the Eucharist for vs, for this fraction or breaking cannot
then was, and yet is a for sundry reasons before (3) mencioned be
sacrifice. referred to the Crosse, but onely to the Sa-

(3) crament, wherein he is said to be so *broken*
See next heretofore *sub-* for vs, in reguard that the external Sacrament
diuis. 1. in the margent vnder which he is really present, (4) *is broken*
at n. (as in like respect *the holy Ghost*, who is in him

(4) selfe inuisible and infinit, and therefore is
He blessed & brake Marc. not seene nor doth discend, is yet in reguard
14. 22. *Math.* 26. 26. of *the doue* descending, and his like presence
and *Luc.* 22. 19. which therwith said in the Scriptures to be (5) *seene*
fraction is so peculiar to *descending)* as also by *S. Luke* who writing in
this Sacrament, that *Pi-* Greeke not onely expresseth *sheeding* in the
scator, and *Amandus Po-* present tense but also referreth it directly to
lanus, do therefore af- the Cup, in like reguard that his bloud there-
firme it to be an essential in contayned is thence powred forth or shed,
rite. See them alledged which sheeding of the cup must needes be
hereafter, *tract.* 5. *sect.* taken as present, for that it cannot by any
1. *initio.* in the margent sleight
at l.   (5)   *He saw the spirit of God descending as a doue. Math.* 3. 16.
in the Protestant treatise entituled *Collat. Cathol. et orthodoxæ Christiano-*
rum fidei. pag. 326. *Iacobus Andræas* saith hereof, *Spiritui sancto prop-*
ter speciem columbæ assumptam tribuitur, quod columbæ proprium est &c.
quemadmodum Ecclesiastici scriptores propter presentiam corporis Christi in
cæna, corpus Christi tractari, dentibus teri, et similia dixerunt &c. And
Caluin in his treatise *de cæna Domini inter opuscula.* maketh his like
application saying, *exemplum valde proprium in re simili habemus &c.*
we haue a maruelouse apt example in the like matter &c. Iohn Babptist
(saith he) *saw the holy Ghost descending, if we consider the matter wel, we*
                                                                                      shal

shal finde that he saw nothing but a doue, for the essence of the holy Ghost is inuisible, yet because he knew wel that vision to be no empty figure, but a more sure signe of the presence of the holy Ghost, he doubted not to affirme that he saw him &c. So in the communion of Christs body & bloud &c. Iustly therfore is the bread called the body of Christ, because it doth not onely figure it, but also present or offer it vnto vs.

sleight of the construction be referred as future to the Crosse, his wordes stand thus after (6) the Greeke, (y) *Hic Calix nouum Testamentum in sanguine meo pro vobis effusus,* in construction of which sentence, the word *effusus,* varieth in casse from *sanguine,* and in gender from *Testamentum,* and agreeth so most euidently onely with *Calix,* and the very same diuersity and agreement is also in the Greeke. A thing so euident that *Castalio* a learned Sacramentarie (whose *translation* is by *D. Humfrey* and other Caluinistes (*) preferred before al others) (a) translateth accordingly, referring this sheding to the Cup. and *Beza* saith thereof, (z) *these wordes (shed for you) if you reguard the plaine construction, do of necessity appertaine not to bloud, but to the*

(6)
(y)

Luc. 22. 20. this place is so strong and euident that *Dauid Chitreus* a famouse Lutheran, *l. de Baptismo & Eucharistia.* printed *Anno.* 1584. *pag.* 295. repeating these wordes in Greeke, withal saith thereof, *singulare et illustre argumentum ex his Lucæ verbis extruit, quæ ita posita sunt vt* To enchunomenon *non possit alio quam ad* Poterion *referri.* and *Ibidem. pag.* 299. he further saith of

S. Luke, Calicem pro nobis effundi scribit, in proofe whereof he there affirmeth that in these foresaid wordes *articulus* To *et participium* Enchunomenon *genere et casu cum nominatiuo* To Poterion, *et non cum datiuo* Aimati *congruunt.* (*) *Humfred. de rat. interpret. l.* 1. *pag.* 62. and 63. and 189. affirmeth *Castolios translation to be most throughly conferred, examined, and published.* And *Gesnerus in Bibliotheca. Sebast. Castalion.* saith of him, *vertit biblia ita diligenter ac summa fide ad Hebraica et Græca exemplaria &c. vt omnes omnium versiones hactenus æditas longo post se interuallo reliquisse videatur.* And *Fredericus Furius* saith, *quid de Castalionis translatione dicam? An non hic omnes interpretes, quicunq; libros sacros in latinū conuerterūt, ita vicit, vt soli ipsi prima merito deferri debeant?* See his wordes *in Sebast. Castal. defens. pag.* 236. (a) *Castal. in Nou. Test.* printed *Basileæ. Anno.* 1556. *in Luc.* 22. 20. translateth thus, *hoc poculum est nouum fædus quod fit per meum sanguinem, quod est*

Qq 2   *pro vobis pro vobis effundendum,* wherein he referreth *quod* and *effundendum,* to *poculum,* and not to *sanguinem.* (z) *Beza Annot. in Luc.* 22. 20. saith hereof, *quum hæc verba, si constructionem spectemus, necessario non ad sanguinem sed ad poculum pertineant &c.*

(a)

M. Whitaker in his answeare to *M. Raynoldes* refutation. *pag.* 210. saith, *the wordes in Luke* 22. 20. *in the greeke that Beza tranflated, by construction indeede require, that the cup is called the new Testament should be shed for vs: in which respect Beza traslateth them otherwise &c.*

(b)

Euthimius, in Luc. 22. saith, *quod vero dicitur, quod pro vobis effunditur ad poculum referrendum est.*

to the cup. And the fame is yet further affirmed by *M.* (a) *Whitaker,* and that ould greeke writer (b) *Euthimius:* In so much that *Beza* hath no other anfweare thereto, but to fay, that it is either (c) *manifeftum folecophanes, a manifeft folecophanes,* or *incongruity* in greeke, for fo doth the learned Caluinistes (d) vnderstand him, or els which he rather (e) thinketh (as being perhaps vpon better consideration abashed to charge *S. Luke* with incongruity) that it is a corruption crept into the margent, & *from thence into the text;* which latter is fo improbable and without al proofe, that his owne brother (f) *Craftonius* doth therefore deny the fame, as alfo manifeft truth enforceth *Beza* him felfe to fay to the contrary of the greeke text as it is now extāt, (g) *neuerthelesse al our old auncient bookes had*

(c) *Beza, in Annot. in nou. Testam. Anno.* 1556. (d) *Andreas Craftonius de opificio Missæ contra Bellarminum. l.* 2. *pag.* 237. faith hereof, *Beza non propter appellationem testamenti vt tu existimas, sed propter poculi effusionem solecismum inesse diuinat.* And *Daniel Camierus* in his epistola Iesuitica, parte altera. pag. 54. faith likewife hereof, *Beza censuit in ea oratione esse solecophanes, hoc est in ipsa quidem gramatica verborum constructione solacismum,* which he would fondly there afterwardes make excusable. And fee *M. Whitaker* againft *M. Saunders* rocke, *pag.* 308. and *Hospinianus in histor. facram. l.* 5. *c.* 1. *pag.* 443. faith hereof, *ad hoc responsum est iam ante a nostris, aut solacismum commissum esse a Luca, neq̨ id mirum &c. vel si hoc impium et blasphemum videtur dicere in Luca esse solæcophanes aliquod, respondetur hanc particulam* To vper vmon enchunomenon, *ex margine insertum esse in Luca contextum, vel casu perperam a librarijs (quamuis consentiant exemplaria) mutatum.* (e) *Beza in Annot. nou. Testam. Anno.* 1556. (f) *Craftonius, de opificio missæ, l.* 2. *pag.*

pag. 237. faith, *omnino autem aut folæcifmus eft, aut ex margine in contextum annotata, aut prefens pro futuro pofitum eft, duo priora non admittimus, tertium ergo relinquitur:* but this *thirde* helpeth not, for it is againft *Craftouius* and his brethren to fay of the cup, or of that which was therein contayned, that it fhould be fhed on the Croffe, for that would argue clearly againft them that Chriftes bloud was in the cup. (g) *Beza vbi fupra.* faith, *omnes tamen vetufti noftri codices ita fcriptum habebant.* and *Hofpinian.* as next before faith, *quamuis confentiant exemplaria.*

(3) And whereas our aduerfaries do further anfweare hereto that *S. Bafile* readeth as thus, (h) *in fanguine meo pro vobis effuffo,* referring fo the fheeding to the bloud, which may be referred to the Croffe: We reply, *firft,* that if *S. Bafile* had red fo, yet may not his onely priuate reading preuaile againft al other confeffed copies in general. *Secondly* we fay, that *S. Bafile* cyted not the text of the Euangeliftes but the fence, which (1) *Beza* him felfe noteth to be the often cuftome of the Fathers. *Thirdly* we fay, *S. Bafile* is not againft vs, for that in thefe forefaid wordes of his *(in fanguine meo pro vobis effufo)* it is not by him determined, but left in fence indifferent or doubtful, whether the word *fhed,* referred there to *bloud, fhould fignify the bloud fhed in the Chalice,* or on the *Croffe.* And we hope that *S. Luke* referring the fheeding thereof fo exprefly to the *cup,* is fufficient to determine that Ambiguitie. And we further fay, that *S. Bafile* him felfe vfing there the word *fhed* in the prefent tenfe, doth fo determine or reftraine the fame, as it cannot be referred to the fheeding on the *Croffe,* becaufe that fheeding was not then *prefent* but *future.* And where our aduerfaries do further vrge that to fay *the cup is fhed,* is *figuratiue,* we reply that in deede by the cup is meant, as (k) *Beza* faith, *that which was contained therein,* (*) *by a kinde of fpeach* (faith he) *common and familiar to euery language;* and therefore that this figure was fo plaine and perfpicuoufe, as ned no expofition, and is therefore impertinent; Alfo we retort this moft fully againft our aduerfaries; for whereas *Luke,* and *Paul,*

had it thus written.

(g) *Beza vbi fupra.* faith, *omnes tamen vetufti noftri codices ita fcriptum habebant.* and *Hofpinian.* as next before faith, *quamuis confentiant exemplaria.*

(h)
Bafil. in his *moral.* 21. *definit.*

(1)
Beza in prefat. in nou. Teftamentum. Anno Domini. 1556.

(k)
Beza, in Math. 26. *verf.* 28.

(*)
Vulgata et trita omnibus linguis confuetudine loquendi. Beza. ibidem.

(2) *Luc.*

faying

(2) *Luke*. 22. 20. and 1. *Cor*. 11. 25.

(3)
Hic est sanguis meus. *Math*. 26. 28. *Marc*. 14. 24.

(*)
Luc. 22. 20. and 1. *Cor*. 11. 25.

(1)
Luc. 22. 20.

(4)
To geue a breife touch of those *sundry reasons*, two thinges may be properly called by the name of *Testament*. first, the wil of the testator, disposing of the inheritance, and so it is vsed. *Hebr*. 9. 24. where it is said, *this is the bloud of the new Testament*, wherby is meant, this is the bloud whereby is established and confirmed the testament, wil, and promise of God. and according to this sence is Circumcision called *the signe of the couenant*. *Gen*. 17. 10. *Secondly*, that which is the authentical instrument contayning the wil of the testator or

saying, (2) *this cup*, are by our aduersaries affirmed, as before, to speake figuratiuely, *Mathew*, and *Marke*, saying not *this cup*, but instede therof (3) *this bloud* or *this is my bloud*, do thereby sufficiently explaine what is meant in *Luke*, and *Paul*, by *the cup*, for seeing that one and the same holy spirit speaketh here by seueral writers of one and the same thing, saying by two of them *this cup*, which is by our aduersaries confessed for an vsual and ordinary figure, signifying as *Beza* confesseth *that which was contained in the cup*, and by other two *this bloud*, or *this is my bloud*, how can it be doubtful, but that hereby the *cup*, is meant the *bloud* therein contayned, which point is also more sufficiently to the same effect explained euen by S. *Luke*, and S. *Paul* themselues, in their calling of (*) *the cup, the new Testament in his bloud*. So plainly are our aduersaries conuinced by their owne obiection.

And where our aduersaries do further obiect, that for so much as S. *Luke* speaketh figuratiuely saying, (1) *the cup is the new Testament in my bloud*, (for say they, neither the cup, nor that which was therein, whether it were bloud or wine, was the new testament) therefore his other foresaid wordes of *the cup shed for vs* are also to be taken figuratiuely; I answeare therto, first, that though I might wel affirme these wordes of S. *Luke*, *this cup is the new Testament in my bloud*, to be not figuratiue, which answeare I am forced to omit, for that the (4) *sundry reasons* therof are

by which the heire is entytled to his right, may also (and that not improperly) be called *a testament*, in this sort is the holy Bible contayning Gods wil, called the ould and new *Testament*, and so also is the

blessed

bleſſed Sacrament called *the new Teſtament,* as being the authentical
inſtrument, whereeby is aplied to vs our right of inheritance, and in
this ſort is it here by *S. Luke,* and alſo by *S. Paul.* 1. *Cor.* 11. 25.
called *the new teſtament,* and ſo alſo *Circumciſion,* which according to
the other former vnderſtanding, was properly called *the ſigne of the couenant,* is yet according to this ſence (as being the Sacrament wherby
was geuen to the *Hebrewes* their right to the land of promſe) called
in like ſort, and that properly alſo by the name of *Teſtament,* or *couenant. Eccleſiaſt.* 44. 20. *Gen.* 17. 10. 13. and ſo accordingly our
aduerſary *Iacobus Andreas,* affirmeth that *Circumciſion doth not onely ſignify the couenant, but was alſo in very deede the couenant. in confut. diſput.*

are longer then can agree with the other intended methode of this ſhorter treatiſe. yet
admitting the ſame wordes to be figuratiue,
it is neuertheleſſe inpertinent to helpe our
aduerſaries, becauſe that the ſame wordes
though admitted for figuratiue, are yet (as
is wel obſerued by our other (5) aduerſaries)
ſufficiently explained by *S. Mathew,* and
Marke, who inſteede of thoſe wordes (*this
cup is the new Teſtament in my bloud*) do explaine and ſay, (m) *this is my bloud of the new
Teſtament:* whereas none of the Euangeliſtes
explaineth or reſtrayneth the foreſaid *ſheeding,*
from *the cup.* Secondly I ſay, that howſoeuer
we graunt (which our aduerſaries ſo greedily vrge) that *S. Luke,* ſaying the *cup* was
ſhed for vs, ſpake figuratiuely, yet can this
by no expoſition that may be deuiſed be reduced to helpe them; for (to forbeare what
haith bene already (6) retorted hereupon
againſt our aduerſaries by allegation from
S. Mathew, and *Marke,* in ful explanation
of this figure, and conuincing thereby of our
aduerſaries) whereas both they, and we, do
as before, acknowledge an ordinary figure,
vnderſtanding ſo by (n) *the cup, that which
is con-*

Ioannis Iocobi Grinæi. pag.
209.

(5)
Mathias Hoe Auſtriacus,
in his *tractatus duo &c.*
tract. 2. *pag.* 185. ſaith,
*Etſi enim Lucas, et Pau-
lus ab ea locutionis formula
non nihil recedant qua Ma-
thæus, et Marcus, et quod
hi ſanguinem Teſtamenti
dicunt, illi teſtamentum in
ſanguine appellant, conſtat
tamen eandem eſſe vtrobiq,
ſententiam, nempe in cæna
verum Chriſti ſanguinem
exhiberi &c.*

(m)
Math. 26. 28. *et Marc.*
14-24.

(6)
See next heretofore in
this preſent 3. ſubdiuiſion, next after the letter
k. at the figures 2. 3.

(n)
Next *heretofore, ſudiuiſ.*
3. at

3. at the letter k.

(o)

Craſtouius, l. 2. de opificio miſſe. pag. 295. ſaith, *ſi vero Allegorica interpretatio aliam habebit interpretationem, non erit interpretatio, ſiue rei obſcura declaratio, ſed rei manifeſta obſcuratio, at ſeptem candelabra, ſeptem Eccleſiæ ſunt dixit Angelus, ſi ergo aliquis ſeptem Eccleſias allegoricæ adhuc voluerit intelligere, quis tandem eſſet finis allegoriarum.* And ſo accordingly in this other place of *Luke* if by *the cup ſhed for vs,* be ſignifyed (moſt clearly) *that which was contained in the cup.* and that this explication hereof muſt not ſtay heare, but that by this ſence alſo which is not yet ſo much as expreſſed, but onely vnderſtoode , muſt againe be yet further ſignifyed or vnderſtood *the Sarcrament of his bloud* to be

is *contained in the cup;* which as the text ſaith, was *ſhed for vs,* they wil not I hope ſay that the wine contayned in the cup was *ſhed for vs.* And if in preuention thereof our aduerſaries would enforce *a ſecond* or further figure as firſt that by *the cup,* ſhould be meant the thing therein contaiend, and then ſecondly that by this implied explication or ſence of the thing contayned in the *cup* ſo *ſhed for vs,* ſhould againe be yet further vnderſtoode *the Sacrament of his bloud,* which ſhould be afterwardes *ſhed for vs* (which hath a diſceaſe that al the tropes and figures which I haue reade are neuer able to cure) beſides that this were ouer violent or rather infinite, and (as our aduerſarie *Craſtouius* ſaith, in an other example of like pretended double figuratiue expoſition of one and the ſame wordes) *(o) were to make no end of figures:* it were yet alſo neuertheleſſe impertinent, for that the cup whereto onely the wordes *ſhed for vs,* haue for al this moſt plaine and reſpectiue referrence, & that alſo in the *preſent tenſe,* cannot (vnleſſe we inuent yet further a third & fourth figure, ſuch as neuer was heard) be reduced by this or any other conſtruction to the *Croſſe.* To conclude therefore with this point: *firſt,* our aduerſaries confeſſe (p) that the gramatical conſtruction (which they in other pointes (q) greatly reſpect) refer-

reth

ſhed for vs afterwardes vpon the Croſſe, then (as *Craſtouius* ſaith) *this were to make no end of figures.* (p) See *Beza,* and *M. Whitaker,* next heretofore *ſubdiuiſ.* 2. at the letter z. and a. In ſo much as *Euthimius* alledged there at b. affirmeth this conſtruction, and *Beza* him ſelfe, as appeareth there at c. d. thinketh it otherwiſe to be *a ſoleciſme* or in congruity . (q) *Zanchius, de ſacra Scriptura. pag.* 388. concludeth from certaine alledged examples of Scripture ſaying,

Arguitur

Aguitur ergo in omnibus ignoratio Grammaticæ, regula igitur necessaria est &c. And *Melancthon* in *l.* 1. *epistolarum.* printed 1570. *in epist. Iusto Iona.* pag. 453. faith, *exigua laus esse ducitur non falli in Grammatica, sed tamen vtilitas est amplissima &c. animaduersa enim Grammatica sententia postea mediocriter doctus videre potest ad quos locos dictum accommodari debeat.* and *ibidem.* pag. 455. he further faith, *multas enim magnas res antea inuolutas Syntaxis profert et exponit.* Also *M. Whitaker de sacra Scriptura contra Bellarminum.* controu. 1. quæst. 4. pag. 392. faith, *qui enim post Grammaticum scripturæ sensum vbiq̑, assequi,* is optime *potest proculdubio scripturas explanabit atq̑ interpretabitur.*

reth this sheeding to the cup. (2) Also this sence is agreeable with our Sauiours (r) foresaid *promise,* when he said, *the bread which I wil gene is my flesh.* (3) It agreeth likewise whith the foresaid relation of the demonstratiue *this,* which (s) pointeth not to *bread* and *wine,* but most directly to *body and bloud.* (4) It is likewise consonant with our Sauiours foresaid other saying in the present tense, (t) *is geuen for you, is shed for many.* (5) The Apostle also in his explanation maketh wholly for it, calling therefore (u) *the cup, the communication of Christes bloud.* (6) The euations which our aduersaries seeke whereby to auoide this, are enforced, racked, and miserable, and being strongly examined, can make nothing for them. (7) Our sence is so plaine, easie, and coherent, that the (x) *Lutheranes* do therefore vrge this very sheeding, referred thus by *S. Luke,* to the cup, as a strong and vnanswearable argument for their real presence. (8) The foresaid iudgement of the Fathers affirming, (7) *that our Sauiour sacrificed him selfe for vs at his last supper,* and the confessed practise of so many precedent ages and by an other Lutheran in the treatise entituled, *Comonefact. cuiusdam theolog. de sacra cæna et cius-*

(r)
See heretofore, *tract.* 2. *sect.* 3. *subd.* 1. throughout.

(s)
Heretofore, *tract.* 2. *sect.* 3. *subdiuis.* 2. and confessed there by *Carolastadius* in the margent at the figure 2. next after d.

(t)
Heretofore *tract.* 2. *sect.* 3. *subdiuis.* 2. in the margent at m. and *tract* 3. *sect.* 3. *subdiuis.* 1. in the margent at n. o. p. and *ibidem. subdiuis.* 2. at y. z.

(u)
See heretofore *tract.* 2. *sect.* 3. *subdiuis.* 3. at r. s.

(x)
It is so vrged by *Chitræus* in *l. de Baptismo, et Euchrist.* pag. 295. & 299.

R r

et eiusdem com. considerat. pag. 183. (7) See this heretofore, tract.
1. sect. 3. subdiuis. 2. at c. d. e. f. g. h. &c.

(y)
See heretofore, tract. 3.
sect. 11. subdiuis. 1. in
the margent at d. and
see further tract. 3. sect.
1. throughout.

(z)
Leo, ser. 11. de passione.

(a)
Ambrose, l. 4. de Sacra-
mentis. c. 5.

(8)
August. epist. 86. ad Ca-
sulanum.

(9)
August. in serm. ad Neo-
phitos, alledged by Iuo
saith, hoc accipite in pane
quod pependit in cruce, et
hoc accipite in calice quod
effusum est in Christi
latere.

(b)
Optatus, l. 6. contra Do-
natist. reporting their
sacriledege saith, quid est
enim Altare nisi sedes et
corporis et sanguinis Christi

ages (y) formerly proued is also agreeable
thereto. (9) And *lastly* (to omit many other
probabilities) this foresaid sence of the *cup*
being *shed* is altogether agreeable with the
Fathers speciall testimonies had of the cup in
particular. To this end S. *Leo* saith, (z) *he*
shed the iust blood, which should be both the price
and the cup to redeeme the world. S. *Ambrose*
saith, (a) *before the wordes of Christ, the cup is*
ful of wine and water, after the wordes of Christ
haue wrought, there is made (present) the blood
which redeemed the people. S. *Augustine* also
instructeth one *Vibichius*, that (8) now also
in the new Testament, no lesse then was before in the old, *we receiue blood in the cup.*
To omit the other no lesse plaine sayinges
of S. (9) *Augustine*, (b) *Optatus*, (c) *Pruden-*
tius, and (d) others. S. *Chrisostome* expounding the Apostles foresaid explication of the
cup to be the communication of Christes blood,
saith vpon those wordes, (e) *the meaning of*
them is that which is in the cup to the same which
flowed from Christes side.

And thus muh from the text to proue that
our Sauiour before his distribution of the
blessed Sacrament to his Apostles, did first
offer

&c. hac omnia furor vester, aut rasit, aut fregit, &c. fregistis etiam Calices
sanguinis Christi portatores. (c) Prudentius, in Peristephanion himn.
2. reporteth how the Tyrant insulted against the holy martir S. Lau-
rence, saying to him, Hunc esse vestris orgiis morem atq́, artem proditum
est, hanc disciplinam foederis habent vt auro Antistites, argenteis Cyphis ferunt libens
fumare sacrum sanguinem. (d)) Theophilact. in Marc. 14. saith,
Christi autem corpus proprie est quod in disco aureo, et sanguis qui in poculo.
(e) Chrisostomus in 1. Cor. hom. 24. saith, eorum (verborum) huiusmodi

modi et sententia hoc est in calice quod e latere fluxit. & *ibidem hom. 27.* he
further faith, *in veteri testamento post sacrificium, sanguinem in calice accipi-*
ebant, brutoru sanguine suu in Calicem (Christus) induxit, et meminit noui
Testamenti, vt opponeret sanguini veteris testamenti qui offerebatur insacrificio.
et ita sacrificabant pro sanguine ~~testis~~

ita sacrificabant pro sanguine

offer it in sacrifice to God (f) *teaching* so
thereby as *Ireneus* faith, *the new oblation of the*
new Testament, which his said offering thereof in sacrifice to God at his last supper as it
is (g) *heretofore* directly and in plaine tearmes
affirmed further by *S. Ciprian, Chrisostome,*
Gregory, Niscene, Hesichius, &c. So likewise
(ouer and besides that which *S.* (*) *Luke* testifyeth of the Apostles) the answearable
practise of the ancient Fathers in offering the
same in like maner to God in euery age since
Christes time, is so plaine and euident, that
it is (h) therefore fully confessed by *Caluin,*
the *Centurie writers,* and sundry other learned Protestantes.

(f) *Ira. l. 4. c. 32.* faith,
eum qui ex creatura panis
est accepit et gratias egit di-
cens hoc est corpus meum,
et calicem similiter &c. sa-
guine suu cofessus est et noui
testam. noua decuit oblatione
&c. (g) See this hertofore
tract. 1. sect. 3. subduis.
2. at c. d. e. h. i. k. l.
(*) *S. Luke, Act. 13. 2.*
faith of the Apostles,
Leitourgounton de auton to
curio cai nesteuonton; a
place so euident that *E-*
rasmus translateth it, sacri-
ficantibus illis Domino et ieiunantibus, while they were doing sacrifice to our
Lord and fasting. And truly the Greeke word *Leiturgia,* doth not signify an internal or priuate minnistery, but as *Melancthon in A-*
polog. confes. August. c. de vocabulis missa. fol. 213. faith, *Lyturgia*
significat publicum ministerium, it signifyeth the Churches publicke ministery, and the same, not in respect of preaching the word, and administring Sacramentes, for neither is the word preached, nor Sacramentes administred vnto God, but to the people, whereas yet the action of ministery here mecioned is directed onely *to the Lord.* And
it wil not suffice our aduersaries to say, that these also are ministred
to *the Lord,* because they are done though to the people, yet in
honor of him; for if this were the proper reason of *S. Lukes* speach,
why then did he in this place ad *fasting,* and the same also without direction thereof to the Lord, nay why did he so much as at al mencion
it, considering that according to the other sence, it was already then
before sufficiently expressed rather then implied in the other foresaid
ministring *to the Lord,* for according vnto that sence to fast to the
Lord, is to minister to the Lord, and so the Apostle faith, *he that*

eateth, eateth to our Lord, and he that eateth not, eateth not to our Lord.
Rom. 14.6. This point is ſo euident that the Greeke Fathers haue
thereupon made the word *Lyturgie* as proper to ſacrifice in the greeke
Church, as the word *Maſſe* ſignifyeth the ſame in the latine Church.
the *Liturgies* of S. *Iames*, *Baſile*, and *Chriſoſtome*, ſignifying the ſame
as properly with them, as the *Maſſes* of *Ambroſe*, and *Gregory*, do
with vs, whereas yet the other publicke functions whether of adminiſtring the word, or the Sacraments, though being publicke actions,
were not yet for al that knowen or tearmed by the name of *Liturgies*, no
more thē in the latin Church they were knowen or tearmed by the name
of *Maſſe*. (h) See this heretofore, *tract. 3. ſect. 2. ſubdiuiſ. 3.* at r.
s. t. x. y. h. i. k. and *ibidem. ſubdiuiſ. 1.* at q.

(i)
Hebr. 9. 20.
(k)
Luc. 22. 20.
(l)
Math. 26. 28.
(*)
Geſnerus, in diſput. 9.
pag. 208. ſaith, *in vete-*
ri teſtamento &c. cum po-
pulus Deo iurabat ſangui-
nem offerebat &c. et cum
vice eiſa verſa, Deus cum popu-
lo paciſcebatur eodem illo
ſanguine populus conſperge-
batur, atꝗ ita verum erat
quod Sacerdos dicebat, hic
eſt ſanguis teſtamenti ſeu
fœderis quod pepigit vobiſ-
cum Deus: eodem modo in
nouo fœdere res habet, et

(4) Hereunto I wil breifly ad the great
coreſpondence that is betweene the wordes
of inſtitution of the ſacrifice of the old law,
and our Euchariſt ; for like as *Moyſes* in the
firſt ſacrifice of the dedication of the old law,
did put bloud into the goblet, ſayıng withal
theſe formal wordes, (i) *this is the bloud of*
the Teſtament which God haith appointed vnto you.
So our Sauionr in like manner in his promulgation of the new Teſtament ſaid ouer his
cup, (k) *this cup is the new Teſtament in my*
bloud, or as (l) *Mathew* ſaith almoſt in *Moy-*
ſes wordes, *this is my bloud of the new teſtament*
which is ſhed for many. So anſwearably it is
(as our aduerſary (*) *Geſnerus* hereupon obſerueth that the new teſtament was as (m)
Tertulian, & *Chriſoſtome*, do ſignify) begunne,
and dedicated in our Sauiours bloud contained in the Chalice, no leſſe truly then was
the

niſi adſit ſanguis fœdus fieri et ſanciri non poteſt, proinde cum Chriſtus dicit
hunc eſſe ſanguinem noui teſtamenti, ſequitur duplici reſpectu ſanguinem Chriſti
in cœna adeſſe primum eo quo nos cum Deo paciſcimur, deinde eo quo Deus
remiſſionem peccatorum nobis offert et exhibet, quorum neutrum ſine interue-
niente ſanguine fieri poteſt: Ac ſi Iſraelita non poterint ſine ſanguine cum Deo
paciſci

pacisci imo non audebant sine sanguine in conspectum Dei venire quantum magis nobis opus est sangine quando ad Thronum gratiæ accedere volumus &c. sine quo (Christi sanguine in cæna) nec Deus nobiscum pacisci et remissionem peccatorum exhibere et applicare, nec nos cum Deo possumus. And to the like effect see *Mathias Hoe,* (an other Proteftant writer) *in trct. duo &c. tract.* 2. *pag.* 185. and 186. (m) *Tertulian, l.* 4. *contra Marcionem* faith, *in Calicis mentione testamentum suum constituit sanguine suo obsignatum.* and *Chrisostom. in* 1. *Cor. hom.* 27. accordingly, *quid significat hic calix nouum testamentum est? In veteri testamento post sacrificium sanguinem in calice accipiebant, et ita sacrificabant, pro sanguine brutorum, sanguinem suum (in calicem Christu) induxit et meminit noui testamenti vt opponeret sanguini veterio testamenti qui offerebatur in sacrificio.*

the old law begun and dedicated (2) in the bloud of calues, for this title of *the new testament* being thus plainly referred, not to Baptifme, but onely to the Euchariſt, and withal ſo manifeſtly matched or oppoſed with like reſemblance of wordes to the other former dedication of the old teſtament, it is thereby euident that the Euchariſt was inſtituted as the proper external ſacrifice of the *new teſtament,* no leſſe truly then were the other ſacrifices of the law inſtituted for the proper ſeruice of the old. As for the ſacrifice of our Sauiours death vpon the Croſſe, though it be the moſt perfect and ſoueraigne conſummation of either teſtament as being common to both, and geuing al grace, and working to either in their kind, yet was not it ſo apointed to be the proper cotinued external ſeruice of *the teſtament* as appeareth manie wayes, *firſt,* in that it was not called *the new teſtament,* as was moſt expreſly the Euchariſt. *Secondly,* in that our Sauiour at his ſufferinges vpon the Croſſe did not ſo much as then mencion or profeſſe to make or didicate his *new teſtament,* which thing yet he did moſt plainly in his inſtitution of the Euchariſt, and that alſo (for

(2)
Habr. 9. 12. 18. 19. 20.

(3)
For where there is a teſtament, the death of the teſtator muſt of neceſſity come betweene, for a teſtament is confirmed in the deade being yet of no value whiles he that made the teſtament is a liue. Habr. 9. 16. 17.

(4)
Muſculus, in locis com. cap. de cæna Dom. num. 2. faith, *Chriſt in his laſt ſupper being neare his death made his teſtamet &c. to the confirmation & ratifying of a teſtament, is required the death of the teſtator*

R r 3 more

testator, *so Christ the next day after the testament was made, dyed on the Crosse &c.* And see the like affirmed by *Bullingers* Decades in englilh. pag. 1064.

(5)
Hereof see the Fathers, alledged hereafter, *tract. 3. sect. 5. subdiuis. 4.* in the margent vnder the letter e. and heretofore *tract. 3. sect. 3. subdiuis. 1.* next after m. in the margent at *.

(6)
See heretofore, *tract. 3. sect. 1. subdiuis. 1.* in the margent at g.

(7)
See heretofore, *tact. 3. sect. 1. subdiuis. 1.* in the margent at the letter m.

(8)
See there in the margent at n.

(9)
See heretofore, *tract. 1. sect. 3. subdiuis. 2.* at e. f. g. h. &c.

(10)
Chrisost. in 1. Cor. hom. 24.

perspicuity) euen with allufió or refemblance to the very fame wordes almoft wherewith *Moyses* dedicated the old. *Thirdly,* in that the (3) Apoftle him felfe fpeaking hereof fignifyeth moft pertinently and plainly that *the testament* which our Sauiour inftituted, was precedent to his death vpon the Croffe, and was therefore fo by him in his faid death *confirmed* rather then inftituted, which thing is also in like manner acknowledged by learned (4) Proteftantes: vpon al which it ineuitably followeth that our facrifice of the Eucharift (which our Sauiour in his inftitution of *the new testament* ordained to (5) continue and apply to vs our redemption by him wrought vpon the Croffe) is (as the Fathers (6) affirme) *a true facrifice,* euen (7) *the facrifice of the new testament,* which (8) *fucceeded al the facrifices of the old testament.* And that our Sauiour (9) *facrifycing him felfe in the fupper of the Apoftles* (did thereby) (10) *chaunge the* (former old) *facrifice, and with al infteede of brute beaftes* (fo before time) *killed in facrifice, commaunded him felfe to be offered.* So properly and truly is our Eucharift a facrifice, no leffe then were the former facrifices of the old teftament; which thing appeareth as yet otherwife more manifeftly in that the Apoftles doubted not vpon this ground, not onely to compare or match our *Eucharift* with the facrifices of the *Hebrewes,* and *Gentiles,* and our *table* with their *Altar* faying.
touching

And *Leo, serm. 7. de passione Dom.* speaking of our Sauiours inftitution of the Sacrament after his celebration of the pafcal lambe faith likewife, *the old obferuance is taken away by the new Sacrament* (hostia in hostiam transit) *one facrifice paffeth into another,* (sanguis excludit sanguinem) *one bloud excludeth an other, and the legal ceremony*

ceremony while it is chaunged is fulfilled. And *Hesichius in Leuit . l . 2 .*
c . 8. faith, *Christ at his last supper hauing first eaten the figuratiue lambe*
with his Apostles, afterwardes offered his owne sacrifice. et vide . l . 6 . c . 23 .
and fee *Augustine in Psal . 33 . con . 2.* alledged hereafter *tract . 3 .*
sect . 4. subdiuis . 1. in the margent vnder the letter d. And fee *Au-*
gustine epist . 86 . ad Casulanum . And fee further heretofore, *tract . 3 .*
sect . 1 . subdiuis . 1 . in the
margent at n.

touching the Hebrewes (n) *are not they which*
eate the sacrifice pertakers of the Altar? And
concerning the Gentiles *the* (o) *thinges which*
the Gentiles offer, in sacrifice they do to deuils, and
therefore (p) *you may not be pertakers of the*
Lords table, and the table of deuiles . but also
further profecuteth the fame argument of di-
fwading *the Hebrewes* from their rites and facrifices by the forefaid example of ours ,
whereof they might not be pertakers if they
frequented the other, to which end he faith,
(q) *wee haue an* (*) *Altar whereof they may*

(n)
1 . *Cor* . 10 . 18 .
(o)
1 . *Cor* . 10 . 20 .
(p)
1 . *Cor* . 10 . 21 .
(q)
Hæbr . 13 . 10 .
(*)
So did *Ignatius*, the A-
postles owne scholer *in*
epist . ad Philadelph . vfe

the very fame word, and which is more, did with al refer it to the
table, wereupon the Sacrament is celebrated as is confessed by *M .*
Iacob in his reafons &c. *pag . 58* . As also *Dionisius Areopagita* conuerted by *Paul, Act . 17 . 34* . whose writinges are proued heretofore *in præfat* . to the reader. *sect . 5 . 6 . 7 .* &c. doth in like manner
in his *c . 4 . de Ecclesiastica Hierarchia* . mencion not onely the *Alter*
whereupon the Eucharist is celebrated, but also *the consecration thereof*
with infusion of holy oyle. And *S . Gregory Nazianzen in Iulianum*, doth
accordingly most pertinently mencion and affirme *Alters receiuing their*
name from the most pure and vnbloudy sacrifice, for (as *D . Raynoldes* in his
conference &c. *pag . 572* . confesseth *Altar and sacrifice are by nature*
linked together in relation and mutual dependance . And therefore the A-
postle mencioning fo plainly in this place our *Altar*, doth withal thereby proue our facrifice. And where our aduerfaries would here
(according to their owne wont) turne al to figures, vnderstanding
againft fo euident premifes by the word *Altar*, not a material but a
metaphorical and fpiritual *Altar*, the Apostle mencioning in this place
not onely our *Altar*, but withal alfo our *eating*, or *parting thereof*,
(which

(which like phrase he vseth in his like mencioning elswhere the *Altar* of the old Testament. 1. *Cor*. 9. 13. and 1. *Cor*. 10. 18. alluding also therein to the like pertaking of (our) *table*. 1. *Cor*. 10. 21. doth thereby explaine him selfe as yet more fully, to meane aswel in this place as he doth in the other, an external and proper *Altar*.

(2)

In præfatione operis Vrbani Regij de prophetijs veteris Testamenti. and *operum part. 3. fol. 78.*

(3)

Vrbanus Regius 1. part. *operum de missa negotio. fol. 65.* saith, *manie there are who thinke a sacrifice to be proued by the Apostle. 1. Cor. 10. where he dehorteth from the society of such as sacrifice to Idols by argumentes taken from the faith of the sacrifice vsed by the Iewes and Gentiles, for he seemeth to compare sacrifice to sacrifice, as Chrisostome teacheth, and his comparison so to stand, that by it is gathered Christians in the Lords supper, to haue a certaine peculiar sacrifice, whereby they are made pertakers of our Lord,*

may not eate who serue the tabernacle ; which foresaid frequent opposition or matching of our *Eucharist* with the *sacrifices* of the Hebrewes and the heathen, and of our *Altar* with theirs , the Apostle most euidently vrgeth as being proportionable betweene *Altar* and *Altar*, *sacrifice* and *sacrifice* which thing that learned Protestant *Vrbanus Regius* reputed for a man of *infinite* (2) *learning* , (and) *the Euangelist and cheife superintendent of the Churches of Christ in the duchy of Luneburge,* doth plainly (3) acknowledge rather then deny : And thus much breifly from the writinges of the new Testament.

That the Scriptures of the old Testament are likewise agreeable thereto.

SECTION. 4.

ANd for so much as according to *S. Augustines* saying, (1) *our sacrifice receiueth demonstration, not onely from the Euangelical*

as the Idolaters by their abhominable *sacrifice, are made pertakers of diuels* ; which thing if it be so, me seemeth it may be answeared, that in the supper of Christians are the *body and bloud of Christ, which are a holy sacrifice but commemoratiue,* so plainly doth he acknowledge the Eucharist to be though a *commemoratiue,* yet a *true sacrifice,* no lesse truly and properly then were the sacrifices vsed by the Iewes during the old Testament, which were neuerthelesse true sacrifices though they weare *commemoratiue*

tiue in respect of Christes passion then to come, as ours is now likwise a true sacrifice & yet *comemorautiue*, in reguard of his passió alreadypast. (1) *August . epist .49. quæst . 3 .* saith, *nostrum sacrificium non solum Euangelicis , sed etiam Propheticis libris demostratũ est.*

gelical, *but also from the Prophetical writinges :* I could, as heretofore from the writinges of the new Testament, so likewise make further proofe thereof from the predictions of the old . To geue onely a breife touch or taist of them : *First* then concerning *Melchisadech ,* (2) *of whom the Apostle had great speach to vtter which he omitteth as being* (3) *inexplicable because the Hebrewes were become weake to heare :* it is yet thus far confessed as that he was (s) *a Preist,* that also (which thing the Apostle (t) proueth) (u) *he offered sacrifice,* and no sacrifice of his can be named other then when (x) *bringing forth bread and wine ,* to the refection of Abraham, he first (as both the *Rabines* and *Fathers* do (4) testify) offered the same in sacrifice to God being therefore thereupon called (y) *the Preist of the most high God*

(2)
Habr . 5 . 11 .
(3)
Habr . 5 . 11 . whereupon *S. Hierome , epist . 126 .* saith, *he spake to the Hebrewes , that is to the Iewes, and not to the faithful men to whom he might haue beene bould to vtter the Sacrament .*
(s)
Gen . 14 . 18 . and *Psal . 109 . 4 . et Habr . 5 . 6. et 7 . 17 .*
(t)
Euery high Preist is ordained to offer sacrifice . Habr .

5 . 1 . et 8 . 3 . (u) *M. Whitaker* in his answeare to *M. William Raynoldes . pag . 63 .* saith, *we neuer denyed but that Melchisadech execu ted the office of a Preist which cheisly consisteth in sacrifice .* and *ibidem. pag . 409 . post med. I say no doubt Melchisadech did sacrifice otherwise he had beene no Preist.* And see *M . Bilson* in his true difference, part . 4 . pag . 513 . (x) *Gen . 14 . 18 .* (4) *Rabby Samuel in c . 14 . Gen .* saith herof, *he setteth forth the actes of Preisthood for he was sacrifycing bread & wine to God & Rabby . Phinees* saith, *at the time of Messias al sarifices shal cease, but the sacrifice of the bread and wine shal not cease, as it is said . Gen . 14 . &c.* and *Melchisadeches* sacrifice in bread and wine is yet further testifyed by *Rabby, Moyses, Hadarsan, in Bereschit Rabba, ad c . 14 . Gen .* As concerning the *Fathers , M . Fulke* against *Heskines, Saunders &c . pag . 99 .* saith, *I confesse that diuers of the old Fathers were of opinion that the bread and wine brought forth by Melchisadech was sacrifyced by him .* And see him against the Rhemish Testament in *Habr . c . 7 . sect . 8 . fol . 405 .* and the same is no lesse plainly confessed by *M . Whitaker contra Duræum .*

l. 9. *pag.* 818. *et* 819. and by *Caluin. in coment. in Habr. c.* 7.
(y) *Gen.* 14. 18.

(z)
Psal. 109. 4. and see further hereof hereafter *tract.* 3, *sect.* 5. *subdiuis.* 3. in the magent at *. next after h.

(5)
Habr. 5. 1. *et* 8. 3.

(a)
Oechumenius, in c. 5. *ad Habr.* saith hereof, *non ad ipsam tantum qua a Deo semel facta est hostiam et oblationem dixit, in aeternum, sed ad nostri temporis Sacerdotes inspiciens per quos Christus et sacrificat et sacrificatur.*

(6)
Arnobius ~~Ambrose~~ *in Psal.* 109. saith, *per misterium panis et vini factus est Sacerdos in aeternum secundum ordinem Melchisadech.*

God. And for so much now as our Sauiour was foretould to be a (z) *Preist for euer according to the order of Melchisadech, and that* (5) *euery high Preist is ordained to offer sacrifice:* This title therfore of *a Preist for euer* argueth a sacrifice according to that order which must continue and be offered for euer; and therefore cannot as *Oecumenius* (a) obserueth appertaine to him, in reguard of his blouddy sufferinges vpon the Crose, because that those were, though in virtue and efficacie *permanent*, yet in action of sacrifice, but transitory and now past, and had also no resemblance to any sacrifice mecioned to be offered by *Melchisadech*; therefore the foresaid title *of a Preist for euer &c.* was geuen him onely in (6) respect of the Churches (7) *dayly sacrifice* of the Eucharist, offered continually vnder the formes of bread and wine, which *Melchisadech* himselfe vsed in his foresaid (8) *onely sacrifice.* This demonstration is so euident that it is acknowledged for true by the *Iewish* (b) *Rabines* and also by the

(7) Of the Eucharist being called by the Fathers, *the dayly sacrifice.* see heretofore, *tract.* 3. *sect.* 1. *subdiuis.* 1. in the margent at h.
(8) *Onely sacrifice,* for there is no testimony in Scripture of any other sacrifice vsed by *Melchisadech.* In so much as *Euseb. demonst. Euang. l.* 5. *c.* 3. saith hereof, *quemadmodum Melchisadech Sacerdos gentium nusquam videtur corporalibus sacrificiis functus, sed vino solo et pane &c.* (b) *Theodorus Bibliander,* a learned Protestant *l.* 2. *de summa Trinitate. pag.* 89. after the *Basile,* print, 1555. confesseth this in the Rabbines saying, *erat apud veteres Hebraeos dogma receptissimum, in aduentu Messiae cessatura esse omnia legalia sacrificia, tantumq, celebrandum sacrificium thodah. gratiarum actionis &c. et illud peragendum pane et vino, sicut Melchisadech &c. panem et vinum protulit.* And see *Rabby Phinees vt supra.*

(c) M.

the (c) *auncient Fathers*, who doubt not hereupon to affirme (d) *the sacrifice of Christes body and bloud* (in the Eucharist) *according to the order of Melchisadech.* In so much that whereas our aduersaries are not abashed to teach that (e) *Melchisadeches bread and wine pertaineth not to his Preisthood, neither did he offer it to God,* also that (f) *Melchisadech did not by any thing, wherein he so sacrificed, prefigure the sacrifice and Preisthood of Christ.* *Andræas Crastouius* a learned Caluinist (and by *M. Sutliue*

(c)
M. Fulke againſt *Heskins, Saunders &c. pag.* 100. saith, *it is graunted that Ciprian thought the bread and wine brought forth by Melchisadech to be a figure of the Sacrament, and that her ein also he resembled the Preisthood of Christ.* And againſt the Rhemiſh Teſtament, *in Habr. c. 7.*

fol. 405. he saith, *manie auncient Fathers without ground of Scripture sought a resemblance of the bread and wine which Melchisadech brought forth, vnto the bread & wine which Christ instituted &c.* And see this point further confessed by Caluin, *in omnes Pauli epistolas, in Habr. c. 7. vers. 9. pag.* 924. where he saith, *quo magis tot veteres Ecclesiæ doctores hac opinione occupatos fuisse miror, vt in oblationem panis et vini insisterant, sic autem loquuntur, Christus Sacerdos est, secundũ ordinē Melchisadech atqui panē et vini Melchisadeh obtulit, ergo panis et vini sacrificiũ sacerdotio Christi cõuenit.* (d) *S. Aug. de ciuit. l.* 17. *c.* 20. *circa med.* saith, *agnoscimus Dei sapientiã &c. mensam in vino et panibus preparasse vbi apparet etiam sacerdotiũ secundũ ordinem Melchisadech &c. quam* (*mensam*) *Sacerdos ipse mediator Testamenti noui, exhibet, secundum ordinem Mechisadech de corpore et sanguine suo, id enim sacrificium successit omnibus illis sacrificijs veteris testamenti, quia pro omnibus illis sacrificijs corpus eius offertur, et participantibus ministratur.* and againe in *Psal.* 33. *conc.* 2. alluding to the history of *Dauid* chaunging his countenance in the sight of king *Achis.* 1. *Reg.* 21. 13. mencioneth our Sauiours chaunging of the sacrifice of the old Testament saying of him, *coram regno Patris sui mutauit Christus vultum suum et dimisit eum et abijt, quia erat ibi sacrificium secundum ordinem Aaron, et postea ipse de corpore et sanguine suo instituit sacrificium secundum ordinem Melchisadech; mutauit ergo vultum suum in sacerdotio et dimisit gentem Iudæorum.* And *S. Ciprian,* speaking of the Sacrament, *l.* 2. *epist.* 3. *paulo post med.* saith, *in sacerdote Melchisadech sacrificij Dominici Sacramentum prefiguratum videmus secundum quod Scriptura diuina testatur, et dicit, et Melchisadech rex Salem protulit panem et vinum &c. et obtulit* (*Christus*) *hoc idem quod Melchisadech obtulerat, id est panem et vinum,*

suum

ſuum, ſcilicet corpus et ſanguinem.   (e)   *M . Fulke* againſt the Rhemiſh Teſtament, *in Hæbr.* 7. *ſect.* 8. *fol.* 406. and *M . Willet* in his ſinop-ſis, *pag.* 478.   (f)   *M . Whitaker* in his anſweare to *M . Raynoldes,* pag . 67. and *M . Willet* in his ſinopſis, *pag.* 478.

(*)

M . Sutliue de miſſa Papi- | *liue* greatly (*) commended) acknowled-
ſtica &c . printed 1603. | ging in his treatiſe thereof againſt *Bellarmine*
l . 5. *c .* 16. *fol.* 161. | this other foreſaid general conſent (g) of the
ſaith, *Craſtouius vir pius et* | Fathers to the contrary, haith vpon a ſecond
doctus magno volumine ac- | and better coſideration yealded thereupon
curate de hac re edito &c . | ſo far as to acknowledge likewiſe againſt
(g) | his other brethren that (h) *Melchiſadech did*
Andræas Craſtouius de opi- | *ſacrifice bread and wine,* and therein (i) *prefigu-*
ficio miſſæ . l . 1 . *ſect.* 66. | *red the Euchariſt,* that alſo the Euchariſt *is pro-*
pag . 28. ſaith hereof, | *perly* (k) *a ſacrifice,* an (l) *external ſacrifice,* and
conſenſum porro et interpre- | (m) *a ſacrifice according to the order of Melchiſa-*
tationis harmoniam Chiſti- | *dech:* to which his opinion (*) *Martin Lu-*
anis Paſtoribus abijcere non | *ther,* M . (n) *Iewel,* and (o) *Melancthon ,*
licet idq̃, cum propter A - | ſeeme

poſtolici ſeculi vicinitatem tum *propter ſingularem omnium concordiam &c .* hic *omnium veluti conſpiratione oblatio Melchiſadechi ſacra proponitur vt non tantum Abrahæ militibuſq̃, ſed etiam Deo incruentum ſacrificium ſimbolice oblatum videatur .* and preſently after he preuenteth our aduerſaries com-mon obiection from the Fathers, ſaying, *quod ſi quibuſdam non-nulli doctores Melchiſadechum panem et vinum Abrahæ dediſſe aſſerunt primariam tamen illam oblationem quæ fit Deo non negant .*   (h)   *Chra-ſtouius de opificio miſſæ . l .* 1 . *ſect .* 66. *pag .* 28.   (i)   *Craſtouius, ib -ſect .* 217. *pag .* 119. *et ſect.* 289 . *pag .* 162 .   (k)   *Ibidem .ſect.* 119. *pag .* 51. *ſacrificium proprie dictum ſignificat et pag .* 162. *et ſect.* 132. *pag .* 60.   (l)   *Ibidem . pag .* 162. and *pag .* 51 .   (m)   *Ibidem . pag .* 58. and 102 . and *ſect .* 302 . *pag .* 171.   (*)   *Luther, ad Pſal .* 110. *tom .* 8. *fol .* 579 . ſaith, *Melchiſadech rex erat et Sacerdos, obtulit panem et vinum etiam pro Patriarcha Abraham et eius familia &c . quid eſt vero ob-latio panis et vini pro Abrahamo? Hoc exprimit ſacerdotium Chriſti ab hoc tempore vtq̃, finem mundi, quo myſticum Altaris ſacramentum pratioſi corpo-ris et ſanguinis ſui offert Eccleſia .* See this thus alledged by *Coccius* in his *Theſaurus &c . tom .* 1. *pag .* 1051.   (n)   *M . Iewel* in his reply, art . 2. *diuiſ .* 5. in *M . Whitakers* tranſlation *pag .* 9. And ſee alſo *M .*

Iewels

Iewels reply in englifh, pag. 7. where he acknowlegeth, that *Melchifadech by his bread and wine fignifyed the facrifice of the holy communion.* and fee *Illiricus in Habr. c. 17.* (o) *Melancthon in concil. theolog. part. 2. pag. 373.* faith, *excipit Melchifadech redeuntem ex prelio Abraham et eum ad facrificium admittit, eig̃ benedicit.*

(p)

feeme for to encline : fo euidently is the Catholicke doctrine of the Maffe eftablifhed in Gods iuft iudgement by thofe very aduerfaries who moft impugne the fame ; as *firft,* by *Luther,* and the *Lutheranes,* who not by ouerfight but after frequent (p) difputation and confideration had of our aduerfaries reafons made to the contrary, do acknowledge the real prefence, as a truth moft manifeft and not to be (q) doubted of, and that our Sauiours wordes are to be take litterally. *Secondly,* by *M.* (r) *Latimer,* the diuines of (s) *Genena,* (t) & *others,* who affirme that therupon trafubftantiation, adoration, and facrifice, do necefarily follow ; in fo much as *D. Barnes,* one of their *martires,* did at the time of his death openly

Hereof fee *Conradus Sclufelburg. in catal. haret. l. 13. et vlt. pag. 835. 836.* and 837. and *M. Couper* in his Cronicle, *fol. 290.* And fee *Iacobus Andraas his epitom. Colloq. Montisbelgar.*

(q)

See *Luther, l. verborum can.* This point is made manifeft in diuers hundreth feueral treatifes written by *Luther,* & the *Lutheranes,* againft the *Caluiniftes.* (r) *Latimer in Act. mon. pag.*

981. faith, *I neuer could perceiue how Luther could defend his opinion without trafubftantiation.* (s) *The diuines of Genena,* in their *Apolog. modefta ad acta conuentus quindecim theologorum torga nuper habit. pag. 18.* fay, *fi fimpliciter accipiantur verba Chrifti confequi necefario tranfubftantiationis delirium & reliquas idololatria fpecies necefe eft.* (t) See *Caluin, l. contra Weftphalum* and *Beza l. contra Hefhutium,* alfo *Grinaus* in the treatife entituled, *confut. difput. Ioan. Iocobi Grinai, autbore Iacobo Andraa pag. 279.* faith, *fcriptum in verbis Domini, fi quis fequatur papiftica potius tranfubftantiatio quam confubftantiatio confirmabitur.* And the learned Proteftant *Eufebius Altkircherus, de miftico et incruento Ecclefia facrificio aduerfus abominandam pontificia miffa fuperftitionem.* printed *Neuftadij Palatinorum.* 1584. *pag. 2.* faith, *ex hoc fundamento (corporalis prefentia & manducationis) necefario tam adorationem quam oblationem corporis et fanguinis Chrifti in facrificium confequi et concedi oportere.* And *ibidem. pag. 3.* he alledgeth in further proofe hereof, *Melancthon,* recyting thefe his

wordes

wordes *nisi tollatur realis coniunctio corporis cum pane nullum super esse firmum & solidum fundamentum contra Pontificiorum argutias quibus receptissimum suum in sacrificando morem ornare & fucare possint, nam si Christus inclusus continetur in pane, cur adorandus et offerendus non esset?* thus far *Melancthon.* And see heretofore, *tract. 2. sect. 9. subdiuis. 2.* in the margent at *. next after b.

(u)
The wordes of *D. Bar-nes* at his death were, *I declared and said that the Sacrament being rightly v-sed according to the Scrip-ture, doth after the word spoken by the Preist chaunge the substance of the bread and wine into the very body and bloud of Christ; were not these my wordes saith he, yes said M. Pope, then beare me witnesse that I erre not in the Sacrament.* these wordes of *D. Bar-nes* being in *the protesta-tion of Robert Barnes &c.* published at that time by one of his followers, and yet extant in *the re-proofe* of the same then written and published by *D. Standish,* are frau-dulently omitted by *M. Foxe, act. mon. pag. 611.* who omitting this, alled geth al the residue (both before & after) of the said protestation *verbatim.*

openly professe to beleeue (u) the doctrine of *transubstantiation.* *Thirdly,* by *Crastouius,* as learned (as the best of them) who (toge-ther with *M. Iewel*) acknowledgeth it as be-fore to be properly *a sacrifice,* which foresaid *three* seueral conclusions, thus acknowledged by our learned aduersaries, do comprehend in them the very ful essence of our Catho-licke Masse.

(2) *Secondly,* the Prophet *Malachie* spea-king in the person of God to the Prestes of the old law, foretelleth the reiecting of their sacrifice saying, (x) *I haue no pleasure in you, saith the Lord of hostes, neither wil I accept any offering at your handes:* and foretelling then after the sacrifice of the new Testament, he saith, (y) *from the rysing of the sunne to the go-ing downe thereof my name is great among the Gentiles and in euery place incense shal be offered to my name and a pure oblation &c.* I am not ignorant that our aduersaries, not being able to deny this *pure* oblation to be by the Pro-phet meant of the time of the new Testament, do yet seeke to euade in (z) answearing that the Prophet in this place speaketh not pecu-liarly of our Prestes, nor of a sacrifice to be offered onely by them, but of al Christians ingeneral

(x) *Malach. 1. 10.* (y) *Malach. 1. 11.* (z) *M. Bilson* in his true difference be-tweene Christian subiection, and Antichristian rebellion, *part. 4. pag. 517.* and *M. Fulke* against *M. Heskins, Saunders &c. pag. 121.*

and

ingeneral and of the spiritual sacrifices of prayer and thankes-geuing which they offer vnto God, being therefore called (a) *a holy Preisthood to offer vp spiritual sacrifices acceptable to God.* But the answeare (being directly against (2) *S. Chrisostome* is false and many waies defectiue; for it appeareth: *First,* that the Prophet directed his foresaid speach of reiecting the Iewish sacrifices not to the people of the old Testament ingeneral, but onely to the *Preistes* beginning his discourse, (b) *o you Preistes that dispise my name &c. you offer vncleane bread vpon my Altar.* And therupon then foretelleth as before, the reiecting of their sacrifice, and his allowance in steede thereof, of the new and *pure oblation* of the new Testament: by which opposition of the Prophet thus plainly signifyed, he must in al due proportió be thought to meane that as in reiecting the Preistes of the old law, & their *sacrifice,* he spoke not of al the people ingeneral, but onely of Preistes in special, and of their external sacrifices so reiected. So likewise in his prediction of *a pure oblation* (3) *to succeede* in place of the other, he meant in like manner (4) *an external worship* or sacrifice to be offered, not by al Christians in common, but (as was before in the old Testament) by peculiar order of people therto specially appointed. This point is so euident and agreeable with the circumstance of the text, that *Andræas Crastouius* a learned Caluinist doth therefore acknowledge (c) the same.

and 122. And *M. Whitaker contra Duræum l. 9. pag. 753. and *M. Bel* in his suruey of Poperie, part. 3. c. 10. pag. 469.

(a)
1. Pet. 2. 5.

(2)
See *S. Chrisostomes* wordes next hereafter in the margent at n.

(b)
Malach. 1. 6.

(3)
Aug. de ciuit. Dei, l. 17. c. 20. post. med. saith, *ad participationem mensæ huius pertinet quam sacerdos ipse mediator noui Testamenti exhibet secumdum ordinem Melchisadech de corpore et sanguine suo id enim sacrificium successit omnibus illis sacrificijs veteris Testamenti &c. quia pro illis omuibus sacrificijs corpus eius offertur et participantibus ministratur.*

(4)
Caluin in his disputation with the Iewes extant in *Ioannes Buxdorfius.* his *sinagoga Iudaica, pag. 555.* saith hereof, *Malachias quoq, discrimen locorum tollens ait quod in locis omnibus nomini diuino suffit us sacrificiumq, purum cibarium fieri debeat; whereof he inferreth, that thereby* mutatio cultus externi sub Christo regnante plane clareq, persignificata fuerit. And see the same in Caluines latine epistles pag. 683. (c)

Crastouius.

Craftouius, l. 1. de opificio missæ, sect. 132. et pag. 60. saith concerning this place of Malachie, Antithesis profecto sacerdotum, eiusmodi proprie dictum sacrificium hoc loco requirit. And see him farther acknowleging *Malachies* prophecy *to be meant of the Eucharist, sect. 139. and 144. and 127.*

(d)
See D. *Raynoldes* conference &c. *pag. 546.* And the english bible of **1576.** in the contentes and marginal notes of the 3. chapter of *Malachie.*

(e)
Malach. 3. 3.

(f)
D. Raynoldes in his conference, *pag. 546.*

(g)
See *the marginal notes of the english bible of 1576. in Malachie. c. 3. verf.* 3. whereupon it is said, *he beginneth at the Preistes that they might be lightes & shine to others,* so plainly & truly do our aduersaries distinguish these Preistes from the other people.

(h)
Esay. 66. 21.

(i)
D. Raynoldes in his conference &c. *pag. 544.*

fame. *Secondly,* it apeareth yet moreplainly in that the same Prophet foretelling afterwardes by whom this cleane oblation is to be offered (d) *in the time of the Gospel,* as D. *Raynoldes* and others vnderstand, affirmeth & saith, (e) *the Lord shal fine the sonnes of Leui and purify them as gold and siluer, that they may offer an offering to God in righteousnesse :* whereby is signifyed that not al persons indifferently were to offer this foresaid *pure oblation or offering to God in righteousnes.* but onely a peculiar fort chosen to sacrifice, whom he therefore figuratiuely tearmeth *the sonnes of Leui,* becaufe that by their sacrifice and Preisthood, they should abolish the preisthood & sacrifice of *Leui,* and succeede in place thereof. And that here by *the sonnes of Leui he meant not al the people* (as D. (f) *Raynoldes* would enforce) appeareth yet further as wel by our aduersaries owne marginal (g) notes vpó the same words as also by cóferéce of this place which the Prophet *Esay,* who likewise vnder the same word, foretelleth the Preisthood of the new Testament saying, (h) *and I wil choose out of them Preistes, and Leuites,* in which place the word *Leuites* signifyeth not al Christians, but onely as D. *Raynoldes* him selfe & others graunt, the (i) *Ecclesiasticaf minister* of the new Testament. *Thirdly,* it is yet

saith in an other place of *Esay,* I graunt the name of Preist is genen to *Paftors, where speaking of the conuersion of the Gentils and of them* (saith he) *I wil take for Preistes for Leuites, faith the Lord.* and see the english

lish Bible of 1576. in the marginal notes vpon *Eſay* 66.¦21. and
M. Hooker in his ecclesiastical pollicy, l. 5. *pag.* 236.

is yet further ſtrong againſt our aduerſaries
that by this foreſaid *pure oblation* or *offering*
to God in righteouſnes, ſhould not be meant the
ſpiritual ſacrifice of prayer and thankeſge-
uing becauſe that according to their (k) *doc-*
trine in thoſe and al other our beſt workes
is not any *righteouſnes, but impurity* and *ſinne*.
To which end they (l) vrge that (m) *our*
righteouſnes is (called) *a defyled cloath. Fourthly*
and *laſtly* (to forbeare the (n) *aduantage* in
this behalfe of this word *incenſe*) the other
foreſaid wordes of *Malachy* infer not onely
a pure oblation, but alſo a new oblation to
ſucceede in place of the other oblation then
reiected, which the text ſaith, (o) *God would*
not receiue at thier handes, but would in lew
thereof accept of this *new* oblation: therefore by this new oblation, cannot be meant
the ſpiritual ſacrifices of prayer and thankeſ-
geuing, becauſe that theſe were not in *any*
(p) *ſence new,* but were heretofore offered by
the Fathers of the old Teſtament, no leſſe
then now by vs.

(k)
Whitaker contra Durænm,
l. 8. *pag.* 572. ſaith,
Sanctorum opera propter in-
herens vitium aliqua pecca-
ti labe polluuntur. And ſee
Luther in aſſertionibus art.
31. *quod in omni opere bo-*
no Iuſtus peccat.

(l)
Vrged by *Luther in aſ-*
ſertionibus.

(m)
Eſay, 64. 6.

(n)
Aduantage, for the ſpiritual ſacrifices of prayer
are here ſignifyed by the
word *incenſe* according to
the like vnderſtanding of
the ſame word. *Apoc.* 8.
3.4. Therefore the Pro-
phet here foretelling
both *incenſe,* and *a pure*
oblation, as thinges diffe-

(3) *Thirdly,* the *pure oblation* is to be diſtinguiſhed
rent it is thereby apparent, that\the *pure oblation* is to be diſtinguiſhed
from the ſpiritual ſacrifice comprehended vnder the word *incenſe*; which
diſtinction S. *Chriſoſtome* obſerueth ſaying in *Pſal.* 95. of the foreſaid
pure oblation. See how manifeſtly and plainly he haith expreſſed the miſti-
cal table which is the vnbloudy ſacrifice, the incenſe alſo he calleth the ſacred
praiers which are offered after the ſaid ſacrifice. and S. *Chriſoſtome* in the
ſame place diſtinguiſheth alſo this *vnbloudy ſacrifice* yet more expreſly
from the ſpiritual *ſacrifices of prayers, almes, preaching, &c.* in that he
there nu mbreth vp theſe, and making this in expreſſe tearmes, a ſpecial
and diſtinct ſacrifice from the other. (o) *Malach.* 1. 10. (p) *Not*
in any ſence new, for if theſe ſpiritual ſacrifices be reguarded *ſimple* by

T t   them

them selues, they were so offered by the Fathers of the new Testament as wel as by vs, and if we respect them as being (which some
Protestantes answeare hereto) *exhibited* or ioyned with the celebration of the *Eucharist*, yet can they not in this sence be new, because
that the rites and *Sacramentes* of the old law, were accompanied likewise with the spiritual
sacrifices of praier and
thankesgeuing.

(q)
Daniel. 12. 11.

(r)
Chemnitius in his examen,
part. 2. pag. 156. and
157.

(s)
Compare the computa-
tion of time mencioned
in *Apoc. 12. 14.* and
11. 3. and *13. 5.* with
Daniel 12. 7. and *7. 25.*

(t)
2. Thes. 2. 4. confer
the Temple of God there
mencioned with *the holy
place in Math. 24. 15.*
in which *the abhominable
desolation foretold by Daniel must stand.*

(u)
Math. 24. 15.

(x)
Daniel. 12. 2.

(y)
*Vide August. de ciuit.
Dei. l. 20. c. 23.*
and *c. 8.* and *Hierom.
in Danil. c. 11.* and *Chrisost. opere imperfecto, hom. 49.*

(3) *Thirdly,* the Prophet *Daniel* foretelleth likewise how that at *Antichristes* comming (q) *the dayly sacrifice shal be taken away
and the abominable desolation set vp.* And where
our aduersaries do (r) answeare hereto that
this was spoken litterally of *Antiochus* who
was before Christes time, and is not referred
to Antichrist, but by an Allegory, which
kinde of argument say they, is of no force.
I reply hereunto that the accomplishment of
this Prophecy was prefigured rather then fulfilled by *Antiochus;* & therefore I vrge not
this place as being an allegory, but in reguard that according to the litteral sence
therof, the foresaid chapter of *Daniel* is explained by (s) S. *Iohn,* and (t) S. *Paul,* as
concerning the time of the new Testament &
is also further referred to the time of vs Christians by our (u) Sauiour him selfe by those
wordes of (x) *Daniel* which concerne the
consummation of the world by the exposition of the auncient (y) *Fathers,* and by the
marginal (z) *notes* of our aduersaries owne
english Bibles.
And where our aduersaries do further (a)
answeare that though this place of *Daniel*
should concerne the time of Christians, yet it
may be wel vnderstood, not of any one external sacrifice, but of the spirittal sacrifices
of prayer and thankes-geuing, or els of the
preaching

and *Hipol, l. de Antichristo.* (z) See
the

the marginal notes of the englifh Bible in *Daniel, c . 12 .*

preaching of the word and *adminiftration* of
the Sacraments which fay they fhal *vpon An-*
tichriftes comming be either taken away or
at leaft greatly corrupted, as now they be
in their opinion, by the Pope: *I reply* therto,
Firft, concerning prayers and thankef-geuing,
that perfecution fhal perfect thefe rather
then abolifh them, and therefore that
thofe cannot be vnderftood by the dayly facrifice which Antichrift by his perfecution
is foretold to take away . *Secondly,* concerning the preaching of the word and adminiftration of the Sacraments, for them to be
taken a way is directly againft our aduerfaries them felues, who hold not onely that
the true Church and the preaching of the
word muft (b) *euermore continue,* euen (c)
during the raigne of Antichrift, but alfo that
the adminiftration of the word and Sacraments,
are the (d) *effential* notes thereof *without*
which

(a) *Chem-*
nitius examen, part . 2 .
pag. 157.

(b)
M . Whitaker, againft *M .*
William Raynoldes, in his
anfweare to the preface
pag . 33 . and *D . Fulke,*
againft the Rhemifh Te-
ftament in *Ephef. 4. fol.*
335. and *Caluin inftit .*
printed, *Geneua.* 1550.
c . 8 . de fide, fect . 37 .
38. *pag .* 233. and 234.
and *Melancthon, loc . com .*
(*adit .* 1561.) *c. de Ec-*
clefia. And fee the harmony of confeffions in
englifh, *pag . 306. 321 .*
323. 324. 325. 473 .

(c)
M . Whitaker againft *M .*
Raynoldes, in his anfweare

to the preface, *pag. 34.* faith, *notwithftanding this general difperfion and*
flight of the Church vnder Antichrift, the Catholicke Church fhal for al that
continue. And *M . Fulke* againft the Rhemifh Teftament in 2. *Thef .*
2. *fect . 5 . fol. 354.* faith, *the true Church though obfcure, and as it were*
driuen into wildernes by Antichrift, yet ftil continue difperfed ouer the world
&c. And *ibidem. fol.* 355. he faith, *finally we acknowledge that the true*
Church did not faile in the time of Antichrift nor was driuen into any corner
of the world, but was, is, and fhal be, alwaies difperfed in many nations .
and fee there *fol .* 477. Alfo that preaching of the word fhal continue *during al the time of Antichriftes raigne,* is affirmed by *M . Gyfford*
vpon the reuelations, *ferm . 21 . pag.* 191. and by *M . Fulke* againft
the Rhemifh Teftament *in reuelat . c . 11 . fect . 4 . fol.* 475. and by
Szegedinus in tabul . Analitic. pag. 368. where he faith, *predicent verbi*
Dei miniftri toto tempore quo Antichriftus templum et ciuitatem fanctam
calcabit. (d) *Whitaker contra Duraum . l . 3 . pag.* 260. faith of them,

funt

sunt Ecclesiæ proprietates Ousiodeis. And M. Whitguift in his defence &c. pag. 81. saith, the essential notes of the Church be these onely, the true preaching of the word of God and the right administration of Sacramentes.

(e)
Affirmed by M. Whitaker who contra Duræum. l. 3. pag. 249. saith, si adsunt, Ecclesiam constituunt, et tollunt si auferantur. And M. Willet in his sinopsis, pag. 71. saith, these markes cannot be absent from the Church, and it is no longer a true Church then it haith these markes. and pag. 69. he saith, the onely absence of them doth make a nullitie of the Church.

(*)
See the title of the dayly sacrifice geuen to the Eucharist by S. Augustine, Ciprian, the Tolletan councel, Eusebius Emissen, and Origen, alledged heretofore, tract. 3. sect. 1. subdiuis. 1. in the margent at h.

(f)
In the english Bible of 1576. in the marginal notes vpon Daniel. cap. 12. verf. 11. at the letter l. wherto also Chemnitius in his examen, part.

which it is no Church. And as to the supposed corrupting of the by the people, though it were true, it is yet impertinent for that our question vpon the Prophets wordes falleth out to be, not of their being corrupted, but of their being taken away. Thirdly I say, that for so much as the word sacrifice, being as here vsed by the Prophet in the singular number and without any explication following, doth euermore in the Scriptures vsually signify that which is properly a sacrifice, therefore by the daily sacrifice here mencioned, Daniel vnderstandeth not those other so many spirituall sacrifices, but one singular and proper sacrifice, which is by the auncient Fathers accordingly tearmed (*) the dayly sacrifice. And where our aduersaries being thus beaten backe do lastly answeare that this taking away of the dayly sacrifice foretold by Daniel, is not meant of Antichrist, but our Sauiour (f) Christ who by his sacrifice, shal take away the sacrifice and ceremonies of the law: I reply thereto that this answeare is exceeding daungerous and inconsiderate, by reason of the other wordes there next following; for the text is, the dayly (g) sacrifice shal be taken away and the abhominble desolation set vp, which the same Prophet explaineth yet more fully elswheare saying, (h) they shal take away the dayly sacrifice, and shal set vp the abhominable desolation; which to apply to our Sauiours passion were great blasphemie. For

lo

2. pag. 157. agreeth saying there hereof, nec quod (Daniel. 12.) ab-
latio

latio iugis sacrificij cum posita abominationis desolatione coniungitur quicquam promissa sacrificio facit, intelligitur enim de abrogatione cultus leuitici. (g)

so much now as it appeareth (al these answeares notwithstanding) that it is foretold
as proper vnto Antichrist that he (as (i) *Hipolitus* expoundeth) shal take away this our
owne singular and dayly saccrifice of Christians, I do hereupon exhort our aduersaries at
the least to greater moderation then as pre-
cursors so plainly to prepare the way to that
foretold so great defection. And pardon me
gentle reader in that I haue bene so much
longer then needed in shewing that these predictions of the prophets do proue our now
sacrifice : for I acknowledge that it had bene
sufficiet for me but to haue told thee in shorter tearmes that the foresaid *pure oblation* and
dayly sacrifice, foretold by *Malachie* and
Daniel, are in shew of wordes (which no man
may deny) indifferent at the least to signify
one singurlar and proper external sacrifice
of Christians, rather then those other so many and improper spiritual sacrifices of praier,
thadkes-geuing, preaching &c. which thing
onely being but admitted, the exposition
thereof must then in al probability be restrained not after their forbidden (k) *priuate interpretation* but according to the (l) *heretofore
confessed* practise and reuerenced (m) iudgement of the Primatiue Church and al other
succeeding ages.

Daniel. 12. 11. (h) *Daniel.* 11. 31.

(i)

*Hippolitus de consummati-
one mundi.* saith, *Luge-
bunt Ecclesia luctum mag-
num quia nec oblatio nec suf-
fitus fiet , nec cultus Deo
gratus, sed Ecclesiarum a-
des Tigurij instar erunt pre-
tiosumq̃ corpus et sanguis
Christi non extabit in diebus
illis, Liturgia extingue-
tur &c.*

(k)

2 . *Pet.* 1. 20. and see
Chemnitius, vpon these
wordes in his examen.,
part. 1. *pag.* 63.

(l)

See heretofore, *tract.* 2.
sect. 11. *sub diuis.* 1. in
the margent at the letter
d. and see the practise
of sacrifice, *tract.* 3.
sect. 1. throughout, and
sect. 2. throughout.

(m)

That the interpretation
of the primatiue Church
is to be receiued, the

Obiections

confession of Bohemia, in the english *harmony* of confessions, *pag.* 400.
saith *the Primitiue Church is the true and best mistris of posterity, and going
before leadeth vs the way.* And *Chemnitius* in his examen, *part.* 1. *pag.*
74. saith, *nullum enim est dubium primatiuam Ecclesiam accepisse ab A-
postolis et viris Apstolicis non tantum textum (sicut loquimur) Scriptura,*

verum actium

verumetiam legitimam et natiuam eius interpretationem &c. and *ibidem. pag.* 64. he faith, *veteris Ecclefiæ teftimonijs in vero et fano Scripturæ fenfu nos non parum confirmari fatemur.* And M. *Bilfon* in his perpetual gouernement of Chriftes Church, *c.* 13. *pag.* 285. faith to the Puritanes, *If we prefer the vniuerfal iudgement of the Primatiue Church in expounding the Scriptures touching the power and function of Bifhops before your perticular and late dreames you muft not blame vs, they were nearer the Apoftles times and likelier to vnderftand the Apoftles meaning &c.* And *Doctor Sarauia* in defenf. *tract. de diuerfis miniftrorum gradibus. pag.* 8. faith, *fpiritus fanctus qui in Ecclefijs præfidet verus eft Scripturarum interpres, ab eo igitur petenda eft vera interpretatio, et cum is fibi non poteft effe contrarius qui Primatiuæ Ecclefiæ præfedit et per Epifcopos eam gubernauit,*

ipfos nunc abijcere confentaneum veritati non eft, qua propter vniuerfalem praxim omnium locorum, omnium temporum, omnium Ecclefiarum tanquam certiffimum interpretem fequendam arbitror.

(2)
Efay. 43. 25. and 44. 22. and *Hieremie.* 31. 34.

(3)
Math. 2. 7.

(4)
Math. 9. 6. and *Mar.* 2. 10.

(5)
Math. 9. 8.

(6)
Ioan. 20. 21. 22. 23.

(7)
Ambrof. l. 1. *de peniten-tia. c.* 2. faith of the nouatians, *fed aiunt fe Domino deferre reuerenti-am*

Obiections againft facrifice taken from the Scriptures anfweared.

SECTION. 5.

HAuing hitherto fpoken in proofe of the Churches external facrifice, I wil now to auoide al difficulty and fcruple, laftly examine and anfweare thofe few cheife obiections wherewith our aduerfaries feeke to dilude and blinde their ignorant hearers. The firft is, that the facrifice of the Maffe is iniurious and difhonourable to Chriftes facrifice vpon the Croffe, whereto it might be anfweared, that the power of the Ecclefiaftical minifter *to forgeue finnes*, may be likewife pretended to be iniurious to the remiffion of finnes geuen by God, for although it be faid (2) *God onely forgeueth finne*, whereupon the Scribes wrongfully infifted faying, (3) *who can forgeue finnes but onely God?* yet did our Sauiour miraculoufly cure the paraliticke (4) *that they might know that the fonne of man alfo had power in earth to forgeue finnes* where-

upon

upon the multitude (5) glorifyed God that gaue such power (euen) vnto men . And as our Sauiour claimed and excercised this power as being man, so also did he without any dishonour to God communicate the same ouer to his Church, saying vnto his Apostles (6) *as my Father sent me, I also send you &c. receiue you the holy Ghost, whose sinnes you forgeue they are forgeuen.* And as hereupon the auncient Fathers doubted not to (7) reproue the heretickes of their times. And sundry of our learned aduersaries (8) reproue now in like manner certaine other of their owne brethren for denying this power of Preistes to remit sinne, vnder pretence forsooth that *God onely* is said *to forgeue sinne.* So also haue we no lesse cause to reproue our now aduersaries

am cui soli remittendorum criminum potestatem reseruant, Imo nulli maiorem iniuriam faciunt, quam qui eius volunt mandata rescindere, nam cum ipse in Euangelio suo dixerit Dominus, accipite spiritum sanctum quorum remiseritis peccata remittuntur eis &c . quis est ergo qui magis honorat vtrum qui mandatis obtemperat an qui resistit ? and *c . 7.* he further saith, *Cur baptizatis si peccata per hominem dimitti non licet &c.* Also *Pacianus in epist. 1. ad Simphronianum nouatianum .* saith, *nunquam Deus non poenitenti comminaretur nisi ignosceret poenitenti: solus hoc (inquies) Deus poterit , verum est, sed et quod per Sacerdotes suos facit ipsius potestas est, nam quid est illud quod Apostolis dicit , quae ligaueritis in terris &c.* In like manner *Socrates in hist. tripart. l. 2. c. 13. fine.* reproueth *Acesius* the nouatian, for that he taught concerning such as fel in persecution, *inuitandos quidem ad poenitentiam , spem vero remissionis non a Sacerdotibus, sed a Deo solummodo sustinere qui potestatem habet peccata remittere, haec cum dixisset Acesius Imperator ait : O Acesi pone scalam et si potes ascende solus in coelum .* So strange in those times was this opinion. And see further *hist. tripart. l. 8. c. 9. prope initium .* (8) *Lobechius,* Doctor and publicke professor in the Protestant vniuersity of *Rostoche,* in his *disput. theolog. pag. 301.* reproueth the Caluinistes, repeating their objection and saying, *est quidem solius Dei a peccatis absoluere, sed ita vt hoc faciat alias immediate &c. alias mediate per suos ministros condonando nobis culpam &c. errant ergo Caluiniani qui &c. obsolutioni ministri verbi illam efficaciam detrahant &c. contendentes ministrum absoluere tantum vt internuncium .* And in like plaine manner are they reproued, and their pretence of God onely forgeuing sinne refelled by sundry other Protestantes, as namely by *Andraeas Althemerus, in conciliat. locorum Scripturae pugnantium &c. loc 194. fol.*

194. *fol.* 218. and *by Iacobus Heilbrunerus, in Schwenfeldio Caluinis-pag.* 55. And hence it is that in the now english Communion booke *in the visitation of the sicke,* is set dowen the forme of the ministers ab∫o: lution geuen vpon the parties *confession* in these wordes, *our Lord Ie-fus who left power to his Church to absolue al sinners &c. forgeue thee &c. and by his authority committed to me I absolue thee from al thy sinnes &c.* And *M. D. Andrews* in his sermon preached *Anno.* 1599. mantai-

(n)   ned publickly the foresaid doctrine hereof.

Chemnitius, examen. part. 2. *pag.* 21. faith, *Deus in ijs quæ ad salutem nostram pertinent per certa media vult nobiscum agere.* and *Ibidem. pag.* 23. he faith, *non vno tantum modo sed per media quæ ad hunc v-sum instituit, vult gratiam suam exhibere, conferre, applicare &c.* and *pag.* 53. he faith, *Deus saluat non sine medijs, sed per la-uacrum regenerationis. tit.* 3. *et vide pag.* 17.

(o)

M. Whitguift in his de-fence of the answeare to the admonition. *pag.*

faries in their thus reiecting the facrifice of Chriftes body offered in the Church vnder like pretence of honouring his oblation thereof made vpon the Croffe. Therefore in more ful explanation of this point I further answeare. *First,* that as it is our conftant be-leefe that our Sauiours paffion vpon the Croffe, is in it felfe the fufficient and moft ac-complifhed price of our redemption: So a-gaine it is no leffe manifeftly acknowledged by our aduerfaries that our Sauiour doth im-part to vs the benefit thereof, not without meanes, but by (n) fpecial meanes in that behalfe fubordinate, as not onely by faith & preaching of the word, but alfo according to the iudgement of our aduerfaries both (o) *Caluinistes,* and (p) *Lutherans,* by his Sacramentes

527. affirmeth that *the effectual applying of the death and paffion of Chrift vnto the comunicantes is the effect of that Sacrament.* And *M. Carthwriht ibidem. pag.* 532. faith that *we receiue life from Chrift the head by the Arteries, and Conduites, of the fupper of our Lord.* And fee the like affir-med more fully by *M. Bilfon, M. Whitaker,* and *Hierome Zanchius,* alledged hereafter in this prefent fection *fubdiuif.* 2. in the margent vnder the letter t. and *M. Whitaker* in his *difput. de facra Scriptura.* printed, *Herbonæ. in præfat. ad auditores. fol.* b. v. And fee *Caluines* wordes heretofore, *tract.* 2. *fect.* 10. *fubdiuif.* 1. in the margent at the letters e. and k. And *M. Hooker* in his *Ecclefiaftical pollicy l.* 5. *fect.* 57. *pag.* 127. and 128. and, 132. (p) *Chemnitius,* examen
part.

part. 2, *pag*. 53. faith, *Baptismus est medium seu organon per quod sit communicatio beneficiorum Christi*. and *ibidem*. *pag*. 21. he faith, *Sacramenta sunt causæ instrumentales, ita quod per illa media seu organa &c. sibi vult meritum suum communicare credentibus*. And fee *Chemnitius* his more plaine fayings to this purpose alleged next herafter in this present fection *subdinis*. 2. in the margent vnder u. And the very fame doctrine is at large further affirmed by *Iacobus Andræas in confut*. *disput*. *Ioan*. *Iacobi Grinæi*. *pag*. 187. 188. and 210. and *in epitom*. *colloquij Montisbelgar*. &c. *pag*. 58. *et pag*. 42. and by *Adamus Francisci* in his *Margarita theologica*. *pag*. 221. and by *Haffenrefferus in loc*. *theolog*. *l*. 3. *pag*. 315. and al the other Lutherans.

mentes, and fo most especially in our opinion by the facrifice of the Masse, which we affirme our Sauiour haith instituted to be to vs not any new redemption (with which mistaken opinion our aduersaries charge vs, contrary to our knowen (q) writinges and the confession had of vs in this behalfe to the contrary by their owne (r) brethren) but onely as cheife meanes appointed to continue the memory of his oblation vpon the Crosse, and the confessed (*) application of againe *sacrificium Missæ non iustificat homines immediate, sed impetrat vt ea merito sacrificij Crucis detur hominibus &c*.

(q) *Bellarmine, de missa, l.2. c.4*. expresseth our doctrine faying, *sacrificium missæ vim habet per modum impetrationis, eius propria efficacia est impetrare* &c. and before in the fame chapter, *sacrificium Missæ vim suam habet a sacrificio Crucis*. and a gaine (r) *Vrsinus*, in his treatife entituled, *commonefactio cuiusdam theologi, et eiusdem commonefact*. *considerat*. faith, *pag*. 289. thus of our doctrine, *Aiunt illi se non denuo sacrificare Christum ad impetrandum remissionem peccatorum, sed victimam illam vnicam semel oblatam ab ipso Christo in Cruce, nunc suis manibus offerre hoc est, sistere et monstrare ac presentare Patri, et petere vt propter hanc ipsis et alijs sit propitius, et ratio ipsorum hæc vbicunq, Christus est corporaliter presens ibi se sistit et presentat in conspectu Patris ad impetrandam nobis salutem propter sacrificium suum semel oblatum in Cruce*. And a litle after expressing our oppinion of the difference which we make betweene Christes oblation made vpon the Crosse, and in the Masse, he faith, we thinke it was *crueuta et meritoria salutis in Cruce*. and that it is *incruenta et illius commemoratiua, seu representatiua et applicatoria in Missa*. (*) *Sigwartus*, Doctor and publique professor at *Tubinge*, in his disputations *Theologica*, *disput*. 16. *pag*. 146. affirmeth, that this

Sacrament is *Organum medium et instrumentum per quod beneficia Christi conferantur et applicentur.* And *M. Whitguift* in his defence &c. pag. 527. affirmeth, that *the effectual applying of the death and passion of Christ vnto the communicantes is an effect of this Sacrament.* And *M. Fulke* in his retentiue against Bristowes motiues. *pag.* 24. saith, *euery Protestant doth acknowledge the ministration of the Sacrament to be a dispensation of the sacrifice of Christes death.* And *Chemnitius* in his examen, part. 2. pag. 153. saith of the Sacrament, *ibi dispensatur et sumitur victima quæ pro peccatis nostris semel in cruce oblata est.* and *Caluin,* in 1. Cor. c. 11. vers. 24. pag. 323. saith of the Sacrament, *per quod redemptionis sumus participes et sacrificij beneficium nobis applicatur.* And *Andreas Crastouius* (a learned Caluinist) de opificio *Missæ. l. 1. sect.* 291. pag. 164. saith, *cum Calix dicatur esse nouum Testamentum, hinc apparet promissiones noui Testamenti applicari fidelibus (non sacrificio Missæ sed) sacramento cænæ sacrificio impetratur applicatio meriti et efficaciæ passionis Christi non vero fit ipsa applicatio.* Therefore this foresaid application to vs of the benefit of Christes death by the Eucharist being thus euident, and confessed, the onely question now remaining, is whether it performe the same to vs as being *a Sacrament,* or a *sacrifice,* that is, whether the Preist may in, or by his oblation thereof, so apply it for vs, or but we onely for our selues in our communicating thereof, whereof see next hereafter *subdiuision 4. fine.* in the answeare to the fourth obiection.

(s)
See *Gesnerus* his wordes alledged heretofore. *tract. 3. sect. 3. subdiuis.* 4. after l. in the margent there at this marke *.

(t)
`M. D. Couel,` in his defence of *M. Hooker &c.*

the general virtue thereof to our particuler necessities, from which doctrine some of our (s) aduersaries do not altogether abhorre. (2) Which foresaid oppinion of referring grace, whether to Sacramentes or in this sort to the Maße, is so far from being dishonowrable to Christes death, that to the cótrary our learned aduersaries both (t) Cal- uinistes

publißhed by authority, and printed, 1603. *art.* 14. pag. 96. saith, *that sauing grace which Christ originally is, or hath, for the general good of his whole Church, by Sacramentes he seuerally deriueth into euery member thereof &c. now agent causes we know are of two sortes, the principal which worketh by vertue of his forme, as fier maketh hot, and thus nothing can cause grace but God him selfe the instrumental which worketh, not as the other &c.*

but

but onely by that motion which it haith from the principal and first agent, *thus do Sacramentes worke.* and *pag.* 98. he further faith, *for God doth* *iustify by the Sacramentes &c.* and *pag.* 99. he yet further faith, *that Sa-* *cramentes passiuely may by the worke done afford grace, for in that iustifica-* *tion and meanes of righteousnes whereof man is made pertaker by the Sacra-* *mentes many thinges do concurre. First, on Gods behalfe a wil that we should* *vse those sensible elements; on Christes behalfe his passion, from which the* *Sacramentes haue their vertue &c. in respect of the Sacrament it selfe the* *external action which ariseth out of the fit application of the matter and forme* *of Sacramentes: now that which in al this actually and instrumentally brin-* *geth grace, is the external action which is commonly called the Sacrament.* In this respect *Andreas Crastonius* (a learned Caluinist) in his booke *de opificio missa. l. 1. sect. 292. pag.* 164. faith, *Euchariftia vt Sa-* *cramentum, est organum iustificationis.* And *M. Bilson* in his true diffe-rence &c. printed. 1586. *part. 4. pag.* 539. faith, *his truth is an-* *nexed to the Sacraments and his power vnited to the creatures after a wonder-* *ful and vnspeakeable manner by the mighty working of the holy Ghost.* and *pag.* 592. he argueth against *them which defend that the Sacrament doth* *onely figure, not offer, signify, not exhibit grace,* affirming there further, *the visible signes to be in signification mysteries, in operation and vertue the* *thinges them selues.* in so much as *pag.* 368. he doubteth not to af-firme that *original sinne is not remitted* (to Children) *but in Baptisme,* and that *they be new borne of water and the holy Ghost. Ioan.* 3. Also *M. Whitakers contra Camp. rat.* 8. teacheth, that *Baptisme is the con-* *duit of grace, it deriue h Christes merites to vs, neither doth it onely signify* *saluation, but doth also performe and bring the same.* in so much as *contra* *Duraeum,* printed 1583. *l.* 8. *pag.* 664. he professeth to alow *(Alani* *sententiam)* the opinion of Doctor *Allon,* affirming there with him, that *Deus operatur &c. God doth worke grace in the soule of man by his Sacra-* *mentes, as by an instrumental cause and no otherwise, nor lesse truly then a* *man is said to write by his penne.* In like manner *Zanchius, in epist. ad* *Ephes.* printed *Neustadij.* 1600. *in c.* 5. *pag.* 564. *sect.* 65. faith, *Baptismus non (est) nudum signum sed rerum omnium exhibitium quorum* *signum est.* And *Ibidem. pag.* 570. *sect.* 3. he further faith, *dubitan-* *dum igitur non est quin Baptismus organum sit spiritus sancti per quod aterno* *faedere Christo incorporamur.* And agane *pag.* 571. *sect.* 11. *est igitur* *Baptismus organum regenerationis nostrae, qua de causa lauacrum regenera-* *tionis vocatur. tit.* 3. hitherto of the Caluinistes.

(u) *Labechius Doctor* & profefforin the vniuerfity of *Roftoch*, in his *difput theolog. &c. pag.* 331.. and 332. faith, *nullo negotio foluitur Suinglianorū obiectio, fi inquiunt Sacramenta conferunt gratiam et promiffionem gratiæ applicant et faluant, tunc exequanda* ᵴᵘⁿᵗ *exunt cum ipfo fpiritu fanĉto et cum merito Chrifti &c. Refpondeo caufa efficiens falutis eft folus Deus, caufa materialis eft folus Chriftus*

5. *Obiections* anfweared Subd. 2. uiniftes, and (u) *Lutherans*, do in the behalfe of grace wrought and conferred by Sacramentes, vndertake to explaine how that the *Godhead, Chriftes paffion*, and the *Sacraments*, do each of them in their degree concurre in working of grace; the Godhead as being the *principal agent*, and without difhonour to Chriftes paffion, his paffion as being *the inftrument* conioyned to the Godhead, & working without offence, or difhonour thereto, and laftly *Sacraments* as being the *feperated inftrument* conferring grace truly, and in their kinde by grace and vertue from the God-head, and Chriftes paffion, & without difho- *Elafterion caufæ* Organicai *mediæ feu inftrumentales, per quas Deus Pater gratiam fuam credentibus communicat, fpiritus fanĉtus efficatiam fuam exercet ad falutem omni credenti* ₐ *funt Sacramenta: confert ergo Deus gratiam fuam, conferunt et Sacramenta &c. duplex ergo eft caufa agens &c. principalis et inftrumentalis.* And *Chemnitius* in his examen, *part.* 2. *pag.* 17. faith, *ea quæ ad falutem neceffaria funt, diftinguenda funt, vt Chriftus promerens pater Dominus organa feu Sacramenta &c. per quæ fpiritus fanĉtus beneficia illa noui Teftamenti offert, applicat &c. fingula hæc fuo modo et in fuo gradu ad falutem noftram ordinata funt &c. non fequitur facramenta funt ad falutem neceffaria, ergo non folus Chriftus fuo merito nobis eam acquifiuit &c. et vide ibidem. pag.* 21. where hauing renewed the like wordes he concludeth faying, *hoc modo manet Deo gloria fua &c.* and fee the like explanation made by *Haffenrefferus, in loc. theolog. l.* 3. *pag.* 277. where he in like manner explaineth how and in what manner, *faluamur per Chrifti meritum, faluamur per facramenta, faluamur per fidem, fuo vbiᵍᵈ feruato peculiari refpeĉtu &c.* And fee the like in the Proteftant writer *Andreas Althamerus, in conciliat. locorum pugnantium. fol.* 218. and *fol.* 212. In fo much as *Chemnitius* in his examen, printed, 1578. *part.* 2. *pag.* 53. faith, *Baptifmus eft medium feu organon per quod fit communicatio beneficiorum Chrifti nam per Baptifmum Chriftus mundat et fanĉtificat. Eohef.* 5. *&c.* and *pag.* 20. he faith, *manifefta funt Scriptura teftimonia quæ vt negari non poffunt, ita eludi non debent. tit.* 3. *Baptifmus vocatur Lauacrum regenerationis. Ephef.* 5. *mundans eam Lauacro aqua in verbo Ioan.* 3. *nifi quis renatus fuerit ex aqua et fpiritu fanĉto &c. Aĉt.*

exhibet filius merix=tū fuum credentibʒ

22. *Baptizare et abluere peccata tua.* 1. *Pet.* 3. *loquens de aqua &c. inquit, quæ aqua archæ antitipon saluos nos facit Baptisma &c.* and then concludeth, *hæc manifestissima testimonia, quæ diserte Sacramentis efficaciam tribuunt, et qualis ea sit explicant, non sunt per tropos peruertenda a simplici et genuina significatione quam propria vocabulorum significatio præbet, et ita veteres hæc testimonia simpliciter sicut sonant intellexerunt.*

nour to either. And if our very aduersaries (both *Caluinistes*, and *Lutherans*) do truely and according to the Scriptures acknow-ledge thus much due to Sacramentes and without al iniury to Christes passion, why then should not our foresaid doctrine of Masse, and sacrifice, being grounded in like manner vpon (r) euident Scriptures, and the (y) confessed answearable practise of the Primatiue Church, be holden likewise freed from al imputation of being dishonourable to Christ. *Secondly*, I say in further explana-tion hereof, that our (z) aduersaries & we do both of vs acknowledge how that Christes sacrifice vpon the Crosse and the force there-of did extend aswel to the people that liued before the same, as it doth now to vs that liue after it; whereupon I infer that our now sacrifice of the Masse may as wel stand with the honour and sufficiency of Christes passion, as before time did the (a) *sacrifices for sinne,* and other sacrifices vsed in the old Testament

(x)
See heretofore, *tract.* 3. *sect.* 3. & 4. through-out.

(y)
See heretofore, *tract.* 3. *sect.* 2. throughout. and see *Caluins* cófession *tract.* 3. *sect.* 2. *subdiuis.* 3. at h. i. k. l. and *subdi-uis.* 4. at b.

(z)
To this end our aduersa-ries do vrge that Christ is called *the Lambe slaine from the beginning of the world. Apoc.* 13. 8. see *M. Fulke* in his confuta-tion of Purgatory, *pag.* 57. where he saith, *to what end was Christ cal-led the Lambe slaine from the beginning of the world, but that the benefit of his*

passion extendeth to the Godly of al ages a like? (a) *Exod.* 29. 36. *et Leuit.* 7. 2. *et Num.* 28. 22. and *Iob.* 1. 5. and. *Habr.* 5. 1. 2. the instance of these *sinne offeringes* of the old Law (whereof *M. Fulke* against the Rhemish Testament in *Habr.* 7. *vers.* 12. *sect.* 7. *fol.* 405. a. *post. med.* saith *the Church vnder the Law had an external Preist=hood to offer vp bloudy sacrifices both, propitiatory and Eucharistical,* are (as the point now in question) so probable that *Andreas Chrastoui-us* (a learned Caluinist) *de opificio Missæ. l.* 1. *sect.* 289. *pag.* 161. onely answeareth to *Bellarmine* alledging the same, *demonstret (Bel-*

Larminus) *institutionem et promissionem Dei, vbi expiatio humana oblationi et orationi Sacerdotis æque ascribatur sicut de mosaicis hostijs frequenter legimus &c.* So as his conceiued scruple, is not of the sacrifice vpon the Crosse, being dishonoured more by the Masse then by the sacrifices for sinne offered during the law, but onely whether the Scripture be as plaine for to proue the Masse propitiatory, as it doth the other foresaid sacrifices of the old law: which point see proued from the wordes of the institution, heretofore, *tract. 3. sect. 3. subdiuis. 1.* at o. and *subdiuis. 2.* at 2. *. y.* and from the abounding testimony of the Fathers, alledged heretofore *tract. 3. sect. 1. subdiuis. 3.* in the margent at r. s. *. t. u. x. &c.

(b)
Habr. 8. 6.

(c)
Habr. 7. 24.

(d)
In *M. Fulkes* translation against the Rhemish Testament.

(e)
In the english Bible of *Anno* 1576.

(f)
D. *Whitaker* against *M. Raynoldes, pag.* 84. and 85. and the marginal notes of the english bible of *Anno* .1576. *in Habr.* 7. 24. at the letter k.

(g)
The Apostle *ibid.* in the wordes next before saith *verf.* 23. of the Preistes of the old Law, among them *many were made*

Testament. And that as those sacrifices of the old testament receiued their force from Christes death and sacrifice vpon the Crosse then to come, and without al dishonour therto: so likewise in the new Testament, (b) *which is established in better promises,* our now sacrifice doth without any dishonour to Christ, confer more abundantly efficacy and vertue, from his said death and passion now past.

(3) *The second* obiection of our aduersaries is, that our Sauiours Preisthood is called (c) *Aparabaton* which our aduersaries translate in one of their english Bibles (d) *vnchaungeable* in an other (e) *euerlasting,* whereupon they vrge (f) that our now Catholicke preisthood is dishonorable, and against Christes Preisthood. Albeit that this friuolous obiection be vnworthy of answeare as being sufficiently (g) *explained* by the *circumstance* of the text, yet I say thereto: *First,* that for so much as according to *M. Whitakers* owne exposition

Preistes because that by death they were prohibited to continue. and then *verf.* 24. *But Christ continueth for euer, hauing an euerlasting Preisthood.* the sence whereof is manifest that as Christ had many excellent prerogatiues

rogatiues aboue the Preistes or Preisthood of *Aaron*. So among many other this was one, that whereas *Aarons* Preisthood passed from one to an other, from father to sonne, by reason of death, Christ to the contrary neuer dying, but euer liuing, neuer departeth from his Preisthood but remaineth *a Preist for euer*. And so accordinly *Caluin in Habr. 7. 24. pag. 929*. collecteth hereupon saying, *veteres ideo plures fuerunt (Sacerdotes) quia mors sacerdotium finiebat, nulla est mors quæ impediat Christum a sua functione, ergo vnus est ac perpetuus*.

position (h) *that properly is Aparabatos that passeth not away from one to an other*, the place is therefore wholly impertinent: for which of vs did euer affirme that Christes preisthood is departed away from him? Do we not acknowledge to the contrary that he is *a Preist for euer according to the order of Melchisadech*. Secondly, (to forbeare in this short intended discourse, the (*) *retorting* otherwise against our aduersaries of Christes confessed *Preisthood for euer*) if the argument be good, that because *Christ is a Preist for euer*, therefore there are no Preistes, then is the argument likewise good that because Christ is (i) *a King for euer*, therefore we must depose

(h)
M. *Whitaker* in his answeare to M. *Raynoldes*, pag. 85.

(*)
Retorting, for if Christ be a *Preist for euer*, then for so much as according to the Apostle, *euery high Preist is apointed to offer sacrifice, therefore of necessity he also must haue some thing to offer. Habr. 8. 3*. which cannot be his sacrifice vpon the Crosse, because that offering is now past, wheras he, being *a Preist*

for euer, must, according to the Apostle, euermore *haue some thing to offer* neither may it be said to be any offering of himselfe in heauen to God the Father by his dayly representing to him his passion for vs; for though our aduersaries now would assent to say that he doth dayly so offer him selfe for vs in heauen: Which his further or renewed oblation is at other times by them selues gainsaid vnder pretext of *Habr. 9. 25*. by them to such purpose vrged and alledged, yet may they not affirme that such representation or any further efficacy of his passion is properly a sacrifice, neither can it be as M. *Fulke* would in these straites euade, that he *excerciseth his continual Preisthood in presenting his Church before God, and making continual intercession for vs. Fulke*, against the Rhemish Testament *in Habr. c. 8. sect. 5. fol. 409.* for neither also is this intercession any proper sacrifice, as appeareth by the by the confeſſed examples, not onely of laye people in this life, but alſo *of Sainctes and Angels in heauen praying*, or making interceſſion *for the Church.* Whereof ſee the Harmony of confeſſions in engliſh, *pag*. 43. and *Bullingers Deeades, pag.* 665. Therefore this *Preiſthood for euer* being alſo further limited to be *according to the order of Melchiſadech. Pſal.* 109. 4. argueth a ſpecial external ſacrifice *for euer* according to that order mencioned heretofore, *tract*. 3. *ſect*.4.*ſubdiuiſ*. 1. at z. 5. a. 6. 7. and by the Fathers therefore tearmed *the dayly ſacrifice,* whereof ſee heretofore, *tract*. 3. *ſect*. 1. *ſubdiuiſ*. 1. in the margent at h. (i) *Eſay*. 9. 7. and *Daniel*. 2. 44. and *Luc*. 1. 33. and *Hæbr.* 1. 8.

(k)
Math. 23. 10.

(l)
Math. 23. 8.

(m)
Eſay. 40. 11. *et Math*. 26. 31. and *Ioan*. 10. 11. 14.

(n)
Luc. 4. 18. *et Epheſ*. 2. 17. and *Hæbr*. 2. 3. and *Eſay*. 61. 1.

(o)
M. Whitguift, in his defence &c. *pag*. 300. proueth that though S. *Peter* cal Chriſt *Archſheapheard or Archbiſhop*,

poſe Princes alſo becauſe he is our (k) *Doctor,* (l) *Maiſter,* (m) *Paſtor,* (n) *Preacher*. Therefore now we muſt haue none, for as Chriſt haith in a moſt excellent ſort his Preiſthood; ſo likewiſe haith he to be a *King,* a *Doctor, Paſtor, Maiſter,* and *Preacher:* al which agree to him *eternally and vnchaungable.* *Thirdly,* I ſay that the ordinary example of the authority of Princes communicated to inferior magiſtrates without iniurie to the Prince, ſheweth ſufficiently (which thing *my Lord of* (o) *Canturbury* acknowledgeth in other matters) how the power of Chriſt may be in like manner communicated to his Preiſtes without any iniury to him or his Preiſthood: as in like reſpect the power of (p) *working miracles,* and (q) *remitting ſinne*, was

yet the name of Archbiſhop may be tranſlated to *other then Chriſt,* and he explaineth there at large how *names proper to God may in ſome reſpect be attributed to others,* affirming that *they belong to God properly, and to man, but in reſpect he is the miniſter of God.* (p) *Math.* 10. 1. *Marc.* 13. 15. *et Act.* 3. 4. (q) *Ioan.* 20. 23. and ſee 2. *Cor.* 2. 10. and thereupon the Proteſtant diuines of *Bohemia* in the engliſh harmony of confeſſions, *pag.* 537. and *pag.* 526. and ſee the forme of abſolution in the Communion booke *in the viſitation of the ſicke,* where it is thus ſet dowen: *By his authority committed to me I abſolue thee from*
al thy

al thy *sinnes &c.* And see sundry other Protestantes as namely *Iacobus Heilbrunerus, l. Schwenkfeldio, Caluin. &c.* pag. 55. and *Lobechius in disput. theolog. &c.* pag. 295. and 301. And *Andræas Althamerus in conciliat. locorum Scripturæ pugnant &c.* sect. 194. fol. 218. and *Sarcerius in loc. com. de confessione,* fol. 289. and 294. who al affirme that not onely God, but also the Ecclesiasticall minister by power and authority geuen from him, do truly remit sinne. (r)

was comunicated by him to his Apostles. This point did the Fathers specialy discerne concerning euen the matter now eutreated affirming therefore of *Preistes,* that (r) *they proceede from Christ,* do (s) *truly execute his* (t) *place offering sacrifice vnder Christ the high Preist,* and *in our* (u) *Lords steede:* in so much as in reguard of this our delegate or ministeriall Preisthood, they doubt not to cal our Sauiour (z) *Principem Sacerdotum &c.* the high *Preist* whom our (inferior) *Preistes* are to follow in offering sacrifice for the people, being so thereby (?) *Christes image in respect of his Preisthood,* affirming yet also further that euen (x) *Christ him selfe* first *instituted and offered this sacrifice.*

(r)
Euseb. l. 5. *demonst. Euang. c.* 3. saith, *Christus ipsius Melchisadech ritu ea quæ ad Sacerdotium in hominibus gerendū speccant, per suos ministros perficit &c. primus ipse saluator ac Dominus noster, deinde qui ab ipso profecti sunt Sacerdotes in omnibus gentibus spiritale secundum Ecclesiasticas sanctiones Sacerdotij munus obeuntes &c.*

(s)
Ciprian. l. 2. *epist.* 3. alledged heretofore, *tract.* 3. *sect.* 2. *subdiuis.* 4. at o. p. (t) *August. de ciuit. Dei, l.* 17. *c.* 17. *circa med.* saith. *vbiq; offertur. sub Sacerdote Christo quod protulit Melchisadech quando benedixit Abraham.* (u) *Ambros. in* 1. *Tim. c.* 4. *vers.* 14. saith, *manus impositiones verba sunt mistica, quibus confirmatur ad hoc opus electus accipiens authoritatem teste conscientia sua vt audeat vice Domini sacrificium Deo offerre* (z) *Ambros. in Psal.* 38. saith, *vidimus principem Sacerdotum ad nos venientem, vidimus, et audiuimus offerentem pro nobis sanguinem suum, sequamur vt possumus Sacerdotes, vt offeramus pro populo sacrificum etsi infirmi merito tamen honorabiles sacrificio, quia etsi Christus non videtur offerre, tamen ipse offertur in terris, quando Christi corpus offertur.* And *Cipriau. l.* 2. *epist.* 3. alledged heretofore, *tract.* 3. *sect.* 2. *subdiuis.* 4. at o. doth in like manner cal our *Sauiour the high Preist* whom our now *Preistes* do *imitate* (in doing) *that which Christ did, offering the* (so) *in the Church a true and*

W w   *ful*

ful *sacrifice &c.* (3) *Ignatius in epist. ad Smirnenses.* see this heretofore *tract.* 1. *sect.* 3. *subdiuis.* 2. atq. r. (x) See heretofore *tract.* 1. *sect.* 3. *subdiuis.* 2. *prope finem.* at e. f. g. h. i. k. m.

(y)
Hæbr. 10. 14.
(z)
Hæbr. 9. 25.
(a)
Hæbr. 10. 18.
(1)
Thou art a Preist for euer according to the order of Melchisadech. Psal. 109. 4. *et Hæbr.* 7. 17.
(2)
Hæbr. 8. 1.
(3)
Hæbr. 8. 3. in so much as Caluin *in omnes Pauli epistolas &c. in c.* 8. *ad Hæbr. pag.* 931. *b. post med.* saith, *vnde liquet inanem fore Sacerdotij titulum sine sacrificio.* and *ibidem. pag.* 932. he further saith, *in Christo cum Sacerdotis nomine sacrificandi officium coniungi debet.*
(4)
Hæbr. 8. 3.
(5)
Bullinger, in his Decades in english. *Decad.* 4. *serm.* 7. *pag.* 707. b.
(6) *Ibidem. pag.* 707.

(4) *The third* obiection is, how the Apostle affirmeth to the Hebrewes that our Sauiour (y) *haith with one oblation consecrated vs,* that (z) *Christ should not offer him selfe often,* and therefore that (a) as now there is no more *offering for sinne;* whereunto I say that al this is to be vnderstood as being onely exclusiue to the bloudy offering of his often dying, for to vnderstand it otherwise were against his confessed (1) *Presthood for euer* which euidently argueth his dayly oblation for our Sauiour (as the same Apostle affirmeth of him) being (2) *a high Preist set on the right hand of God,* (3) *it is of necessity that he also haue somewhat to offer,* & for this (their) expressed reason because that (4) *euery high Preist is appointed to offer;* whereupon our learned aduersaries do affirme that as now also in heauen (5) *Christ our Lord sacrifyceth for vs, and offereth a sacrifice for sinnes vnto the liuing God,* (euen) *him selfe, alwaies an effectuall sacrifice,* and continuing stil (6) *our Preist executeth his office* (of Presthood) *before God in heauen;* al which is so directly against that other sence, which our aduersaries do now enforce from the Apostles other foresaid sayinges, that them selfe do acknowledge to their Lutheran brethren, that (7) *wheresoeuer Christ is present there he doth offer him selfe in the sight of his Father to obtaine vs remission, for his sacrifice once offered vpon the Crosse,* and therefore

(7) *Vrsinus* in his *commonefactio cuiusdam theologi et eiusdem commonefactionis considerat.* printed, 1583. *pag.* 290. argueth thus as in our behalf saying, *ratio ipsorum hæc est; vbicunq, Christus est cor-*

est corporaliter presens ibi se sistit et presentat in conspectu Patris, ad impetrandam nobis propter sacrificium suum semel oblatum in Cruce &c. In Missa est presens corporaliter, ergo in pane presentat se Patri ad salutem nostram non minus quam in calo: hic nostri minorem negant qua sublata corruit vno impetu, adoratio et oblatio pontificia, et qua concessa quā non facile sit has euertere &c.

fore that (8) *the real presens but admitted, the sacrifice of Christes body doth thence necessarily follow,* so litle thereto (in their opinion) is the other obiection of his not being *often offered.* Therefore in some more ful explication of this point I do yet further answeare, that the Apostle doth in this epistle to the Hebrewes prosecute the many excellent prerogatiues of Christes Preisthood and sacrifice vpon the Crosse, aboue the Preisthood and sacrifice of *Aaron;* shewing amongst other that whereas the Preistes of the old law offered at seueral times sacrifices, Christes oblation though but once made vpon the Crosse was sufficient without his often dying: And to this effect where he saith as before is obiected that Christ *should not offer him selfe often* it is explained by the same Apostle saying, (b) *not that he should offer him selfe often, as the high Preist entred into the holy place enery yeare in the bloud of others, for then must he haue often suffered.* So plainly doth he professe to speake (not against the Churches now sacrifice, which the Fathers do to this purpose in special distinction from his other sacrifice of the Crosse, tearme to the great dislike of (*) *Caluin, the vnbloudy sacrifice,* but) onely against

(8)

Vrsinus vt supra, at **7.** and see the same fully & directly affirmed by *Eusebius Altkircherus* and *Melanchthon,* alledged heretofore, *tract.* 3. *sect.* 4. *subdiuis.* 1. in the margent vnder **t.** and by the Diuines of *Wittenberge,* alledged hertofore, *tract.* 2. *sect.* 9. *subdiuis.* 2. in the margent, and next after **b.** at *.

(b)

Habr. 9. 25. 26.

(*)

The auncient Fathers in reguard of the maner of Christes presence and oblatió in the Eucharist different from his other violent and bloudy sacrifice vpon the Crosse, haue

this purpose tearmed the Eucharist the *vnbloudy sacrifice.* So the general *Councel of Ephesus, in declar. Annthematismi vndecimi.* saith, *we celebrate in the Church the holy life-geuing and vnbloudy sacrifice, beleeuing that which is set before vs, not to be the body of a common man like to vs &c. but rather we receiue that, as the proper body and bloud of the word which*

W w 2

geueth

geueth life &c. and the *firſt Nicene Councel* (in a ſpecial Canon mentioned and acknowledged by *Oecolampadius in lib. epiſt. Oecolamp. & Swing. pag.* 667. by *Caluin inſtitut. l. 4. c.* 17. *ſect.* 36. by *M. Iewel* in his Apollogie of the Church of England by *M. D. Bilſon,* in his true difference &c. *part.* 4. *pag.* 555.) ſaith of the Altar, *let vs by faith vnderſtand to lye vpon that holy table the Lambe of God that taketh away the ſinnes of the world, ſacrifyced by Prieſtes without killing* (or effuſion of bloud, or as tranſlateth *Oecolampadius vbi ſupra. pag.* 668. *non victimarum more) and that we do receiue truly the pretious body and bloud of the ſaid Lambe &c.* And the greate *Councel of Calcedon,* conſiſting of 360. Biſhops. *art.* 3. tearmeth the Euchariſt *the vnbloudy hoſt offered in the Church the vnbloudy and dreadful ſacrifice.* And ſo likewiſe doth the *ſixt Councel of Conſtantinople in trullo. can.* 28. & 32. tearme it *the vnbloudy ſacrifice.* and *Nazianzen in orat. in Iulianum,* alledged heretofore *tract.* 1. *ſect.* 2. *ſubdiuiſ.* 1. after z. at *. tearmeth it *the vnbloudy ſacrifice.* and alſo *in carminibus,* where he ſaith, *O ſacrificia mittentes incruenta Sacerdos* (o *magni figmentum Dei in manibus veſtris ferentes.* and *Damaſcen. in vita Barlaam. c.* 12. & 19. & 29. tearmeth it *the vnbloudy ſacrifice,* and ſo likewiſe doth *S. Chriſoſtome,* alleged heretofore, *tract.* 3. *ſect.* 4. *ſubdiuiſ.* 2. in the margent at n. And *Cirillus Alex. epiſt.* 10. *ad Neſtorium,* tearmeth it *incruentum cultum,* which foreſaid diſtinction ſo made by the Fathers betweene the *bloudy ſacrifice* of the Croſſe, but once offered, and the Churches other *vnbloudy ſacrifice* dayly celebrated, is ſo proper to explaine the point now in hand, that *Caluin in epiſt. ad Hæbr. in c.* 9. *verſ.* 26. *pag.* 947. *b. fine, et a. initio.* hauing vrged the very argument now obiected, and withal recited our foreſaid diſtinction (taken in anſweare thereto from the Fathers) of *bloudy and vnbloudy oblation,* replyeth ſaying, *nec moror quod ſic loquuntur veteres &c. I reguard not the auncient Fathers ſo ſpeaking of vnbloudy ſacrifice, for it is not in mens liberty to feaine ſacrifices at their pleaſure.* And in his booke *de vera Eccleſia reformandæ ratione.* he further ſaith, *whereas the Papiſtes obiect that the auncient Fathers according to the Scriptures profeſſe, that in the Church there is an vnbloudy ſacrifice in the one part they erre, in the other they lie, for Scriptures they haue none, as for the authority of the Fathers it ſkilleth not, neither is it reaſon that we depart from the eternal truth of God for their ſakes, and therefore that vnbloudy ſacrifice which men haith deuiſed let them hardly reſerue and take it to them ſelues.*

(c) *Hæbr.*

against al *bloudy* sacrifice of his often dying, in the excellency of Christes sacrifice vpon and as thereupon to perswade the Hebrewes the Crosse, aboue their legal sacrifices (c) *in which there was (by reason of their imper-* *fection as the Apostle saith) a remembrance* *againe of sinnes euery yeare;* whereas Christes passion vpon the Crosse though but once suffered is yet sufficient without al iteration or repetition thereof by his dying againe, the *force* thereof enduring for euer: & so our selues do accordingly acknowledge that the grace and efficacy of al our Baptismes, sacrifice, and Sacramentes, do flow from thence. As also we hold that in our now sacrifice of the Masse there is not any worke or sacrifice of any second or new redemption, but (as our aduersaries them selues do acknowledge of vs) we do therein (d) onely *offer, commemo-* *rate, and apply the other (foresaid) oblation of* *the Crosse.* And to this effect do the aumcient (e) Fathers specially defend and answeare (for our Preistes now sacrifycing) against the

(c)
Hæbr. 10. 3.

(d)
Vrsinus in commonefact. cu- *iusda theologi de sacra cœna* *et eiusdem commonefact.* *considerat.* pag. 289. al-ledged next heretofore, *subdiuis.* 1. in the margent at the letter r.

(e)
S. Ambros. in c. 10. *Hæbr.* saith, *quid ergo nos* &c. *what then do we, do* *we not offer euery day? we* *offer truly, but this sacri-* *fice is an exemplar of that,* *for we offer alwaies the selfe* *same, & not now one lambe,* *to morrow an other, but al-* *waies the selfe same thing,* *therefore this is one sacrifice,* *otherwise by this reason, be-* *cause it is offered in many*

places there should be many Christes, not so, but it is one Christ in euery place, *here whol and there whol one body, but this which we do is done for a com-* *memoration of that which was done, for we offer not an other sacrifice as the* *high Preist of the old Law but alwaies the selfe same &c.* And see the like solution in *Theodiret, in epist. ad Hæbr. c.* 8. and in *Chrisostom. hom.* 17. *in epist. ad Hæbr.* also *Primasius in Hæbr. c.* 10. saith, *what then* *shal we say, do not our Preistes the same thing dayly whiles they offer sacri-* *fice continually, they offer indeede but in remembrance of his death, and be-* *cause we sinne dayly, & haue dayly neede to be cleansed, and because he cannot* *now dye, he hath geuen vs this Sacrament of his body and bloud, that as his* *passion was the redemption and absolution of the world, so also this oblation* *thereof may be redemption and clensing to al that offer it in truth and verity.* And *Primasius* saith yet further in the same place, *the diuinity of the* *word of God which is euery where, maketh that there are not many sacrifices,*

but

but one, *although it be offered of many and that as it is one body, which he tooke of the virgines wombe, not many bodies euen ſo alſo one ſacrifice, not diuers, as thoſe of the Iewes were:* vpon which premiſes it is to be noted that if in the Fathers iudgement the Euchariſt had beene onely a commemoration of Chriſtes body, and ſacrifice vpon the Croſſe, & not alſo his very body and properly a ſacrifice in it ſelfe, the forenamed Fathers in their foremencioned expounding the foreſaid wordes obiected from the epiſtle to the Hebrewes, would neuer thereupon then haue made ſuch doubt with ſpecial anſweare thereto, as before is alledged, how the often offering of the Euchariſt in ſacrifice may ſtand with that *one* ſacrifice vpon the Croſſe. And how alſo it may auoide, in reguard of it being offered *in many places*, the foremencioned ſeeming ſequele of *many Chriſtes*, and *many bodies*, for there could not be any cauſe of doubt but that the onely often commemoration might wel enough ſtand with the other (*one*) oblation, becauſe that *one* thing, though a thouſand times remembred, remaineth yet vndoubtedly *one* and the ſame thing ſtil, their ſayinges therefore do infer not onely commemoration, but alſo external and real ſacrifice of Chriſtes very body, which they affirme to be in it ſelfe ſtil but one, notwithſtanding the diuers offering thereof *in many places*.

(*)

Direttly proueth, as where it affirmeth *Chriſts Preiſt-hood for euer according to the order of Melchiſadech*, (*Habr.* 7. 17. which argueth a dayly offering of ſacrifice according to that order whereof to ſpeake particularly the Apoſtle ſignifyeth his reſpectiue forbearing *becauſe the Hebrewes were become weake to heare*. (*Habr.* 5. 11.) and yet in general fully ſignifyeth the ſame in affirming our Sauiours yet continued ſacrifycing *Habr.* 8. 3. and the Churches yet

the foreſaid obiection taken from the epiſtle to the Hebrewes: which ſaid epiſtle is ſo far from inpugning our ſacrifice, that to the contrary it rather (*) *direttly proueth* and eſtabliſheth the ſame. *A fourth obertion*, or difficulty is, that howſoeuer the communicant may be ſaid to apply by faith Chriſtes death to him ſelfe, yet it ſeemeth hard and vnexplicable that the Preiſt ſhould in his oblatiõ make application of the benefit thereof, to or for any other: In explanation whereof I breifly anſweare that the ſpecial efficacy which our diuines do attribute as proper to the ſacrifice of the Maſſe, being not any new redemption but only (as the ſchoolemen ſay) yet like continuing *Altar. Hebr.* 13 . 10 . whereof fee heretofore, *tract.* 3 . *fect* . 3 . *fubdiuif.* 4 . next after q. at *. in the margent.

say) (f) *per modum impetrationis* (as appeareth yet more plainly by that which our aduerfaries do (g) *report* of vs) is not hard or inexplicable, but reafonable and eafie to be conceiued; the fame being (in reguard of the like peculiar effect) femblable (though in far tranfcendent fort) vnto *praier,* which profiteth, not onely the party praying, (*) but others alfo for whom praier is made accordingly as (in fome like refemblance thereof) the Scriptures witnes how that *Iob* (h) *offered burnt offeringes* for his abfent childreen *according to the number of them,* for (faith he) *it may be that my fonnes haue finned.* The other like examples whereof are frequent in the (*) writinges of the old Teftament. Thus our Sauiour inftituted in his moft holy fupper with his Apoftles, geuing as then, his moft bleffed body, not onely to them, but (i) *for them.* And thus the auncient Fathers of the Primitiue Church practifed offering this moft acceptable facrifice, not onely for the (k) *liuing,* but alfo (l) *for the deade.*

Of the

(f)
See *Bellarmine de Miffa, l.* 2 . *c.* 4 . *circa med.*

(g)
Hereof fee heretofore, *tract.* 3 . *fect.* 5 . *fubdiuif.* 1 . at r. in the margent at the letter r.

(*)
Go to my feruant · Iob he fhal pray for you , him wil I accept. Iob. 42 . 8 . the Apoftle, *hoped by the praiers of others to be geuen to them. Philemon verf.* 22 . *helpe me with your praiers. Rom.* 15 . 30 . *pray one for an other.* and for this reafon there expreffed, *for the feruent praier of the iuft auaileth much' Iacob .* 5 . 16 . how much more then is this moft acceptable facrifice auailable for others, whe

it is (according to Chriftes inftitution) by the Preift offered and prefented for the to God. (h) *Iob.* 1 . 5 . (*) In refpect of the facrifices for finne mencioned, *Exod.* 29 . 36 . *& Leuit* . 7 . 2 . *et numer.* 28 . 22 . the Apoftle faith, that *euery Preift is ordained for men in thinges pertaining to God that he may offer guiftes and facrifices for finnes.* and not onely for *him felfe, but alfo for the people. Habr.* 5 . 1 . 3 . (i) *Is geuen for you. Luc.* 22 . 20 . *Is fhed for many vnto remiffion of finnes. Math.* 26 . 28 . and fee *Marc.* 14 . 24 . and *Luc.* 22 . 20 . (k) See heretofore, *tract.* 3 . *fect.* 1 . *fubdiuif.* 3 . in the margent there at the letters r. and . s. (l) See heretofore, *tract.* 3 . *fect.* 1 . *fubdiuif.* 3 . at the letters t . u . x . c.

pag. 283.

(m) Of the

(m)
Of the miracles concer-
ning the real presence,
see heretofore, *tract. 2.*
p. 187. sect. 6. throughout.
And concerning adora-
tion, see heretofore *tract.*
2. sect. 8. & sect. 9.
p. 198. 218. throughout.

(n)
August. de ciuit. Dei l.
22. c. 8. circa med.

(*)
Perrexit vnus obtulit ibi
sacrificium corporis Christi
&c.

(o)
Gregor. hom. 37. in E-
uang. et vide Greg. l. 4.
dial. c. 57.

(p)
Beda, hist. l. 4. c. 22.
ante med.

(*)
Beda vbi supra.

(q)
Eum vxor sua cum ex ea-
dem captiuitate non recipe-
ret, extinctum putauit,
pro quo iam velut mortuo
hostias hebdomadibus sin-
gulis curabat offerri.

(r)
Beda, l. 4. c. 22. post
med.

(s)
Greg. hom. 37. in Euang.
(t) *Beda*

Of the miracles shewed by God in behalfe of
Masse, and sacrifice: and of Luthers in-
struction against it from the Deuil.

SECTION. 6.

ANd as almighty God haith (for our
confirmation in the true faith) vouchsaifed to shew vndoubted *miracles* in proofe
of the real presence and adoration of the
blessed Sacrament sundry of which miracles,
are (m) *heretofore* reported: So haith he in
like manner approued our Catholicke doctrine of Masse and sacrifice, with his like
powerful testimonies, of wich many, I wil
onely alledge some few, and those taken,
not from fabulous legendes, but from most
graue authority, S. *Augustine* reporteth of
his owne time, and country, how that a certaine *worshipful man* called (n) *Hesperius, who*
(saith he) *haith a peece of gold* ground *with vs, in his*
territory of Fussala called Cuber, when he vnder-
stood his house to be infested with wicked spirites to
the affliction of his beastes, and seruantes, he desired
in my absence certaine of our Preistes that some
of them would go thither &c. one went (*) *and*
offered there the sacrifice of the body of Christ
praying what he might that the vexation might
cease, and God being thereupon merciful it ceased.
also S. (o) *Gregory* and (p) S. *Bede* make
report of two seueral persons who be-
ing *taken prisoners in the warres* and so detai-
ned in prison were by their frendes thought
to be slaine: In so much as a certaine Preist
brother (as S. *Bede* reporteth) to the one
of them, (*) *pro absolutione anima eius sepius*
Missas facere curauit, caused Masse to be often
said.

said for pardon of his soule. And the like (as reporteth S. *Gregory*) was procured in behalfe of the other by (q) *his wife,* whereupon it hapened that at *certaine howers the Irons did without any* outward meanes or helpe, *fal louse from the said imprisoned persons:* And afterwardes they being set at liberty, and returned home it fel out vpon accompt and obseruation of time that as S. *Bede* saith of thone *(r) his handes were loased specially at those times when Masse was celebrated for him.* and as S. *Gregory* saith of the other, (s) *his wife calling to memory the daies and howers, acknowledged him to be loased* (of his Irons) *euen then when for him she remembred the sacrifice to be offered.* S. *Bede* in his report mencioned withal the names of the partie and of his said brother the Preist, and the place of his aboade, affirming further that it was reported to him by credible (t) *persons who heard it from the party him selfe,* whereupon (saith he) *hauing so good proofe I thought good to insert the same without any doubt into my Ecclesiastical history.* And the other miracle was so certainly knowen that S. *Gregory* beginning to speake thereof saith, (u) *dearly beloued I am perswaded that many of you do know that whereof now I wil remember you.* In like manner doth (x) *Simeon Metaphrastes* make like report of an other prisoner thought to be slaine, whose bandes were in like sort loased in time of sacrifice offered for him. And S. (y) *Gregory* reporteth an other like miracle concerning a *Mariner* who being left in extrame daunger of drowning in the middest of the Seas, was thereupon thought to be drowned, whereupon (saith *Gregory) a certaine Bishop commaundeth to offer vnto God in absolution of his soule, the sacrifice of the healthful host:* and afterwardes the party him selfe escaping most miraculously from drowning, tould the same Bishop how that *when he was in the middest of the Sea, one appeared to him and refreshed him with bread,* and that afterwardes he escaped saife to land, which thing (saith *Gregory) when the Bishop heard, he enquired of the time, and found it to be that day in which the Preist offered for him to almighty God, the sacrifice of the holy oblation.* In this report S. (*) *Gregory*

X x   mecioneth.

(t)
Beda, l. 4. c. 22. fine.

(u)
Gregorius, vbi supra.

(x)
Simeon Metaphrastes, in vita Ioannis Eleemozinarij, apud Surium, tom. 1.

(y)
Greg .l.4. Dial. cap. 57.

(*)
The parties name was *Baraca,* the Bishop was called *Agathus* and was *Panormitanus Episcopus.* and of the said *Baraca Gregorie* saith, *nunc eiusdē Ecclia clericatus officio fungitur.*

(z) See

mencioneth the parties name, the Bishops name, and the place of their dwelling affirming further that the party him selfe (*nunc vsq̃, testatur*) *was then liuing and did testify the same.* Hereunto might be added aswel the foresaid vision of *Angels* in time of sacrifice reported heretofore by *S. Chrisostome,* from (z) *a holy man to whom* (saith he) *many reuelations were seene.* And further testimony of like vision, shewed to (a) *S. Chrisostome* him selfe, and by him *declared in priuate to his spiritual frendes.* As also that which (b) *Simeon Metaprastes* mencioneth concerning the like visió of *Angels,* appearing in time of sacrifice, with such light to the behoulders that *they cast thē selues prostrate vpon the earth as not being able to behold the splendor that thence proceeded,* whereunto I might likewise ad that memorable vision of *Gemmes,* appearing with great luster and glory vpon S. *Martins* hand when he was offering sacrifice to God, and reported by three sundry auncient Fathers, namely by *Seuerus* (c) *Sulpitius,* (d) *Paulinus Nolanus,* and (e) *Fortunatus.* I am not ignorant how prophainly & contemptuously our hardned aduersaries do thinke and speake of this foresaid miracle, (f) *I waye not worth a flie* (saith *M. Fulke*) *that tale you tel out of Beda, of him that had his chaines falen of in Masse time, that credulous and superstitiouse age had many such fained miracles. And the like* (g) *fable* (saith he) *telleth Gregory, hom.* 37. *in Eaung.* thus basely thinketh he of S. *Beda,* who by
the

(z) See heretofore, *tract.* 2. *sect.* 8. *subdiuis.* 2. in the margent at the letter r.

(a) *Nilus Monachus, in epist. ad Anastasium Episcopum.* saith hereof, *Ioanes Sacerdos admirandum Ecclesiæ Constātinopolitanæ &c. videbat domum Domini refertam Angelorum cætu et tunc in primis cum diuinum et incruentum sacrificium offerebatur, quo quidem tempore stupore ac letitia plenus, rem precipuis amicis spiritualibus priuatim enarrauit &c.*

(b) *Simeon Metaphrastes in vita Sancti Clementis Ancirani.*

(c) *Seuerus Sulpitius de vita Martini. dial.* 2. *et* 3. saith, *testatur Arborius expræfectus vidisse se Martini manum, sacrificium offerentis vestitam quodammodo nobilissimis gemmis luce micare &c.* (d) *Paulinus vita Sancti Martini, l.* 5. saith, *Arborius vidit fulgentem luce micantem gemmarum dum sancta Deo solemma defert Martini rutilasse manum lumenq̃, coruscum &c.* (e) *Fortunatus, l.*4. *vitæ sancti Martini,* maketh like mencion of this miracle. (f) *M. Fulke* in his confutation of Purgatory, pag. 333. (g) *M.*

(g) *M. Fulke* againſt the Rhemiſh Teſtament. *in. Habr. c.* 10. *verſ.* 11. *fol.* 416.

the iudgement euen of Proteſtantes was (h)
for his learning and Godly life renowmed in al the
world, and therefore ſurnamed (i) *the reuerend*
Beda. As alſo of *S. Gregory,* of whom Proteſtantes them ſelues ſay, (k) *that bleſſed and*
holy Father S. Gregory &c. and againe (l)
Gregory great in name and great in deede, a man
adorned with many and great guiftes of diuine
grace. Therefore I doubt not Chriſtian reader (this mans inſolence notwithſtanding)
but that the graue and credible teſtimonies
of *S. Beda, Gregory, Chriſoſtome,* and thoſe
other auncient Fathers before herein alledged ſhal incite and ſtir up to due and anſwearable conſideration.

(2) Onely now in the meane time I am
to requeſt thy patience, whiles I report to
thee out of our aduerſaries owne wordes,
ſuch there pretended miracles againſt the
Maſſe as are extant in their owne writinges :
To begin with *Martin Luther,* he did continue his accuſtomed ſaying of *Maſſe* vntil that
(among the (m) ſeueral apparitions hapned to
him, not of Angels, for therein he ſpecially
(*) diſclaimeth, but of wicked ſpirites wherwith he was infeſted or haunted, whereof
one was ſo feareful that *he was almoſt* (n) caſt

(h)
See *M. Coupers* Cronicle
at *Anno Dom.* 734. *fol.*
168. & *Hollinſhead* Cro-
nicle of the laſt edition,
vol. 2. *pag.* 130. and
M. Foxe, act. mon. pag.
128.

(i)
Vbi ſupra.

(k)
So ſaith *M. Godwine* in
his Catallogue of the
Biſhops of England *pag.*
3.

(l)
So ſaith *D. Humfrey* in
Ieſuitiſmi. part. 2. 5. *rat.*
5. *pag.* 624.

(m)
Manlius, Luthers ſcholer
teſtifyeth this in *Loc.*
com. pag. 42. and ſee
alſo the Alphabetical
table of that booke at the
letter l. where it is ſet
dowen, *Luthero ſæpius*
ſpectra apparuerunt. And

Luther 1. *Teutonic. ad Senat. ciuit. Germ.* ſpeaking of other ſectaries (to
wit the *Swinkfeldians,* & *Anabaptiſtes,* who bragged of voices & apparitions) confeſſeth of him ſelfe ſaying, *ego quoq̃ fui in ſpiritu, atq̃ etiã vidi*
ſpiritus (ſi omnino de proprijs gloriandum eſt) forte pluſquam ipſi intra annum
videbunt. (*) Luther, *in Lutheri loc. com. claſ.* 4. *pag.* 39. ſaith,
nullas apparitiones Angelorum habeo. and *Ibidem. pag.* 40. he further
ſaith, *pactum feci cum domino Deo meo ne vel viſiones, vel ſomnia, vel eti-*
am Angelos mihi mittat. and ſee further there *pag.* 40. (n) *Manlius*
in locis

X x 2

in locis communibus, *pag.* 42. and 43.

(o)
Luther, tom. 7. *Witten-berg. Anno.* 1588. *in libro de Missa priuata et vnctione Sacerdotum fol.* 443. and *tom.* 6. *Germ. Genens. fol.* 28. *in libro de Missa angulari.* Also Luthers wordes hereof are acknowledged and set dowen in the trea-tise *against the defence of the censure. pag.* 234. 235. & 236.

(p)
So is it answeared in the *treatise against the defence of the censure. pag.* 234. and by sundry others.

(q)
Next heretofore at the letter o.

(r)
Luther, speaking there further of this his confe-rence with the deuil saith, *et ego plane per-swasus sum Emserum, et Oecolampadiū et similes his ictibus, horibilibus et quas-sationibus subito extinctos esse: nec enim humanum cor horrendum hunc et in effabilem impetum, misi Deus illi adsit perferre potest.* (s) *Hic certe sudor mihi erupit, habet diabolus grauem et fortem vocem, atq; ego tum bene expertus sum quomodo*

into a *sound,* in remedy wherof *oyle was distilled into his eare, & his feete rubbed with hot cloathes*) it hapned that (o) *vpon a certaine time* (as him selfe reporteth) *he was sodainly awaked a-bout midnight,* then, saith he, *Satan began this disputation with me saying, harken right learned Doctor Luther, thou hast said priuate Masse by the space of fifteene yeares, almost euery day, what if such priuate masses were horrible Idolatry?* and then the Deuil laieth dowen sundry long ar-gumentes against the Masse, after which *Lu-ther* mencioneth his owne answears thereto, and the deuils reply; to which in the end *Lu-ther* yealdeth, the *Deuil* being so the first that diswaded *Luther* frō further saying of Masse. I know right wel that our learned aduersa-ries being greatly ashamed of Luthers first proceeding in this sort against the Masse, do vse sundry sleightes in excuse thereof which for the readers further satisfaction I wil breif-ly examine. Their cheife answeare or rather colour is, that Luther in his foresaid saying meant onely (p) *a spiritual tentation of minde and not any sensible conference had with the Deuil.* But the contrary is many waies euident: as *first* by Satans foresaid preface to him, calling him as before (q) *right learned Doctor Luther. Secondly,* in that Luther saith thereof ther in the same place, (r) *I am verily perswaded that Emser, Oecclampadius, and such like were sodain-ly slaine with these horrible stripes and shakinges &c.* which argueth more then onely a spiri-tual temptation. *Thirdly,* by Luthers discri-bing there the *sound* of Satans voice whereof he faith, (s) *here sweate did burst forth of me,*
the

mane homines in lecto mortui inueniuntur. These wordes of Luthers concerning the *Deuils voice*, are purposly and deceiptfully omitted by the Protestants, in their latter edition of *Wittenberge,* but are yet stil ex-stant in the more auncient edition of Luthers workes. *Tom. 6. len. Germ . fol . 28.*

the deuil haith a great and strong voice, and I, (t) *as then wel, learned how in the morning early* Next heretofore at the *men are found dead in their bed. Fourtly,* by letters m. n. report of other like sensible apparitiōs testi- (u) fyed as (t) *before,* not by any supposed Papist, *Luther in colloquijs mensa-* but by *Ioannes Manlius* Luthers owne scholer, *libus Germanice editis fol .* and also by *Martin Luther* him selfe . *Fiftly,* 275 . by *Luthers* report elswhere, of (u) *the deuils* (x) *often walking with him in his bedchamber . Sixt-* *Tigurin . in confessione* ly, as wel by the *Tigurine Caluinists,* who *Germanica impres . Tigur .* therefore obiected against *Luther* (x) *his di-* *Anno . 1544. vide ibid.* *sputation had with the Deuil.* Also by *Baldui-* *fol. 275.* *nus* the Lutheran confessing this disputation (z) of *Luther* with the deuil to haue bene by him *Balduinus, in. l . de dispu-* written neither (z) *in iest nor hiperbolically,* *tatione Lutheri cum diabo-* *but historically and seriously. Seauenthly* and *lo &c . pag. 83 . saith* lastly hereof, *fateor disputatio-*

nem illam esse veram et neq, ioco, neq, hiperbolice, sed serio et historice scriptam. And the like he affirmeth futher in the same booke, *pag. 75. & 76.* And wheras this *Balduinus* perceiuing the vanity of the other answeares, seeketh to euade by his late inuented answeare not yet mentioned, as namely, that for so much as Luther had before the time of his di-sputation geuen ouer saying of Masse, the deuil yet now alledgeth out of the Scriptures true argumēts against the Masse not to diswade frō the Masse, but therebyto set forth the greeuousnes of *Luthers* former sinne in hauing said Masse, & so therby to driue him into dispaire . *Ibid. pag.* 91 . 92. 105. *&c .* the falshood of this answeare consisting only vpon this point, that *Luther* had before the time of this disputatiō geuen ouer the Masse, is many waies discouerable . As *first,* in that it is but mere fiction whithout any testimony of *Luthers* wordes to iustify the same. *Secondly,* in that Satan most plainly to the contrary speaketh of *Luthers* estate not onely as past, but also as then present, saying and obiecting to *Luther* in that disputation there recyted by *Balduinus, tu impius et ig-*

narus stas ibi solus, et putas Christum propter te instituisse Sacramentum, et protinus in tua priuata Missa te conficere corpus et sanguinem Domini, cum non sis membrum sed hostis Christi &c. tu solus in angulo tuo tacens et mutus comedis solus, bibis solus. Ibidem. pag. 44. 45. 46. and *sicut tu facis in missa. pag.* 51. and *nunc annos quindecim totos, semper solus priuatim pro te in Missa vsus es Sacramento. pag.* 38. And againe *quare ergo in missa priuata blaspheme contrauenis claris verbis et ordinationi Christi, et postea tuo mendacio tuæ impietati pratexis nomen et intentionem Ecclesiæ, et misero hoc fuco ornas comentum? pag.* 58. 59. and see the like *pag.* 56. Al which had beene improper and impertinently vrged by *Satan,* had *Luther* then long before geuen ouer his accustomed saying of Masse. *Thirdly,* this appeareth yet more manifestly by *Luthers* then defending against the deuil his foresaid saying of Masse in these wordes, *cui ego respondi, sum vnctus Sacerdos, accepi vnctionem et consecrationem ab Episcopo, et hæc omnia feci ex mandato et obedientia maiorum, quare non consecrassem cum verba Christi serio pronunciarim, et magno serio missam celebrarim? pag.* 31. And againe, *in hoc agone volebam retundere hostem armis quibus assuetus eram sub Papatu, obyciebamq́, intentionem et fidem Ecclesiæ. pag.* 55. *initio.* Thus euidently did *Luther* in the beginning of this disputation vndertake to defend his saying of Masse, and to answeare the deuils argumentes; whereas if *Balduinus* answeare were true, he should insteed therof haue alledged against the deuil, that he had already then before geuen ouer saying of Masse, and had also repented him for saying thereof. *Fourthly,* the other forealledged Protestantes would neuer (as before) haue so denyed *Luthers* sensible conference with the deuil and betaken themselues to their other foresaid answeares had this pretended answeare of *Balduinus* beene either true or probable.

(y)
Sutliue, l. de vere Catholica Christi Ecclesia. pag. 298. saith, *per somnum tantū diabolū secū colloqui visum, dicit Lutherus.* and *pag.* 299. *paulo ante med.* he futher saith hereof, *Lutherus autem nihil aliud*

lastly this answeare or rather euasion of spiritual temptation to be hereby onely meant, is so false that *M. Sutliue* inuenteth therefore an other further shift, answearing that *Luther* in his foresaid saying, setteth downe onely (y) *his dreame*; but that is as false as is the other, & directly against Luthers owne wordes, which are, that he was first (z) so
dainty

pecauit quam quod vt homo Germanus et non ita pridem Monachus qui has
de diabolo-

de diabolorum apparitionibus Monasticas fabulas e mente adhuc eiecerat, (non) *omnium narrat erasso filo, quare si nullum habeant aliud huius calumniæ juramentum præter somnium quod ipsi etiam male detorquent, nihil est quod &c.*

danly awaked about midnight: and that thereupon then afterwardes *Satan began disputation with him &c.* As also the other premises of *Luthers* supposing (3) *Emser, and Oecolampadius,* to haue bene *sodainly slaine* with such like *horrible encounters* argue more then a *dreme* for it were strange to thinke that men should be *slaine by dreaming*: and so likewise doth our other aduersaries former confession to the contrary, and further forbearing to make this answeare. Ad but now hereunto that *Ioannes Regius,* a Protestant writer of principal note, seeing the matter so plaine and no excuse left for *Luther,* vndertaketh therfore insteede of excuse to iustify the same, answering thereto, either that *(4) the spirit (which thus appeared to Luther, and whom Luther affirmeth to haue bene Satan) was no wicked spirit, or if he were that, yet it followeth not that he should lye to Luther,* in his foresaid instructing him gainst the Masse, so variable, perplexed, & miserable, or rather recreant, is their defence of *Luther* in this behalfe. A thing so euident that *Hospinianus* though a learned Caluinist and honouring Luther for *(5) a man adorned by God with most excellent virtues and light of heauenly doctrine &c.* doth yet in ful andplaine tearmes acknowlege that *(6) Luther being taught by the deuil that the Masse was a wicked thing and bing ouercome with the deuils arguments,* did

(z) See next *heretofore* at the letter o.

(3)
See next heretofore at the letter r.

(4)
Ioannes Regius, in l. Apologetico pro Ecclesia angustanæ confessionis &c. pag. 123. saith hereof to Bellarmine obiecting the same, quid hoc administerium seu doctrinam verbi diuini per Lutherum restauratum euertendum aut ad Missæ etiam veritatem stabiliendam? et vnde constat tibi malum ipsum fuisse spiritum qui hoc dixerit? et posito licet malus fuisset, non sequitur tamen mox eum mentitumfuisse quia et vera interdum diaboli loquuntur.

(5)
Hospinian. in hist. sacram. part. 2. in Prolegomen. fol. 2. saith of Luther, Suinglius, and Caluin, hos tres viros nosco a Deo ornatos fuisse multis excellentibus donis et virtutibus &c. Luce diuinitus formatos & excitatos ad Ecclesiam Christi &c.

ce doctrinæ cælestis &c. Zelo gloriæ Dei &c. citatos ad Ecclesiam Christi &c.　　(6) Hospinian. ibidem. fol. 131. saith, narrat Lutherus se a diabolo edoctum esse quod missa priuata in primis fit res *fit res mala, & rationibus diaboli coniunctum aboleuisse eam*. And *Ibidem. fol. 131. a circa med.* he further saith, *in lucem quoq̃ emisit hoc anno Lutherus librum de missa priuata & Sacerdotum cosecratione, in quo statim ab initio describit colloquium a se cum diabolo in tempesta nocte habitum in eoq̃ se de multis abusibus Missæ priuatæ præcipue a cacodemone admonitum fatetur*. And in the margent there he setteth downe, *Colloquium Lutheri cum diabolo, a quo instituitur de erroribus mis-*

(*)
Melancthon apud Hospinianum in hist. sacram. part. 2. fol. 108. saith, *præterrem tumultuatur Suinglius in alijs quibusdam articulis videtur in homine magis heluoticus quidam quà Christianus esse spiritus*

(a)
Suinglius, l. de subsid. Euchar. And see these wordes alledged & confessed *in the treatise against the defence of the censure, pag. 249. and 250.*

(*)
Ibi visus est monitor adesse, ater fuerit an albus nihil memini.

(b)
Suinglius vbi supra.

(c)
Iacobus Andræas in confut. disput. Ioannis Iacobi Grinæi. pag. 304. saith, *Lutherus Ecclesiam Dei grauiter et seueriter monuit vt sibi a spiritu inquam Suingli-*

did (thereupon) abandon the same.

(3) Hereunto I wil ad the like supposed miraculouse apparition which hapned to *Suinglius*, a man greatly disliked (*) of *Melancthon*, when he laboured the abolishing of the Masse at *Zurich*; the which I wil deliuer from his owne wordes, wherein it appeareth that *Suinglius* disputing thereof as then with a certaine Scribe (a) *was prouoked to bring forth examples which were ioyned with no parrable therefore we began* (saith he) *to thinke of al that we could, but yet no other example came to minde &c. but when the 13. day of April drew nere I tel the truth, and that so true as though I would conceale it my conscience compelleth me to vtter what the Lord bestowed vpõ me &c. me thought as I was on sleepe I was againe disputing with my aduersary the Scribe, and my mouth so stopped that I was not able to speake &c. then sodainly there was seene* (*) *an admonisher to be present with me, whether he were blacke or white I remember not &c.* which said, *why doest thou not coward answeare him that which is written. Exod. 12. for it is the Pascal which is the pasouer of the Lord: Imediatly as this sight appeared I a wooke and lept out of my bed and fi st I considered the place in the seauenty interpreters on euerey side, and thereof before the whol Congregation I preached, which sermon when it was heard droue away al mist &c.* Thus was *Suinglius* his foresaid proceeding against the Masse, furthered with nightly instruction

struction in his dreame by an admonisher, *whether blacke or white he remembreth not,* wherof though he made seriouse and great accompt affirming it to be no (b) *light matter which* (saith he) *I learned by this dreame thankes be to God &c.* yet is the same discouered & derided for a mere illusion by *Martin Luther,* and (c) *Iacobus Andreas,* by (d) *Conradus Sclhusselburge,* and sundry (e) *other* learned Protestants. To this which haith bene said concerning *Luther,* and *Suinglius,* might also be added a third example of (*) *that epicurian gospellar Carolastadius,* (so *M. Fulke* tearmeth him) the (¶) *first beginner* in that age of the Sacramentary doctrine, of whom a learned Protestant writer of our nation witnesseth saying, (f) *amongst others Carolastadius, a preacher professing the gospel &c.* attributed *much to Cabinet teachers in priuate conuenticles and vnto visions and pretended conferences with God:* Thus was this daughter of eternal dakenes, I meane the Sacramentary error (so directly impugning our blessed sacrifice of the

Suinglianorum caueant, ex cuius reuelatione in somnio facta Suinglius gloriatus est, se interpretationem verborum Testamenti Christi a se confictam didicisse, neq, tamen meminisse ait, atir an albus fuerit, de quo Lutherus predixit, quod non minores turbas Ecclesiae et Reipub. sit daturus quam spiritus Anabaptistaru &c. et vide Ibidem. pag. 120. et pag. 254. (d) *Schlusselburg. in theologia Caluinistarum in proem. fol. 3. saith, notetur quam trepidante conscientia Suinglius hanc causam facrimentariaagit &c. modo enim affirmat sibi Dominu Deum istam suam doctrinam de Sacramento impertisse, modo asserit se ignorare, an ater vel albus spiritus, hoc est num vel bonus Angelus vel ipse diabolus fuerit qui per somnium et haresim de Sacramentis suggessit: certissi num autem est &c. malu Angelum fuisse monitorem istum qui Suinglio in somnio dogma Sacramentarium eiusq, in crastinationem reuelauit.* In proofe whereof he there setteth dowen sundry reasons at large. (e) The like is affirmed by *Bedneict. morgensterne in tract. de Ecclesia. pag. 68.* and by *Dauid Rungius in disputationibus &c. disput. 11. part. 1. sect. 8.* and by *Iacobus Heilbrunerus in Schwenckfeldio, Caluinismo &c. in præfat.* (*) *M. Fulke in his reioynder to Bristowes reply &c. pag. 420..* (¶) *Melancthon, in epist. ad Fridericum Michonium,* saith hereof, *Carolastadius primum excitauit hunc tumultum &c. Carolastadius* first of al in our memory raised vp this stir aboute the Sacrament a rude sauage man &c. so far of it is that euer any signe of Gods spirit appeared in him. (f) In the booke entituled *Conspiracy for pretended reformation. pag. 83.* And

Luther

Luther in his booke *contra caelestes Prophetas*, the second part *tom.* 3.
Ieneus. fol. 68. And *Chemnitius* in his booke *de cæna Domini. pag.* 214.
affirmeth, that *Carolastadius was instructed by the deuil, and that him selfe*
was wont to boast among his frendes that a certaine strange man came to him
and taught him, how to intarpret the wordes of the supper, this is my body,
which man Carolastadius thought to be a Prophet sent from heauen, but saith
Luther, vel diabolus fuit vel diaboli mater, it was the deuil or the deuils
damme. And see further hereof the Protestant writer *Albertus contra*
Carolastadianos. z. 4. *pa.* 1. and y. 2. *pa.* 1. And *Luther in colloq.*
mensal. fol. 367. and 371.

(*)
Luther cōfesseth this saying, *pactū feci cū Domino*
ne Angelos mihi mittat,
alledged next hereto-
fore, *subdiuis.* 2. in the
margent at *. next af-
ter m.

(g)
Hereof see heretofore,
tract. 2. *sect.* 8. *subdiuis.*
2. in the margent at r.
and *tract.* 3. *sect.* 6.
subdiuis. 1. at a. b..

(h)
Daniel. 12. 11. & here-
of see *heretofore pag.*

(i)
Mathew, 24. 15. wher-
by it is signifyed that
Daniels Prophecy is to
be fulfilled towardes the
latter end of the world,
and so concerneth the
taking away of the Christians *dayly sacrifice* .

(k)
Many doubt that this

the Masse) brought forth to the world in
this last age, not (*) *with vision of Angels* or
other miracle from heauen, *heretofore* (g)
mencioned by S. *Chrisostome*, and other Fathers in behalfe of our Churches sacrifice,
but in lew thereof with infernal nightly and
ghostly apparition, and haith so accordingly
euer since raged through the world like a
fatal *Erinnis*, breathin for the ouerthrow of
religiouse houses, & other monuments of piety erected by our Catholicke ancestors together also with the Churches further vastety
and direct course of preparatiō to (h) *the*
taking a way of the dayly sacrifice, and setting vp
so the abominable desolation foretold by (i) *Da-*
niel.

That the impugners of the Masse in the ages be-
fore Luther, were al of them in other mat-
ters confessed heretickes.

SECTION. 7.

A Nd like as such haith bene the prodi-
giouse begunning and diuulging of our
aduersaries doctrine in this last age, so also it
is worthy of obseruation to remember that
although

although the enemy haith in the former ages before *Luther* busily laboured to set it a-broach, yet the Patrons and publishers therof to the world in those times, (the chosen instrumentes for such a purpose) were al of them in other pointes of faith grosse heretickes whose memories remaine yet to this day accordingly branded with the hatful note of sundry confessed and execrable errors. To make some litle examination hereof, although we should (k) admit for true, the writinges now extant vnder the name of *Bertram* who liued *Anno. Domini.* 840. to haue bene written by him, and though likewise we should suppose that his meaning thereby had bene to haue gainsaid our now professed Catholicke doctrine of the Sacrament; which thing the Century writers vtterly deny, charging that very booke to the contrary with (l) transubstantiation, for so much yet (al this suppo-sed notwithstanding) as the author thereof whosoeuer he were, appeareth euidently to haue bene (to speake the least) so fearfully (m) *ambiguouse*, and doubtful in his couert manner of writing and to haue purposly vsed therein such an affected kind of reseruati-on as no man might be able directly to charge him

booke *de corpore et san-guine Domini* now extant vnder *Bertrams* name should be none of his, for it was first published of late by *Oecolampadius.* And *Pantaleō* in his *Chronogr. pag.* 65. mencioning *Bertram*, and his other writinges forbea-reth yet to mencion this. As also *Illuricus* forbea-reth to mention *Berthrā* in his *catologue* of (Pro-testant) *witnesses.* As for the auncient booke writ-ten indeede by *Bertram* vnder this very title, it is vnlike that it were ex-tant, it should make a-gainst Masse and the re-al presence, because that it is mencioned and com-mended by our knowen cōfessed Catholicke wri-ters of auncient times & also euen by *Tritbemias,* (*in libro de scriptoribus Ec-*

clesiasticis. at *Anno Domini.* 840.) who liuing but some 120. yeares since, would neuer haue so commended any booke written against the knowen doctrine of that time. (1) *The Century writers, cent.* 9. *c .4 .col.* 212. saith, *transubstatiationis semina habet Bertramus, vtitur enim vocabulis, permutationis commutationis & conuersionis &c.* (m) *Ambi-guouse,* as where he saith, *sub velameuto corporei pants spiritualiter corpus et sanguis Christi existunt.* and againe, *corpus et sanguis Christi dicuntur, quia non quod exterius videntur, sed quod interius diuino spiritu operante facta sunt, accipiuntur; et quia longe aliud per spiritualem potentiam existunt, quam corporaliter apparent.* yet more *ex his omnibus qua hactenus dicta sunt mon-*

strant.

stratum est quod corpus et sanguis Christi quæ fidelium ore in Ecclesia perci-piuntur, figura sunt secundum speciem visibilem, at vero secundum spiritu-alem substantiam, id est diuini potentiam verbi, corpus et sanguis Christi vere existunt. who reading these can thinke otherwise but his meaning to be that Christes body is really and truly present vnder the exter-nal & outward Sacramēt.

(n) Open Patrons of that opi-nion there were then none, for *Pascasius* who liued *Anno*. 880. some *fourty yeares* after *Bertram* and wrote a peculiar booke *de corpore et sangui-ne Domini*. wherein he so euidently affirmeth our doctrine of real pre-sence, that he is therfore reiected & charged with real presence, and tran-substantiation by *M. Fulke*, *Oecolampadius*, *Crispinus*, *Prætorius*, and the Century writers, al-ledged heretofore, *tract.*

him with ful and plaine impugning of the real presence, I wil therefore forbeare to al-ledge him for any of those who were (n) o-pen Patrons and publishers to the world of our aduersaries doctrine: And obseruing (as not improper) the foretould (*) *letting loose of Satan after the end of the (first) thousand yeares*, wil begin with *Berengarius from whom* (as our aduersaries themselues do confesse) (o) *the first publicke conflict did spring, Anno Dom*. 1050. This man beginning to diuulge and publish the innouation of his Sacramen-tary error, which was then in him gainsaid (p) by the whol Christian world confessed-ly withal taught sundry grosse errors, for (q) *he denyed the grace of Baptisme ; denyed (also that men committing mortal sinne could euer ob-taine pardon therefore ; and besides this he was an enemy*

2. *sect*. 2. *subdiuis*. 2. at g. h. i. *. doth in his said booke affirme of our said doctrine of real presence, saying, *there is none who doth o-penly contradict this which the whol world beleeueth*. (*) *Reuelat*. 20. 3. (o) *Ioachim Chamerarius*, a learned Protestant in his *Historica narra-tio de Ecclesijs fratrum in Bohemia &c*. pag. 161. saith euen of tran-substantiation, *post Annum Christi*, 850. *tanquam in quieta possessione mansit (dogma transubstantiationis) vsq̃ ad Berengarij tempora, & annum Christi circiter* 1050. *nam etsi antea priuatis scriptis quorundam notata res fuit, publica tamen* Surrazis *a Berengario primæ extitit*. (p) *Papir Mas-son. Annal. Francorum. l.* 3. *in Henrico Rege*. saith, *Berengario illius temporis theologi bellum omnes indixere*. And see the further testimony herein of *Lanfrancus*, who wrote against *Berengarius*, alledged here-tofore, *tract*. 2. *sect*. 2. *subdiuis*. 1. at e. *. (q) *Papir Masson, in Annalibus*

Annalibus Francorum. l . 3 . in Hugone, et Roberto. Also *Oecolampadius in libro epistolarum Occolampadij, et Sningly, l . 3 . pag .* 710 . saith yet further *Berengarius nonnulla affirmabat aduersus contugium, et Baptismum Paruulorum .* and *pag .* 711 . he yet further saith, *deinde etiam Berenga- rius parum candide incessisse deprehenditur .* and *pag . 712 . damnata est Berengarij opinio nimirum Sacerdotio parum Christiano minus tribuens.* And *Chrispinus* the Caluinist, in his booke of the estate of the Church, pag . 289 . saith, *although Beregarius had the truth of his side, yet had he a certain hatred against Lanfrancus & Rogerius mingled with glory &c. he migled withal certaine speaches of mariage, and the Baptisme of litle Children &c. so it cometh to passe when without the Lords feare we wil mantaine the cause of the Gospel .*

enemy to mariage &c. Onely in this he was happy , that he (r) *recanted* and some what before his death (s) *heartily repented* him of his said sacramentary and other errors, and finally dyed in the bosome of the Catholicke Church, in respect of which his said conuer- sion and others his excellent guiftes of nature (common for the most part to most Arch- heretickes) sundry of our writers afford him that commendable memory, which is by our aduersaries so often mistaken, and imperti- nently alledged.

This being the end of *Berengarius* and his said Sacramentary error , being in respect of publicke dispute with him extinct, it was next afterwardes publickely reuiued about *Anno Dom .* 1218. by *the waldenses,* and (t) *Albigenses,* men liuing in one time, and of *one* (u) *sect* onely diuersifyed in name, according to

penitentiam vt spero ad gloriam &c. see this also more fully in *Papir Masson . in Annal . Francorum . l . 3 . in Philip . Rege.* and in *Vincentius, l . 25 . c . 30.* and in *Malmesbury, l . 3 . c . 58. & 59.* (t) The Caluinistes in their *Catalogus testiu veritatis. tom .* 2 . printed, *Anno .* 1597 . pag . 535 . do alledge the *Waldenses* opinion to be *omnes missas & præ- cipue pro mortuis impias affirmant.* and *Hospinian , in hist . Sacram . part . 1 .*

(r)

His recantation is recor- ded *verbatim* by the Cen- tury writers, *cent .* 11 . *c . 9. col .* 458.

(s)

Berengarius as lying mor tally sicke and at the point of death is thus reported of by *the Cen- turistes, cent .* 11 . *col .* 657 : *moriens autem Berengari- us die Epiphaniorum gemi- tuq producto recordatus quot miseros quondam ado- lescentiæ primo erroris calore secta infecerit . Hodie in- quit in die apparitionis suæ apparebit mihi Dominus noster Iesus Christus propter*

pag. 343. faith, *Waldenses repudiarunt aperte corporalem Christi in pane præsentiam &c.* And fee *Chrispinus* of the eſtate of the Church, *pag.* 371. *fine.* & *Chrispinus ibidem. pag.* 350. *ante med.* faith of the *Albigenses,* they oppoſed them ſelues *againſt tranſubſtantiation &c.* (u) *Of one ſect,* to this end M. *Sparke* in his anſweare to M. *Iohn D. Albines, pag.* 58. faith to *Albines* of theſe men, *your frendes cal them Waldenses, Albigenses &c· chaunging their titles and names according to the diuerſity of places and times they liued in, howſoeuer their religion was al one.* and the like is afterwardes affirmed by M. *Fulke, de ſucceſſione Eccleſiaſtica, contra Stapletonum. pag.* 332. & *vide Ibidem. pag.* 359. and 333.

(x)
See this in *Guido,* and *Antoninus, de Waldenſibus,* and *Aneas Siluicus,* in his *Bohemica hiſtoria de Waldenſium dogmatibus.* and *Luxemb. in har. Paup. de Lugduno.*

(y)
Illiricus in his *catal. teſt. pag.* 735.

(z)
Illir. ibidem. pag. 748.

(a)
Foxe. Act. mon. pag. 41. and fee *Simon de Voyon,* in his diſcourſe vpon the catallogue of the Doctors of the Church, *pag.* 134.

to the ſeueral places of their aboad, ſo as what is alledged in diſcouery of the one, is thereby ſufficient to charge the other, but to offend in ſurpluſage, and for the auoiding of al ſcruple to ſpeake ſeuerally of them both, and firſt concerning *the Waldenſes* commonly called *Pauperes de Lugduno,* it is abundantly teſtifyed by the (x) writers next thoſe times that they denyed (y) *al iudgement to bloud* and impugned alſo (z) *the Saboath* being therefore called (a) *inſabatiſtes* and to alledge further the very teſtimony of *Reinerus,* (whom our aduerſaries do vnworthily alledge in their excuſe) it appeareth by that auncient (*) examination of them by him written, and by (c) *Illiricus* ſithence publiſhed

(b) M. *White* in his way to the true Church. *pag.* 321. and M. *Welſh,* in his reply againſt M. *Gilbert Browne* Preiſt, *pag.* 188. *circa med.* do both of them alledge maſ=medly and by *peecmele, Reinerus* affirming, that *the Waldenſes beleeued al thinges wel of God, and al the articles contained in the creede &c.* apud *Illir. in catal. teſt. pag.* 727. which thinges many other heretikes did, and ſo accordingly that notwithſtanding, the ſame *Reinerus* ſetteh dowen in his wordes there next following, their many other hereſies by him vtterly condemned, affirming of them in his wordes there next before thoſe alledged by M. *White,* and M. *Welſh,* that *non eſt ſecta perni-*

permisosior Ecclesiæ Dei quam pauperum de Lugduno, tearming allo their opinions in his other wordes a litle there after following *nefandissimas blasphemas,* and *spurc ssimos errores.* (*) *Rejnerus apud Illiricum, in catal.* pag. 726. saith, *inquisitioni et examinationi frequenter interfui &c.*

shed that they further taught that (d) *laye men and women might consecrate the Sacrament, and preach,* that (e) *men ought not to sweare in any case, they condemned* (f) *Iudges,* also (g) *they condemned the Sacrament of mariage,* affirming that those (h) *married persons mortally sinned, who accompained together without hope of issue ;* and affirmed also that (i) *neither Preist, nor ciuil magistrate, being guilty of mortal sinne, did inioy their dignity, or were to be obeyed :* And to omit much more they were confessedly (k) *dissemblers* of their faith and religion; & for such (l) condemned by Protestantes them selues, al this being in it selfe euident, and by our very aduersaries reported. I wil now speake of the *Albigenses* whose execrable errors the Protestant writer *Osiander,* repor-

(c) See it in *Illir. catal.* test. pag. 724. & 725. &c.

(d) *Illir. ibidem.* pag. 731. & 745. & 730. & 732. & 740.

(e) *Illir. ibidem.* pag. 735. & 756. & 752.

(f) *Illir. ibidem.* pag. 735.

(g) *Illir. ibidem.* pag. 751. & 743.

(h) *Illir. ibidem.* pag. 743.

(i) *Illir. ibidem.* pag. 760.

teth *Illir. ibidem.* pag. 760. & 740. and see this foule error testifyed of them by *Osiander, cent.* 9. 10. 11. *&c.* pag. 440. and by *M. Foxe, act. mon.* pag. 44. in the latine *Articles.* (k) *Illir.* pag. 734. it is there said of them, *ipsi etiam ad Ecclesiam ficte vadunt, offerunt, & confitentur & communicant ficte.* And *Illiricus* him selfe, *ibidem.* pag. 722. saith of them, *non est quidem id omnino probandum quod in multis locis diu sine vlla publica confessione fuerint.* And *Ioachim Camerarius* (a learned Protestant writer) in his *Historica narrat de fratrum orthodox. Ecclesijs in Bohemia.* pag. 273. saith vpon the credit of auncient testimony, *sed hoc docere possumus, cum nostris Ecclesijs, illos (Waldenses) nunquam coaluisse, neq, nostros vnquam cum his se coniunxisse voluisse; & duabus quidem de causis sicut in Annalibus nostris legimus, primum enim offendebantur nostri in Waldensibus, quod nulla publica extare vellent doctrinæ et fidei suæ testimonia atq, ita occultare veritatem viderentur &c. Secundo quod missa Pontificia quam idolatricam esse scirent et profiterentur, pacis tamen et tranquillitatis causa vterentur atq, ita*

atq; ita hac in parte cum Pontificijs *colludentes scandalo assent alijs &c.*
(l) *Condemned,* for *Melancthon, in concil . theologic . part. 2. pag . 152.*
writeth to a frend of his saying, *gaudeo te de summa doctrinæ nobiscum
sentire Waldenses scio dissimiles esse, et quidem nimis morose defendunt quadam de quibus aliquando cum eis rixatus sum ; quidam nolunt absoluere lap-
sos qui ad penitentiam redeunt &c.* And *Benedict . Morgenstern .* (a learned Proteitant) *in tract . de Ecclesia. pag . 79 . paulo post med.* faith of
the Waldenses, that they be *falsi fratres quia lucem doctrinæ diuinitus ac-
censsam hoc seculo, superciliose neglexerunt et errors crassissimos etiam ab ipso
Luthero, Anno 1523. monstratos &c. clam scriptis apud suos mordicus de-
fenderunt, id quod demum post obitum Lutheri innotuisse D . D . Ioannes Hede-
ricus scribit &c .* & see there *pag . 154 . & 216.* Selnecerus his teitimony
of the *Waldenses* grosse errors
not to be suffered.

(m)
Osiander in his *epitom .
histor . Ecclef . cent . 13.
l . 1 . c . 4 . pag . 329 .*
faith , *exorta eft hæresis
Albigensium &c . dogma-
ta hæc illis attribuuntur,
duo esse principia, Deum ,
viz . bonum, et Deum ma-
lum, hoc eft diabolum, qui
omnia corpora creet, bonum
aut Deu creare animas &c.
Baptismum abijciant ire in
Ecclesias vel in ijs orare nihil prodesse &c . matrimo-
nia damnabant promiscuos
concubitus , eosq; nefarios
sanctos ducebant, corporum resurrectionem negant &c . quod Christus non fuerit verus homo, nec vere comederit &c .* (n) A litle after *Osiander*
further faith of them, *Hæ propositiones cum sint absurdæ, impiæ, et hære-
tica &c . cum Albigenses admonitiones non admitterent sed in erroribus et
sceleribus persisterent &c .* (o) He further there faith, *fuit enim Albigensis furor Anabaptisticus qualis Anno . 1534. nostro seculo Anabaptistarum
monasteriensium erat .* (p) *Iewel,* in his defence of the Apologie *pag . 48.*
(q) *Pantaleon*

teth to be as following *viz .* (m) they held
two beginninges a good God, and an il God, namely
the deuil : that the good God created our soules,
and the deuil our bodies &c . they reiected Baptifme, and praier in Churches &c . they condemned Matrimony and vsed promiscuoufe and wicked
filthines, they denyed the resurrection of our bodies ;
and affirmeth, that *Christ was not truly man ,
nor did truly eate* ; (n) they persisted (faith *Osiander*) in their errors and wickednes , admitted
no admonition, but were faith he, (o) an Anabaptistical fury, such as was at munster in our owne
age . *Anno . 1534.* In so much as *M . Iewel*
difclaymeth in the *Albigenses.* faying exprefly
of them, (p) *they be none of ours .* and in like
manner are they reiected by (q) *Pantalion,*
and fundry other (r) Proteitant writers .

Next

(q) *Pantaleon, in Cronograph. pag. 98.* numbreth them among *Heretickes.* (r) *M. Marbech,* in his common places, *pag. 22.* expresly censureth them for *hereticks,* withal recyting certaine of their foresaid heresies. And see in the *Century writers cent. 13. col. 555.* and *col. 558.* they say thereof, *durauit ista hæresis ab Anno septimo &c.*

Next after these did *the Apostolici,* publish their opinion against (s) *Masse* and reai presence about *Anno Dom.* 1163. and what were they? most execrable Hereticks, for as the Protestant writer *Osiander* confesseth and reporteth of them they taught amongst many other that (t) *Infantes were not to be Baptised, that virgins were onely to be maried; that a sinner could not be a Bishop; they forbad to eate any thing that came of generation; they affirmed oathes to be vnlawful &c.* in so much as *Osiander* him selfe saith of them, (u) *although they did in some thinges rightly impugne the Papistes, yet in most thinges their opinions were fantastical, Anabaptistical, and to be condemned.* And *M. Iewel* in like sort saith expresly of them (x) *they be none of ours;* as also they are directly writen against, and condemned for heretickes by (y) *S. Barnard,* who liued in the same time with them, *M. Fulke* him selfe thereupon reiecting and condemning them likewise for (z) Heretickes.

(2) About these times were also one *Henrie,* and *Peter Bruis,* two (a) *fellow Gospellers*

(s)
Of *the Apostolici,* impugning *Masse, M. Symonds vpon the reuelations, pag.* 143. alledging them saith, *there were also such as were called Apostolical,* they denyed the *Masse to be a sacrifice, as Berengarius did, they held against real presence &c.*

(t)
Osiander, cent. 12. pag. 291. saith, *extiterunt hoc tempore hæretici qui Apostolici vocati sunt &c. eorum hæc fuerunt dogmata infantes non esse Baptisandos &c. virgines tantum matrimonio copulandas &c. Episcopum esse non posse qui peccator sit &c. omne quod ex coitu procreatur non comedendum &c. iuramenta esse illicita dicunt.* And *S. Bernard* who liued with them and wrote specially against them geueth like testimony of their errors *in serm. 66.* saying of them, *Apostolicos se nominant &c. Irrident nos quia Baptizamus Infantes &c.* and after much more, *multa quidem et alia huic populo stulto et insipienti a spiritibus erroris in hipocrisi loquentibus mendacium mala persuasa sunt, sed non est respondere ad omnia &c.* and see the *Century writers, cent. 12. cap. 5. col. 843. & 844.* (u) So saith *Osiander, cent. 12. pag. 291.* (x) *M. Iewel,* in his defence of the

Apology

Apology, *pag*. 48. (y) *Bernard, serm*. 66. *vt supra*. at t. (z) *M. Fulke* in his retentiue against *Bristow*, *pag*. 124. further saith, *the very same doth Bernard report of the heretickes called Apostolicke &c*.

(a)

Hospinian . in hist . sacram .
part . 1 . *pag* . 361. saith,
Henricus quidam cum Pe-
tro Bruis circa Annum
1140 . *docere cæpit, semel*
tantum in ipsa, nempe vl-
tima Domini cæna Aposto-
lis Christi corpus vere da-
tum sub specie panis deinceps
autem meram deceptionem
esse quod Sacerdotum mi-
nisterio dicitur aut creditur,
testis est et refutator huius
erroris Petrus Cluniacensis,
qui eodem tempore floruit .
And the Caluinistes in
their *catalog. testium ve-*
ritatis, tom. 2 . printed
1597. *pag* . 561. Ioyne

lers, who indeede published to the world
their denyal of (b) masse, & real presence but
their other condemned heresies are yet knowen
and them suruiuing ; for (c) *they denyed* (both)
the Baptisme and saluation of Infantes ; and further affirmed that *Churches ought not to be buil-*
ded, that *the Sacrament ought not as now to be*
ministred, because that Christ at his last supper
gaue it to his Apostles once for al ; they denyed
the actes of the Apostles, and other Scriptures,
besides much more vnworthy to be rehearsed.
In like sort also did (about these times) one
Peter (d) *Abaylardus,* impugne openly the
doctrine of Masse and real presence, but his
monstruouse errors were so grosse as I wonder that any of our learned aduersaries would
euer alledge him : for euen *Oecolampadius*
(who should most excuse him) disclaimeth
in him

them together as fellow Gospellers . and *Osiander, cent*. 12. *pag*. 282.
saith, *Petrus de Bruis , et Henricus ipsius socius &c*. (b) *M. Symondes*
vpon the reuelations. *pag*. 143. alledgeth *Peter Bruis , as differing*
from the Romaines in the doctrine of the Sacrament. and the said last foremencioned treatise of *catal* . *test* . *l* . 15 . *pag*. 561 . reporteth their o-
pinion to be *corpus et sanguinem Christi in theatrica Missa non offerri* . & so
likwise doth *Osiand. Cent* . 12 *pag*. 282. (c) *Osiand. cent*. 12. *l*. 3 . *c*. 3.
pag. 282. saith of the, *in sequentibus aute videtur hi hæretici Baptismu paruul oru*
improbasse &c. *canam sacram non dandam nunc hominibus quia semel data sit*
tantum Apostolis a Christo &c. And see ful testimony of al these errors
geuen by him who liued in the same time with them, namely *Petrus*
Cluniacensis, contra Henricianorum, & Petro Brusianorum hæreses Epistola
duæ. and in his booke *de sacrificio missæ initio*. and see next heretofore
at a. and see them also in the *Centurie writers cent* . 12. *col*. 833. & 834.
(d) *M. Symondes,* vpon the reuelations, *pag*. 142. alledgeth *Pe-*
trus.

trus Abailardus, a man (faith he) *of a moft fubtil witte oppofing him felfe againft the Sacrament of the Altar, he made his Apology in which he defendeth his inocency &c.*

in him, confeffing that (e) *Abailardus denyed the fumme of faith, namely that Chrift fatisfyed for our finnes; euacuating the price of our redemption:* and his many other groffe errors are fo knowen and (f) confeffed that *M. Foxe, Illiricus, Crifpinus,* and other, do therefore forbeare to rancke him in their Catalogues of Proteftant witneffes. in or about this age alfo ftept forth one *Almericus,* publickly inueying (g) againft Maffe and real prefence, but his other damnable errors are likewife knowen and confeffed, for he taught *that* (h) *the omnipotency of* (God) *the Father ceafed by the comming of Chrift, he denyed Baptifme, and the refurrection of our bodies,* and alfo *hel* it felfe: befides his diuers other abfurd monftruous opinions, vnworthy of recital. In refpect whereof *M. Iewel* faith exprefly of him and others

Church, in the table vnder the letter p. fetteth him dowen *Peter de Baylarde hereticke pelagian.* and *Ofiander, cent.* 12. *pag.* 264. faith, *hoc anno fuit Petrus Alaybardus infignis Philofophus fed hæreticus &c. Hos promulgauit errores.* recyting there in particular his monftruous errors: and fee his groffe errors reported by the *Centurie writers. cent.* 12. *col.* 849. in fo much as he was fpecially contradicted by *S. Bernard,* witneffe hereof *M. Simondes,* and *Pantaleon vbi fupra.* and the *Century writers. cent.* 12. *col.* 850. and *Ofiander, in cent.* 12. *pag.* 265. faying, *D. Bernardus Clareualenfis, contra Petrum Abalardum, erudite difputauit.* (g) *Almericus* is alledged as impugning our Churches Catholicke doctrine of the Sacrament by *Pantaleon in cronograph. pag.* 98. by *M. More* in his table, *pag.* 174. And by *Hofpinian* who in his *hift. facram. part.* 1. *pag.* 439. claimeth and alledgeth him faying, *circa An.* 1203. *claruit Almericus qui et tranfubftantiationem et corporalem illam Chrifti in miffa prefentiam aperte negauit, fideiq, fua confeffionem vitâ et fanguine fuo confirmauit.* (h) *Ofiander, cent.* 13. *l.* 1. *c.* 3.

(e)
In libro Epiftolarum Suinglij, et Oecolampadij. pag. 716. *Oecolampadius* faith, *Abelhardus fummam fidei negauit nempe, Chriftum fatisfeciffe pro peccatis noftris &c. precium redemptionis euacuans &c.*

(f)
Pantaleon in cronograph. at *Anno.* 1145. placing him in the rancke of heretickes faith, *Petrus Abailardus præter creatorem et creaturas aliud quiddam ponit et præter Deum aliud ponit æternum.* and *Crifpinus* of the eftate of the

pag. 326. faith, *Almaricus hæreticus parisys ſua dogmata ſparſit ſenſerunt autē Almaricani hæretici &c.* *Patris omnipotentiam Chriſti aduentu deſuſſe Baptiſmum &c. in Eccleſia amplius locum non habere &c. omnem turpitudinem perpetrabant hi hæretici pratextu charitatis reſurrectionem corporum futurum non credebant Paradiſum, & infernum negabant.* And ſee like report made by the *Centurie writers, cent.* 13. *col.* 558. *&* 559. And ſee his groſſe errors further reported by the more auncient writers that liued in, or neare to thoſe times, as namely by *Ceſarius l. dial. d.* 5. and by *Vincentius, Lucelburg. Aquinas, Ganguinus,* and others in their ſeueral reportes of *Almaricus.*

(i)
M. *Iewel, in his defence of the Apology. pag.* 48.
(k)
Oſiander, vt ſupra at h. and *Pantaleon in cronograph. pag.* 98. ranketh him in his Catalogue of *heretickes* ſaying further of him, that *aliquot errores docens comburitur pariſys.* and the *Centurie writers, vbi ſupra.* do implace him in their *fift chapter de hæreſibus.* and ſee *Criſpinus* of the eſtate of the Church, *pag.* 349.
(2)
M. *Simondes* vpon the reuelations, *pag.* 187.
(3)
M. *Willet* in his *tetraſtalon, part.* 3. *pag.* 163.
(4) *Cent.* 13. *c.* 5.

others, (i) *of them we haue no skil they are none of ours.* And other Proteſtant (k) writers do accordingly reiect him for a barbarous and condemned hereticke. about theſe times alſo did appeare the *Beguardes,* whom *M. Symondes* alledgeth as (2) *houlding againſt adoration of the Euchariſt at the eleuation*; but *M. Willet* acknowledgeth and tearmeth them (3) *Heretickes that held diuers heretical and monſtruous opinions:* which their erronious opinions are particularly recyted and confeſſed by the (4) century writers. Laſtly did ariſe vp our country man *Iohn Wicliue* (l) impugning openly the Churches then receiued doctrine of Maſſe and real preſence. And was he otherwiſe cleare? nothing leſſe but deeply ſtained with the blemiſh of ſundry confeſſed and knowen hereſies, for, faith *Melancthon* of him, (m) *he ſcoulded plainly, ſophiſtically, & ſediciouſly, concerning the ciuil magiſtrate,* teaching that (n) *there is no ciuil magiſtrate whileſt he is in mortal ſinne,* and that (*) *the people may at their pleaſure correct Princes when they do offend,* from whence proceeded the many

col. 564. ſaying there further in general of them, *ad vitæ licentiam pleraq̃, eorum dogmata pertinent.* (l) So alledged by *Hoſpinian. in hiſt. ſacram. part.* 1. *pag.* 441. in this point as being euident I wil not vſe

further

further proofe . (m) *Melancthon in epist. ad Fred. Michonium ex-tant in libro epistolarum Oecolampadij, et Suingly. pag. 622.* faith, *de dominio ciuili fophistice et plane feditiofe rixatur.* (n) See this as one of *Wicliues* articles, condemned in the Councel of *Constance. Sef. 8. art. 15.* and reported by *Ofiander, cent. 15. pag. 454.* And *Melanc-thon de iure magistratuum,* faith hereof, *infanijt Wicleuus qui fensit impios nullum dominium habere.* (*) *Ofiander. cent. 15. pag. 455. art. 17.*

(¶)

ny barroufe knowen (¶) rebellions commit-ted by his followers: In fo much as *Melanc-thon* chargeth him with (o) *stirring vp traga-dies,* and withal vndertaketh to confute and (p) *recite Wicliues fophistical reafons in proofe of his opinion* ; in like maner is it confeffed and yet further collected and reported by Prote-ftantes them felues out of *Wicliues* owne wri-tinges how that he tauhgt, that (q) *if a Bi-fhop, or Preist, be in deadly finne, he doth not or-der, confecreate, nor Baptife.* that (r) *Ecclefiasti-cal ministers fhould not haue any temporal poffeffi-ons or* (s) *property in any thing but* (t) *fhould beg,* alfo (u) *he condemned lawful oathes* confeffedly (x) *fauoring therein of Annabaptifme :* and re-newing the blind error of the Stoickes, he further taught that (y) *al thinges come to paffe by abfolute neceffity.* and laftly defended (z) *Humaine merites,* as did the damnable here-ticke

Hereof fee *M. Stowes Annals, pag. 550. & 566. & 551. Wicleuus qui fensit impios nullum Dominium habere.*

(o)

Melancthon in commentar. ad politica Aristotelis. faith, *miras tragedias ex-citauit Wicleuus qui conten-dit eos qui non habent fpi-ritum fanctum amittere do-minium et colligit multas fophisticas rationes ad con-firmandum hoc dogma &c. recitabimus quædam argu-menta Wicleui &c.*

(p)

Melancthon vt fupra.
(q) *M. Foxe act. mon. pag. 96. art. 4. & art. 15.* And *Ofiander, cent. 15. pag. 452. art. 4.* (r) *Act. mon. pag. 96. & 93. art. 12. & Ofiander, Cent. 15. pag. 453. art. 10. & pag. 458. art. 36.* (s) *Melancton, in epist. ad Frederic. Micon.* (extant) *in libr. epist. Oecolampadij, et Suingly. pag. 622.* faith, *Infpexi Wicleunm &c. contendit Prefbiteris non licere vt poffi-deant quicqam proprium.* (t) *Melancthon, in loc. com. de poteftate Ec-clefia ante med.* faith, *illa Wicleuita fuperstitio perniciofa et fuperstitiofa est qua adigit ministros Ecclefia ad mendicitatem & negat eis licere proprium habere.* (u) *Ofiander cent. 15. pag. 459. art. 43.* (x) *Ofiander, ibidem.* faith thereof, *hic articulus probari non potest quia Anabaptifmum*

fapit,

sapit. (y) *Osiander, ibidem.* pag. 457. in so much as *Osiander* saith thereof, *hic articulus explicatione indigebat ne Stoicum fatum statueretur.* (z) Hereof see *Waldensis,*

tom. 3. *c.* 7. 8. 9.

(a)
Melancthon in epist. ad Fred. Micon. in libro e-pist. Suingly, et Oecolam-padij. pag. 622. saith of *Wicliue, prorsus nec intel-lexit nec tenuit fidei insti-tiam.*

(b)
Melancthon, ibidem. saith, *deprehendi in eo multa alia errata de quibus iudicium de eius spiritu fieri potest.*

(c)
Ioachim Vadian de Eucha-ristia, l. 5. *pag.* 168. saith of *Wiclife, in nonnul-lis fide lapsus est &c.* he *was foully ouer seene in sun-dry pointes of religion, and more geuen to bable then became a sober diuine.*

ticke *Pelagius* hould them, in respect where-of *Melancthon* saith of *Wiclife,* (a) *verily he did not vnderstand nor hould the iustice of faith,* saying withal, (b) *I haue found in him many er-rors wherby one may iudge of his spirit.* And in like plaine manner is he yet further reiected & có-demned for a confessed (c) *hereticke* by *Va-dianus* the *Suinglian,* *Pantaleon,* and *Mathias Hoe,* al of them learned Protestantes. Ad but now hereto his often *recantation* and kno-wen dissembling of his religion by him at seueral times confessedly (d) practised some what before his death, by meanes whereof he so escaped the daunger and trouble other-wise perhaps ensuing against him, that (e) he returned againe to his parish of *Lutherworth* (in *Licester shire*) whereof he was person, and quietly there (saith *M. Foxe*) slept in the Lord vpon S. *Siluesters* day. *Anno.* 1387.

Thus far onely am I able to proceede be-fore *Luthers* time, for as concerning *Ihon Husse* And *Pantaleon in cronogr.* pag. 110. placeth *Wi-clife* in the rancke of *herertickes* saying withal, *Ioannes Wicleuius cum Lothardis in Anglia suam hæresim prædicat.* And *Mathias Hoe* in his *tract. duo &c. tract.* 1. *de disput.* pag. 27. expresly placeth and num-breth the *Wicleuites* in the *rancke of heretickes,* calling them, and others by him there named, *most monstruous monsters.* (d) *M. Foxe, act. mon.* pag. 95. saith *Wicliue being beset with troubles was forced once againe to make confession of his doctrine; in which confession as occasion serued for to auoide the rigor of thinges he answeared with intricate wordes &c. Anno.* 1381. And *pag.* 91. he signifyeth *Wicliues* often recantation alledging *Wicliue* saying: *and now againe as before also I do reuoke and make retrac-tation &c.* by meanes whereof as *M. Foxe* confesseth a litle there be-fore *Wicliue wonde him selfe out of the Bishops snares. Anno.* 1377. and *pag*. 846. it is teſtifyed how that *Wicline*, in an *epiſtle written by him ad Iohannem Epiſcopum Lincolinenſem*, retracted his former doctrine againſt the real *preſence of Chriſtes body in the Sacrament and in the Maſſe*, reconciling him ſelfe in that *article* to the Romaine Church. And *pag*. 98. & 99. it appeareth that *Wicline Anno*. 1384. (not three yeares before his death in *Anno*. 1387.) *in his epiſtle to Pope Vrban doth purge him ſelfe to the Pope*, acknowledging that *the Biſhop of Rome is the vicar of Chriſt here vpon earth*, with much further like diſſimulation.

Huſſe, he did (f) acknowledge the Maſſe, & if any other impugned the ſame, it was the followers of ſome, or other the perſons before named who alſo they likwiſe imitated in their other foremencioned errors no leſſe then in their impugning of the Maſſe: ſo as our aduerſaries are not for ſo many confeſſed ages paſt & before *Luthers* time, able to alledge ſo much as one Patron & publiſher of their doctrine againſt Maſſe and real preſence, who was ~not~ alſo in other ſubſtantial pointes of faith confeſſedly euen in their owne opinion a knowen and condemned hereticke. And for ſo much as according to the Apoſtle, Chriſt hath placed in his Church (g) *Paſtors, and Doctors*, to continue *to the conſummation of Sainctes*, and as *Caluin* & others do hereupon confeſſe (h) *for euer*, and as *M. Fulke* ſaith euen (i) *from Chriſtes time to Luthers age*. And ſeeing alſo there is ſuch a mutual reſpectiue dependance or relation betweene doctrine, and Doctor, as that the one argueth the being of the other, for as it is witten-(k) *faith commeth by hearing, and hearing by the word of God*: (*) *and how ſhal they heare withſide, ſect*. 37. 38. *pag*. 233. & 234. And *M. Fulke* againſt the Rhemiſh Teſtament *in Epheſ*. 4. *ſect*. 4. *fol*. 335. and *Melancthon in loc. com. edit*. 1561. *c. de Eccleſia*. (i) *M. Fulke* againſt *Heſkins, Saunders &c. pag*. 569. and *ibidem. pag*. 536. he further ſaith, *it is true that*

(e)
So teſtifyeth *M. Foxe*, *act. mon. pag*. 98.

(f)
That *Huſſe* acknowleged *tranſubſtantiation*. ſee *act. mon. pag*. 209. & *pag*. 197. And concerning Maſſe. *M. Foxe, in Apoc. c*. 11. *pag*. 290. ſaith, *quid vnquam docuit aut in concilio defendit Huſſius in quo non cum Papiſtis potuis ſuperſtitioſe conſentire videbatur? quid de tranſubſtantiatione ſtatuit fides Pontificia quod ipſe pariter cum iſdem Pontificiis non confirmauit? quis miſſas illo religioſius celebrauit &c*.

(g)
Epheſ. 4, 11. 12. 13.
(h)
Caluin inſtitut. printed, *Geneuæ*. 1550. *c*. 8. *de*

that Pastors, and Doctors must stil be to the end of the world in the Church.
(k) *Rom.* 10. 17. (*) *Rom.* 10. 14.

(l)

M. Fulke, in his an-
sweare to a counterfeate
Catholicke, *pag.* 100.
saith of Pastors, *truth
cannot be continued in the
world but by their mini-
sterie.*

(m)

*Certaine ages before and af-
ter Bertram*, for as ap-
peareth next heretofore,
subdiuis. 1. in the margent vnder n. & in *Ber-
trams* time the doctrine
of real presence was ge-
neral and but couertly
and doubtfully (if so
much at al) impugned by
Bertram. and it also appeareth further hereto-
fore *tract.* 2. *sect.* 2.
subdiuis. 1. in the margent at d. by testimony
there alledged of *M.*

out a preacher? It hereof followeth that the
doctrine of Christes Church deliuered by
his Apostles must euer continue in being, &
(l) *preserued* by the preaching and instruction of the Churches true Pastors, and Doctors: And that aswel the Church which haith
at any one time wanted al being therin
of such Doctors, cannot possibly be the true
Church, as also that the doctrine which haith
not accordingly beene by them preserued in
continual being, but haith at some season
failed, or for the time ceased to be so taught
and professed, cannot possibly be that doctrine which was deliuered and taught by the
Apostles. Which point being so necessarily
deduced from so euident premises of our learned aduersaries owne assertions & the sacred
text it selfe. What now may the indifferent
reader in al probability of reasonable consequence, thinke concerning our aduersaries
foresaid doctrine against the Masse, wherof
for (m) *certaine ages* before and after *Bertram*
vntil *Berengarius*, no one Doctor & publicke
profesfor

Foxe, and *Ioachim Camerarius*, that it likewise continued no lesse general til the *first conflict* or breach made by *Berengarius*, whose doctrine
was so singular, as he was therefore the *first* that *was accompted an hereticke for the same. Ibidem.* in the text at d. our other doctrine being then *general ouer the whol* (*Christian*) *world. Ibidem.* at e.*. Also
it appeareth hertofore, *tract.* 3. *sect.* 2. *subdiuis.* 2. at l. n. that frō the
time of *Gregory the first*, which is now a ful thousand yeares since *the
Masse haith raigned as a puissant Empresse in al Churches &c.* and the same
is yet further confessed, *Ibidem.* after q. at the figure 4. which point
being so euident and our aduersaries being vnable to shew during al
those meane ages any knowen Doctors of their doctrine, other then
onely

only those hertofore mencioned & confessed for hereticks which were since the time of *Berengarius* who liued almost *sixe hundreth yeares* after such first (confessed) vniuersality of the *Masse* how can this foresaid knowen want of their Doctors and professed doctrine, so many ages before *Berengarius* time, agree with that which the Scripture, and our learned aduersaries them selues do teach to the contrary, concerning the foresaid perpetual cõtinuance in the Church *for euer*, euen *frõ Chrifts time to Luthers age*, both of *Doctors, and doctrine*.

professor can be named: & which againe (n) from *Berengarius, to Luther*, was at certaine seueral times so quit extinct, that not any testimony thereof can be then produced. And concerning *Berengarius*, and those other that are knowen to haue at certaine times professed and taught the same, they were not the Churches true Doctors but were confessedly in other material pointes of faith al (o) of them execrable and condemned heretikes: which thing but duly obserued together with that which haith bene (p) heretofore not by way of amplification, but historically and truly deliuered from the conftant report of our learned aduersaries them selues concerning afwel *Suinglius*, and *Carolaftadius*, as also *Luthers* impugning the Masse by instructiõ & fenfible conference had with the deuil, who difcerning his endeauours of former times attempted by his myftical agentes not to be so succeful, did in this laft age (God in his iuftice fo permitting) vndertake (as in (*) other pointes fo in this) the matter in his owne person. Let the attentiue reader in Gods name vpon the peril of his foule, now aduife whether he may with faifty ther-

(n)

Frõ *Berengarius*, to *Luther*, many meant & long currentes of time paffed wherein no inftance can be geuen of any impugning the Masse, as namely for many yeares next before *Wicliue*.

(o)

This appeareth in this prefent feauenth fection in the forefaid feueral examples of *Berengarius the Waldenfes*, *Albigenfes*, *Apoftolici*, *Henrie*, *Peter Bruis*, *Abaylardus*, *Almericus*, and *Wicliue* whofe feueral herefies are recyted & fet dowen in particular.

(p)

See *heretofore, tract.* 3. *fect.* 6. *fubdiuif.* 2. & 3. throughout.

of (*) See the Proteftant treatife entituled *Apocalipfis infignium, aliquot harifarcharum qua vifiones et in fomnia ipfis per fomnia patefacte, blafphemias puta inauditas ac deliramenta Euthufiaftica reuelantur &c.* printed *Lugduni Batauorum.* cɪɔ.ɪɔ.c.vɪɪɪ.

A a a

a cheife

A cheife point of these mens doctrines and reuelations were *occide*, *iugula sufaq deq, monachos omnes, Papas omnes*. *Ibidem. D. 2. & D. 5.*

(q)

See concerning *S*. *Ber-* of abandon the Masse, which hauing bene
nard, heretofore, *tract.* professed by *S*. (q) *Bernard, S*. (*) *Au-*
2. *sect.* 11. *subdiuis.* 3. *gustine*, and so many other confessed (r)
in the margent at 11. *Sainctes*, and confirmed with so many (s)
z. 12. And *Tindal, in* miracles, and no (t) time of it nouel begin-
Act. mon. pag. 1338. ning knowen, haith yet further bene (to
saith, *I doubt not but S*. speake the least) the knowen ackowledged
Bernard, Francis, Domi- doctrine of the whol Christian world for
nicke, and many other holy these (u) *thousand yeares* last past; vnto the
men erred as concerning publicke profession whereof so many (x) *fore-*
Masse. *tould* Kinges and kingdomes of the Gentiles,

(*) haue in that meane time bene accordingly
Heretofore, *tract.* 3. (y) *conuerted*, and so neuer embraced our ad-
sect. 2. *subdiuis.* 3. in uersaries other negatiue doctrine impugning
the margent vnder the *Masse*, which haith receiued it abortiue be-
figures 11. (r) *Tin-* ginninges and vntimely further groweth in
dal, vt supra. at q. and   manner

Luther in colloquijs Germanicis, c. de missa. saith, *Missa priuata &c. priuate*
Masse haith deceiued many Sainctes and carried them away into errors from
the time of Gregory, for 800. *yeares*. (s) See these miracles alledged heretofore *tract.* 3. *sect.* 6. *subdiuis.* 1. throughout. (t) See
this confessed heretofore, *tract.* 3. *sect.* 2. *subdiuis.* 2. *fine.* at the figure 5. after q. (u) See this confessed heretofore, *tract.* 3. *sect*
2. *subdiuis.* 2. at l. n. and afterwardes at the figure 4. after q.
(x) *Foretould by Esay.* 49. 23. & 60. 10. 11. 16. & 62. 2. &
Psal. 102. 15. (y) Of the Kinges and kingdomes conuerted to
the publicke profession of Christian religion within these last thousand yeares in which Masse was confessedly vniuersal. see the Protestant writer D. *Ioannes Pappus*, in his epitome, *historie Ecclesiasticae.*
printed *Witteberga, Anno.* 1604. in a special tract there entituled
historia conuersionis gentium. from pag. 88. 89. &c. vntil pag. 132.
wherein is set dowen in perticuler the publicke conuersion of most
Kinges and kingdones that became Christian, for albeit the Christian
faith was priuatly or vnder persecution professed in many kingdomes,
and nations, during the other *first sixt hundreth yeares* after Christ, yet
                                                                    the

the special accomplishment of those foresaid Prophecies which concerning the publicke conuersion of kinges and their kingdomes, and
the great encrease and number of them, neither was nor could be accomplished during the great persecution of the *first* 300. *yeares*, nor
during the smale time of the other next ensuing 300. *yeares*, but haith
beene hitherto principally or rather almost wholly performed within the last thousand yeares, as appeareth by the many particuler examples thereof set dowen by *Ioannes Pappus, vbi supra.* and more large
in the firster part of *the Protestantes Apology of the Roman Church. tract.*
2. *cap.* 1. *sect.* 4.

manner (z) before mencioned so strange ,   (z)
forbindden, feareful, and prodigious : And *Of Luthers* first straunge
thus much concerning sacrifice .   and fearful beginning a-
                                 gainst the Masse. see
heretofore *tract* . 3. *sect.* 6. *subdiuis.* 2. throughout. And concerning the like impugning thereof in like straunge sort begunne
by *Suinglius,* and *Carolastadius.* see there *sect.* 3. throughout. And concerning the publicke impugning there-
of in former ages begunne and prosecuted
onely by such as were in other pointes
al of them confessedly heretickes.
see in this present *seauenth section.*
subdiuis. 1. *&* 2. throughout.

That Communion of the Euchariſt vnder both kindes vnto the Laity, is neither commaunded by Chriſt, in it ſelfe neceſſary, or otherwiſe expedient.

TRACT. 4.

The true ſtate of the queſtion and the doƈtrine of both Catholickes, and Proteſtantes is plainly ſet dowen.

SECTION. 1.

FOr my clearer proceeding in this ſo waighty a controuerſy, and the better diſcouery of ſundry greauous calumnies and moſt hateful imputations, iniuriouſly laid vpon the Charholicke Church ; I am to premoniſh the reader, that the true ſtate of the queſtion now in diſpute is, not whether Chriſt our Sauiour did inſtitute the Euchariſt vnder both kindes, or whether him ſelfe did in ſuch ſort receiue or adminiſter the ſame vnto his Apoſtles ; or whether his Apoſtles, and their ſucceſſors, the reuerend Biſhops, and Preiſtes, of the Primitiue Church, did in like manner at ſundry times make ſemblable vſe and praƈtiſe thereof, for al this the Catholicke Church doth willingly admit and graunt .

Wherefore the true and maine point in controuerſy is, whether Chriſt our Sauiour gaue abſolute commaunde vnto his Apoſtles and their ſucceſſors, of adminiſtring the ſaid Sacrament vnder both kindes, to wit, of bread and wine, when ſo euer the ſame was to be geuen to the people ; in ſo much as the miniſtring only vnder one, ſhould be a tranſgreſſion of his law, a maming of his Sacrament, and a depriuing of his people of much grace and comforth they might enioy thereby ; or els that the ſame he left onely as a thing indifferent, and therefote ſuch as his deareſt ſpouſe the holy Catholicke Church might abſolutly limit and determine, according to the direƈtion of the holy Ghoſt, and ſundry important reaſons mouing her thereto.

The Catholicke doƈtrine.
(a) Concil. Conſtantienſe. Seſ.

In this caſe the Councel of (a) Conſtance vpon information that ſome taught that it was a thing ſacrilegious to deny the people the

the vse of both kindes, and in such sort *Sef.* 13.
therefore did minister the same, did thereu-
pon *after mature deliberation had of many Doctors, aswel diuines, as lawiers, declare, decree, and define &c. that though in the Primitiue Church this Sacrament was receiued by the faithful vnder both kindes, afterwardes it was to be receiue by those that consecrate vnder both, and by the Laity onely vnder the forme of bread; seeing it is firmely to be beleeued, and no wayes to be doubted, that the whol body and bloud of Christ is truly contained, aswel vnder the forme of bread, as vnder the forme of wine: wherefore seeing this custome vpon good reason was brought in by the Church, and holy Fathers, and haith bene long obserued, it is to be accompted for a law* . And then afterwardes it censureth such for *Heretickes and greauously to be punished* who
shal obstinatly affirme or practise the opposite to the premises.

And though it was graunted by the Councel of *Basil*, to the *Bohe-*
mians vpon special occasions that they might lawfully minister and receiue the Communion vnder both, yet the like decree to the former
of *Constance* is made at large, and almost in   (b)
the same wordes by the said (b) Councel *Concil. Basil. Sef.* 30.
of *Basil*   (c)

The Councel of (c) *Florence* declared, *Concil. Florent. in decret.*
and that with the assent of the *Armenians*, *Eugeny Papæ,* 4.
that *by vertue of the wordes the substance of*
bread, is turned into the body of Christ, and the substance of the wine into his
bloud, yet so as Christ is contained whol vnder the forme of bread, and whol
vnder the forme of wine, as also whol vnder euery part of the Hoast consecra-
ted, and the wine consecrated, seperation being made .

Protestancy (as a straunge monster appearing in the world) presently
the Councel of (d) *Trent*, in destruction and   (d)
ruine thereof, amongst other thinges decreed *Concil. Trident. Sef.* 21.
that *the Laity are not bound vnder any diuine* ca. *primo.*
precept to Communicate vnder both kindes. Also   (e)   *Cap.* 3.
that (e) *vnder either kinde whol Christ and the*
true Sacrament is receiued, and therefore as concerning the fruictes thereof,
such as receiue only one kinde are not defrauded of any grace necessary to sal-
uation; and the contrary doctrine it condem-   (f)
neth (f) of *heresie*, and so by these expresse *Can.* 1. 2. 3.
& absolute decrees of so many general Coun-
cels our Catholicke doctrine is plainly made knowen.

Al this

The Protestant doctrine.

(h)
De formula Missæ.

(i)
Caluin, l. 4. *instit.* c. 17. *parag.* 47. 48. 49. So *Hamelmanus l. de comun. sub. vtraq̃. spe. Chemnitius in* 2. *par. Conc. Trident. Sess.* 21. *Brentius, in Apol. pro confes. Wittenberg. in* 2. *Pericopes* . and sundry others.

Al this notwithstanding, to the contrary, *Martin Luther* teacheth that (h) *simply according to the institution of Christ, both kindes are to be seeked for and administred: neither in these thinges which manifestly are the Gospel, wil we* (saith he) *expect or heare Councels*. The like is the doctrine of (i) *Caluin*, and most other protestants, who labour by sundry argumēts to disproue the decrees of the foresaid Councels, as opposite to the commandement & institution of Christ, and preiudicial, and iniurious to the faithful communicantes.

The doctrine of both sides and the true state of the question being thus faithfully set dowen, for the cleare discussing of sundry difficulties pretended, in the residue of this discourse, I intend briefly to proue these pointes following : *First*, that vnder either kind Christ is truly and wholly contained, as also the true essence of the Sacrament, and consequently that the people by receiuing vnder one kinde are not depriued of any grace necessary to saluation, or the Sacrament made imperfect, maymed, or iniuried,. Secondly that Christ our Sauiour gaue no commaundement of administring the Sacrament vnto the people vnder both kindes. Thirdly, that the practise of the Primitiue Church was not alwaies vnder both, but promiscuouse, somtimes vnder one, and sometimes vnder both. Fourtly that euen by the confession of Protestantes, it is a matter of indifferency. Fiftly, that therefore it is lawful for the Church vpon iust reasons to determine it to either part.

That vnder either kinde whol Christ is truly contained, and the true Essence of the Sacrament preserued, and consequently that neither the people are depriued of any grace necessary to saluation, nor the Sacrament therby made impefect or mamed .

SECTION. 2.

VV Hereas Protestantes ordinarily obiect against Catholikes that by ministring the Sacrament vnder one kinde they do
maime

maime it, and geue it onely halfe and imperfe ct, thereby depryuing the people of the great fruict which were to be reaped thereof. In ful confutation of this false surmise, and in deede in perfect clearing of almost al difficulties that are apprehended in this question, I wil endeauour breifly to proue two thinges: The first wherein not onely al Catholicke diuines do ioyntly agree, but which (as before) is already determined by sundry general Councels which is, that vnder either kinde is truly contained whol Christ, to wit, body, bloud, soule, and diuinity. The second, that the true essence of the Sacrament is found in either kinde; from which wil euidently follow that neither irreuerence is offered to the Sacrament, nor iniury to the receiuers.

Wherefore concerning the firster, my first reason in proofe therof shal be drawen from 3. principles of faith: *first* (as haith bene formerly proued) that by reason of those wordes of Christ; *this is my body which shal be genen for you*, that in the Eucharist is truly and really the very body of Christ. The second, that Christ our Sauiour after his resurrection from death was neuer to dye againe, according to those wordes of S. Paul, (b) *Christ rising againe from the deade, now dyeth no more, death shal no* (b) *Rom.* 6. 9. *more haue dominion ouer him*: fro whence it necessarily followeth, that vnder the forme of bread is not the body of Christ without bloud, and soule, for so it should be without life, & consequently deade. The third, that Christ is one diuine person subsisting in two natures, from whence it immediatly ariseth, that seeing the body of Christ haith no other subsistence then that of his Godhead, which really is al one with his essence, that therefore wheresoeuer his body is, there also is his diuinity: This argument, supposing these three principles, doth euidently conuince; and for the two latter, I doubt not but most Protestantes wil admit, and the first is acknowledged for true by al *Lutherans*. And although it is already proued, yet in deede it is to be supposed in this controuersy, for altogether immaterial it were in respect of any fruict or profit to be obtayned thereby, whether we receiue vnder one or both kindes, if that which we receiue be but onely a peece of bread and a cup of wine, and that without any grace or vertue exhibited therwith: both which such Protestantes auouch as deny the real presence of Christes true body in the Sacrament.

Secondly

Secondly the same truth is further proued by these wordes of (c) Christ, *he that eateth me, the same also shal liue by me,* for Christ is not eaten but vnder the forme of bread, wherefore vnder that forme is not onely his sacred body without his blessed soule & precious bloud, but euen whol Christ, for of his body onely he would neuer haue said, *he that eateth me;* and *I am the bread of life which descended from heauen,* or *this is the bread which descended from heauen.*

(c)
Ioan. 6. 57.

Thirdly the same is confirmed by the general beleefe of the Primitiue Church. In the first Council (d) of Nice, were taught to beleeue that *in the sacred table is placed the Lambe of God which taketh away the sinnes of the world.* now to say that the Lambe is vpon the Altar partly in the bread, and partly in the wine, is to say contrary to the Councel, that there is not the true and perfect lambe of God, but the body of the lambe, & the bloud of the lambe seuered, and without soule, which doth not make, but rather destroy the lambe of God, Christ.

(d)
Conc. Nicen. 1. ad (secund. Pisanum) l. 3. decret. de diuina mensa. This decree is ackuowledged so authentical by *Oecolampadius dial. cid. Nathaniel.* By *Caluin, l. 4. instit. c. 17. parag. 36.* by *Boouinns, de cana Domini. contra Heshusium.* and by *Klebitius l. de victoria veritatis solut. 32. Aig.*

S. *Ciril* of *Hierusalem* saith, (¶) *we shal be called Chrisostofers, that is, bearers of Christ, when we shal receiue his body and bloud.*

(¶)
Catech. mistag. 4.

S. (d) *Ambrose* inferreth that *in this Sartamēt Christ is, because it is the body of Christ:* rightly gathering whol Christ to be there where one part is, from whence the rest cannot be seuered.

(d)
L. d. initiandis minister. c. 9. ante fin.

S. *Hierome,* auoucheth of our Sauiour (e) that he is *the guest, and the banquet, he that eateth and he that is eaten;* and reprehending those who after the act of mariage durst not receiue in the Church, and yet receiued at home demaundeth (f) *whether there be one Christ in publicke and another at home.*

(e)
Epist. ad Hediliam. q. 2.

(f)
Apol. pro lib. in Iouin.

S. *Chrisostome* assureth thee, that (g) *thou seest him, thou touchest him, thou eatest him.* and that (h) *thou receiuest not the sonne of a king, but the onely*

(g)
Hom. 83. in Math.

(h) Hom. 24. in 1. Cor.

S. *Augustine* teacheth that (i) *Christ bore him selfe in his owne handes*, when he said, *this is my body*. The like might be shewed through sundry other Fathers, who vniformely teach that it is Christ our Sauiour whom we eate and receiue in this blessed Sacrament, which were manifestly false, if vnder either kind whol Christ were not contained.

My fourth reason is taken from the common conceipt of Christians, who beleeue that in the Eucharist, they receiue true, liuely, and entyre, Christ, and not onely a deade body voide of sence and life, whereas according to such Protestantes as beleeue the real presence, and deny the entyrenes thereof vnder either kinde, not onely a dead body is onely receiued, but so often as their ministers do celebrate their Lords supper, so often they slay Christ our Sauiour, seperating his body, bloud, and soule, a sunder, or at least beleeue they do so, which is most impious and absurd.

Fiftly, miracles shewed by God do forcibly confirme the same, for that at the breaking of the hoste at sundry times great copy of bloud haith issued out, it is a thing formerly testifyed (*) by many writers of learning and credit, & with that relation of so many particuler circumstances of the very time, place, number of persons, seuere execution in publicke of the offenders, and sundry other such accidentes, as to cal the same in question, is to lobour, not onely to dissolue the deserued aucthority of the most approued histories which antiquity haith left vs, but also of sundry Protestant writers.

(*) *Tract*. 2. *sect*. 6. And see *comment*. *Surij*. *Anno*. 1510. and 1556. *Vincent*. *in speculo*, *hist*. *l*. 30. *c*. 24. *Alex*. *Halens*. *q*. 11. *mem*. 2. *art*. 4. *parag*. 3. *Fulgosius*, *l*. 6. *c*. 6. *Nauterus Generat*. 44. *Ciantzuis*, *hist*. *Vand*. *l*. 8. *c*. 8. & many others.

Lastly al Lutheran Protestantes, who generally teach the vbiquity of Christes humanity; 1. that the humanity of Christ is euery where present with his Godhead, must needes acknowledge this our Catholicke doctrine, for if Christes humanity be whol & entire in euery place, the is it whol in the host & whol in the Chalice, and so accordingly confesse the Protestant writers, (k) *Luther*, *Brentius*, and *Kemnitius*: Thus we see the cheifest

(k) *Luther in assert*. *art*. *Bren*. *in confes*. *Witteberg*. *art*. *de Euchar*. *Kemnit*. *in fine disput*. *de vtraq̃ specie in examine Concil*. *Trident*. *Pro*. 2.

B b b　　　　　　　　　point

point of al this controuersy fully confirmed by strongest arguments from Scripture, Fathers, miracles, and the forced confession of the aduersaries them selues.

Concerning the second, to wit the essence of this Sacrament, the same is truly (l) found in either kinde, for in a Sacrament is onely required that it be a signe, and cause of grace; the signe in the Eucharist, as it is a Sacrament is twofould : The 1. of internal refection according to those wordes of Christ. *Ioan*. 6. *my flesh is truly meate*. The second, of vnion of the faithful amongst them selues, and with Christ, whereof S. (m) *Paul* saith, *for being many we are one bread, one body, al that participate of one bread* ; now both these significations are found in either kinde, for as for spiritual refection it only importeth the refection of the soule, which whether it be by way of meate, or drinke, or both, is altogether impertinent, seeing in spiritual refections one and the selfe same thing is said to be meate & drinke : So of iustice our Saviour saith, (n) *blessed are they who hunger and thirst iustice, for they shal be filled*. And of wisdome the wise man saith, (o) *they that eate me shal yet hunger, and they that drinke me shal yet thirst* ; wherefore as our Saviour said, *my flesh is truely meate*, and *my bloud is truly drinke* ; so also in the same place he said, *he that eateth this bread shal liue for euer*. and *he that eateth me shal liue by me*. See this expresly taught by S. *Ciprian*, *sermo de cœna Dom*. And by S. *Augustine*, vpon that of the *Psal*. 103. *bread confirmeth the heart of man*.

(l)
*Concil. Trident. Ses. 21.
c. 3.*
(m)
. Cor. 10. 17.
(n)
Math. 5. 6.
(o)
Eccliest. 24. 29.

The second signification of the vnion of the faithful amongst them selues, is also expressed by the many graines of corne wrought together, and with Christ, by the making thereof with flower and water, as S. *Ciprian* also testifyeth. *l. 2. epist. 3. ad Cecilium*. And the like may be shewed in the wine, composed of many grapes, and mingled with water in the Chalice.

The causality likwise requisite in a Sacrament is found in either kind, for that proceedeth from Christ who vnder either forme is whol and entyre as I haue proued before.

Neither doth it follow from hence that because the Sacrament is essentially contained vnder either kind, that therefore the Preist receiuing

ceiuing vnder both, receiueth two Sacraments, for being receiued both at once they make but one, as being ordained to one refe&ion, fignifying one thing, and producing one effe&; euen as fixe or feauen difhes of meate fet vpon a table, do but make one dinner, whereas part thereof being but ferued one day, and the reft an other, they would make two; and the reafon why Preiftes receiue vnder both kindes, is becaufe they offer vp a facrifice which reprefenteth the facrifice of Chrift vpon the Croffe, which were not perfe&ly reprefented but by both kindes, for the onely forme of bread, would not reprefent Chrift as deade, without fome figne of bloud, nor the onely forme of wine, would fufficiently reprefent him as facrificed, feeing onely wine is not an hofte or thing to be facrificed, wherfore alfo in this fort was it prefigured in the facrifice of *Melchifadech*, offering vp both bread and wine.

Hauing thus proued the piemifes, to wit, that whol Chrift is contained vnder either kinde and the true effence of the Sacrament: from hence it dire&ly followeth that neither irreuerence is offered to the Sacrament, not being indeede as was obie&ed, geuen halfe or mamed, but effentially whol, nor iniury to the people by depriuing them of any grace neceffary to faluation, feeing the very fountaine of grace is no leffe receiued vnder either kinde then vnder both.

That Chrift our Sauiour gaue no commaund of receiuing vnder both kindes,
it is proued by the facred Scriptures, and by his owne, and his bleffed
Apoftles examples.

SECTION. 3.

Though in this queftion it belongeth to our aduerfaries to proue, and to vs onely to anfweare, they affirming, and we denying, yet in more ful demonftrance of the truth, I wil alledge fundry reafons in proofe that Chrift our Sauiour gaue no commaundement of receining vnder both kindes.

And firft as there were figures which did reprefent this Sacrament vnder both kindes, fo alfo there were others which did the fame onely vnder one, as the Pafchal lambe; for the bloud which was fprinkled vpon the poftes, did not prefigure the bloud in the Cha-

lice

(a)
Auguft. 1. 12. *contra*
Fauft. *c*. 30. *Hier*. *in c*.
66. *Efa*. *Cirprian*, *in tract*.
c. *Demet*. *Ifidorus in c*.
12. *Exod*.

(b)
1. *Cor*. 10. 3. 4.

(c)
Exod. 16. 1. 4.

(d)
Exod. 17. 1.

(e)
Ioan. 6. 49.

(f)
Ioan. 6. 57. 58.

(g)
Luc. 24. 30.

(h)
Lib. 3. *de confenf*. *c*. 25.
Auth. *operis imperf*. *in*
Math. *hom*. 17. *Hie-*
rom. *Epitaph*. *Paulæ*. *Be-*
da et Theophil. *in hunc* *loc*.
Lucæ.

(i)
Melancthon, *apol*. *confef*.
Auguft. *in art*. *de vtraq̨*
fpecie.

(k)
Act. 2. 42.
Act. 20. 7.

lice, but (as auncient (a) Fathers teach) the
figne of the Croffe, for that bloud was not
drunke, nor geuen to others, but the poftes
were fprinkled therewith, and that before
the lambe was eaten. So alfo Manna was geuē
without drinke, for though *S*. (b) *Paul* faith,
*al did eate the fame fpiritual foode, and al drnuke,
the fpiritual drinke* yet they were two diftinct
figures & geuen at diuerftimes ; *Manna* being
geuen in the (c) *defert fin*, & afterwardes water
frō the (d) *Rocke in Raphydim* : and fo our Sauiour
our (e) comparing *Manna* with the *Eucharift*
maketh yet no mencion of water.

Secondly as our Sauiour fomtimes doth
mention both kindes, fo alfo often he mentioneth but one, as (f) *he that eateth me*. *the
fame alfo fhal liue by me*, *this is the bread that
came dowen from heauen*. *he that* (g) *eateth this
bread fhal liue for euer*, and the like.

Thirdly the practife of our Sauiour is beft
witneffe of his doctrine, *S*. *Luke* relateth of
him, that being with two of his Difciples at
fupper in *Emaus*, he tooke bread, and *bleffed
and brake, and did reach to them*; by which
bread is vnderftood the Eucharift, not onely
by *S*. (h) *Auguftine* and the other Fathers,
but euen by (i) Proteftant writers, and yet
he maketh here mention of wine, or the cup,
but rather by the wordes and circumftances
of the want thereof, for it is faid, (k) *and it
came to paffe whileft he fate at the table with
them he tooke bread, and bleffed and brake, and
did reach to them, and their eyes were opened, and
they knew him, and he vanifhed out of their fight*, fo ioyning to the *reaching
of the bread* & their *knowing him*, his *vanifhing away*, not leauing any
time for the benediction and confecration of the Chalice.

Fourtly in like fort alfo was the practife of the Apoftles after
Chriftes time, for *S*. *Luke* fpeaking of the faithful affirmeth that *they
were*

were perseuering in the doctrine of the Apostles, and in the communication of breaking of bread and prayers, where also by *breaking of bread,* is vnderstoode the *Eucharist,* aswel in that it is ioyned with doctrine and praier, as also in that it had bene rather a dispraise then praise, to report of the faithful that they were perseuering in corporal dinners and suppers. And so also is vnderstood by (l) Fathers, & Protestant (*) writers, and yet neither here is there any mention of wine.

(l) *Author. operis imperf. in Math. hom.* 17. *Beda ad c.* 20. *Act.*

To answeare with *Chemnitius,* that by breaking of bread, is vnderstood also the geuing of the Chalice, by the figure *Sinecdoche,* by the part vnderstanding the whol; This I say is insufficient as being an answeare onely imaginary and not grounded, & such as by the like liberty, any doctrine though neuer so impious or absurd, might easily be maintayned against al Scripture though neuer so plaine.

(*) *Luther, ser. de Eucharist. Caluin. l.* 4. *iustit.* 17. *parag.* 35. *Chemnitius in examen. conc. Trident. Ses.* 21. *part.* 2. *examinis.*

Neither is it any thing confirmed by affirming that if the Chalice be not vnderstood, that then would follow thereof, that the Apostles did but consecrate vnder one kind, which yet Catholickes do not admit: for *S. Luke* doth not set dowen what the Apostles but what the people did, and therefore they might consecrate vnder both, though they did administer vnto the people onely vnder one.

And this yet further may be established in that there were many (m) Christians in *Hierusalem,* who in these beginning times in sundry thinges did Iudaize, the Apostles permitting them; amongst whom were the (n) *Nazarites* who drunke no wine, nor shaued their heades vntil the time of their vow was expired: now it is not credible that these against their vow drunke of the Chalice, or probable that they abstained altogether from communion.

(m) *Act.* 21. 24. 26.

(n) *Num.* 6. 3. 4. 5. 18.

Lastly *Andreas Friccius* a Caluinist (whom *Peter Martir* calleth (o) *an excellent learned man*) writeth thus, (p) *Christ at his last supper ioyned wine with bread, if therefore the Church seperate these, she is not to be heard. the Church of Hierusalem did seperate these;*

(o) *Com. pla. in* English *part.* 4. *pag.* 77.

(p) *Lib.* 2. *de Eccles. c.* 2. *pag.* 411.

Iæme

Iames (as some dare affirme) gaue onely one kind to the people of Hierusalem, what then? The word of God is plaine and manifest, eate and drinke; this is to be heard of vs and preferred before al Iameses, and wordes of the Church. So cleare and confessed then it is that S. Iames the Apostle, and the Church of *Hierusalem,* in his time administred the communion vnder one kinde, that no other answeare is left to this Protestant, then onely to make the Scriptures and the Apostles prac-tise one contrary to the other, then ~~with~~ *which* what more impious or absurd.

That the practise of the Primitiue Church was promiscuous, some-times vnder one kinde and sometimes vnder both.

O SECTIN. 4.

THat which Protestantes so much vrge to wit, the example and practise of the Primitiue Church, doth likewise make in proofe of our Catholicke vse, for though we do not deny but in those firster times the Laity did often receiue vnder both kindes, yet that neither that vse was vniuersal in respect of time or place, or obser-ued as a matter of necessity, which is the matter onely controuersal, let these obseruations following beare ful testimony.

1   The *Manachees* the better to conceale their heresy, receiued often amongst Catholickes, and yet they (*) only receiued vnder the forme of bread, as thin-king wine to be the (a) gaule of the Prin-ces of drunkenes; and withal denying the true death of Christ our Sauiour: now if it had bene as the a general vse at Rome, & obserued as a precept of christ for euery one to receiue vnder both kindes, their abstinence from the one, insteede of concealement would haue serued for a most pre-sent and certaine discouery of their heresie. And at this day wheras the *Grecians* stil continew in schime against the latine Church, and rest most wacthful and greedy to obiect what soeuer may be pretended against vs, yet our cotrary custo to theirs herein, they neuer as yet accused for error or innouation.

(*) *Leo ser. 4. de Quadrag.*

(a) *August. l. de hæres. c. 46.*

(6) *Hier. patr. resp. ad Pro-test. c. 21.*

it was

2   It was as then a general vse to (c) referue
the Sacrament, which referuation to haue
bene for the moſt part onely of the hoſt, and
not of the Chalice is manifeſt, in that yet
was often referued for a (d) long time, euen
for the ſpace of a yeare (which likewiſe the
Grecians to this day obſerue) whereas wine
in a litle quantity, could not haue bene ſo
referued without congelation, or corruption
and ſowering, and yet I do not deny but that
the Chalice was (e) ſomtimes referued for a
ſmaler time.

3   The auncient Chriſtians did alſo vſe to
cary the Euchariſt home to their (f) houſes,
that ſo they might receiue it when they
thought fit, which was onely vnder the forme
of bread, for that onely was geuen into their
handes, the bloud they receiuing from (g) the
Chalice, neither had they at home any (h)
Chalices or ſacred veſſels wherein the bloud
ſhould be kept. A thing ſo certaine that (i)
Chemnitius confeſſeth the vſe of one kind in
priuate houſes, and onely anſweareth that
thoſe who receiued in their houſes vnder the
forme of bread, receiued before in the Church
vnder the forme of wine; and that the controuerſy is not of what was vſed in priuate
houſes, but in the publicke adminiſtration of
this Sacrament: but doth not this man ouerthrow him ſelfe, for if they receiue it in the
Church onely vnder one kinde, and at home
vpon different dayes vnder the other; doth
not this euidently proue that at neither time
in that caſe they receiued vnder both, the
ſaid communions being two, & moſt diſtinct.
And if in priuate horſes it was lawful to
receiue vnder one, doth not this vnanſwearably conuince that Chriſt
had geuen no abſolute commaund of both.

(c)
Conc. Nicen. 1. *can.* 12.
& 14. *alias* 18. *alias.* 20.
Nazian. orat. in Gorgon.
Ambroſ. orat. de obitu
Satiri. c. 7. *Chriſoſt. ep.* 1.
ad Innocent. P. Hier. ep.
ad ruſticum. and many
others. ſee alſo Caluin,
l. 4. *inſtitut. c.* 17. ſee
39. *Chemnit. in examen.*
ſeſ. 8. *can.* 1.

(d)
Amphilochius, in vita S.
Baſilij. Sophronius in Prato
ſpirit. c. 79.

(e)
Hierom. epiſt. ad Ruſt.
Chriſoſt. epiſt. 1. *ad In-*
nocent. P. Iuſt. apol. 2.

(f)
Tertul. l. 2. *ad vxor. &*
l. de corona mil. clem. A-
lex. l. 1. *ſtcom. Ciprian.*
ſer. de lapſis. Hier. in A-
pol. pro lib. c. Iouin. Aug.
ſer. 252. *de tempore.*

(g)
Ciril. catech. 5. *miſtag.*

(h)
Athanaſius Apol. 2. *cont.*
Arianos.

(i)
Exam. part. 2. *diſput. de*
vtraq̃ ſpecie.

4   In

(k)
Ciprian. *fer. de lap*. 4.
Dionif. *c*. 7. *de Ecclef.*
Hierar.

(*)
Conc. Carthag. 4. *c*. 76.
Conc. Tol. 11. *c*. 11.
conc. Rhem. *c*. 2. *Eu-*
feb. hift. l. 6. *c*. 36.
Pauling. *in vita S. Am-*
brof. Amphiloch. *in vita*
S. *Bafily* Amalarius de of-
fic. Ecclef. l. 3. *c*. 35.
Microlog. de rebus Ec-
clef. c. 17.

(1)
Felix. 3. *epift*. 1. *c*. 2.
Siricus, *epift*. 1. *c*. 11.
Conc. Elibert. *can*. 76.
conc. Sardic. *c*. 2. *Aga-*
thenfe. c. 25. 50. Cipri.
l. 4. *epift*. 2.

(m)
Melancton *in Apol .confef.*
Auguft.

(n)
Felix. *f*. 3. *vbi fupra.*

(o)
Conc. Sardic. *cap*. 2.

4 In thofe times alfo were Infants fometime communicated, and that onely vnder
the forme of wine, by (k) inftilling fome
few dropes of the bloud into their mouthes;
neither could they haue poffibly caufed them
to haue fwallowed the bread being but Infants.

5 The ficke were vfed to receiue & that
for the moft part vnder one kind, whereof
plentiful examples are to be found in feueral (*) authors .

6 It was impofed often vpon the cleargy
(1) in a penalty for fome crime committed,
that they fhould receiue after the manner of
the Laity, which was not (as (m) fome pretend) onely to debar them from the confecrating, for this penalty was inflicted for the
moft part vpon Deacons, and other inferior
cleargy men, who neuer had power to confecreate, neither was it in reguard of time or
place, becaufe the Laity did reciue in a lower
part of the Church and after the Cleargy for
often were they prohibited to receiue but
onely at the (n) hower of their death; and
fometimes (o) neither then was it permitted: now at the hower of their death, and
that in a priuate chamber, no diftinction
could be made either of time or place be-
twixt the Cleargy, and the laity, wherefore
that onely was called the communion of the
Laity, which was permitted by them to be touched, and caried away
if they would, which onely was the facred hoft, which was geuen into their handes for though thofe that would, might drinke of the
Chalice in the Church, yet might they not touch the Chalice, much
leffe cary it away.

(p)
Innocent. *epift*: 1. *c*. 4.
liber Sacramentorum S .
Greg-

7 It haith bene a moft auncient Cuftome
(p) and that without any knowen beginning euen for the Preift himfelfe vpon good
fryday

fryday onely to receiue vnder one kind.

8 Yea the vſe and practiſe of receauing vnder one kind is ſo confeſſedly auncient, as that *Vrbanus Regius* a Proteſtant writer, acknowledgeth that the hereticke (*) *Neſto-rius communicated the Laity vnder both kindes,* (but) *the councel of Epheſus reſiſted him* ; which Councel was one of the foure firſt general Councels, celebrated in the pureſt times of the Primitiue Church.

9 And that communion vnder one kind haith bene vſed in ſundry countries for many hundreth yeares, ſundry (r) Councels and writers do largely teſtify.

Now whereas *D. Morton* relateth that (s) *M. Whitaker did note the adminiſtration of the Sacrament but in one kind, now vſed in the Romiſh Church, to haue had the original from the Ma-nichees,* and further vrgeth that Catholickes *haue not anſweared hereunto,* but rather *willing-ly concealed it* : we haue and do anſweare that the *Manichees* were iuſtly condemned; firſt for that with them the Preiſtes alſo refuſed the cup. Secondly for that as (t) *Chemni-tius,* and other Proteſtantes are forced to relate the truth, *the Manichees, becauſe they deteſted wine as a thing abhominable, and feaned the body of Chriſt* (as in their opinion) but fantaſtical, *not to haue had true bloud, they endeauored to bring in the receauing of only one kind;* which how impertinently and vnconſcionably it is vrged againſt vs, *D. Mor-ton* him ſelfe ſhal plead in our behalfe ſaying, (u) *knowing the Mani-chees, did heretically celebrate the Euchariſt onely in one kind the bread, but the wine they did not allow, becauſe they imagined wine to haue bene created by an euil ſpirit, and were therefore aunciently* (x) *condemned for heretickes, would now the Apologiſts* (that is Catholickes) *hould it concionable in Proteſtantes to accuſe the Romaniſtes of that hereſy of the Manichees becauſe they diſtribute not the Euchariſt in both the elements bread and wine? nay would they not rather reiect this accuſation as altogether iniurious, ſaying, it is*

Gregor. in officio Paraſce-ues. ordo Romanus anti-quus in officio euſdemnei. Rabanus l. 2. de inſtitut. c. 37. Microlog. l. de Ec-cleſ. obſeruat. c. 19.

(*)
Loc. com. f. 56.

(r)
Con. Conſtant. ſeſ. 13. Baſilienſe ſeſ. 30. S. Tho-mas 3. p. q. 80. art. 12. Alcuinus c. de ordine cele-brand. Miſſam.

(s)
Proteſt. Appeal. l. 4. c. 15. p. 505.

(t)
Exam. part. 2. p. 145. Zepperus de ſacram. p. 41.

(u)
Proteſt. Apeal l. 2. c. 4. p. 139. 140.

(x)
Leo ſerm. 4. Quadrag.

C c c

not rather reiect this accusation as altogether iniurious saying, it is not the Manichees abstinence from the wine, but the reason of that forbearance which was iudged heretical? So clearly doth *D. Morton* cleare vs from this foule and falſe imputation vrged againſt vs by *D. Whitakers*, and him ſelfe; and ſo clearly doth he contradict him ſelfe, in one place accuſing vs, in an other excuſing vs, in one and the ſame reſpect: of which foule fault of contradiction in ſo great a *Rabbin*, when he cleareth him ſelfe, inſteede of being Biſhop of *Liechfilde*, and *Couentry*, he ſhal be to me euer *magnus Apollo*.

That communion vnder one kinde is of it ſelfe a matter of indifferency, not prohibited, and ſo lawful, it is further proued by the confeſſion of Proteſtantes.

SECTION. 5.

AMongſt many other arguments which might be produced in proofe of this matter I haue euer eſteemed this one, moſt cleare and conuincing, which is the confeſſion of our aduerſaries them ſelues, who indeed not laying any firme ground wherupo to found their conceipts neither vſing any certaine ſquare or rule wherby to direct them in their proceedinges, do, as in moſt other cheifeſt pointes of faith and religion, ſo in this, not onely directly contradict one an other, but euen one and the ſelfe ſame man doth make domeſtical war with him ſelfe.

Martin Luther, the firſt founder of Proteſtancy plainly acknowledgeth that Chriſt haith geuen no commaundment hereof; his wor-

(a)

Ep. ad Bohem. et in declarat. Euchar. et in ſerm. de Euchar.

(b)

De captiuit. Babil. c. de Euchar.

des (a) *although truly it were an excelleut thing to vſe both kindes in the Euchariſt, and Chriſt in this thing haith commaunded nothing as neceſſary, yet it were better to follow peace and vnity which Chriſt hath comanded vs to follow, then to contend about the kindes.* And againe (b) *they ſinne not againſt Chriſt, who vſe one kind, ſeeing Chriſt haith not commaunded to vſe it, but haith left it to the wil of euery one, ſaying as often as you ſhil do theſe, you ſhal do them in memory of me.*

He teacheth further that it is onely a matter of indifferency, *I am*

no

not (c) author (faith he) that the Bohemians be
compelled to the one part of the Sacrament, but
that they be left to that manner which they wil
them felues. Let the Bifhop onely take care that
difcord rife not by the manner of receiuing, but
let him inftruct them familiarly that neither is
ioyned with error, euen as it is free from error,
that Preiftes vfe a different habit from the Laity.
As alfo (d) if thou fhalt come to a place in which
one onely kinde is miniftred, take onely one, as
they there receiue, if two be offered, take two,
neither bring in any thing fingular, or opofe thy
felfe to the multitude. And (e) further I haue not faid, nor conceiued, *counfailed* neither
is it my intention that one or more Bifhops by their proper authority may begin
to minifter to any both kindes, vnleffe it fhould be fo ordained or commaunded
by fome general Councel.

Hofpinian alledgeth *Luther* faying, (f) it is not needful to geue both
kindes, but the one alone fufficeth: the Church
haith power of ordaining onely one, and the people
ought to be content therewith, if it be ordained by
the Church. And Hofpinian further reporteth
that certaine (g) Proteftantes anfweared that
they beleeued and confeffed whol Chrift to be real-
ly prefent, exhibited, and receiued vnder euery kinde, and therefore vnder
the onely forme of bread, neither did they iudge thofe to do euil who communicated vnder one kinde. Thus Catholickly doth doctor *Luther* teach
communion vnder both kindes not to be commaunded by Chrift, to
be a thing indifferent of it felfe, and as now not lawful by any priuate authority to adminifter it vnder both.

Philip *Melancthon*, a pryme man amongft Proteftantes, writeth thus,
(h) concerning both kindes of the Lords fupper
we fee many tumults to haue beene renewed &c.
but the Pope without any hurt might eafily helpe
thefe inconueniences, if taking away the prohibition, he would leaue the vfe free. And this liberty
&c. would nothing hurt any, and the whol bufi-
nes is in the Popes handes. Againe he compa-
reth the indifferency hereof with our liberty of eating or abftaining

(c)
*Lib. ad Chriftianam nobi-
litatem.*

(d)
*Tom. 2. Germ. f. 100.
et in alia edit. tom. 7. f.
360. l. de vtraq; fpecie
Sacramenti.*

(e)
*In declarat. in ferm. de
Euchar.*

(f)
*Hift. Sacram. part. 2.
fol. 12.*

(g)
Ibidem. fol. 112.

(h)
*Cent. epift. Theol. epift.
74. pag. 251. 252.*

(i)
*In 2. edit. loc. com. im-
pref. Argent. An. 1525.
fol. 78.*

from swines flesh, (i) *he erreth* (saith he) *that thinketh it impious to eate swines flesh ; as also he erreth who thinketh it impious to abstaine from swines flesh : these thinges ar indifferent and placed in our power, and so I iudge of the Eucharist, that they sinne not who knowing and beleeuing this liberty, do vse either part of the signe.* And whereas *M. Harding* alledgeth this last saying of *Melancthon,* as also *Bucer,* aduising and wishing *that the holy Church would geue free power of receauing this Sacrament vnder one or*

(k)   *both kindes &c.* M. (k) *Iewel* cannot deny
Reply, pag. 108. 109.   these testimonies so alledged by *M. Harding,*
110.   but acknowledgeth them for truly alledged.

Amongst the articles of the conference at *Katesbone* which *Bucer* allowed, one was, that *for the decyding of the controuersy of one or both kindes, it would cheifly auaile if the holy Church would geue free choice of receiuing this Sacrament vnder one or both kindes :* which referring the matter to the Church doth euidently suppose that Christ our Sauiour had geuen no absolute commaund thereof.

Iohn Przibram, a Bohemian Protestant, after endeauour to proue com-
(l)   munion vnder both, yet concludeth saying,
De professione fidei Cathol. (l) *here fearing God and taking heede of the euil*
c. 19.   *customes of others, I do confesse that I do not intend*
to condemne or censure for heretickes any such persons of the Church as do
impugne the communion of the faithful vnder both kindes; which yet of
necessity he must if he had thought that Christ had commaunded it.

And the like confession might be shewed from others of their brethren ; but from hence wil I infer two thinges : first that communion vnder one, or both kindes, being a thing confessedly of it selfe indifferent, that then the vse thereof vnder one, or both, cannot possibly be censured of sacriledge in reguard of Christes institution, or of any hurt or preiudice to the faithful receiuers. The second that then also was it lawful for the Church of God vpon iust occasions absolutely to determine or limit the vse thereof, of which point I wil now further treate.

That communion vnder one or both kindes being a thing indifferent, the
Church might lawfully determine the same: and of the reasons
that moued the Church in limitation thereof.

SECTION. 6.

Although we were not thus stored with such plentiful and pregnant proofes, as in sundry other high mysteries of our faith
we are not, nor with reason can expect, yet the doctrine of the vniuersal Church inspired by the holy Ghost, and made knowen vnto vs
by the absolute and infallible decrees of sundry general Councels,
might sufficiently serue to free the vnderstanding of any man from
error, or his conscience from sinne; for it may not be auouched without great temerity, either that she should so haynously trespasse a-
gainst the sacred lawes of her dearest spouse, or so vnnaturally and
vncharitably, depriue her owne children of necessary blessinges and
helpes bequeathed vnto them; yea in the end it would redound to
the blemish of Christ him selfe, if he should suffer his Church so
daungerously to erre in a matter of that moment.

Wherefore in this present case we are to assume, that she onely
expresseth that power which she haith euer had, to wit (a) *in dispen-*
sing of the Sacraments, their substance (or es-
sence) being preserued, to ordaine or alter what   (a)
soeuer shee shal iudge more expedient for the   *Concil. Trident. sess. 21.*
profit of the receiuers, or reuerence of the Sacra-   *c. 2.*
ments, according to the variety of thinges, times,   (b)
and places: which her authority *the Apostle*   1. *Cor.* 4. 1.
seemeth not obscurely to insinuate, when he said,   (c)
(b)*so let a man esteme vs as the ministers of Christ,*   1. *Cor.* 11. 34.
and the dispensors of the mysteries of God, and   (d)
him selfe to haue vsed this power, it is manifest   *Math.* 28. 19.
both in many other thinges, as also in this Sacra-   (e)
ment, when hauing ordained some thinges concer-   *Can. Apost. can.* 49.
ning the vse thereof, (c) *the rest saith he, I wil dispose when I come.* Christ
our Sauiour said to his Apostles (d) *going teach ye al nations, Baptising*
them in the name of the Father, and of the Sonne, and of the holy Ghost. and
yet the Church commaundeth Infants to be baptised, who are not ca-

C c c 3   pable

pablic of teaching. So in the Primitiue Church vpon certaine occasion (e) Baptisme was commaunded to be ministred with threefould immersion; and yet the same Church, iust reasons requiring the contrary rite, haith limited it onely to one. In like sorte the Church haith lawfully decreed (f) certaine impediments of mariage, which yet neither the law of nature nor any positiue diuine law exacted.

And not onely in the Sacraments, but also in other thinges haith the Church vpon iust occasions exercysed her said aucthority, by reducing thinges of their owne natures indifferent, to be matter of precept and necessity : so the Apostles them selues imposed vpon the *Gentils* for a time, a new law of abstinence (g) *from the thinges immolated to Idols, and bloud, and that which is strangled &c.* which yet Christ him selfe had neuer imposed, but left the eating of them a matter indifferent, whereas after the Apostles decree, the said eating had bene sinne, and abstinence necessary, as is manifest by those wordes (h) *it seemeth good to the holy Ghost, and to vs, to laye no further burden vpon you then these necessary thinges, that ye abstaine from thinges immolated to Idols &c.* And so of S. (i) *Paul* it is said, that he walked *through Syria, and Cilicia,* confirming the Churches, commaunding them to keepe the precepts of the Apostles, and the auncients. And in the Primitiue Church it was not onely thought (k) vnlawful to violate the said law, but also seuere (l) punishment was inflicted vpon the transgressors thereof, yea there haith bene scarce any councel in the Church of God, which haith not commaunded or forbidden vnder sinne, somthing which before the said Councel was free and indifferent.

Wherefore communion vnder one or both kindes, being proued and acknowledged to be a thing of indifferency, the Church in fulnes of her power might lawfully permit or limit the same; and yet her decree once past, the violating therof is vndoubtedly

Marginal notes:

(f)
See S. *Augu∫t. l. 15. de ciuit. c. 16. S. Ambro∫. epi∫t. 66. ad Patern. S. Greg. l. 12. Regi∫t. epi∫t. 31. ad Fælicem.*

(g)
Act. 15. 29.

(h)
Ver∫. 28. 29.

(i)
Act. 15. 41. & 16. 4.

(k)
Tertul. in Apol. c. 9. Origen. l. 8. cont. Cel∫. Ciril. catech. 5. Aug. ep. 154. Leo, epi∫t. 79. c. 5. Con. Gang. c. 2.

(l)
Can. Apo∫t. c. 62. Con. 2. Aurelianes. can. 19. 20.

(m)
De precepto & di∫pen∫.

tedly sinne. So S. (m) *Bernard* saith, *although the quality of the worke enioyned, of it selfe be free from fault, yet the waight of authority adioyned maketh it subiect to commaund, and the commaundement subiect to sinne.*

Yea D. *Whitguift* teacheth that (n) *thinges indifferent of them selues do after a sort chaunge their nature, when by some commaundement they are commaunded or forbidden,* and (o) *they remaine indifferent til the Church haith taken order in them, which being done they are no more indifferent.* with him agreeth (p) *Beza* affirming *that thinges of them selues indifferent do in a manner chaunge their natures when they are commanded or forbidden by any lawful commaund.* yea pag. 7 saith M. *Powel,* (q) *such indifferent thinges as by the Church haith bene lawfully and orderly instituted and approued, are so far humane, as that they are also diuine, and therefore haue more then humane authority, yea plainly diuine &c. therefore the precepts of the Church in thinges indifferent are both true and holy:* and consequently seeing the Church haith determined receauing of the Sacrament to be vnder one kinde, which was formerly indifferent, it is now vnder sinne accordingly to be vsed and obserued.

(n)
Defence &c. pag. 258.
(o)
Ibidem. pag. 92.
(p)
Epist. theol. epist. 24. pag. 155.
(q)
Of thinges indifferent.

Now the reasons that moued the Church to the restraint therof were many and forcible; as first to preuent thereby the occasion of error, for whereas in the beginning of the Church the vse of one or both kindes was indifferent, as haith bene shewed heretofore in condemnation of the *Manichees,* who abstained from wine, as a thing of it selfe vnlawful, holy Bishops did much commend the vse of the Chalice, but this error being extinguished, & an other arising against the integrity of Christ vnder either kinde, as also auouching the absolute necessity of both; the Church of God hereu-

(r)
Æneas Siluius, hist. Bohem. c. 35.

pon began more vniuersally to practise the communion vnder one, & withal in declaration of the truth, and preuention of schisme & scandal, did absolutely decree the lawfulnes thereof, with prohibition to the contrary. So in auncient times when the *Ebionites* taught vnleauened bread to be necessary in consecratiõ of the *Eucharist,* the Church commaunded consecration to be made in leuened bread, and when the hereticke *Nestorius,* denyed our B. Lady to be the Mother of God, and onely to be called the mother of Christ, the Church condemned
him.

and commaunded the contrary, so that no courfe haith euer beene found more effectual for confutation and vtter extirpation of error & herefy, then by contrary decrees to declare & to eftablifh the truth.

The fecond reafon mouing the Church was the deferued reuerence of this higheft Sacrament; in due confideration whereof the holy Fathers (s) did carefully prefcribe moft dilige̅t care to be vfed, left any litle particle of the hofte, or drop of the Chalice fhould fal vpon the ground, mnch vnlike to the Proteftant minifter who in diftribution of his communion letting one morfel cafually fal, tould the communicant offering to take it vp, that jt was not needful, for fome dog, might afterwardes take it, now the multitude of Chriftians being very great, and their negligence in facred thinges through want of zeale and deuotion notorious, it could not morally be poffible but that frequent fpilling of the bloud would happen, if the Chalice were ordinarily to be geuen to the people, of which (t) prophanations ouer frequent experience haith beene had.

(s)
Aug. l. 5. homil. 26. hom. 25. Ciril. catech. 5. miftag. Orig. hom. 13. in Exod.

(t)
Æneas Siluius, ep. 130. de errore Bohemorum. et narratio de Bohemis ad Concil. Bafil.

To thefe I may ad, that many in hot countries do abftaine from wine fró their childhood, and either by nature or education do abhor it fo much as they connot endure to taift it. Alfo in fome countries wine is fo fcarce and deare, as that fufficient cannot be prouided for al the people: now as thefe to be debarred wholly from reeeauing were a thing lamentable, fo is it moft improbable that the wifdome of Chrift would bind his feruants to fo great inconueniences.

An examination of such argumentes as are drawen from sacred Scrip-
tures in proofe that Christ gaue conmaund vnto his Apostles & their
successors to administer the Sacrament of the Eucharist vnder
both kindes to the laity.

SECTION. 7.

THe cheifeſt cauſe of difficulty in this queſtion, and that which
geueth our aduerſaries the beſt colour for impugning the truth,
and perſiſting in their error, is, as they pretend, certaine texts of ſacred Scripture, wherefore I wil indeuour by ſundry forcible reaſons
to lay open the true ſence, ſcope, and vnderſtanding thereof, and therby to diſcouer the inſufficency and weakenes of al ſuch their groundes
as they mainly inſiſt on.

The places are theſe (a) *vnleſſe you eate the fleſh of the ſonne of man,*
and drinke his bloud, you ſhal not haue life in you.   (a)
And taking (b) *the Chalice, he gaue thankes* Ioan. 6. 53.
and gaue to them, ſaying, drinke you al of this.   (b)
I receiued of our Lord (c) *that which alſo I haue* Math. 26. 27.
deliuered vnto you, that our Lord Ieſus &c. tooke   (c)
bread and geuing thankes, brake, and ſaid, take 1. Cor. 11. 23. 24. 25.
ye and eate, this is my body which ſhal be deliuered
for you. this do ye for the commemoration of me.   In like manner alſo the
Chalice, after he had ſupped, ſaying, this Chalice is the new teſtament in my
bloud, this do ye as often as you ſhal drinke for the commemoration of me.

From theſe texts Proteſtants infer three thinges: *firſt,* that we are not
commaunded only to eate, but likewiſe, and that expreſly, to drinke.
Secondly that his commaund of drinking is not geuen only to Preiſtes,
but extended to al, it being plainly ſaid, *drinke ye al of this.* And thirdly that the inſtitution by Chriſt was vnder both kindes which we are
bound not to alter, but ſtrictly to imitate.

This notwithſtanding I anſweare, theſe places to be vrged as concerning their preſent purpoſe, moſt impertinently and inſufficiently,
and that for ſundry cauſes: And firſt touching thoſe wordes of Chriſt,
vnleſſe (d) *you eate the fleſh of the ſonne of man*   (d)
and drinke his bloud, you ſhal not haue life in Ioan. 6. 53.
you. I affirme that ſeeing according to the doctrine of the learned

(e)
Lurber de captiuit. Babil.
c. 1. Suing. l. de vera &
falſa relig. c. de Euchar.
Chemnit. 2. part. exam.
pag. 657. ad s. 1. ſeſ.
21. Conc. Trid. Caluin.
inſtit. l. 4. c. 17. parag.
33. Pet. Mart. l. cont.
Gardin. part. 1. ad ſolut.
32. obiect.

(e) Proteſtantes, nothing in the ſaid 6. chapter of *S. Iohn* concerneth the Sacrament of the Euchariſt, but al their ſaid eating and drinking, is onely to be vnderſtood of beleeuing in Chriſt, that therefore according to them nothing can be produced from thence, for communion vnder one or both kindes, ſeeing nothiog therein concerneth the ſame.

2 Yet according to the true doctrine & generall opinion of Catholickes teaching the ſaid wordes & ſundry other in the ſaid 6. chapter, truly & properly to côcerne only the Euchariſt

I anſweare, that the wordes obiected do not neceſſarily import a precept ; for which wee are to note, that not alwaies in the doctrine of Chriſt that byndeth of neceſſity and vnder ſinne, which ſeemeth to haue the marke or badge of a precept, but in ſundry caſes for the attaining of the true ſence and vnderſtanding, we are to make recourſe to the intention of the ſpeaker. So our Sauiour him ſelfe hauing cured two

(f)
Math. 9. 30. 31.
(g)
Mar. 10. 4. 5.
(h)
Ioan. 13. 14.

blind men, (f) *he threatned them ſaying, ſee that no man know it, but they went forth and bruted him in al that countrey,* & yet none houldeth that either hereby they ſinned , or that Chriſt intended any ſuch bound . The bil of diuorſe which *Moyſes* permitted Chriſt expreſly calleth (g) *a commaund and preecpt,* he likewiſe tould his Apoſtles (h) *they ought to waſh one an others feete,* and yet neither by them nor vs ſince, was it houlden for a matter of neceſſity, and ſundry other ſuch like .

Thirdly, but ſuppoſing for the preſét, that it includeth a precept, yet the precept therin implied is not in the maner of receiuing, but in the thing receiued, for therin was contained one of the principal meanes or remedies whereby to preſerue our ſpiritual life obtained by Baptiſme, which meanes conſiſt not in the formes or manner of receauing, but in receauing of the body and bloud of Chriſt, which in either kind we do (as is formerly proued) no leſſe then in both, and thus accor-

(i)
Ioan. 6. 57.

dingly he declared him ſelfe ſaying, (i) *he that eateth me the ſame alſo ſhal liue by me,* which alſo further may be illuſtrated by heedful conſideration of theſe circumſtances

cumstances following: As 1. the occasion of the wordes obiected, which was the incredulity of the *Chapharnaites*, whose doubt was not whether the Sacrament was to be receiued vnder one or both kindes, but as Protestantes stil doubt, whether he could *geue vs his flesh to eate*. The second is the manner of his speach, which was not by making mention of either forme or kind in the said wordes, but onely of the thinges them selues; al which are contained in either kinde: yea in other places of the same chapter where he maketh mention of either kind, it is onely of the bread and none at al of the wine; and wheras somtimes he maketh mention both of eating and drinking, yet much more often doth he onely mention eating. Lastly to be considered, is the conclusion of his speach,   (k)
which was that (k) *he that eateth this bread Verf.* 58.
shal liue for euer: from al which it followeth that the Iewes not doubting of the manner of receiuing vnder one or more kindes, but of the possibility of the thinges to be receiued; and Christ our Sauiour thereupon assuering not onely the said possibility, but also the necessity therof to our spiritual life, did therefore intend no other thing but the instruction of the Iewes and declaration of the neede and profit thereof, al which is performed no lesse by receauing one then both kindes of the Sacrament.

    Fourtly it is vsual in sacred Scriptures for the coniunction copulatiue (*et and*) to be taken for a disiunctiue;   (l)
so it is said, (l) *he that shal strike his father & Exod.* 21. 15.
mother, shal dye; Also (m) *gold and siluer I*   (m)
haue not, and sundry other such like; wherin *Act.* 3. 6.
it is manifest the sence is disiunctiue, to wit,   (n)
he that shal strike his father or mother shal dye; 1. *Cor.* 11. 29.
and gold or siluer I haue not. And as *S. Paul*
speaking of this very Sacrament said (n) *he that eateth and drinketh vnworthyly eateth and drinketh iudgement to him selfe:* so also he said (o)
whosoeuer shal eate this bread or drinke the Cha-   (o)
lice of our Lord vnworthely &c.   *Verf.* 27.

    And wee are also further to obserue that the particle (*nisi vnles*) including in it a negation, as *vnles you shal eate*, is al one to say, *as if you shal not eate*; that the said negation put in the begining of a proposition coppulatiue, doth deny both partes, and according to the Hebrew phrase (which not onely latin interpreters do imitate, but euen

S. *Iohn*, who writ in Greeke is noted by his expoſition (often to follow) is vnderſtood twice, to wit, as repeated in both partes, ſo according to the Hebrew it is ſaid, (p) *the*
wicked do not riſe in iudgement, and the ſinners
in the councel of the iuſt, which yet by the latin
interpreters is truly and properly tranſlated,
the wicked do not riſe in iudgement, nor ſinners in
the councel of the iuſt ; as alſo (g) *gold and ſiluer I haue not* 1. *neither*
gold nor ſiluer I haue, ſo in the preſent, *vnles you ſhal eate the fleſh of the*
ſonne of man, and drinke his bloud, you ſhal not haue life in you, is al one
with *if you ſhal not eate the fleſh of the ſonne of man, or if you ſhal not drinke*
his bloud, you ſhal not haue life in you; according to which ſence he is
onely excluded from life, who ſhal neither eate his fleſh nor drinke
his bloud: and from this negatiue copulatiue propoſition doth directly follow this affirmatiue diſiunctiue, *he that ſhal eate the fleſh, or ſhal*
drinke the bloud of our Lord ſhal haue life. And that this is the true
ſence of the words, it is manifeſt by theſe textes, precedēt *I am the liuing*
bread that came dowen from heauen, if any ſhal eate of this bread he ſhal liue
for euer. and theſe ſubſequent, *he that eatethme the ſame alſo ſhal liue by me,*
he that eateth this bread ſhal liue for euer: By al which places it is euident, that the receiuing vnder the forme of bread is ſufficient to life.
beſides it is plaine to the reader, that in this whol chapter, Chriſt
taketh for the ſame *bread, his fleſh, his fleſh and bloud, and him ſelfe*.
And promiſeth to euery one of them the ſame reward, to wit, *life*
euerlaſting, and ſo to *eate bread, to eate fleſh, and to eate fleſh and drinke*
bloud, is nothing els but to eate *Chriſt*, ſeeing whether he be receiued
vnder one or both kindes, nothing geueth life but *Chriſt*. And ſo I
may laſtly infer, that the ſaid ſayinges were plainly falſe if the foreſaid wordes, *vnleſſe you ſhal eate &c.* were to be taken copulatiuely,
not diſiunctiuely; or which is al one, if Chriſt had geuen therby a
commaund of both kindes. And thus we ſee this firſt obiection according to the doctrine of Proteſtants, altogether impertinent, and
according to the truth for ſundry reaſons moſt inſufficient.

Concerning the ſecond taken from theſe
wordes of Chriſt, (r) *drinke you al of this,*
from whence Proteſtantes would likewiſe in-
fer an vniuerſal commaund not onely of eating, but likewiſe of drinking ; I anſweare, the word (*al*) is not alwaies taken in Scripture moſt
                                                                    vniuerſally

(p)
Pſal. 1 . 5.
(q)
Act. 3 . 6.

(r)
Math. 26. 27.

vniuersally for al men, or al thinges, but often for al of some certaine kinde ; for otherwise that of *S. Paul*, (s) *al seeke the thinges which are their owne*, should include the most iust, & that *(t) al haue sinned*, should comprehend Christ, and that (u) *al cryed crucify him*, and the like, should belong to the Apostles, which yet are most vntrue ; and so if in the wordes obiected the word *(al)* should be taken vniuersally for al, then the Sacrament were to be geuen to Turkes, Iewes, Heathens, Infants, and such as cannot drinke wine, these being men, al which Protestantes exclude : wherefore the word (al) being to be restrained, it is cleare it concerneth here the twelue Apostles who as then onely (x) sate with Christ at the table. *S.* (y) *Marke* most answearably, and in direct tearmes affirming of the Apostles that *they al dranke of it*. And this sence also do al circumstances of the place conuince, as when (a) *it was euening he sate dowen with his twelue Apostles &c. and whiles they were at supper Iesus tooke bread and blessed, and brake, and gaue to his Disciples and said, take ye and eate &c. And taking the Chalice he gaue thankes, and gaue to them saying, drinke ye al of this &c. And an himne being said, they went forth vnto mount Oliuet, then Iesus said vnto them al you shal be scandalized in me in this night.* Al which do ioyntly conspire in prouing the word *(al)* to concerne here onely al the twelue Apostles. Now from the example or fact of the Apostles drinking or receiuing vnder both kindes, to infer a necessity for the laity to do the like, no argument wilbe of force, as shal be hereafter most clearly conuinced.

But though this explication be most litteral and agreable with the Scriptures, yet Protestants obiect sundry thinges against it, as *first* (b) that Christ foreseeing that some would deny the vse of the Chalice to al, did therfore say, *drinke ye al of this*, wheras he said not of thother kind, *eate yee al of this*: but the answeare is easy, for though not by the written word, yet by Apostolical tradition, the Church placeth in the Cannon of the Masse these wordes, *eate you al of this*.

(s)
Phil. 2. 21.
(t)
Rom. 3. 23.
(u)
Math. 27. 22.
(x)
Mar. 14. 17. 18. *and when euening was come, he cometh with the* 12. *and when they were sitting at the table and eating &c.*
(y)
Cap. 14. 23.
(a)
Math. 26.
(b)
Luther, l. de captiuit. Babil. c. de Euchar. Caluin, in Antido. artic.

(c)
S. Ambros. l. 4. de Sa-crament. c. 5. see the like in paschal l. de corpore Chrifti c. 15.

(d)
Cap. 22. 17.

And fo S. Ambrofe fetting downe the inftitution of this Sacrament (c) bringeth in our Sauiour faying to his Apoftles, *take yee and eate yee al of this.* And though it were certaine that Chrift had not faid fo, yet it auayleth nothing, the difparity, being manifeft, for Chrift geuing one and the fame Chalice, that al of them might drinke thereof he might wel fay, *drinke yee al of this,* that fo the firft might know he was not to drinke al, but was to leaue fo much as would fuffice for al the reft, which forme of fpeach he vfed moft plainly a litle before in the fupper of the Pafche ; for as S. Luke (d) faith, *taking the Chalice he gaue thankes and faid, take and diuide among you,* wheras breaking the bread him felfe, and geuing to euery one his part, not the whol to be diuided amonft them, there was no fuch neceffity of the forefaid wordes.

But *Luther* further argueth, that to the fame is faid, *eate,* to whom *drinke,* wherfore the whol Sacrament is either to be geuen only to Preiftes, or alfo to the laity, if alfo to thefe, then to al it is faid, *eate and drinke,* if onely to Preiftes then it is not lawful differently from the inftitution of Chrift, to geue any part thereof to the laity; and of this argument he thus infulteth, *I confeffe my felfe to be ouercome with this vnanfwearable reafon, neither haue I read, heard or found what to fay againft it.* But that you may fee the weaknes of *Luther* fo eafily ouercome, and how fmal and fuperficial his reading, hearing, or fynding haith bene, I anfweare, admitting that to the fame was faid, *eate,* to whom *drinke,* to wit, to the Apoftles. As alfo I graunt that the whol Sacrament is to be geuen not onely to Preiftes but alfo to the laity ; but that which is inferred hereof is moft falfe, to wit, that if the whol Sacrament be to be geuen to the laity, then they are to drinke, for I haue already demonftrated that the whol Sacrament is truly and effentially vnder either kind, neither did it further follow that if the whol Sacrament vnder both kindes was geuen onely to Preiftes by Chrift, and not to the laity, that then it may not now be geuen to them vnder one, for though Chrift him felfe did not geue it, yet did he no where prohibit it, yea elfwhere he commaunded it, when he faid,

(e)
Luc. 22. 19.

(e) *do this* which wordes imediatly follow the confecration of the bread, and no where
repeated

repeated by any of the *Euangelistes* after con- (f) }
secration of the Chalice; and though *S. Paul* 1 . *Cor* . 11 . 25 .
saith, (f) *this do yee as often as you shal drinke*
&c. yet these wordes are not absolute, but with this restraint, to
wit, *as often as you shal drinke,* thereby signifying not the necessity of
drinking, but the manner and end thereof, to wit, *in commemoration of*
Christ . So easily might Luther haue found what to haue said against
his so vnanswearable a reason.

But yet not satifyed, he further replyeth that seeing Christ said, *this*
is my bloud which shal be shed for you and for many, that therefore it is to
be geuen to al for whom it was shed, in which number no doubt the
laity is contained. And of this reason he thus triumpheth, *this of al*
cheifly vrgeth, and altogether concludeth me, and so indeede he may for a
singuler asse, for if the bloud were to be geuen to al for whom it was
shed, then were it to be geuen to Iewes, Turkes, Heathens, Infants,
and most abhominable sinners; for al (g)   (g)
whom no doubt Christ spent his precious 1 . *Tim* . 4 . 10 . *we hope*
bloud; wherefore the wordes obiected one- *in the liuing God which is*
ly conclude (and that most manifestly against *the Sauiour of al men, espe-*
Protestantes) that in the Chalice was truly *cially of the faithful.* 2 .
bloud, seeing Christ said thereof, *this is my* *Pet* . 2 . 1 . *In you there*
bloud which shal be shed for you and for many . *shal be lying maisters which*

Lastly some reply that though it be true *shal deny him that hasth*
that Christ spake vnto his Apostles when he *bought them, the Lord brin-*
said, *drinke yee al of this,* yet the Apostles as *ging vpon them selues spidy*
then representing al the faithful, al the faith- *perdition.* and see the like
ful therefore did drinke in them, and there- 1 . *Cor* . 8 . 11 . *Rom* .
fore now are to do it in them selues. *An-* 14 . 15 . *Herb* . 10 . 29 .
swere: But this auaileth not, for besides that
it is but onely imagined and not proued, that al the faithful were as
then represented in the Apostles, yet thence might we gather that now
they are not bound to the chalice, seeing that precept they haue already either fulfilled in the Apostles, or at the least that sufficiently
they fulfil the same stil in Preistes who drinke of the chalice, and whom
the Apostles as then did indeede truly represent.

The third principal obiection is taken from the first institution of
this Sacrament, which was by Christ our Sauiourr vnder both kindes,
and vnder the said both kindes geuen to the present communicants,
the

the 12. Apoftles: wherefore to communicate vnder one kind feemeth to alter the inftitution of Chrift, and therefore is vnlawful. The weakenes of this obiection is prefently difcouered, if onely we obferue the true natures of an inftitution, & of a precept, which of them felues are matters moft diftinct, for an inftitution is onely a certaine produc-tion of a thing whereby the nature and fubftance of the thing is efta-blifhed and ordained: and though the inftitution in the end be refer-red to the vfe of the thing, in that euery thing is for his vfe, yet the inftitution of it felfe commaundeth nothing concerning the vfe, wher-as a precept further prefcribeth, whether, and how the thing of ne-ceffity is to be vfed. *Matrimony* for example, is a thing ordained by God; and yet therefore al are not bound to marry, neither yet being married are they bound to vfe the fame, at al times, or in al fortes, which according to Goddes inftitution they lawfully might: And fo al creatures were by God ordained to ferue man and yet al men are not bound thereby to vfe them al. The like is in the prefent, Chrift inftituted the Eucharift vnder both kindes, but thereupon it doth not follow, that therefore euery one is in fuch fort to receiue it, no more then becaufe Chrift inftituted this Sacrament after wafhing of his Di-fciples feete, and after fupper, and fo gaue the fame to his Difciples not fafting, that therefore the like circumftances now are to be obferued in the adminiftration thereof; fo exceeding careful are our Proteftants of their cup of wine and careleffe of the reft.

Certaine breife rules whereby fuch places as are obiected from Fathers,
may eafily be anfweared.

SCTION. 8.

I am not ignorant that many thinges alfo are pretended from an-tiquity in defence of communion vnder both kindes, the which hauing examined very particularly and diligently my felfe, I finde the feueral difcuffion thereof would proue a labour both tedious and fruciles; tedious, in reguard of the great multitude of places obiec-ted; and fruciles, in that being duly confidered, they clearly appeare to be thinges either falfe and corrupt, or at the leaft altogether im-pertinent.

Wherefore

Wherefore I wil propofe certaine breife obfcruations, which being carefully remembred wil eafily folue al difficulties whatfoeuer arifing from Scriptures or Fathers.

And firft wheras fundry places offacred (a) Scriptures, and holy Fathers, do fpeake indifferently, or onely make mention of communion vnder both kindes, or affirme the vfe thereof to be lawful from thence yet cannot be inferred any precept of Chrift, or necefsity to faluation.

(a)

1. *Cor*. 11. *Chrifoft. hom*. 18. *in* 2. *epift. ad Cor. Ignat. epift. ad Pphiladelp. Theophil in* 1. *Cor*. 11.

Secondly, and when other places contained in them a precept, yet the fame are either vnderftood (b) of Preiftes who do facrifice, whofe bound (as before) is different from theirs of the laity, or els they concerne only the time, (d) and place, when and where, that cuftome of both kindes was obferued by al ; for the cuftome of the Church, whether it be general in the whol Church, or in fome notable part thereof, as in a Country, Kingdome, Prouince, or Diocefſe, haith

(b)

Math. 26. 27. *& Gelafius, dift*. 2. *can. comperimus*.

(d)

Ciprian. l. 1. *epift*. 2. *Pafchafius de corp. et fang. Chrifti*.

(e)

Auguft. epift. 84. *ad Cafulanum*.

the bynding (e) force of a law or precept; and fo it is vnlawful for any priuate man by word or deede knowingly to tranfgreffe the faid cuftome, in fuch place as it is generally kept and vfed, and yet the fame cuftome once ceafing, the bound and truth of al aucthorities produced in defence and confirmation of the faid cuftome do likewife ceafe.

Thirdly, fo alfo in the allegatió of any aucthority we are diligétly to obferue whether the fame maketh mentió of the formes or kindes, to wit, of bread and wine, or onely of the thinges contained vnder the faid kindes, to wit, the body and bloud of Chrift : for in the examples of the firfter we fhal feldome or neuer finde any one which importeth a precept or necefsity. And if by chaunce any one fuch fhould occurre, then it were to be fquared by the fecond and laft obferuations ; and though of the latter innumerable may (f) be brought, yet they are al impertinent, feeing the body and bloud of Chrift are as truly receiued vnder either kind, as vnder both, and the precept in that cafe

(f)

Ioan. 6. 53. *Auguft. queft*. 57. *in Leuit*.

determi-

determineth onely the thing and not the kinde.

Fourtly, as Chrift our Sauiour and the holy Fathers do ordinarily take for the fame thefe tearmes following, *bread, flefh, flefh and bloud, & Chrift him felfe,* promifing to any one thereof the like reward as to al the reft; fo alfo *by eating of the body and, drinking of the bloud,* they vnderftand in general the receauing of both, which moft truly and entyrely is performed by the receiuing of one. And if we fhould at-tend to the propriety of fpeach, neither is the bloud properly ~~drinke~~ drunke out of the Chalice, but onely the forme of wine, feeing the bloud in the Chalice haith the fame manner of exifting, as vnder the forme of bread, to wit, not diuided or feperated from the body, but inclu-ded in the vaines, and they in the body.

Fiftly, many authorities alledged for laical communion vnder both kindes, are vnderftood onely (g) of fpiritu-al, not Sacramental receauing, as when the Preift confecrating at the Altar vnder both, the people prefent with faith and deuotion, do with the mouth of their heartes, through pious thonghtes and meditations, eate the body and drinke the bloud of Chrift fpiritually, fo vniting them felues vnto him by the facred effect of trueft charity.

(g)
Auguft. l. 4. q. 9. 57. in Leuit.

Sixtly, though the Fathers fome times fignify the communion to be moft complete and perfect, when it is adminiftred and receiued vnder both kindes, in reguard that then the effectes thereof are more liuely expreffed, which yet is onely an accidental perfection, yet from thence may not be inferred a precept or neceffity for innumerable thinges there are which accidentally would conduce to grace & faluation which yet do not fal vnder any bound or commaund.

Seauenthly, The Fathers fometimes repro-uing fuch as abftained from the Chalice, do onely fpeake againft the (h) *Manichees,* and other heretickes, who vpon certaine fuper-ftition abhorred wine, as foolifhly thinking it to be (i) *Gaul of the deuil,* and withal de-nying Chrift our Sauiour to haue had true bloud, which nothing concerneth our Catho-licke doctrine and practife or reafons thereof.

(h)
Leo fer. 4. de Quadrag. Gelafius, apud Gratian. de confecrat. dift. 2. can. comperimus.
(i)
Auguft. l. de heref. c. 46.

Eightly, and it is greatly to be marked, that whereas the onely point in controuerfy is, whether Chrift our Sauiour gaue abfolute command commaund, not onely to Preiſtes, but alſo to the laity, to receaue vnder both kindes, as alſo whether the Primitiue Church did vniuer-ſally for time, and place, and as matter of neceſſity, obſerue the ſame, yet no one teſtimony of Scripture, or Doctor, can be produced, ei-ther expreſly, or by neceſſary conſequence affirming the ſame.

Laſtly, though any aucthority could be produced from a Doctor moſt auncient and learned, which expreſly and in direct tearmes ſhould contradict our Catholicke doctrine, yet the ſame with any man of iudgement and vertue, could beare no force againſt the infallible de-crees of the Oecumenical Councels, and the general practiſe of the Church of God, ſeeing not the Church vnto Doctors, but them ſelues and their writinges ought, and are to be ſubmitted to her, as might eaſily be proued by ſundry demonſtrations.

The concluſion of this treatiſe containing certaine rules which the greateſt Doctor S. Auguſtine gaue to his ſcholer Ianuarius, for his ſureſt direction in matters of faith and religion.

SECTION. 9.

BVt though theſe and ſundry other reaſons produced by Catho-lickes were not ſo pregnant, yet I am to geue notice to a Chriſti-an minde, that it is not our partes ſo much to diſcuſſe and enquire the cauſes mouing the Church herein, as rather to ſuppoſe the equi-ty thereof, and ſimply to obey her wholſome decrees; euer mindful of that heauenly precept, (a) *thou ſhalt do what*   (a) *ſoeuer they ſhal ſay who beare rule in that place*   *Deut.* 17. 10. *which our Lord haith choſen,* as alſo that the   (b) Church (b) *is the piller & ground of truth:* And   1. *Tim.* 3. 15. therfore that thoſe who (c) wil not heare or   (c) obey the *Church, are to be accompted as heathens*   *Math.* 18. 17. *and publicans.*

Werefore for my concluſion, that we may not be ſeduced either in this or any other point of controuerſy, I wil onely propoſe certaine general rules which the auncient and greateſt Doctor S. *Auguſtine,* gaue to his ſcholer *Ianuarius,* who had writ vnto him for the reſolu-tion of certaine doubtes; wherefore concerning the aucthority of Ec-

cleſiaſtical

cleſiaſtical traditions and general Councels. The firſt inſtruction was

(d)

Auguſt. epiſt. 118. ad Ianuarium, c. 1. 2.

that (d) *thoſe thinges which we keepe not writ-ten but deliuered, which are obſerued al ouer the world, are geuen to be vnderſtood, to be retained as commaund d and ordained either from the A-poſtles, or general Councels, whoſe aucthority in the Church is moſt ſound. So our Lords Paſſion, Reſurrection, Aſcention into heauen, and the comming of the holy Ghoſt, are celebrated with yearely ſolemnity, and if any other ſuch thing ſhal happen which is kept by the vniuerſal Church whether ſoeuer it ſhal dilate it ſelfe. But other thinges which are varied according to places and countries; as that ſome faſt vpon the Saboath, others not &c. al theſe kinde of thinges haue free obſeruation, neither is there in theſe any order better for a graue and prudent Chriſtian, then to do in ſuch ſort as he ſhal ſee the Church to which he ſhal hap to come &c.*

2 Then ſpeaking of the ſacred Scriptures he affirmeth that (e)

(e)

Ibidem. c. 5.
(f) *Ep. 119. c. 19.*
(g) *Epiſt. 118. c. 6.*

if aucthority of diuine Scripture preſcribe which of theſe thinges is to be done, it is not to be doubted but that ſo we ought to do as we reade &c. From thence proceeding to ſpeake of the Church, he ſaith, *in like ſort if any of theſe thinges the vniuerſal Church doth frequent, for to diſpute whether as then it is to be done, is moſt inſolent madnes.*

3. But leſt any ſhould doubt that the Church in ſome caſes might erre, he therefore further teacheth vs, (f) *that the Church of God, placed amongeſt much chaffe and cockle, doth tollerate many thinges yet thinges againſt faith, or good life ſhee doth not approue, ſhe doth not conceale, ſhe doth not.*

4. And this her certainty and freedome from error he attributeth to the holy Ghoſt, for hauing obiected that the Apoſtles at the laſt ſupper receiued not faſting, he anſweareth, (g) *muſt we therefore calumni-ate the vniuerſal Church that (this Sacrament) is alwaies receaued of thoſe who are faſting: And this pleaſed the holy Ghoſt, that in honour of ſo great a Sacrament, our Lords body ſhould enter into the mouth of a Chriſtian before al other meates. for therfore is this cuſtome obſerued through the whol world &c. And for this cauſe (our Sauiour) commaunded not in what order af-terwardes it ſhould be taken, that ſo he might reſerue this to his Apoſtles by whom he was to diſpoſe his Churches, for if he had admoniſhed this, that after other meates it ſhould alwaies haue bene receiued, I beleeue that no man*

would

would haue altered that custome.

Hauing thus informed vs what to beleeue, he passeth to the contrary, instructing vs what not to be beleue   (h)
saying, (h) *al such thinges which are neither* Epist. 119. c. 19.
contained in the aucthority of sacred Scriptures,
nor found ordained in the Councels of Bishops, nor strengthned with the custome
of the vniuersal Church, but varied infinite waies with the diuers customes of
diuerse places &c. where power is, I thinke without al doubt they are
to be cut of.

If these admonitions of so great a Doctor might be accompted sound doctrine in a Protestant schoole, as in al schooles of true learning and iudgement perforce they must, then would our controuersy be presently decyded, for no first knowen beginning of our
Catholicke practise can be instanced, sundry general councels haue confirmed it, the vniuersal Church haith vsed
it, and if Christ had commaunded the contrary,
I may say with *S. Augustine* in the like case,
that I beleue no (Catholicke) *man would*
haue altered it.

Of the ceremonies after sacrifice, and namely of fraction of the Sacrament, and the kisse of peace, and the recciuing fasting.

TRACT. 5.

SECTION. 1.

(k)
He tooke bread blessed, and brake, Math. 26. 26. & *Marc.* 14. 22. *and Luc.* 22. 19. *and* 1. *Cor.* 11. 23. *they knew him in the breaking of bread. Luc.* 22. 35. *& vide* Act. 2. 42. *and* 20. 7.

(l)
Piscator in volum. 1. *Thesium, Theologic. loc.* 25. *pag.* 418. *&c. And A-mandus Polanus in Siloge thesium theologic. pag.* 304. *saith, fractio igitur panis est de essentia cænæ.*

(m)
1. *Cor.* 10. 16.

(n)
Chrisost. in 1. *Cor. hom.* 24.

(*)
Ioan. 19. 36.

(o)
Germanus in theoria rerum Ecclesiasticarum.

(p)
It was knowen and vsual *Anno.* 700. in the time of *Pope Sergius,* as appeareth

Among the sundry ceremonies obserued after sacrifice, followeth to be spoken of the Preiftes fraction, or breaking of the Sacrament, the same being done, not as is pretended, for diftribution thereof only to the people, but in the special hofte which the Preist him selfe offereth and receiueth, and is also so done on it in reguard of special myftery & fignification. The (k) Scriptures do make such mention of fraction in general, that our aduerfaries do therefore thinke it to be an (l) effential rite. And S. *Chrifoftome* also writing of these wordes of the Apoftle (m) *the bread which we breake &c.* saith thereupon (n) *why doth the Apoftle ad, which we breake? this in the Eucharift may be seene, but on the Croffe not, but altogether contrary, for a bone of him* (saith the (*) text) *you shal not breake therefore what he did not suffer on the Croffe, that doth he* (by way of miftery, and fignification) *suffer in the facrifice.* And (o) *Germanus* Bifhop of *Conftantinople,* saith likewise hereof, *after eleuation, partition is made of the diuine body, but though it be diuided into partes, yet in euery part so diuided it remaineth whol.* And like mention is made of this fraction, in the auncient Liturgies of S. *Iames,* and S. *Chrifoftome,* as also of latter time by *Pope* (p) *Sergius,* who mentioneth not onely the diuiding thereof in *three partes*

(q) *partes*, as our Preiftes of the Latin Church yet vfe, but alfo the *commixtion* or dipping of one of thofe partes in to the Chalice: of which *commixtion* further mention is like wife (r) made by S. *Chrifoftome*, and other Fathers. After this the Preift pronounceth the *pax* or preace, as is plentifully teftifyed by *Dionifius* (s) *Areopagita*, S. (t) *Anguftine*, and the auncient (*) *Lyturgies*; and thereupon then followeth *the kiffe of peace* amongft the people. *Iuftinus martir*, difcribing in part the Liturgy of that firft time, maketh mention hereof faying, (u) *after prayer we mutual-ly falute one another with a kiffe*: And like mention is made thereof *By Dionifius*. To omit many other (x) teftimonies hereof S. *Chri-foftome* difcribeth the vfage of the *Greeke Church*

appeareth by *M. Foxe*, *Act. mon. pag.* 897.

(q.)
See *Gratian. de confecra-tione diftinct. 2. c. trifor:* and *Hofpinianus in hiftoria facramentaria l. 3. pag.* 193. alledgeth *Amalari-us, Rabanus, Micrologus*, and *Iuo Carnotenfis*, ma-king at large fpecial mention and explication of this trinal fraction of the Hofte.

(r)
Chrifoft. in Liturg. faith, at *ille patitur portionem fanctam in quatuor partes*

ponens eas in modum Crucis fuper Patenam, et vnam quidem partium mit-tit in Calicem, dicens &c. and in the Liturgy of S. *Iames* it is faid, *deinde Sacerdos frangit panem &c. et quod tenet manu dextra immergit in Calicem dicens &c.* And fee further *Micrologus, c.* 18. and 19. (s) *Dionifius de Ecclefiaftica Hierarchia. c. 3.* faith, *ad hæc venerandus Antiftes &c. pacem fanctam omnibus nunciat, et cum fe mutuo omnes faluta-uerint.* (4) *Aug. in ferm. de vigil. Pafchæ.* faith, *poft orationem do-minicam dicitur pax vobifcum, et ofculantur fe Chriftiani in ofculo fancto.* (*) In *Bafils* Lyturgy it is faid, *pax omnibus et dant omnes pacem.* And in *Chrifoftoms* Liturgy, the Preift faith, *peace to al &c.* and the Dea-cons *kiffe one an other* and after the *kiffe of peace geuen &c.* And the like is to be feene in the auncient Liturgies of other remote nations, as in the Liturgy of the *Æthiopians* it is faid, *Diaconus dicit, orate pro pace perfecta falutifera & Apoftolica; falutate vos inuicem, qui communicare non vult difcedat.* And in the Lyturgy of the *Armenians* the Deacon admonifheth faying, *falutate inuicem ofculo fancto.* (u) *Iuftinus mar-tir apolog. 2. fine.* faith, *poft precationem, nos falutamus ofculo mutuo, de-inde offertur precipuo fratri panis et calix aqua dilutus.* (x) The *Loa-dicen* councel, *can.* 19. decreeth faying, *tunc fideles orare debebunt &c. et tunc demum ofculum pacis dari debere, et poftquam Prefbiteri Epifcopo pacem dederint, tunc etiam Laicos dare et tunc oblatio offeratur.* Alfo *Ter-*

tulian de orat. c. 14. ſaith, *ſubtrahunt oſculum pacis quod eſt ſigna-*
culum orationis, quando autem magis conferenda cum fratribus pax eſt, niſi
cum oratione commendabilior aſcendit &c. quale ſacrificium eſt a quo ſine
pace receditur? And ſee further *Germanus in theoria.* and *Sedulius in*
epiſt. ad Rom. c. 16. and *Maximus in expoſitione Lyturgiæ. c. 13.*

(y)
Chriſ. l. 1. de. com-
punctione cordis ſaith, *oſculũ*
pacis porrigere tempore quo
munera offeruntur in vſu
eſt, ſed vereor ne forte plu-
res ex nobis labys hoc tan-
tummodo faciant.

(z)
Innocentius epiſt. ad De-
centium c. 1. ſaith, *pacem*
ergo aſſeris poſt confecta
miſteria quoſdam populis
imperare, vel ſibi inter Sa-
cerdotes tradere, cum poſt
omnia quæ aperire non de-
bet pax ſit neceſſaria iudi-
cenda per quam conſtat po-
pulum ad omnia quæ in mi-
ſterijs aguntur, atq; in Ec-
cleſia celebrantur præbuiſſe
conſenſum, ac finita eſſe pa-
cis concludentis ſignaculo
demonſtrentur.

(a)
The third councel of
Carthage, can. 29. de-
creed ſaying, *Sacramen-*
ta Altaris non niſi a ieiu-
nis hominibus celebrentur
&c. and ſee further here-
of heretofore, *tract. 2. ſect. 8. ſubdiuiſ. 3.* in the margent at the letters f. i. (b) See there at h. both the text and margent. (i) *Concil.*
Agathenſ.

Church ſaying, (y) *it is vſual to deliuer the*
kiſſe of peace, at the time when the (holy) *guiftes*
are offered. And *Innocentius* the firſt who
liued in the ſame time with *Chriſoſtome* geueth like teſtimony for the Latin Church
ſaying, (z) *the kiſſe of peace is to be geuen after*
the miſteries are finiſhed &c. Next after followeth the Preiſtes communion, and the further
communion of ſuch perſons then preſent as
are prepared and willing to receiue, at what
time it is ſpecially obſerued, that the bleſſed
Sacrament be receiued (a) *faſting,* as *S.*
Auguſtine, and others geue the reaſon (b)
in honour of ſo great a Sacrament.

Of the Preiſtes benediction vpon Maſſe ended.

SECTION. 2.

THe Maſſe or publicke Liturgy being
thus ended, the Preiſt diſmiſſeth the
people, *bleſſing them:* which *benediction* is by
the people acknowledged and receiued with
inclining or bowing downe of their heades. Hence
it was that the old Councel of *Agatha* decreed ſaying, (i) *we commaund ſecular perſons*
to continue at Maſſe vpon our Lords day ſo as
                                                    the

Agathenſ. can. 47. *in Iſidore.* ſaith, *miſſas die dominica ſecularibus totas tenere ſpeciali ordine præcipimus, ita vt ante benedictionem Sacerdotis egredi populus non praſumat &c.*

the people do not preſume to depart before the Preiſtes benediction. And an other Councel decreed in like manner, (k) *when the people is aſſembled to Maſſe let them not depart before the ſolemnity of Maſſe be ended, and if a Biſhop be not preſent let the receiue benediction of the Preiſt.* And S. *Chriſoſtome* ſaith accordingly, that (l) *Laye perſons do receiue bleſſing from Preiſtes;* which *bleſſing of the Preiſt* is yet further mencioned by other (m) *Fathers;* in ſo much as they alſo mention the peoples foreſaid receiuing thereof with bowing dowen of their heades. S. *Clement* the Apoſtles ſcholer ſaith hereof (n) *bowe dowen and receiue bleſſing,* and againe (o) *let the Biſhop bleſſe them they bowing dowen their heades.* And *Ceſarius Arelatenſis* ſaith accordingly, (p) *I admoniſh you brethren that at bleſſing you ought to bow dowen, and faithfully to decline your bodies and heades, becauſe that bleſſing is geuen vs, though by man, yet not from man:* which kind of benediction was not wanting in the old law, euen with ſtretching forth of the Preiſtes hand, accordingly as is now vſed as

(k)
Concil. Aurelianenſ. can. 22. ſaith, *cum ad celebrandas miſſas in Dei nomine conuenitur, populus non ante diſcedat quam miſſæ ſolennitas compleatur: & vbi Epiſcopus non fuerit, benedictionem accipiat Sacerdotis.*

(l)
Chriſoſt. orat. 4. *aduerſos Iudeos poſt med.* and in *Liturgia.* it is ſaid, *tunc Sacerdos populum benedicit.*

(m)
Auguſt. epiſt. 59. *ad Paulinum. quæſt.* 5. ſaith, *poſtulationes fiunt cum populus benedicitur. et vide Concil.* 4. *Toletanum, can.* 17. decreeth ſaying, *nonnulli Sacerdotes poſt dictam orationem dominicam*

ſtatim communicant, & poſtea benedictionem populo dant, quod deinceps interdicimus, ſed poſt orationem dominicam benedictio in populum ſequatur. (n) *Clemens, l.* 8. *Apoſt. conſtit. c.* 23. and *c.* 5. *fine.* according to the *Antwerpe* print of *Anno.* 1564. ſaith, *inclinamini et benedictionem accipite.* (o) *Clemens. l.* 8. *c.* 5. *fine.* it is ſaid, *Inclinantibus autem ipſis capita, benedicat ijs ordinatus Epiſcopus.* and *Ibidem. c.* 9. *fine.* it is ſaid, *inclinantes ſe benedicantur ab Epiſcopo.* And according to the laſt edition in the Councels. See *l.* 8. *c.* 6. *poſt. med. & c.* 7. *fine.* (p) *Cæſarius Arelatenſis.* who liued *Anno Dom.* 470. in *hom.* 30. *de genibus flectendis in oratione.* ſaith, *et illud ſimiliter ad-*

Eff
mones

moneo fratres chariſſimi, quoties diaconus clamauerit vt vos ad benedictio-
nem inclinare debeatis, & corpora et capita fideliter inclinetis, quia benedictio
nobis licet per hominem non tamen ab homine datur, nec attendatis ſi forte
negligens eſt qui tranſmittit, benedictio enim qua vobis datur, ros et pluuia cæ-
leſtis eſſe cognoſcitur.

(q)
Leuiticus. 9. 22.

(r)
In *Chriſoſtomes Liturgy*,
printed at *Antwerpe An-*
no. 1560. *fol.* 52. it is
ſaid, *tunc vadit, et cum in-*
clinauerit ſancto Altari at-
q̃ ipſum deoſculatus fuerit
&c. and ſee *fol.* 50.
where it is ſaid, *tribus*
viſcibus ſimul inclinans.
& vide fol. 62. *et* 65. and
ſee further mention of
this ceremonie in the
Liturgies of *S. Iames*, &
S. Baſil, then printed.
fol. 19. and 20. and
21. and 26. and 28.
and 36. and by *Germa-*
nus in Theoria. who ex-
preſſeth the ſignifica-

as appeareth in *Leuiticus* where is mentioned
how that (q) *Aaron* after his oblation made,
liſt vp his band towardes the people and bleſſed
them.

A recytal of ſundry other ceremonies repea-
ted or often vſed in ſeruice time.

SECTION. 3.

Nely now I wil laſtly mencion ſundry
O other ceremonies and behauiours of
the Preiſt by him at ſeueral times vſed or repeated during his celebration of ſeruice.
As for example, his (r) *praying with bowing*
dowen his head at certaine times; his (s) *tur-*
ning towardes the people and ſigning them with
the ſigne of the Croſſe; his *praier made ſomtimes*
in (t) *ſecret,* whereof the old Lyturgies and
ancient Fathers geue ful teſtimony, of his (u)
contuntion of his breſt with his handes, his
eleuation

tion thereof ſaying, *etenim quod pronus Sacerdos diuinam miſtagogiam fa-*
ciat id declarat eum inuiſibiliter cum ſolo Deo colloqui. (s) In *Baſils* Lyturgy, *fol.* 38. it is ſaid, *conuertit ſe Pontifex ad popolum et facit tres cruces*
ſuper eum. alſo in *Chriſoſtomes* Liturgy *fol.* 52. it is ſaid, *et ſignat*
preſbiter populum tertio. and *fol.* 63. *deinde facit crucem ſuper populum.*
(t) In *Baſils* Liturgy it is ſaid, *tunc eleuans manus Pontifex dicit ſe-*
certe. *fol.* 38. *et vide ibidem fol.* 36. 39. 40. 42. 43. *&c.* and
this ceremony is further mencioned in *Chriſoſtoms* Lyturgy. *fol.* 56.
and 61. and the auncient *Laodicen* Councel. *can.* 19. ſaith hereof,
tres orationes fiant, prima per ſilentiam, ſecunda, et tertia, per vocis pro-
nuntiationem, et tunc demum oſculum pacis dare debere. And ſee *In-*
nocentius

nocentius, epist . 1 . ad Decentium, c. 1 . whose testimony in this point is so plaine, that *Hutterus de sacrificio Missatico, pag. 590.* answearing thereto saith thereof, *Innocenty primi authoritatem merito explodimus, quippe ab hoste veritatis petitum.* And before al these see *S. Clement* (the Apostles scholer) *in constit. Apost.* after the *Antwerpe* print of 1604. *l. 2. c. 61. fol. 56.* (u)   *August. ex lib. 50. homiliarum. hom. 10.* saith, *quotidie tundimus pectora, quod nos quoq̃ Antistites ante Altare assistentes cum omnibus facimus &c.* And *Maximus Taurinensis. hom. 3. de quadragessima.* saith, *recte contundis manibus pectus si omnem*

inde furorem malignæ voluntatis excusseris.

(x) *eleuation,* and (y) *streeching abroad of his handes in forme of a Crosse,* his (z) *kissing of the booke,* and of the *Altar,* his pronouncing of *Amen,* and *Alleluia,* as sacred or mystical, & not to be translated, whereof *S. Augustine* saith, (a) *sciendum est &c. it is to be knowen that al nations do sing Amen and Alleluia in the Hebrew wordes, which neither the latin man nor the barbarouse may translate.* And the cause why they may not be translated, is (as he saith elswhere) (b) *propter sanctiorem authoritatem &c. for the more sacred authority of the wordes* so remaning. As also the like obseruation of the Greeke wordes, *Kyrie eleison* is mentioned by *S.* (c) *Gregory* and other more auncient (d) Fathers. Hereunto might be annexed the sundry other ceremonies heretofore mencioned from the auntient Liturgies of *S. Basile,* and *Chrisostome;* whereto also I finally ad aswel (which our learned aduersaries themselues haue heretofore (e) confessed) that

(x)
Maximus   Taurinensis, hom. 2. de cruce et sepultura Domini. saith, *ipsius enim incessus hominis cum manus leuauerit crucem pingit, atq̃ ideo eleuatis manibus orare precipimur.* And *S. Ciprian. in serm. de cæna Domini, post med.* saith, *Hierarcha pius eleuatione manuum crucis misterium representans confidenter orat &c.* and *Basil in Liturg. fol. 38.* saith, *tunc eleuans manus Pontifex &c. et vide fol. 47. et Chrisost. ad Pop. hom. 69.*   (y)
Petrus Damianus de dominico Lori(c)ato. c. 12. saith,

extensis in crucis effigiem brachys Psalterium capi &c. And *Micrologus in Ecclesiasticis obseruationibus, c. 16.* saith, *Sacerdos in expansione manuum Christi extensionem in cruce designat.* (z) In *Chrisostomes* Lyturgy *fol. 52.* it is said, *cum inclinauerit sancto Altari et ipsum deosculatus fuerit.* and a litle after, *osculanturq̃, in manibus Diaconi sacerdotes sanctum Euangelium quo finito librum seorsum deponit.* (a) *August. epist. 178.*

and

and *Alleluia* is vsed in the Lyturgies of *Basil, fol.* 37. and of *Chri-softome, fol.* 51. and see *Gregory, l.* 27. *Moral. c.* 6. (b) *August. l.* 2. *de doctrina Christiana. c.* 11. (c) *Greg. l.* 7. *epist.* 63. (d) *August. tom.* 2. *altercatione cum pascentio quæ habetur inter epistolas. numer.* 178. and *Concil. valens. can.* 5. see this heretofore in the preface to the reader *sect.* 14. throughout. (e) See heretofore *tract.* 3. *sect.* 2. *subdiuis.* 2. at d. *. e. f. g. n. o.

(f)

Szegedin. in specula ponti- | that our now Catholicke (or as they tearme
ficum pag. 68. saith, *Mis-* it Popish Masse, with the forme and ceremo-
so papistica Architecti Cle- monies thereof, hath had an acknowledged
mens, Anacletus, Alexan- continuance for these *thousand yeares* last past.
der &c. and the French As also that *Szegedinus* a learned *Caluinist,*
Protestant writer in his and others, vndertaking to set dowen the
sixe godly treatizes &c. framers or *Architectes of the Popish Masse,* be-
tranflated (with much ginneth therein with the **(f)** Fathers, from
commendation thereof the Apostles times, and the more auncient
in the translators pre- **(g)** Courcels of the Primitiue Church : wher-
face) into english and vnto might be added the like further acknow-
printed, 1608. hauing ledgement

said, *pag.* 48. *let no man thinke it straunge if the successors of the Apostles from time to time haue corrupted the true vse of this holy Sarament,* in pretended proofe thereof chargeth *Alexander the first in the yeare of Christ* 114. *with corrupting of the holy Sacrament, in ordayning to mixe water with wine. pag.* 52. *et* 62. also with *consecrating of holy water. pag.* 92. *&* 62. in like manner doth he charge, *Sixtus Bishop of Rome in the yeare of Christ,* 121. (with) *instituting corporasses of fine linnen, to lay vp the consecrated hoastes, and also Albes and other vestimentes of Preistes their sacrifices &c. pag.* 65. chargeth *in like manner Pius Bishop of Rome, in the yeare of Christ* 144. *with ordaining of the consecrated bread and wine falling vpon the ground should be left to the sacrificer, and the rest remaning should be burn'd and the ashes laid vp among the reliques. pag.* 65. and after much other alledged matter, concludeth against al the Roman Bishops during the whol first 300 yeares saying, *how was it then possible that the first Bishopes of Rome should draw the Princes, Senators, and Romaines, vnto the law of the Gospel, during* 300. *or* 400. *yeares after Christ, seeing they did not labour but to corrupt the vse of the holy Sacramentes, and to restore the iudaical Ceremonies &c.* This being his opinion of the Romane

mane

man Church in these first times, which of al Churches in the world
is confessed to haue beene then most pure, by *Ridley Act. mon. pag.*
1359. and by *M. Iewel* in his reply, *pag.* 268. what is then to be
thought of the other Churches of those said first times, is easily con-
iectured· (g) *Szegedin. ibidem. pag.* 69. saith, *concilia Epscoporum*
pro missa Papistica, Ephesium, Antiocheum, Carthaginense secundum, Con-
stantinopolitanum, Arela-
ledgement made by (*) *Theodore, Beza, and* *tense &c.*
Iohn (¶) *Caluin.*

(*)

Beza in epist. theolog. ep.
8 : pag. 84. saith, *plerig,*
tamen ex vetissimis illis
An answere to those who affirme the cere-   *(Patribus) Christianorum*
monies of the Masse to be a wilworship &   *sacra non alter quam cere-*
against Scripture, with an explication   *ris misteria quædam occul-*
of that point from Scriptures, Fa-   *tanda censuerunt, adeo vt*
thers, and learned Protestantes.   *ne catechumenos quidem ad*
spectandum admiserint, et
totam illam actionem in qua

SECTION. 4.   *quicquid paucis et simplici-*
bus simbolis figurabatur,

BVt for so much as not any prescription   *verbo suo clare et ea lingua*
of time though continued vp to the   *neuer quæ ab omnibus intellige-*
purest, nor any Fathers, or Councels, though
retur explicato palam predicari & promulgari voluit ac precepit Dominus,
sicut et insemet fecit auit in Aporreta *quidem et in ipsis quidem mistis ple-*
riq. intellecta sacra transformarunt. And *pag.* 82. he taxeth herein both
the auncient and new Lyturgies, as wel of the east, as of the west. and *pag.*
8*3.* he saith, *introducta sunt paulatim pro m nsis Altaria &c. at qui pri-*
mam hanc arrapuit occasionem Satan, *sacram istam actionem non dandi sed*
accipiendi Christi causa institutam in sacrificium etiam Ilasticon *transfor-*
mandi; non placuerunt vulgares & simplices himni &c. non placuit simpex et
communis apparatus idcirco conquiri marmora inaurati parietes, vasa aurea
& argentea comparari, pretiose etiam et pontificales atq, adeo imperatoriæ ve-
stes ministris circundari ceperunt, honorandi scilicet Sacramenti causa, ro-
tundi panes singuli porrigi capti & ritus a Domino institutus abrogatus; non
placuit vel sedentibus vel stantibus panem in manum porrigi vt olim fiebat, sed
attolli panem quasi venerandum &c. And *pag.* 79. he saith, *totum illum*
apparatum quo vetustissimi etiam illi, Baptismum et cœnam Domini se exora-
re pose

re poſſe putarunt non ſatis mirari poſſum &c. (¶) See *Caluins* wordes alledged next here-

after in the margent af-
ter u. at the figure 3.

(h)
M. Raynoldes in his conference with *M. Hart,*
pag. 570. and 571.

(i)
Exod. 30. 7.

(k)
Exod. 28. 4. and 39.
2. 3. *&c.*

(l)
Exod. 30. 20.

(m)
Exod. 25. 10. 17.

(n)
Exod. 16. 33.

(o)
Exod. 30. 23.

(p)
Numer. 19. 9.

(q)
Numer. 17. 10.

(r)
Exod. 25. 31. and 27.
20.

(s)
Exod. 30. 26.

(t)
Numer. 8. 7.

(u)
1. *Reg.* 6. 32.

(2)
D. Samuel Gardener in
his dialogue betweene
Ireneus, and *Antimachus,*
of

neuer ſo auncient can ſatisfy our aduerſaries in the foreſaid ceremonies of our Church ſeruice, which becauſe they are not parti-cularly mencioned in the Scriptures are by them reie&ed as being a ſelfe deuiſed *wil-worſhip,* or *ſtagelike ſpe&ackle:* I wil there-fore now end with examination and proofe that our ſaid ceremonies haue ſnfficient groundworke from Scriptures, and from the learned Proteſtantes them ſelues. In ful ex-plication whereof I wil firſt alledge from the old teſtament, euen that which *D. Raynoides* is not abaſhed to obie& againſt vs ſaying, (h) *as the Preiſt with them was ſeuered from the people by the diuiſion of the ſanctuary and court of the Temple, ſo with you by the Chancel and body of the Church ; as with them he (i) burned incenſe at the altar, ſo with you he doth; as with them he (k) was clad in an Ephod. a myter, a brode-red coate, a girdle, a breſtplate, and a robe, and they who ſerued him were in their linnen coates, ſo with you he muſt haue an Amice, an Albe, a Girdle, a Fanel, a Chiſible, and a Stole, and they who are about him haue Surpleſes, yea Coapes, alſo their Preiſtes had a (l) Luar, whereat they muſt waſh before they ſacrificed, ſo haue yours , your pixe with the Sacrament, reſembleth their (m) Arke with the mercy ſeate, your phila&ery with the Sainctes reliques, and their pot with (n) Manna &c. your holy oyle of Balme, and theirs of (o) Myrhe with ſpices , their puriſring (p) water made of the aſhes of an heffer, and yours of other aſhes with water, wine, and ſalt &c. their (q) rod of Aaron, and your Croſſe of Chriſt; fi-nally your candles, & their (r) Candleſtickes with Lampes, your conſecrating of Biſhopes, of Chur-ches*

ches, *of Alters, Paten, Chalices, by* (s) *annointing them according to the order of Aaron and the Tabernacle, your shaning, as of* (t) *Leuites, your imagery as from* (u) *Salamon &c.* with sundry other rytes by him there mentioned, resembled to other like, vsed in the old Testament, such confessed groundworke haue our foresaid ceremonies of the Masse from the writinges of the old testament: but for that our aduersaries extreamest refuge or endeauour is to retort this vpon vs, inferring hereupon that we may not vse any such ceremonies as were vsed in the old testament. I alledge against this, *first*, that it is their onely bare assertion without al testimony of Scripture, for as our aduersarie (2) *D. Gardner* wel answeareth hereunto, the Iewish ceremonies which haue ceased and may not now be reteyned or borowed, are most properly those which were ordained to signify some thing as being future, and to be accomplished in Christ: as for example, *the Paschal lambe*, which signifyed his passion to come, may not as now be obserued, by reason of the false signification which thence would follow: But as concerning the ceremonies of other kind, that in the auntient Fathers iudgement they might be lawfully reteyned, or vsed, and so accordingly were by them vsed in their celebration of the publicke Liturgie is in it selfe euident, and by (3) *Caluin* confessed. *M. Carwright* him selfe also not

of the rytes and ceremonies of the Church of England, printed at London 1605. fol. b. 3. saith, *I thus answeare, there were Sacramentes, by which it pleased God to consigne his promisses of Christ that was to come; al which are repealed &c. But yet notwithstanding there were then some actions that serued for decency, that may be reuyued and reteyned*; wherof he there geueth sundry examples, as in *tythes of festiual dayes &c.* wherof saith he, *shal we abolish al these because they haue so nigh neighbourehood and cognation with the old legal and leuitical ceremonies?* affirming further *fol. c. 1. that our Bishops robes are taken vp in imitation of the high Priestes robes enioyned at the apointment of God by Moyses.*

(3)

Caluin. de cæna Domini, in tract. theologic. printed 1597. pag. 7. reprehendeth the Fathers her-

in saying, *neq; tamen possum veteris Ecclesiæ consuetudinem excusare, quod gestu ac ritu suo speciem quandam sacrificij figuraret, ijsdem fere ceremonijs quæ sub veteri Testamento in vsu erant, eo excepto, quod panis hostia animalis loco vtebantur, quod cum nimis ad Iudaismum accedat, nec Domini institutioni consentaneum sit minime probo.* (*) In *M. Whitguiftes* defence. pag.

pag. 322.

(4)

Hereof fee *D. Gardener* in his dialogue &c. *fol.* **b.** 3. vpon the **b.** fide.

(x)

Exod. 23. 16. & 34. 2. and *Numer.* 29. 7. 8.

(y)

1. *Cor.* 16. 8. and *Act.* 20. 16.

(z)

Exod. 13. 6. and *Leuit.* 23. 5. and *Numer.* 9. 2.   (a)

Exod. 9. 29. 33. and 17. 10. 11. *&c.* and 3. *Reg.* 8. 54. and 2. *Par.* 6. 13. and 1. *Efdra.* 9. 5. *Pfal.* 87. 10. & *Pfal.* 140. 2.   (b)

3. *Reg.* 8. 54. and 2. *Par.* 6. 13. and *Daniel.* 6. 10.

(c)

1. *Tim.* 2. 8. (5) *Act.*

not denying, but affirming that (*) *the Lord tranflated diuers thinges out of the law into the Gofpel. Secondly* we geue inftance of fundry ceremonies vfed during the old Teftament, and yet now retained: the *Temple* of the old Teftament maketh not againft our now *Churches,* northeir then (4) *tenthes,* againft our now *tything,* their *holy dayes* then, nothing againft *ours* now, not their (x) *Penticoft* a-gainft our (y) *Pentecoft,* not their feaft of (z) *Pafche,* againft ours, their then (a) *eleuation of handes,* and (b) *genuflection* in time of prayer, nothing againft our now like (c) *eleuation of handes,* and (5) *genuflection*; the *Canonical houres,* or appointed times of prayer in the old (6) *Law,* not againft the like vfage ther-of in the (7) *new,* and laftly the *impofition of handes* then (d) vfed, nothing againft the like vfage thereof now in the new (e) *tefta*-ment.

2. *Thirdly,* that the Church of Chrift might, and euen in the Apoftles times, did borow rites from the old Teftament is made euident, and fo by *Caluin, Beza,* and fundry other learned Proteftantes (f) confeffed in

the

7. 60. and *Act.* 21. 5. and *Ephef.* 3. 14. (6) *Daniel.* 6. 10. and fee *Hierome* thereupon. (7) *Act.* 3. 1. and *Act.* 10. 9. (d) *Numer* 27. 23. (e) *Act.* 6. 6. and 8. 17. and 13. 3. and 19. 6. and 1. *Tim.* 4. 14. and 5. 22. and 2. *Tim.* 1. 6. alfo *M. Carthwright* in his fecond reply, *part.* 1. *pag.* 138. affirmeth that, *impofition of handes haith a profitable aduertifement* (or fignification) *and contayning an affurance of the Lords hand muft needes be houlden ftil for ordinary.* (f) *Auguftinus Marolet* in his *Enchirid. locorum com. &c. pag.* 222. faith of *impofitoin of handes, ab Hebrais fluxit, qui hac ceremonia folebant vti &c. quem ritum deinde feruauit Ecclefia Chriftiana in miniftris ordinandis &c.* And *Mathias Hoe* in his *tract. duo de difputationibus theologicis &c. part.* 2. *pag.* 162. faith, *manuum impofitio in-nuebat.*

nuebat esse eum qui ordinebatur Deo et Ecclesiæ consecratum &c. qui ritus est ex veteri testamento desumptus &c. And *Caluin, inst. l. 4. c. 3. sect. 16.* saith, *constat Apostolos non alia cæremonia vsos esse cum aliquem ministerio admonebant quam manuum impositione, hunc autem ritum fluxisse arbitror ab hæbreorum more &c. quare Apostoli per manuum impositionem eum se Deo offerre significabant, quem initiabant in ministerium?* hereof see further the english Bible of 1576. in the marginal notes in *act. c. 6. vers. 6.* & *Beza in act. c. 6.* who there saith hereof, *hic totus ritus ab hæbrais fluxit, qui hac formula vtebantur &c. hunc ritum seruauit Ecclesia. 1. Tim. 5. 22. &c.* and see the like testimony of *Aretius in loc. com. loc. 65. pag. 204.*

the very foresaid example of *imposition of handes*; in so much as *Peter Martir* doubeth not to acknowledge, (g) *many thinges which the Church haith borowed of the decrees of Moyses, yea and that from the first times,* in profe wherof he vouchsaifeth sundry (h) examples; to which his opinion *Bullinger,* and *Gualter* do professe for to (*) assent; if therefore the Iewish (2) *ceremonies* had (as *Bullinger* affirmeth) *sundry and godly significations, the end of those ordinances being for glory and comlines sake, and they inuented partly for aduancement of religion, because* (saith he) *the thinges are most regarded that are set out with great solemnity.* why then may not the Church now vpon the very same ground, and to the same like end, either retaine sundry of those, or els institute other like, as to her graue and spiritu-al

(g)

Peter Martir in his epistles annexed to his common places in english, pag. 118.

(h)

Peter Martir; Ibidem pag. 118. saith, *tythes are instituted at this day to maintaine the ministers of the Church.* and pag. 118. *we haue feast dayes in remembrance of the Lords Resurrection, of the Natiuity, of Whitsontide, and of the death of Christ: should al these thinges be abolished, because they be steps of the old Law.* (*) *Bullin-*

ger, and *Gualter,* in their epistle extant after the end of *Bullingers Decads* in english (*ante med. epist.*) professe to answeare to the very question hereof with *Peter Martir* saing, *there were in the Leuitical law certaine actions of that nature which &c. serued to decency &c. these I suppose may be brought in and also retained &c.* And hauing recyted some examples of certaine thinges now retained in imitation of the old Law, they conclude saying, *shal al these be abolished because they are tokens and reliques of the old Law? you see therefore al thinges of the Leuitical law are*

not so

not so abrogated that none of them may be used: Thus far *Bullinger, Gualter,* & *Peter Martir.* (2) *Bullinger* in his Decades in english, pag. 335.

(3)
Leo in ieiun. menf. fept. ferm. 9. alledged by *M. Hooker* in his Ecclesiastical pollicy, *l.* 4. *fect.* 11. *pag.* 192.

(4)
M. Hooker in his third booke of Ecclesiastical pollicy. *fect.* 11. and *pag.* 164. saith, *if al thinges must be commaunded of God, which may be practised of his Church, I would know what comaundement the Gileadites had to erect that Altar which is spoke of in Iosua.* 22. *&c. I would know what comandement the women of Israel had yearly to mourne in memory of Iephtaes daughter.* Iudic. 11. 40. *what commandement the Iewes had to celebrate their feast of dedication neuer spoken of in the law, yet solemnised by our sauiour himselfe Io.* 10. 22. *what Commandement finally they had for the ceremony of odors used about the bodies of the dead afterwhichcustom our Lord was contented that his owen most pretiouse body should be entombed.* Iohn. 19. 40. and *pag.* 138. he geueth like instance of sundry other like vnwritten ceremonies obserued by the Iewish Church in Christes time. Also *Bullinger,* and *Gualter,* in their epistle *post med.* extant after the end of *Bullingers* Decades in english, answearing the question *whether any new ceremonies may be encreased besides the expresse word of God* do graunt that, *new may be deuised for order and discipline*; in proofe whereof they do alledge saying, *Christ himselfe celebrated the feast or ceremony of the dedication, and yet we reade not that the same was commaunded by the law.* (i) *Hierom.* 35. 14.

al iugemeut may seeme most conuenient? Very aptly to this purpose (as *M. Hooker* obserueth) saith *S. Leo,* (3) *the Apostolical ordinance, knowing that Christ came not into this world to vndoe the law, hath in such fort distinguished the misteries of the old Testament, that certaine of them it hath chosen to benefit Euangelical knowledge withal, and for that purpose appointed that those thinges which before were lewish might now be Christian customes:* and if against al this any man do here vrge that the foresaid ceremonies of the old law were prescribed by God him selfe whereas our Sauiour Christ haith not commaunded any such in the new Testament, and that therefore the Church may not as now by her authority appoint any such to be obserued without direct warrant of Christes expresse commaundement, to omit the (4) *sundry examples* geuen to the contrary by *M. Hooker,* I answeare and alledge further in the same kind, that *the sonnes of Ionadab,* were for euer by their Fathers onely commaundement prohibited (i) *from wine* and they (k) commended for their obseruing thereof: also *Mardocheus* appointed a new (l) *festiual day to be for euer* celebrated, and so likewise did (m) *Iudas Machabeus, and his brethren for their time.* Like further example whereof appeareth also in (n) *Iudith,* vpon the slaughter of *Holifernes,* & al these without any expresse comandemēt signifyed from God. In likemaner god did not cōmand (o) *the sacrifice offered to him by Abel,* neither *the stone (p) which Iacob set vp as a piller, and powred oyle vpon the top of it,* nor do we finde any commaundement geuen by Christ to his Apostles for their foresaid retayning of *imposition of handes:* very wel therfore doth *Peter Martir* affirme that (q) *it is lawful for the Church to ad vnto ceremonies deliuered to vs by the word of God, both time, manner, and place, yea and some ceremonies as wel for ornament, as for edifying of the faithful.* In like manner D. *Witguift* saith to *M. Carthwright,* (5) *you and I agree in this that the Church haith authority to ordaine ceremonies, and make orders which are not expressed in the word of God.* In like sort *Suinglius* affirmeth (6) *that in external thinges and matters of ceremonies many thinges are to be vsed in the Church, which be not contained in the Scriptures.* To which end in the late conference before his Maiesty M. (7) *Deane of the Chapel* remembred the practise of the Iewes, *who vnto the institution of the Pasouer prescribed by Moyses, added, as the Rabbins witnes, both signes and wordes eating sowre hearbes, and drinking wine, with these wordes to both, take and eate these in remembrance &c. drinke this in remembrance &c.* vpon which *addition and tradition of theirs,* our *Sauiour instituted the Sacrament of his last supper in celebrating it with the same wordes, &* after the same manner, thereby approuing that

(k)
Hierom. 35. 18. 19.
(l)
Hester. 9. 21. 31.
(m)
1. *Machab.* 4. 59.
(n)
Iudith. c. 16. *vers.* 31. after *Hieroms* translation it is said, *dies victoriæ huius festiuitatis hebræis in numero sanctorum dierum accipitur et colitur a Iudæis ex illo tempore vsq̄ in presentem diem.*
(o)
Gen. 4. 4. and *Hæbr.* 11. 4.
(p)
Gen. 28. 18. 22.
(q)
Peter Martir, in his other collection &c. annexed to his common places in english *pag.* 166.
(5)
M. *Whitguift* in his defence of the answeare &c. *pag.* 88. and see further there *pag.* 94.
(6)
Suinglius de Baptis. alledged by M. *Whitguift* vbi supra. *pag.* 126.
(7)
In the some of the conference before the kinges Maiesty at *Hampton* court 1603.

Obieƈtions againſt the ceremonies Subd. 2.

that faƈt of theirs in particuler, wherupon (ſaith the booke) M. Deare cócluded, (8) *generally that the Church may inſtitute and retaine a ſigne ſignificant which ſatisfyed his Maieſty exceeding wel.* Alſo M. D. Couel poſſeſſeth to diſlike the ſingular (r) *oppinion of ſome, who thinke that thoſe ceremonies ordained by Chriſt and his Apoſtles, are fit enough to be retained in the Church, but the reſt as being made without warrant haue no warrant to remaine ſtil;* whereto ſaith he, (s) *we anſweare* (affirming) *the Churches lawful ordaining of ceremonies for ends ſpiritual* (as) *firſt for ornament &c. Secondly to ſtir vp deuotion &c.* for (t) (ſaith he) *the principal exerciſe of our religion being ſpirttual is not eaſily obſerued of the greateſt number which are carnal, & therefore we propound not naked miſteries, but cloath them, that theſe offering to the ſences a certaine maieſty may be receiued of the minde with greater reuerence;* and vpon this ground it is that the Church of England doth as yet retain *Coapes, Surpleſſes,* and ſuch like Church (u) apparel, acknowwledging that it (x) *ſerueth to edification,* and carrieth with it (y) *a fit and profitable ſignification,* in defence wherof Peter Martir ſaith, (z) *how can we depriue the Church of this liberty, that it may not ſignify ſome thing*

without good and proper ſignification, for the linnen garment is a ſimbole and ſigne of innocency and purity, whereof it is ſaid in the reuelation of the Sainƈtes that they ſhal be cloathed with long white robes. (z) Peter Marter, in his epiſtles annexed to his common places in engliſh, pag. 119. and ſee M. Whitguiſt vbi ſupra pag. 290. and M. Carthwright in M. Whitguiſtes defence &c. pag. 599. ſpeaking of *ſitting at Communion,* ſaith that *in receiuing ſitting we ſignify reſt that is a ful finiſhing through Chriſt of al the ceremonial Law.* and ibidem. poſt med. he affirmeth it to be, the reaſon of two notable learned men Ioannes Alaſco, and M. Hooper. Alſo Caluin inſtit. l. 4. c. 10. ſeƈt. 14. ſaith, *ergone* (inquies)
nihil

Marginal notes:

1603. pag. 67. and 68.
(8)
Ibidem. pag. 68.
(r)
M. D. Couel in his modeſt examination, pag. 63.
(s)
M. Couel. Ibidem. and pag. 64.
(t)
M. Couel ibidem. pag. 66.
(u)
See M. Whitguiſtes defence of the anſweare to the admonition, pag. 268. 269. 270.
(x)
Ibidem. pag. 286. and 287. and 288. &c.
(y)
Ibidem. pag. 270. and D. Samuel Gardner in his dialogue betweene Antimachius, & Ireneus &c. fol. c. 1. ſaith of Church veſtimentes, they are not

nihil ceremoniarum rudioribus dabitur adiuuandam eorum imperitiam, id ego non dico omnino enim vtile illis esse sentio hoc genus adminiculi, tantum hic contendo, vt is modus adhibeatur qui Christum illustret non obscuret. requiring in his wordes there following as necessary to such ceremonies (*in significatione dignitatem*) *worthines of signification.* and ibidem. *sect.* 15. he chalengeth our ceremonies onely as defectiue through pretended want of signification, therefore (though vntruly) tearming them, *signa omni significatione carentia*, so fully did he acknowledge *signifying ceremonies.* And *Zanchius in compend. loc.* 16. *pag.* 639. saith, *ceremoniæ sunt pietatis exercitia qui sua significatione ducunt nos ad Christum.* alledged to this purpose by *M. Powel, de Adiaphoris theses &c.* printed *Londini* 1606. *pag.* 105. in the margent.

(a)
Germanus Constantinop. who liued 900. *yeares since in his Theoria rerum Ecclesiasticarum* saith, *tonsura capitis Sacerdotis & rotunda eius pilorum media sectio vice coronæ est spineæ quam Christus gestauit &c.*

thing by her *actions and rites*? If now we do but accordingly enter into examination of our other Church apparel vsed in the Masse, we shal finde that euery part thereof was instituted with a most holy and profitable *signification*, no lesse then were the *Coape*, and *Surplesse*.

(3)   And so accordingly the auncient writers that liued many ages since do (a) explaine, that thereby is represented *the sacred tragedy*

rubedo vestimentorum eius indicat tinctam Christi stolam carnis in sanguine in eius immaculata cruce, i-

temá, quia etiam coccineam chlamidem gestauit in passione Christus &c. Tunica quæ alba est, diuinitatis splendorem indicat, et Sacerdotis splendidam conuersationem, lora tunicæ quæ sunt ad manum, significant vinculum Christi, vinctum enim eum abduxerunt ad Caipham &c. Lora quæ sunt transuersa sanguinem significant qui fluxit ex latere Christi in cruce, peritrachelion est fasciola quæ producebatur a Pontifice vinctus et tractus in interiorem partem per collum Christus ad patiendum ipse, proficens epitracheli dextera pars denotat arundinem quam dederunt illudentes dextræ Christi. leua pars crucis est gestatio super humeris eius &c. Causula denotat coccineam purpuram, quam Iesu illudentes gestandam impij dederunt &c. incensum autem representat aramata illa quæ offerebant sepeliendo domino. and hauing explained diuers other he saith, *Agnoscite igitur omnes Sacerdotes qui sacro Altari assidetis, et incruentam victimam sacrificatis, quod viuas passiones Christi annuncietis &c.* Thus far *Germanus* explaining the rites and significations

of the Greeke Church. And for the Latin Church, see the signification of the Church apparel and other rites explained also aboue
800. yeares by *Alcuinus, de diuinis officijs, c* . 38. *quid significent vestimenta.* and by *Amalarius, de Ecclesiasticis officijs, l*. 2. *c*. 15. 17. 18.
19. 20. 21. & *l*. 3. *c*. 19. and by *Rabanus Maurus, l*. 1, *de instit.
cler. c*. 15. *et sequentibus.*

(b)
Where can our aduersa-
ries finde in the text any
explanation made of the
significatiōs of the Preistly apparel and other ce-
remonies of the old law?
which yet are confessed
and explained by *D.
Babington Bishop of Wor-
cester,* in his notes vpon
Exodus &c. pag. 408.
409. 411. 412. 414.
419. 420. 428. 431.
& 387. and by *Bullin-
ger* in his decades in en-
glish, 3. *decade,* 5. *sermon.* throughout.

tragedy of our Sauiours passion with other
mistical significations, which though they
were not knowen to al (as neither (b) were
the confessed significations of the Preistly apparel and other ceremonies in the old law
knowen to the vulgar of those times) yet
is this no more now then it was during the
old law, any let to the profitable retaining &
vsage of them, as is 1400. yeares since and
aboue, precisely to this point obserued of
ceremonies in general by (c) *Origen,* and *Dionisius* (d) *Areopagita,* and afterwardes by
S. (e) *Augustine.* A thing so euident that
sundry (f) Protestant diuines of great esteeme
haue professed stil to retaine the *accustomed
ceremonies*

(c) *Origen. hom.* 5. *in
nummer.* saith, *in Ecclesiasticis obseruationibus nonnulla sunt huius modi quæ
omnibus quidem facere necesse est, nec tamen ratio eorum omnibus patet &c.
cuncta ergo hæc et horum similia congerimus, v c tamen eorum assequimur rationem.* (d) *Dionisius Areopagita de Eccles. Hierarch. cap. vlt.* saith
of signifying ceremonies, *plurima ex his quæ ignoramus causas habent dig-
nissimas nobis quidem ignoratas, verum præstantioribus ordinibus cognitas &c.*
(e) *Aug. de doctrina Christiana. l. 3. c. 9.* saith, *qui autem non intelligit quid significet signum, et tamen signum esse intelligit nec ipse premitur
seruitute, melius est autem vel premi incognitis sed vtilibus signis quam inu-
tiliter ea interpretando a iugo seruitutis eductam ceruicem laqueis erroris in-
ferere.* (f) Their most famous confession of *Ausburge* in the English
harmony of confessions. *pag*. 433. saith, *our Churches are wrongfully accused to haue abolished the Masse, for the Masse is retained stil amongst vs,
and celebrated with great reuerence, yea and almost al the ceremonies that are
in vse &c. for therefore we haue neede of ceremonies that they may teach
&c.* And

&c. And see further there *pag.* 440. And *Melancthon* in his *Apologia confes. August.* persisteth in defence therof saying yet further, *non a-bolemus Missam, sed eam religiose retinemus ac defendimus, fiunt enim apud nos Missæ singulis dominicis diebus &c. et seruantur vsitata ceremoniæ pub-licæ, ordo lectionum, orationum, vestitus, et alia similia.* in so much as *Ho-spinian. in histor. Sacram. part. 2. fol.* 120. hauing recyted these wordes saith thereof, *nec quicquam aliud in doctrina Pontificiorum de Missa reprehendit Apologia quam quod celebratur latina tantum lingua, quod doce-tur ceremonias prodesse ex opere operato* (wherein he belyeth the Catho-licke doctrine) *quod docetur etiam Missam sacrificium esse propitiatorium pro viuis ac mortuis &c.* And see *Hutterus* alledged next herafter, after m. at *. And *M. CarthWright,* and *M. Whitguift,* do both of them con-fesse in the examination of places after the end of *M. Whitguiftes* de-fence, *pag. penult.* that *the Lutherans do obserue images and al the Popish apparel vsed in the Masse.* And *Zepperus* the Caluinist in his *politia Ec-clesiastica &c.* printed *Herbonæ.* 1607. *pag.* 9. saith, *Altaria hostiæ seu panes numularij, corporalia & Calices consecrati &c. habitus ille ministrorum Aaronicus, & sacerdotalis, cerei ardentes, idola et imagines &c. hisq́ simi-lia, quorum colluuies et sordes in plurimis Euangelicorum Ecclesijs secun-dum magis et minus etiam nunc hodie inueniuntur.* and *Hutterus* Doctor and publicke professor in the vniuersity of *Wittenberge. de sacrificio Missatico. l. 2. c.* 13. *pag.* 614. saith, *In Missa multa occurrunt cere-moniæ quæ natura sua sunt liberæ et indifferentes &c. quales sunt vestes sacræ, vasa sacra, cerei, thymiamata, et id genus aliæ ceremoniæ, quarum vsus in Ecclesijs etiam Lutheranis non plane exoleuit.*

(g)

cermonies of our *Masse* and Church *apparel. Hulldricke* (g) *Suinglius* geuing withal his spe-cial allowance of our Church vestimentes in respect of such their foresaid signification, whereby is so represented to vs the manner and memory of our Sauiours sufferinges; where-

Suinglius in epicher. de Ca-none Missæ. tom. 1. fol. 187. speaking of our Church apparel saith, *vestes quibus amicitur cæ-lestis mensæ minister non ad-modum damnamus quoad formam attinet: nam quem*

non moueat caput ad eum morem velatum quo Christus velebatur in Caphæ domo? &c. poderis quam nos albam vocamus, eam vestem referat, qua Chri-stus ab Herode ad ludibriam donatus est, vnde eam fluere mallem quam cinctam esse in propter operationem colligamus: Clamidem quoq́ purpuream quouis tem-pore oportet esse non secus ac poderam albam, Pusillum hoc quod in manu si-

nistra

nistra gestatur, si ad statuam alligationis ad quam flagris casus est simbolum sit, probatur: similiter hoc quod nunc stolam vocamus (quamuis reuera stola non sit) si reliqua vincula representet &c. Thus far *Suinglius* in allowance of our Church apparel, and the sinification thereof, euen in that very Treatise which he wrote purposly against the Masse.

(h)
See heretofore, *tract.* 1. *sect.* 5. *subdiuis.* 2. at g. h. i. k. l. m. n. o.

(i)
See heretofore *tract.* 1. *sect.* 5. *subdiuis.* 1. before x. at the figure 2.

(k)
See there at the. figure 3. (l)
See next hertofore *tract.* 5. *sect.* 5. *subdiuis.* 2. at y. z.

(*)
Peter Martir in his collection annexed to his common places in english, *pag.* 160. affirmeth that *in the old ceremonies was first set forth Christ, and the redemption which should be made by him.* and in his common places englished, *pag.* 580. he further affirmeth that *euery ceremony (of the old law) was a token & shadow of Christ.*

(m)

whereunto the remote Churches also of (h) *Grece,* (i) *Armenia,* and (k) *Ethopia,* do assent; neither may this signification of our Sauiours sufferinges thus represented by the foresaid rites and ceremonies of our Masse, seeme to our other aduersaries either strange or improbable, for seeing it is heretofore made so cleare, & by the selues (l) confessed, that the Church haith authority & power to institute signifying ceremonies, can any ceremony or signification be thought more choice & worthy, then that, whereby is represented the manner and progresse of our Sauiours painful agonies for vs sustaiued. May those sacred and deare remembrances of our accomplished redemption behoulden to vs so vngrateful or in them selues so vnworthy, or prophane, as that the Church of Christ may not now by her fewer ceremonies prescribed in her publicke Liturgy, geue signification of his death and passion already past, which the Iewish (*) Church haith formerly by her many moe ceremonies, represented and signifyed as being then future and to come? And seeing that ceremonies, though of their owne nature indifferent, being yet once commaunded by the Church, do thereby confessedly (m) *loase the nature of indifferency,* and are

M. Whitguift in his defence &c. *pag.* 92. setteth dowen in his margent there, *thinges indifferent loase the nature of indiferency when they are commaunded.* and in his text there doth prosecute the proofe thereof
at large

at large further there pag. 93. that *willingly to breake the order appointed by the Church in such matters is sinne.* And *Ibidem.* pag. 258. he further saith, *in the confession of the Duch Church which is allowed by the Church of Geneua, and diuers other reformed Churches, it is thus writen of thinges indifferent, thinges otherwise indifferent of them selues after a sort chaunge their nature when by some commaundement they are either commaunded or forbidden, because that neither they can be omitted contrary to the commaundement, neither done contrary to the prohibition.* Also M. *Powel* in his booke of thinges indifferent. printed, 1607. *c. 2. pag.* 7. saith, *such indifferent thinges as by the Church haue beene lawfully and orderly instituted and approued &c. haue more then humane authority yea plainly diuine, the reason hereof is, because the Church is directed by the spirit of Christ who is truth, therefore the preceptes of the Church in thinges indifferent are both true and holy.*

(*)

are in respect of such commaundement become necessary. And seeing also that the foresaid ceremonies of our publicke Lyturgy being of like (*) *indifferency* are matters, not of our late inuention, but (as appeareth by the (n) premisses) were obserued and to vs deliuered by (o) *the Primitiue Church, the true and best mistris to posterity, which going before leadeth vs the way.* with what spirit of contradiction & innouation may we then thinke those possessed who not reguarding the example and authority of the auncient Church (which them selues (p) acknowledge for the true

Of like indifferency, and so confessed by Hutterus, Doctor & publicke professor in *Wittenberge* in his booke *de sacrificio missatico. c. 13. pag.* 614. *saying, in Missa multæ occurrunt ceremoniæ quæ natura sua sunt liberæ et indifferentes, quippe neq, a Christo neq, ab Apostolis præceptæ vel prohibitæ, quales sunt vestes sacræ, vasa sacra, cerei, thymiamata, et id genus aliæ ceremoniæ, quorum vsus in Ecclesijs etiam Lutheranis non plane exoleuit.* (n) See the ceremonies of the Masse mencioned by the auncient Fathers, alledged heretofore in the preface to the reader. *sect.* 12. at *. next after p. and *sect.* 14. throughout, and in the body of the booke, *tract.* 1. *sect.* 2. throughout and *sect.* 5. throughout. and *tract.* 2. *sect.* 1. *subdiuis.* 1. throughout and *tract.* 4. *sect.* 1. throughout. and *sect.* 3. throughout. and *sect.* 4. *subdiuis* 1. *prope et paulo post initium.* (o) So saith the confession of *Bohemia* in the english harmony of confessions, *pag.* 400. And M. *Bilson* in his perpetual gouernement of Christes Church. *c.* 13. *pag.* 285. doth

H h h

285. doth *prefer the iudgement of the Primitiue Church &c.* becaufe faith he, *they were nearer the Apoftles times, and likelier to vnderftand the Apoftles meaning then thofe that come after &c.* (p) *M. Iewel* in his publicke chalenge at Paules Croffe, appealed to the firft 600. yeares, as being the true Church. And *M. Whitaker contra Camp. rat.* 5. reneweth that chalenge faying further thereof that, *ea eft noftrum omnium profeffio.* And *M. White* in his way to the true Church, pag. 385. faith, *in the firft 600. yeares there was no fubftantial or fundamental innouation receiued into the Church.*

(q) That the Maffe with the now vfual ceremonies therof, haith confeffedly continued and beene generall for thefe laft thoufand yeares, fee heretofore, *tract.* 3. *fect.* 2. *fubdiuif.* 2. at l. m. n. & there alfo at the figures 4. 5. next after q. of their yet further antiquity in the times of *Bafile,* and *Chrifoftome,* fee in the preface to the reader. *fect.* 14. throughout. and *M. Powels* teftimony there towardes the end of that fection at t. where he only excepteth againft the truth of thofe Lyturgies, acknowledging otherwife in them *the forme of our Maffe.* which other point concerning the true authors of the faid Liturgies, is likewife confeffed from his owne brethren *Ibidem. fect.* 12. at s. t. (r) The *Century writers* writing of the eight Century or age, whofe beginning was 900. yeares fince, do confeffe that then preuailed, *theatricum fpectaculum, & facrificium pro viuis et mortuis. centur.* 8. *col.* 361. *& cent.* 9. *col.* 245. they tearme the thē publicke Lyturgy, *theatricū fpectaculū* recyting vp in particuler there *col.* 245. *& 246* the Maffing rites and ceremonies yet to this day vfual, they and others acknowledging yet further that in the 7. Century or age, which began a thoufand yeares fince was *Maffe celebrated in latine.*

true Church) in her (q) confeffed retaining of the faid ceremonies haue not forborne to reiect and condemne them for fuperftitious, and (r) *ftagelike.*

4 Hitherto is entreated of the Maffe and ceremonies, therof only now remaneth as yet vnfpoken of, the language in which it is by vs celebrated: concerning which no longe difcourfe fhal be needful; *firft* becaufe that *Martin* (s) *Luther* him felfe confeffed that the language wherein the publicke Liturgy is to be celebrated, is but a matter in it felfe indifferent. *Secondly,* it is (t) heretofore proued (from our aduerfaries owe confeffion) that the publicke Liturgy haith for thefe thoufand yeares laft paft bene celebrated in Latin, euen

in latin. see this heretofore, *tract* . 3 . *sect* . 2 . *subdiuis* . 2 . in the margent at g. And *M. Sparke,* against *M. Iohn D. Albines . pag.* 160 . confessed that, *the Masse now vsed commonly called S. Gregories Masse, was receiued Anno .* 780 . *Before which time* (saith he) *S. Ambrose Liturgy* (being the very same with the other almost in euery ceremony) *was much in vse.* (s) *Hospinianus in histor . Sacramentar. part .* 2 . *fol .* 33 . saith, *docet (Lutherus) librum esse siue in vulgari siue in peregrina lingua Missam celebrare.* (t) See this heretofore, *tract* . 3 . *sect* . 2 . *subdiuis* . 2 . in the margent vnder g.

(u) euen in such nations as vnderstood not the latin language, and it is in it selfe euident that the english nation was aboue 1000 . yeares since conuerted by *S. Gregory* to latin (u) seruice, the which haith euer since accordingly continued as the publicke Liturgy of this nation. *Thirdly,* the more auncient proofe and reason thereof is established and certaine, for seeing it is heretofore made plaine that in the other much more auncient times, the Chauncel in which the Preist did celebrate the publicke Liturgy, was so (x) seueral to the Cleargy, as that the Laye people might not enter thereto, and that also diuers partes of the publicke prayers vsual there in Masse time, were (y) *pronounced in secret,* it is thereby made vndoubted that the publicke Liturgy was not then made audible and common to the Laye people. *Fourtly,* there is not any appearing necessity herein of the vulgar language for seeing that the Preistes proper and principal end in his celebrating of Masse and sacrifice, is therby not to instruct the people, but to worship God (as faith *S. Augustine* thereof (z) *cultu latria)*

(u) Our conuersion by *S. Gregory* being somwhat aboue 1000 . yeares since, *M. White* in his way to the true Church. *pag .* 378 . confesseth that *the latin language came in in the time of Gregory.*

(x) See this heretofore, *tract* . 1 . *sect* . 2 . *subdiuis* . 1 . in the margent at m . n . o. and see the auncient testimony of *Dionisius Areopagita,* in the preface to the reader *sect.* 7 . *initio.* at e.

(y) Of this see heretofore in the auncient Liturgies of *S. Basile,* and *Chrisosteme,* in the preface to the reader, *sect.* 14 . at the second h. and see also heretofore, *tract* . 5 . *sect* . 4 . *subdiuis.* 1 . in the margent vnder t. the fur-

ther testimonies herein of *Innocentius,* and the *Laodicen Councel;* hereto also is not impertinent the *varle* vsed of auncient in the *Greeke*

Church

Church, wherewith the Preift was for the time compaffed about, whereof fee heretofore, *tract*. 2. *fect*. 7. *initio*. at z. (z) See this heretofore, *tract*. 3. *fect*. 1. *fubdiuif*. 2. at f.

(a)

Hierom. in c. 1. *ad Titum* faith, *quid de Epifcopo fentiendum eft, qui quotidie pro fuis populiq̃ peccatis illibatas Deo oblaturus eft victimas*. And *Ambrofe, in Pfal.* 38. faith, *vidimus principem Sacerdotum ad nos venientem, vidimus et audiuimus offerentem pro nobis fanguinem fuum: fequamur vt poffumus Sacerdotes vt offeramus pro populo facrificium, etfi infirmi tamen honorabiles facerdotio.* and *Nazianzen. epift.* 8. *ad fimpliciū.* tearmeth the Preift

latria) and to make (a) oblation and praiers for him felfe and the people, it is fufficient that God vnderftandeth what is therein faid and done by the Preift, as for the people, the Preiftes acte of celebrating of publicke facrifice for them, dependeth not vpon the corefpondence of their particular vnderftanding no more then doth his like confeffedly practifed oblation (b) for the deade, depend vpon corefpondence held with them, but is in it felfe accomplifhed and perfect, as was the Preiftes facrifice in the old law for him felfe & the whol congregation, whereat the people (c) *might not be prefent.* And fo accordingly *Theodore* (*) *Beza*, confeffeth of the publicke liturgies celebration had in the times of the moft auncient Fathers. *Fiftly*, the inconuenience

the mediator betweene God and man. And *Ignatius* in *epift. ad Smirnenf.* faith, *in the Church nothing is greater then the Bifhop who facrifjceth to God for the faifty of the world.* and *Chrifoftome, de Sacerdot. l.* 6. *c.* 4. *initio.* faith, *nam eum qui pro omni ciuitate (quid autem dico pro ciuitate?) Immo pro vniuerfo mundo ligatione fungitur, et deprecatur iniquitatibus omnium propitium Deum fieri, non folum viuentium fed etiam mortuorum, qualem putas effe debere?* and fee the Liturgies of *S. Bafile*, and *Chrifoftome*, alledged heretofore in the preface to the reader. *fect.* 14. in the margent at the firfter r. And the Apoftle, *habr.* 5. 1. 3. teacheth accordingly that *euery Preift is ordained for men in things pertaining to God, that he may offer guiftes and facrifices for finnes &c. as for the people, fo alfo for him felfe.* (b) Of the Preiftes oblation for the deade practifed in the Primitiue Church, fee pregnant teftimony thereof from *S. Auguftine* and others, alledged heretofore, *tract.* 3. *fect.* 1. *fubdiuif.* 3. next after the letter s. in the margent at the figures 4. 5. & there at t. u. x. y. z. a. b. &c. whereby is fufficiently proued that the

Primitiue

Primitiue Church held the Preistes celebration absolute in it selfe without any necessity of the peoples particuler vnderstanding. (c) *And there shal be no man in the tabernacle of the Congregation, when he goeth in to make an attonement in the holy place, vntil he come out, and haue made an attonement for him selfe, and for his houshould, and for al the Congregation of Israel. Leuiticus. 16. 17.* (*)

ence of the vulgar language seemeth great aswel in respect of the (d) chaunge and degenerating, dayly incident to those languages as also in regard of the communion of dispersed Churches in forraine nations, which is preserued by latine seruice, so as in what cuntry soeuer of the latine Church any stranger soiourneth, he is yet in regard of the Church seruice & publicke worship of God, as though he were at home, & so accordingly the *Italian* Preist may ce'ebrate his publicke Liturgy aswel in *France*, and *Germany*, as in *Italie*, and the like may be said of other people and nations; the contrary whereof falleth out vpon the variable and diuers celebration of the publicke Liturgy according to the diuersity of rites and vulgar languages variably obserued in feueral nations. *Sixtly*, the auncient presidentes of pub'icke liturgies within the first 600. yeares, are worthy of obseruation herein, for the Liturgies in those auncient times vsed by the oriental Churches are either *Greeke*, or *Caldee*, as liewise al the like auncient Liturgies of the west Church are onely latine, which argueth that vpon the first conuersion of nations, the publicke Liturgy was not diuersly first taught and celebrated accoding to the diuersity of vulgar languages.

And whereas our aduersaries do no lesse vehemently then vsually obiect to the con-

See *Bezas* wordes heretofore, *tract. 4. sect. 4. fine. at* *. in the margent.

(d)
The chaunge of vulgar languages appeareth by example of our owne so greatly altered from the first old english, as that ours now vsed, is almost become an other language. A thing so incident to other nations, that *M. D. Morton, in apolog: cath. part. 1. c. 10. pag. 25.* saith, *tu igitur tempus primum demonstra, quo vernacula græca, Romana, Habrea, primo ceperint a natiua sua integritate degenerare.*

(e)
1. *Cor.* 14. 15.

(f)
See the Annotations of the Rhemish Testament vpon this place.

(g)
I would that you al spoke strange langueges, but rather that you prophecyed for greater is he that prophyseseth

H h h 3   trary

cyeth then he that speketh
with tongues, except he expound it that the Church
may receiue edification.
verf. 5. euen so you, for so
much as you couet spirituall
guiftes seeke that you may
excel vnto the edifying of
the Church. verf. 12.
whereby, & yet further
by the 23. 26. 27. &
28. verses, is made eui-
dent that the Apostles
discourse is not of vulgar
languages, but onely of
such tongues as then
were geuen by miracle,
before which he here
preferreth the guift of
interpretation: As also
the praier in a straunge
tongue here mencioned
verf. 14. concerneth
likewise the spirituall praiers then vttered in a
strange tongue geuen by
extraordinary and mira-
culous guift, and is therfore impertinent to the
point now properly issu-
able.

(h)

*If I pray in an vnknowen
tongue my spirit pra eth but
my vnderstanding is with-
out fruict. 1. Cor. 14.
14.* wherein it is to be
obserued, that the A-
postle

trary that which the Apostle writeth to the
Corinthians of (e) *prayer with vnderstanding*.
To forbeare that longer discourse had in explication thereof by our other (f) writers,
I briefly answeare: *first* that though we
should suppose it were ment of our ordinary
praiers, (as indeede it is onely spoken of
languages (g) geuen in those first times by
miracle) yet is it in such sort defectiue as
against vs, as wel for that our now question
is onely of the Churches publicke Liturgy
celebrated by the Preist, who vnderstandeth
the same, and not concerning the Primitiue *primate*
praiers of the faithful, whom to vnderstand
their praiers we do not forbid: As also for
that concerning praiers though not vnderstoode, the Apostle doth not there forbid &
condemne them, but to the contrary in the
same place expresly (h) affirmeth that the spirit
and affection of the party so praying, doth
pray wel towardes God, although his vnderstanding be not thereby instructed. *Secondly*, though we should for the time yet further
suppose with our aduersaries that the Apostles
saying did concerne the prayers made in the
Churches publicke Liturgy, yet so also it
maketh nothing for them; for thus much
though supposed, at the most but proueth,
that the Cleargy celebrating this Liturgy
should vnderstand the same: As for the other
question of the Laye peoples actuall ioyning
with the Preist in his celebration thereof
that is nothing at al hereby inferred or proued, but at the most (the premisses though
supposed notwithstanding) remaneth in question stil as before; nay the Apostle him selfe
(his saying being so vnderstoode) seemeth
rather to signify the contrary, in his affirming
tha.

that not al the vulgar or vnlearned, but (i) one specially appointed *to supply their place*, must for them al *answeare Amen*; so as the laye peoples ioynt action herein with the Preist, is by the Apostles wordes (according to this supposed vnderstanding of the place) rather excluded then directly proued.

postle here saith, that not the praier but the vnderstanding is vnfruitful, affirming plainly, that neuerthelesse the deuotion or *spirit* of the party so praying is acceptable, or (as the marginal notes of the english Bible of 1576. vpon this place at 1. are) doth his part. (i) *If thou blesse in the spirit how shal he that supplyeth the place of the vulgar say Amen vpon thy blessing, seeing he vnderstandeth not what thou sayest.* 1. *Cor.* 14. 16.

F I N I S.

A TABLE OF THE CONTENTES
IN THE PREFACE TO THE READER.

(1) THe Epiftles of S. Ignatius the martir proued to be his. 9.

(2) Anfweare to an obiection againft them, of corruptions inferted by example of their fo earneft prohibiting to faft vpon Sunday. 11.

(3) Anfweare to the like obiected prohibition to keepe Eafter daye with the Iewes. 14.

(4) Anfweare to an obiection that *Theodoret*, and *Hierome*, do alledge certaine fentences from *Ignatius* which are not found in thefe epiftles. 15.

(5) *Dionifius Areopagita* his writinges proued. 16. &c.

(6) Anfweare to the obiection that *Eufebius*, and *Hierome*, do not mencion them. 21.

(7) Anfweare to the obiection of Churches and Chancels mentioned in them. 22.

(8) Anfweare to their like obiected mencioning of Monkes. 24.

(9) Anfweare to *Dionifius* his mencioning him felfe to be prefent at our B. Ladyes death. 30.

(10) Anfweare to *Dionifius* his cyting of a faying of *Ignatius* fuppofed to haue beene written by *Ignatius* after *Dionifius* his death with further anfweare to his fuppofed mifnaming the then Bifhop of *Ephefus*. 33.

(11) Anfweare to the obiection that *Dionifius* maketh no remembrance of his M. S. Paul, & affirmeth the Apoftles to haue beene inftructed by old tradition : with a breefe repetition of certaine Catholicke doctrines contained in the writinges of *Dionifius*. 38.

(12) The Lyturgies of S. *Bafile*, and *Chrifoftome* proued. 41.

(13) Anfweare to the obiection of mencion made in *Chrifoftomes* Lyturgy afwel of *Alexias*, and *Nicholas*, who liued long after *Chrifoftome*, as alfo of *Crifoftome* him felfe as then deade. 44.

(14) A breefe recytal of many ceremonies mencioned in thofe Lyturgies. 48.

(15) Certaine writinges of S. *Ciprian*, and *Ambrofe*, proued. 51.

(16) A like proofe of S. *Gregories Dialogues*, and the *Catechefes* of *Cirillus Herofolimitanus*: alfo of *Eufebius Emiffenus* his homilie

I i i   *de Pafch.*

de Pafch. of the Lyturgy of *S . Iames*, of *Policarpus*, his epiftle. of the Paffion of *S . Andrew*. of *S . Clements* booke of *Apoftolicke conftitutions*. of the Apoftles Canons ; and of *Hipolitus* his booke of the end of the world.　　　　　　　54 . &c.

A TABLE OF THE CONTENTES

OF EVERY SEVERAL TRACT AND SECTION.

TRACT. 1.

(1) OF the antiquity of the word Maffe.　　　*pag*. 59.

(2) Of the defcription of the Church, and how it was folemnly dedicated and alfo confecrated, and furnifhed with Chancel, Altar, holy water, reliques of Sainctes, lightes, and pictures.　　　　　61.

(3) Of the Preift and that he was appointed to offer facrifice. 70.

(4) That the Preift might not be fuch a one as before his orders taken was *Bigamus*, and that after his orders taken he might not marrie.　　　　　77.

(5) Of Preiftes, the ordaining, his vnction, tonfure, and apparel vfed in the holy Maffe.　　　　86.

TRACT. 2.

(1) OF the Preiftes beginning to fay Maffe, and the fundry ceremonies vfed before confecration, and of his confecration of the Sacrament.　　　　　93.

(2) That after confecration the real prefence was acknowledged, with a continued courfe of confeffed teftimonies in that behalfe from this age vp to the Apoftles.　　　　106.

(3) That the Scriptures are agreeable to that fence, fully prouing the real prefence of Chriftes body & bloud in the Eucharift. 127.

(4) That the real prefence is not impoffible, nor to faith abfurd. 146.

(5) Of the contradiction and abfurdity of the Proteftants real prefence.　　　　　167.

(6) Of the miracles fhewed by God in teftimony of the real prefence.

prefence. 187.

(7)   That after confecration the Sacrament was fhewed to the people, with eleuation thereof. 196.

(8)   That the Sacrament was adoared with a continued courfe of teftimonies thereof vp to the Apoftles age. 198.

(9)   That no firft beginning of adoration of the Sacrament can be found, and how forcibly that argueth, and of certaine miracles in proofe of adoration. 218.

(10)   Obiections againft the real prefence taken from the Scriptures, anfweared. 228.

(11)   Obiections againft the real prefence taken from the Fathers anfweared. 238.

T R A C T. 3.

(1)   THat the wordes concerning facrifice in the now Miffal are agreeable with the forme vfed in the auncient Lyturgies and with the practife of the auncient Fathers. 270.

(2)   A further demonftration of facrifice practifed in euery age vp to the Apoftles. 285.

(3)   That the Scriptures of the new Teftamēt are agreable therto. 316.

(4)   That the Scriptures of the old Teftament are likewife agreeable thereto. 334.

(5)   Obiectiōs againft facrifice takē frō the Scriptures anfweared. 348.

(6)   Of the miracles fhewed by God in behalfe of Maffe and facrifice, and of *Luthers* inftruction againft it from the Deuil. 366.

(7)   That the impugners of the Maffe in the ages bofore *Luther*, were al of them in other matters confeffed heretickes. 376.

T R A C T. 4.

Sect. 1.   THe true ftate of the queftion concerning Communion vnder one or both kindes and the doctrine of both Catholickes, and Proteftants, is plainly fet downe. p. 394.

(2)   That vnder either kind whol Chrift is truly contained, and the true effence of the Sacrament preferued, and confequently that neither the people are depriued of any grace neceffary to faluatiō, nor the Sacrament thereby made imperfect or mamed. 396.

(3)   That Chrift our Sauiour gaue no commaund of receiuing vnder both

    der both

der both kindes, it is proued by the sacred Scriptures, and by his owne and his blessed Apostles examples . 401 .

(4) That the practise of the Primitiue Church was promiscuous, somtimes vnder one kind and somtimes vnder both . 404 .

(5) That Communion vnder one kind is of it selfe a matter of indifferency, not prohibited, and lawful, it is further proued by the confession of Protestantes . 408 .

(6) That Communion vnder one or both kindes being a thing indifferent, the Church might lawfully determine the same : and of the reasons that moued the Church in limitation therof. 411 .

(7) An examination of such arguments as are drawen from sacred Scriptures in proofe that Christ gaue commaund vuto his Apostles and their successors to administer the Sacrament of the Eucharist vnder both kindes to the laity . 415 .

(8) Certaine breife rules whereby such places as are obiected from Fathers may easily be answeared . 422 .

(9) The conclusion of this treatise containing certaine rules which the greatest Doctor S . Augustine gaue to his scholer Ianuarius, for his suerest direction in matters of faith and religion . 425 .

TRACT. 5.

(1) OF the ceremonies after sacrifice, and namely of fraction of the Sacrament, and the kisse of peace, and the receiuing fasting . 428 .

(2) Of the Preistes benediction vpon Masse ended . 430 .

(3) A recytal of sundry other ceremonies repeated or often vsed in seruice time . 432 .

(4) An answeare to those who affirme the ceremonies of the Masse to be a wil-worship, and againt Scripture, with an explication of that point from Scriptures, Fathers, and learned Protestantes. 435 .

A

A Baylardus his errors.   384. d.
   Abſolution from ſiane geuen by Preiſtes.   348. at 2.
Abſurdity pretended agamſt Catholicke real preſence, anſweared.   146.
Abſurdity of Proteſtants real preſence proued.   181. *.
Accidentia non entis affirmed by Proteſtantes.   177. s.
Accolites.   71. z.
Admimniſtration of the word and Sacraments muſt euer continue.   345. b.
Adoration of the Euchariſt neceſſarily followeth vpon real preſence. 223. *.
   taught by Luther, and the vniuerſal Church in his time. 199. l. &c.
   And before the time of Honorius the 3. 201. at 4. Taught by the aur.ci-
   ent Fathers. 203. with a preſcript forme of praier. 198. f. 204. x. 217.
   z. 212. *. and proſternation. 205. d. 206. g. 212. v. external circum-
   ſtances obſerued in the Primitiue Church prouing the ſame 212. x. Miracles alſo in proofe thereof. 212. *. 226. f. Adoration euer practiſed
   without any knowen beginning.   218.
Æthiopians, Indians, Armenians, Greeians, conuerted in the Apoſtles times.
   288. They agree with vs in the ſacrifice of the Maſſe.   289.
Albigenſes their errors.   382. m.
Alleluia anciently vſed. 49. d. Alleluia & Amen not to be tranſlated. 433. a.
Alexander the firſt charged with ſacrifice. 308. c. with mingling wine and
   water in the Chalice. 95. l. And with holy water.   93. b.
Almaricus his errors.   385. g.
Ambroſe his writinges proued not to be counterfeate.   53.
S. Andrewes Paſſion writte by his diſciples proued not to be counterfeate. 309. *.
   it maketh for ſacrifice.   310. o.
Angels and Sainctes, inuocated in Maſſe time. 49. t. 99. ſ. Angels pre-
   ſent at Maſſe.   368. z.
Anthropophagie obiected againſt the auncient Chriſtians in reguard of the Sa-
   crament.   121. at 2.
Antichriſt wil at his comming take away ſacrifice.   344. q. 383. s.
Aplication of ſacrifice made by the Preiſt.   348. &c. 363. e.
Apoſtolicy their errors.   383. s.
Argument drawen from computation of time vncertaine.   30. &c.

Auerroes his testimony for adoration of the Sacrament vniuersally vsed in his time.   203. at 10.

Altars in the first times of the Primitiue Church vsed. 64. J. 310. o. *so named in respect of sacrifice.* 64. z. 115. at 5. 333. *. *mencioned in the new Testament.* ib. at n. *aunciently consecrated with the signe of the Crosse, and Chrisme.*   66. c.

Austerity of life vsed by S. Iames, by S. Iohn Baptist, & by S. Timothy. 29. a.

S. *Augustines sermons de tempore proued to be his 60.* g. *his saying, non hoc corpus quod videtis manducaturi estis &c. answeared.* 250. n. *He & the other Primitiue Fathers confessed by Protestantes for the Masse.* 296. &c.

Authors vsually alleged by Protestants against their knowen meaning 262. q. 266. p.

B

B *Asils Liturgy proued.*   41. k.

Beguardini *their errors.*   386. at 2.

Benediction of the Preist anciently vsed at the end of the Masse. 430. *And the peoples then bowing of their heades.*   431.

Berengarius his impugning of real presence, singular at that time in him. 107. d. *his other errors.*   378. *.

Bernard a Roman Catholicke. 263. at 11. *his doctrine of real presence.* ib. at z. *He reporteth a miracle done in confirmation thereof.*   195. q.

Bertram whether against the real presence.   377. k.

Beza his desperate euasion from the real presence.   322. c.

Bigami forbidden in a Preist. 77. q. *Also in a professed Widow.* 77. q.

Bloud in the Chalice.   328. z.

C

C *Aluin reiecteth the Fathers for their doctrine of sacrifice.* 301. k. 307. b. *His straunge deuised real presence.*   169. &c.

Camel to passe trough an neeldes eye possible.   152. at 5.

Canon of the Masse how auncient. 271. at 3. *Pronounced in secret.* 50. o.

Canons of the Apostles proued.   82. f.

Capernaites vnderstood Christ as speaking of corporal eating. 128. a. *They beleeued not therefore his wordes.* ib. k. *And are thereupon reproued, not for their misunderstanding, but for their misbeleeuing his wordes.* ib. r.

Carolastadius his expositiō of Christs words 138. d. *His pretēded visiōs.* 375. f.

Catechumens remoued in Masse time 40. at 18. 98. at 2. 215. k. *Holy bread prepared for them in lieu of the Sacrament.* 215. m. *Yet for their cure are somtimes brought in presence of the mysteries.* 98. at 3. *A mira-culous*

culous difpoffeffing fo done by S. Bernard. Ib. at 4.

Centuriftes difcliamed from by Sutline. 307. a.

Ceremonies though not commaunded by God may be appointed by the Church. 440. at 4. 442. s. May be borrowed from the Iewes. 427. at 2. 3. fundry of whofe are ftil retained. 438. at 4. &c. ordained to fignify and ftir vp deuotion. 439. at 2. 441. q.

Ceremonies of the now Maffe aunciently vfed. 40. 48. 93. 432. Vpon what ground they be inftituted. 436. h. Allowed by Proteftantes. 442. u.

Ceremonies of Baptifeme auncient. 40. at 14.

Chalice how called the Teftament. 324. at 4. fpecially confecrated. 67. *. It containeth Chriftes bloud. 328. z. by teftimony of S. Luke. 321. y.

Chancels aunciently vfed in the Church. 23. e. 62. m.

Chaunge of facrifice vpon chaunge of the law. 274. n. 332. at 6.

Chrifoftomes Liturgy proued. 41. &c. Obiections pretended againft it anfweared. 44. The ceremonies of our now Maffe mencioned therein. 48.

Chrift his promife of his body to be eaten. 127. &c. His anfwearable performance. 135. &c. S. Pauls anfwearable explication. 145. The Fathers agreeable doctrine. 106. confirmed with miracles. 187.

Chriftes wordes confeffedly plaine for real prefence. 146. y. Proteftantes affirming them figuratiue cannot agree thereof. 140. f. That they are not figuratiue. ib. *.

Chrift offered the facrifice of the body and bloud at his laft fupper. 76. 77. 316. His faid facrifice not difhonourable to his facrifice of the Croffe. 348. His Preifthood being aparabaton. 356. c. often offered explained. 360. y. A Preift for euer according to the order of Melchifadech in refpect of the Eucharift. 335. at 2. His body in many places at once. 162. h. 363. e. 149. at 3. 209. o. 210. at b. 236. b. The natural properties of his body, as circumfcription, vifibility, quantity, &c. fufpended. 147. at 8. 151. at 4.

Churches had in the Apoftles times. 22. h. confecrated by the figne of the Croffe and holy water. 64. r. Dedicated in honour of Sainctes. 63. p. Builded towardes the eaft 62. at b. furnifhed with Altars, fee Altar, with holy water. fee confecration of water, with lightes. 70. t. with images. ib. s. with reliques. ib. m. with veftrie. 48. o. with holy Corporals, Paten, Turible, ib. l. with veftments. ib. o.

Circumcifion tollerated by the Apoftles for a time. 14. 1.

Circulation of Proteftantes in their difputes of the real prefence. 154. at 7.

Ciril. Hierofol. his Catechefis proued. 55. t. plaine for real prefence. 116. at 2.

at 2. 246. *t*. 269. *n*. *and for sacrifice for the deade* . 301. *at* 16.
Clemens constitutions proued . 311. *x*.
Commixtion or putting of one part of the Hoaste into the Chalice . 415.
Communion vnder one or both kindes; the state of the question set dowen . 394.
Communion vnder one decreed by Councels . 395 . *impugned by Protestants* .
396 . *vnder one whol Christ, and the sacrament preserued*. 397 . *vnder both*
not commaunded by Christ. 401. *The Primitiue Church somtimes vsed only*
one . 404. *The Manichees heresy herein* . 404 . 407. *Protestants allow*
communion vnder one. 408. *Reasons mouing the Church to one* . 413. *Ob-*
iections from Scriptures answeared. 415. *From Fathers answeared* . 422.
Consecration of water in Baptisme with the signe of the Crosse . 64. *n*. *Of*
holy water . 93 . *b*. *of holy bread* 215. *m*. *Of monkes*. 39. *at* 4. *Of*
Candles . 70. *t*. *Of incense*. 49. *y*. *Of Altar*. 66. *c*. *Of Chalice and*
corporal. 67. ***. *Of Churches* . 63. *p*.
Consecration of the Sacrament 99 . *z*. *made by wordes* . 100.
Corporals . 48. 67. 97. ***.
Corpus connot in Christes wordes signify figura corporis . 138. ***.
Crosse, see signe of the Crosse .
Ciprians workes defended. 51. *y*. *His plaine sayinges for real presence*. 116.
h. *And for sacrfice* . 303. *m*.

D

Aniels Prophecy of sacrifice . 344.
Dayly sacrifice taught by the Fathers . 273. *h*.
Deacons a seueral order from Preisthood. 71 . *a*. *they might distribute the*
Sacrament, but not offer sacrifice. *ib*. *and* 275. *q*.
Dionisius Areopagita his writinges proued. 16. *Obiections against them an-*
sweared 21. *His Catholicke doctrines therein taught*. 39.
Disputation betweene Luther and the Deuil, see Luther .
Distribution of the Sacrament to the Communicants is distinct from oblation
of sacrifice. 275. ***.

E

Asters obseruation not to be according to the Iewes. 14.
Eleuation of the Sacrament. 51. *p*. 196. *c*.
Epithites of sacrifice geuen by the Fathers. 273. 278.
Errors of the Waldenses, Albigenses, &c. who impugned the Masse . 376.
Esayes Prophecy of Preistes . 74. *l*.
Essees mencioned by Philo, were Christians . 26.
Est, cannot in Christes wordes import significat . 140. *g*.

Euchrist

Euchariſt how a Sacrament & ſacrifice. 316.l. See real preſence and ſacrifice.

Euſebius Emiſſen. his writinges proued. 55. z.

Exorciſt an order or degree to Preiſthood. 71. y.

F

Aſting on Sunday and Chriſtmas day forbidden. 11.

Faſting preſcribed before receiuing of the Sacrament. 214.f.430.a.

Fathers obſcure ſayinges how to be vnderſtood. 252.r. 240. at 10. Alleá-ged by Proteſtantes againſt their knowen meaning. 262. Their wary writing of the Sacrament, as norunt fideles. 238. at 8. They are charged by Pro-teſtantes with error in real preſence. 106. In Tranſubſtantiation 109. 112. *. 116. *. In ſacrifice. 293. 296. 302.

Figuratiue ſayinges proue not. 184.

Figure excludeth not verity. 244. p.

Firſt 600. yeares acknowledged by Proteſtantes. 294. h.

Fleſh profiteth nothing, anſweared. 131. l. r.

Fraction of the Sacrament. 51. q. 428. How affirmed by the Apoſtle 320. at 2. How affirmed of Chriſtes body. ib. at 5.

G

Oſpel read the people ſtandeth vp. 49. c. 94. *. A waxen Candle then lighted. 94. g.

Grace conferred by Sacramentes. 350. n. p. 352. t.

Grammatical ſenſe of Scripture holden beſt. 326. q. It proueth real preſence. ib. p. and 146. y.

Greeke Church aunciently vſed Maſſe and the ceremonies thereof, as appea-reth by the Lyturgies of Baſil and Chriſoſtome 48. at this day alſo it conti-nueth the ſame beleefe. 202. at 6. 288. *.

Gregory the great, one of thoſe Fathers to whom Iewel appealed. 294. h. Con-uerted vs Engliſh men to Maſſe. 294. l. 296. at 5. Taught Maſſe in latine. 293. g. & Priuate Maſſe. 295. o. for the liuing and the deade. 294. l. Miracles by him reported in proofe thereof. 366. o. his Dia-logues proued. 54.

H

Allowed Candles, ſee confecration.

Heathen, in the auncient Church charged Chriſtians with adoring Chriſt in the Sacrament. 203. at 10. 207. *. Their obiecting of Anthropophagy 121. at 2.

K k k

Heresy euer at it first appearing contradicted. 219. *f.* *yet confessedly no first*
appearing or beginning knowen of real presence. 126. *x.* *Of adoration of*
the Sacrament. 218. *Of Masse.*   314. *g.*
Hipolitus his booke proued.   304. *y.*
Holy bread, see consecration.
Holy water, see consecration.
Honorius the third did not first bring in adoration.   201. *at 4.*

I

I Am a doore &c. explained.   229. *t.*
Iewish Rabins for sacrifice according to the order of Melchisadech. 336. *b.*
Iewes charged Christiaus with offering a child in sacrifice. 285. **. Their*
malice against the blessed Sacrament miraculosly discouered. 188.
Iewish ceremonies may some of them be retained.   437. 438.
Images aunciently placed in Churches.   69.
Incense aunciently vsed in Masse time.   40. *l.* 94. *d.*
Indifferent thinges once commaunded do thereby loose the nature of indiffe-
rency.   411. 412. 413. 446. *m.*
Infants communion in the Primitiue Church, a proofe of real presence. 117.
q. Not taught as necessary to saluation.   118. *s.*
Inuocation in Masse time of our B. Lady S. Mary, of S. Michael, and o-
ther Sainctes.   49. 94.

K

Kisse of peace aunciently vsed in Masse time. 429. *As also kissing of the*
booke and Alter.   49. *a.* 94. *s.* *h.* 433. *z.*
Kyrie eleison aunciently vsed.   433. *c.*

L

L anguage vulgar if necessary to the publicke Liturgy 448. *s.* *Obiection*
answeared.   452. *e.*
Latine seruice how auncient.   293. *g.*
Latria requireth external sacrifice.   279. *f.*
Law translated argueth sacrifice.   274. *n.* 332. *at 9.*
Laye persons prohibited to touch the Chalice, Corporal &c. 68. *k. And to*
enter into the Chancel.   62. *m.*
Lightes in the Church. 70. *t. consecrated.*   *ib.*
Logomachia condemned.   61. *at 4.*
S. Luke plaine for real presence and sacrifice. 321. *y. in answeare thereto he*
is charged with incongruity, or false Greeke.   322. *c.*
                                                              Luther

Luther his desire to alter his opinion against the real presence. 188. *at* 6.
He dissented from Suinglius in the real presence 266. *his disputation of Masse had with the deuil.* 369.
Liturgies of S. Basil, and S. Chrisostome proued. 41. *obiections to the contrary answeared.* 44. *Their ceremonies and Catholicke doctrines.* 48.
Liturgy of S. Iames, and the antiquity thereof. 56. *.
Liturgies of Æthiopia, Hierusalem, Alexandria, Constantinople, Syria, and the Latine, al of them make for sacrifice. 287. *p. their confessed antiquity.* 288. *q.*

M

Alachias his Prophecy of the sacrifice of the new Testament. 309. *z.* 307. *b.* 340. *x.*
Malachias his miracle in proofe of real presence. 195. *q.*
Manna inferior in efficacy to the Eucharist. 133. *at* 8.
Marriage of Preistes forbidden. 77. *in reguard of their dayly offering sacrifice.* *ib. i. and* 84. *z.*
S. Maries death. 30. 31. *she was called by the Fathers, the mother of God.* 158.
Martialis his writinges proued. 309. *m.*
Mathew Paris commended by Protestantes. 193. *.
Masse, the word thereof how auncient. 59. *celebrated in Latine.* 293. *g.* 448. *r. vniuersally professed* 1000. *yeares since. ib. l. and at* 4. *continued and deduced from these times til the Apostles times.* 291. 434. *f. confessedly no beginning thereof knowen.* 314. *g. Proued from the Scriptures of the new Testament.* 316. *from the Scriptures of the old Testament.* 334. *affirmed and proued in it seueral partes by the very impugners therof.* 339. *p. vsd vniuersally ouer the whol Christian world at Luthers first appearing.* 286. *. *Al auncient Liturgies make for it.* 48. 270. 288. *p. miracles make for it.* 366. *It haith beene impugned openly before Luthers time onely by confessed Hereticks.* 376. *obiections against it answeared.* 348. *Luther being instructed against it by sensible conference with the deuil thereupon abandoned it.* 369. *Suinglius also* 374. *Carolastadius.* 375.
Melchisadech his sacrifice of breade and wine prefigured the sacrifice of the new Testament, affirmed from the Scriptures. 335. *from the Rabines.* 336. *b. from the Fathers.* 337. *c. And from Protestants.* 338. *h.*
Miracles in proofe of real presence. 187. 399. *. *of adoring the Sacrament.* 225. *of receiuing of the Sacrament.* 188. *l.* 194. *n.* 212. *u.* 163. *. *Of Masse and sacrifice.* 366.
Mixture of water with wine in the Chalice anciently vsed. 48. 95.

Monkes how auncient. 24. *their austerity*.

N

Abuchodonosors *fierie furnace* .   163. k.
Names proper to God, communicated to creatures. 358. o. *Names of Sainctes taken in the Apostles times in their honour & imitation* . 36.
Natural properties may be suspended from a body. 147. *at* 8. *and so were in Christes body*.   151. *at* 4.
Nicen first Councel distinguisheth distribution of the Sacrament from the sacrifycing thereof.   275. q.
Nicholas the Pope mistaken by Iewel .   44. x.
Nunnes see Virgins sacred .

O

Biections *from the Scriptures against real presence answeared*. 131. i. 228. *from the Fathers*.   228.
Obiections against Masse and sacrifice answeared, as namely, that is dishonorable to his sacrifice vpon the Crosse . 248. *That Christes Preisthood passeth not away*. 356. r. *That Christ should not be often offered*. 360. y. *applyed for others* .   363. d.
Omnipotency of God impugned by Protestantes in their denyal of real presence. 146. z. *And yet in the Caluinistes pretended real presence more depended vpon, then do the Catholickes in theirs*.   177. s.
Orders thought by the Fathers to be a Sacrament .87. r. *geuen by a Bishop only*. 86. *with imposition of handes* 87. p. *& fasting* 87. *they confer grace*. 87. *the seueral degrees thereof*.   71. y.

P

Arables *expounded by Christ*. 133. s. *and by his Euangelistes*. ib.*.
Christes wordes. Ioan. 6. 55. *are denyed to be parabolical by S. Chrisostome* .   230. h.
Paten aunciently vsed .   48. 67.
Paul expounder of our Sauiours wordes 145. q. *His comparing our sacrifice and Altar, with the sacrifices & Altars of the Iewes, and Gentils*. 333. n.
Pax, see kisse of peace.
Perfection of life practised in the Apostles times.   29.
Peter Bruis his errors.   383. a.
Philo his testimony of religious Essees, concerneth Christian Monkes . 26.
Pilgrimage to holy places. 68 p. *to Hierusalem*. 286. m. *It proueth the vniuersality of Masse throughout the whol Christian world*. 287. *.
                                                                   an ar-

an argument that Masse is Apostolicke. 290. *.

Pix for reservation of the Sacrament . 212 . x . certaine knowen miracles reported thereof. 163 . *.

Policarpe his epistle proued . 10.

Possessed persons deliuered by the sacrifice of the Masse, & the B. Sacramēt. 98.

Prayer in Masse time to our Lady, S. Michael, and Sainctes, see inuocation.
and for the deade. 39 . at 7 . 283 . u . of prayer in an vnknowen tongue .

Prayers in Masse time somtimes vsed in secret. 432 . t .

Prescription whereof no beginning since the Apostles times is knowen in real
presence . 127 . y . In adoration of the Sacrament . 218 . a . in the round
forme thereof . 97 . p . In Masse. 314 . g .

Preistes the word how auncient . 70 . Properly so called in the new Testament .
74 . they do truly sacrifice . 73 . so explained by the Fathers . 75 . foretold
by Esay. 74 . They offer sacrifice in Christes steede . 75 . a . 383 . o . Christ
him self first executed this Preisthood and sacrifice . 76 . e . Preisthood deriued from Christ . 259 . r . Preisthood for euer according to the order of
Melchisadech, is onely in reguard of the Eucharist . 235 . Preistes haue power to forgeue sinne . 348 . at 2 . they may not marrie . 79 . their marriage
forbidden in reguard of their dayly offering of sacrifice . 84 . They celebrated Masse fasting . 88 . they are consecrated onely by a Bishop . 86 . i . m .
Their tonsure . 39 . 88 . Their vnction . 88 . t . Preistly vestments in Masse
time . 88 . 89 . They turne somtimes towardes the people in Masse time .
432 . s . bow their heads . 432 . r . And signe the people with the signe of
the Crosse . 432 . s .

Primitiue Church commended . 347 . m . 447 . o . The first 600 . yeares after Christ acknowledged . 294 . h . 447 . p .

Propitiatory Sacrifice, see sacrifice.

R

R Eal presence in the Sacrament confessedly possible . 146 . Christs wordes
confessedly plaine for it . 146 . 225 . promised by our Sauiour. 127 .
A nswerably performed in the Sacrament . 135 . explained accordingly by S .
Paul. 145 . Confirmed with many miracles . 187 . seuerally beleeued
throughout the whol Christian world for these last 1000 . yeares . 106 . 108 .
k Deduced by successiue testimonies from the more auncient Fathers vp to
the Apostles times . 109 . &c . confessedly no first beginning thereof knowen .
126 . Adoration and sacrifice do necessarily follow and depend vpon it . 225 . *.
Obiections against it answeared, see Obiections. Real presence graunted, no
dishonour thereby followeth to Christ. 156 .

K k k d

Real presence affirmed by Protestantes. 170. *. *Euen to the vnworthy re-ceiuer*. 171. o. *It is confessedly aboue al vnderstanding and thought*. 175. g. *more wonderful then the other Catholicke presence* 177. y. *It is supposed to containe many miracles*. 177. u. *It is in it selfe repugnant*. 178. *And absurd*. 181. *. *and for such reiected by other Protestants*. 185. u.

Reliques aunciently placed in the Church. 68. *Pilgrimage thereto*. ib. *miracles shewed thereat*.   69. y.

Reseruation of the sacrament how auncient. 102. 125. *confirmed with many miracles*. 188. l. 194. n. 212. u. 163. *. *the denyal thereof condemned for heresy* ·   103. h.

Rules from S. *Augustine for our direction in matters of doubt concerning religion*.   425.

S

Acraments their number. 39. *at* 8. *They confer grace*. 350. n. 352. t. *Sacrament blessed by Christ*. 103. *round in forme*. 96. n. *consecrated* 100. z. *care that no part thereof fal to the ground* 215. *may be reciued in one kinde*.

How it is both a figure and truth. 244. p. *It is not bread*. ib. n. *How it is both a Sacrament and sacrifice*. 316. l. *It is receiued fasting*. 214. c.

Sacrifice, the forme of wordes the same for it in the auncient Liturgies that are now. 270. a. *offered actually to God*. 275. *why directed to God the Father*. 280. 303. *offered for the liuing*. 281. 282. 308. d. *for the deade*. 283. *at* 4. 304. *for the Emperour, for the sicke, for the fruicles of the earth*. 281. *against euil spirits*. 282. *It is distinct from distribution to the people*. 275. *. *the signifying Epithets thereof vsed by the Fathers*. 273. g. 278. *at* 5. *first instituted and executed by Christ*. 75. 76. 317. n. 322. *at* 9. 359. x. *proued from the writinges of the new Testament*. 316. *Obiections against it answeared, see obiections*. *Proued from this last age vp to the Apostles times*. 291. *No first beginning therof since the Apostles time knowen*. 314. g. *and see Altars*.

Sainctes, see inuocation.

Scriptures to be taken in their plaine litteral, and vsual sense in articles of faith. 155. k. *so taken they proue the real presence*. 146. y. *alledged for real presence*. 127. *for sacrifice*. 216. *their seeming repugnances*.   37.

Signe of the Crosse vsed in the signing the Sacrament. 50. n. 95. k. *signing the people*. 50. k. *vsed in Baptisme*.   40. *at* 14.

Spiritual receiuing how vnderstood by Protestantes. 173. *Receiuing by faith how*.   178.

Subdeacons

Sub *deacons* .　　　　　　　　　　　　　　　71 . *y* .

Suinglus *his opinion concerning Christes wordes* . 167 . *he translateth, this signifyeth my body* . 140 . *at* 4 . *His pretended vision against the Masse* . 374 . *a. condemned for an illusion* .　　　　　　ib . c .

T

T On*sure of Preistes aunciently vsed* .　　　39 . *at* 10 . 88 . *n* .

　Traditions vnwritten .　　　　　　　　39 . *at* 2 .

Tran*substantiation proued from* Scriptures. 136 . *a. from the Fathers*. 109 . *m*. 112 . * . 116 . *h*. 244 . *n. Pretended to be first taught in the time of the Lateran Councel*. 127 . *at* 3 . *at the time of the said Councel it was vniuersal* . 107 . *e . & therefore the deny al thereof was then before condemned as a nouelty in Berengarius. ib . d . It followeth necessarily vpon real presence* . 329 . *r . And confessedly entred early into the Church* 126 . *x . It is also taught by Protestantes* .　　　　　　　　339 . *r* .

V

V Aile *vsed in the Greeke Church in time of consecration* .　197 . *z* .

　Vestiments, *see Preistly vestments* .

Vestrie .　　　　　　　　　　　　　　　48 . *o* .

Virgins *sacred* .　　　　　　　　　　　29 . *g* .

Vnbloudy *sacrifice* .　　　　　　　　　361 . * .

Vnction *of Preistes* .　　　　　　　　　88 . *t* .

Vniuersality *of doctrine a strong argument* .　290 . *b* .

Voluntary *pouerty* .　　　　　　　　　　29 . *e* .

Vowed *chastity* .　　　　　　　　　　　79 . *b* .

W

VV Afer *cakes how auncient* .　　　96 . 308 . *at* 23 .

　　Waldenses *their errors* .　　　　379 . *t* .

Washing *the Preistes fingers in Masse time* .　50 . *l*. 94 . *i* .

Water *consecrated, see consecration* .

Widowes *professed vowed chastity* .　　　　79 . 80 .

Wordes *of consecrating the Sacrament*. 100 . *Holden operatory* .　103 .

Writinges *of* Ignatius *proued*. 9 . *Of* Policarpus . 10 . *at i. Of* Dionisius A-reopagita . 16 . *The Liturgies of* Basil *and* Chrisostome . 41 . *The writinges of* Ciprian, *&* Ambrose . 51 . *of* Gregory *the great,* Ciril *of* Hierusalem, *&* Eusebius Emissen . 54 . *The Liturgy of* S . Iames . 56 . * . *The passion of* S . Andrew *written by his Disciples* 309 . * . *The Apostles Canons*. 82 . *q* . Clemens *Apostolicke constitutions* . 311 . *x* . Hipolitus .　　304 . *y* .
　　　　　　　　　　　　　　　　　　　　386 . *l* .

Wuliffe *his errors* .

FINIS.

The Printers ignorance in our language, must intreat the curteous Readers
excuse for the faultes escaped : yet those which are most materiall
are here obserued ; where the first figures signify the page,
the second the line, and the wordes or figures following,
the correction to be made .

Pag. 21. 24. workes. 26. 8. life. 29. 5. of S. ib. 29. 1. 7. example. 31. 2. meane.
32. 26. matters specially. 36. 25. kinde 40. 18. vncouering. 52. 16. Ciprian 73.
31. sacrificer. 90. 22. Infula. 116. 10. vnanswearably. 146. 15. Ridley. 146. 16. for
Christ to. 159. 18. Valentinus 160. 4. reiecting. ib. 16. reiect. 206. 3. priority. 209.
4. greatest. 243. 17. foode 249. 15. could 250. 23. followeth. 251. 11. lecludeth. 260.
24. his. 261. 21. it. Ib. 10. as. 267. 14. life. 273. 16. Epithets. 278. vlt. of Christians.
286. 8. descent. 287. 2. Moscouites. 288. 9. faith 291. 25. stagelike. 293. 5. stagelke.
295. 10. west part. 303. 4. & 328. 22. is 332. 11. ineuitably. 333. 4. offer to. 346.
2. Pope. 350. 11. impart. 354. 10. offence. 366. 15. ground. 369. 14. the vp. 377. 20.
Transubstantiation. ib. 27. affected. 389. 12. not also. 395. b. receiued. 404. 8. which.
405. 4. it. 409. 13. counsailed. 411. 15. exercyseth. 414. 2. to declare. 415. 18. textes.
416. 13. not necessaryly. 417. 17. answering. 418. 1. expositors. 420. 31. haue already.
424. 8. the. 451. 17. variably. 452. 13. priuate.

Corrections in the margent .

17. 20. Aerius. 16. 4. vnde. 18. 28. 917. ib. 34. hac re scripsit. 19. 7.
in diuersos. ib. 15. diuinitas. ib. 25. Tou oranou. ib. 29. 540. 20. 4. A-
nastasius ib. Odega. 21. 6. 26. ib. 14. sequuntur. 25. 26. testantur. 26.
23. aliquo. 27. 27. fax. 30. 2. it not. ib. 4. conference. ib. 9. in his sermon of 35. 5. saith. 38. 31. are. 39. 7. ridentes. 40. 3. ratione. ib. 21.
iubet ac. 46. 10. sint. 47. 27. editionibus. 48. vlt. dignos offerre. 55.
30. secreta. 59. 4. 1593. 62. 22. scripto. 63. 9. quousque. 64. 26.
qua regenerantur. 67. 1. sanctissimi. 69. 13. cæcus. ib. 30. 20. 74. 27.
& the. 78. vlt. 84. 82. (*) Tim. 5. 22. (0) Tit. 1. 7. 8. and Hier.
vpon this place. 83. 9. then. 85. 18: 3. 86. 27. Turacoxensers. 89. 29.
Talaris. 90. 10. Talaris. 91. 1. 2. ib. 21. alledged. ib. 24. 286. 91.
32. et 95. 19. Crux. 96. 32. drawne 97. 21. 259. 98. 19. vos 99.
7. confessione. 101. 37. fas. 104. 29. Eucharistethenta. 107. 22. 1050.
ib. 25. priuato. ib. 33. hanc. 110. 3. postea. ib. 24. commode. 111. 4.
496. ib. proposita. ib. 19. ipse. ib. 21. et ib. 23. manaui. 112. 12. would.
ib. trauuled. 113. 4. commendando. ib. vlt. apposita. 114. 1. convertens
117. 23. supposititia. 119. 17. præsente. 122. 8. et. ib. 36. proditum. 123.
32. peperat. 127. 3. maturo. 130. 33. the truth. 132. 9. torquens. ib.
15. profit. 133. 3. 262. 138. 28. neutrum. 142. 22. geminum. 164.
25. frater. 169. 27. totam 186. 10. uisi. 192. 30. confessione. 195. 10.
desfieni. 207. 10. liberum. ib. 11. libero. 209. 24. volis. 210. 34. depre-

cantes. 211. 18. tali. 221. 35. be houlden. 223. 5. et adorabile. and 225. 25. eosdem. 237. 3. sacris. 245. 8. that they. 255. 30. 3. 262. 31. absit. 263. 18. 324. ib. 30. quæ. 267. 19. 370. 268. 22. phanasticall. 271. 35. clarissime. 274. vlt. cederet. 275. 5. transisse. ib. 8. 23. 276. 4. decreed by. 277. 25. constiterit. ib. 34. 12. 279. 15. perrexit. ib. 31. præcepit. ib. 32. debent. 283. 3. significatur in. ib. 25. offeretur. 284. 29. 71. 285. 8. se manasse. 287. 21. Almanæ. 288. 4. expressior. 287. 27. indutum. 290. 13. 1548. ib. 31. Missa. 294. 4. Idolo. ib. 23. 406. 295. 32. 47. 9. 299. 19. totius. 301. 12. latenter. 302. 23. erant. ib. 24. 17. 304. 27. chield. ib. 32. notwithstanding. 306. 9. Hipolitum. 308. 11. deleri. 313. 26. fide. 315. 22. inuersa. 316. 3. me 317. penult. Clomenon. ib. vlt. broken. 321. 28. polished. 322. 13. which is. ib. 27. hoc. 324. 19. the testament. ib. 29. is the. 327. 9. potest. 328. 27. libent. 329. 3. et ita sacrificabant pro sanguine brutorum. ib. 4. opponeret. 330. 13. 20. ib. 21. vico. 331. 12. Christus. 333. 26. 552. 336. 17. Arnobius. 337. 17. insisterent. 344. 1. old. 350. 4. absolution. 354. 14. causa. ib. 17. exhibet filius meritum suum credentibus. ib. 22. dominus. 367. 12. Ecclesiæ. clericatus. 373. 1. non eiecerat. 379. 10. of. 380. 28. affirming. ib. 33. them. 382. 4. sentire. ib. 35. Albigensis 386. 29. 113. 400. 2. c. 3. 402. 16. hunc. 424. 1. 4. 429. 15. partitur. 433. 4. ab. ib. 27. for their 436. 8. 30. 429. 5. Deo offerre. 442. 4. necessary. ib. 10. nos. ib. 31. proficiscens. 445. 22. l. 2. 447. affirming further. 449. 7. liberum. 450. 17. infirmi. ib. 26. legationi.

The other onely litteral faultes of lesse moment the reader may easily
perceiue and amend.

D E O G R A T I A S.